GW00658735

What the Bible Says About

WHAT THE BIBLE SAYS ABOUT

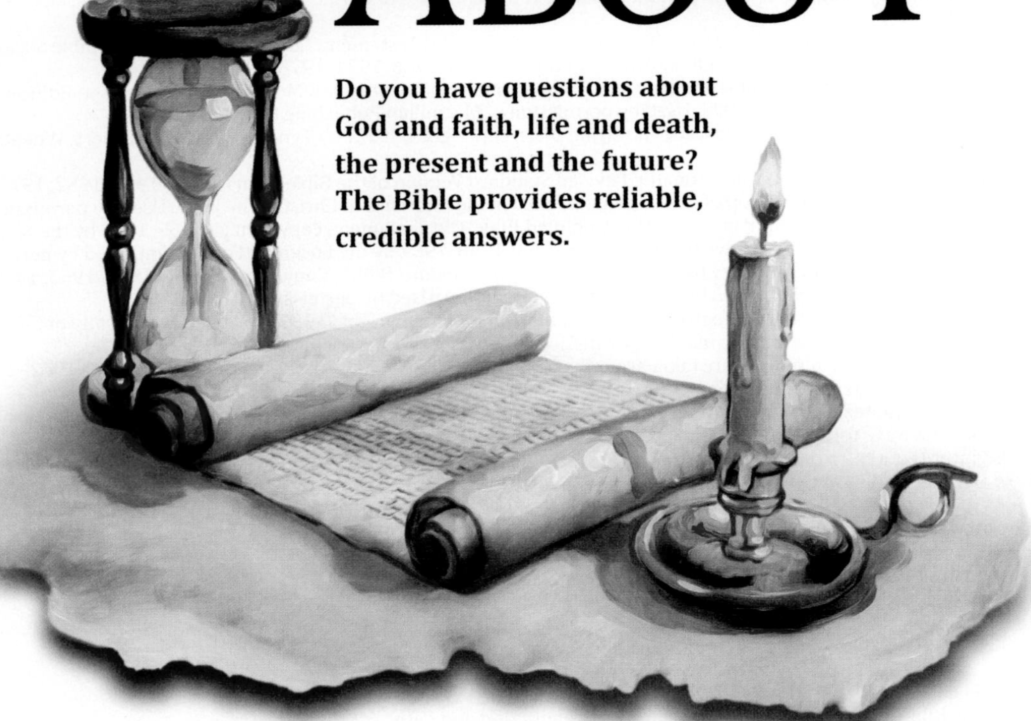

Do you have questions about God and faith, life and death, the present and the future? The Bible provides reliable, credible answers.

MARK A. FINLEY

Pacific Press® Publishing Association
Nampa, Idaho
Oshawa, Ontario, Canada
www.pacificpress.com

Hart Research Center

Cover design by Gerald Lee Monks
Cover illustrations by Marcus Mashburn
Inside design by Kristin Hansen-Mellish
Inside illustrations by Marcus Mashburn

Additional copies of this book are available by calling toll-free 1-800-765-6955
or by visiting http://www.adventistbookcenter.com.

Library of Congress Cataloging-in-Publication Data:

Finley, Mark, 1945-
What the Bible says about : do you have questions about God and faith, life and death, the present and the future? : the Bible provides reliable, credible answers / Mark A. Finley.
p. cm.
ISBN 13: 978-0-8163-3403-2
ISBN 10: 0-8163-3403-X
1. Bible—Miscellanea. I. Title.
BS612.F49 2012
220.6—dc23

2012023585

13 14 15 16 • 5 4 3 2

Contents

What the Bible Says About

CHAPTER 1

What the Bible Says About Itself

The blazing Palestinian sun beat mercilessly down on a young Arab boy herding his few sheep in a remote area by the Dead Sea. It was just another ordinary day in his life. Each morning he led the sheep across the burning desert sands in search of a few morsels of food. He had no idea that this day would change the world.

When one of his sheep wandered away into a cave, he attempted to scare it out by throwing a stone into the cave. To his surprise, he heard the sound of breaking pottery. Thinking he had discovered some valuable hidden treasure, he raced home to tell his father. What they discovered in the cave that day was far more valuable than some ancient nobleman's riches. There, on the shores of the Dead Sea, in 1947, the Dead Sea Scrolls were discovered. The clay jars in the cave did contain a treasure. They contained the oldest Bible manuscript in existence. These scrolls were written by the Qumran community approximately 150 years before Christ. These people were called "Essenes." They spent hours hand copying the Bible. To ensure accuracy, their copying laws were extremely strict. Some of the world's most outstanding Bible scholars and specialists in the ancient biblical languages have pored over these manuscripts for decades. These ancient scrolls eloquently testify to the accuracy and reliability of the Bible. They contain every book in the Old Testament.

Down through the millenniums, God's Word has been accurately passed from one generation to the next. From the Bible's first book, Genesis, to its last, Revelation, it answers our deepest questions and speaks to our heart's deepest needs. The Bible was written over a span of fifteen hundred years by more than forty authors. Many of these authors did not know one another. They lived in different places, spoke different languages, and were products of different cultures, yet each one, writing under the inspiration of the Holy Spirit, clearly presents God's eternal plan for the human race. There is no contradiction on these main themes of Scripture. There is an amazing unity of thought throughout the Bible. There is an incredible unity of purpose throughout the pages of Scripture. The Bible reflects the thoughts of a divine mind. In three thousand places, the Bible writers declare "and God said," "and the Lord spoke," or similar phrases. The Bible writers believed they were inspired by God, and the internal evidence within Scripture reveals that the messages are of divine origin. Discoveries in archaeology and the fulfillment of numerous biblical prophecies reveal the truthfulness of Scripture.

The main purpose of the Bible is to unfold God's eternal plan of salvation. The Bible contains history, but it is not primarily a history book. The Bible touches on science, but it is not a scientific textbook. The Bible provides insights into the human mind, but it is not a treatise on psychology. Although God's Word touches on a variety of disciplines, it is first and foremost a revelation of God's will revealing God's eternal truths to the human race. The Bible answers the three great questions of life: "Why am I here?" "Where did I come from?" and "What does the future hold?" It provides hope and courage for each of us.

You may have had questions for years about God and faith, life and death, the present and the future. The Bible provides reliable, credible answers. *What the Bible Says About* is especially designed to provide you with the answers you are looking for. This volume is organized in a very simple way. It takes a single topic and explores what the Bible has to say about that topic. You may have questions, such as:

- If God is so good, why is the world so bad?
- Why is there so much suffering in the world?
- How can I live forever?
- What do Revelation's prophecies mean?
- How can I know my sins are forgiven?
- What did Jesus say about signs of the end?
- What happens after we die?
- What does Bible prophecy predict about the end of the world?

Or you may have a host of other questions. You will find Bible answers here. In each chapter, you will discover your questions answered directly by the Bible. These are not the opinions of men, but answers directly from God's Word. If you have never studied the Bible before, you will be amazed at how clear and powerful it is. No other book has such life-changing power. No other book so satisfies the mind and transforms the heart.

As you begin this journey of discovery, why not offer a simple prayer and ask God to give you understanding of His Word? The One who inspired the Bible will inspire you as you read it. This first chapter is titled "What the Bible Says About Itself." In it we will discover how God communicated to the human race through His Word and how to understand the Bible for ourselves. So let's begin.

01 How did God communicate His plan for the entire world through the centuries?

Before Adam and Eve sinned, God communicated with them directly. But after sin, He revealed His will through the biblical prophets in visions and dreams and by the direct impressions of the Holy Spirit. God moved upon the prophets' minds, and they wrote down what He showed them in vision or the thoughts He impressed upon them. The Bible is the authoritative revelation of God's will. It is God speaking to us through His Word.

"Prophecy never came by the will of man, but holy men of God spoke as they were moved by the Holy Spirit" **(2 PETER 1:21).**

"Hear now my words: If there be a prophet among you, I the LORD will make myself known unto him in a vision, and will speak unto him in a dream" **(NUMBERS 12:6, KJV).**

"And Moses said: 'By this you shall know that the LORD has sent me to do all these works, for I have not done them of my own will' " **(NUMBERS 16:28).**

The patriarch David said, "The Spirit of the LORD spoke by me, and His word was on my tongue" **(2 SAMUEL 23:2).**

"He [the Lord God] spoke by the mouth of His holy prophets, who have been since the world began" **(LUKE 1:70).**

"Surely the Lord GOD does nothing, unless He reveals His secret to His servants the prophets" **(AMOS 3:7).**

God spoke through His Holy Spirit and inspired the prophets to write down His messages. Although they recorded these messages in their own words, the message of the Bible comes directly from God. The Bible is God's Word.

02 Is the Bible really God's Word or is it merely a book written by men who were the product of their culture?

"All Scripture is given by inspiration of God, and is profitable for doctrine, for reproof, for correction, for instruction in righteousness" **(2 TIMOTHY 3:16).**

"For the word of God is living and powerful, and sharper than any two-edged sword, piercing even to the division of soul and spirit, and of joints and marrow, and is a discerner of the thoughts and intents of the heart" **(HEBREWS 4:12).**

"The Holy Scriptures . . . are able to make you wise for salvation through faith which is in Christ Jesus" **(2 TIMOTHY 3:15).**

"Jesus answered and said to them, 'Are you not therefore mistaken, because you do not know the Scriptures nor the power of God?' " **(MARK 12:24).**

"The grass withers, the flower fades, but the word of our God stands forever" **(ISAIAH 40:8).**

Both the Old and New Testaments are inspired by God. The Old Testament consists of the first thirty-nine books of the Bible from Genesis to Malachi. It reveals God's plan for His people before Jesus' birth. The New Testament, the last twenty-seven books of the Bible (from Matthew to Revelation), reveals the birth, life, death, and resurrection of Jesus. It especially describes God's instructions to His church today.

03 Can we really trust the Bible? Has it been changed through the centuries?

The great theme of the Bible is Jesus Christ. He is the great mountain peak of Scripture. All Scripture testifies of Jesus' love, grace, mercy, power, and desire to save us. He is the Bible's central figure.

"The words of the LORD are pure words, like silver tried in a furnace of earth, purified seven times. You shall keep them, O LORD, You shall *preserve* them from this generation forever" **(PSALM 12:6, 7; EMPHASIS SUPPLIED).**

"Who made heaven and earth, the sea, and all that is in them; who keeps [preserves] truth forever" **(PSALM 146:6).**

Jesus said, "The Scripture cannot be broken" **(JOHN 10:35).**

Peter said, "This Scripture had to be fulfilled, which the Holy Spirit spoke" **(ACTS 1:16).**

"The Jews have been entrusted with the very words of God" **(ROMANS 3:2, NIV).**

"Heaven and earth will pass away, but my words will never pass away" **(MATTHEW 24:35, NIV).**

The same Holy Spirit who inspired the Bible has preserved it throughout the centuries. Recent archaeological and historical discoveries have further confirmed its accuracy and reliability. God's Word is a safe, reliable guide.

04 What are God's purposes in giving us the Bible?

"Your word is a lamp to my feet and a light to my path" **(PSALM 119:105).**

"The entrance of Your words gives light; it gives understanding to the simple" **(PSALM 119:130).**

"Whatever things were written before were written for our learning, that we through the patience and comfort of the Scriptures might have hope" **(ROMANS 15:4).**

Paul told Timothy, "From childhood you have known the Holy Scriptures, which are able to make you wise for salvation through faith which is in Christ Jesus" **(2 TIMOTHY 3:15).**

God's Word is the clearest revelation of His eternal plan of salvation. Although nature, our conscience, and life's circumstances reveal God's workings, the Bible reveals His plans more clearly than any other source. It is God's authoritative word to us.

05 Isn't it easy to misunderstand the Bible? Are there keys to understanding and interpreting it correctly?

"Knowing this first, that no prophecy of Scripture is of any private interpretation" **(2 PETER 1:20).**

"You shall not add to the word which I command you, nor take from it" **(DEUTERONOMY 4:2).**

"Whatever I command you, be careful to observe it; you shall not add to it nor take away from it" **(DEUTERONOMY 12:32).**

"Do not add to His words, lest He rebuke you, and you be found a liar" **(PROVERBS 30:6).**

"I testify to everyone who hears the words of the prophecy of this book: If anyone adds to these things, God will add to him the plagues that are written in this book; and if anyone takes away from the words of the book of this prophecy, God shall take away his part from the Book of Life, from the holy city, and from the things which are written in this book" **(REVELATION 22:18, 19).**

To understand God's Word, it is essential to listen to all of His teaching on a given subject. We avoid "private" interpretation by letting the Bible explain itself. The Bible is its own interpreter. By allowing one passage of Scripture to explain another we discover God's interpretation. We cannot pick and choose what sections or passages of the Bible to accept or reject. If we want to understand the Bible, it is vital to approach it with honest hearts and minds willing to do what whatever God says.

06 Is truth a matter of personal opinion? What is the source of truth?

Praying to His Father, Jesus said, "Sanctify them by Your truth. Your word is truth" **(JOHN 17:17).**

"The entirety of Your word is truth" **(PSALM 119:160).**

"O Lord GOD, You are God, and Your words are true" **(2 SAMUEL 7:28).**

"It is impossible for God to lie" **(HEBREWS 6:18).**

We live "in hope of eternal life which *God, who cannot lie*, promised before time began" **(TITUS 1:2; EMPHASIS SUPPLIED).**

"O LORD, . . . all Your commandments are truth" **(PSALM 119:151).**

07 What did Jesus declare about truth?

Jesus declared, "I am the way, the truth, and the life" **(JOHN 14:6).**

Jesus said, "You shall know the truth, and the truth shall make you free" **(JOHN 8:32).**

From what did Jesus come to make us "free"? *From the shackles of sin and the prison house of false teachings.* The gospel prophet Isaiah predicted: "The Spirit of the Lord GOD is upon Me, because the LORD has anointed Me to preach good tidings to the poor; He has sent Me to heal the brokenhearted, *to proclaim liberty to the captives, and the opening of the prison to those who are bound*" **(ISAIAH 61:1; EMPHASIS SUPPLIED).**

LUKE 4:18–22 records that when the Lord Jesus read this verse from Isaiah in the house of worship and applied it to His ministry, His Jewish listeners were astonished, for they knew that this was the work of the promised Messiah—and that by reading this verse, Christ was thereby claiming to be the Messiah!

"I will walk at liberty, for I seek Your precepts" **(PSALM 119:45).**

"The Lord is the Spirit; and where the Spirit of the Lord is, there is liberty" **(2 CORINTHIANS 3:17).**

"Show me Your ways, O LORD; teach me Your paths. Lead me in Your truth and teach me, for You are the God of my salvation; on You I wait all the day. . . . Good and upright is the LORD; therefore He teaches sinners in the way. The humble He guides in justice, and the humble He teaches His way" **(PSALM 25:4–9).**

08 What attitude is essential in understanding Bible truth?

"If anyone wants to do His will, he shall know concerning the doctrine, whether it is from God or whether I speak on My own authority" **(JOHN 7:17).**

The Revised English Bible renders **JOHN 7:17** as: "*Whoever chooses to do the will of God* will know whether my teaching comes from him or is merely my own" **(EMPHASIS SUPPLIED).**

Those who want to do God's will "are those who, having heard the word with a noble and good heart, keep it and bear fruit with patience" **(LUKE 8:15).**

Wouldn't it be nice if these simple words could describe us—"He will teach us His ways, and we shall walk in His paths" **(MICAH 4:2)**?

"The humble He guides in justice, and *the humble He teaches His way*. . . . Who is *the man that fears the LORD*? Him shall He teach in the way He chooses" **(PSALM 25:9, 12; EMPHASIS SUPPLIED).**

An understanding of the Bible largely depends on a willingness to do whatever God requires. Bible study is not simply a mental exercise. It is a heart experience. If you are willing to do whatever God asks you in His Word, He will guide you into all truth.

09 Why do some people have difficulty discovering Bible truth?

Because our natures are fallen, "the heart is deceitful above all things, and desperately wicked" **(JEREMIAH 17:9).**

"All we like sheep have gone astray; we have turned, every one, to his own way; and the LORD has laid on Him the iniquity of us all" **(ISAIAH 53:6).**

"There is a way that seems right to a man, but its end is the way of death" **(PROVERBS 16:25).** This verse is repeated in the Bible in **PROVERBS 14:12.**

Some people who have a haughty, unreceptive attitude are "always learning and never able to come to the knowledge of the truth" **(2 TIMOTHY 3:7).**

"Therefore, as the Holy Spirit says: 'Today, if you will hear His voice, do not harden your hearts' " **(HEBREWS 3:7, 8).**

Understanding the Bible is difficult for some people because of their unwillingness to give up their own ideas. God invites us to seek His way, not our own. He invites us to turn from the pride of our own understanding to humble acceptance of His revealed will in His Word.

It is very important to study the Bible for yourself. You can't rely on what others tell you. God invites you to go on a personal discovery of truth from His Word.

10 What method of Bible study is especially helpful to keep us from misunderstanding the Bible and falling into error?

"Whom will he teach knowledge? And whom will he make to understand the message? Those just weaned from milk? Those just drawn from the breasts? For precept must be upon precept, precept upon precept, line upon line, line upon line, here a little, there a little" **(ISAIAH 28:9, 10).**

"These things we also speak, not in words which man's wisdom teaches but which the Holy Spirit teaches, comparing spiritual things with spiritual" **(1 CORINTHIANS 2:13).**

"But the natural man does not receive the things of the Spirit of God, for they are foolishness to him; nor can he know them, because they are spiritually discerned" **(1 CORINTHIANS 2:14).**

Paul testified, "My speech and my preaching were not with persuasive words of human wisdom, but in demonstration of the Spirit and of power, that your faith should not be in the wisdom of men but in the power of God" **(1 CORINTHIANS 2:4, 5).**

Let's suppose you are putting together a jigsaw puzzle. Do you come to a conclusion regarding what the finished picture will look like without looking at the original picture? Certainly not! It's the same with God's Word. God invites us to study all the texts on a given subject before coming to a conclusion regarding what the Bible teaches on a particular topic.

11 Whom did Jesus promise to send to guide us into truth? What promises did He give to ensure that we will be led into His truth as we study the Bible with an open mind and sincere heart?

"*When He, the Spirit of truth, has come, He will guide you into all truth;* for He will not speak on His own authority, but whatever He hears He will speak; and He will tell you things to come" **(JOHN 16:13; EMPHASIS SUPPLIED).**

"But the Helper, the Holy Spirit, whom the Father will send in My name, He will teach you all things, and bring to your remembrance all things that I said to you" **(JOHN 14:26).**

As the Holy Spirit leads us in our Bible study, interpreting line upon line and text after text, we will know the truth of God. God has not left us alone in our pursuit of truth. He has promised the Holy Spirit's guidance.

12 What is the main purpose for studying the Bible? Whom does the Bible reveal?

"You search the Scriptures, for in them you think you have eternal life; and these are they which testify of Me" **(JOHN 5:39).**

"Philip found Nathanael and said to him, 'We have found Him of whom Moses in the law, and also the prophets, wrote—Jesus of Nazareth, the son of Joseph' " **(JOHN 1:45).**

"Beginning at Moses and all the Prophets, He [Christ] expounded to them in all the Scriptures the things concerning Himself. . . . Then He said to them, . . . 'All things must be fulfilled which were written in the Law of Moses and the Prophets and the Psalms concerning Me' " **(LUKE 24:27, 44).**

The apostle Paul stood before King Agrippa, "saying no other things than those which the prophets and Moses said would come—that the Christ would suffer, that He would be the first to rise from the dead, and would proclaim light to the Jewish people and to the Gentiles" **(ACTS 26:22, 23).**

13 As we study the precious promises of God's Word, what impact will they have on our lives?

"His divine power has given to us all things that pertain to life and godliness, through the knowledge of Him who called us by glory and virtue, by which have been given to us exceedingly great and precious promises, that through these you may be partakers of the divine nature, having escaped the corruption that is in the world through lust" **(2 PETER 1:3, 4).**

"We may be partakers of His holiness" **(HEBREWS 12:10).**

"We all, with unveiled face, beholding as in a mirror the glory of the Lord, are being transformed into the same image from glory to glory, just as by the Spirit of the Lord" **(2 CORINTHIANS 3:18).**

The apostle Paul urges us to "be renewed in the spirit of your mind, and that you put on the new man which was created according to God, in true righteousness and holiness" **(EPHESIANS 4:23, 24).**

"As many as received Him [Jesus], to them He gave the right to become children of God, to those who believe in His name" **(JOHN 1:12).**

The Scriptures testify or bear witness of Jesus. As we study the Bible, the power of the living Christ will transform us. Open your mind to God's Word. Allow the Holy Spirit to teach you through the pages of Scripture. Let God guide you in a deeper understanding of His truth. As you do, your life will be changed.

The most important directions in life involve getting from earth to heaven.

CHAPTER 2

What the Bible Says About the Future

Surveys regarding people's confidence in the future reveal a great concern. Unprecedented natural disasters, conflict in the Middle East, financial uncertainty, international terrorism, and the instability of numerous governments around the world have millions of people worried about the future. What does the future hold? Is some great catastrophe coming soon upon this world? Will the future usher in a new world order of peace? Or will it bring destruction, devastation, and disaster to our planet?

Bible prophecy reveals that God is in ultimate control of the future. Although many things happen that are not in harmony with His will, He will soon right every wrong and establish His everlasting kingdom. Throughout history, the Bible's predictions of the future have proven reliable. Bible prophets have accurately foretold future events. The predictions of the book of Daniel give us courage for our times. They have been amazingly accurate for the last twenty-five hundred years. They speak with particular meaning to a twenty-first-century generation. They reveal God is in charge of history.

In this chapter, we will explore together Daniel's inspired outline of world history. But before we actually turn to the book of Daniel, we need to discover a few things about Bible prophecy.

01 According to the Bible, who only can reveal the future?

"Remember the former things of old, for I am God, and there is no other; I am God, and there is none like Me, declaring the end from the beginning, and from ancient times things that are not yet done, saying, 'My counsel shall stand, and I will do all My pleasure' " **(ISAIAH 46:9, 10).**

"Blessed be the name of God forever and ever, for wisdom and might are His. And He changes the time and the seasons; He removes kings and raises up kings; He gives wisdom to the wise and knowledge to those who have understanding. He reveals deep and secret things; He knows what is in the darkness, and light dwells with Him" **(DANIEL 2:20–22).**

The great God who holds the future in His hand, who knows that omniscience is an acid test of divinity, boldly challenges the false, pagan gods of wood and stone to "show us what will happen; . . . or declare to us things to come. Show the things that are to come hereafter, that we may know that you are gods" **(ISAIAH 41:22, 23).**

"Known to God from eternity are all His works" **(ACTS 15:18).**

The true God is able to "utter things kept secret from the foundation of the world" **(MATTHEW 13:35).**

In contrast to all false gods, God knows "the end from the beginning." He alone has the ability to consistently reveal the future.

02 What is God's method of revealing the future?

"Surely the Lord God does nothing, unless He reveals His secret to His servants the prophets" **(AMOS 3:7).**

"Holy men of God spoke as they were moved by the Holy Spirit" **(2 PETER 1:21).**

"Hear now My words: If there is a prophet among you, I, the LORD, make Myself known to him in a vision; I speak to him in a dream" **(NUMBERS 12:6).**

"And Moses said: 'By this you shall know that the LORD has sent me to do all these works, for I have not done them of my own will' " **(NUMBERS 16:28).**

The patriarch David said, "The Spirit of the LORD spoke by me, and His word was on my tongue" **(2 SAMUEL 23:2).**

"He [the Lord God] spoke by the mouth of His holy prophets, who have been since the world began" **(LUKE 1:70).**

God has the ability to look into the future and foretell what is going to take place centuries before the events come to pass. He revealed the mysteries of the future to the Bible prophets. These Bible prophets share God's messages of the future with us. As we see these prophecies fulfilled, our faith in God increases. One of the Bible's most significant prophecies regarding the future is found in Daniel 2.

03 How did God reveal the destiny of this world to the king of Babylon?

"Now in the second year of Nebuchadnezzar's reign, Nebuchadnezzar had dreams; and his spirit was so troubled that his sleep left him" **(DANIEL 2:1).**

"I saw a dream which made me afraid, and the thoughts on my bed and the visions of my head troubled me" **(DANIEL 4:5).**

Nebuchadnezzar had a dream of great significance, but when he woke up the next morning he couldn't remember it. He was greatly troubled. We all have had similar experiences but this dream had divine consequences.

04 How did Nebuchadnezzar, the Babylonian king, attempt to discover the dream and its meaning?

"Then the king gave the command to call the magicians, the astrologers, the sorcerers, and the Chaldeans to tell the king his dreams. So they came and stood before the king. And the king said to them, 'I have had a dream, and my spirit is anxious to know the dream' " **(DANIEL 2:2, 3).**

"Therefore I issued a decree to bring in all the wise men of Babylon before me, that they might make known to me the interpretation of the dream" **(DANIEL 4:6).**

Throughout the Bible God gave dreams at particular times to communicate His will.

In Genesis 40, Pharaoh's butler and baker had dreams that Joseph interpreted. God also gave dreams to Mary's husband, Joseph, to flee with Mary and Jesus to Egypt because Herod would attempt to kill the infant Jesus. John received dreams of the future on the island of Patmos. These are just a few examples of God using dreams to communicate His will.

Miraculously, God hid this dream from Nebuchadnezzar's mind. If the king could have remembered the dream, the psychics would have been able to make up a plausible interpretation. But the wise men of Babylon utterly failed to tell the king what he had dreamed.

05 When the wisest men in his kingdom could not reveal the king's dream, what did Nebuchadnezzar do?

"For this reason the king was angry and very furious, and gave a command to destroy all the wise men of Babylon. So the decree went out, and they began killing the wise men; and they sought Daniel and his companions, to kill them" **(DANIEL 2:12, 13).**

Daniel and his companions were counted among the so-called wise men in the king's court. In those days, the king held in his hands the absolute power of life and death. (**SEE DANIEL 3:19, 20,** which tells of Shadrach, Meshach, and Abed-Nego being cast into a fiery furnace, and **DANIEL 6:6–16,** which tells of Daniel being cast into a den of lions.)

The angry king condemned all the wise men of Babylon to death when they could not tell him what he had dreamed. Daniel was a Hebrew captive in the king's court and educated in the "University of Babylon." He, too, was considered one of Babylon's wise men.

06 How did Daniel respond?

"So Daniel went in and asked the king to give him time, that he might tell the king the interpretation. Then Daniel went to his house, and made the decision known to Hananiah, Mishael, and Azariah, his companions, that they might seek mercies from the God of heaven concerning this secret, so that Daniel and his companions might not perish with the rest of the wise men of Babylon" **(DANIEL 2:16–18).**

In this crisis, Daniel and his companions fervently prayed to God, as did Queen Esther and her people in the crisis of her day. **(SEE ESTHER 4:13–17.)**

"Call upon Me in the day of trouble; I will deliver you, and you shall glorify Me" **(PSALM 50:15).**

"He [the believer who prays in fervent faith] shall call upon Me, and I will answer him; I will be with him in trouble; I will deliver him and honor him" **(PSALM 91:15).**

Just as Jeremiah heeded God's command to "call to Me, and I will answer you, and show you great and mighty things, which you do not know" **(JEREMIAH 33:3),** Daniel's companions earnestly sought God as well. They followed David's example: "I waited patiently for the Lord; and He inclined to me, and heard my cry" **(PSALM 40:1).**

07 How did God answer Daniel's prayer? What does this teach us about answers to our own prayers?

"Then the secret was revealed to Daniel in a night vision. So Daniel blessed the God of heaven" **(DANIEL 2:19).**

God caused the king to forget his dream, because if the king had told his "wise men" his dream, they could have made up a meaning or interpretation. Any dream you have, just tell me, and I'll tell you what it means! I may not know, but I can guess, right? Anyone can guess. Psychics can guess; astrologers can guess; fortune-tellers can guess. But God doesn't need to guess—God knows. If the king's astrologers and magicians couldn't tell him what he had dreamed a few hours before, how could they possibly tell him what the dream meant twenty-five hundred years in the future? So the king realized they were impostors and prepared to execute them. But the dream was revealed to Daniel, who sought "mercies from the God of heaven concerning this secret, so that . . . [he] and his companions might not perish with the rest of the wise men of Babylon" **(DANIEL 2:18).**

GOD PROMISES TO ANSWER OUR PRAYERS TOO

"Call to Me, and I will answer you, and show you great and mighty things, which you do not know" **(JEREMIAH 33:3).**

"The righteous cry out, and the LORD hears, and delivers them out of all their troubles" **(PSALM 34:17).**

"Evening and morning and at noon I will pray, and cry aloud, and He shall hear my voice" **(PSALM 55:17).**

"Cast your burden on the LORD, and He shall sustain you; He shall never permit the righteous to be moved" **(PSALM 55:22).**

08 According to Daniel's own testimony, who revealed the dream to him?

"There is a God in heaven who reveals secrets" **(DANIEL 2:28).**

Daniel didn't say, "King Nebuchadnezzar, there might be a God up there." He didn't say, "King Nebuchadnezzar, perhaps there may be a God up there." He said with assurance: "There is a God in heaven." And He's in control of this world.

Furthermore, Daniel's reply shows his humble, honest character. As the human instrument of God, he took no credit for himself, but gave all the glory to the God of heaven.

"The king answered Daniel, and said, 'Truly your God is the God of gods, the Lord of kings, and a revealer of secrets, since you could reveal this secret' " **(DANIEL 2:47).**

In an earlier incident, Pharaoh's butler and baker said to Joseph, " 'We each have had a dream, and there is no interpreter of it.' So Joseph said to them, 'Do not interpretations belong to God?' " **(GENESIS 40:8).**

"Then Pharaoh said to Joseph, 'I had a dream last night, and no one here can tell me what it means. But I have heard that when you hear about a dream you can interpret it.'

'It is beyond my power to do this,' Joseph replied. 'But God can tell you what it means and set you at ease' " **(GENESIS 41:15, 16, NLT).**

Joseph exhibited the same humility shown by Daniel. He rightly gave all the praise and honor to God.

Remember, the prophet Isaiah said that God is the only One who knows all things. The God of the universe is the only One who can reveal the future. **(SEE ISAIAH 46:9, 10.)**

09 To what period of time does Nebuchadnezzar's dream especially apply?

"He [God] has made known to King Nebuchadnezzar what will be in the latter days. Your dream, and the visions of your head upon your bed, were these" **(DANIEL 2:28).**

Other modern translations are more clear. Instead of the phrase, "in the latter days," the New International Version reads, "in days to come." The New Revised Standard Version reads, "at the end of days." The New Living Translation plainly states, "in the future."

The book of Daniel especially reveals events in the last days of earth's history. The king's dream focuses on the end times. It foretells events that occur at the close of this earth's history.

10 How did Daniel describe King Nebuchadnezzar's dream?

"You, O king, were watching; and behold, a great image! This great image, whose splendor was excellent, stood before you; and its form was awesome. This image's head was of fine gold, its chest and arms of silver, its belly and thighs of bronze, its legs of iron, its feet partly of iron and partly of clay. You watched while a stone was cut out without hands, which struck the image on its feet of iron and clay, and broke them in pieces. Then the iron, the clay, the bronze, the silver, and the gold were crushed together, and became like chaff from the summer threshing floors; the wind carried them away so that no trace of them was found. And the stone that struck the image became a great mountain and filled the whole earth" **(DANIEL 2:31–35).**

11 What explanation of the dream did Daniel give the king?

"Wherever the children of men dwell, or the beasts of the field and the birds of the heaven, He has given them into your hand, and has made you ruler over them all—you are this head of gold. But after you shall arise another kingdom inferior to yours; then another, a third kingdom of bronze, which shall rule over all the earth. And the fourth kingdom shall be as strong as iron, inasmuch as iron breaks in pieces and shatters everything; and like iron that crushes, that kingdom will break in pieces and crush all the others" **(DANIEL 2:38–40).**

The four metals in the image represent four "kingdoms"—three of these world empires were yet future in Daniel's day. Compare this modern version of these same verses: "He has made you the ruler over all the inhabited world and has put even the wild animals and birds under your control. You are the head of gold. But after your kingdom comes to an end, another kingdom, inferior to yours, will rise to take your place. After that kingdom has fallen, yet a third kingdom, represented by bronze, will rise to rule the world. Following that kingdom, there will be a fourth one, as strong as iron. That kingdom will smash and crush all previous empires, just as iron smashes and crushes everything it strikes" **(DANIEL 2:38–40, NLT).**

According to Daniel's interpretation of Nebuchadnezzar's dream, each metal represents a corresponding kingdom that would rule the world. Beginning with Babylon, the prophet traces the destiny of the nations through the centuries.

12 Here are the metals that made up the image the king saw in his dream.

Head .... Fine Gold

Breast and arms .... Silver

Belly and thighs................. Bronze

Legs............................... Iron

Feet ....Part Iron/Part Clay

"This image's head was of fine gold, its chest and arms of silver, its belly and thighs of bronze, its legs of iron, its feet partly of iron and partly of clay" **(DANIEL 2:32, 33).**

IDENTIFYING THE KINGDOM

13 Whom does the Bible identify as the head of gold? What kingdom does this head of gold represent?

"Wherever the children of men dwell, or the beasts of the field and the birds of the heaven, He [God] has given them into your hand, and has made you ruler over them all—you are this head of gold" **(DANIEL 2:38).**

"You, O king, are a king of kings. For the God of heaven has given you a kingdom, power, strength, and glory" **(DANIEL 2:37).**

Daniel, under his Babylonian name, "Belteshazzar" **(SEE DANIEL 1:7; 10:1)**, told Nebuchadnezzar, "It is you, O king, who have grown and become strong; for your greatness has grown and reaches to the heavens, and your dominion to the end of the earth" **(DANIEL 4:22).**

The Babylonian monarchy, over which Nebuchadnezzar was the only king of note, at one time extended throughout Chaldea, Assyria, Arabia, Mesopotamia, Palestine, Syria, Egypt, and Libya. Babylon was the dominant world empire from 605 B.C. until 538 B.C. Gold was a fitting symbol of Babylon. It was lavishly used in Bel Marduk's temple. Bel Marduk was the chief god of Babylon. He sat in a golden temple, on a golden throne, before a golden table by a golden candlestick.

14 In the image, what metal followed gold? What kingdom would arise next? What nation conquered Babylon?

"But after you shall arise another kingdom inferior to yours; then another, a third kingdom of bronze, which shall rule over all the earth" **(DANIEL 2:39).**

"Your kingdom has been divided, and given to the Medes and Persians" **(DANIEL 5:28).**

The Medes and Persians overthrew the Babylonians in 539 B.C. Under the leadership of the Persian king, Cyrus, they ruled from 539 B.C. to 331 B.C. Both of these empires were dominant world powers that aggressively oppressed God's ancient people.

15 What metal followed silver? What kingdom would overthrow the Medes and Persians?

"Then another, a third kingdom of bronze, which shall rule over all the earth" **(DANIEL 2:39).**

The nation of Greece overthrew the Medes and the Persians in 331 B.C. The prophet Daniel describes the Greeks in two ways. First, as the bronze kingdom in the image of Daniel 2. The Greeks were known for their bronze-plated armor. Second, in chapter 8, the prophet describes a fierce battle between a ram and a he-goat. There he clearly identifies Greece as the goat that tramples down Media-Persia, the ram.

16 How is the fourth dominant world power described?

"And the fourth kingdom shall be as strong as iron, inasmuch as iron breaks in pieces and shatters everything; and like iron that crushes, that kingdom will break in pieces and crush all the others" **(DANIEL 2:40).**

The Bible testifies—and history verifies—that one by one, the empires of Babylon, Media-Persia, and Greece passed from the scene and were finally succeeded by the Roman Empire. So inescapably did Daniel's prophetic portrayal match its historical fulfillment that the great English historian Edward Gibbon, though not a Christian or Bible believer himself, used scriptural language in his monumental *History of the Decline and Fall of the Roman Empire* when he wrote: "The images of gold, of silver, of brass, that might serve to represent the nations and their kings, were successively broken by the IRON monarchy of Rome" ([London: Methuen & Co., 1898], vol. 4, chap. 38; general observations at the end of the chapter, para. 1, p. 161).

The complementary, parallel prophecies in chapters 2 and 7 of Daniel's wonderful book have long been recognized as confirmed by later historical events. For instance, the ecclesiastical writer Hippolytus, who was killed as a martyr in A.D. 235, wrote: "The golden head of the image and the lioness denoted the Babylonians; the shoulders and arms of silver, and the bear, represented the Persians and Medes; the belly and thighs of brass, and the leopard, meant the Greeks, who held sovereignty from Alexander's time; the legs of iron, and the beast dreadful and terrible, expressed the Romans, who hold sovereignty at present; the toes of the feet which were part clay and part iron, and the ten horns, were emblems of the kingdoms that are to rise; the other little horn that grows up among them meant the Antichrist in their midst; the stone that smites the earth and brings judgment upon the earth was Christ. . . . Rejoice, blessed Daniel! thou hast not been in error; all these things have come to pass. . . . Already the iron rules; . . . already we see these things ourselves. Now we glorify God, being instructed by thee" (Hippolytus, *Treatise on Christ and Antichrist,* sect. 28, 32, 33, translated in *Ante-Nicene Fathers,* vol. 5, p. 201).

The Roman Empire conquered the Greeks in 168 B.C. The Romans ruled the world during the time of Christ.

17 According to the king's dream, what significant events would occur next? Would a fifth world-ruling empire arise to overthrow Rome?

"Whereas you saw the feet and toes, partly of potter's clay and partly of iron, the kingdom shall be divided; yet the strength of the iron shall be in it, just as you saw the iron mixed with ceramic clay" **(DANIEL 2:41).**

"The kingdom shall be divided," says the pen of inspiration. The mighty Roman Empire was to disintegrate into smaller kingdoms symbolized not only by the ten toes of **DANIEL 2:41, 42,** but also by the "ten horns" of **DANIEL 7:7, 24**—and it did! True to God's Word, those nations of modern Europe remain "divided"—separate but adjacent, like the ten toes of the feet.

The prophet Daniel predicted that the Roman Empire would be divided. The breakup of the empire occurred from A.D. 351 to A.D. 476. Daniel continued, "But they will not adhere to one another" **(2:43).** History has followed this prophecy like a blueprint. Dictators and rulers have attempted to unite Europe through the centuries, but have absolutely failed. The Roman Empire was divided. The divisions of the empire into the eastern and western sections formed the foundation of the nations located in Europe today.

18 Will the nations of Europe ever be united into one cohesive, enduring political unit again?

"And as the toes of the feet were partly of iron and partly of clay, so the kingdom shall be partly strong and partly fragile. As you saw iron mixed with ceramic clay, they will mingle with the seed of men; but they will not adhere to one another, just as iron does not mix with clay" **(DANIEL 2:42, 43).**

The nations of modern Europe vary in their economic strength and military might. They are "partly strong and partly fragile" **(VERSE 42)**, just as the Bible says.

"They will mingle with the seed of men" **(VERSE 43)**. What does that mean? Intermarriage. Mingling the seed of one royal throne with the seed of another royal throne. So the king of France married the heir-apparent, or queen, of Austria. The king of England intermarried with the royal family of Spain. Queen Victoria, with more truth than poetry, was sometimes called "the Grandmother of Europe." By the early part of the twentieth century, it was said that all the European royal families were related to one another by intermarriage. They had "mingled their seed" in an attempt to unite Europe. But all those attempts were doomed to failure, for God says, "they will not adhere to one another, just as iron does not mix with clay" **(VERSE 43).**

It's a mistake for some to teach that there will be "a revived Roman Empire." Heaven knows men have tried to weld those "iron-clay" nations into a superstate. Some have tried by intermarriage, as mentioned above. Statesmen have also tried, using such diplomatic means as the League of Nations and the United Nations. Then, too, tyrants and dictators have resorted to military might to achieve that end. Charlemagne tried it around A.D. 800; Charles V, about 1500; Napoleon Bonaparte, about 1800. Kaiser Wilhelm II's attempt led to World War I, and Adolf Hitler's led to World War II. But all these attempts failed miserably. "All the king's horses and all the king's men" couldn't put the Roman Empire back together again. God's Word still stands regarding the nations: "They will not adhere to one another" **(VERSE 43)**. The European Common Market has not been successful in bringing unity among its member states. Europe is still divided by language, culture, politics, and ideals.

Oppression of God's people does not last forever. Although the Roman Empire lasted longer than any prior empire—no small feat in and of itself—God saw that oppressive regimes would ultimately collapse. God's Word is clear. These seven prophetic words, "They will not adhere to one another," have stopped every would-be conqueror of Europe through the centuries. Throughout history, political leaders such as Charlemagne, Charles V, Louis XIV, Napoleon, Hitler, and Stalin have attempted to dominate by uniting Europe. Each has desperately failed. Communism stretched its tentacles across Europe. One nation after another fell into its grasp. But communism failed. The Berlin Wall came down. Freedom triumphed! Bible prophecy is accurate. The future is in God's hands. He can be safely trusted. He will guide us safely into the twenty-first century.

19 According to God's revelation to Daniel in this prophecy, what is the next great event on history's horizon?

"And in the days of these kings the God of heaven will set up a kingdom which shall never be destroyed; and the kingdom shall not be left to other people; it shall break in pieces and consume all these kingdoms, and it shall stand forever. Inasmuch as you saw that the stone was cut out of the mountain without hands, and that it broke in pieces the iron, the bronze, the clay, the silver, and the gold—the great God has made known to the king what will come to pass after this. The dream is certain, and its interpretation is sure" **(DANIEL 2:44, 45).**

Inspiration says, "In the days of these kings the God of heaven will set up a kingdom"—His eternal kingdom. In the days of which kings? The kings, or leaders, of the nations of modern Europe. Today democratic societies often call their leaders "president" or "prime minister," although a few kings or queens are still around. But the take-home message from this lesson is that we—you and I—are living in the days of those very nations. We're living not just in the toes, but in the very toenails of the image in Nebuchadnezzar's dream! Divine prophecy is shouting at us: "In the days of these kings [in the days of a "divided" empire, when misguided men try but fail to reunite Europe politically by conquest or economically by the European Common Market], the God of heaven will set up a kingdom which shall never be destroyed." How do we know? Because "the dream is certain, and its interpretation is sure" **(VERSE 45).**

Along with the Bible prophets and apostles, we can look forward to the "blessed hope and the glorious appearing of our great God and Savior Jesus Christ" **(TITUS 2:13).**

The rock that struck the image on its feet represents the coming kingdom of God. Soon all wickedness, evil, and rebellion will be gone forever. The forces of evil will be crushed, destroyed, and broken in pieces. God will establish His everlasting kingdom forever. You can face the future with confidence. The twenty-first century is bright with the promises of God. The future is in His hands. Hope is on the way.

Throughout history the Bible has proven its accuracy in predicting the future.

CHAPTER 3

What the Bible Says About Signs of the End

World conditions are uncertain! Political leaders are seeking answers to some of the greatest problems society has ever faced. The future is cloudy for many. Our global problems defy human solutions. The stock market rises and falls at the whim of the investors. The interdependent world economy is on shaky ground. Moral conditions are rapidly deteriorating. School violence is rampant. Weather patterns seem out of control. World hunger is increasing. Tens of thousands of refugees cross international borders seeking a safe sanctuary. People everywhere are asking, "What do these things mean?" The Bible presents an answer. There is help on the way. There is hope on the horizon.

The second coming of Christ is one of the Bible's most important truths. It is mentioned 250 times in the New Testament alone—once in every twenty-five verses. The second coming of Christ has encouraged Christians through the centuries. For every prophecy in the Old Testament about the first coming of Christ, there are eight on His second coming.

In Matthew's Gospel, Christ clearly indicated the signs that would precede His return. Looking at the temple in Jerusalem, He declared, "See! Your house is left to you desolate" **(MATTHEW 23:38).** Jesus then predicted, "Not one stone shall be left here upon another, that shall not be thrown down" **(MATTHEW 24:2).** The disciples thought that an event as cataclysmic as the destruction of the temple at Jerusalem must be the end of the world. In a magnificent prophecy, Jesus answered their questions about the destruction of Jerusalem and also about the end of the world.

01 When Jesus described the destruction of Jerusalem to His disciples, what questions did they ask Him?

"Now as He sat on the Mount of Olives, the disciples came to Him privately, saying, 'Tell us, when will these things be? And what will be the sign of Your coming, and of the end of the age?' " **(MATTHEW 24:3).**

The disciples actually asked two questions: (1) "When will these things be?"—that is, "When will Jerusalem be destroyed?" (2) "What will be the sign of Your coming and the end of the world?" In His answer, Jesus blended these two events. Events that led up to the destruction of Jerusalem by Titus in A.D. 70 mirrored events that would occur on a larger, grander scale just before the return of our Lord.

02 Does the Bible reveal the exact time and day of Christ's coming? What does it teach about the timing of Jesus' coming? Can we know anything about the time He will come or is it all a mystery?

"But of that day and hour no one knows, not even the angels of heaven, but My Father only" **(MATTHEW 24:36).**

"Watch therefore, for you know neither the day nor the hour in which the Son of Man is coming" **(MATTHEW 25:13).**

"But of that day and hour no one knows, not even the angels in heaven, nor the Son, but only the Father. Take heed, watch and pray; for you do not know when the time is" **(MARK 13:32, 33).**

"And He said to them, 'It is not for you to know times or seasons which the Father has put in His own authority' " **(ACTS 1:7).**

"Therefore you also be ready, for the Son of Man is coming at an hour you do not expect" **(LUKE 12:40).**

In His mercy, God has not revealed the exact time of His second coming. Think of the despair of early Christians if they had thought Christ's coming was hundreds of years in the future. Anyone who claims to know just when Christ will return is teaching falsehood.

03 How can we prepare for the return of our Lord if we don't know when it will happen?

"Watch therefore, and pray always that you may be counted worthy to escape all these things that will come to pass, and to stand before the Son of Man" **(LUKE 21:36).**

"Therefore let us not sleep, as others do, but let us watch and be sober" **(1 THESSALONIANS 5:6).**

"But the end of all things is at hand; therefore be serious and watchful in your prayers" **(1 PETER 4:7).**

Give glory "to Him who is able to keep you from stumbling, and to present you faultless before the presence of His glory with exceeding joy" **(JUDE 24).**

"And now, little children, abide in Him, that when He appears, we may have confidence and not be ashamed before Him at His coming" **(1 JOHN 2:28).**

Our Lord advises us to "watch" and "pray," or be ready at all times. The great evangelist Dwight L. Moody, in his book *The Second Coming of Christ,* wrote, "The proper attitude of a Christian is to be always looking for his Lord's return" (p. 9). Christ's counsel is to live in a state of expectation. Live your life with a sense of the nearness of the Second Coming.

04 We may not know the exact time of Jesus' coming, but is it possible to know that the end is near?

"When it is evening you say, 'It will be fair weather, for the sky is red'; and in the morning, 'It will be foul weather today, for the sky is red and threatening.' Hypocrites! You know how to discern the face of the sky, but you cannot discern the signs of the times" **(MATTHEW 16:2, 3).**

"Now learn this parable from the fig tree: When its branch has already become tender and puts forth leaves, you know that summer is near. So you also, when you see all these things, know that it [the end] is near—at the doors!" **(MATTHEW 24:32, 33).**

"Then He spoke to them a parable: 'Look at the fig tree, and all the trees. When they are already budding, you see and know for yourselves that summer is now near. So you also, when you see these things happening, know that the kingdom of God is near' " **(LUKE 21:29–31).**

"But concerning the times and the seasons, brethren, you have no need that I should write to you. For you yourselves know perfectly that the day of the Lord so comes as a thief in the night. . . . But you, brethren, are not in darkness, so that this Day should overtake you as a thief" **(1 THESSALONIANS 5:1, 2, 4).**

"For yet a little while, and He who is coming will come and will not tarry" **(HEBREWS 10:37).**

The signs Jesus gave do not reveal He is here. They tell us He is near. A good farmer knows that summer will produce a harvest. He watches the crop carefully. Growing plants, opening buds, ripening fruit all indicate harvest time is near. Jesus' end-time signs in **MATTHEW 24** clearly reveal a ripening harvest. The darkening sky reveals a storm is coming. The darkening horizon of this world reveals troublous times ahead, but beyond the dark clouds is a ray of hope. Jesus is coming!

05 What amazing signs in the religious world indicate Jesus' coming is drawing near?

"For many will come in My name, saying, 'I am the Christ,' and will deceive many. . . . Then many false prophets will rise up and deceive many. . . . For false christs and false prophets will rise and show great signs and wonders to deceive, if possible, even the elect" **(MATTHEW 24:5, 11, 24).**

"And the LORD said to me, 'The prophets prophesy lies in My name. I have not sent them, commanded them, nor spoken to them; they prophesy to you a false vision, divination, a worthless thing, and the deceit of their heart' " **(JEREMIAH 14:14).**

False prophets have troubled God's people through the centuries. Jesus predicted that their numbers would increase just before the end.

"For some time ago Theudas rose up, claiming to be somebody. A number of men, about four hundred, joined him. He was slain, and all who obeyed him were scattered and came to nothing. After this man, Judas of Galilee rose up in the days of the census, and drew away many people after him. He also perished, and all who obeyed him were dispersed" **(ACTS 5:36, 37).**

"But there was a certain man called Simon, who previously practiced sorcery in the city and astonished the people of Samaria, claiming that he was someone great, to whom they all gave heed, from the least to the greatest, saying, 'This man is the great power of God' " **(ACTS 8:9, 10).**

"I have come in My Father's name, and you do not receive Me; if another comes in his own name, him you will receive" **(JOHN 5:43).**

As the end approaches, the devil will double his efforts to deceive. Millions will turn to counterfeit sources of truth. Falsehood will abound. Lies will be accepted as truth. False religious leaders will deceive. The occult and astrology will capture the imagination of gullible people who are looking for answers to life's deepest questions. The New Age movement, with its subtle deceptions, will lead many from God's Word. Interest in cults and false religions will explode.

06 What prediction did Jesus make regarding international conflicts, political upheaval, and war?

"And you will hear of wars and rumors of wars. See that you are not troubled; for all these things must come to pass, but the end is not yet. For nation will rise against nation, and kingdom against kingdom" **(MATTHEW 24:6, 7).**

"But when you hear of wars and commotions, do not be terrified; for these things must come to pass first, but the end will not come immediately" **(LUKE 21:9).**

Wars have occurred throughout history. There is nothing special about a single war. Jesus is not speaking here about an individual war. He is speaking about *wars*—nation rising against nation and kingdom against kingdom. The twentieth century has witnessed the horrors of World War I and World War II. The Korean War, the Vietnam War, the Indochina War, the Iran-Iraq War, Kuwait, the Balkans, Iraq, and tribal battles too numerous to mention. In the twenty-first century, we continue to experience political conflicts in Iraq, Afghanistan, and throughout Africa. Each of these speaks eloquently of the fulfillment of Christ's words.

07 How does the Bible describe the unprecedented dangerous situation among the nations of the world prior to the return of Christ?

"The nations were angry, and Your wrath has come, and the time of the dead, that they should be judged, and that You should reward Your servants the prophets and the saints, and those who fear Your name, small and great, and should destroy those who destroy the earth" **(REVELATION 11:18).**

"And there will be . . . on the earth distress of nations, with perplexity, the sea and the waves roaring; men's hearts failing them from fear and the expectation of those things which are coming on the earth, for the powers of the heavens will be shaken. Then they will see the Son of Man coming in a cloud with power and great glory" **(LUKE 21:25–27).**

"Proclaim this among the nations: 'Prepare for war! Wake up the mighty men, let all the men of war draw near, let them come up. Beat your plowshares into swords and your pruning hooks into spears; let the weak say, "I am strong." ' Assemble and come, all you nations, and gather together all around.

Cause Your mighty ones to go down there, O LORD. 'Let the nations be wakened, and come up to the Valley of Jehoshaphat; for there I will sit to judge all the surrounding nations. Put in the sickle, for the harvest is ripe. Come, go down; for the winepress is full, the vats overflow—for their wickedness is great.' Multitudes, multitudes in the valley of decision! For the day of the Lord is near in the valley of decision" **(JOEL 3:9–14).**

Jesus will come at a time when the human race has the ability to destroy all life on planet Earth. With nuclear weapons, we now have the capacity for self-destruction. This is certainly one of the greatest signs of the return of Jesus. Broadcasting from Hiroshima in 1945 after the atomic bomb was dropped, William Ripley stated, "I am standing on the place where the end of the world began." The problem is that more and more nations are quietly building their nuclear arsenals. The nuclear secrets have been unlocked, and there is no way to totally prevent these weapons from getting into the wrong hands. Our hope is anchored in Jesus' promise, "I will come again" **(JOHN 14:3).**

08 In spite of the buildup of thermonuclear weaponry, what will the nations be saying in the last days?

"For when they say, 'Peace and safety!' then sudden destruction comes upon them, as labor pains upon a pregnant woman. And they shall not escape" **(1 THESSALONIANS 5:3).**

" 'Come,' one says, 'I will bring wine, and we will fill ourselves with intoxicating drink; tomorrow will be as today, and much more abundant' " **(ISAIAH 56:12).**

"In the measure that she glorified herself and lived luxuriously, in the same measure give her torment and sorrow; for she says in her heart, 'I sit as queen, and am no widow, and will not see sorrow' " **(REVELATION 18:7).**

09 What signs will occur in nature and our environment before the coming of Christ?

"And there will be signs in the sun, in the moon, and in the stars; and on the earth distress of nations, with perplexity, the sea and the waves roaring; men's hearts failing them from fear and the expectation of those things which are coming on the earth, for the powers of the heavens will be shaken. Then they will see the Son of Man coming in a cloud with power and great glory" **(LUKE 21:25–27).**

Jesus predicted, "There will be famines, pestilences, and earthquakes in various places" **(MATTHEW 24:7).**

"There will be earthquakes in various places, and there will be famines and troubles. These are the beginnings of sorrows" **(MARK 13:8).**

Due to crop failure, the politics of greed, growing population, and food distribution problems, world famine is still a major problem. Ten thousand people a day, or more than 3.5 million per year, die of starvation. In the past hundred years there have been 1.5 million fatalities from earthquakes alone. Thousands of earthquakes occur each year. Tornadoes, hurricanes, cyclones, and tsunami disasters are commonplace. The unusual has become ordinary and the exception the rule. As the apostle Paul so clearly stated, "The whole creation groans and labors with birth pangs together until now" **(ROMANS 8:22).** Jesus' words are certainly being fulfilled. "Now when these things begin to happen, look up and lift up your heads, because your redemption draws near" **(LUKE 21:28).**

10 Will economic conditions stabilize before the coming of our Lord? What can we expect to happen to the world's monetary systems?

"Come now, you rich, weep and howl for your miseries that are coming upon you! Your riches are corrupted, and your garments are moth-eaten. Your gold and silver are corroded, and their corrosion will be a witness against you and will eat your flesh like fire. You have heaped up treasure in the last days. Indeed the wages of the laborers who mowed your fields, which you kept back by fraud, cry out; and the cries of the reapers have reached the ears of the Lord of Sabaoth. You have lived on the earth in pleasure and luxury; you have fattened your hearts as in a day of slaughter. You have condemned, you have murdered the just; he does not resist you. Therefore be patient, brethren, until the coming of the Lord. See how the farmer waits for the precious fruit of the earth, waiting patiently for it until it receives the early and latter rain" **(JAMES 5:1–7).**

"In that day a man will cast away his idols of silver and his idols of gold, which they made, each for himself to worship, to the moles and bats" **(ISAIAH 2:20).**

"Do not lay up for yourselves treasures on earth, where moth and rust destroy and where thieves break in and steal; but lay up for yourselves treasures in heaven, where neither moth nor rust destroys and where thieves do not break in and steal. For where your treasure is, there your heart will be also" **(MATTHEW 6:19–21).**

"The fruit that your soul longed for has gone from you, and all the things that are rich and splendid have gone from you, and you shall find them no more at all. . . . 'For in one hour such riches come to nothing' " **(REVELATION 18:14, 17).**

We are told to seek "an inheritance incorruptible and undefiled and that does not fade away, reserved in heaven for you" **(1 PETER 1:4).**

The Bible predicts there will be a sudden economic collapse. We are admonished to place our priorities on eternal values. Jesus said, "Seek first the kingdom of God and His righteousness, and all these things shall be added to you. Therefore do not worry about tomorrow, for tomorrow will worry about its own things. Sufficient for the day is its own trouble" **(MATTHEW 6:33, 34).**

11 What will the social conditions be like before Christ returns?

"But know this, that in the last days perilous times will come: For men will be lovers of themselves, lovers of money, boasters, proud, blasphemers, disobedient to parents, unthankful, unholy, unloving, unforgiving, slanderers, without self-control, brutal, despisers of good, traitors, headstrong, haughty, lovers of pleasure rather than lovers of God" **(2 TIMOTHY 3:1–4).**

"For all seek their own, not the things which are of Christ Jesus" **(PHILIPPIANS 2:21).**

"They are without excuse, because, although they knew God, they did not glorify Him as God, nor were thankful, but became futile in their thoughts, and their foolish hearts were darkened. Professing to be wise, they became fools, and changed the glory of the incorruptible God into an image made like corruptible man—and birds and four-footed animals and creeping things. Therefore God also gave them up to uncleanness, in the lusts of their hearts, to dishonor their bodies among themselves, who exchanged the truth of God for the lie, and worshiped and served the creature rather than the Creator, who is blessed forever. Amen. For this reason God gave them up to vile passions. For even their women exchanged the natural use for what is against nature. Likewise also the men, leaving the natural use of the woman, burned in their lust for one another, men with men committing what is shameful, and receiving in themselves the penalty of their error which was due. And even as they did not like to retain God in their knowledge, God gave them over to a debased mind, to do those things which are not fitting; being filled with all unrighteousness, sexual immorality, wickedness, covetousness, maliciousness; full of envy, murder, strife, deceit, evil-mindedness; they are whisperers, backbiters, haters of God, violent, proud, boasters, inventors of evil things, disobedient to parents, undiscerning, untrustworthy, unloving, unforgiving, unmerciful; who, knowing the righteous judgment of God, that those who practice such things are deserving of death, not only do the same but also approve of those who practice them" **(ROMANS 1:20–32).**

Read the morning newspaper of any major city, and you will note the sordid catalog of sins mentioned in this Bible passage. The Bible predicts waning moral values just before the coming of Christ. Perilous or dangerous times, the disintegration of the family unit, "lovers of money," "lovers of pleasure," "without self-control" are word pictures describing life in the twenty-first century.

"And as it was in the days of Noah, so it will be also in the days of the Son of Man: They ate, they drank, they married wives, they were given in marriage, until the day that Noah entered the ark, and the flood came and destroyed them all" **(LUKE 17:26, 27).**

"But as the days of Noah were, so also will the coming of the Son of Man be. For as in the days before the flood, they were eating and drinking, marrying and giving in marriage, until the day that Noah entered the ark, and did not know until the flood came and took them all away, so also will the coming of the Son of Man be" **(MATTHEW 24:37–39).**

God "did not spare the ancient world, but saved Noah, one of eight people, a preacher of righteousness, bringing in the flood on the world of the ungodly" **(2 PETER 2:5).**

"The world that then existed perished, being flooded with water" **(2 PETER 3:6).**

With some concern, Jesus asked, "When the Son of Man comes, will He really find faith on the earth?" **(LUKE 18:8).**

There is certainly nothing wrong with eating and drinking. Jesus is speaking of overindulgence, an obsession with eating and drinking. Eating, drinking, and marrying are all part of life's routine. Here Jesus describes people swallowed up in life's routine—oblivious to the fact that His return is near.

12 What is the final sign before Jesus' return?

"And Jesus went about all Galilee, teaching in their synagogues, preaching the gospel of the kingdom, and healing all kinds of sickness and all kinds of disease among the people" **(MATTHEW 4:23).**

"Then Jesus went about all the cities and villages, teaching in their synagogues, preaching the gospel of the kingdom, and healing every sickness and every disease among the people" **(MATTHEW 9:35).**

"And this gospel of the kingdom will be preached in all the world as a witness to all the nations, and then the end will come" **(MATTHEW 24:14).**

"Then I saw another angel flying in the midst of heaven, having the everlasting gospel to preach to those who dwell on the earth—to every nation, tribe, tongue, and people—saying with a loud voice, 'Fear God and give glory to Him, for the hour of His judgment has come; and worship Him who made heaven and earth, the sea and springs of water' " **(REVELATION 14:6, 7).**

"And He said to them, 'Go into all the world and preach the gospel to every creature' " **(MARK 16:15).**

"But you, Daniel, shut up the words, and seal the book until the time of the end; many shall run to and fro, and knowledge shall increase" **(DANIEL 12:4).**

"After these things I saw another angel coming down from heaven, having great authority, and the earth was illuminated with his glory" **(REVELATION 18:1).**

"For the earth will be filled with the knowledge of the glory of the Lord, as the waters cover the sea" **(HABAKKUK 2:14).**

The rapid spread of the gospel throughout the world is one of the clearest indications that Christ is coming soon. Consider the impact of Jesus' teaching in the first century and compare that to what He predicts will happen at the end of time. In the twenty-first century, our world has become a "global village." The gospel is now going to all the world with a speed that would have left the apostle Paul amazed. Sophisticated satellite communication systems such as the Internet, satellite technology, interlinking computers, the World Wide Web, and mass media television and radio communications are in reality a gift that God is using to communicate the gospel with incredible speed to the world. The technological revolution has provided a setting to rapidly spread the gospel.

13 How did Jesus tell us we should react to all the signs of His return?

"Now when these things begin to happen, look up and lift up your heads, because your redemption draws near" **(LUKE 21:28).**

"So you also, when you see all these things, know that it is near—at the doors!" **(MATTHEW 24:33).**

"It will be said in that day: 'Behold, this is our God; we have waited for Him, and He will save us. This is the LORD; we have waited for Him; we will be glad and rejoice in His salvation" **(ISAIAH 25:9).**

For those who are unprepared, the second coming of Christ may be very frightening. But the experience of those who love Him and long for His return is dramatically different. Their hearts are filled with eager anticipation. They joyfully await His coming. Their Savior, Lord, and King already rules in their hearts. Now they eagerly welcome Him as King and Ruler of this world.

CHAPTER 4

What the Bible Says About Christ's Return

As the world races through the twenty-first century, have you ever considered what our greatest need is? What do men and women living in the twenty-first century need most? If you were starving, it might be food. If you were homeless, it might be a place to live. If disease ravaged your body, it might be medicine. If you were lonely and discouraged, it might be love. But is there one thing more than any other that could take you through *any* difficulty you might face in life? Is there one thing that can make the human spirit soar? All over the world people are desperately looking for hope. Someone has well said, "What oxygen is to the lungs, hope is to the human spirit." We can live days without food, hours without water, a few minutes without air, but no time at all without hope. Hope buoys up our spirits. It lifts our vision from what is to what will be. It is a candle in the darkness. It is like water in the desert or food to a starving man. It provides encouragement for the future. The Bible is filled with the best hope of all—the hope of our Lord's return. The apostle Paul states, "For whatever things were written before were written for our learning, that we through the patience and the comfort of the Scriptures might have hope" **(ROMANS 15:4).**

01 Just before He returned to heaven, what hopeful promise did Jesus give His disciples to fill their hearts with hope?

"Let not your heart be troubled; you believe in God, believe also in Me. In My Father's house are many mansions; if it were not so, I would have told you. I go to prepare a place for you. And if I go and prepare a place for you, I will come again and receive you to Myself; that where I am, there you may be also" **(JOHN 14:1–3).**

Christ's comforting words are like a promissory note. Jesus said He would return—and we can bank on it!

"[The angels] said, 'Men of Galilee, why do you stand gazing up into heaven? This same Jesus, who was taken up from you into heaven, will so come in like manner as you saw Him go into heaven' " **(ACTS 1:11).**

Just before Jesus ascended to heaven, He assured His followers, "I will come again" **(JOHN 14:3).** The fact that Jesus is coming to the world a second time is as certain as the reality that He lived on this earth two thousand years ago. There is hope on the way.

The apostle Paul speaks of "the coming of our Lord Jesus Christ and our gathering together to Him" **(2 THESSALONIANS 2:1).**

"Christ was offered once to bear the sins of many. To those who eagerly wait for Him He will appear a second time, apart from sin, for salvation" **(HEBREWS 9:28).**

On the last page of the Bible—in the last chapter of the last book—Jesus promises: "Behold, I am coming quickly, and My reward is with Me, to give to every one according to his work" **(REVELATION 22:12).**

02 How does the apostle Paul describe the hope of the second coming of Christ?

"Looking for the blessed hope and glorious appearing of our great God and Savior Jesus Christ" **(TITUS 2:13).**

The apostle Paul says, "We were saved in this hope, but hope that is seen is not hope; for why does one still hope for what he sees? But if we hope for what we do not see, we eagerly wait for it with perseverance" **(ROMANS 8:24, 25).**

"Now may the God of hope fill you with all joy and peace in believing, that you may abound in hope by the power of the Holy Spirit" **(ROMANS 15:13).**

"To them God willed to make known what are the riches of the glory of this mystery among the Gentiles: which is Christ in you, the hope of glory" **(COLOSSIANS 1:27).**

We are told to "lay hold of the hope set before us. This hope we have as an anchor of the soul, both sure and steadfast" **(HEBREWS 6:18, 19)**.

Peter describes our hope in Jesus' return this way: "Blessed be the God and Father of our Lord Jesus Christ, who according to His abundant mercy has begotten us again to a living hope through the resurrection of Jesus Christ from the dead, to an inheritance incorruptible and undefiled and that does not fade away, reserved in heaven for you" **(1 PETER 1:3, 4)**.

03 Notice how the Bible prophets have predicted the second coming of Christ throughout Scripture. Every book in the Bible except one mentions the return of our Lord.

The psalmist David wrote many hundreds of years ago, "Our God shall come, and shall not keep silent; a fire shall devour before Him, and it shall be very tempestuous all around Him" **(PSALM 50:3)**.

"Now Enoch, the seventh from Adam, prophesied about these men also saying, 'Behold, the Lord comes with ten thousands of His saints, to execute judgment on all, to convict all who are ungodly among them of all their ungodly deeds which they have committed in an ungodly way, and of all the harsh things which ungodly sinners have spoken against Him' " **(JUDE 14, 15)**.

"And it will be said in that day: 'Behold, this is our God; we have waited for Him, and He will save us. This is the LORD; we have waited for Him; we will be glad and rejoice in His salvation' " **(ISAIAH 25:9)**.

"For behold, I create new heavens and a new earth; and the former shall not be remembered or come to mind. But be glad and rejoice forever in what I create" **(ISAIAH 65:17, 18)**.

"Put in the sickle, for the harvest is ripe. Come, go down; for the winepress is full, the vats overflow—for their wickedness is great. Multitudes, multitudes in the valley of decision! For the day of the LORD is near in the valley of decision" **(JOEL 3:13, 14)**.

"Of this salvation the prophets have inquired and searched carefully, who prophesied of the grace that would come to you, searching what, or what manner of time, the Spirit of Christ who was in them was indicating when He testified beforehand the sufferings of Christ and the glories that would follow. To them it was revealed that, not to themselves, but to us they were ministering the things which now have been reported to you through those who have preached the gospel to you by the Holy Spirit sent from heaven—things which angels desire to look into. Therefore gird up the loins of your mind, be sober, and rest your hope fully upon the grace that is to be brought to you at the revelation of Jesus Christ" **(1 PETER 1:10–13)**.

John the revelator, exiled to the lonely Isle of Patmos, wrote these words: "Behold, He is coming with clouds, and every eye will see Him, even they who pierced Him. And all the tribes of the earth will mourn because of Him. Even so, Amen" **(REVELATION 1:7).**

Jesus says, "Behold, I am coming quickly, and My reward is with Me, to give every one according to his work" **(REVELATION 22:12).**

Bible writers down through the ages have predicted the coming of the Lord. For every prophecy in the Old Testament predicting the first coming of Jesus as a babe in Bethlehem's manger, there are eight foretelling the second coming of Christ. His coming is mentioned in every book of the New Testament except the little book of Philemon.

04 How will Christ return? Will we see Him when He returns? Will His coming be a real event or simply a spiritual coming into our hearts?

"Now when He [Jesus] had spoken these things, while they [the disciples] watched, He was taken up, and a cloud received Him out of their sight. And while they looked steadfastly toward heaven as He went up, behold, two men [angels] stood by them in white apparel, who also said, 'Men of Galilee, why do you stand gazing up into heaven? This same Jesus, who was taken up from you into heaven, will so come in like manner as you saw Him go into heaven' " **(ACTS 1:9–11).**

Don't miss the fact that on this occasion angels, as heavenly messengers from God, confirmed Christ's promise and testified to its literal truthfulness: "This same Jesus," was not a ghostly spirit but had "flesh and bones," to use His own words—and an appetite **(SEE LUKE 24:36–43.)** He "will so come in like manner" as He ascended to heaven. What manner was that? Visibly—"you saw Him go into heaven" **(ACTS 1:11).**

Here is an interesting fact. When the disciples asked Jesus, "What will be the sign of Your coming, and of the end of the age?" **(MATTHEW 24:3),** the Greek word translated "coming" is *parousia.* This same word is used in **1 CORINTHIANS 16:17** for the coming of Paul's friends, Stephanas and Fortunatus, to see him. His friends were literally coming. They were not some shadowy spirits. When a king or a royal dignitary came to town, the word *parousia* was used. It always means a literal, real coming or presence.

God, through Paul, tells us "to wait for His Son from heaven, whom He raised from the dead, even Jesus who delivers us from the wrath to come" **(1 THESSALONIANS 1:10).**

Jesus' ascension to heaven was a real, literal event. And His return will likewise be a very real, literal event.

05 How many people will see our Lord when He returns? Will the entire human race see Him or only a few people?

"Behold, He is coming with clouds, and every eye will see Him, even they who pierced Him. And all the tribes of the earth will mourn because of Him. Even so, Amen" **(REVELATION 1:7)**.

Every eye will see Jesus when He returns. The eyes of the young and the eyes of the old. The eyes of the educated and the eyes of the uneducated, the eyes of the rich and the eyes of the poor. People from all cultures, nationalities, languages, groups, and countries will see Him come.

Evidently a special resurrection of the wicked men "who pierced Him" will enable them to witness Christ's return. Note the following text in connection with **REVELATION 1:7**. "But He [Christ] kept silent and answered nothing. Again the high priest asked Him, saying to Him, 'Are You the Christ, the Son of the Blessed?' Jesus said, 'I am. And you will see the Son of Man sitting at the right hand of the Power, and coming with the clouds of heaven' " **(MARK 14:61, 62)**.

"Then they will see the Son of Man coming in the clouds with great power and glory. And then He will send His angels, and gather together His elect from the four winds, from the farthest part of earth to the farthest part of heaven" **(MARK 13:26, 27)**.

"Then the sign of the Son of Man will appear in heaven, and then all the tribes of the earth will mourn, and they will see the Son of Man coming on the clouds of heaven with power and great glory. And He will send His angels with a great sound of a trumpet, and they will gather together His elect from the four winds, from one end of heaven to the other" **(MATTHEW 24:30, 31)**.

This passage refutes the teaching of the "secret rapture" that misleads so many Christians today. For not only does it emphasize that Christ will come "with power and great glory," but it states that His return will be arrestingly audible, accompanied by the "great sound of a trumpet"—the noisiest of all musical instruments! Furthermore, teachers of the secret rapture claim that the *redeemed* may see the Lord return, but the *wicked who are lost* do not. Yet both this verse and **REVELATION 1:7** speak of the wicked—those who "mourn" when they "see the Son of Man coming . . . with power and great glory" to "gather" His saints!

Both the righteous and the wicked will see Jesus coming in the clouds of the sky when He returns again the second time. Every living inhabitant of our globe will witness the Second Coming. Christ's return will overshadow every other event on planet Earth. No one will need to tell you when Jesus returns. You will see His coming!

06 To what does the Bible compare Jesus' coming?

"For as the lightning comes from the east and flashes to the west, so also will the coming of the Son of Man be" **(MATTHEW 24:27)**.

"For as the lightning that flashes out of one part under heaven shines to the other part under heaven, so also the Son of Man will be in His day" **(LUKE 17:24)**.

Anyone who has seen lightning brightly flash against the dark night sky knows how dazzlingly brilliant it is! The Lord uses such breathtaking imagery as "lightning" to describe His return and the glorious rapture that accompanies it.

07 Will Christ's return be a secret, silent coming?

"For the Lord Himself will descend from heaven with a *shout,* with the *voice* of an archangel, and with the *trumpet* of God. And the dead in Christ will rise first. Then we who are alive and remain shall be caught up together with them in the clouds to meet the Lord in the air. And thus we shall always be with the Lord" **(1 THESSALONIANS 4:16, 17; EMPHASIS SUPPLIED)**.

This text, the key scripture dealing with the rapture of the saints, both living and dead, also happens to be the *noisiest* passage in all the Bible! Think of it: A "shout" is not silent. A "voice" is not silent. Neither is a "trumpet." The Greek word translated *voice* is from the word *phone*, from which we get our English word *telephone.* Who ever heard of a silent phone? We wouldn't even hear it when it rings! And a trumpet is the loudest, most piercing of all musical instruments. Quite clearly, then, the rapture of God's saints will be *far from silent*!

Another text Paul wrote about Christ's second coming makes conspicuous mention of the trumpet blast accompanying that glorious event: "Behold, I tell you a mystery: We shall not all sleep, but we shall all be changed—in a moment, in the twinkling of an eye, at the last trumpet. For the trumpet will sound, and the dead will be raised incorruptible, and we shall be changed. For this corruptible must put on incorruption, and this mortal must put on immortality" **(1 CORINTHIANS 15:51–53)**.

The psalmist, David, wrote, "Our God shall come, and shall not keep silent; a fire shall devour before Him, and it shall be very tempestuous all around Him. He shall call to the heavens from above, and to the earth, that He may judge His people: 'Gather My saints together to Me, those who have made a covenant with Me by sacrifice' " **(PSALM 50:3–5)**.

Jesus' coming will be like a mighty blast of a trumpet. Everyone everywhere will hear it.

08 Who will join Jesus when He returns?

"For the Son of Man will come in the glory of His Father with His angels, and then He will reward each according to his works" **(MATTHEW 16:27).**

"When the Son of Man comes in His glory, and all the holy angels with Him, then He will sit on the throne of His glory" **(MATTHEW 25:31).**

The second coming of Christ is the grand climax of time and eternity which all creation has been eagerly anticipating! The heavenly angels—not the fallen ones—have been impatiently waiting for and working toward that great event. Do you think any one of them would like to be told, "You stay here while all the rest of us go and rescue the redeemed?" You know the answer, and this text declares that none will be disappointed. John the revelator and Daniel no doubt felt the impotence of mere human language when trying to describe how many heavenly messengers they saw in vision: "Then I looked, and I heard the voice of many angels around the throne, . . . and the number of them was ten thousand times ten thousand, and thousands of thousands" **(REVELATION 5:11).** "A thousand thousands ministered to Him; ten thousand times ten thousand stood before Him" **(DANIEL 7:10).** Truly, the angels are indeed "innumerable" **(HEBREWS 12:22).**

"For whoever is ashamed of Me and My words in this adulterous and sinful generation, of him the Son of Man also will be ashamed when He comes in the glory of His Father with the holy angels" **(MARK 8:38).**

God desires "to give you who are troubled rest with us when the Lord Jesus is revealed from heaven with His mighty angels" **(2 THESSALONIANS 1:7).**

"Mighty" is putting it mildly, for angels excel in strength and command supernatural power. We read that at the time of Christ's resurrection "there was a great earthquake; for an angel of the Lord descended from heaven, and came and rolled back the stone from the door, and sat on it. His countenance was like lightning, and his clothing as white as snow. And the guards shook for fear of him, and became like dead men" **(MATTHEW 28:2–4).** If a single angel can cause a great earthquake, roll back the massive stone sealing the tomb as if it were a pebble, and cause seasoned Roman guards to tremble in fear and fall down "like dead men," imagine what innumerable angels could do!

Jesus' second coming will be the mighty climax of all the ages. He will be surrounded by all His holy angels. Try to imagine what that glorious scene will be like.

09 How does the Bible describe the awesome majesty of our Lord's return?

"Then the sign of the Son of Man will appear in heaven, and then all the tribes of the earth will mourn, and they will see the Son of Man coming on the clouds of heaven with power and great glory" **(MATTHEW 24:30).**

"For whoever is ashamed of Me and My words, of him the Son of Man will be ashamed when He comes in His own glory, and in His Father's, and of the holy angels" **(LUKE 9:26).**

Consider the mind-boggling effect of this threefold glory: First, Christ returns "in His own glory"—the glory of God the Son. Second, He returns "in His Father's" glory—the glory of God the Father. And third, He returns in the glory "of [all] the holy angels." Beyond all question, this dazzlingly spectacular event will be breathtakingly glorious!

"Then they will see the Son of Man coming in the clouds with great power and glory" **(MARK 13:26).**

"Then they will see the Son of Man coming in a cloud with power and great glory" **(LUKE 21:27).**

Jesus came silently once. Although angels sang "glory to God in the highest" in shepherds' fields outside of Bethlehem, only a few people had any idea the Baby born in Bethlehem was the eternal Son of God. When He comes the second time, He will come in "power and great glory" in spectacular splendor visible to the entire world.

10 Should we believe anyone who tells us that Christ's coming will be in secret?

"Then if anyone says to you, 'Look, here is the Christ!' or 'There!' do not believe it" **(MATTHEW 24:23).**

"Therefore if they say to you, 'Look, He is in the desert!' do not go out; or 'Look, He is in the inner rooms!' do not believe it" **(MATTHEW 24:26).**

No one—not a single individual in the whole world—will need to be told about Christ's cataclysmic return. And we won't need to read about it in the newspaper or see it on television. It will be witnessed firsthand by everyone alive on the entire earth, for "every eye will see Him" **(REVELATION 1:7).**

11 What amazing dramatic event will take place when Christ returns?

"The dead in Christ will rise first. Then we who are alive and remain shall be caught up together with them in the clouds to meet the Lord in the air. And thus we shall always be with the Lord" **(1 THESSALONIANS 4:16, 17).**

"Behold, I tell you a mystery: We shall not all sleep, but we shall all be changed—in a moment, in the twinkling of an eye, at the last trumpet. For the trumpet will sound, and the dead will be raised incorruptible, and we shall be changed. For this corruptible must put on incorruption, and this mortal must put on immortality" **(1 CORINTHIANS 15:51–53).**

"There will be a resurrection of the dead, both of the just and the unjust" **(ACTS 24:15).**

"You shall be repaid at the resurrection of the just" **(LUKE 14:14).**

"Do not marvel at this; for the hour is coming in which all who are in the graves will hear His voice and come forth—those who have done good, to the resurrection of life, and those who have done evil, to the resurrection of condemnation" **(JOHN 5:28, 29).**

"Your dead shall live; together with my dead body they shall arise. Awake and sing, you who dwell in dust; for . . . the earth shall cast out the dead" **(ISAIAH 26:19).**

"For as in Adam all die, even so in Christ all shall be made alive. But each one in his own order: Christ the firstfruits, afterward those who are Christ's at His coming" **(1 CORINTHIANS 15:22, 23).**

You may have confidence "knowing that He who raised up the Lord Jesus will also raise us up with Jesus, and will present us with you" **(2 CORINTHIANS 4:14).**

12 How will people respond when Jesus comes?

What will be the reaction of the lost?

"Then the sky receded as a scroll when it is rolled up, and every mountain and island was moved out of its place. And the kings of the earth, the great men, the rich men, the commanders, the mighty men, every slave and every free man, hid themselves in the caves and in the rocks of the mountains, and said to the mountains and rocks, 'Fall on us and hide us from the face of Him who sits on the throne and from the wrath of the Lamb!' " **(REVELATION 6:14–16).**

"Then I saw a great white throne and Him who sat on it, from whose face the earth and the heaven fled away. And there was found no place for them" **(REVELATION 20:11).**

"Then they will begin to 'say to the mountains, "Fall on us!" and to the hills "Cover us!" ' " **(LUKE 23:30).**

Filled with guilt and fear, the unsaved run from the Christ who loves them and longs to save them. They have rejected His mercy and turned their backs on His love. Now frightened, they flee to shield themselves from His glory. What a tragic ending!

What will the reaction of the righteous be?

"And it will be said in that day: 'Behold, this is our God; we have waited for Him, and He will save us. This is the LORD; we have waited for Him; we will be glad and rejoice in His salvation' " **(ISAIAH 25:9).**

"He will swallow up death forever, and the Lord GOD will wipe away tears from all faces; the rebuke of His people He will take away from all the earth; for the LORD has spoken" **(ISAIAH 25:8).** (NOTE: This verse tells why the righteous react to Jesus' coming as described in verse 9 above.)

The saved long for His return. Their hearts are filled with joy. Jesus is their Friend, their Savior, their Lord, and their King. They delight in His presence here on earth, and they will delight in it through all eternity.

13 When is the time to prepare for the coming of the Lord?

"Therefore you also be ready, for the Son of Man is coming at an hour you do not expect" **(MATTHEW 24:44).**

"Watch therefore, and pray always that you may be counted worthy to escape all these things that will come to pass, and to stand before the Son of Man" **(LUKE 21:36).**

"For He says: 'In an acceptable time I have heard you, and in the day of salvation I have helped you.' Behold, now is the accepted time; behold, now is the day of salvation" **(2 CORINTHIANS 6:2).**

"Therefore, as the Holy Spirit says: *'Today, if you will hear His voice, do not harden your hearts as in the rebellion, in the day of trial in the wilderness.'* . . . Beware, brethren, lest there be in any of you an evil heart of unbelief in departing from the living God; but exhort one another daily, while it is called *'Today,'* lest any of you be hardened through the deceitfulness of sin. . . . While it is said: *'Today, if you will hear His voice, do not harden your hearts as in the rebellion.'* . . . Again He designates a certain day, saying in David, *'Today,'* after such a long time, as it has been said: *'Today, if you will hear His voice, do not harden your hearts'* " **(HEBREWS 3:7, 8, 12, 13, 15; 4:7; EMPHASIS SUPPLIED).**

Down the corridors of time, that timely word *today* echoes and re-echoes from God's throne, emphasizing the urgency of our choosing right now—today—which master we'll follow.

14 To what event does Jesus compare His coming? Why?

"Watch therefore, for you do not know what hour your Lord is coming. But know this, that if the master of the house had known what hour the thief would come, he would have watched and not allowed his house to be broken into" **(MATTHEW 24:42, 43).**

"Behold, I am coming as a thief. Blessed is he who watches, and keeps his garments, lest he walk naked and they see his shame" **(REVELATION 16:15).**

This verse is one of the few Bible texts used by teachers of the secret rapture theory to prove their points, for they can't find many scriptures in their favor. They teach that these texts indicate Jesus will return secretly—like a thief quietly entering a home to steal. However, in these texts Jesus is warning us about the unexpectedness of His return and the need to be prepared—not that He will return secretly. The New Living Translation expresses **REVELATION 16:15** this way: "Look, I will come as unexpectedly as a thief! Blessed are all who are watching for me, who keep their clothing ready so they will not have to walk around naked and ashamed." Secret rapture advocates think this text means that Jesus will return secretly, silently, the way a thief surreptitiously goes about his dishonorable work. But is that what the Bible really teaches? Let's look at similar texts and *let the Bible explain itself*.

"For you yourselves know perfectly that the *day* of the Lord so comes as a thief in the night" **(1 THESSALONIANS 5:2; EMPHASIS SUPPLIED).**

"But the *day* of the Lord will come as a thief in the night, in which the heavens will pass away with a great noise, and the elements will melt with fervent heat; both the earth and the works that are in it will be burned up" **(2 PETER 3:10; EMPHASIS SUPPLIED).**

It's important for us to understand that the two verses above are not saying that the *Lord* will come as a thief in the night, but that the *day* of the Lord will come unexpectedly. In each case, the subject of the sentence is "day," and "of the Lord" is just a prepositional phrase used to designate which day is being referred to. In the same way, if I say, "The father of the bride was state boxing champ," are you to understand that the bride was good with her fists? Of course not! The subject of the sentence is "father," and "of the bride" simply tells us which father we mean. In these texts, both Peter and Paul are discussing not the *manner*, but the *time* of Christ's return. They're giving insight into *when* Christ will return, not *how*. We know this, because Paul specifically states in **1 THESSALONIANS 5:1,** the verse immediately preceding the one quoted above, that this passage deals with "the times and the seasons." It's not the *Lord* who comes as a thief—it's the *day* of the Lord, the *time* of His return, that sneaks up and surprises those in the world who fail to watch. Then in verse 4, Paul concludes his message to Christian believers: "But you, brethren, are *not* in darkness, so that this Day should overtake you as a thief" **(1 THESSALONIANS 5:4; EMPHASIS SUPPLIED).** There's no reason in either logic or Scripture for Jesus to come for His faithful people in the manner of a sneaky thief.

Jesus compared His coming to a thief breaking into a house. This does not mean that Christ will come secretly. It means He will come swiftly, quickly, at a time we least expect Him.

15 Since Jesus is coming unexpectedly, what counsel does He give us?

"Therefore you also be ready, for the Son of Man is coming at an hour you do not expect" **(MATTHEW 24:44).**

"And while they [the foolish virgins] went to buy, the bridegroom [Jesus] came, and those who were ready went in with him to the wedding; and the door was shut. . . . Watch therefore, for you know neither the day nor the hour in which the Son of Man is coming" **(MATTHEW 25:10, 13).**

"The Lord is at hand" **(PHILIPPIANS 4:5).**

"Be patient. Establish your hearts, for the coming of the Lord is at hand. . . . Behold, the Judge is standing at the door!" **(JAMES 5:8, 9).**

To be ready for the coming of Jesus means to eagerly anticipate His coming. It means a heart-longing for His return. It involves a life committed to doing His will. Love for Him leads us to long to be with Him throughout eternity.

The Bible is filled with the best hope of all—the hope of our Lord's return.

Some Commonly Asked Questions Regarding Jesus' Second Coming

Isn't Jesus coming secretly? Doesn't the Bible say, "There will be two in the field, one taken and one left"? (SEE MATTHEW 24:40.)

The Bible makes it abundantly plain that Jesus' coming is not a secret event **(SEE REVELATION 1:7; PSALM 50:3; 1 THESSALONIANS 4:16, 17; MATTHEW 24:27).** When the Bible speaks of those who are left, it does not say they will be left alive on earth. The extended passage in **LUKE 17:26–37** describes the event in detail. In Noah's day there were two classes, one taken (saved), and one left (destroyed by the Flood) **(SEE VERSE 27).** In Lot's day there were two classes (one taken out of the city and saved, and one left in the city and consumed by the fire). It will be similar when Jesus comes **(SEE LUKE 17:30–37).** One class will be taken to heaven with Jesus (saved), and the other class will be left behind (destroyed). In **LUKE 17:37**, the question is raised, "Where, Lord?" That is, "Where are these people left?" The Bible's answer is plain, "Wherever the body is, there the eagles will be gathered together." **REVELATION 19:11–18** clarifies the point that the wicked are destroyed when Jesus comes **(SEE ALSO 2 THESSALONIANS 1:7–9; 2:8).**

Doesn't the Bible teach that Jesus is coming as a thief? (SEE 1 THESSALONIANS 5:2.)

Each Bible reference to Jesus coming as a thief is in reference to the unexpected *time* of Jesus' coming, not the *manner* of His coming. He comes quickly as a thief, unexpectedly as a thief, but He also comes in glorious splendor, as lightning in triumphant glory **(SEE MATTHEW 24:42–44; 1 THESSALONIANS 5:1–5; MATTHEW 24:27).**

Do God's people live through the coming Tribulation or are they raptured before the Tribulation?

The experiences of ancient Israel were examples given by God for His people living at the close of time. Just as Israel was delivered from Egyptian bondage after the plagues, so God's church will be protected through the plagues and be delivered from the hand of the oppressor **(SEE 1 CORINTHIANS 10:11; PSALM 91:4–6)**. Shadrach, Meshach, and Abed-Nego entered the flames of the fiery furnace when they refused to yield to the universal death decree of Babylon's king. In those flames God miraculously delivered them. Their death-defying faith faced the flames **(SEE DANIEL 3:16–28)**. Jesus comes as a thief after the plagues have fallen on the earth **(SEE REVELATION 16:15)**. What sense would it make to declare "Behold I come as a thief" after six plagues are already poured out if He had already come as a thief before they were poured out? **REVELATION 15:8** emphatically declares, "No man can enter the [heavenly] temple until the plagues are completed." In **2 THESSALONIANS 2:1–3** the Bible makes it plain that the antichrist is revealed before Jesus comes and is destroyed by the brightness of His coming **(SEE VERSE 8)**.

Does the Bible teach that the righteous receive their reward when they are raptured at the beginning of a seven-year tribulation, but that the unrighteous are destroyed at the end of the seven-year tribulation?

The parables of Jesus make it plain that the second coming of Jesus is a divine climactic event—men and women are either saved or lost when Jesus comes. There is no seven-year period to reconsider our lives. Now is the day of salvation **(SEE 2 CORINTHIANS 6:2)**. In **MATTHEW 13:30**, both wheat and tares—the righteous and the wicked—grow together until the harvest. The righteous are saved, and the unrighteous are lost. In the parable of the unfaithful servant, there is no second chance. The unfaithful are lost when the Lord of the household comes unexpectedly **(SEE MATTHEW 24:44–51)**. In the parable of the sheep and the goats, men and women are either saved or lost when Jesus comes **(SEE MATTHEW 25:31–46)**.

Remembering the *Titanic*

On April 15, 2012, the world commemorated the one-hundredth anniversary of the sinking of the *Titanic.* On that fateful night a century before—on April 15, 1912—the unsinkable *Titanic* sank.

The *Titanic* was an engineering masterpiece. So carefully had this great nine-hundred-foot-long sailing ship been constructed, with sixteen watertight compartments in a one-sixth-mile long hull, that the captain had made a pre-voyage boast, "Not even God Himself could sink her." The engineers had calculated that even if four of the sixteen compartments should burst, the ship would still float! But on that starry night of April 14, when the luxury liner, with 2,223 people aboard, made a direct hit on an unseen iceberg, five of the compartments were split open and began to suck in the icy sea water. Within a relatively short time, the unsinkable *Titanic* sunk in the frigid waters of the North Atlantic.

Before the crash there was no sign of danger. The cold, dark sea was calm, as smooth as glass, beneath the star-studded heavens. It was an hour before midnight. Some people had gone to bed and slipped into a serene sleep. Others ate in the luxurious dining room, listening as the band played soothing songs beneath the decks in the first-class lounge. They were totally unaware that the greatest maritime tragedy in the history of sailing, stealthily, silently awaited them in the ice-strewn midnight waters of the North Atlantic. They were totally oblivious to the fact that two-thirds of the people on that mighty ship would be dead before the night was over.

The crew of the *Titanic* received multiple messages of icebergs in the area. Were they so overconfident in the ship's ability to withstand any crash that they ignored them? Were they too busy with their routine duties to heed the messages? Were they overtired, drowsy, or just plain sleepy because of the lateness of the hour? Only eternity will tell. But this one fact is certain—every person aboard the *Titanic* was incredibly surprised with the outcome. Not one of them expected the ship to sink and hundreds of lives to be lost.

Now Is the Time

What's the Second Coming going to be for you? It matters whether you are prepared for that surprise of a lifetime. It's one of the things that matters most. Please don't be caught sleeping on that most important date in history. Please take responsibility for your own spiritual state right now. Please don't assume someone else can take care of it. Don't be swallowed up by the routine. Make God a priority in your life right now. Jesus urged men and women in His day to make their priorities right. He admonished them to "seek ye first the kingdom of God, and his righteousness" **(MATTHEW 6:33, KJV)**. Is the kingdom of God a priority in your life? Is a personal relationship with Jesus supremely important to you? Have the things of time crowded out the things of eternity or does heaven have first place in your heart?

A saving relationship with Jesus will not come by chance. You've got to decide to do it. You've got to allow Jesus to get into your heart and into your life. If you don't decide, you'll end up sleeping, and you'll wake up to the most terrifying surprise of your lifetime.

It's so much better to wake up now. It's so much better to acknowledge what's most important now—rather than later when it's too late.

CHAPTER 5

What the Bible Says About Eternal Life

For generations explorers have searched for the fountain of youth—a legendary spring that reputedly restores health and vitality. Anyone who drinks of its waters is supposedly healed of disease, relieved of suffering, and infused with life. The legend became particularly prominent in the sixteenth century. Rumors flooded the Caribbean about a land called Bimini, a land of wealth and prosperity with a curative spring of healing waters. Ponce de Leon organized an expedition to find the fountain in A.D. 1513. He landed near the site of what is now St. Augustine, Florida. He did not realize he had landed in North America. He thought he had landed on the famed island of Bimini. If you happened to visit St. Augustine, Florida, today, you might visit the fountain of youth, a popular tourist attraction. People who drink from its refreshing waters still get sick, their hair still grays, their skin still wrinkles, and their bodies still age. The fountain of youth is certainly not a tonic of longevity. It certainly is not a magic formula for long life.

Have you ever wondered why millions of people do everything they can to keep from aging. Wrinkle-free creams are a multimillion dollar industry. It is difficult for most people to accept the fact that they are getting old. As one senior citizen said, "Aging is no fun; I want to live forever." Living forever is the heart cry of both young and old. In this chapter, we will discover the secret of living forever.

01 How are each of us affected by the consequences of sin? With what kind of nature are we born?

"All we like sheep have gone astray; we have turned, every one, to his own way" **(ISAIAH 53:6).**

"The heart is deceitful above all things, and desperately wicked" **(JEREMIAH 17:9).**

"But we are all like an unclean thing, and all our righteousnesses are like filthy rags; we all fade as a leaf, and our iniquities, like the wind, have taken us away" **(ISAIAH 64:6).**

"In sin my mother conceived me" **(PSALM 51:5).**

02 How does all the world stand before God?

"Now we know that whatever the law says, it says to those who are under the law, that every mouth may be stopped, and all the world may become guilty before God" **(ROMANS 3:19).**

"And do you think this, O man, you who judge those practicing such things, and doing the same, that you will escape the judgment of God?" **(ROMANS 2:3).**

"Though they join forces, the wicked will not go unpunished; but the posterity of the righteous will be delivered" **(PROVERBS 11:21).**

The reason we lack inner peace is a sense of guilt. Whether we always realize it or not, there is something eating away at us inside. Unless we deal with the problem of guilt, we will never have real peace. The root of our guilt is separation from God—or sin **(SEE ISAIAH 59:1, 2).**

03 How universal is the problem of guilt and sin?

"For all have sinned and fall short of the glory of God" **(ROMANS 3:23).**

"And even as they did not like to retain God in their knowledge, God gave them over to a debased mind, to do those things which are not fitting; being filled with all unrighteousness, sexual immorality, wickedness, covetousness, maliciousness; full of envy, murder, strife, deceit, evil-mindedness; they are whisperers, backbiters, haters of God, violent, proud, boasters, inventors of evil things, disobedient to parents, undiscerning, untrustworthy, unloving, unforgiving, unmerciful; who, knowing the righteous judgment of God, that those who practice such things are deserving of death, not only do the same but also approve of those who practice them. . . . Therefore you are inexcusable, O man, whoever you are who judge, for in whatever you judge another you condemn yourself; for you who judge practice the same things" **(ROMANS 1:28–32; 2:1).**

"For there is not a just man on earth who does good and does not sin" **(ECCLESIASTES 7:20).**

"For God has committed them all to disobedience, that He might have mercy on all" **(ROMANS 11:32).**

"But the Scripture has confined all under sin, that the promise by faith in Jesus Christ might be given to those who believe" **(GALATIANS 3:22).**

"If we say that we have no sin, we deceive ourselves, and the truth is not in us. . . . If we say that we have not sinned, we make Him a liar, and His word is not in us" **(1 JOHN 1:8, 10).**

04 What are the wages—or end result—of sin?

"For the wages of sin is death" **(ROMANS 6:23).**

"Through one man [Adam] sin entered the world, and death through sin, and thus death spread to all men, because all sinned" **(ROMANS 5:12).**

"But of the tree of the knowledge of good and evil you shall not eat, for in the day that you eat of it you shall surely die" **(GENESIS 2:17).**

"In the sweat of your face you shall eat bread till you return to the ground, for out of it you were taken; for dust you are, and to dust you shall return" **(GENESIS 3:19).**

"Woe to the wicked! It shall be ill with him, for the reward of his hands shall be given him" **(ISAIAH 3:11).**

"The soul who sins shall die. The son shall not bear the guilt of the father, nor the father bear the guilt of the son. The righteousness of the righteous shall be upon himself, and the wickedness of the wicked shall be upon himself" **(EZEKIEL 18:20).**

"Do you not know that the unrighteous will not inherit the kingdom of God? Do not be deceived. Neither fornicators, nor idolaters, nor adulterers, nor homosexuals, nor sodomites, nor thieves, nor covetous, nor drunkards, nor revilers, nor extortioners will inherit the kingdom of God" **(1 CORINTHIANS 6:9, 10).**

"Do not be deceived, God is not mocked; for whatever a man sows, that he will also reap" **(GALATIANS 6:7).**

"Then, when desire has conceived, it gives birth to sin; and sin, when it is full-grown, brings forth death" **(JAMES 1:15).**

"But the cowardly, unbelieving, abominable, murderers, sexually immoral, sorcerers, idolaters, and all liars shall have their part in the lake which burns with fire and brimstone, which is the second death" **(REVELATION 21:8).**

Left to ourselves, we are caught in a vicious cycle. We are separated from God. Our hearts are filled with guilt. We are restless and lack inner peace. We feel guilty, unaccepted, and unloved. And without God we are powerless to change our condition.

05 How does sin affect our relationship with God?

"But your iniquities have separated you from your God; and your sins have hidden His face from you, so that He will not hear" **(ISAIAH 59:2).**

"The LORD is far from the wicked, but He hears the prayer of the righteous" **(PROVERBS 15:29).**

"Your iniquities have turned these things away, and your sins have withheld good from you" **(JEREMIAH 5:25).**

"The High and Lofty One who inhabits eternity, whose name is Holy" says of the foolish sinner, "For the iniquity of his covetousness I was angry and struck him; I hid and was angry, and he went on backsliding in the way of his heart" **(ISAIAH 57:15, 17).**

"Then My anger shall be aroused against them in that day, and I will forsake them, and I will hide My face from them, and they shall be devoured. And many evils and troubles shall befall them, so that they will say in that day, 'Have not these evils come upon us because our God is not among us?' And I will surely hide My face in that day because of all the evil which they have done, in that they have turned to other gods" **(DEUTERONOMY 31:17, 18).**

"And He said: 'I will hide My face from them, I will see what their end will be, for they are a perverse generation, children in whom is no faith' " **(DEUTERONOMY 32:20).**

"The Gentiles shall know that the house of Israel went into captivity for their iniquity; because they were unfaithful to Me, therefore I hid My face from them. I gave them into the hand of their enemies, and they all fell by the sword. According to their uncleanness and according to their transgressions I have dealt with them, and hidden My face from them" **(EZEKIEL 39:23, 24).**

"Then they will cry to the LORD, but He will not hear them; He will even hide His face from them at that time, because they have been evil in their deeds" **(MICAH 3:4).**

God is the Source of life. And because sin separates us from God, it separates us from the only Source of life. The plan of salvation is God's process to bridge the gap caused by sin. Through Christ we are reunited with God.

06 What is God's solution to the sin problem?

"For God so loved the world that He gave His only begotten Son, that whoever believes in Him should not perish but have everlasting life" **(JOHN 3:16).**

Here is a gospel acrostic.

For **G**od so loved
The w**O**rld that He gave
His only begotten **S**on, that whoever
believes in Him
Should not **P**erish
But have **E**verlasting
Life.

JOHN 3:16 is likely the most quoted text in the Bible. It reveals the greatest love, the greatest gift, the greatest sacrifice, the greatest penalty, and the greatest reward this world has ever seen. It reveals the incredible good news that Jesus Christ, the Divine Son of God, has provided salvation for us.

Abraham's willingness to sacrifice his own son, Isaac, gave him—and us—insights into God's incomparable sacrifice in giving up Jesus to die for us. "And He [God] said [to Abraham], 'Do not lay your hand on the lad, or do anything to him; for now I know that you fear God, since you have not withheld your son, your only son, from Me' " **(GENESIS 22:12).**

In His parable of the vineyard, Jesus taught, "Therefore still having one son, his beloved, he also sent him to them last, saying, 'They will respect my son' " **(MARK 12:6).**

"In this the love of God was manifested toward us, that God has sent His only begotten Son into the world, that we might live through Him. In this is love, not that we loved God, but that He loved us and sent His Son to be the propitiation for our sins. . . . We love Him because He first loved us" **(1 JOHN 4:9, 10, 19).**

"He who did not spare His own Son, but delivered Him up for us all, how shall He not with Him also freely give us all things?" **(ROMANS 8:32).**

"For if when we were enemies we were reconciled to God through the death of His Son, much more, having been reconciled, we shall be saved by His life" **(ROMANS 5:10).**

"God demonstrates His own love toward us, in that while we were still sinners, Christ died for us" **(ROMANS 5:8).**

"Glory to God in the highest, and on earth peace, goodwill toward men!" **(LUKE 2:14).**

Paul confessed, "This is a faithful saying and worthy of all acceptance, that Christ Jesus came into the world to save sinners, of whom I am chief. However, for this reason I obtained mercy, that in me first Jesus Christ might show all longsuffering, as a pattern to those who are going to believe on Him for everlasting life" **(1 TIMOTHY 1:15, 16).**

07 Was Jesus' death on the cross really necessary? Wasn't it enough that He lived a perfect life as an example to us?

"But we see Jesus, who was made a little lower than the angels, for the suffering of death crowned with glory and honor, that He, by the grace of God, might taste death for everyone. . . . Inasmuch then as the children have partaken of flesh and blood, He Himself likewise shared in the same, that through death He might destroy him who had the power of death, that is, the devil" **(HEBREWS 2:9, 14).**

Paul speaks of Christ Jesus, "who, being in the form of God, did not consider it robbery to be equal with God, but made Himself of no reputation, taking the form of a bondservant, and coming in the likeness of men. And being found in appearance as a man, He humbled Himself and became obedient to the point of death, even the death of the cross. Therefore God also has highly exalted Him and given Him the name which is above every name" **(PHILIPPIANS 2:6–9).**

Speaking to the diabolical and dishonest serpent in Eden, God said, "I will put enmity between you [Satan, in the guise of a serpent] and the woman [Eve], and between your seed and her Seed [Jesus Christ]; He shall bruise your head, and you shall bruise His heel" **(GENESIS 3:15).**

This text, so close to the beginning of the Bible, was the first of many that foretold and foreshadowed the promised Messiah. This promise—that Christ would come and conquer evil—helped sustain Adam and Eve after their fall. (The New International Version and The New Living Translation say that Christ will "crush" the serpent's head.)

"For what the law could not do in that it was weak through the flesh, God did by sending His own Son in the likeness of sinful flesh, on account of sin: He condemned sin in the flesh" **(ROMANS 8:3).**

"The next day John [the Baptist] saw Jesus coming toward him, and said, 'Behold! The Lamb of God who takes away the sin of the world!' " **(JOHN 1:29).**

The people of God were taught to bring a sacrificial *lamb* to the sanctuary when they had sinned. There the priest would have the sinner *confess* his or her sins over the head of the innocent lamb. Then the priest would hand the repentant sinner a sharp knife, and the sinner—with his or her own hand—would have to *kill* the lamb by cutting its throat. This act taught ancient Israel the seriousness of sin: "The wages of sin is death" **(ROMANS 6:23).**

But an ordinary lamb could atone only for the sins of one sinner, and besides, the sacrificial system came to a dramatic end at the moment when Jesus died on the cross as shown by the fact that just as He died, the temple veil was torn in two from top to bottom by an unseen heavenly hand. "And Jesus cried out again with a loud voice, and yielded up His spirit. Then, behold, the veil of the temple was torn in two from top to bottom; and the earth quaked, and the rocks were split" **(MATTHEW 27:50, 51).** All those animal sacrifices had simply pointed forward to the one great Sacrifice to take place when God's dear Son died on the cross for you and me. Now the true Lamb of God has been offered, once and for all, and His divine death is sufficient to take away the sins of the whole world, as John the Baptist so eloquently put it in this majestic verse. But the efficacy of the saving blood from that great Sacrifice can be applied only to those sinners who accept Jesus as their Savior.

"He died for all, that those who live should live no longer for themselves, but for Him who died for them and rose again" **(2 CORINTHIANS 5:15).**

"The Man Christ Jesus . . . gave Himself a ransom for all" **(1 TIMOTHY 2:5, 6).**

"He Himself is the propitiation [the atoning sacrifice] for our sins, and not for ours only but also for the whole world" **(1 JOHN 2:2).**

"And they sang a new song, saying: 'You [the Lamb of God] are worthy to take the scroll, and to open its seals; for You were slain, and have redeemed us to God by Your blood out of every tribe and tongue and people and nation' " **(REVELATION 5:9).**

Salvation "has now been revealed by the appearing of our Savior Jesus Christ, who has abolished death and brought life and immortality to light through the gospel" **(2 TIMOTHY 1:10).**

Because God's nature is love, He would not leave us to perish without hope. He took the penalty of sin upon Himself. In His death on the cross He broke the stronghold of death.

08 How is it possible for Jesus' death on the cross to atone for our sins?

"Surely He has borne our griefs and carried our sorrows; yet we esteemed Him stricken, smitten by God, and afflicted. But He was wounded for our transgressions, He was bruised for our iniquities; the chastisement for our peace was upon Him, and by His stripes we are healed. All we like sheep have gone astray; we have turned, every one, to his own way; and the LORD has laid on Him the iniquity of us all. . . . Therefore I will divide Him a portion with the great, and He shall divide the spoil with the strong, because He poured out His soul unto death, and He was numbered with the transgressors, and He bore the sin of many, and made intercession for the transgressors" **(ISAIAH 53:4–6, 12).**

"He was cut off from the land of the living; for the transgressions of My people He was stricken. . . . My righteous Servant [Jesus] shall justify many, for He shall bear their iniquities" **(ISAIAH 53:8, 11).**

The apostle Peter speaks of Jesus, "who Himself bore our sins in His own body on the tree, that we, having died to sins, might live for righteousness—by whose stripes you were healed" **(1 PETER 2:24).**

"The Son of Man did not come to be served, but to serve, and to give His life a ransom for many" **(MATTHEW 20:28).**

The apostle Paul speaks of Jesus, "who was delivered up because of our offenses, and was raised because of our justification" **(ROMANS 4:25).**

"For when we were still without strength, in due time Christ died for the ungodly. For scarcely for a righteous man will one die; yet perhaps for a good man someone would even dare to die. But God demonstrates His own love toward us, in that while we were still sinners, Christ died for us. Much more then, having now been justified by His blood, we shall be saved from wrath through Him. For if when we were enemies we were reconciled to God through the death of His Son, much more, having been reconciled, we shall be saved by His life" **(ROMANS 5:6–10).**

"Not with the [sacrificial] blood of goats and calves, but with His own blood He entered the Most Holy Place once for all, having obtained eternal redemption" **(HEBREWS 9:12).**

"Christ also suffered once for sins, the just for the unjust, that He might bring us to God, being put to death in the flesh but made alive by the Spirit" **(1 PETER 3:18).**

The Old Testament prophet Isaiah uses these expressions to describe Jesus' sacrificial death: "wounded for our transgressions," "bruised for our iniquities [sins]," "numbered with the transgressors," and "bore the sin of many." In the plan of salvation, Jesus bears the guilt of our sins. He credits His perfect righteousness to our account. We owe a sin debt that we can never pay. Jesus paid the enormous debt through the shedding of His blood. He died the death we deserve so we might live the life He deserves.

09 What really happened at the Cross? What did Jesus actually accomplish for us?

"For He [God] made Him who knew no sin [His only Divine Son] to be sin for us, that we might become the righteousness of God in Him" **(2 CORINTHIANS 5:21).**

Through Divine Inspiration and a visit by the angel Gabriel, the prophet Daniel was led to predict two vital facts about the Messiah, the Prince of God: (1) the very time when the Messiah would begin His great work, and (2) the time when He would be cut off out of the land of the living—or killed: "Seventy weeks are determined for your people [Daniel's people, the Jews] and for your holy city [Jerusalem]. . . . Know therefore and understand, that from the going forth of the command to restore and build Jerusalem [which was then lying in ruins, having been destroyed by the Babylonians] until Messiah the Prince, there shall be seven weeks and sixty-two weeks; the street shall be built again, and the wall, even in troublesome times. And after the sixty-two weeks Messiah shall be cut off, but not for Himself" **(DANIEL 9:24–26).**

"Walk in love, as Christ also has loved us and given Himself for us, an offering and a sacrifice to God for a sweet-smelling aroma" **(EPHESIANS 5:2).**

"Christ also suffered once for sins, the just for the unjust, that He might bring us to God, being put to death in the flesh but made alive by the Spirit" **(1 PETER 3:18).**

"My little children, these things I write to you, so that you may not sin. And if anyone sins, we have an Advocate with the Father, Jesus Christ the righteous. And He Himself is the propitiation for our sins, and not for ours only but also for the whole world" **(1 JOHN 2:1, 2).**

The angel of the Lord told Joseph, "And she [the Virgin Mary] will bring forth a Son, and you shall call His name JESUS, for He will save His people from their sins" **(MATTHEW 1:21).**

The name *Jesus* very appropriately means "Savior." The title "Christ" means "king" or "anointed one," as kings even today are anointed with a few drops of oil at their coronation ceremony. Jesus was anointed by the Holy Spirit at His baptism as He was about to inaugurate His ministry: "When He had been baptized, Jesus came up immediately from the water; and behold, the heavens were opened to Him, and He saw the Spirit of God descending like a dove and alighting upon Him. And suddenly a voice came from heaven, saying, 'This is My beloved Son, in whom I am well pleased' " **(MATTHEW 3:16, 17)**. Thus the humble Babe in Bethlehem was destined to be both our Savior and King, our Lord and Master.

Jesus never sinned. He became sin or accepted the guilt of our sin voluntarily. When Christ died on Calvary's cross, He willingly assumed all the guilt of our sins. As the Divine Son of God, He became a human being, lived the perfect life we should have lived, and died the death we should have died. He is our loving Savior.

10 Although it is unthinkable, what did Jesus, the perfect, righteous Son of God, become for us?

"Christ has redeemed us from the curse of the law, having become a curse for us (for it is written, 'Cursed is everyone who hangs on a tree')" **(GALATIANS 3:13)**.

"If a man has committed a sin deserving of death, and he is put to death, and you hang him on a tree, his body shall not remain overnight on the tree, but you shall surely bury him that day, so that you do not defile the land which the LORD your God is giving you as an inheritance; for he who is hanged is accursed of God" **(DEUTERONOMY 21:22, 23)**.

"[Jesus] Himself bore our sins in His own body on the tree, that we, having died to sins, might live for righteousness—by whose stripes you were healed" **(1 PETER 2:24)**.

A beautiful statement on this point is provided in the following words from an insightful biography of the Lord: "Christ was treated as we deserve, that we might be treated as He deserves. He was condemned for our sins, in which He had no share, that we might be justified by His righteousness, in which we had no share. He suffered the death which was ours, that we might receive the life which was His. 'With His stripes we are healed' " (Ellen G. White, *The Desire of Ages,* p. 25).

Jesus became a curse for us. All of the guilt of sin rested upon Him when He died on the cross. He bore sin's curse of condemnation. Everything I deserved, He received.

11 Is salvation something we earn by our good works?

"For by grace you have been saved through faith, and that not of yourselves; it is the gift of God" **(EPHESIANS 2:8)**.

Repentant sinners are "justified freely by His grace through the redemption that is in Christ Jesus" **(ROMANS 3:24)**.

Mary Magdalene knew she was a sinner. "She began to wash His [Jesus'] feet with her tears, and wiped them with the hair of her head; and she kissed His feet and anointed them with the fragrant oil. . . . Then He said to her, 'Your sins are forgiven.' And those who sat at the table with Him began to say to themselves, 'Who is this who even forgives sins?' Then He said to the woman, 'Your faith has saved you. Go in peace' " **(LUKE 7:38, 48–50).**

"The Son of Man [must] be lifted up [on a cross], that whoever believes in Him should not perish but have eternal life. For God so loved the world that He gave His only begotten Son, that whoever believes in Him should not perish but have everlasting life. For God did not send His Son into the world to condemn the world, but that the world through Him might be saved. He who believes in Him is not condemned; but he who does not believe is condemned already, because he has not believed in the name of the only begotten Son of God. . . . He who believes in the Son has everlasting life; and he who does not believe the Son shall not see life, but the wrath of God abides on him" **(JOHN 3:14–18, 36).**

"Most assuredly, I say to you, he who hears My word and believes in Him who sent Me has everlasting life, and shall not come into judgment, but has passed from death into life" **(JOHN 5:24).**

"This is the will of Him who sent Me, that everyone who sees the Son and believes in Him may have everlasting life; and I will raise him up at the last day" **(JOHN 6:40).**

"If you confess with your mouth the Lord Jesus and believe in your heart that God has raised Him from the dead, you will be saved. For with the heart one believes unto righteousness, and with the mouth confession is made unto salvation" **(ROMANS 10:9, 10).**

"How then shall they call on Him in whom they have not believed? And how shall they believe in Him of whom they have not heard? And how shall they hear without a preacher? . . . So then faith comes by hearing, and hearing by the word of God" **(ROMANS 10:14, 17).**

"But as many as received Him, to them He gave the right to become children of God, to those who believe in His name: who were born, not of blood, nor of the will of the flesh, nor of the will of man, but of God" **(JOHN 1:12, 13).**

12 What question did a heathen jailer ask Paul and Silas two thousand years ago that speaks for all of us?

"And he brought them out and said, 'Sirs, what must I do to be saved?' "**(ACTS 16:30).**

This is the most important question in life. It is the eternal question. It keeps coming back throughout the Bible.

"Now when they [those listening to Peter's sermon] heard this, they were cut to the heart, and said to Peter and the rest of the apostles, 'Men and brethren, what shall we do?' "**(ACTS 2:37).**

Saul, the horrible persecutor of Christians, became Paul, the great apostle to the Gentiles, after he encountered Christ in a dazzling vision on the road to Damascus. "So he, trembling and astonished, said, 'Lord, what do You want me to do?' Then the Lord said to him, 'Arise and go into the city, and you will be told what you must do' " **(ACTS 9:6)**.

Paul related his conversion experience to others, testifying, "So I said, 'What shall I do, Lord?' And the Lord said to me, 'Arise and go into Damascus, and there you will be told all things which are appointed for you to do' " **(ACTS 22:10)**.

The patriarch Job asked, "How then can man be righteous before God? Or how can he be pure who is born of a woman?" **(JOB 25:4)**.

John the Baptist gave instruction in practical Christian living: "The people asked him, saying, 'What shall we do then?' He answered and said to them, 'He who has two tunics, let him give to him who has none; and he who has food, let him do likewise.' Then tax collectors also came to be baptized, and said to him, 'Teacher, what shall we do?' And he said to them, 'Collect no more than what is appointed for you.' Likewise the soldiers asked him, saying, 'And what shall we do?' So he said to them, 'Do not intimidate anyone or accuse falsely, and be content with your wages' " **(LUKE 3:10–14)**.

13 What response did Paul give the Philippian jailer?

"Believe on the Lord Jesus Christ, and you will be saved, you and your household" **(ACTS 16:31)**.

"Now when they heard this, they were cut to the heart, and said to Peter and the rest of the apostles, 'Men and brethren, what shall we do?' Then Peter said to them, 'Repent, and let every one of you be baptized in the name of Jesus Christ for the remission of sins; and you shall receive the gift of the Holy Spirit' " **(ACTS 2:37, 38)**.

"Nor is there salvation in any other [than Jesus], for there is no other name under heaven given among men by which we must be saved" **(ACTS 4:12)**.

When Philip, led by the Spirit, encountered an Ethiopian eunuch who was treasurer of the Ethiopian queen, he preached Christ to him. "Now as they went down the road, they came to some water. And the eunuch said, 'See, here is water. What hinders me from being baptized?' Then Philip said, 'If you believe with all your heart, you may.' And he answered and said, 'I believe that Jesus Christ is the Son of God' " **(ACTS 8:36, 37)**.

"He who believes and is baptized will be saved; but he who does not believe will be condemned" **(MARK 16:16)**.

The Emperor of the universe proclaims, "Look to Me, and be saved, all you ends of the earth! For I am God, and there is no other" **(ISAIAH 45:22)**.

"As many as received Him, to them He gave the right to become children of God, to those who believe in His name" **(JOHN 1:12).**

"This is the will of Him who sent Me, that everyone who sees the Son and believes in Him may have everlasting life; and I will raise him up at the last day. . . . Most assuredly, I say to you, he who believes in Me has everlasting life" **(JOHN 6:40, 47).**

"Jesus said to her [Martha, mourning over the death of her brother, Lazarus], 'I am the resurrection and the life. He who believes in Me, though he may die, he shall live. And whoever lives [at the time of My second coming] and believes in Me shall never die. Do you believe this?' " **(JOHN 11:25, 26).**

"These are written that you may believe that Jesus is the Christ, the Son of God, and that believing you may have life in His name" **(JOHN 20:31).**

"Therefore, having been justified by faith, we have peace with God through our Lord Jesus Christ, through whom also we have access by faith into this grace in which we stand, and rejoice in hope of the glory of God" **(ROMANS 5:1, 2).**

Believing is simply receiving the grace God so freely offers. God's plan for saving us is simple. It is so simple that anyone can understand it. Often it has been made so complicated that few can understand it. There are four basic steps in receiving Christ. Let's look at each one of them.

Step 1: BELIEVE—JOHN 3:16
"For God so loved the world that He gave His only begotten Son, that whoever believes in Him should not perish but have everlasting life."

Step 2: REPENT—ACTS 3:19
"Repent therefore and be converted, that your sins may be blotted out."

Step 3: CONFESS—1 JOHN 1:9
"If we confess our sins, He is faithful and just to forgive us our sins and to cleanse us from all unrighteousness."

Step 4: RECEIVE—REVELATION 3:20
"Behold, I stand at the door and knock. If anyone hears My voice and opens the door, I will come in to him."

The Bible teaches us four simple steps of salvation. First, believe that God loves you and wants to save you through Jesus Christ. Second, let the Holy Spirit lead you to repentance. Repentance is to turn away in sorrow from sin that separates you from God. Third, confess your sins and admit you are a sinner and need Jesus Christ. And fourth, receive Jesus into your heart today. Believe He lives in your heart, because He has promised to do so when you sincerely ask Him. Don't doubt it. Don't question it. Believe that Jesus Christ now reigns in your heart because in simple faith and commitment you asked Him to come in. As you believe, repent, confess, and receive Jesus Christ into your life, you will have personal peace. "However sinful, however guilty you may be, you are called, you are chosen. Draw nigh to God and He will draw nigh to you" (Ellen G. White, *Fundamentals of Christian Education,* p. 33).

14 What promise does Jesus give to those who receive Him as their personal Savior and accept His gift of salvation by faith?

"This is the testimony: that God has given us eternal life, and this life is in His Son. He who has the Son has life; he who does not have the Son of God does not have life. These things I have written to you who believe in the name of the Son of God, that you may know that you have eternal life, and that you may continue to believe in the name of the Son of God" **(1 JOHN 5:11–13)**.

"And this is the promise that He has promised us—eternal life" **(1 JOHN 2:25)**.

Jesus, the Good Shepherd, declares, "My sheep hear My voice, and I know them, and they follow Me. And I give them eternal life, and they shall never perish; neither shall anyone snatch them out of My hand" **(JOHN 10:27, 28)**.

In His beautiful prayer to His heavenly Father, Jesus prayed, "You [God the Father] have given Him [God the Son] authority over all flesh, that He should give eternal life to as many as You have given Him. And this is eternal life, that they may know You, the only true God, and Jesus Christ whom You have sent" **(JOHN 17:2, 3)**.

"So that as sin reigned in death, even so grace might reign through righteousness to eternal life through Jesus Christ our Lord" **(ROMANS 5:21)**.

"The wages of sin is death, but the gift of God is eternal life in Christ Jesus our Lord" **(ROMANS 6:23)**.

"Keep yourselves in the love of God, looking for the mercy of our Lord Jesus Christ unto eternal life" **(JUDE 21)**.

To receive Jesus is to receive His gift of eternal life. If we have accepted Jesus and by faith believe He is our personal Savior, we can have the assurance of eternal life. Guilt is gone. According to God's Word, we are "accepted in the Beloved" **(EPHESIANS 1:6)**. "We have redemption through His blood" **(EPHESIANS 1:7)**. We are adopted into the family of God and are now part of the royal family of heaven. Would you like to open your heart right now and receive the gift of eternal life Christ so freely offers?

A Commonly Asked Question Regarding the Divinity of Christ

Doesn't the Bible teach that Jesus was the "Firstborn" of all creation and as such a created being, not coexistent with the Father from eternity?

The text in question is **COLOSSIANS 1:15**, which calls Jesus "the firstborn over all creation." The Greek word used here is *prototokos* meaning "the pre-eminent one"—the one who has the privileges and prerogative of God. Jesus is the Firstborn not in the sense of time, but in the sense of privilege. All the privileges of the Firstborn are His. David was the eighth son of Jesse, yet he was called the firstborn. Jesus declared that He is the "I AM" **(JOHN 8:58)**, meaning the Self-Existent One. He said, "Before Abraham was, I AM." Isaiah, the prophet, calls Him the "everlasting Father" **(ISAIAH 9:6)**. Micah declares that His origin is from everlasting **(SEE MICAH 5:2)**. John affirms, "In the beginning was the Word, and the Word was with God, and the Word was God" **(JOHN 1:1)**. Jesus had the privileges and prerogatives of God. Yet He thought equality with God not a thing to be grasped while the world was lost, so He voluntarily left heaven to become a man. He dwelt in human flesh, fought temptation's battles as we fight them, and overcame in our behalf **(SEE PHILIPPIANS 2:5–11; HEBREWS 2:14, 17)**.

A Commonly Asked Question Regarding Salvation

Doesn't the Bible teach that once you come to Jesus you can never lose your salvation? (SEE JOHN 10:28.)

We receive the gift of eternal life by coming to Jesus, accepting His forgiveness by faith, and receiving His grace **(SEE EPHESIANS 2:8; ROMANS 3:22–25)**. Salvation is a free gift. It is not something we earn by our obedience. Salvation is by grace through faith. When the Philippian jailer asked, "What must I do to be saved?" Paul responded, "Believe on the Lord Jesus Christ" **(ACTS 16:30, 31)**. Belief is a function of the will. The same mind that chooses to believe can choose to disbelieve, and unbelief leads to spiritual death **(SEE HEBREWS 3:12–14)**. If we do not hold our confidence in God to the end, we will develop a heart of unbelief. "He who endures to the end shall be saved" **(MATTHEW 24:13)**. We are saved only if we keep in memory what was preached and live the life of faith **(SEE 1 CORINTHIANS 15:1, 2)**. It is always possible to return to the old life of sin, have our names blotted out of the book of life, and be eternally lost **(SEE 2 PETER 2:19–22; REVELATION 3:5; 1 CORINTHIANS 9:27)**. The Greek word Paul uses for "castaway" in **1 CORINTHIANS 9:27 (KJV)** is the same word that is used in **JEREMIAH 6:30** for those who are burned and ultimately lost. **JOHN 10:28** declares that when we come to Jesus, we receive eternal life. Just as His coming into our hearts by faith brings life, our unbelief brings spiritual death. We cannot be unborn, but we can die. Nothing can take us from His hand except our own choices.

CHAPTER 6

What the Bible Says About Prayer

Prayer is opening our hearts to God as a friend. It enables us to share with Him our joys and sorrows, our strengths and weaknesses, our victories and defeats, and our successes and failures. There is nothing that concerns us that He is uninterested in. Prayer is not a sanctified gift list presented to God as children present their Christmas list to a fictional Santa Claus. Prayer is intimate communion with God.

Through prayer we discover what is on God's mind, and we share with Him what is on ours. Prayer may include praise, confession, repentance, petition, thanksgiving, and intercession. Our heavenly Father longs for us to come to Him in prayer. In prayer we acknowledge our absolute dependence on Him.

01 What divine invitation does Jesus personally give to us?

"Ask, and it will be given to you; seek, and you will find; knock, and it will be opened to you. For everyone who asks receives, and he who seeks finds, and to him who knocks it will be opened" **(MATTHEW 7:7, 8).**

"And whatever you ask in My name, that I will do, that the Father may be glorified in the Son. If you ask anything in My name, I will do it" **(JOHN 14:13, 14).**

"Seek the LORD while He may be found, call upon Him while He is near" **(ISAIAH 55:6).**

"Call to Me, and I will answer you, and show you great and mighty things, which you do not know" **(JEREMIAH 33:3).**

"Watch therefore, and pray always that you may be counted worthy to escape all these things that will come to pass, and to stand before the Son of Man" **(LUKE 21:36).**

02 What promise does our Lord give us when we pray?

"Then you will call upon Me and go and pray to Me, and I will listen to you. And you will seek Me and find Me, when you search for Me with all your heart" **(JEREMIAH 29:12, 13).**

"It shall come to pass that before they call, I will answer; and while they are still speaking, I will hear" **(ISAIAH 65:24).**

"The Lord is good to those who wait for Him, to the soul who seeks Him" **(LAMENTATIONS 3:25).**

"They will call on My name, and I will answer them. I will say, 'This is My people'; and each one will say, 'The LORD is my God' " **(ZECHARIAH 13:9).**

"The eyes of the LORD are on the righteous, and His ears are open to their cry. . . . The righteous cry out, and the LORD hears, and delivers them out of all their troubles" **(PSALM 34:15, 17).**

03 What role does faith play in answered prayer?

"All things, whatsoever ye shall ask in prayer, believing, ye shall receive" **(MATTHEW 21:22, KJV).**

"Therefore I say to you, whatever things you ask when you pray, believe that you receive them, and you will have them" **(MARK 11:24, 25).**

"But let him ask in faith, with no doubting, for he who doubts is like a wave of the sea driven and tossed by the wind. For let not that man suppose that he will receive anything from the Lord" **(JAMES 1:6, 7)**.

"But without faith it is impossible to please Him, for he who comes to God must believe that He is, and that He is a rewarder of those who diligently seek Him" **(HEBREWS 11:6)**.

"So Jesus said to them, 'Because of your unbelief; for assuredly, I say to you, if you have faith as a mustard seed, you will say to this mountain, "Move from here to there," and it will move; and nothing will be impossible for you' " **(MATTHEW 17:20)**.

Faith is not a magic formula to manipulate God into doing what we want. Faith is having a relationship with God just like we would with a well-known friend. Faith believes, hopes, and trusts knowing that God desires only our best good. It seeks His will not our own. What does Jesus mean when He says, "If you have enough faith you can move mountains"? If you have faith—trust in God—the challenge you are facing will either be divinely removed through His supernatural power or He will give you the strength to cope with it. To put it in Jesus' language of mountains, the Master will either miraculously move your mountain or He will give you the strength, to climb it. In our own strength, small hills appear as mountains. In Jesus' strength, mountains appear as small hills. Through faith we are more than conquerors.

"Yet in all these things we are more than conquerors through Him who loved us" **(ROMANS 8:37)**.

As we pray in faith, divine power flows into our lives. Through prayer we unite our weakness with God's strength, our ignorance to His wisdom, and our frailty to His enduring might. Prayer unites us with the will of God and the power of God.

04 How does Jesus' prayer life provide us with a model for our own prayer lives?

"Now in the morning, having risen a long while before daylight, He went out and departed to a solitary place; and there He prayed" **(MARK 1:35)**.

"So He Himself often withdrew into the wilderness and there prayed" **(LUKE 5:16)**.

"And it happened, as He was alone praying, that His disciples joined Him, and He asked them, saying, 'Who do the crowds say that I am?' " **(LUKE 9:18)**.

"As He prayed, the appearance of His face was altered, and His robe became white and glistening" **(LUKE 9:29)**.

"Now it came to pass, as He was praying in a certain place, when He ceased, that one of His disciples said to Him, 'Lord, teach us to pray, as John also taught his disciples' " **(LUKE 11:1).**

"Who, in the days of His flesh, when He had offered up prayers and supplications, with vehement cries and tears to Him who was able to save Him from death, and was heard because of His godly fear, though He was a Son, yet He learned obedience by the things which He suffered" **(HEBREWS 5:7, 8).**

Jesus placed priority on prayer. Each day He set aside a specific time to pray. Early in the morning, He spent time alone with His heavenly Father to receive strength for the day. Jesus also had special places set aside to pray. He often spent time in nature communing with His heavenly Father. In the Garden of Gethsemane, in the shadow of the olive trees, was one of His favorite places to pour out His heart to God. Jesus regularly prayed out loud. When the disciples heard Him baring His soul to God in intimate communion, they requested that He "teach" them to pray just like He prayed. An effective prayer life requires that we, too, set aside specific times for prayer when we can be alone with God in our place of prayer to pour out our hearts to Him. **(SEE MATTHEW 26:39; HEBREWS 5:7.)** Secret prayer need not necessarily be silent prayer. Although it is certainly appropriate to pray silently at times, praying aloud focuses our thoughts and helps to keep our minds from wandering. The great biblical prayers of Moses, Daniel, David, and, of course, Jesus were all prayed aloud before God.

05 How does the Holy Spirit cooperate with us in our prayer lives?

"The Spirit also helps our weaknesses. For we know not what we should pray for as we ought, but the Spirit Himself makes intercession for us with groanings which cannot be uttered" **(ROMANS 8:26).**

"For through Him we both have access by one Spirit to the Father" **(EPHESIANS 2:18).**

"But you, beloved, building up yourselves on your most holy faith, praying in the Holy Spirit" **(JUDE 20).**

"Praying always with all prayer and supplication in the Spirit, being watchful to this end with all perseverance and supplication for all the saints" **(EPHESIANS 6:18).**

The Holy Spirit leads us to prayer, guides us in prayer, and reassures us after prayer. The role of the Holy Spirit in our prayer lives is indispensible. As we come to God with our fallen humanity, the Holy Spirit interprets our hearts' desires and takes our feeble words and presents them in the language of heaven to our lovingly heavenly Father. The Holy Spirit convicts us of our need of prayer. He constantly reveals our spiritual helplessness without the power of God. The Holy Spirit is constantly drawing our hearts out to God.

06 What elements help make our prayer lives effective?

Pray with thanksgiving

"So I will go about Your altar, O LORD, that I may proclaim with the voice of thanksgiving, and tell of all your wondrous works" **(PSALM 26:6, 7)**.

"Oh come, let us sing to the LORD! Let us shout joyfully to the Rock of our salvation. Let us come before His presence with thanksgiving" **(PSALM 95:1, 2)**.

"Be anxious for nothing, but in everything by prayer and supplication, with thanksgiving, let your requests be made known to God" **(PHILIPPIANS 4:6)**.

"Continue earnestly in prayer, being vigilant in it with thanksgiving" **(COLOSSIANS 4:2)**.

Pray with perseverance

"Pray without ceasing, in everything give thanks; for this is the will of God in Christ Jesus for you" **(1 THESSALONIANS 5:17, 18)**.

"Praying always" **(EPHESIANS 6:18)**.

"Continue earnestly in prayer" **(COLOSSIANS 4:2)**.

"Then He spoke a parable to them, that men always ought to pray and not lose heart" **(LUKE 18:1)**.

Pray fervently

"The effective, fervent prayer of a righteous man avails much" **(JAMES 5:16)**.

Pray confidently

"Let us therefore come boldly [confidently] to the throne of grace, that we may obtain mercy and find grace to help in time of need" **(HEBREWS 4:16)**.

"Let us draw near with a true heart in full assurance of faith, having our hearts sprinkled from an evil conscience and our bodies washed with pure water. Let us hold fast the confession of our hope without wavering, for He who promised is faithful" **(HEBREWS 10:22, 23)**.

To pray without ceasing means to be always in a frame of mind or atmosphere of prayer. In other words, there should never be a time in our lives when prayer is inappropriate. If our minds are in harmony with Jesus, we will turn to Him naturally throughout the day. There are three powerful elements of our prayer lives listed in the passages above. As we approach God *confidently* with hearts full of *thanksgiving* and fervently *present* our needs before Him, He will answer our prayers in the way He knows is best for us.

07 Are there some things that hinder our prayers?

"If I regard iniquity in my heart, the Lord will not hear. But certainly God has heard me; He has attended to the voice of my prayer" **(PSALM 66:18, 19).**

"If My people who are called by My name will humble themselves, and pray and seek My face, and turn from their wicked ways, then I will hear from heaven, and will forgive their sin and heal their land" **(2 CHRONICLES 7:14).**

"But let him ask in faith, with no doubting, for he who doubts is like a wave of the sea driven and tossed by the wind. For let not that man suppose that he will receive anything from the Lord; he is a double-minded man, unstable in all his ways" **(JAMES 1:6–8).**

"You ask and do not receive, because you ask amiss, that you may spend it on your pleasures" **(JAMES 4:3).**

If we cherish sin in our hearts, live hypocritical lives, and use prayer as a method simply to get what we want from God, we will miss the precious relationship He desires—and we certainly will not get answers to our prayers.

08 Where does our confidence rest when we pray, and what is our focus in prayer?

"Now this is the confidence that we have in Him, that if we ask anything according to His will, He hears us" **(1 JOHN 5:14).**

"He went a little farther and fell on His face, and prayed, saying, 'O My Father, if it is possible, let this cup pass from Me; nevertheless, not as I will, but as You will' " **(MATTHEW 26:39).**

"I always do those things that please Him" **(JOHN 8:29).**

"Then I said, 'Behold, I have come—in the volume of the book it is written of Me—to do Your will, O God' " **(HEBREWS 10:7).**

As we pray, our confidence does not rest in our faith, our goodness, or our prayers. Our confidence is in God's goodness. It is in His gracious mercy to us. As we pray, the Holy Spirit interprets our prayers before God's throne. The righteousness of Jesus is mingled with our prayers to make them acceptable to God, since even our best efforts are tinged with our sinful humanity. As we pray, our prayers are united with Jesus' prayers in our behalf. Jesus is praying for us in heaven's sanctuary daily.

The goal of all prayer is to lead us into a closer relationship with Jesus and to instill within us a deeper desire to do His will. The purpose of prayer is not to get our way, but to do His will. As you enter into an ever-deepening relationship with Jesus through prayer, you will enter into life's greatest joy and deepest delight. Your soul will be at rest, and your heart will find peace.

CHAPTER 7

What the Bible Says About Worry

Many Christians are crippled by worry. Fear projects a worst case scenario on the screens of their minds. These two twin enemies of faith—worry and fear—rob them of their joy in the Christian life. Hope dances away like a shadow, and they live in the gloomy pessimism of their fearful thoughts. Fear and worry can eat the heart out of your joy. They can destroy your happiness and keep you in constant turmoil. Does God have an answer for worried minds and troubled hearts? Does He have a solution for anxiety and fear? He certainly does.

First, let's remember that all of us worry at times. Worry is a part of life in a fallen world. We may be concerned about our health, our children, or our finances. But worry and fear become negative forces in our lives when we focus on them and are consumed by them. In this chapter, we will learn how to shift our focus to the reality of God's love, care, and presence in our lives. We will discover His ultimate solution to the problem of worry and fear.

01 Consider the experience of the disciples overwhelmed by a storm on the Sea of Galilee. Why were the disciples so fearful, and why was Jesus so calm?

"And a great windstorm arose, and the waves beat into the boat, so that it was already filling. But He [Jesus] was in the stern, asleep on a pillow. And they [the disciples] awoke Him and said to Him, 'Teacher, do You not care that we are perishing?' Then He arose and rebuked the wind, and said to the sea, 'Peace, be still!' And the wind ceased and there was a great calm. But He said to them, 'Why are you so fearful? How is it that you have no faith?' " **(MARK 4:37–40).**

The disciples were consumed with fear because they were focused upon the storm. Jesus' mind was filled with faith, because He had absolute assurance that His heavenly Father was in control of the storm. Jesus looked at the Father's power. The disciples looked at the storm's power. Jesus' heart was filled with faith. The disciples' hearts were filled with fear. Jesus had peace in the storm, because the Father's peace filled His life every moment of the day.

Jesus offers us His peace. He says, "Peace I leave with you, My peace I give to you; not as the world gives do I give to you. Let not your heart be troubled, neither let it be afraid" **(JOHN 14:27).**

"These things I have spoken to you, that in Me you may have peace. In the world you will have tribulation; but be of good cheer, I have overcome the world" **(JOHN 16:33).**

Throughout the Bible God offers His peace and presence to those who trust Him.

"Yea, though I walk through the valley of the shadow of death, I will fear no evil; for You are with me" **(PSALM 23:4).**

"My heart shall not fear; though war may rise against me, in this I will be confident. One thing I have desired of the LORD, that will I seek: that I may dwell in the house of the LORD all the days of my life" **(PSALM 27:3, 4).**

"I will hear what God the LORD will speak, for He will speak peace" **(PSALM 85:8).**

"Have I not commanded you? Be strong and of good courage; do not be afraid, nor be dismayed, for the LORD your God is with you wherever you go" **(JOSHUA 1:9).**

02 What invitation does our Lord give us when we are overburdened with care, worry, and fear?

"Casting all your care upon Him, for He cares for you" **(1 PETER 5:7).**

The original Greek word translated "casting" really means "throwing your full weight upon something." So Peter's passage might be translated, "Throw the entire weight of all of your worries and anxieties upon Jesus. He is fully able to handle them."

Jesus says, "Come to Me, all you who labor and are heavy laden, and I will give you rest" **(MATTHEW 11:28).**

"I sought the LORD, and He heard me, and delivered me from all my fears. They looked to Him and were radiant, and their faces were not ashamed" **(PSALM 34:4).**

"But immediately Jesus spoke to them, saying, 'Be of good cheer! It is I; do not be afraid.' And Peter . . . said, 'Lord, if it is You, command me to come to You on the water.' So He said, 'Come' " **(MATTHEW 14:27–29).**

The real issue of fear is focus. Fear torments us when we consider all of the bad things that can happen. In any given situation, if we consider all of the negative possibilities that might crush us, we will be left in despair. Jesus speaks to each of our hearts just as He encouraged Peter: "Be of good cheer. Do not be afraid. I have everything under control." As long as Peter kept His eyes upon Jesus, he remained calm. When he turned his attention to his own strength to cope with the elements, he began to sink beneath the waves, and Jesus had to miraculously rescue him. Keeping our eyes on Jesus, we are secure.

"Wait on the LORD; be of good courage, and He shall strengthen your heart; wait, I say, on the LORD" **(PSALM 27:14).**

03 What is the result of casting all of our care upon Jesus, trusting that He is fully capable of handling it?

"You will keep him in perfect peace, whose mind is stayed on You, because he trusts in You. . . . For in YAH, the LORD, is everlasting strength" **(ISAIAH 26:3).**

The main word translated "peace" in the Old Testament is the Hebrew word *shalom.* It means a complete sense of harmony, completeness, security, and restfulness. Throughout the Bible, peace is a gift from God. It is not something we can manufacture or produce. We cannot make ourselves peaceful. Only God can give us peace.

"The LORD will give strength to His people; The LORD will bless His people with peace" **(PSALM 29:11).**

"In returning and rest you shall be saved; in quietness and confidence shall be your strength" **(ISAIAH 30:15).**

The apostle Paul typically opens his New Testament epistles with these words, "Grace to you and peace from God the Father and our Lord Jesus Christ" **(GALATIANS 1:3). (SEE EPHESIANS 1:2; PHILIPPIANS 1:2; COLOSSIANS 1:2; 1 THESSALONIANS 1:1; 2 THESSALONIANS 1:2; 1 TIMOTHY 1:2; 2 TIMOTHY 1:2; TITUS 1:4; PHILEMON 3.)**

For the apostle Paul, peace had its source in the heart of God. If early Christians were going to receive peace, it must come from Him. God is still the Source of peace for our troubled hearts today.

04 We cannot necessarily control every thought that flashes through our minds. When worry rushes in, what counsel does Jesus give us?

"Therefore I say to you, do not worry about your life, what you will eat or what you will drink; nor about your body, what you will put on. Is not life more than food and the body more than clothing? . . . Now if God so clothes the grass of the field, which today is, and tomorrow is thrown into the oven, will He not much more clothe you, O you of little faith? Therefore do not worry, saying, 'What shall we eat?' or 'What shall we drink?' or 'What shall we wear?' . . . For your heavenly Father knows that you need all these things" **(MATTHEW 6:25, 30–32).**

"But seek first the kingdom of God and His righteousness, and all these things shall be added to you. Therefore do not worry about tomorrow, for tomorrow will worry about its own things. Sufficient for the day is its own trouble" **(MATTHEW 6:33, 34).**

Jesus' counsel is clear. It is a matter of priority. Focus your mind on Jesus. He loves you. He cares for you. He will provide life's basic needs. He longs for you to have a happy, abundant life. Tomorrow's troubles will come, but He is fully capable of handling them. In His strength, deal with the challenges you face today, and you will be equipped to handle whatever life brings tomorrow.

"Be anxious for nothing, but in everything by prayer and supplication, with thanksgiving, let your requests be made known to God; and the peace of God, which surpasses all understanding, will guard your hearts and minds through Christ Jesus" **(PHILIPPIANS 4: 6, 7)**.

05 Where do we find strength to deal with our deepest fears?

"There is no fear in love; but perfect love casts out fear, because fear involves torment. But he who fears has not been made perfect in love. We love Him because He first loved us" **(1 JOHN 4:18, 19)**.

Strength to deal with fear and worry is found in God's love. Knowing He loves us and resting in that love delivers us from the paralyzing and tormenting effects of fear.

"Do not fear, little flock, for it is your Father's good pleasure to give you the kingdom" **(LUKE 12:32)**.

We need not fear any earthly calamity or disaster, because through the death of Jesus on the cross we are sons and daughters of God, heirs of an eternal kingdom.

"You drew near on the day I called on You, and said, 'Do not fear!' O Lord, You have pleaded the case for my soul; You have redeemed my life" **(LAMENTATIONS 3:57, 58)**.

06 Where does fear come from? Is God the originator of fear, worry, and anxiety?

"For God has not given us a spirit of fear, but of power and of love and of a sound mind" **(2 TIMOTHY 1:7)**.

God is not the originator of our worries and fears. Sometimes worry is the result of circumstances in life beyond our control. Other times it may be an emotion which we ourselves have cultivated for years. Of course, Satan is behind all negative emotions, seeking to rob us of life's true joy. The power of God is sufficient to give us a "sound" or healthy frame of mind free from the torment of worry. Tormenting fear originates with Satan himself.

"Finally, my brethren, be strong in the Lord and in the power of His might. Put on the whole armor of God, that you may be able to stand against the wiles of the devil. For we do not wrestle against flesh and blood, but against principalities, against powers, against the rulers of the darkness of this age, against spiritual hosts of wickedness in the heavenly places" **(EPHESIANS 6:10–12).**

07 How does the apostle Paul describe God's ultimate goal for each committed Christian?

"Now may the God of hope fill you with all joy and peace in believing, that you may abound in hope by the power of the Holy Spirit" **(ROMANS 15:13).**

"Therefore, having been justified by faith, we have peace with God through our Lord Jesus Christ, through whom also we have access by faith into this grace in which we stand, and rejoice in hope of the glory of God" **(ROMANS 5: 1, 2).**

"For whatever things were written before were written for our learning, that we through the patience and comfort of the Scriptures might have hope" **(ROMANS 15:4).**

"Since we heard of your faith in Christ Jesus and of your love for all the saints; because of the hope which is laid up for you in heaven, of which you heard before in the word of the truth of the gospel" **(COLOSSIANS 1:4, 5).**

"This hope we have as an anchor of the soul, both sure and steadfast, and which enters the Presence behind the veil, where the forerunner has entered for us, even Jesus, having become High Priest forever according to the order of Melchizedek" **(HEBREWS 6:19, 20).**

"Looking for the blessed hope and the glorious appearing of our great God and Savior Jesus Christ" **(TITUS 2:13).**

The Bible mentions hope 128 times. God longs for us to be filled with hope, not fear. His goal for our lives is joy and peace. Why not give Him all your worries and fears today by praying this simple prayer?

"Dear Lord, I confess that at times I focus on the problem more than the solution. Sometimes I am overwhelmed with worry and fear. Right now I choose to cast all of my cares upon You. I believe You are fully capable of handling them. By faith I receive the peace, joy, and hope that You are giving me right now. In Jesus' name, Amen.

CHAPTER 8

What the Bible Says About a Changed Life

Have you ever wondered how you can become the person you really want to be? Why is it that when we try so hard we fail so often? At times we seem to be prisoners of our habits—chained in the dungeon of evil desires.

Unaided by the grace of God, we are all helpless prisoners. We are captives of our fallen sinful nature. We may desire to change, but we don't have the power to change. Separated from God, we are subject to death. The death of Jesus paid the penalty of sin for every person. However, this gift must be accepted individually. It becomes effective when a person chooses to acknowledge Jesus as Savior. God's grace provides pardon from the penalty of sin. It also provides a new power for living. In this chapter, we will discover the real secret of power for living in the twenty-first century.

01 What marvelous promise does Jesus give to those who choose to follow Him totally and surrender to His will?

"Therefore, if anyone is in Christ, he is a new creation; old things have passed away; behold, all things have become new" **(2 CORINTHIANS 5:17).**

God urges "that you put off, concerning your former conduct, the old man which grows corrupt according to the deceitful lusts, and be renewed in the spirit of your mind, and that you put on the new man which was created according to God, in true righteousness and holiness" **(EPHESIANS 4:22–24).**

"Then I will give them one heart, and I will put a new spirit within them, and take the stony heart out of their flesh, and give them a heart of flesh, that they may walk in My statutes and keep My judgments and do them; and they shall be My people, and I will be their God" **(EZEKIEL 11:19, 20).**

"Cast away from you all the transgressions which you have committed, and get yourselves a new heart and a new spirit. For why should you die, O house of Israel?" **(EZEKIEL 18:31).**

"I will give you a new heart and put a new spirit within you; I will take the heart of stone out of your flesh and give you a heart of flesh. I will put My Spirit within you and cause you to walk in My statutes, and you will keep My judgments and do them" **(EZEKIEL 36:26, 27).**

"Then I will give them a heart to know Me, that I am the LORD; and they shall be My people, and I will be their God, for they shall return to Me with their whole heart" **(JEREMIAH 24:7).**

This new heart the Bible talks about is really a new appreciation for divine truth, a new love for Jesus, and a new commitment to follow Him.

"Do not remember the former things, nor consider the things of old" **(ISAIAH 43:18).**

"Do you not know that as many of us as were baptized into Christ Jesus were baptized into His death? Therefore we were buried with Him through baptism into death, that just as Christ was raised from the dead by the glory of the Father, even so we also should walk in newness of life. For if we have been united together in the likeness of His death, certainly we also shall be in the likeness of His resurrection, knowing this, that our old man was crucified with Him, that the body of sin might be done away with, that we should no longer be slaves of sin" **(ROMANS 6:3–6).**

"For in Christ Jesus neither circumcision nor uncircumcision avails anything, but a new creation" **(GALATIANS 6:15).**

"Do not lie to one another, since you have put off the old man with his deeds, and have put on the new man who is renewed in knowledge according to the image of Him who created him" **(COLOSSIANS 3:9, 10).**

02 Is it possible to accomplish this change in our own strength without divine aid?

"Who can bring a clean thing out of an unclean? No one!" **(JOB 14:4).**

"Can the Ethiopian change his skin or the leopard its spots? Then may you also do good who are accustomed to do evil" **(JEREMIAH 13:23).**

" 'Though you wash yourself with lye, and use much soap, yet your iniquity is marked before Me,' says the Lord GOD" **(JEREMIAH 2:22).**

"The heart is deceitful above all things, and desperately wicked; who can know it?" **(JEREMIAH 17:9).**

"Create in me a clean heart, O God, and renew a steadfast spirit within me" **(PSALM 51:10).** (The King James Version of **PSALM 51:10** reads: "renew a right spirit within me.")

"When His disciples heard it, they were greatly astonished, saying, 'Who then can be saved?' But Jesus looked at them and said to them, 'With men this is impossible, but with God all things are possible' " **(MATTHEW 19:25, 26).**

"Those who are in the flesh cannot please God. But you are not in the flesh but in the Spirit, if indeed the Spirit of God dwells in you. Now if anyone does not have the Spirit of Christ, he is not His" **(ROMANS 8:8, 9).**

03 How did Jesus describe this change to Nicodemus, a Jewish religious leader?

"There was a man of the Pharisees named Nicodemus, a ruler of the Jews. This man came to Jesus by night and said to Him, 'Rabbi, we know that You are a teacher come from God; for no one can do these signs that You do unless God is with him.' Jesus answered and said to him, 'Most assuredly, I say to you, unless one is born again, he cannot see the kingdom of God.' Nicodemus said to Him, 'How can a man be born when he is old? Can he enter a second time into his mother's womb and be born?' Jesus answered, 'Most assuredly, I say to you, unless one is born of water and the Spirit, he cannot enter the kingdom of God. That which is born of the flesh is flesh, and that which is born of the Spirit is spirit. Do not marvel that I said to you, "You must be born again." The wind blows where it wishes, and you hear the sound of it, but cannot tell where it comes from and where it goes. So is everyone who is born of the Spirit' " **(JOHN 3:1–8).**

04 What word does the Bible use to describe what Jesus Christ offers us?

"For by grace you have been saved through faith, and that not of yourselves; it is the gift of God, not of works, lest anyone should boast" **(EPHESIANS 2:8, 9).**

"Not by works of righteousness which we have done, but according to His mercy He saved us, through the washing of regeneration and renewing of the Holy Spirit" **(TITUS 3:5).**

"Every good gift and every perfect gift is from above, and comes down from the Father of lights, with whom there is no variation or shadow of turning" **(JAMES 1:17).**

"But the free gift is not like the offense. For if by one man's offense many died, much more the grace of God and the gift by the grace of the one Man, Jesus Christ, abounded to many. And the gift is not like that which came through the one who sinned. For the judgment which came from one offense resulted in condemnation, but the free gift which came from many offenses resulted in justification" **(ROMANS 5:15, 16).**

"For the wages of sin is death, but the gift of God is eternal life in Christ Jesus our Lord" **(ROMANS 6:23).**

Jesus' words to the Samaritan woman by the well speak powerfully to each of us today. "Jesus answered and said to her, 'If you knew the gift of God, and who it is that says to you, "Give me to drink," you would have asked Him, and He would have given you living water' " **(JOHN 4:10).**

Jesus is still heaven's priceless Gift. He is the Gift beyond compare that satisfies the longings of our souls and provides us eternal life, full and free, through His selfless sacrifice on the cross.

05 When we surrender our lives to Christ, how does this life transforming change take place in us?

"I have been crucified with Christ; it is no longer I who live, but Christ lives in me; and the life which I now live in the flesh I live by faith in the Son of God, who loved me and gave Himself for me" **(GALATIANS 2:20).**

"Knowing this, that our old man was crucified with Him, that the body of sin might be done away with, that we should no longer be slaves of sin. For he who has died has been freed from sin. Now if we died with Christ, we believe that we shall also live with Him, knowing that Christ, having been raised from the dead, dies no more. Death no longer has dominion over Him. For the death that He died, He died to sin once for all; but the life that He lives, He lives to God. Likewise you also, reckon yourselves to be dead indeed to sin, but alive to God in Christ Jesus our Lord" **(ROMANS 6:6–11).**

"As many as received Him, to them He gave the right to become children of God, to those who believe in His name" **(JOHN 1:12).**

"Abide in Me, and I in you. As the branch cannot bear fruit of itself, unless it abides in the vine, neither can you, unless you abide in Me" **(JOHN 15:4).**

"This is the covenant that I will make with the house of Israel after those days, says the LORD: I will put My laws in their mind and write them on their hearts; and I will be their God, and they shall be My people" **(HEBREWS 8:10).**

"This is the covenant that I will make with them after those days, says the LORD: I will put My laws into their hearts, and in their minds I will write them" **(HEBREWS 10:16).**

"Those who are Christ's have crucified the flesh with its passions and desires" **(GALATIANS 5:24).**

"God forbid that I should boast except in the cross of our Lord Jesus Christ, by whom the world has been crucified to me, and I to the world" **(GALATIANS 6:14).**

You were "buried with Him in baptism, in which you also were raised with Him through faith in the working of God, who raised Him from the dead. And you, being dead in your trespasses and the uncircumcision of your flesh, He has made alive together with Him, having forgiven you all trespasses" **(COLOSSIANS 2:12, 13).**

"But God, who is rich in mercy, because of His great love with which He loved us, even when we were dead in trespasses, made us alive together with Christ" **(EPHESIANS 2:4, 5).**

"If then you were raised with Christ, seek those things which are above. . . . Set your mind on things above, not on things on the earth. For you died, and your life is hidden with Christ in God" **(COLOSSIANS 3:1–3).**

Jesus wants us to "know that I am in My Father, and you in Me, and I in you" **(JOHN 14:20).**

When we are fully surrendered to Christ the desire of our heart is "that the life of Jesus also may be manifested in our body. For we who live are always delivered to death for Jesus' sake, that the life of Jesus also may be manifested in our mortal flesh" **(2 CORINTHIANS 4:10, 11).**

"Though He was crucified in weakness, yet He lives by the power of God. For we also are weak in Him, but we shall live with Him by the power of God toward you. Examine yourselves as to whether you are in the faith. Test yourselves. Do you not know yourselves, that Jesus Christ is in you?" **(2 CORINTHIANS 13:4, 5).**

Paul prayed "that Christ may dwell in your hearts through faith" **(EPHESIANS 3:17).**

"God willed to make known what are the riches of the glory of this mystery among the Gentiles: which is Christ in you, the hope of glory" **(COLOSSIANS 1:27).**

God redeems a sinner "that he no longer should live the rest of his time in the flesh for the lusts of men, but for the will of God" **(1 PETER 4:2).**

When an individual surrenders totally to God, the Holy Spirit takes possession of the life. The result is a mysterious union with God. The person becomes a new individual.

He or she is now under the control of a completely new nature **(SEE ROMANS 6:6–11)**. By receiving Christ, a person receives power for victorious living **(SEE JOHN 1:12)**, and, day by day, as he abides in Christ, the Holy Spirit writes the principles of the law upon the heart **(SEE JOHN 15:4; HEBREWS 8:10)**.

06 What role does faith play in our salvation and in the change by which we become children of God?

"Where is boasting then? It is excluded. By what law? Of works? No, but by the law of faith. Therefore we conclude that a man is justified by faith apart from the deeds of the law" **(ROMANS 3:27, 28)**.

"Therefore by the deeds of the law no flesh will be justified in His sight, for by the law is the knowledge of sin. But now the righteousness of God apart from the law is revealed, being witnessed by the Law and the Prophets, even the righteousness of God, through faith in Jesus Christ, to all and on all who believe. For there is no difference" **(ROMANS 3:20–22)**.

"If Abraham was justified by works, he has something to boast about, but not before God. For what does the Scripture say? 'Abraham believed God, and it was accounted to him for righteousness.' Now to him who works, the wages are not counted as grace but as debt. But to him who does not work but believes on Him who justifies the ungodly, his faith is accounted for righteousness" **(ROMANS 4:2–5)**.

"Therefore, having been justified by faith, we have peace with God through our Lord Jesus Christ" **(ROMANS 5:1)**.

"He [Jesus] spoke this parable to some who trusted in themselves that they were righteous, and despised others: 'Two men went up to the temple to pray, one a Pharisee and the other a tax collector. The Pharisee stood and prayed thus with himself, "God, I thank You that I am not like other men—extortioners, unjust, adulterers, or even as this tax collector. I fast twice a week; I give tithes of all that I possess." And the tax collector, standing afar off, would not so much as raise his eyes to heaven, but beat his breast, saying, "God, be merciful to me a sinner!" I tell you, this man went down to his house justified rather than the other; for everyone who exalts himself will be humbled, and he who humbles himself will be exalted' " **(LUKE 18:9–14)**.

"What do you have that you did not receive? Now if you did indeed receive it, why do you boast as if you had not received it?" **(1 CORINTHIANS 4:7)**.

"For by grace you have been saved through faith, and that not of yourselves; it is the gift of God, not of works, lest anyone should boast. For we are His workmanship, created in Christ Jesus for good works, which God prepared beforehand that we should walk in them" **(EPHESIANS 2:8–10)**.

"Knowing that a man is not justified by the works of the law but by faith in Jesus Christ, even we have believed in Christ Jesus, that we might be justified by faith in Christ and not by the works of the law; for by the works of the law no flesh shall be justified" **(GALATIANS 2:16).**

"This is the testimony: that God has given us eternal life, and this life is in His Son. He who has the Son has life; he who does not have the Son of God does not have life" **(1 JOHN 5:11, 12).**

"Most assuredly, I say to you, he who hears My word and believes in Him who sent Me has everlasting life, and shall not come into judgment, but has passed from death into life" **(JOHN 5:24).**

"Therefore let it be known to you, brethren, that through this Man is preached to you the forgiveness of sins; and by Him everyone who believes is justified from all things from which you could not be justified by the law of Moses" **(ACTS 13:38, 39).**

"And such [wicked sinners] were some of you. But you were washed, but you were sanctified, but you were justified in the name of the Lord Jesus and by the Spirit of our God" **(1 CORINTHIANS 6:11).**

"Therefore the law was our tutor [schoolmaster] to bring us to Christ, that we might be justified by faith" **(GALATIANS 3:24).**

Paul's wish was "that I may gain Christ and be found in Him, not having my own righteousness, which is from the law, but that which is through faith in Christ, the righteousness which is from God by faith" **(PHILIPPIANS 3:8, 9).**

"Having been justified by His grace we should become heirs according to the hope of eternal life" **(TITUS 3:7).**

Salvation is totally of grace, never of works. By faith we receive God's grace. Even when the born-again Christian obeys God, it is Christ who empowers him to obey. We only cooperate with Christ and let Christ work in us. Our responsibility is to be willing to do anything Christ asks us to do. Love is the motive for obedience. Christ will never ask us to do anything that He will not provide us the power to do.

07 If salvation is by faith, how can I receive Jesus' power to overcome sin and temptation in my life?

"But as many as received Him, to them He gave the right to become children of God, to those who believe in His name" **(JOHN 1:12).**

In this verse, the Greek word translated "right" (the right to become children of God) is *exousia*. It can mean both "authority" and "power." When we receive Jesus as our Savior, God gives us both the authority and the power to become His child.

"Likewise you also, reckon [count] yourselves to be dead indeed to sin, but alive to God in Christ Jesus our Lord" **(ROMANS 6:11).**

"But where sin abounded, grace abounded much more" **(ROMANS 5:20).**

"If anyone is in Christ, he is a new creation; old things have passed away; behold, all things have become new" **(2 CORINTHIANS 5:17).**

"Therefore 'Come out from among them and be separate, says the Lord. Do not touch what is unclean, and I will receive you. I will be a Father to you, and you shall be My sons and daughters, says the LORD Almighty' " **(2 CORINTHIANS 6:17, 18).**

"For you are all sons of God through faith in Christ Jesus" **(GALATIANS 3:26).**

As a child of God, you become heir "to an inheritance incorruptible and undefiled and that does not fade away, reserved in heaven for you" **(1 PETER 1:4).**

"Behold what manner of love the Father has bestowed on us, that we should be called children of God!" **(1 JOHN 3:1).**

To receive Christ is to receive this power. As He enters our lives, He is the power for victory. In our natural state, we are incapable of doing good. When we want to do what is right, another power seems to take possession of us. Through Jesus we have the power to overcome. We no longer need to fail again and again, fixed in the rut of perpetual discouragement. Now we can be victorious.

08 When Jesus enters our hearts through the Holy Spirit, what does He give us?

"But if the Spirit of Him who raised Jesus from the dead dwells in you, He who raised Christ from the dead will also give life to your mortal bodies through His Spirit who dwells in you" **(ROMANS 8:11).**

"This is the testimony: that God has given us eternal life, and this life is in His Son. He who has the Son has life; he who does not have the Son of God does not have life. These things I have written to you who believe in the name of the Son of God, that you may know that you have eternal life, and that you may continue to believe in the name of the Son of God" **(1 JOHN 5:11–13).**

"We are in Him who is true, in His Son Jesus Christ. This is the true God and eternal life" **(1 JOHN 5:20).**

"In this the love of God was manifested toward us, that God has sent His only begotten Son into the world, that we might live through Him" **(1 JOHN 4:9).**

"In Him [Jesus] was life, and the life was the light of men" **(JOHN 1:4).**

"Jesus said to her [Martha, sorrowing at the death of her brother Lazarus], 'I am the resurrection and the life. He who believes in Me, though he may die, he shall live. And whoever lives [when I return] and believes in Me shall never die. Do you believe this?' " (JOHN 11:25, 26).

Jesus declared, "I am the way, the truth, and the life. No one comes to the Father except through Me" (JOHN 14:6).

"If we have been united together in the likeness of His death, certainly we also shall be in the likeness of His resurrection" (ROMANS 6:5).

09 What is the greatest evidence that Christ dwells in our hearts?

The greatest evidence that Christ dwells in our hearts is a transformed life. To "crucify the flesh" is to voluntarily go through the pain of surrendering our will to Christ.

"Those who are Christ's have crucified the flesh with its passions and desires. If we live in the Spirit, let us also walk in the Spirit" (GALATIANS 5:24, 25).

A converted, born-again Christian has become a new person: "You have put off the old man with his deeds, and have put on the new man who is renewed in knowledge according to the image of Him who created him" (COLOSSIANS 3:9, 10).

This was the experience of the apostle Paul, who testified, "The world has been crucified to me, and I to the world" (GALATIANS 6:14).

"Knowing this, that our old man was crucified with Him, that the body of sin might be done away with, that we should no longer be slaves of sin" (ROMANS 6:6).

"For if you live according to the flesh you will die; but if by the Spirit you put to death the deeds of the body, you will live" (ROMANS 8:13).

Paul appeals to us, "Put on the Lord Jesus Christ, and make no provision for the flesh, to fulfill its lusts" (ROMANS 13:14).

And Peter echoes, "Beloved, I beg you as sojourners and pilgrims, abstain from fleshly lusts which war against the soul" (1 PETER 2:11).

10 What was the one guiding principle of Jesus' life that influenced all of His decisions?

"Then I said, 'Behold, I have come—in the volume of the book it is written of Me—to do Your will, O God' " (HEBREWS 10:7).

In the previously quoted words, the writer of Hebrews records Christ's fulfillment of a Messianic prophecy containing these beautiful words: "Then I said, 'Behold, I come; in the scroll of the book it is written of me. I delight to do Your will, O my God, and Your law is within my heart' " **(PSALM 40:7, 8).**

"He who sent Me is with Me. The Father has not left Me alone, for I always do those things that please Him" **(JOHN 8:29).**

Jesus' longing was to do the Father's will. His heart's desire was to please God. The heart desire of every Christian who has been transformed by God's grace is to do God's will.

"Jesus said to them, 'My food is to do the will of Him who sent Me, and to finish His work' " **(JOHN 4:34).**

"I do not seek My own will but the will of the Father who sent Me" **(JOHN 5:30).**

"I have come down from heaven, not to do My own will, but the will of Him who sent Me" **(JOHN 6:38).**

"That the world may know that I love the Father, and as the Father gave Me commandment, so I do" **(JOHN 14:31).**

"If you keep My commandments, you will abide in My love, just as I have kept My Father's commandments and abide in His love" **(JOHN 15:10).**

The guiding principle of Jesus' life was His desire to please His Father in all things. The passion of His life was to do His Father's will. His highest delight was obedience to His Father's commands and revealing His Father's love.

What divine commendation follows such an attitude? "Suddenly a voice came from heaven, saying, 'This is My beloved Son, in whom I am well pleased' " **(MATTHEW 3:17).**

In His victorious life, lived to please God, Jesus "was in all points tempted as we are, yet without sin" **(HEBREWS 4:15).**

11 When Jesus breaks the bondage of sin, what wonderful privilege does He offer us? What does He call us?

"As many as are led by the Spirit of God, these are sons of God. For you did not receive the spirit of bondage again to fear, but you received the Spirit of adoption by whom we cry out, 'Abba, Father.' The Spirit Himself bears witness with our spirit that we are children of God, and if children, then heirs—heirs of God and joint heirs with Christ" **(ROMANS 8:14–17).**

Abba is an Aramaic term used in direct address for the title "father." But more than that, it was a commonly used colloquialism for the close, warm relationship between children and their father. As such, it is equivalent to our English term "Daddy."

What a wonderful privilege to know we are an adopted son or daughter of God through Christ! We are part of God's royal family with all the rights and privileges of a family member. We never need to feel lonely, insecure, or uncertain again. Jesus is our older Brother; God is our wonderful, loving heavenly Father; the Holy Spirit is our Counselor and Guide; and the angels are our protectors.

12 What does Christ promise to do deep within us through the power of His Holy Spirit?

"This is the covenant that I will make with the house of Israel after those days, says the LORD: I will put My laws in their mind and write them on their hearts; and I will be their God, and they shall be My people" **(HEBREWS 8:10).**

The same thought expressed above is *repeated* for emphasis two chapters later in these words: "This is the covenant that I will make with them after those days, says the LORD: I will put My laws into their hearts, and in their minds I will write them" **(HEBREWS 10:16).**

In the two texts listed above, the inspired writer of Hebrews—who most Christians believe was the apostle Paul—was quoting this verse from the prophet Jeremiah: "This is the covenant that I will make with the house of Israel after those days, says the LORD: I will put My law in their minds, and write it on their hearts; and I will be their God, and they shall be My people" **(JEREMIAH 31:33).**

"Behold, the days are coming, says the LORD, when I will make a new covenant with the house of Israel and with the house of Judah" **(JEREMIAH 31:31). (COMPARE ALSO HEBREWS 8:8.)**

"The LORD your God will circumcise your heart and the heart of your descendants, to love the LORD your God with all your heart and with all your soul, that you may live" **(DEUTERONOMY 30:6).**

"You are our epistle written in our hearts, known and read by all men; clearly you are an epistle of Christ, ministered by us, written not with ink but by the Spirit of the living God, not on tablets of stone but on tablets of flesh, that is, of the heart" **(2 CORINTHIANS 3:2, 3).**

The old covenant was written on tablets of stone *by the finger of God* **(SEE EXODUS 24:12; 31:18; 32:16).** The new covenant is written on tablets of flesh, that is, of the heart, *by the Spirit of God.*

"But if the ministry of death, written and engraved on stones, was glorious, so that the children of Israel could not look steadily at the face of Moses because of the glory of his countenance **(SEE EXODUS 34:29–35),** which glory was passing away, how will the ministry of the Spirit not be more glorious?" **(2 CORINTHIANS 3:7, 8).**

The Old Testament prophet, Ezekiel, was led by God to write of this miraculous change of heart: "Then I will give them one heart, and I will put a new spirit within them, and take the stony heart out of their flesh, and give them a heart of flesh, that they may walk in My statutes and keep My judgments and do them; and they shall be My people, and I will be their God" **(EZEKIEL 11:19, 20).**

Ezekiel repeats this glorious thought some chapters later in his book: "I will give you a new heart and put a new spirit within you; I will take the heart of stone out of your flesh and give you a heart of flesh. I will put My Spirit within you and cause you to walk in My statutes, and you will keep My judgments and do them" **(EZEKIEL 36:26, 27).**

The apostle Peter speaks of "the Holy Spirit whom God has given to those who obey Him" **(ACTS 5:32).**

Jesus taught us, "If you love Me, keep My commandments. And I will pray the Father, and He will give you another Helper, that He may abide with you forever—the Spirit of truth, whom the world cannot receive, because it neither sees Him nor knows Him; but you know Him, for He dwells with you and will be in you" **(JOHN 14:15–17).**

God promises to change us from within. He will place His law in our mind so we know it. He will also write it in our hearts so we love it. When God changes us inside, we will love to do His will.

13 When will this miraculous new birth take place?

"Behold, I stand at the door and knock. If anyone hears My voice and opens the door, I will come in to him and dine with him, and he with Me" **(REVELATION 3:20).**

The Lord Jesus, being a perfect gentleman, will never force Himself upon us. Rather than kick in the doors of our hearts, He patiently waits for us to open them and welcome Him into our lives. The choice is ours and ours alone.

"Jesus answered and said to him, 'If anyone loves Me, he will keep My word; and My Father will love him, and We will come to him and make Our home with him' " **(JOHN 14:23).**

Jesus urges, let "yourselves be like men who wait for their master, when he will return from the wedding, that when he comes and knocks they may open to him immediately. Blessed are those servants whom the master, when he comes, will find watching" **(LUKE 12:36, 37).**

"What then shall we say to these things? If God is for us, who can be against us? He who did not spare His own Son, but delivered Him up for us all, how shall He not with Him also freely give us all things? . . . Yet in all these things we are more than conquerors through Him who loved us" **(ROMANS 8:31, 32, 37).**

Jesus delights in giving us new power for living. As we consciously choose to invite Him to become the Lord of our lives, His dynamic, life-transforming power changes us. He lifts us from our human weakness and gives us His divine strength. No longer must we battle the desires of our human nature alone. We are now conquerors through Jesus Christ our Lord. In Christ we are free to become the people we were born to be.

Amazed at Bethlehem

A careful look at Jesus' life leaves even skeptics amazed. The teachings of Jesus are amazing. His parables are amazing. His miracles are amazing. When Mary and Joseph found Him teaching on the wonders of grace in the temple at only twelve years of age, Luke's Gospel records, "Everyone who heard him was amazed . . ." **(LUKE 2:47, NIV)**. Some of the most incredible events in Jesus' life surrounded His birth. Matthew's genealogy of Jesus, Joseph's faith, Mary's submission, and Christ's incarnation are simply amazing. At Bethlehem, there are significant spiritual insights to discover. There is a depth of truth to mine. There are practical lessons of faith to learn.

Amazed at Jesus' Genealogy

Genealogies are not usually the most interesting part of the Bible. We tend to skip over them quickly. The long list of names of who "begot" who can seem either quite daunting or downright boring. But before we pass over Jesus' genealogy too rapidly, here are a few thoughts to keep in mind. Matthew's Gospel was written to a Jewish audience to present indisputable evidence that Jesus was the Messiah. Every Jew was interested in their pedigree. A person's genealogy was an essential part of their life. The Jews placed extreme importance on the purity of one's lineage. The Sanhedrin kept impeccably accurate records of each Jewish leader's genealogy.

Jesus' genealogy ends with these significant words: "So all the generations from Abraham to David are fourteen generations, from David until the captivity in Babylon are fourteen generations, and from the captivity in Babylon until the Christ are fourteen generations" **(MATTHEW 1:17)**.

Christ's genealogy summarizes the three great stages of Jewish history. The first fourteen generations lead us from Abraham through the rise of Israel to the nation's greatest king, David. These are Israel's glory days. The pinnacle of Israel's history was David's reign. The next fourteen generations take us from David through Israel's shame and defeat to the Babylonian captivity. This is the bondage or captivity period. The last fourteen generations guide us to Israel's Messiah or Deliverer, Jesus Christ. This is the time of liberation.

Matthew's genealogy is really the story of the plan of salvation in three stages.

The human race was created in the "image of God" destined for greatness. We are not what we were created to be. Through our own free choice, we have rebelled against our Maker. The fall brought guilt, shame, and condemnation. It resulted in disease, disaster, and death. Even then God did not abandon us. He did not leave us to our own folly. He provided a way of escape. Jesus Christ, the Divine Son of God, was born as a babe in Bethlehem's manger; He entered this snake pit of a world, filled with selfishness and greed and revealed the Father's heart. He is our Liberator. He "sets the captives free."

Here at the birth of Christ—gathered around the cradle of the Messiah—we find enough grace for us all. Now that's pretty amazing! But it is just the beginning of the story. There are three central figures in the story that we must consider further—Joseph, Mary, and the Christ child.

Amazed at Joseph's Faith

Think of the thoughts that must have raced through Joseph's mind when he discovered that Mary was pregnant. He must have been astonished, confused, bewildered, and perplexed. The scripture declares that "Mary was betrothed to Joseph" **(MATTHEW 1:18)**. What does this mean? What exactly is betrothal? In Jewish society in the days of Jesus, there were actually three steps to consummate a marriage. First there was engagement. Typically the parents chose the marriage partner for their son or daughter. There was an agreement between the parental parties that their children would one day marry. This contract between the two families when the boy and girl were young was termed engagement. The engagement could be broken if the girl eventually refused to marry.

The engagement was followed by betrothal. The couple now formally accepted the engagement and entered into one year of betrothal. During this year, the couple was committed to marriage. In a sense, they functioned as husband and wife although they did not yet enter into the privileges of a married couple. If the betrothal bond was ever to be broken, the couple must register for a legal divorce.

After the one year betrothal, the man and woman sealed their love in the wedding ceremony. Now they were free to enter into the privileges of marriage as they consummated their relationship on their wedding night. It was a great embarrassment for the family for a woman to become pregnant during the betrothal period. It was a shame both for the family and for the couple.

This is precisely why Joseph was quietly seeking the necessary legal divorce or way out of the marriage contract when the angel appeared and explained, " 'do not be afraid to take to you Mary your wife, for that which is conceived in her is of the Holy Spirit. And she will bring forth a Son, and you shall call His name JESUS, for He will save His people from their sins' " **(MATTHEW 1:20, 21)**. Joseph's response is amazing. "Then Joseph, being aroused from sleep, did as the angel of the Lord commanded him and took to him his wife" **(MATTHEW 1:24)**. Joseph trusted God and did exactly what God asked him to do.

What faith! This is precisely what faith is all about. Faith is trusting God and doing what He says. It is not based on some sentimental, emotional feeling. It is grounded in His Word.

As in our minds we come to Bethlehem to view the Christ child, the words of the angel to Joseph speak to our hearts. "You shall call His name Jesus and He shall save His people from their sins." By faith we grasp the reality of His grace. By faith we understand the majesty of His love. By faith we accept the purpose of His mission. By faith, in His presence, we realize that our hopes and dreams are fulfilled in Him and we stand amazed.

Amazed at Mary's Submission

If Joseph was perplexed at the angel's announcement, how do you think Mary reacted? She must have been absolutely astonished when the angel appeared to her and declared, " 'Rejoice, highly favored one, the Lord is with you; blessed are you among women!' " **(LUKE 1:28)**. The record affirms that she was "troubled." The angel continues, " 'And behold, you will conceive in your womb and bring forth a Son, and shall call His name JESUS. He will be great, and will be called the Son of the Highest; and the Lord God will give Him the throne of His father David. And He will reign over the house of Jacob forever, and of His kingdom there will be no end' " **(LUKE 1:31–33)**.

At this point, Mary was absolutely astonished. Imagine her thoughts. *Could this really be happening? How could I become pregnant with the Messiah?*

I have never known a man. How will I explain this to my parents? What will they think? I will be the laughing stock of Nazareth. The angel continued his explanation, " 'The Holy Spirit will come upon you, and the power of the Highest will overshadow you; therefore, also, that Holy One who is to be born will be called the Son of God' " **(LUKE 1:35).**

Mary's response is classic. It echoes through the centuries and speaks to us today. "Then Mary said, 'Behold the maidservant of the Lord! Let it be to me according to your word' " **(LUKE 1:38).** Essentially Mary responded, "Lord, I do not understand all of this. I am confused. I do not have all the answers. I don't even understand what questions to ask, but if this is Your will, I accept it." Mary's submission is an amazing thing. She said, "Whatever God says, I will do."

At Bethlehem's manger, we stand amazed at a teenage girl, Mary, totally committed to doing God's will whatever it takes. Our faith is increased and in our imagination we, too, kneel on the straw in submission.

Amazed at Jesus' Incarnation

The most amazing fact about Bethlehem is the Baby in the manger. God chose to reveal Himself among the animals in a barn. God chose to speak to the human race in the innocence, the gentleness, and helplessness of a baby. The Creator of the universe identifies with His creation. The King of kings tabernacles in human flesh and is born in a stinking, smelling stable. He comes to reveal the Father's love. He comes to face the temptations of Satan head-on. He comes to live and die for us. He comes to bear the condemnation and guilt of our sins. He comes to die the death that was ours so we can live the life that was His. He comes to hang on the cross in shame so we can sit with Him upon His throne in glory. Love knows no other way.

There in Bethlehem, in that Baby lying in the straw, we, too, discover that the essence of life is giving, not getting. Life takes on new meaning as our hands are unselfishly open to give, not selfishly reaching out to grasp for more.

There at Bethlehem, we fall on our knees to worship Him once again. Like Joseph, we kneel in faith, believing. Like Mary, we kneel in submission, surrendering. With millions of every nation, kindred, tongue, and people, we kneel in adoration, amazed.

CHAPTER 9

What the Bible Says About the Great Controversy Between Good and Evil

God has left His fingerprints across our world. The dazzling splendor of a sunset, the majesty of snowcapped mountain peaks, the glory of a starlit night, the beauty of an opening rosebud, and the carefree laughter of children playing—all speak to us of a loving God who delights in making His people happy.

But other fingerprints give evidence that someone else stalks our planet. Ours is a world in trouble—a world consumed with war, famine, and poverty; a world writhing in sickness, disease, and sorrow.

Rising from this troubled planet like an incense of doom is the persistent question: Why? Why war and suffering and heartache and death?

Doesn't God care? Are we only a forgotten cinder out on the edge of an unimportant galaxy? A world that doesn't matter? If God is a God of love, why is there so much suffering in our world? Why do the good suffer as well as the bad?

The Bible draws aside the curtain on one of life's greatest dramas, allowing us to look behind the scenes in the great controversy between good and evil. This chapter will provide a clear answer to the question of who is responsible for this world's suffering. It will also reveal God's ultimate solution to the problem of why innocent people suffer.

01 What is God's fundamental nature? Is He responsible for the sin and suffering in our world?

"The LORD has appeared of old to me, saying: 'Yes, I have loved you with an everlasting love; therefore with lovingkindness I have drawn you' " **(JEREMIAH 31:3).**

"We love Him because He first loved us" **(1 JOHN 4:19).**

"But the mercy of the LORD is from everlasting to everlasting on those who fear Him, and His righteousness to children's children" **(PSALM 103:17).**

" 'With a little wrath I hid My face from you for a moment; but with everlasting kindness I will have mercy on you,' says the LORD, your Redeemer" **(ISAIAH 54:8).**

"Now may our Lord Jesus Christ Himself, and our God and Father, who has loved us and given us everlasting consolation and good hope by grace, comfort your hearts and establish you in every good word and work" **(2 THESSALONIANS 2:16, 17).**

"But God, who is rich in mercy, because of His great love with which He loved us, even when we were dead in trespasses, made us alive together with Christ (by grace you have been saved)" **(EPHESIANS 2:4, 5).**

Note the beautiful paradox in Paul's counsel "to know the love of Christ which passes knowledge; that you may be filled with all the fullness of God" **(EPHESIANS 3:19).**

"Thus says the LORD: 'Let not the wise man glory in his wisdom, let not the mighty man glory in his might, nor let the rich man glory in his riches; but let him who glories glory in this, that he understands and knows Me, that I am the LORD, exercising lovingkindness, judgment, and righteousness in the earth. For in these I delight,' says the LORD" **(JEREMIAH 9:23, 24).**

"For we ourselves were also once foolish, disobedient, deceived, serving various lusts and pleasures, living in malice and envy, hateful and hating one another. But when the kindness and the love of God our Savior toward man appeared, not by works of righteousness which we have done, but according to His mercy He saved us, through the washing of regeneration and renewing of the Holy Spirit" **(TITUS 3:3–5).**

"Blessed be the God and Father of our Lord Jesus Christ, who according to His abundant mercy has begotten us again to a living hope through the resurrection of Jesus Christ from the dead" **(1 PETER 1:3).**

"He who does not love does not know God, for God is love" **(1 JOHN 4:8).**

"We have known and believed the love that God has for us. God is love, and he who abides in love abides in God, and God in him" **(1 JOHN 4:16).**

Moses asked the Lord, "Please, show me Your glory." "And the LORD passed before him and proclaimed, 'The LORD, the LORD God, merciful and gracious, longsuffering, and abounding in goodness and truth, keeping mercy for thousands, forgiving iniquity and transgression and sin, by no means clearing the guilty, visiting the iniquity of the fathers upon the children and the children's children to the third and the fourth generation' " **(EXODUS 33:18; 34:6, 7).**

"For You, Lord, are good, and ready to forgive, and abundant in mercy to all those who call upon You. . . . But You, O Lord, are a God full of compassion, and gracious, longsuffering and abundant in mercy and truth" **(PSALM 86:5, 15).**

"Finally, brethren, farewell. Become complete. Be of good comfort, be of one mind, live in peace; and the God of love and peace will be with you" **(2 CORINTHIANS 13:11).**

"But God, who is rich in mercy, because of His great love with which He loved us" **(EPHESIANS 2:4).**

The essence of God's nature is love. He desires only what is best for us. All of His actions toward us are loving. They are designed to produce lasting happiness. God would never do anything that is not ultimately for our best good. For God to act any other way than in love would be to act contrary to His very nature.

02 If God is not responsible for the evil in our world, who is?

"Another parable He [Jesus] put forth to them, saying: 'The kingdom of heaven is like a man who sowed good seed in his field; but while men slept, his enemy came and sowed tares among the wheat and went his way. But when the grain had sprouted and produced a crop, then the tares also appeared. So the servants of the owner came and said to him, "Sir, did you not sow good seed in your field? How then does it have tares?" He said to them, "An enemy has done this." The servants said to him, "Do you want us then to go and gather them up?" ' " **(MATTHEW 13:24–28).**

"Be sober, be vigilant; because your adversary the devil walks about like a roaring lion, seeking whom he may devour" **(1 PETER 5:8).**

"So the great dragon was cast out, that serpent of old, called the Devil and Satan, who deceives the whole world; he was cast to the earth, and his angels were cast out with him" **(REVELATION 12:9).**

"But I fear, lest somehow, as the serpent deceived Eve by his craftiness, so your minds may be corrupted from the simplicity that is in Christ" **(2 CORINTHIANS 11:3).**

"You once walked according to the course of this world, according to the prince of the power of the air, the spirit who now works in the sons of disobedience" **(EPHESIANS 2:2).**

"Put on the whole armor of God, that you may be able to stand against the wiles of the devil. For we do not wrestle against flesh and blood, but against principalities, against powers, against the rulers of the darkness of this age, against spiritual hosts of wickedness in the heavenly places" **(EPHESIANS 6:11, 12).**

03 What are some of the names of this enemy of God and man? What tactics does he use?

Jesus continues His explanation of the parable: "The enemy who sowed them [the tares] is the devil, the harvest is the end of the age, and the reapers are the angels" **(MATTHEW 13:39).**

"Be sober, be vigilant; because your adversary the devil walks about like a roaring lion, seeking whom he may devour" **(1 PETER 5:8).**

"So the great dragon was cast out, that serpent of old, called the Devil and Satan, who deceives the whole world; he was cast to the earth, and his angels were cast out with him" **(REVELATION 12:9).**

"But I fear, lest somehow, as the serpent deceived Eve by his craftiness, so your minds may be corrupted from the simplicity that is in Christ" **(2 CORINTHIANS 11:3).**

"You once walked according to the course of this world, according to the prince of the power of the air, the spirit who now works in the sons of disobedience" **(EPHESIANS 2:2).**

"Put on the whole armor of God, that you may be able to stand against the wiles of the devil. For we do not wrestle against flesh and blood, but against principalities, against powers, against the rulers of the darkness of this age, against spiritual hosts of wickedness in the heavenly places" **(EPHESIANS 6:11, 12).**

04 Where did sin originate?

"He who sins is of the devil, for the devil has sinned from the beginning. For this purpose the Son of God was manifested, that He might destroy the works of the devil" **(1 JOHN 3:8).**

"You are of your father the devil, and the desires of your father you want to do. He was a murderer from the beginning, and does not stand in the truth, because there is no truth in him. When he speaks a lie, he speaks from his own resources, for he is a liar and the father of it" **(JOHN 8:44)**.

"So the great dragon was cast out, that serpent of old, called the Devil and Satan, who deceives the whole world; he was cast to the earth, and his angels were cast out with him" **(REVELATION 12:9)**.

"God did not spare the angels who sinned, but cast them down to hell and delivered them into chains of darkness, to be reserved for judgment" **(2 PETER 2:4)**.

"The angels who did not keep their proper domain, but left their own abode, He has reserved in everlasting chains under darkness for the judgment of the great day" **(JUDE 6)**.

"And He [Jesus] said to them, 'I saw Satan fall like lightning from heaven' " **(LUKE 10:18)**.

"Now is the judgment of this world; now the ruler of this world will be cast out" **(JOHN 12:31)**.

The Holy Spirit will convict the world "of judgment, because the ruler of this world is judged" **(JOHN 16:11)**.

It is shocking but true. Satan's rebellion began in heaven. Evil originated there. The devil had his beginning in the heavenly courts. Oh, he was not a devil when God created him! Many people imagine the devil as dwelling in some hot spot of burning flames deep within the bowels of the earth. On the contrary, the devil fell from heaven.

05 Did God create a devil?

"Son of man, take up a lamentation for the king of Tyre, and say to him, 'Thus says the Lord God: "You were the seal of perfection, full of wisdom and perfect in beauty. You were in Eden, the garden of God; every precious stone was your covering: the sardius, topaz, and diamond, beryl, onyx, and jasper, sapphire, turquoise, and emerald with gold. The workmanship of your timbrels and pipes was prepared for you on the day you were created. You were the anointed cherub who covers; I established you; you were on the holy mountain of God; you walked back and forth in the midst of fiery stones. You were perfect in your ways from the day you were created, till iniquity was found in you" ' " **(EZEKIEL 28:12–15)**.

God inspired Ezekiel to rebuke "the king of Tyre," who was a wicked agent of the devil. But as the prophet proceeded, he shifted his focus to Satan himself, who as "*the anointed cherub*" in heaven was "*perfect* in [his] ways from the day [he was] created, till iniquity was found in [him]." This shift in subject—from the king of Tyre to the devil—is clearly seen when we read that "*you were in Eden*, the garden of God." That cannot be said of the king of Tyre, but it well describes Satan who visited the Garden in his diabolical role of the tempting serpent who seduced our mother Eve!

"Son of man, say to the prince of Tyre, 'Thus says the Lord GOD: "Because your heart is lifted up, and you say, 'I am a god, I sit in the seat of gods, in the midst of the seas,' yet you are a man, and not a god, though you set your heart as the heart of a god" ' " **(EZEKIEL 28:2).** This text shows the devilish pride in the heart of the prince, or king, of Tyre—overwhelming pride inspired by Satan in the heart of a mere mortal.

"Now the serpent was more cunning than any beast of the field which the LORD God had made. And he said to the woman, 'Has God indeed said, "You shall not eat of every tree of the garden?" ' And the woman said to the serpent, 'We may eat the fruit of the trees of the garden; but of the fruit of the tree which is in the midst of the garden, God has said, "You shall not eat it, nor shall you touch it, lest you die." ' Then the serpent said to the woman, 'You will not surely die. For God knows that in the day you eat of it your eyes will be opened, and you will be like God, knowing good and evil.' So when the woman saw that the tree was good for food, that it was pleasant to the eyes, and a tree desirable to make one wise, she took of its fruit and ate. She also gave to her husband with her, and he ate" **(GENESIS 3:1–6).**

God promises, "To him who overcomes I will give to eat from the tree of life, which is in the midst of the Paradise of God" **(REVELATION 2:7).**

"You shall make a mercy seat of pure gold; two and a half cubits shall be its length and a cubit and a half its width. And you shall make two cherubim of gold; of hammered work you shall make them at the two ends of the mercy seat. Make one cherub at one end, and the other cherub at the other end; you shall make the cherubim at the two ends of it of one piece with the mercy seat. And the cherubim shall stretch out their wings above, covering the mercy seat with their wings, and they shall face one another; the faces of the cherubim shall be toward the mercy seat" **(EXODUS 25:17–20).**

"The mercy seat" in the sanctuary Moses built on earth represented God's throne in heaven. Thus the cherubim sculpted of solid gold, whose wings stretched out over the mercy seat, represented the special angels favored to be closest to God and His throne. This, then, was the exalted position occupied by Lucifer in heaven **(SEE EZEKIEL 28:12–15).** But even this blessing was not enough to satisfy his prideful heart, and he rebelled against his Creator, as **REVELATION 12:7–9** tells us.

God created Lucifer a beautiful, glorious angel. He was perfect in his ways. God gave this magnificent angel the capacity to choose. To remove the power of choice is to remove the power to love. Genuine love is not forced or coerced; it springs from divine love. To destroy the ability to love is to deny the opportunity to be fully happy and completely free. Since God longs for all His creatures to be fully happy and free, He has given them the power of choice.

06 What thoughts, deep within Lucifer's mind, led him into rebellion against God?

"How you are fallen from heaven, O Lucifer, son of the morning! How you are cut down to the ground, you who weakened the nations! For you have said in your heart: 'I will ascend into heaven, I will exalt my throne above the stars of God; I will also sit on the mount of the congregation on the farthest sides of the north; I will ascend above the heights of the clouds, I will be like the Most High' " **(ISAIAH 14:12–14).**

This illuminating passage shows us the selfish pride that motivated the once-noble Lucifer and caused him to fall into sin, making him the embodiment of evil we call Satan. Lucifer may have had twenty-twenty vision, but he had "I" trouble—big time! Note the personal pronouns so prominent in his thinking and expressed in the words quoted above: It is "MY throne"—not God's—that this devil-in-the-making wants to exalt. Then, five times in as many sentences, he voices the personal pronoun "I . . . I . . . I . . . I . . . I," boldly boasting what he hoped to accomplish by his blasphemous plans. Talk about ungodly ambition!

"And another sign appeared in heaven: behold, a great, fiery red dragon having seven heads and ten horns, and seven diadems on his heads. His tail drew a third of the stars of heaven and threw them to the earth" **(REVELATION 12:3, 4).**

Many Bible scholars believe this verse teaches that Satan deceived as many as one-third of the heavenly angels into following him in his rebellion against God! They base this conclusion on the statement: "His tail drew a third of the stars of heaven and threw them to the earth." **REVELATION 12:9 AND 20:2** explicitly state that "the dragon" is "the Devil and Satan," and **REVELATION 1:20** explains that stars are used to represent angels.

07 Where did this rebellion lead? As a result, what eventually happened to Satan?

"And war broke out in heaven: Michael and his angels fought with the dragon; and the dragon and his angels fought, but they did not prevail, nor was a place found for them in heaven any longer. So the great dragon was cast out, that serpent of old, called the Devil and Satan, who deceives the whole world; he was cast to the earth, and his angels were cast out with him" **(REVELATION 12:7–9).**

Satan, the name of God's archenemy, means "adversary." Satan, the great adversary of both God and man, is also known as the *devil* **(MATTHEW 4:10, 11)**, *Beelzebub* **(MATTHEW 12:24)**, *Belial* **(2 CORINTHIANS 6:15)**, the *tempter* **(MATTHEW 4:1, 3)**, the *enemy* **(MATTHEW 13:28, 39)**, the *wicked one* **(MATTHEW 13:38)**, the *serpent* or *dragon* **(REVELATION 12:3, 9, 17; 20:2; GENESIS 3:1–6)**, the *accuser* **(REVELATION 12:10; ZECHARIAH 3:1–4; JOB 1:6–12; 2:1–6)**, and the *adversary* **(1 PETER 5:8)**.

"For we do not wrestle against flesh and blood, but against principalities, against powers, against the rulers of the darkness of this age, against spiritual hosts of wickedness in the heavenly places" **(EPHESIANS 6:12)**.

"Then Jesus said to him, 'Away with you, Satan! For it is written, "You shall worship the LORD your God, and Him only you shall serve" ' " **(MATTHEW 4:10)**.

Every angel chose either the path of loyalty or rebellion. The same option is available to every human being. There are only two ways: the way of loyalty to God or the way of rebellion against God.

08 How did our world become involved in this great controversy between good and evil?

"Therefore, just as through one man sin entered the world, and death through sin, and thus death spread to all men, because all sinned" **(ROMANS 5:12)**.

"Therefore, as through one man's offense [Adam's] judgment came to all men, resulting in condemnation, even so through one Man's [Christ's] righteous act the free gift came to all men, resulting in justification of life. For as by one man's disobedience many were made sinners, so also by one Man's obedience many will be made righteous" **(ROMANS 5:18, 19)**.

"For since by man [Adam] came death, by Man [Christ] also came the resurrection of the dead. For as in Adam all die, even so in Christ all shall be made alive" **(1 CORINTHIANS 15:21, 22)**.

"So when the woman saw that the tree was good for food, that it was pleasant to the eyes, and a tree desirable to make one wise, she took of its fruit and ate. She also gave to her husband with her, and he ate" **(GENESIS 3:6)**.

God explicitly warned, "But of the tree of the knowledge of good and evil you shall not eat, for in the day that you eat of it you shall surely die" **(GENESIS 2:17)**.

There was nothing really wrong with the tree God chose to use as a test for Adam and Eve. The fruit was not poisoned or tainted with some dread disease. It was not contaminated with evil. God wanted a simple test by which our first parents could prove their loyalty to Him and demonstrate their inward allegiance by the outward act of obedience. God gave them everything: "Of every [other] tree of the garden you may freely eat" **(GENESIS 2:16)**. In love and wisdom, He gave them free choice. But to exercise that choice and to show their love to Him, He *had* to give them one childishly easy test. Yet they were overcome by Satan and fell into sin.

"Therefore the LORD God sent him [Adam] out of the garden of Eden to till the ground from which he was taken. So He drove out the man; and He placed cherubim at the east of the garden of Eden, and a flaming sword which turned every way, to guard the way to the tree of life" **(GENESIS 3:23, 24).**

"Then, when desire has conceived, it gives birth to sin; and sin, when it is full-grown, brings forth death" **(JAMES 1:15).**

"For the wages of sin is death, but the gift of God is eternal life in Christ Jesus our Lord" **(ROMANS 6:23).**

Through deliberate disobedience, Adam, the head of the human family, opened a door God desired forever shut. His conscious choice to disobey separated him from God and resulted in death. Our world was not created as a "dumping-off" place for Satan. It was created perfect **(SEE GENESIS 1:31).** Through sin, Adam's dominion was forfeited. But we must not lay all the responsibility for sin upon our first parents. The apostle Paul writes, "For all have sinned and fall short of the glory of God" **(ROMANS 3:23).** We are sinners by birth. We inherited a sinful nature from Adam. We are also sinners by choice. Through our own deliberate disobedience, we have participated in Adam's sin of rebellion against God.

09 As a result of our fall, what claim does Satan make?

Satan even tried to tempt Jesus: "Then the devil, taking Him up on a high mountain, showed Him *all the kingdoms of the world* in a moment of time. And the devil said to Him, 'All this authority I will give You, and their glory; for *this has been delivered to me, and I give it to whomever* I wish' " **(LUKE 4:5, 6; EMPHASIS SUPPLIED).**

"Now is the judgment of this world; now the ruler of this world will be cast out" **(JOHN 12:31).**

Paul speaks of those "whose minds the god of this age has blinded, who do not believe, lest the light of the gospel of the glory of Christ, who is the image of God, should shine on them" **(2 CORINTHIANS 4:4).**

"You once walked according to the course of this world, according to the prince of the power of the air, the spirit who now works in the sons of disobedience" **(EPHESIANS 2:2).**

When God created Adam and Eve, He gave them dominion over this planet. As the result of their disobedience, they lost this dominion. Satan now became the prince of this world. The evil one usurped the authority of our first parents. Before the entire universe he claimed that this earth was his. Jesus entered into the arena of human affairs to break the stranglehold of Satan and restore everything lost by sin.

10 What self-sacrificing efforts has God made to redeem this planet in rebellion?

"The son of Man has come to seek and to save that which was lost" **(LUKE 19:10).**

"You were not redeemed with corruptible things, like silver or gold, . . . but with the precious blood of Christ, as of a lamb without blemish and without spot" **(1 PETER 1:18, 19).**

"None of them can by any means redeem his brother, nor give to God a ransom for him—for the redemption of their souls is costly, and it shall cease forever" **(PSALM 49:7, 8).**

"Therefore take heed to yourselves and to all the flock, among which the Holy Spirit has made you overseers, to shepherd the church of God which He purchased with His own blood" **(ACTS 20:28).**

"The Son of Man did not come to be served, but to serve, and to give His life a ransom for many" **(MATTHEW 20:28).**

"This is My blood of the new covenant, which is shed for many for the remission of sins" **(MATTHEW 26:28).**

"Not with the blood of goats and calves, but with His own blood He entered the Most Holy Place once for all, having obtained eternal redemption. For if the blood of bulls and goats and the ashes of a heifer, sprinkling the unclean, sanctifies for the purifying of the flesh, how much more shall the blood of Christ, who through the eternal Spirit offered Himself without spot to God, cleanse your conscience from dead works to serve the living God?" **(HEBREWS 9:12–14).**

"The blood of Jesus Christ His Son cleanses us from all sin" **(1 JOHN 1:7).**

"And if anyone sins, we have an Advocate with the Father, Jesus Christ the righteous. And He Himself is the propitiation for our sins, and not for ours only but also for the whole world" **(1 JOHN 2:1, 2).**

"For you were bought at a price; therefore glorify God in your body and in your spirit, which are God's" **(1 CORINTHIANS 6:20).**

"You were bought at a price; do not become slaves of men" **(1 CORINTHIANS 7:23).**

"[Jesus] Himself bore our sins in His own body on the tree, that we, having died to sins, might live for righteousness—by whose stripes you were healed" **(1 PETER 2:24).**

"Christ also suffered once for sins, the just for the unjust, that He might bring us to God, being put to death in the flesh but made alive by the Spirit" **(1 PETER 3:18).**

"In Him we have redemption through His blood, the forgiveness of sins, according to the riches of His grace" **(EPHESIANS 1:7).**

The apostle Paul writes of God's dear Son that in Him "we have redemption through

His blood, the forgiveness of sins" **(COLOSSIANS 1:14).**

John the revelator praises "Jesus Christ, the faithful witness, the firstborn from the dead, and the ruler over the kings of the earth. To Him who loved us and washed us from our sins in His own blood" **(REVELATION 1:5).**

With a heart of inexhaustible, infinite love God decided to pay the price of sin Himself. Jesus Christ, the eternal Son of God, came to this sin-cursed world. He entered into the arena of human affairs to redeem us from the curse of sin.

11 What hopeful promises does God give His children, who are caught in the grip of suffering and injustice?

"No temptation has overtaken you except such as is common to man; but God is faithful, who will not allow you to be tempted beyond what you are able, but with the temptation will also make the way of escape, that you may be able to bear it" **(1 CORINTHIANS 10:13).**

"Our soul has escaped as a bird from the snare of the fowlers; the snare is broken, and we have escaped. Our help is in the name of the LORD, who made heaven and earth" **(PSALM 124:7, 8).**

"For I know the thoughts that I think toward you, says the LORD, thoughts of peace and not of evil, to give you a future and a hope" **(JEREMIAH 29:11).**

The Lord Jesus told Peter, "I have prayed for you, that your faith should not fail" **(LUKE 22:32).**

"The Lord knows how to deliver the godly out of temptations" **(2 PETER 2:9).**

"For I, the LORD your God, will hold your right hand, saying to you, 'Fear not, I will help you' " **(ISAIAH 41:13).**

"Fear not, for I am with you; be not dismayed, for I am your God. I will strengthen you, yes, I will help you, I will uphold you with My righteous right hand" **(ISAIAH 41:10).**

"The eternal God is your refuge, and underneath are the everlasting arms; He will thrust out the enemy from before you, and will say, 'Destroy!' " **(DEUTERONOMY 33:27).**

In his last letter Paul testifies, "At my first defense no one stood with me, but all forsook me. May it not be charged against them. But the Lord stood with me and strengthened me, so that the message might be preached fully through me, and that all the Gentiles might hear. And I was delivered out of the mouth of the lion" **(2 TIMOTHY 4:16, 17).**

In the midst of our personal suffering, God promises to be with us. He promises never to allow any temptation of the evil one to overwhelm us. He promises to provide strength to meet the temptations of each day. In tones of tenderest love, He encourages us with these simple words, "Fear not, I will help you."

12 What is Satan's ultimate fate?

"By the abundance of your trading you became filled with violence within, and you sinned; therefore I cast you as a profane thing out of the mountain of God; and I destroyed you, O covering cherub, from the midst of the fiery stones. Your heart was lifted up because of your beauty; you corrupted your wisdom for the sake of your splendor; I cast you to the ground, I laid you before kings, that they might gaze at you. You defiled your sanctuaries by the multitude of your iniquities, by the iniquity of your trading; therefore I brought fire from your midst; it devoured you, and I turned you to ashes upon the earth in the sight of all who saw you. All who knew you among the peoples are astonished at you; you have become a horror, and shall be no more forever" **(EZEKIEL 28:16–19).**

In these words the Lord of eternity describes the fate of Satan, once the "covering cherub" nearest God's throne. He who knows the end from the beginning uses the past tense to describe a doom we know is yet in the future—that's how certain it is!

" 'Behold, the day is coming, burning like an oven, and all the proud, yes, all who do wickedly will be stubble. And the day which is coming shall burn them up,' says the LORD of hosts, 'that will leave them neither root nor branch. . . . You shall trample the wicked, for they shall be ashes under the soles of your feet on the day that I do this,' says the LORD of hosts" **(MALACHI 4:1, 3).**

The apostle Peter speaks of God "turning the cities of Sodom and Gomorrah into ashes, condemned them to destruction, making them an example to those who afterward would live ungodly" **(2 PETER 2:6).**

"Wait on the LORD, and keep His way, and He shall exalt you to inherit the land; when the wicked are cut off, you shall see it" **(PSALM 37:34).**

"Then the beast was captured, and with him the false prophet who worked signs in his presence, by which he deceived those who received the mark of the beast and those who worshiped his image. These two were cast alive into the lake of fire burning with brimstone" **(REVELATION 19:20).**

"Then Death and Hades were cast into the lake of fire. This is the second death. And anyone not found written in the Book of Life was cast into the lake of fire" **(REVELATION 20:14, 15).**

"For evildoers shall be cut off; but those who wait on the LORD, they shall inherit the earth. For yet a little while and the wicked shall be no more; indeed, you will look carefully for his place, but it shall be no more. . . . The wicked shall perish; and the enemies of the LORD, like the splendor of the meadows, shall vanish. Into smoke they shall vanish away. . . . Yet he passed away, and behold, he was no more; indeed I sought him, but he could not be found" **(PSALM 37:9, 10, 20, 36).**

Satan is soon to be defeated and destroyed. Through Calvary's cross he has been proven a liar. God is love. The principles of His government will ensure the happiness of His creatures throughout all eternity. You can be on the winning side. Why not tell Jesus, "Lord, I choose to stand with You. I accept Jesus as my Lord and Savior. I invite You to enter my life as my King"?

13 How will God eventually restore this planet to its basic roots?

"But the day of the Lord will come as a thief in the night, in which the heavens will pass away with a great noise, and the elements will melt with fervent heat; both the earth and the works that are in it will be burned up. . . . Nevertheless we, according to His promise, look for new heavens and a new earth in which righteousness dwells" **(2 PETER 3:10, 13).**

"Then He who sat on the throne said, 'Behold, I make all things new' " **(REVELATION 21:5).**

"For behold, I create new heavens and a new earth; and the former shall not be remembered or come to mind" **(ISAIAH 65:17).**

" 'For as the new heavens and the new earth which I will make shall remain before Me,' says the LORD, 'so shall your descendants and your name remain' " **(ISAIAH 66:22).**

"Now I saw a new heaven and a new earth, for the first heaven and the first earth had passed away. Also there was no more sea" **(REVELATION 21:1).**

In the earth as we know it today—cursed by sin, disease, and death—the sea may be beautiful to behold, but a problem in other ways: (1) Its bountiful water is not fit to drink; (2) its great expanse takes up much of the earth's surface, which might otherwise be given to land useful for living space or agriculture; and (3) its watery boundaries present a great barrier, often separating us from loved ones. But none of this will be true in the new earth, where we're promised there will be "no more sea"—just beautiful lakes and ponds and sparkling streams and brooks! "And he showed me a pure river of water of life, clear as crystal, proceeding from the throne of God and of the Lamb" **(REVELATION 22:1).**

God has left His fingerprints across the world.

Thriving in Life's Toughest Times

During the 1980s, Peter Rumachik endured great hardships, locked up in a harsh prison in the Soviet Gulag. Because he refused to renounce his Christian faith, Peter was often placed in punishment cells or kept in solitary confinement. Confined by iron and concrete, suffering cold and hunger, he became so sick on several occasions that he could barely breathe.

No one thought the man could survive. This was his fifth imprisonment for preaching the gospel. Peter was a gifted speaker, and the authorities wanted him silenced.

But this pastor's spirit couldn't keep quiet. The other men in neighboring cells began to hear the most unexpected sound coming from Peter's dark, dank cell. He was singing hymns. He was lifting up praises to God.

After a bit, Peter stopped and called out, "Do you want me to sing some more?"

The others replied in awe, "Yes, if you have strength, sing some more."

And so Pastor Rumachik's voice continued echoing through the prison. The thieves, murderers, and rapists around him had never heard words like these. Peter sang hour after hour as they listened, enraptured.

He was singing because God's hand was there with him in that terrible place. He was singing because, as he put it, "My heart enjoyed the presence of God."

And before Peter's unexpected release in 1987, he had led several fellow prisoners to repentance and faith in Jesus Christ.

God's hand stretches from century to century. It touches people in every place, in every situation. It gives us peace and hope.

The foundation of hope in the twenty-first century is this: God's hand stretches into the future. The Almighty can touch our lives in the decades ahead. That's why we can have hope. We can have hope because God has a plan.

The writers of Scripture tell us over and over that God's right hand holds us up, that God's right hand lifts us high, that God covers us with the shadow of His hand, that we can become a royal diadem in His hand.

In fact, one psalmist gives us this wonderful picture: "You open Your hand and satisfy the desire of every living thing" **(PSALM 145:16).**

This is the hand that is stretched into the future, into the twenty-first century. As the prophet Isaiah assures us, "His hand is stretched out, and who will turn it back?" **(ISAIAH 14:27).**

The psalmist went through a period of anguish and perplexity. But in this dark time, he did find one important answer. This is what he discovered: "I am continually with You; You hold me by my right hand. You will guide me with Your counsel, and afterward receive me to glory" **(PSALM 73:23, 24).**

In Psalm 139, we find the same belief expressed in a different way. Verse 10 expresses the psalmist's assurance of what he could always count on: "If I ascend into heaven, You are there; if I make my bed in hell, behold, You are there. If I take the wings of the morning, and dwell in the uttermost parts of the sea, even there Your hand shall lead me, and Your right hand shall hold me" **(PSALM 139:8–10).**

God's hand stretches out to us no matter where we are. And it stretches out into the future. It will be there to care for us. That's why we can have hope no matter what happens in the next millennium.

And there's something very important you need to understand about that hand, the hand of God. It doesn't just move events in general; it's not just nudging the big picture here and there. The hand of God touches individual lives; it touches your life. Jesus has never lost a battle with Satan yet. In the great controversy between good and evil, Jesus wins and Satan loses. We are on the winning side.

CHAPTER 10

What the Bible Says About Revelation's End-Time Message

The book of Revelation is one of the most important books in the entire Bible. Its main theme, or central focus, is the return of Jesus Christ. Revelation unmasks the deceptive plans of Satan. And it unfolds God's plans for these last days.

In **REVELATION 14,** Jesus Christ is clearly pictured as the Son of man coming on a cloud to reap the harvest of the earth **(SEE VERSES 14–16).** Before He returns, He sends a special message to prepare a people for His coming. We find this message in **VERSES 6–12**.

01 How does Jesus describe the critical importance of His last-day message of REVELATION 14:6–12?

"Then I saw another angel flying in the midst of heaven, having the everlasting gospel to preach to those who dwell on the earth—to every nation, tribe, tongue, and people" **(REVELATION 14:6).**

It's interesting that some angels have six wings! Isaiah describes some angels he saw in vision called *seraphim* (the Hebrew plural of *seraph*): "Each one had six wings: with two he covered his face, with two he covered his feet, and with two he flew" **(ISAIAH 6:2).** Also, these heavenly beings of dazzling brightness can run like lightning: "The living creatures ran back and forth, in appearance like a flash of lightning" **(EZEKIEL 1:14).**

Christ is spoken of as "so much better than the angels, as He has by inheritance obtained a more excellent name than they" **(HEBREWS 1:4).**

"And I looked, and I heard an angel flying through the midst of heaven, saying with a loud voice, 'Woe, woe, woe to the inhabitants of the earth, because of the remaining blasts of the trumpet of the three angels who are about to sound!' " **(REVELATION 8:13).**

Throughout the book of Revelation, angelic messengers are pictured as bearing a message to earth. The fact that angels are pictured as bearing this message reveals its urgent heavenly importance. Jesus commissioned His angelic messengers to impress the mind of His prophet John with heavenly visions of end-time events. John recorded these messages in the Bible's last book, Revelation.

02 How expansive and international is this end-time message?

"Then I saw another angel flying in the midst of heaven, having the everlasting gospel to preach to those who dwell on the earth—to every nation, tribe, tongue, and people" **(REVELATION 14:6).**

The apostle John saw an angel flying swiftly in the heavens, quickly carrying God's last-day message to the entire world. Noah preached a message of urgent importance for men and women soon to face a universal flood, and God sent a message through Joseph warning of an Egyptian famine. The messages of Noah and Joseph were sent by a loving God to prepare His people for overwhelming events that would profoundly affect millions. Once again in our day God has a special message for His people. It is a message of urgent importance.

"And he said to me, 'You must prophesy again about many peoples, nations, tongues, and kings' " **(REVELATION 10:11).**

Throughout the Bible, God's plan of salvation has always been for all peoples. Speaking to ancient Israel, our Lord declared, "For My house shall be called a house of prayer for all nations" **(ISAIAH 56:7).**

"Then King Darius wrote: To all peoples, nations, and languages that dwell in all the earth: Peace be multiplied to you. I make a decree that in every dominion of my kingdom men must tremble and fear before the God of Daniel. For He is the living God, and steadfast forever; His kingdom is the one which shall not be destroyed, and His dominion shall endure to the end" **(DANIEL 6:25, 26).**

The great desire of the apostle Paul was "to *make all see* what is the fellowship of the mystery, which from the beginning of the ages has been hidden in God who created all things through Jesus Christ" **(EPHESIANS 3:9; EMPHASIS SUPPLIED).**

God's plans and purposes are everlasting:

God's everlasting covenant .... **2 SAMUEL 23:5; HEBREWS 13:20**

God's everlasting righteousness .... **PSALM 119:142**

God's everlasting way .... **PSALM 139:24**

God's everlasting kingdom .... **PSALM 145:13**

God's everlasting word .... **ISAIAH 40:8**

God's everlasting salvation .... **ISAIAH 45:17**

God's everlasting purpose .... **EPHESIANS 3:11**

God's everlasting gospel .... **REVELATION 14:6**

03 What is the major focus of God's last-day message?

There is only one gospel—the gospel of Christ. The apostle Paul testified, "I am not ashamed of the gospel of Christ, for it is the power of God to salvation for everyone who believes" **(ROMANS 1:16).** With earnest conviction he warns, "I marvel that you are turning away so soon from Him who called you in the grace of Christ, to a different gospel, which is not another; but there are some who trouble you and want to pervert the gospel of Christ. But even if we, or an angel from heaven, preach any other gospel to you than what we have preached to you, let him be accursed. As we have said before, so now I say again, if anyone preaches any other gospel to you than what you have received, let him be accursed" **(GALATIANS 1:6–9).**

This "gospel of Christ" is the "everlasting gospel," as John puts it in **REVELATION 14:6.**

It was first announced in Eden when God told the diabolical serpent: "I will put enmity between you [Satan] and the woman [Eve], and between your seed and her Seed [Christ]; He shall bruise your head, and you shall bruise His heel" **(GENESIS 3:15).**

It was preached to Abraham. "And the Scripture, foreseeing that God would justify the Gentiles by faith, preached the gospel to Abraham beforehand, saying, 'In you all the nations shall be blessed' " **(GALATIANS 3:8).** This gospel was also preached to the children of Abraham: "Therefore, since a promise remains of entering His rest, let us fear lest any of you seem to have come short of it. For indeed the gospel was preached to us as well as to them; but the word which they heard did not profit them, not being mixed with faith in those who heard it" **(HEBREWS 4:1, 2).**

It has since been proclaimed anew to every generation.

The heart of God's last-day message is the "everlasting gospel." The gospel is the good news about Jesus. It is the story of the Cross. It is the story of Jesus' love, His forgiveness, His grace, and His mercy. The gospel is "the power of God to salvation" **(ROMANS 1:16).** It speaks of a love that transforms our lives and makes us into new persons in Christ.

04 To what specific end-time event does this message draw our attention?

John heard this angel "saying with a loud voice, 'Fear God and give glory to Him, for the hour of His judgment has come' " **(REVELATION 14:7).**

God is willing to put Himself—His character, His motives, His actions—on trial before the entire universe. With infinite patience, the Lord of love has borne the lying charges and slanders of Lucifer/Satan. But instead of instantly blotting the devil out of existence, He has allowed the evil one's own diabolical deeds to unmask his wicked heart. An old saying tells us: "Give a man enough rope, and he'll hang himself." And that's what God in His wisdom has done. He's given the devil enough rope and enough time to hang himself, to blow his cover, to show to the watching universe the true depth of his unspeakable malignity. Now the righteous character of God will be forever vindicated before all creation.

C. S. Lewis (1898–1963) was perhaps the most influential Christian writer of the twentieth century. Among his many insightful writings, he left us a little essay called "God in the Dock," using a British term for someone on trial in a courtroom. There Lewis makes this observation: "The ancient man approached God (or even the gods) as the accused person approaches his judge. For the modern man the roles are reversed. He is the judge: God is in the dock. He is quite a kindly judge: if God should have a reasonable defense for being the god who permits war, poverty, and disease, he is ready to listen to it. The trial may even end in God's acquittal. But the important thing is that Man is on the bench and God is in the Dock" (*The Collected Works of C. S. Lewis* [New York: Inspirational Press, 1996], p. 464).

Why is God on trial? Satan has claimed God is unfair and unjust. This diabolical being has challenged God about the way He administers the universe. The judgment will reveal to a waiting world and watching universe God's incredible love, His absolute justice, and His passionate desire to save us.

A time of judgment! "The nations were angry, and Your wrath has come, and the time of the dead, that they should be judged, and that You should reward Your servants the prophets and the saints, and those who fear Your name, small and great, and should destroy those who destroy the earth" **(REVELATION 11:18).**

"The end of all things is at hand; therefore be serious and watchful in your prayers" **(1 PETER 4:7).**

Notice the tense of the verb describing the judgment in **REVELATION 14:7.** The text clearly says, "The hour of [God's] judgment *has* come!" **(EMPHASIS SUPPLIED).** Some translations declare, "The hour of [God's] judgment is come." In other words, it is here. It has arrived.

05 What does the Bible declare regarding the reality and nature of the judgment?

Jesus says, "But I say to you that for every idle word men may speak, they will give account of it in the day of judgment" **(MATTHEW 12:36).**

"Now as he reasoned about righteousness, self-control, and the judgment to come, Felix was afraid and answered 'Go away for now; when I have a convenient time I will call for you' " **(ACTS 24:25).**

"Our God shall come, and shall not keep silent; a fire shall devour before Him, and it shall be very tempestuous all around Him. He shall call to the heavens from above, and to the earth, that He may judge His people" **(PSALM 50:3, 4).**

"I said in my heart, 'God shall judge the righteous and the wicked, for there is a time there for every purpose and for every work' " **(ECCLESIASTES 3:17).**

"Rejoice, O young man, in your youth, and let your heart cheer you in the days of your youth; walk in the ways of your heart, and in the sight of your eyes; but know that for all these God will bring you into judgment" **(ECCLESIASTES 11:9).**

"For God will bring every work into judgment, including every secret thing, whether good or evil" **(ECCLESIASTES 12:14).**

"And many of those who sleep in the dust of the earth shall awake, some to everlasting life, some to shame and everlasting contempt" **(DANIEL 12:2).**

The apostle Paul speaks of "the day when God will judge the secrets of men by Jesus Christ, according to my gospel" **(ROMANS 2:16).**

"So then each of us shall give account of himself to God" **(ROMANS 14:12).**

"We must all appear before the judgment seat of Christ, that each one may receive the things done in the body, according to what he has done, whether good or bad" **(2 CORINTHIANS 5:10).**

"I charge you therefore before God and the Lord Jesus Christ, who will judge the living and the dead at His appearing and His kingdom" **(2 TIMOTHY 4:1).**

"It is appointed for men to die once, but after this the judgment" **(HEBREWS 9:27).**

"Then I saw a great white throne and Him who sat on it, from whose face the earth and the heaven fled away. And there was found no place for them. And I saw the dead, small and great, standing before God, and books were opened. And another book was opened, which is the Book of Life. And the dead were judged according to their works, by the things which were written in the books. The sea gave up the dead who were in it, and Death and Hades delivered up the dead who were in them. And they were judged, each one according to his works" **(REVELATION 20:11–13).**

Jesus speaks of the day of judgment in the future. Paul describes "judgment to come." In the days of both Jesus and Paul, the judgment was certainly a future event. However, Revelation's urgent message for us today is: "The hour of [God's] judgment is come." It is here. According to the overwhelming evidence of the Bible, this judgment occurs just before the return of our Lord.

06 What two classes are developed before Jesus comes?

"He who is unjust, let him be unjust still; he who is filthy, let him be filthy still; he who is righteous, let him be righteous still; he who is holy, let him be holy still. And behold, I am coming quickly, and My reward is with Me, to give to every one according to his work" **(REVELATION 22:11, 12).**

"So I gave them over to their own stubborn heart, to walk in their own counsels" **(PSALM 81:12).**

"When the Son of Man comes in His glory, and all the holy angels with Him, then He will sit on the throne of His glory. All the nations will be gathered before Him, and

He will separate them one from another, as a shepherd divides his sheep from the goats. And He will set the sheep on His right hand, but the goats on the left. Then the King will say to those on His right hand, 'Come, you blessed of My Father, inherit the kingdom prepared for you from the foundation of the world:'. . . . Then He will also say to those on the left hand, 'Depart from Me, you cursed, into the everlasting fire prepared for the devil and his angels' " **(MATTHEW 25:31–34, 41)**.

"But evil men and impostors will grow worse and worse, deceiving and being deceived" **(2 TIMOTHY 3:13)**.

"Then one of the elders answered, saying to me, 'Who are these arrayed in white robes, and where did they come from?' And I said to him, 'Sir, you know.' So he said to me, 'These are the ones who come out of the great tribulation, and washed their robes and made them white in the blood of the Lamb. Therefore they are before the throne of God, and serve Him day and night in His temple. And He who sits on the throne will dwell among them' " **(REVELATION 7:13–15)**.

"Blessed are those who hunger and thirst for righteousness, for they shall be filled" **(MATTHEW 5:6)**.

Christ's desire for His church is "that He might present her to Himself a glorious church, not having spot or wrinkle or any such thing, but that she should be holy and without blemish" **(EPHESIANS 5:27)**.

The Lord Jesus desires "to present you holy, and blameless, and above reproach in His sight" **(COLOSSIANS 1:22)**.

Jude speaks of "Him who is able to keep you from stumbling, and to present you faultless before the presence of His glory with exceeding joy" **(JUDE 24)**.

"The wicked is banished in his wickedness, but the righteous has a refuge in his death" **(PROVERBS 14:32)**.

The Lord told His prophet, Ezekiel, "When I speak with you, I will open your mouth, and you shall say to them, 'Thus says the Lord GOD. He who hears, let him hear; and he who refuses, let him refuse; for they are a rebellious house' " **(EZEKIEL 3:27)**.

"Many shall be purified, made white, and refined, but the wicked shall do wickedly; and none of the wicked shall understand, but the wise shall understand" **(DANIEL 12:10)**.

"While they [the foolish virgins or bridesmaids] went to buy [oil for their lamps], the bridegroom came, and those who were ready went in with him to the wedding; and the door was shut. Afterward the other virgins came also, saying, 'Lord, Lord, open to us!' But he answered and said, 'Assuredly, I say to you, I do not know you' " **(MATTHEW 25:10–12)**.

Jesus is coming to give rewards. A judgment must precede His coming to determine what reward each individual is to receive. The destiny of all men and women must be decided before He returns. The reason for this judgment is not because God does not know who is saved or lost. He certainly knows. Remember, a rebel angel has challenged God's character. Lucifer has claimed God is unfair and unjust. He has charged God before the whole universe. The judgment will reveal God's character of love before the whole universe. It will show that those who are lost are lost because of their own choices. God has done everything He could to save them.

When did this judgment begin? What is the nature of the judgment? How can you and I have assurance in the judgment? These and many other questions will be answered in the next two chapters. However, we first need to look further at God's message in Revelation 14.

07 Whom does this message call upon us to worship?

John the revelator heard an angel "saying with a loud voice, 'Fear God and give glory to Him, for the hour of His judgment has come; and worship Him who made heaven and earth, the sea and springs of water' " **(REVELATION 14:7).**

The last part of this urgent verse commands us to worship God as the Creator. But how do we do that? *How* do we worship God as the One who made all things? The answer is: We worship God as the Creator by keeping His law, the Ten Commandments—especially the fourth commandment. The fourth commandment reads: "Remember the Sabbath day, to keep it holy. Six days you shall labor and do all your work, but the seventh day is the Sabbath of the LORD your God. In it you shall do no work: you, nor your son, nor your daughter, nor your male servant, nor your female servant, nor your cattle, nor your stranger who is within your gates. For in six days the LORD made the heavens and the earth, the sea, and all that is in them, and rested the seventh day. Therefore the LORD blessed the Sabbath day and hallowed it" **(EXODUS 20:8–11).**

Please note that God's end-time message, as recorded in the last book of the Bible **(REVELATION 14:7)**—"worship Him who made heaven and earth, the sea and springs of water"—finds an echo here in the fourth commandment. In fact, those words are a "carbon copy" of the words God Himself dictated in the Sabbath command. Is God, through John, trying to tell us something here? He is! All true worship is based on the fact that God created us. We did not evolve. We were created by a loving God. And that's a divine reality calling forth our highest praise. "You are worthy, O Lord, to receive glory and honor and power; for You created all things, and by Your will they exist and were created" **(REVELATION 4:11).**

"By the word of the LORD the heavens were made, and all the host of them by the breath of His mouth. . . . For He spoke, and it was done; He commanded, and it stood fast" **(PSALM 33:6, 9).**

"The sea is His, for He made it; and His hands formed the dry land. Oh come, let us worship and bow down; let us kneel before the LORD our Maker" **(PSALM 95:5, 6).**

"Our help is in the name of the LORD, who made heaven and earth" **(PSALM 124:8).**

"Happy is he who has the God of Jacob for his help, whose hope is in the LORD his God, who made heaven and earth, the sea, and all that is in them; who keeps truth forever" **(PSALM 146:5, 6).**

"You alone are the LORD; You have made heaven, the heaven of heavens, with all their host, the earth and everything on it, the seas and all that is in them, and You preserve them all. The host of heaven worships You" **(NEHEMIAH 9:6).**

"The LORD possessed me at the beginning of His way, before His works of old. I have been established from everlasting, from the beginning, before there was ever an earth. When there were no depths I was brought forth, when there were no fountains abounding with water. Before the mountains were settled, before the hills, I was brought forth; while as yet He had not made the earth or the fields, or the primeval dust of the world. When He prepared the heavens, I was there, when He drew a circle on the face of the deep, when He established the clouds above, when He strengthened the fountains of the deep, when He assigned to the sea its limit, so that the waters would not transgress His command, when He marked out the foundations of the earth, then I was beside Him as a master craftsman; and I was daily His delight, rejoicing always before Him" **(PROVERBS 8:22–30).**

"But the LORD is the true God; He is the living God and the everlasting King. At His wrath the earth will tremble, and the nations will not be able to endure His indignation. Thus you shall say to them: 'The gods that have not made the heavens and the earth shall perish from the earth and from under these heavens. He has made the earth by His power, He has established the world by His wisdom, and has stretched out the heavens at His discretion' " **(JEREMIAH 10:10–12).**

"Men, why are you doing these things? We also are men with the same nature as you, and preach to you that you should turn from these useless things to the living God, who made the heaven, the earth, the sea, and all things that are in them" **(ACTS 14:15).**

The apostle Paul told the men of Athens: "As I was passing through and considering the objects of your worship, I even found an altar with this inscription: TO THE UNKNOWN GOD. Therefore, the One whom you worship without knowing, Him I proclaim to you: 'God, who made the world and everything in it, since He is Lord of heaven and earth, does not dwell in temples made with hands. Nor is He worshiped with men's hands, as though He needed anything, since He gives to all life, breath, and all things" **(ACTS 17:23–25).**

In an age when the evolutionary hypothesis has captured the scientific world, God invites us to worship Him as the Creator. We did not evolve. We were fashioned by a loving God. We are His. The fact that God made us is precisely the reason we worship Him. The basis of all worship is simply this: He is our Life-Giver. Revelation gives an urgent, last-day call to worship Christ as Creator. In a future chapter, we will discover God's end-time sign of last-day allegiance, the symbol of His creative power.

08 The first angel calls us to faithful obedience in the light of the everlasting gospel and the present-tense judgment. It is an appeal to worship the Creator. What is the heart of the second angel's message?

"And another angel followed, saying, 'Babylon is fallen, is fallen, that great city, because she has made all nations drink of the wine of the wrath of her fornication' " **(REVELATION 14:8)**.

Centuries before John wrote, ancient Babylon had been destroyed just as God predicted: "Babylon is fallen, is fallen! And all the carved images of her gods He has broken to the ground" **(ISAIAH 21:9)**.

God effectively used the kingdom of ancient Babylon (626–539 B.C.) as a human instrument to conquer and punish heathen nations and blasphemous practices. For example, God used Babylon in this way against Tyre. "Thus says the Lord GOD: 'Behold, I will bring against Tyre from the north Nebuchadnezzar king of Babylon, king of kings, with horses, with chariots, and with horsemen, and an army with many people' " **(EZEKIEL 26:7)**. He also used Babylon to punish Egypt: "It [Egypt] shall be the lowliest of kingdoms; it shall never again exalt itself above the nations, for I will diminish them so that they will not rule over the nations anymore. . . . Therefore thus says the Lord GOD: 'Surely I will give the land of Egypt to Nebuchadnezzar king of Babylon; he shall take away her wealth, carry off her spoil, and remove her pillage; and that will be the wages for his army' " **(EZEKIEL 29:15, 19)**.

In fact, God used Babylon even against His own people of Israel when they forsook Him and His truth. "The word which came to Jeremiah from the LORD, when Nebuchadnezzar king of Babylon and all his army, all the kingdoms of the earth under his dominion, and all the people, fought against Jerusalem and all its cities, saying, 'Thus says the LORD, the God of Israel: "Go and speak to Zedekiah king of Judah and tell him, 'Thus says the LORD: "Behold, I will give this city into the hand of the king of Babylon, and he shall burn it with fire" ' " **(JEREMIAH 34:1, 2)**.

Finally, however, the Lord destroyed the pagan empire of Babylon itself, for it was wicked and corrupt. "Call together the archers against Babylon. All you who bend the bow, encamp against it all around; let none of them escape. Repay her according to her work; according to all she has done, do to her; for she has been proud against the LORD, against the Holy One of Israel" **(JEREMIAH 50:29)**.

Therefore, when John the revelator penned the words, "Babylon is fallen" **(REVELATION 14:8)**, he was not referring to the literal, historical Babylon of the ancient past. That great city, the capital of the once-mighty Babylonian Empire, had lain in desolate ruins, a ghost town without inhabitants, for centuries. To announce that ancient, literal Babylon was fallen would be "old news," and the prophet was as aware of all this as anyone else when he wrote in the first century. Obviously, therefore, the name "Babylon" here in **REVELATION 14:8,** must have a different meaning—a symbolic meaning—and it does, as we shall see.

09 What final appeal does God give to people in Babylon? Why?

"And I heard another voice from heaven saying, 'Come out of her, my people, lest you share in her sins, and lest you receive of her plagues' " **(REVELATION 18:4).**

"Flee from the midst of Babylon, and every one save his life! Do not be cut off in her iniquity, for this is the time of the LORD's vengeance; He shall recompense her. Babylon was a golden cup in the LORD's hand, that made all the earth drunk. The nations drank her wine; therefore the nations are deranged. Babylon has suddenly fallen and been destroyed" **(JEREMIAH 51:6–8).**

"I will punish Bel in Babylon. . . . Yes, the wall of Babylon shall fall. My people, go out of the midst of her! And let everyone deliver himself from the fierce anger of the LORD" **(JEREMIAH 51:44, 45).**

"Therefore, 'Come out from among them and be separate, says the Lord. Do not touch what is unclean, and I will receive you' " **(2 CORINTHIANS 6:17).**

"Depart! Depart! Go out from there, touch no unclean thing; go out from the midst of her, be clean, you who bear the vessels of the LORD" **(ISAIAH 52:11).**

Who composes Babylon? What does Babylon stand for? The city of Babylon was built on the site of the former Tower of Babel where God confused the languages **(SEE GENESIS 11:1–9).** In Revelation's prophecies, Babylon is a symbol of religious confusion. Revelation's spiritual Babylon represents false religion. It symbolizes a departure from Bible truth. In a future chapter, we will discover just how error has slipped into the Christian church and examine God's call to return to His truth.

10 What critical issue does the third angel's message focus upon?

"Then a third angel followed them, saying with a loud voice, 'If anyone worships the beast and his image, and receives his mark on his forehead or on his hand, he himself shall also drink of the wine of the wrath of God, which is poured out full strength into the cup of His indignation. He shall be tormented with fire and brimstone in the presence of the holy angels and in the presence of the Lamb. And the smoke of their torment ascends forever and ever; and they have no rest day or night, who worship the beast and his image, and whoever receives the mark of his name' " **(REVELATION 14:9–11).**

"He [the power opposed to God] causes all, both small and great, rich and poor, free and slave, to receive a mark on their right hand or on their foreheads, and that no one may buy or sell except one who has the mark or the name of the beast, or the number of his name" **(REVELATION 13:16, 17).**

In a future chapter, we will discover who the beast is and what his mark represents. In this chapter, it is vital to understand that the issue of the mark of the beast is part of earth's final conflict.

"For in the hand of the LORD there is a cup, and the wine is red; it is fully mixed, and He pours it out; surely its dregs shall all the wicked of the earth drain and drink down" **(PSALM 75:8).**

11 How does Revelation describe God's people just before the return of our Lord?

"Here is the patience of the saints; here are those who keep the commandments of God and the faith of Jesus" **(REVELATION 14:12).**

"Blessed are those who do His commandments, that they may have the right to the tree of life, and may enter through the gates into the city" **(REVELATION 22:14).**

"The dragon [the devil] was enraged with the woman [the church], and he went to make war with the rest of her offspring ["the remnant of her seed," KJV], who keep the commandments of God and have the testimony of Jesus Christ" **(REVELATION 12:17).**

The "woman" in **REVELATION 12:17** represents God's church. "The rest of her offspring" (or "the remnant of her seed") refers to God's church in the last days.

Jesus commissioned His church to "go therefore and make disciples of all the nations, baptizing them in the name of the Father and of the Son and of the Holy Spirit, teaching them to observe all things that I have commanded you; and lo, I am with you always, even to the end of the age" **(MATTHEW 28:19, 20).**

"By this we know that we love the children of God, when we love God and keep His commandments. For this is the love of God, that we keep His commandments. And His commandments are not burdensome" **(1 JOHN 5:2, 3).**

"By this we know that we know Him, if we keep His commandments. He who says, 'I know Him,' and does not keep His commandments, is a liar, and the truth is not in him" **(1 JOHN 2:3, 4).**

The apostle Paul, facing martyrdom, could die in peace, knowing that he had been loyal and obedient: "I have fought the good fight, I have finished the race, I have kept the faith" **(2 TIMOTHY 4:7).**

As a result of the proclamation of God's message of **REVELATION 14**, two classes are developed. One receives the mark of the beast. This group persecutes and oppresses the true people of God. Ultimately this group receives the seven last plagues. The other group, sensing it is the judgment hour, loyally stand for their Creator. Through faith in Jesus, they keep the commandments of God. They flee from the falsehoods of spiritual Babylon and are protected from the plagues.

12 What promise does God give to those who study the prophecies of Revelation?

"Blessed is he who reads and those who hear the words of this prophecy, and keep those things which are written in it; for the time is near" **(REVELATION 1:3).**

"Behold, I am coming quickly! Blessed is he who keeps the words of the prophecy of this book" **(REVELATION 22:7).**

"Blessed is the man who listens to me" **(PROVERBS 8:34).**

"And it happened, as He [Jesus] spoke these things, that a certain woman from the crowd raised her voice and said to Him, 'Blessed is the womb that bore You, and the breasts which nursed You!' But He said, 'More than that, blessed are those who hear the word of God and keep it!' " **(LUKE 11:27, 28).**

In future chapters, we will especially study God's urgent last-day messages for today. Why not open your heart to God right now and tell Him that you hunger after the truth of His Word? John the revelator promises that we will receive a triple blessing from reading, understanding, and following Revelation's teachings. God has a special blessing in store for us in the next few chapters.

Revelation unmasks the deceptive plans of Satan.

Faith Not Fear

The island of Patmos is a bit of rock jutting out of the Aegean about forty-five miles southwest of the city of Ephesus. In the first century, it was a Roman place, a place within the long reach of Caesar. And it was a pagan place. A temple to the goddess Artemis had been erected on the island. She was its patron deity.

The apostle John was one of the primary eyewitnesses to the life, death, and resurrection of Jesus Christ. He'd been one of the founders of the Christian church. But now that church faced great perils. It had spread so dramatically that Roman authorities were taking notice. They especially noticed that Christians refused to participate in the cult of emperor worship. These believers would give their absolute allegiance only to a Galilean rabbi called Jesus. This seemed like treason to many Romans. And they came to regard Christianity as a dangerous sect. More than one Roman emperor made attempts to stamp it out.

At various times, Christians would be burned at the stake on city streets, thrown to the lions in the Colosseum, or slaughtered by the sword throughout the empire. Some of the apostles lost their lives to Roman persecution. Other Christian leaders were killed by violent Jewish fanatics.

This was the world in which the apostle John found himself. Years before, as a very young man, he had looked into the face of Jesus on the shores of Lake Galilee—and never looked back. Jesus' invitation, "Follow Me," had become the passion of his life.

But now, John's eyes were dimmed with age. His shoulders slumped a bit; his feet shuffled; his hands weren't as strong and steady as they used to be. John had seen a lot in the last few years, a lot of hardship and suffering. Several of those who'd stood with him as leaders in the early church had met martyrdom.

But the remarkable fact is this: From his exile, from this island of Patmos, the apostle John still managed to inspire us with the book of Revelation. Down through the ages, this unique document has given people great hope about the future. From his dark place in a remote corner of the Roman Empire, John saw an incredibly bright picture.

John saw far beyond the trials of the present. He saw far beyond the vast power of pagan Rome. John saw something glorious coming toward him. And as the scenes described in Revelation were progressively unfolded to John, this picture grew even brighter. Toward the end of the book, he wrote, "Now I saw heaven opened, and behold, a white horse. And He who sat on him was called Faithful and True, and in righteousness He judges and makes war" **(REVELATION 19:11).** Here John saw a militant Christ, a Christ riding to the rescue. On His head are many crowns and He is leading the armies of heaven down to earth.

What is John's message? That Jesus Christ is going to triumph in the end! That all of human history will come to a climax in His return to earth. We have this glorious prospect to look forward to.

It's true there are perils and calamities pictured in the book of Revelation. John didn't close his eyes to hard times. But the image that dominates is this glorified Christ.

He's coming to bring justice and righteousness.

He's coming to take His people home.

He's coming to do away with sin and suffering once and for all.

He's coming to bring the New Jerusalem.

He's coming to make all things new, to create a new heaven and a new earth.

John's picture of the future just keeps getting brighter and brighter in the book of Revelation. It keeps getting brighter until we see believers in a dazzling golden city, rejoicing in the presence of God. He shines so brilliantly that they have no need of the sun.

Do you know what's most remarkable about this document, this book of Revelation, this final voice of witness in the Bible? What's most remarkable is this—its complete lack of fear. You just don't feel fear in this book. Yes, calamities are described. Yes, the powers of darkness will try to do terrible things. But John isn't afraid. He's not afraid of corrupt Babylon. He's not afraid of the roaring beast or the raging dragon. All through the book, John is confident that Jesus is going to be triumphant.

CHAPTER 11

What the Bible Says About the 2,300-Year Prophecy

On August 5, 2010, a vicious underground explosion left thirty-three miners trapped a half mile underground in a Chilean mine. As the drama unfolded, the men waited in the darkness of the mine. They longed for deliverance. Their emotions fluctuated from optimism to despair. Entombed in the bowels of the earth, thirty-three men struggled to survive.

Rescue workers toiled around the clock to discover some way to reach the miners. On Saturday, October 9, there was a major breakthrough. The Schramm T-130 drill carved a twenty-one-inch hole wide enough to pull the men out in a sophisticated rescue capsule similar to the ones used by the American astronauts. A siren sounded outside the mine, echoing through Camp Hope, the tent city where families were holding their vigil, longing for some good news. Shouts of joy filled the air. Word spread from tent to tent. Rescue is on its way! Families and close friends of the miners were overwhelmed with happiness. They would see their loved ones again. The wailing siren was a message of incredible hope.

This world is frantically searching for a message of hope. Like those trapped miners, we too, are doomed unless there is deliverance from above. The Bible's last book, Revelation, unfolds God's last-day message for a fallen world. It reveals a rescue on the way.

In this Bible study, you will discover the incredibly good news of the judgment. Evil will one day be banished from the universe forever. Right will triumph. Righteousness will prevail, and justice will reign. Jesus will come. Our rescue is guaranteed. Our deliverance is certain.

Although Revelation reveals that the hour of God's judgment has come, it does not tell us when that happened. To discover when the judgment began, we must turn to the prophetic book of Daniel. The prophecies of Daniel unlock the mysteries of Revelation. These two Bible books are designed by God to be studied together.

01 What awesome scene did the prophet Daniel witness taking place in heaven? What other Bible prophets saw something similar taking place?

The prophet Daniel, in vision and by divine inspiration, witnessed an awesome scene of judgment in heaven while events still continued on earth: "I watched till thrones were put in place, and the Ancient of Days [God the Father] was seated; His garment was white as snow, and the hair of His head was like pure wool. His throne was a fiery flame, its wheels a burning fire; a fiery stream issued and came forth from before Him. A thousand thousands ministered to Him; ten thousand times ten thousand stood before Him. The court was seated, and the books were opened" **(DANIEL 7:9, 10).**

"I was watching in the night visions, and behold, One like the Son of Man [Jesus Christ], coming with the clouds of heaven! He came to the Ancient of Days, and they brought Him near before Him. Then to Him was given dominion and glory and a kingdom, that all peoples, nations, and languages should serve Him. His dominion is an everlasting dominion, which shall not pass away, and His kingdom the one which shall not be destroyed. . . . Until the Ancient of Days came, and a judgment was made in favor of the saints of the Most High, and the time came for the saints to possess the kingdom" **(DANIEL 7:13, 14, 22).**

The angel directed Daniel's attention to the throne room of the universe. There the prophet saw the supreme court of the universe being set up in heaven's sanctuary.

"In the year that King Uzziah died, I saw the Lord sitting on a throne, high and lifted up, and the train of His robe filled the temple. Above it stood seraphim; each one had six wings: with two he covered his face, with two he covered his feet, and with two he flew. And one cried to another and said:

'Holy, holy, holy is the LORD of hosts; the whole earth is full of His glory!' " **(ISAIAH 6:1–3).**

"Immediately I was in the Spirit; and behold, a throne set in heaven, and One sat on the throne. . . . Around the throne were twenty-four thrones, and on the thrones I saw twenty-four elders sitting, clothed in white robes; and they had crowns of gold on their heads. And from the throne proceeded lightnings, thunderings, and voices. Seven lamps of fire were burning before the throne, which are the seven Spirits of God" **(REVELATION 4:2, 4, 5).**

02 When does this heavenly judgment take place?

"And he [Gabriel] said to me [Daniel], '*For two thousand three hundred days;* then the sanctuary shall be cleansed' " **(DANIEL 8:14; EMPHASIS SUPPLIED).**

"And the vision of the evenings and mornings which was told is true; therefore seal up the vision, for it refers to many days in the future" **(DANIEL 8:26).**

03 What does the prophet Daniel say would happen to the sanctuary at the end of the 2,300 prophetic days?

"And he [Gabriel] said to me [Daniel], 'For two thousand three hundred days; *then the sanctuary shall be cleansed*' " **(DANIEL 8:14; EMPHASIS SUPPLIED).**

The Hebrew word *tsadaq* is translated as "cleansed," which is a good English translation. This word is also sometimes translated as "justified" or "made right."

04 What was the role of God's people, the Israelites, on the Day of Atonement when the ancient sanctuary was being cleansed?

"This shall be a statute forever for you: In the seventh month, on the tenth day of the month, you shall afflict your souls, and do no work at all, whether a native of your own country or a stranger who dwells among you. For on that day the priest shall make atonement for you, to cleanse you, that you may be clean from all your sins before the LORD. . . . The tenth day of this seventh month shall be the Day of Atonement. It shall be a holy convocation for you; you shall afflict your souls, and offer an offering made by fire to the LORD. And you shall do no work on that same day, for it is the Day of Atonement, to make atonement for you before the LORD your God.

For any person who is not afflicted in soul on that same day shall be cut off from his people" **(LEVITICUS 16:29, 30; 23:27–29).**

"I will cleanse them from all their iniquity by which they have sinned against Me, and I will pardon all their iniquities by which they have sinned and by which they have transgressed against Me" **(JEREMIAH 33:8).**

"Then I will sprinkle clean water on you, and you shall be clean; I will cleanse you from all your filthiness and from all your idols. I will give you a new heart and put a new spirit within you; I will take the heart of stone out of your flesh and give you a heart of flesh. I will put My Spirit within you and cause you to walk in My statutes, and you will keep My judgments and do them" **(EZEKIEL 36:25–27).**

"Christ came as High Priest of the good things to come, with the greater and more perfect tabernacle not made with hands, that is, not of this creation. Not with the blood of goats and calves, but with His own blood He entered the Most Holy Place once for all, having obtained eternal redemption. For if the blood of bulls and goats and the ashes of a heifer, sprinkling the unclean, sanctifies for the purifying of the flesh, how much more shall the blood of Christ, who through the eternal Spirit offered Himself without spot to God, cleanse your conscience from dead works to serve the living God?" **(HEBREWS 9:11–14).**

"Wash me thoroughly from my iniquity, and cleanse me from my sin. . . . Purge me with hyssop, and I shall be clean; wash me, and I shall be whiter than snow. . . . Create in me a clean heart, O God, and renew a steadfast spirit within me" **(PSALM 51: 2, 7, 10).**

Jesus Christ "gave Himself for us, that He might redeem us from every lawless deed and purify for Himself His own special people, zealous for good works" **(TITUS 2:14).**

"Now when these things had been thus prepared, the priests always ["every day," Today's English Version] went into the first part of the tabernacle, performing the services. But into the second part the high priest went alone once a year, not without blood, which he offered for himself and for the people's sins committed in ignorance" **(HEBREWS 9:6, 7).**

Each day during the earthly sanctuary service, the Israelites confessed their sins. They came to the sanctuary with their sacrificial animals. Each sacrificial animal represented Jesus. Day-by-day sin was transferred from the sinner to the substitute and through the blood of the sacrificial victim carried into the sanctuary by the Jewish priest. Each priest represented Jesus, our Priest, who represents us in heaven's sanctuary. Once a year, on the Day of Atonement, the sanctuary was cleansed of all the guilt transferred into it by the confessed sins of the Israelites. It was a day of judgment! At the end of the day, the sins of the repentant Israelites were either confessed, forgiven, and renounced—or unconfessed, unforgiven, and cherished. All those who refused to confess their sins were banished from the camp. They were judged.

The cleansing of the heavenly sanctuary takes place at the end of time. It is God's final judgment on sin.

05 To what specific period of time does the vision of the 2,300 days especially apply?

The prophet Daniel tells us: "I heard a man's voice between the banks of the Ulai, who called, and said, 'Gabriel, make this man understand the vision.' So he came near where I stood, and when he came I was afraid and fell on my face; but he said to me, 'Understand, son of man, that the vision refers to the time of the end.' . . . And he said, 'Look, I am making known to you what shall happen in the latter time of the indignation; for at the appointed time the end shall be' " **(DANIEL 8:16, 17, 19).**

"But you, Daniel, shut up the words, and seal the book until the time of the end; many shall run to and fro, and knowledge shall increase. . . . And he said, 'Go your way, Daniel, for the words are closed up and sealed till the time of the end. . . . But you, go your way till the end; for you shall rest [in the grave], and will arise to your inheritance at the end of the days' " **(DANIEL 12:4, 9, 13).**

"The LORD answered me and said: 'Write the vision and make it plain on tablets, that he may run who reads it. For the vision is yet for an appointed time; but at the end it will speak, and it will not lie. Though it tarries, wait for it; because it will surely come, it will not tarry' " **(HABAKKUK 2:2, 3).**

06 Whom did Jesus commission to clearly explain the vision to the prophet Daniel?

Daniel says, "I heard a man's voice [no doubt the Lord's voice] between the banks of the Ulai, who called, and said, 'Gabriel, make this man [Daniel] understand the vision' " **(DANIEL 8:16).**

The angel Gabriel is one of God's special angels to bring His eternal messages to the human race. Gabriel travels swiftly to earth at God's command with urgent messages for God's people.

"Then an angel of the Lord appeared to him [Zacharias, father of John the Baptist], standing on the right side of the altar of incense. And when Zacharias saw him, he was troubled, and fear fell upon him. But the angel said to him, 'Do not be afraid, Zacharias, for your prayer is heard; and your wife Elizabeth will bear you a son, and you shall call his name John. . . . I am Gabriel, who stands in the presence of God, and was sent to speak to you and bring you these glad tidings' " **(LUKE 1:11–13, 19).**

"Thus the Lord has dealt with me, in the days when He looked on me, to take away my reproach among people. Now in the sixth month the angel Gabriel was sent by God to a city of Galilee named Nazareth" **(LUKE 1:25, 26).**

When the angel attempted to explain the vision, Daniel fainted: "And I, Daniel, fainted and was sick for days; afterward I arose and went about the king's business. I was astonished by the vision, but no one understood it" **(DANIEL 8:27).**

When the angel attempted to explain the vision, Daniel fainted. At the end of Daniel, chapter 8, the prophet still did not fully understand the vision.

07 As Gabriel explained the vision to Daniel, the prophet fainted. What events transpired next?

"While I was speaking in prayer, the man Gabriel, whom I had seen in the vision at the beginning, being caused to fly swiftly, reached me about the time of the evening offering. And he informed me, and talked with me, and said, 'O Daniel, I have now come forth to give you skill to understand. At the beginning of your supplications the command went out, and I have come to tell you, for you are greatly beloved; therefore consider the matter, and understand the vision' " **(DANIEL 9:21–23).**

Faithful Daniel heard from the angel Gabriel words that anyone would treasure—"You are *greatly beloved*"! **(SEE ALSO DANIEL 10:11, 19.)**

08 What portion of the prophecy applies directly to Daniel's people, the Jews?

The angel Gabriel informed Daniel, the Jewish prophet: "Seventy weeks are determined for your people [the Jews] and for your holy city [Jerusalem], to finish the transgression, to make an end of sins, to make reconciliation for iniquity" **(DANIEL 9:24).**

The Hebrew word *chatta'th,* translated "sins" in this verse, may mean either "sins" or "sin offerings." Of the 290 times this word occurs in the Old Testament, it has the meaning "sin" 155 times, and "sin offering" 135 times. If "sin offering" is the intended meaning here, we can understand that when Jesus gave Himself on Calvary, it was no longer necessary for sinners to bring sin offerings, as **JOHN 1:29** implies, calling Christ "the Lamb of God who takes away the sin of the world."

The phrase "to make reconciliation" comes from the Hebrew word *kaphar,* generally translated as "to make atonement," as in **EXODUS 30:10 AND LEVITICUS 4:20**. By His vicarious death on Calvary, Christ provided reconciliation for all who accept His atoning sacrifice.

No less a heavenly being than the angel Gabriel was sent to Daniel for the express purpose of explaining to him the point he had failed to understand in the vision of the eighth chapter—the statement relative to time. "For two thousand and three hundred days; then shall the sanctuary be cleansed" **(DANIEL 8:14).** After bidding Daniel to "consider the matter, and understand the vision" **(DANIEL 9:23),** the angel's very first words are: "Seventy weeks are determined for your people and for your holy city" **(DANIEL 9:24).** The word translated "determined" literally means, "cut off." Seventy weeks, representing 490 prophetic days—or literal years, as we'll see in the next question—are declared by the angel to be "cut off" to apply especially to the Jews. But from what were they cut off? As the 2,300 days is the only period of time mentioned in chapter 8, this must be the period from which the seventy weeks are cut off. Therefore, the seventy weeks must be a part of the 2,300 days, and the two periods must begin together. If the starting point for one of these periods could be determined, then the beginning date for the other would also be ascertained.

Gabriel begins his explanation by stating that seventy weeks (490 days) are determined (cut off) from the 2,300 days to apply especially to the Jews **(SEE DANIEL 9:22–24).**

09 In Bible prophecy, what does one prophetic day equal?

"According to the number of the days in which you spied out the land, forty days, for each day you shall bear your guilt one year, namely forty years, and you shall know My rejection" **(NUMBERS 14:34).**

"And when you have completed them, lie again on your right side; then you shall bear the iniquity of the house of Judah forty days. I have laid on you a day for each year" **(EZEKIEL 4:6).**

When we read in **EZEKIEL 4:6** that "I [the Lord] have appointed thee each day for a year" or "a day for each year" (KJV and NKJV), we get the impression that *God is trying to tell us something*! This famous "Year-Day Principle" of prophetic interpretation helps unlock the meaning of time prophecies and enables us to check them against their historical fulfillment.

Through the years, many, if not all, eminent Bible scholars have held and taught that in time prophecies, *a prophetic day* stands for *an actual year.* Just as architects use a scale value of "one quarter-inch equals one foot" on their blueprints, and just as cartographers use a scale of "one inch equals one hundred miles" on their maps, so God uses a scale value of "one day equals one year" in symbolic time prophecies.

For example, E. B. Elliott refers to "two most remarkable symbolic actions of that prophet [Ezekiel, see Ezekiel 4:4–6]. . . . He was on one occasion commanded by God to lie 390 DAYS on his left side before the people; thereby to typify . . . the 390 years of the iniquity and concomitant debasement on the nation of Israel; on another, to lie 40 DAYS on his right side, thereby to typify the 40 last years of Judah's iniquity. And the meaning of these mystical days was declared by God Himself. 'I have laid upon thee the years of their iniquity, according to the number of the days 390 days. I have appointed thee each day for a year.'—A precedent more clear and complete than this could scarce be desired; as a probable key and guide to the meaning of the days in the symbolic visions that we have under consideration" (*Horae Apocalypticae*, 3rd ed., 1847, vol. 3, pp. 226, 227).

But the acid test of the Year-Day Principle is that it works! When put to a practical test and applied to biblical time prophecies such as the coming of the Messiah, it is marvelously precise and a great confirmation of the divine inspiration of the Scriptures.

The entire 2,300 days lead us to the time of the end and the opening of the judgment.

10 When does this prophetic period—the 2,300 days of both Daniel 8 and 9—begin?

"Know therefore and understand, that from the going forth of the command to restore and build Jerusalem until Messiah the Prince, there shall be seven weeks and sixty-two weeks; the street shall be built again, and the wall, even in troublesome times" **(DANIEL 9:25).**

When Daniel wrote this prophecy, he was a prisoner of war, a captive in Babylon. And his Jewish homeland was desolate. Jerusalem lay in ruins. Thus "the command to restore and build Jerusalem" would be a great historical event—to the world in general and to God's people, the Jews, in particular. This royal decree, recorded in Scripture in **EZRA 7:11–26,** was issued by Artaxerxes, king of Persia, in 457 B.C. Actually, three successive Persian kings concurred in passing such a decree. The little book written by Ezra the scribe documents these three royal decrees. The decree of Cyrus is mentioned in **EZRA 1:1, 2, 7–11; 5:13, 17 AND 6:3, 4.** The decree of Darius is mentioned in **EZRA 6:1, 6–13.** And the decree of Artaxerxes is mentioned in **EZRA 7:1–28.** Since the first two decrees were impeded by neighboring forces around Jerusalem—as shown in chapter 4 of Ezra—the work of rebuilding Jerusalem had to "cease." That's why all three decrees were needed, and in fact **EZRA 6:14** refers to all three as *one single* "commandment" to achieve the same end. The third and last of these decrees, the one which not only allowed work to resume but also restored the Jews' civil government in Jerusalem with "magistrates and judges" **(EZRA 7:25),** went into effect "in the seventh year of the king" Artaxerxes' reign **(EZRA 7:8).** Since records confirm that Artaxerxes' first full year on the throne was 464 B.C., his seventh year would be 457 B.C. Therefore that year—457 B.C.—solidly grounded on reliable evidence, is the key date that begins the seventy-week prophecy mentioned in **DANIEL 9:25.**

The entire prophetic period of 2,300 days begins with the command to restore and rebuild Jerusalem. Jerusalem was attacked in 605 B.C. by the Babylonian king, Nebuchadnezzar. In 587–586 B.C., it was largely destroyed. The Medes and Persians overthrew the Babylonians in 539 B.C., and in 457 B.C., the Persian king, Artaxerxes, passed a decree allowing the Jews to return to their homeland to rebuild Jerusalem. You can read about this decree in **EZRA 7:12, 13.**

11 How long would it be from the decree to restore Jerusalem to the anointing of Jesus as the Messiah at His baptism?

"Know therefore and understand, that from the going forth of the command to restore and build Jerusalem until Messiah the Prince, there shall be seven weeks and sixty-two weeks; the street shall be built again, and the wall, even in troublesome times" **(DANIEL 9:25).**

"He [Andrew] first found his own brother Simon, and said to him, 'We have found the Messiah' (which is translated, the Christ)" **(JOHN 1:41).**

Mathematics verifies Jesus as the Messiah. The Year-Day Principle is verified by the fact that Jesus was anointed as Messiah by the Holy Spirit at His baptism in the fall of A.D. 27, just as predicted! Note the arithmetic: Gabriel told Daniel that "from the going forth of the command to restore and build Jerusalem until Messiah the Prince, there shall be seven weeks and sixty-two weeks" **(DANIEL 9:25)**—a total of 69 of the 70 weeks. Because there are seven days in each week, we multiply 69 x 7 = 483 prophetic days, or 483 actual years.

Now 483 years *minus* 457 B.C. = A.D. 27. (In crossing from B.C. to A.D. one year must be *added* because there never was a "zero" year. The year A.D. 1 immediately followed the year 1 B.C.) Thus, in addition to other abundant evidence, mathematics proves Jesus is the Messiah.

Jesus did not assume His role as Messiah until He was anointed, and He was not anointed until His baptism **(COMPARE ACTS 10:38 WITH MARK 1:9–11 AND LUKE 3:22).** Finally, Jesus was baptized "in the fifteenth year of the reign of Tiberius Caesar" **(LUKE 3:1)**, which history records as A.D. 27—*the very year predicted by Daniel centuries before*!

This prophecy points not to Jesus' birth, but to the beginning of His ministry. Just as today individuals must reach a certain age before they qualify to hold public office, so in Bible times priests were anointed at the age of thirty **(SEE NUMBERS 4:3, 23, 30, 35, 39, 43, 47).** As noted above, in A.D. 27, Jesus reached that age, was anointed by the Holy Spirit, and began His ministry as the Messiah. All this explains the otherwise cryptic statement made by Christ when, after His baptism He went into Galilee, "preaching the gospel of the kingdom of God, and saying, '*The time is fulfilled*' " **(MARK 1:14, 15; EMPHASIS SUPPLIED).** How marvelous is God's foreknowledge!

The prophecies of Daniel predict that from the decree to restore and rebuild Jerusalem in 457 B.C. until the coming of the Messiah would be sixty-nine prophetic weeks, or 483 prophetic days (7 x 69 = 483). Since one prophetic day equals one literal year, 483 years would elapse from the going forth of the command to rebuild Jerusalem until the Messiah would appear. The chart below will clarify this prophecy.

Based on Daniel's prophecy, the logical time of the Messiah's anointing (Christ's baptism) is the fall of A.D. 27

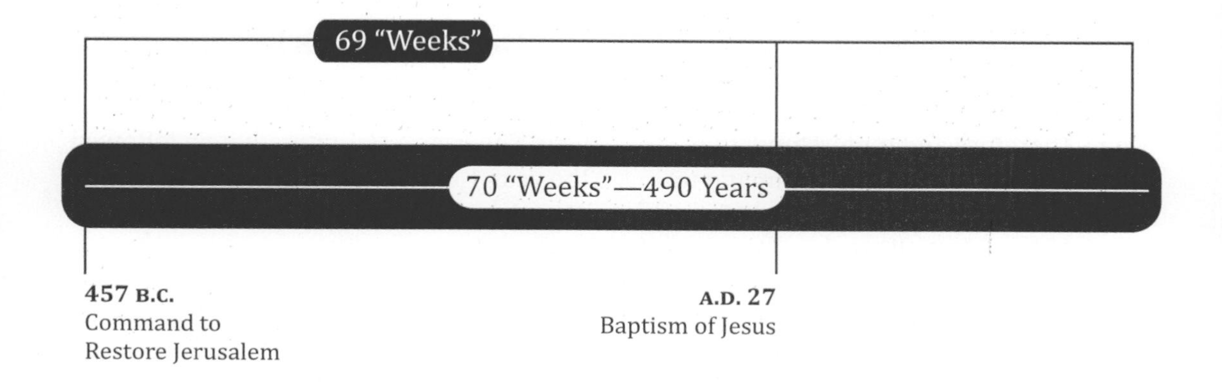

12 What significant event occurred at Jesus' baptism?

"When all the people were baptized, it came to pass that Jesus also was baptized; and while He prayed, the heaven was opened. And the Holy Spirit descended in bodily form like a dove upon Him, and a voice came from heaven which said, 'You are My beloved Son; in You I am well pleased' " **(LUKE 3:21, 22).**

"God anointed Jesus of Nazareth with the Holy Spirit and with power, who went about doing good and healing all who were oppressed by the devil, for God was with Him" **(ACTS 10:38).**

"Then Jesus came from Galilee to John at the Jordan to be baptized by him. And John tried to prevent Him, saying, 'I need to be baptized by You, and are You coming to me?' But Jesus answered and said to him, 'Permit it to be so now, for thus it is fitting for us to fulfill all righteousness.' Then he allowed Him. When He had been baptized, Jesus came up immediately from the water; and behold, the heavens were opened to Him, and He saw the Spirit of God descending like a dove and alighting upon Him. And suddenly a voice came from heaven, saying, 'This is My beloved Son, in whom I am well pleased' " **(MATTHEW 3:13–17).**

"It came to pass in those days that Jesus came from Nazareth of Galilee, and was baptized by John in the Jordan. And immediately, coming up from the water, He saw the heavens parting and the Spirit descending upon Him like a dove. Then a voice came from heaven, 'You are My beloved Son, in whom I am well pleased' " **(MARK 1:9–11).**

Jesus was anointed by the Holy Spirit at His baptism, as the verses quoted above clearly show. The Greek title "Christ" and the Hebrew title "Messiah," both mean "the Anointed One," or "King." Even today the crowned heads of Europe are ceremonially anointed with a few drops of oil upon assuming the throne. The Lord's other name, "Jesus," is a Greek form of "Savior." That's why His mother Mary was told, "You shall call His name JESUS, for He shall save His people from their sins" **(MATTHEW 1:21).** So His full name, " Jesus Christ," honors Him as both our Savior and our King.

13 When would Jesus bring the sacrificial system to an end with His death on the cross?

"Then he shall confirm a covenant with many for one week; but in the middle of the week he shall bring an end to sacrifice and offering" **(DANIEL 9:27).**

"We have been sanctified through the offering of the body of Jesus Christ once for all" **(HEBREWS 10:10).**

Just as **DANIEL 9:27** predicted, Jesus brought "an end to [animal] sacrifice and offering" when He died as the Lamb of God. Chart 2 shows that this occurred precisely on time in A.D. 31.

The first sixty-nine weeks of the seventy-week prophecy ended in A.D. 27 at Christ's baptism. One week, or seven years, remained. In the middle of this last prophetic week, all animal sacrifices would cease. The Messiah would be cut off or crucified. According to the prophecy, Jesus would be crucified three-and-one-half years from His baptism in A.D. 27. This brings us to the spring of A.D. 31. Jesus was crucified at Passover, in the spring, exactly as the prophecy predicted.

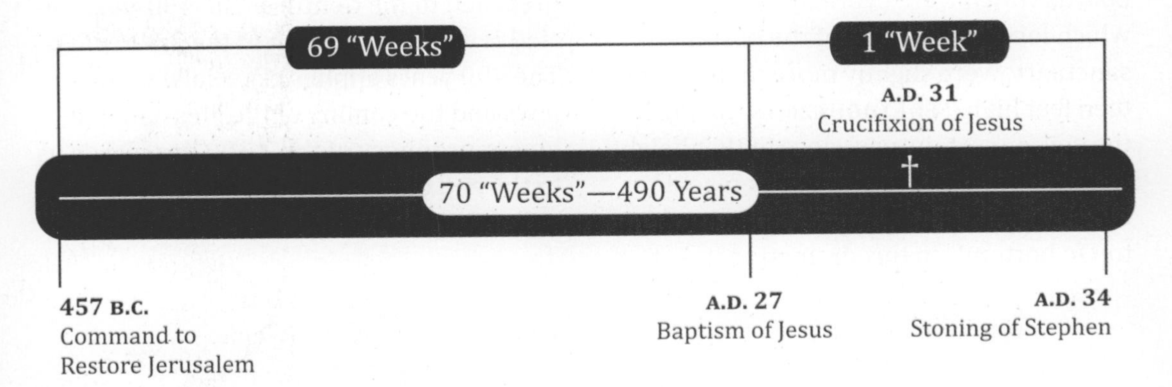

14 What amazing supernatural event occurred in the Jewish temple when Christ died?

"Then, behold, the veil of the temple was torn in two from top to bottom; and the earth quaked, and the rocks were split" **(MATTHEW 27:51).**

"And Jesus cried out with a loud voice, and breathed His last. Then the veil of the temple was torn in two from top to bottom" **(MARK 15:37, 38).**

This veil separated the Holy Place from the Most Holy Place in the magnificent temple in Jerusalem. The tearing of the veil in two is seen as a supernatural, divine act when we understand that the "veil" was a thick, sturdy curtain—like a tapestry. God told Moses: "You shall make a veil woven of blue, purple, and scarlet thread [most translations say "yarn" or "material"], and fine woven linen. It shall be woven with an artistic design of cherubim [angels]" **(EXODUS 26:31).** Such a woven curtain would be very difficult, if not impossible, to tear with human hands.

This curtain was not only quite substantial, it was also of a considerable height. The boards which were overlaid with gold and which formed the walls of the portable sanctuary, were slightly more than seventeen feet high **(SEE EXODUS 26:15, 16, 29).** If the veil, or curtain, was close to that height, it would be far above any man's reach! Yet the Bible says that it was "torn in two from top to bottom!" In this dramatic act—at this climactic moment—God was telling the world in general and the Jews in particular that Jesus' great sacrifice was bringing "an end to sacrifice and offering" **(DANIEL 9:27)** once and for all time. Animal sacrifices were now of no avail, "for it is not possible that the blood of bulls and goats could take away sins" **(HEBREWS 10:4),** since they simply pointed forward to Jesus, "the Lamb of God who takes away the sin of the world!" **(JOHN 1:29).**

The tearing of the veil in the Jewish temple signified the end of the sacrificial system. On Passover of A.D. 31, Jesus Christ, our Passover, was crucified for us. The sacrificial system lost its significance. Christ, our Substitute, was sacrificed in our behalf. Historically, the whole sacrificial system came to an end with the destruction of Jerusalem by Titus in A.D. 70. In A.D. 34, as the prophecy predicted, the Jews finally sealed their doom as a nation. The Jewish high priest, speaking on behalf of the Sanhedrin, the high Jewish council, officially rejected Jesus. Stephen, the first Christian martyr, was stoned, and the gospel was preached to the Gentiles. The 490-year period is a smaller section of the 2,300 days. The 490 years applies especially to the Jews and the coming of the Messiah. The longer prophecy of the 2,300 days leads us to the end of time, the cleansing of the sanctuary and earth's final judgment.

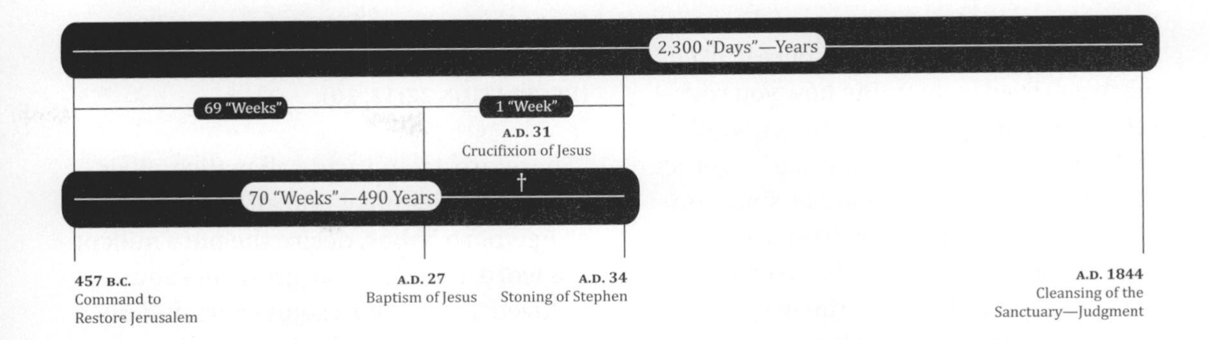

Adding 1810 years to the 490 years which ended in A.D. 34, brings us to the year A.D. 1844. Just as surely as Christ was baptized in A.D. 27 and crucified in A.D. 31, the judgment began in A.D. 1844.

15 How should living in the judgment hour influence the way we live today?

"Do this, knowing the time, that now it is high time to awake out of sleep; for now our salvation is nearer than when we first believed. The night is far spent, the day is at hand. Therefore let us cast off the works of darkness, and let us put on the armor of light. Let us walk properly, as in the day, not in revelry and drunkenness, not in lewdness and lust, not in strife and envy. But put on the Lord Jesus Christ, and make no provision for the flesh, to fulfill its lusts" **(ROMANS 13:11–14).**

"Now when these things begin to happen, look up and lift up your heads, because your redemption draws near" **(LUKE 21:28).**

"But the end of all things is at hand; therefore be serious and watchful in your prayers" **(1 PETER 4:7).**

" 'Cast away from you all the transgressions which you have committed, and get yourselves a new heart and a new spirit. For why should you die, O house of Israel? For I have no pleasure in the death of one who dies,' says the Lord GOD. 'Therefore turn and live!' " **(EZEKIEL 18:31, 32).**

"Have no fellowship with the unfruitful works of darkness, but rather expose them" **(EPHESIANS 5:11).**

"I say then: Walk in the Spirit, and you shall not fulfill the lust of the flesh. For the flesh lusts against the Spirit, and the Spirit against the flesh; and these are contrary to one another, so that you do not do the things that you wish. . . . And those who are Christ's have crucified the flesh with its passions and desires" **(GALATIANS 5:16, 17, 24).**

"Therefore put to death your members which are on the earth: fornication, uncleanness, passion, evil desire, and covetousness, which is idolatry. Because of these things the wrath of God is coming upon the sons of disobedience, in which you yourselves once walked when you lived in them. But now you yourselves are to put off all these: anger, wrath, malice, blasphemy, filthy language out of your mouth. Do not lie to one another, since you have put off the old man with his deeds, and have put on the new man who is renewed in knowledge according to the image of Him who created him" **(COLOSSIANS 3:5–10).**

"Do not love the world or the things in the world. If anyone loves the world, the love of the Father is not in him. For all that is in the world—the lust of the flesh, the lust of the eyes, and the pride of life—is not of the Father but is of the world. And the world is passing away, and the lust of it; but he who does the will of God abides forever" **(1 JOHN 2:15–17).**

"Behold, I am coming quickly, and My reward is with Me, to give to every one according to his work. . . . He who testifies to these things says, 'Surely I am coming quickly.' Amen. Even so, come, Lord Jesus!" **(REVELATION 22:12, 20).**

"Therefore, laying aside all malice, all deceit, hypocrisy, envy, and all evil speaking, as newborn babes, desire the pure milk of the word, that you may grow thereby. . . . Beloved, I beg you as sojourners and pilgrims, abstain from fleshly lusts which war against the soul" **(1 PETER 2:1, 2, 11).**

"You are all sons of light and sons of the day. We are not of the night nor of darkness. Therefore let us not sleep, as others do, but let us watch and be sober. For those who sleep, sleep at night, and those who get drunk are drunk at night. But let us who are of the day be sober, putting on the breastplate of faith and love, and as a helmet the hope of salvation" **(1 THESSALONIANS 5:5–8).**

16 Is the judgment something to terrify us? What assurance does our Lord give us as we face the judgment?

The Lord Jesus is our great High Priest "who does not need daily, as those high priests, to offer up sacrifices, first for His own sins and then for the people's, for this He did once for all when He offered up Himself" **(HEBREWS 7:27).**

"But He [Jesus], because He continues forever, has an unchangeable priesthood. Therefore He is also able to save to the uttermost those who come to God through Him, since He always lives to make intercession for them. For such a High Priest was fitting for us, who is holy, harmless, undefiled, separate from sinners, and has become higher than the heavens" **(HEBREWS 7:24–26).**

"Seeing then that we have a great High Priest who has passed through the heavens, Jesus the Son of God, let us hold fast our confession. For we do not have a High Priest who cannot sympathize with our weaknesses, but was in all points tempted as we are, yet without sin. Let us therefore come boldly to the throne of grace, that we may obtain mercy and find grace to help in time of need" **(HEBREWS 4:14–16).**

"For there is one God and one Mediator between God and men, the Man Christ Jesus" **(1 TIMOTHY 2:5).**

"Now this is the main point of the things we are saying: We have such a High Priest, who is seated at the right hand of the throne of the Majesty in the heavens, a Minister of the sanctuary and of the true tabernacle which the Lord erected, and not man" **(HEBREWS 8:1, 2).**

If any of us had to stand alone, we would have no hope. But Jesus will stand in our behalf in the judgment. What assurance! We can rejoice in the hope of the One who is our best Friend representing us before the throne of God.

What the Bible Says About the Judgment and the 2,300 Days

A number of years ago in the state of Florida, a man named Carl Gibbon performed a petty crime. He broke into a pool room and robbed something and was caught by the police. He was sentenced to five years in prison.

Now Carl had one problem. A homeless wanderer, he didn't have enough money for a lawyer. And so the judge said this crime does not require a man to have a lawyer. Carl was sentenced to prison without ever having a lawyer.

In prison, this homeless man began studying law. He studied the sixth amendment. The sixth amendment says that no American should ever be tried without the right of having a lawyer; somebody who can represent him at the judgment bar. This homeless man appealed his case.

It went all the way to the Supreme Court. And Carl was let free because he did not have a lawyer to defend him. The good news is that right now before God's throne, you and I have a lawyer. "My dear children, I write this to you so that you will not sin. But if anybody does sin, we have one who speaks to the Father in our defense—Jesus Christ, the Righteous One" **(1 JOHN 2:1, NIV).**

God said, "My goal for you is to live a righteous life and obey Me." But, then the Lord says, "If anybody does sin, we have One who speaks to the Father in our defense. Jesus Christ the Righteous One." Ancient Israel gathered around the sanctuary of old and cried, "Oh Lord, cleanse my heart, pardon my sin. Oh Lord, forgive me." Then the high priest went in to that inner Most Holy Place of the earthly sanctuary. He went in there representing all of Israel to God.

So where is Jesus tonight? Tonight Jesus is in the Most Holy Place of heaven's sanctuary.

What is Jesus doing there now? He is securing pardon for you and for me before all the angels. He lifts His hands and He says "This man is one of Mine, that woman is one of Mine." He is sending His Spirit to our hearts.

What is Jesus doing now? He is there in judgment, there where the destinies of the dead are now being decided, there where the destinies of the entire human race will soon be decided. Jesus is there interceding for you and for me.

He is the Author of our faith. He began a good work in you, but He is the Finisher of our faith. He is interceding for you. His arms are outstretched to you tonight.

Jesus longs to represent you before the throne of God, but He can only represent those cases that are given into His hands.

CHAPTER 12

What the Bible Says About the Judgment

We are living in judgment hour. The Bible refers to the judgment more than a thousand times. In 1844, God's prophetic time clock struck the hour. Revelation's angelic messenger announced, "The hour of His [God's] judgment has come" **(REVELATION 14:7)**. In the judgment, Christ is revealed as fully just and loving in His handling of the sin problem. Each case is decided for life or death. The entire universe recognizes that God has done everything possible to save every single person. It is His desire that every person be saved and "come to the knowledge of the truth" **(1 TIMOTHY 2:4)**. God is not willing that any individual be lost; He longs for all to "come to repentance" **(2 PETER 3:9)**.

In the judgment, God's heart of infinite love asks, "Is there anything more I could have done?" There is nothing more. Love has done all it could. The entire universe sings with one accord, "Worthy is the Lamb who was slain to receive power and riches and wisdom, and strength and honor and glory and blessing!" **(REVELATION 5:12)**.

God's matchless love is revealed in the judgment. All of heaven pauses to consider the choices each individual has made in the light of God's incredible desire to save him or her. This Bible study unfolds the importance of our choices in the twenty-first century.

01 How does the Bible describe the awesome scene of God's judgment in the heavenly courts?

"I watched till thrones were put in place, and the Ancient of Days [God the Father] was seated; His garment was white as snow, and the hair of His head was like pure wool. His throne was a fiery flame, its wheels a burning fire; a fiery stream issued and came forth from before Him. A thousand thousands ministered to Him; ten thousand times ten thousand stood before Him. The court was seated, and the books were opened" **(DANIEL 7:9, 10).**

God's beloved prophet Daniel was privileged to witness the opening of the judgment in the heavenly court. The context of the surrounding verses shows that events on earth are still continuing while this divine court is convened. What a scene—breathtaking in its majesty and solemn in its import!

"We have been made a spectacle to the world, both to angels and to men" **(1 CORINTHIANS 4:9).**

The Greek word translated "world" in this verse is *kosmos,* which gives us our English word, *cosmos,* meaning the whole universe. And the word "spectacle" is translated from the Greek term, *theatron,* from which we get our English word, *theater.* So this verse from the inspired pen of Paul is pregnant with meaning. It tells us that the numberless inhabitants of unfallen worlds throughout the universe are intensely interested in the judgment. The attention of the entire universe is riveted on the events unfolding in God's final judgment. In **DANIEL 7:10,** the "ten thousand times ten thousand" heavenly beings may be angels or they may be beings from unfallen worlds, but they are watching to see the choices you make, the choices I make, and the effect those choices have on our ultimate outcome. We can be sure that the drama in this real-life "theater" is far more fascinating than any soap opera!

Here is a brief summary of **DANIEL 7:9, 10:**

- Thrones are placed; the throne is a moveable throne.
- The Ancient of Days is seated, signifying the beginning of the judgment.
- Thousands upon thousands stand before Him. The unfallen world and the angels witness this scene.
- The court is seated. All things are ready.
- The books are opened. The drama unfolds!

All heaven is interested in this judgment. The destiny of the entire human race will be settled forever. The honor of God's throne is at stake.

02 How universal is God's judgment?

"We must all appear before the judgment seat of Christ, that each one may receive the things done in the body, according to what he has done, whether good or bad" **(2 CORINTHIANS 5:10).**

"So then each of us shall give account of himself to God" **(ROMANS 14:12).**

"We shall all stand before the judgment seat of Christ. For it is written: 'As I live, says the LORD, every knee shall bow to Me, and every tongue shall confess to God' " **(ROMANS 14:10, 11).**

"At the name of Jesus every knee should bow, of those in heaven, and of those on earth, and of those under the earth" **(PHILIPPIANS 2:10).**

"And He commanded us to preach to the people, and to testify that it is He who was ordained by God to be Judge of the living and the dead" **(ACTS 10:42).**

"He has appointed a day on which He will judge the world in righteousness by the Man whom He has ordained. He has given assurance of this to all by raising Him from the dead" **(ACTS 17:31).**

03 What records are kept that will provide an accurate description of our lives in the judgment?

"I saw the dead, small and great, standing before God, and books were opened. And another book was opened, which is the Book of Life. And the dead were judged according to their works, by the things which were written in the books" **(REVELATION 20:12).**

"The court was seated, and the books were opened" **(DANIEL 7:10).**

"But there shall by no means enter it [the Holy City, New Jerusalem] anything that defiles, or causes an abomination or a lie, but only those who are written in the Lamb's Book of Life" **(REVELATION 21:27).**

"All who dwell on the earth will worship him [the antichrist/beast power], whose names have not been written in the Book of Life of the Lamb slain from the foundation of the world" **(REVELATION 13:8).**

"At that time Michael shall stand up, the great prince who stands watch over the sons of your people; and there shall be a time of trouble, such as never was since there was a nation, even to that time. And at that time your people shall be delivered, every one who is found written in the book" **(DANIEL 12:1).**

Jesus told His disciples, "Nevertheless do not rejoice in this, that the spirits are subject to you, but rather rejoice because your names are written in heaven" **(LUKE 10:20).**

"Then Moses returned to the LORD and said, 'Oh, these people have committed a great sin, and have made for themselves a god of gold! Yet now, if You will forgive their sin—but if not, I pray, blot me out of Your book which You have written.' And the LORD said to Moses, 'Whoever has sinned against Me, I will blot him out of My book' " **(EXODUS 32:31–33).**

The apostle Paul mentions the "church of the firstborn who are registered in heaven" **(HEBREWS 12:23).**

Millions of pieces of information can be stored in the memory of sophisticated computers. God can easily preserve our character decisions.

04 Whose names are in the book of life?

"And I urge you also, true companion, help these women who labored with me in the gospel, with Clement also, and the rest of my fellow workers, whose names are in the Book of Life" **(PHILIPPIANS 4:3).**

"He who overcomes shall be clothed in white garments, and I will not blot out his name from the Book of Life; but I will confess his name before My Father and before His angels" **(REVELATION 3:5).**

When we accept Jesus, we pass from spiritual death to spiritual life. Without Christ, we are dead in sin. Since the "wages of sin is death" **(ROMANS 6:23)**, we have no possibility of living eternally without Christ. When we come to Jesus, we receive the gift of eternal life from Him, and our names are placed in the book of life.

05 What does God record in His "book of remembrance"?

God clearly records a faithful record of our characters. His record books reveal what we actually are. There is no pretense or make-believe with God.

"Then those who feared the LORD spoke to one another, and the LORD listened and heard them; so a book of remembrance was written before Him for those who fear the LORD and who meditate on His name" **(MALACHI 3:16).**

"You number my wanderings; put my tears into Your bottle; are they not in Your book?" **(PSALM 56:8).**

Earthly kings have very detailed records, and so does God.

"And when an inquiry was made into the matter, it was confirmed, and both were hanged on a gallows; and it was written in the book of the chronicles in the presence of the king" **(ESTHER 2:23).**

"That night the king could not sleep. So one was commanded to bring the book of the records of the chronicles; and they were read before the king. And it was found written that Mordecai had told of Bigthana and Teresh, two of the king's eunuchs, the doorkeepers who had sought to lay hands on King Ahasuerus. Then the king said, 'What honor or dignity has been bestowed on Mordecai for this?' And the king's servants who attended him said, 'Nothing has been done for him' " **(ESTHER 6:1–3).**

These two passages from the book of Esther show the value and importance of even human historical records. How much more infinitely vital, then, are those kept in heaven by the recording angels—the books of the Judge of the universe!

"Oh, that my words were written! Oh, that they were inscribed in a book! That they were engraved on a rock with an iron pen and lead, forever!" **(JOB 19:23, 24).**

06 Are our sins actually recorded before God?

" 'Though you wash yourself with lye, and use much soap, yet your iniquity is marked before Me,' says the Lord GOD" **(JEREMIAH 2:22).**

"For My eyes are on all their ways; they are not hidden from My face, nor is their iniquity hidden from My eyes" **(JEREMIAH 16:17).**

"The sin of Judah is written with a pen of iron; with the point of a diamond it is engraved on the tablet of their heart" **(JEREMIAH 17:1).**

"Do not let your mouth cause your flesh to sin, nor say before the messenger of God that it was an error. Why should God be angry at your excuse and destroy the work of your hands?" **(ECCLESIASTES 5:6).**

God unquestionably keeps careful records. This verse lets us know that no one will justifiably be able to accuse the recording angel of making a mistake. In the end, all will acknowledge the justice of God and praise His name: "Just and true are Your ways, O King of saints! . . . True and righteous are Your judgments" **(REVELATION 15:3; 16:7).**

Neither are our good deeds forgotten: God says, "Is this not laid up in store with Me, sealed up among My treasures?" **(DEUTERONOMY 32:34).**

"The LORD has sworn by the pride of Jacob: 'Surely I will never forget any of their works' " **(AMOS 8:7).**

"You have set our iniquities before You, our secret sins in the light of Your countenance" **(PSALM 90:8).**

"The iniquity of Ephraim is bound up; His sin is stored up" **(HOSEA 13:12).**

These last two verses refer, of course, to sins that are unconfessed, unrepented, unforsaken, and unforgiven. Sins that are forgiven by God are covered by the blood of Jesus and eventually "blotted out" of heaven's record books **(SEE PSALM 51:1, 9; JEREMIAH 18:23)**. The God of mercy "will cast all our sins into the depths of the sea" **(MICAH 7:19)**.

07 How detailed is the judgment? How deeply does it probe into individual lives?

"But I say to you that for every idle word men may speak, they will give account of it in the day of judgment" **(MATTHEW 12:36)**.

"Let us hear the conclusion of the whole matter: Fear God, and keep His commandments: for this is the whole duty of man. For God shall bring every work into judgment, with every secret thing, whether it be good, or whether it be evil" **(ECCLESIASTES 12:13, 14, KJV)**.

"Rejoice, O young man, in your youth, and let your heart cheer you in the days of your youth; walk in the ways of your heart, and in the sight of your eyes; but know that for all these God will bring you into judgment" **(ECCLESIASTES 11:9)**.

Paul reminds us of "the day when God will judge the secrets of men by Jesus Christ, according to my gospel" **(ROMANS 2:16)**.

"Enoch, the seventh from Adam, prophesied about these men also, saying, 'Behold, the Lord comes with ten thousands of His saints, to execute judgment on all, to convict all who are ungodly among them of all their ungodly deeds which they have committed in an ungodly way, and of all the harsh things which ungodly sinners have spoken against Him' " **(JUDE 14, 15)**.

"For there is nothing covered that will not be revealed, nor hidden that will not be known. Therefore whatever you have spoken in the dark will be heard in the light, and what you have spoken in the ear in inner rooms will be proclaimed on the housetops" **(LUKE 12:2, 3)**.

"And I saw the dead, small and great, standing before God, and books were opened. And another book was opened, which is the Book of Life. And the dead were judged according to their works, by the things which were written in the books" **(REVELATION 20:12)**.

"But fornication and all uncleanness or covetousness, let it not even be named among you, as is fitting for saints; neither filthiness, nor foolish talking, nor coarse jesting, which are not fitting, but rather giving of thanks. For this you know, that no fornicator, unclean person, nor covetous man, who is an idolater, has any inheritance in the kingdom of Christ and God. Let no one deceive you with empty words, for because of these things the wrath of God comes upon the sons of disobedience" **(EPHESIANS 5:3–6)**.

08 Will anything remain hidden from God?

"Therefore judge nothing before the time, until the Lord comes, who will both bring to light the hidden things of darkness and reveal the counsels of the hearts. Then each one's praise will come from God" **(1 CORINTHIANS 4:5).**

"Their throat is an open tomb; with their tongues they have practiced deceit; the poison of asps is under their lips" **(ROMANS 3:13).**

"Then you shall again discern between the righteous and the wicked, between one who serves God and one who does not serve Him" **(MALACHI 3:18).**

09 Does God consider the circumstances of our lives in the judgment?

"And of Zion it will be said, 'This one and that one were born in her; and the Most High Himself shall establish her.' The LORD will record, when He registers the peoples: 'This one was born there' " **(PSALM 87:5, 6).**

"Jesus said to them, 'If you were blind, you would have no sin; but now you say, "We see." Therefore your sin remains' " **(JOHN 9:41).**

"And that servant who knew his master's will, and did not prepare himself or do according to his will, shall be beaten with many stripes. But he who did not know, yet committed things deserving of stripes, shall be beaten with few. For everyone to whom much is given, from him much will be required; and to whom much has been committed, of him they will ask the more" **(LUKE 12:47, 48).**

"You are all sons of God through faith in Christ Jesus. For as many of you as were baptized into Christ have put on Christ. There is neither Jew nor Greek, there is neither slave nor free, there is neither male nor female; for you are all one in Christ Jesus" **(GALATIANS 3:26–28).**

"The LORD said to him [an angel or the "man clothed with linen"], 'Go through the midst of the city, through the midst of Jerusalem, and put a mark on the foreheads of the men who sigh and cry over all the abominations that are done within it' " **(EZEKIEL 9:4; SEE ALSO VERSES 1–6).**

"If I had not come and spoken to them, they would have no sin, but now they have no excuse for their sin. He who hates Me hates My Father also. If I had not done among them the works which no one else did, they would have no sin; but now they have seen and also hated both Me and My Father" **(JOHN 15:22–24).**

"Also He spoke this parable to some who trusted in themselves that they were righteous, and despised others: 'Two men went up to the temple to pray, one a Pharisee and the other a tax collector. The Pharisee stood and prayed thus with himself, "God, I thank You that I am not like other men—extortioners, unjust, adulterers, or even as this tax collector. I fast twice a week; I give tithes of all that I possess."

And the tax collector, standing afar off, would not so much as raise his eyes to heaven, but beat his breast, saying, "God, be merciful to me a sinner!" I tell you, this man went down to his house justified rather than the other; for everyone who exalts himself will be humbled, and he who humbles himself will be exalted' " **(LUKE 18:9–14).**

The judgment reveals not only our actions but also our attitudes. It delves into our motives. It considers our opportunities and the privileges God has given us.

10 Who will preside during these proceedings?

"For the Father judges no one, but has committed all judgment to the Son" **(JOHN 5:22).**

God the Father "has given Him [Jesus] authority to execute judgment also, because He is the Son of Man" **(JOHN 5:27).**

"He commanded us to preach to the people, and to testify that it is He [Christ] who was ordained by God to be Judge of the living and the dead" **(ACTS 10:42).**

God "has appointed a day on which He will judge the world in righteousness by the Man whom He has ordained. He has given assurance of this to all by raising Him from the dead" **(ACTS 17:31).**

"Jesus came and spoke to them, saying, 'All authority has been given to Me in heaven and on earth' " **(MATTHEW 28:18).**

"We must all appear before the judgment seat of Christ, that each one may receive the things done in the body, according to what he has done, whether good or bad" **(2 CORINTHIANS 5:10).**

"I charge you therefore before God and the Lord Jesus Christ, who will judge the living and the dead at His appearing and His kingdom" **(2 TIMOTHY 4:1).**

Said Jesus, "All things have been delivered to Me by My Father" **(MATTHEW 11:27).**

"The Father loves the Son, and has given all things into His hand" **(JOHN 3:35).**

"The Son of Man will come in the glory of His Father with His angels, and then He will reward each according to his works" **(MATTHEW 16:27).**

11 Who is our Defense Lawyer?

"My little children, these things I write to you, so that you may not sin. And if anyone sins, we have an Advocate with the Father, Jesus Christ the righteous" **(1 JOHN 2:1).**

"It is Christ who died, and furthermore is also risen, who is even at the right hand of God, who also makes intercession for us" **(ROMANS 8:34).**

"For there is one God and one Mediator between God and men, the Man Christ Jesus" **(1 TIMOTHY 2:5).**

"Seeing then that we have a great High Priest who has passed through the heavens, Jesus the Son of God, let us hold fast our confession. For we do not have a High Priest who cannot sympathize with our weaknesses, but was in all points tempted as we are, yet without sin. Let us therefore come boldly to the throne of grace, that we may obtain mercy and find grace to help in time of need" **(HEBREWS 4:14–16).**

"But He, because He continues forever, has an unchangeable priesthood. Therefore He is also able to save to the uttermost those who come to God through Him, since He always lives to make intercession for them" **(HEBREWS 7:24, 25).**

"For Christ has not entered the holy places made with hands, which are copies of the true, but into heaven itself, now to appear in the presence of God for us" **(HEBREWS 9:24).**

Jesus is both our Lawyer and our Judge. He stands in our behalf in the judgment. Jesus longs for us to be saved. In the judgment He is for us, not against us. He created us. He redeemed us, and now He lives for us. **HEBREWS 7:25** says, "Therefore He is able to save to the uttermost those who come to God through Him, since He always lives to make intercession for them."

12 When Satan condemns us in the judgment, what does Jesus say to him?

"Then he showed me Joshua the high priest standing before the Angel of the LORD, and Satan standing at his right hand to oppose him. And the LORD said to Satan, 'The LORD rebuke you, Satan! The LORD who has chosen Jerusalem rebuke you! Is this not a brand plucked from the fire?' " **(ZECHARIAH 3:1, 2).**

Throughout the Bible, Jesus rebukes demons. He challenges the authority of Satan and delivers His people. Jesus has never lost a battle with Satan yet! Notice these Bible passages that describe Jesus rebuking Satan and remember He will also rebuke him on your behalf in the final judgment.

"Yet Michael the archangel, in contending with the devil, when he disputed about the body of Moses, dared not bring against him a reviling accusation, but said, 'The Lord rebuke you!' " **(JUDE 9).**

"But Jesus rebuked him [the unclean spirit or demon], saying, 'Be quiet, and come out of him!' And when the demon had thrown him in their midst, it came out of him and did not hurt him" **(LUKE 4:35).**

"And as he was still coming, the demon threw him down and convulsed him. Then Jesus rebuked the unclean spirit, healed the child, and gave him back to his father" **(LUKE 9:42).**

"There was a man in their synagogue with an unclean spirit. And he cried out, saying, 'Let us alone! What have we to do with You, Jesus of Nazareth? Did You come to destroy us? I know who You are—the Holy One of God!' But Jesus rebuked him, saying, 'Be quiet, and come out of him!' " **(MARK 1:23–25).**

"So the great dragon was cast out, that serpent of old, called the Devil and Satan, who deceives the whole world; he was cast to the earth, and his angels were cast out with him. Then I heard a loud voice saying in heaven, 'Now salvation, and strength, and the kingdom of our God, and the power of His Christ have come, for *the accuser of our brethren, who accused them before our God day and night,* has been cast down' " **(REVELATION 12:9, 10; EMPHASIS SUPPLIED).**

13 What type of clothing is Joshua wearing and what new clothing does our Lord give him?

"Now Joshua was clothed with filthy garments, and was standing before the Angel. Then He [the Angel or Jesus] answered and spoke to those who stood before Him, saying, 'Take away the filthy garments from him.' And to him He said, 'See, I have removed your iniquity from you, and I will clothe you with rich robes' " **(ZECHARIAH 3:3, 4).**

Only Jesus can place the white robe of His spotless righteousness upon us. Only Jesus' righteousness is sufficient to stand the test of the judgment.

"Then one of the elders answered, saying to me, 'Who are these arrayed in white robes, and where did they come from?' And I said to him, 'Sir, you know.' So he said to me, 'These are the ones who come out of the great tribulation, and washed their robes and made them white in the blood of the Lamb' " **(REVELATION 7:13, 14).**

"And to her [the Lamb's wife, the church] it was granted to be arrayed in fine linen, clean and bright, for the fine linen is the righteous acts of the saints" **(REVELATION 19:8).**

"You have a few names even in Sardis who have not defiled their garments; and they shall walk with Me in white, for they are worthy. He who overcomes shall be clothed in white garments, and I will not blot out his name from the Book of Life; but I will confess his name before My Father and before His angels" **(REVELATION 3:4, 5).**

"Because you say, 'I am rich, have become wealthy, and have need of nothing'—and do not know that you are wretched, miserable, poor, blind, and naked—I counsel you to buy from Me gold refined in the fire, that you may be rich; and white garments, that you may be clothed, that the shame of your nakedness may not be revealed; and anoint your eyes with eye salve, that you may see" **(REVELATION 3:17, 18)**.

"I will greatly rejoice in the LORD, my soul shall be joyful in my God; for He has clothed me with the garments of salvation, He has covered me with the robe of righteousness, as a bridegroom decks himself with ornaments, and as a bride adorns herself with her jewels" **(ISAIAH 61:10)**.

"But the father said to his servants, 'Bring out the best robe and put it on him, and put a ring on his hand and sandals on his feet' " **(LUKE 15:22; SEE ALSO VERSES 11–24)**.

"And such [wicked sinners] were some of you. But you were washed, but you were sanctified, but you were justified in the name of the Lord Jesus and by the Spirit of our God" **(1 CORINTHIANS 6:11)**.

As we commit our lives to Christ, Satan condemns us. He accuses us of all the sins we have ever committed. Jesus stands in our behalf rebuking Satan. Our Savior takes away our filthy garments of sin and clothes us with the garments of His own righteousness.

14 What is God's standard in the judgment?

"So speak and so do as those who will be judged by the law of liberty" **(JAMES 2:12)**.

What is this "law of liberty" by which we "will be judged"? The Bible calls it a "perfect law"—"He who looks into the perfect law of liberty and continues in it, and is not a forgetful hearer but a doer of the work, this one will be blessed in what he does" **(JAMES 1:25)**. And **PSALM 19:7** says, "The law of the LORD is perfect, converting the soul." Furthermore, this same passage in James unmistakably identifies God's standard in the judgment as His moral law of Ten Commandments: "For whoever shall keep the whole law, and yet stumble in one point, he is guilty of all. For He who said, 'Do not commit adultery,' also said, 'Do not murder.' Now if you do not commit adultery, but you do murder, you have become a transgressor of the law" **(JAMES 2:10, 11)**.

"If you really fulfill the royal law according to the Scripture, 'You shall love your neighbor as yourself,' you do well" **(JAMES 2:8)**. "The royal law," of course, is the law of the King.

Jesus said, "If you love Me, keep My commandments" **(JOHN 14:15)**.

We are not saved by obeying God's law. We are saved by God's grace. In the judgment, God does not weigh our good deeds against our bad deeds. We are accepted on the basis of Christ's righteousness, not our own righteousness. However, when Christ accepts us, He leads us to obedience. Obedience is the evidence of a changed life. Obedience is the evidence that our faith is genuine. The basic question asked in the judgment is this: "Has this person accepted the saving grace of Christ? Is this acceptance evidenced by a changed relationship to the law? Is his or her attitude one of obedience or rebellion?"

Those who are saved by grace can say with the psalmist, "I delight to do Your will, O my God, and Your law is within my heart" **(PSALM 40:8).** It hurts them if they hurt Jesus by breaking His law. Deep within their heart they have chosen the way of obedience, not the way of rebellion.

Jesus and His law are inseparable. To willfully disobey His law is to wound Him. Will you not say in your heart, "Lord, I love You. Cover my sins with Your righteousness. Forgive me of my rebellion. Take away my desire to disobey. I choose now to be Your obedient child"?

Why is the moral fabric of society disintegrating? Is there an answer? God's matchless love is revealed in the judgment.

CHAPTER 13

What the Bible Says About the Law of God

The controversy flared. Lines were sharply drawn. There were people with strong opinions on both sides of the question. Roy Moore, chief justice of the Supreme Court of Alabama, refused to remove a monument of the Ten Commandments from the state courthouse despite orders to do so from a federal judge. Two months after his election to the Alabama Supreme Court, Moore began making plans to construct the 2.6-ton stone carving from Vermont granite. He argued that the Ten Commandments provide "the moral foundation of law to our people."

On August 27, the Ten Commandment monument was moved from the Alabama State capitol's rotunda to a side room. It is possible to argue, as some have, that the presence of the granite monument in the rotunda of the Alabama capitol building was a violation of the "establishment clause" of the United States Constitution regarding a separation of church and state. But the removal of the monument is emblematic of something much deeper. Could it be that our society has removed the Ten Commandments to a side room? That we have removed the Ten Commandments from our lives? Is it possible that we have cast off all moral authority? In a society where violent crime, immorality, school violence, corporate greed, drug addiction, alcoholism, and terrorism are rampant, something has gone tragically wrong. The issue is not the removal of a monument of the Ten Commandments from the state capitol of Alabama; it's the removal of the commandments from our hearts and homes. Our society appears to be drifting on an uncharted sea without a moral compass. We seem to be wandering in confusion, desperately looking for some "North Star" to guide us. In this chapter, we will discover the truth about what's gone wrong with our society, and we'll look at God's solution to crime and violence in the twenty-first century.

01 What urgent appeal does God give to a world of changing moral standards and crumbling ethical foundations?

John the revelator heard an angel "saying with a loud voice, 'Fear God and give glory to Him, for the hour of His judgment has come; and worship Him who made heaven and earth, the sea and springs of water' " **(REVELATION 14:7).**

"Fear God and keep His commandments, for this is man's all. For God will bring every work into judgment, including every secret thing, whether good or evil" **(ECCLESIASTES 12:13, 14).**

To fear God is to reverence or respect Him enough to obey Him. In the Bible there is a relationship between fearing God, glorifying His name, and living an obedient life.

"Who shall not fear You, O Lord, and glorify Your name? For You alone are holy. For all nations shall come and worship before You, for Your judgments have been manifested" **(REVELATION 15:4).**

"Then a voice came from the throne, saying, 'Praise our God, all you His servants and those who fear Him, both small and great!' " **(REVELATION 19:5).**

"But the Angel of the LORD called to him from heaven and said, 'Abraham, Abraham!' So he said, 'Here I am.' And He said, 'Do not lay your hand on the lad, or do anything to him; for *now I know that you fear God*, since you have not withheld your son, your only son, from Me' " **(GENESIS 22:11, 12; EMPHASIS SUPPLIED).**

Abraham demonstrated his fear, or respect, for God by obeying Him.

"God is greatly to be feared in the assembly of the saints, and to be held in reverence by all those around Him" **(PSALM 89:7).**

These passages make it clear that to "fear God" means to respect or reverence Him. It is a call to obedience. God's call to judgment implies accountability and moral choices. It is a call to a higher standard—a standard outside of ourselves.

02 Are our minds the ultimate judge of right and wrong?

"The heart is deceitful above all things, and desperately wicked; who can know it?" **(JEREMIAH 17:9).**

"You have done worse than your fathers, for behold, each one follows the dictates of his own evil heart, so that no one listens to Me" **(JEREMIAH 16:12).**

"Then the LORD saw that the wickedness of man was great in the earth, and that every intent of the thoughts of his heart was only evil continually" **(GENESIS 6:5).**

"What is man, that he could be pure? And he who is born of a woman, that he could be righteous? If God puts no trust in His saints, and the heavens are not pure in His sight, how much less man, who is abominable and filthy, who drinks iniquity like water!" **(JOB 15:14–16).**

"Behold, I was brought forth in iniquity, and in sin my mother conceived me" **(PSALM 51:5).**

"Trust in the LORD with all your heart, and lean not on your own understanding" **(PROVERBS 3:5).**

"From within, out of the heart of men, proceed evil thoughts, adulteries, fornications, murders, thefts, covetousness, wickedness, deceit, lewdness, an evil eye, blasphemy, pride, foolishness. All these evil things come from within and defile a man" **(MARK 7:21–23).**

"The carnal mind is enmity against God; for it is not subject to the law of God, nor indeed can be" **(ROMANS 8:7).**

"Truly the hearts of the sons of men are full of evil; madness is in their hearts while they live, and after that they go to the dead" **(ECCLESIASTES 9:3).**

"Beware, brethren, lest there be in any of you an evil heart of unbelief in departing from the living God" **(HEBREWS 3:12).**

Since our natures are fallen, our hearts deceive us at times. It is easy to justify our behavior based on our own personal desires. We need a higher standard outside of ourselves.

03 How does God's Word describe those who trust only in their own judgment in making moral decisions?

"He who trusts in his own heart is a fool, but whoever walks wisely will be delivered" **(PROVERBS 28:26).**

This principle of not trusting one's own moral strength is certainly demonstrated in the life of Peter. When he thought he was strong, he was actually weak.

Peter's bold statement. "Then Jesus said to them [the disciples], 'All of you will be made to stumble because of Me this night, for it is written: "I will strike the Shepherd, and the sheep will be scattered." But after I have been raised, I will go before you to Galilee.' Peter said to Him, 'Even if all are made to stumble, yet I will not be.' Jesus said to him, 'Assuredly, I say to you that today, even this night, before the rooster crows twice, you will deny Me three times.' But he spoke more vehemently, 'If I have to die with You, I will not deny You!' And they all said likewise" **(MARK 14:27–31).**

Peter's later experience. "Now as Peter was below in the courtyard, one of the servant girls of the high priest came. And when she saw Peter warming himself, she looked at him and said, 'You also were with Jesus of Nazareth.' But he denied it, saying, 'I neither know nor understand what you are saying.' And he went out on the porch, and a rooster crowed. And the servant girl saw him again, and began to say to those who stood by, 'This is one of them.' But he denied it again. And a little later those who stood by said to Peter again, 'Surely you are one of them; for you are a Galilean, and your speech shows it.' Then he began to curse and swear, 'I do not know this Man of whom you speak!' A second time the rooster crowed. Then Peter called to mind the word that Jesus had said to him, 'Before the rooster crows twice, you will deny Me three times.' And when he thought about it, he wept" **(MARK 14:66–72).**

When we depend on our own strength, we are destined to failure.

"You have done worse than your fathers, for behold, each one follows the dictates of his own evil heart, so that no one listens to Me" **(JEREMIAH 16:12).**

"Then the Lord saw that the wickedness of man was great in the earth, and that every intent of the thoughts of his heart was only evil continually" **(GENESIS 6:5).**

"What is man, that he could be pure? And he who is born of a woman, that he could be righteous? If God puts no trust in His saints, and the heavens are not pure in His sight, how much less man, who is abominable and filthy, who drinks iniquity like water!" **(JOB 15:14–16).**

"Behold, I was brought forth in iniquity, and in sin my mother conceived me" **(PSALM 51:5).**

"From within, out of the heart of men, proceed evil thoughts, adulteries, fornications, murders, thefts, covetousness, wickedness, deceit, lewdness, an evil eye, blasphemy, pride, foolishness. All these evil things come from within and defile a man" **(MARK 7:21–23).**

"Truly the hearts of the sons of men are full of evil; madness is in their hearts while they live, and after that they go to the dead" **(ECCLESIASTES 9:3).**

"Beware, brethren, lest there be in any of you an evil heart of unbelief in departing from the living God" **(HEBREWS 3:12).**

In Revelation, the Bible's last book, what did John see open in heaven? How do the other Bible prophets cast light on this scene?

"Then the temple of God was opened in heaven, and the ark of His covenant was seen in His temple. And there were lightnings, noises, thunderings, an earthquake, and great hail" **(REVELATION 11:19).**

The prophet Isaiah described his breathtaking experience: "In the year that King Uzziah died, I saw the Lord sitting on a throne, high and lifted up, and the train of His robe filled the temple. Above it stood seraphim; each one had six wings: with two he covered his face, with two he covered his feet, and with two he flew. And one cried to another and said: 'Holy, holy, holy is the LORD of hosts; the whole earth is full of His glory!' " **(ISAIAH 6:1–3).**

"And they shall make an ark of acacia wood; two and a half cubits shall be its length, a cubit and a half its width, and a cubit and a half its height. And you shall overlay it with pure gold, inside and out you shall overlay it, and shall make on it a molding of gold all around. . . . And you shall put into the ark the Testimony which I will give you. . . . You shall put the mercy seat on top of the ark, and in the ark you shall put the Testimony that I will give you. And there I will meet with you, and I will speak with you from above the mercy seat, from between the two cherubim which are on the ark of the Testimony, about everything which I will give you in commandment to the children of Israel" **(EXODUS 25:10, 11, 16, 21, 22).**

In the Most Holy Place of the sanctuary was found "the ark of the covenant overlaid on all sides with gold, in which were the golden pot that had the manna, Aaron's rod that budded, and the tablets of the covenant [the two tablets of stone on which God had written the Ten Commandments with His own finger]" **(HEBREWS 9:4).**

"When He [God] had made an end of speaking with him [Moses] on Mount Sinai, He gave Moses two tablets of the Testimony, tablets of stone, written with the finger of God" **(EXODUS 31:18).**

"Now the tablets were the work of God, and the writing was the writing of God engraved on the tablets" **(EXODUS 32:16).**

When God commanded the Israelites in the Old Testament to build a sanctuary, He commanded them to make the ark of the covenant to contain the tables of stone or the Ten Commandment law. The temple in heaven containing the ark of the covenant contains God's law, the foundation of His character. Revelation's answer to lawlessness is found in heaven at God's throne in His eternal standard of righteousness—His law. The law of God is a transcript of His character, a description of His will. Without the law there is no sin. The apostle Paul states, "For where there is no law there is no transgression" **(ROMANS 4:15).**

05 What role does God's law play in the plan of salvation?

"Therefore by the deeds of the law no flesh will be justified in His sight, for *by the law is the knowledge of sin*" **(ROMANS 3:20; EMPHASIS SUPPLIED).**

"What shall we say then? Is the law sin? Certainly not! On the contrary, *I would not have known sin except through the law.* For I would not have known covetousness unless the law had said, 'You shall not covet' " **(ROMANS 7:7; EMPHASIS SUPPLIED).**

God's Law of Ten Commandments reveals His will for us and tells us what is right and wrong. The apostle Paul explains that, because the law of God is what *identifies* sin, what *defines* sin for us, "where there is no law there is no transgression. . . . Sin is not imputed when there is no law" **(ROMANS 4:15; 5:13).** Even in civil and criminal matters here on earth, no policeman could arrest you, and no judge could convict you, justly, if there were "no law" against what you were doing. These facts, from the Bible and from the court of reason, effectively refute the arguments of those who claim that God's law has been abolished.

The Bible defines sin this way: "Whosoever commits sin also commits lawlessness, and sin is lawlessness" **(1 JOHN 3:4).** The King James Version of this verse says, "sin is the transgression [the breaking] of the law." And I like the way the Phillips translation of this verse puts it, so simply and so directly to the point: "Everyone who commits sin breaks God's law, for that is what sin is, by definition—a breaking of God's law." Sin is simply breaking God's moral law of Ten Commandments. Sin is not a matter of our opinion. Sin is not sin, because I think it is sin. It is sin, because God defines it as sin.

"By this we know that we know Him, if we keep His commandments. He who says, 'I know Him,' and does not keep His commandments, is a liar, and the truth is not in him" **(1 JOHN 2:3, 4).**

"For this is the love of God, that we keep His commandments. And His commandments are not burdensome" **(1 JOHN 5:3).**

06 What is the eternal, unchangeable standard of God's government?

"All His precepts are sure. They stand fast forever and ever" **(PSALM 111:7, 8).**

"My covenant I will not break, nor alter the word that has gone out of My lips" **(PSALM 89:34).**

God's law of Ten Commandments was not only written on stone with His own finger, He also spoke it in thunderous tones with His own voice from the heights of Mount Sinai. **EXODUS 20:1** says, "God spoke all these words, saying: . . ."—then the Ten Commandments follow.

Jesus told us, "Do not think that I came to destroy the Law or the Prophets. I did not come to destroy but to fulfill. For assuredly, I say to you, till heaven and earth pass away, one jot or one tittle will by no means pass from the law till all is fulfilled. Whoever therefore breaks one of the least of these commandments, and teaches men so, shall be called least in the kingdom of heaven; but whoever does and teaches them, he shall be called great in the kingdom of heaven" **(MATTHEW 5:17–19).**

The Master says we shouldn't even "think" He came to destroy the law, let alone teach others that it's been abolished. And I haven't noticed heaven and earth passing away yet, have you? So God's law still must be fully in effect—according to Jesus.

"Do we then make void the law through faith? Certainly not! On the contrary, we establish the law" **(ROMANS 3:31).**

Paul, the apostle to the Gentiles, had high praise for the law of God: "The law is holy, and the commandment holy and just and good" **(ROMANS 7:12).**

"For I am the LORD, I do not change" **(MALACHI 3:6).**

Jesus said, "Heaven and earth will pass away, but My words will by no means pass away" **(MATTHEW 24:35).**

None of Jesus' words will ever pass away. But that's all the more true of His words in the Ten Commandments. The humble Carpenter of Nazareth who walked the dusty roads of Galilee is not only our Creator and Redeemer—as many texts of Scripture testify—but He is also our Lawgiver. Careful comparison of **NEHEMIAH 9:11–15** with **1 CORINTHIANS 10:1–4** proves this fact. The Lord who accompanied His people in the wilderness—who sheltered and guided them in pillars of cloud and fire, who came down on Mount Sinai to give His law, who gave them manna to eat and water to drink—is symbolized in **NEHEMIAH 9:15** as "the rock" from which thirst-quenching water poured. Paul, in **1 CORINTHIANS 10:1–4**, repeats these events and then states explicitly that "that Rock was Christ" **(VERSE 4).** Printers of the Bible capitalize the letter *r* in *Rock* here in **VERSE 4** because they know it refers to Deity. Jesus is the "Rock of Ages" we sing about in church, and He is the Lord who gave the Ten Commandments!

"Every good gift and every perfect gift is from above, and comes down from the Father of lights, *with whom there is no variation or shadow of turning*" **(JAMES 1:17; EMPHASIS SUPPLIED).**

God's law is the basis of His government. It was established to ensure the peace, order, harmony, and unity of the universe. A broken law brings sorrow, suffering, bondage, and death **(SEE PROVERBS 5:22; ROMANS 6:16, 23).**

07 What are a few things the Bible compares God's law to?

God compares His Word/law to a mirror.

"If anyone is a hearer of the word and not a doer, he is like a man observing his natural face in a mirror; for he observes himself, goes away, and immediately forgets what kind of man he was. But he who looks into the perfect law of liberty and continues in it, and is not a forgetful hearer but a doer of the work, this one will be blessed in what he does" **(JAMES 1:23–25).** God's law is a mirror that allows us to see ourselves and recognize our need of saving grace. The law reveals what sin is. It provides a moral structure outside of ourselves.

God compares His Word/law to a musical instrument.

The Lord tells His prophet Ezekiel, "So they come to you as people do, they sit before you as My people, and they hear your words, but they do not do them; for with their mouth they show much love, but their hearts pursue their own gain. Indeed you are to them as a very lovely song of one who has a pleasant voice and can play well on an instrument; for they hear your words, but they do not do them" **(EZEKIEL 33:31, 32).**

God compares His Word/law to a foundation.

"But everyone who hears these sayings of Mine, and does not do them, will be like a foolish man who built his house on the sand: and the rain descended, the floods came, and the winds blew and beat on that house; and it fell. And great was its fall" **(MATTHEW 7:26, 27).**

08 Is God's law still relevant today or does it need changing?

"The law of the LORD is perfect, converting the soul; the testimony of the LORD is sure, making wise the simple" **(PSALM 19:7).**

"The law is holy, and the commandment holy and just and good" **(ROMANS 7:12).**

God's law is His eternal standard of righteousness. It is a reflection of His "holy, just and good" character, so it never needs improvement. You cannot improve upon what is already perfect. You can only strive to understand it better.

09 What is the role of grace in the plan of salvation?

"By grace you have been saved through faith, and that not of yourselves; it is the gift of God" **(EPHESIANS 2:8).**

"What then shall we say that Abraham our father has found according to the flesh? For if Abraham was justified by works, he has something to boast about, but not before God. For what does the Scripture say? 'Abraham believed God, and it was accounted to him for righteousness.' Now to him who works, the wages are not counted as grace but as debt" **(ROMANS 4:1–4).**

"But God demonstrates His own love toward us, in that while we were still sinners, Christ died for us. Much more then, having now been justified by His blood, we shall be saved from wrath through Him. For if when we were enemies we were reconciled to God through the death of His Son, much more, having been reconciled, we shall be saved by His life" **(ROMANS 5:8–10).**

"But God, who is rich in mercy, because of His great love with which He loved us, even when we were dead in trespasses, made us alive together with Christ (by grace you have been saved), and raised us up together, and made us sit together in the heavenly places in Christ Jesus, that in the ages to come He might show the exceeding riches of His grace in His kindness toward us in Christ Jesus. For by grace you have been saved through faith, and that not of yourselves; it is the gift of God" **(EPHESIANS 2:4–8).**

Grace

Grace is God's divine, unmerited, undeserved power. It provides pardon, mercy, and forgiveness for our past—and power for the present. It is a gift of His love.

Grace is God's unmerited favor to bring us back into harmony with Him. The sole basis of our salvation is grace. Grace has always existed. It means pardon, mercy, love, and kindness **(SEE GENESIS 6:8; ROMANS 4:1–4; EPHESIANS 2:4–8).** Grace frees us from the condemnation of the law. By grace we pass from death to life **(SEE ROMANS 5:8–10; 8:1, 2).** By faith we accept the grace of God **(SEE ROMANS 3:28).**

"The grace of God that brings salvation has appeared to all men" **(TITUS 2:11).**

"But Noah found grace in the eyes of the LORD" **(GENESIS 6:8).**

Some people think that grace is a concept known solely in the New Testament. Thus they picture the God of the Old Testament as harsh and unforgiving. But this is an unfortunate mistake. For instance, **GENESIS 6:8,** quoted above, tells us that the grace of God appeared to Noah long ago in Old Testament times. And **TITUS 2:11,** also quoted above, states that God's saving grace "has appeared to all men." The Lord Jesus constantly tried to correct distorted pictures of God: "I do not say to you that I shall pray the Father for you; *for the Father Himself loves you*, because you have loved Me, and have believed that I came forth from God" **(JOHN 16:26, 27; EMPHASIS SUPPLIED).** Both God the Father and God the Son are infinitely loving and gracious. That's why Jesus came to this earth—to reveal God to us. And that's why, when Philip asked, "Lord, show us the Father," Jesus said to him, "Have I been with you so long, and yet you have not known Me, Philip? He *who has seen Me has seen the Father;* so how can you say, 'Show us the Father'?" **(JOHN 14:8, 9).**

Just as "all have sinned and fall short of the glory of God," all who believe and follow God are "justified freely by His grace through the redemption that is in Christ Jesus" **(ROMANS 3:23, 24).**

"Not by works of righteousness which we have done, but according to His mercy He saved us, through the washing of regeneration and renewing of the Holy Spirit" **(TITUS 3:5).**

The closing words of the entire Bible are these all-inclusive ones: "The grace of our Lord Jesus Christ be with you all. Amen" **(REVELATION 22:21).**

Faith

Faith is a relationship of trust with God as a friend. It believes what He says and acts upon it in spite of the circumstances, knowing that God desires only our best and that in the end His plans and purposes will triumph. Faith is the hand that reaches out to receive His grace.

"For God so loved the world that He gave His only begotten Son, that whoever believes in Him should not perish but have everlasting life. . . . He who believes in Him is not condemned; but he who does not believe is condemned already, because he has not believed in the name of the only begotten Son of God. ... He who believes in the Son has everlasting life; and he who does not believe the Son shall not see life, but the wrath of God abides on him" **(JOHN 3:16, 18, 36)**.

"Most assuredly, I say to you, he who hears My word and believes in Him who sent Me has everlasting life, and shall not come into judgment, but has passed from death into life" **(JOHN 5:24)**.

"And this is the will of Him who sent Me, that everyone who sees the Son and believes in Him may have everlasting life; and I will raise him up at the last day" **(JOHN 6:40)**.

"And he brought them out and said, 'Sirs, what must I do to be saved?' So they said, 'Believe on the Lord Jesus Christ, and you will be saved, you and your household' " **(ACTS 16:30, 31)**.

"Now to him who works, the wages are not counted as grace but as debt. But to him who does not work but believes on Him who justifies the ungodly, his faith is accounted for righteousness" **(ROMANS 4:4, 5)**.

"If you confess with your mouth the Lord Jesus and believe in your heart that God has raised Him from the dead, you will be saved. For with the heart one believes unto righteousness, and with the mouth confession is made unto salvation" **(ROMANS 10:9, 10)**.

"Therefore we conclude that a man is justified by faith apart from the deeds of the law" **(ROMANS 3:28)**.

10 How are we justified or made right with God? Does keeping the law form the basis of our salvation?

"Knowing that a man is not justified by the works of the law but by faith in Jesus Christ, even we have believed in Christ Jesus, that we might be justified by faith in Christ and not by the works of the law; for by the works of the law no flesh shall be justified. ... I do not set aside the grace of God; for if righteousness comes through the law, then Christ died in vain" **(GALATIANS 2:16, 21)**.

"But to him who does not work but believes on Him who justifies the ungodly, his faith is accounted for righteousness" **(ROMANS 4:5)**.

"Therefore, having been justified by faith, we have peace with God through our Lord Jesus Christ" **(ROMANS 5:1)**.

"Not by works of righteousness which we have done, but according to His mercy He saved us, through the washing of regeneration and renewing of the Holy Spirit, ... that having been justified by His grace we should become heirs according to the hope of eternal life" **(TITUS 3:5, 7)**.

Paul's earnest prayer was that he might "be found in Him [Christ], not having my own righteousness, which is from the law, but that which is through faith in Christ, the righteousness which is from God by faith" **(PHILIPPIANS 3:9)**.

"Therefore let it be known to you, brethren, that through this Man is preached to you the forgiveness of sins; and by Him everyone who believes is justified from all things from which you could not be justified by the law of Moses" **(ACTS 13:38, 39)**.

11 If we are saved by grace, do we have the freedom to break God's law?

"Do we then make void the law through faith? Certainly not! On the contrary, we establish the law" **(ROMANS 3:31)**.

Obviously, it's only those who are faithful—not the infidel, atheist, or libertine—who cooperates with God and obeys Him. Thus faith, far from voiding God's divine requirements, establishes them in our hearts.

"What then? Shall we sin because we are not under law but under grace? Certainly not!" **(ROMANS 6:15)**.

This wonderful text has a comforting message for all forgiven sinners, but it's important to understand what Paul means by the expression "not under law but under grace." The phrase "under the law" can have two legitimate, possible meanings—but neither means we have a license to sin! This phrase could mean "under [the *jurisdiction* of] the law" or it could mean "under [the *condemnation* of] the law."

To be under the jurisdiction of the law means we are *subject* to the law and must obey it. Everyone in the United States is under the jurisdiction of the laws of the United States. A person living in California is under the jurisdiction of the laws of that state, but he or she would not be subject to the laws of Illinois or Oklahoma.

To be under the condemnation of the law means that when we *break* the law, we fall under its condemnation and must *pay its penalty*. God's Word says, "Sin is the transgression of the law," and the penalty or "wages of sin is death" **(1 JOHN 3:4, KJV; ROMANS 6:23)**.

But this is where grace comes in. The grace of God operates to free repentant sinners from the condemnation of the law. Since Jesus died in the sinner's place, the death penalty is paid for all who accept Him as their Savior. Every sin they've ever committed is forgiven. At that moment they have a clean record in the books of heaven because they enjoy "the remission of sins that are past" **(ROMANS 3:25, KJV)**. But they are still under the jurisdiction of God's law and may not break it without incurring sins in the future.

Happily, however, the good news of the gospel is that God's grace operates in both areas of a believer's life—not only to cover *past* sins by cancelling the condemnation of the law, but also to prevent future sins by helping us cope with the jurisdiction of the law!

"What shall we say then? Shall we continue in sin that grace may abound? Certainly not! How shall we who died to sin live any longer in it?" **(ROMANS 6:1, 2)**.

"It is time for You to act, O LORD, for they have regarded Your law as void" **(PSALM 119:126).**

"How can you say, 'We are wise, and the law of the LORD is with us'? Look, the false pen of the scribe certainly works falsehood. The wise men are ashamed, they are dismayed and taken. Behold, they have rejected the word of the LORD; so what wisdom do they have?" **(JEREMIAH 8:8, 9).**

"Do not think that I came to destroy the Law or the Prophets. I did not come to destroy but to fulfill" **(MATTHEW 5:17).**

"He [Jesus] answered and said to them, 'Why do you also transgress the commandment of God because of your tradition? . . . Thus you have made the commandment of God of no effect by your tradition. . . . And in vain they worship Me, teaching as doctrines the commandments of men" **(MATTHEW 15:3, 6, 9).**

"What shall we say then? Is the law sin? Certainly not! On the contrary, I would not have known sin except through the law. For I would not have known covetousness unless the law had said, 'You shall not covet.' . . . Therefore the law is holy, and the commandment holy and just and good" **(ROMANS 7:7, 12).**

"If you really fulfill the royal law according to the Scripture, 'You shall love your neighbor as yourself,' you do well; but if you show partiality, you commit sin, and are convicted by the law as transgressors. For whoever shall keep the whole law, and yet stumble in one point, he is guilty of all. For He who said, 'Do not commit adultery,' also said, 'Do not murder.' Now if you do not commit adultery, but you do murder, you have become a transgressor of the law. So speak and so do as those who will be judged by the law of liberty" **(JAMES 2:8–12).**

Paul prays "that the righteous requirement of the law might be fulfilled in us who do not walk according to the flesh but according to the Spirit" **(ROMANS 8:4).**

"For Christ is the end of the law for righteousness to everyone who believes" **(ROMANS 10:4).**

"Owe no one anything except to love one another, for he who loves another has fulfilled the law. For the commandments, 'You shall not commit adultery,' 'You shall not murder,' 'You shall not steal,' 'You shall not bear false witness,' 'You shall not covet,' and if there is any other commandment, are all summed up in this saying, namely, 'You shall love your neighbor as yourself.' Love does no harm to a neighbor; therefore love is the fulfillment of the law" **(ROMANS 13:8–10).**

Our attitude should be like that of Christ: "I delight to do Your will, O my God, and Your law is within my heart" **(PSALM 40:8).**

"This is the covenant that I will make with them after those days, says the LORD: I will put My laws into their hearts, and in their minds I will write them" **(HEBREWS 10:16).**

"This is the covenant that I will make with the house of Israel after those days, says the Lord: I will put My law in their minds, and write it on their hearts; and I will be their God, and they shall be My people" **(JEREMIAH 31:33).**

"The LORD is well pleased for His righteousness' sake; He will exalt the law and make it honorable" **(ISAIAH 42:21).**

"I say to you, that unless your righteousness exceeds the righteousness of the scribes and Pharisees, you will by no means enter the kingdom of heaven" **(MATTHEW 5:20).**

"For the grace of God that brings salvation has appeared to all men, teaching us that, denying ungodliness and worldly lusts, we should live soberly, righteously, and godly in the present age, looking for the blessed hope and glorious appearing of our great God and Savior Jesus Christ, who gave Himself for us, that He might redeem us from every lawless deed and purify for Himself His own special people, zealous for good works" **(TITUS 2:11–14).**

"Certain men have crept in unnoticed, who long ago were marked out for this condemnation, ungodly men, who turn the grace of our God into lewdness and deny the only Lord God and our Lord Jesus Christ" **(JUDE 4).**

12 What is the converted person's relationship to God's law?

"I delight in the law of God according to the inward man" **(ROMANS 7:22).**

"Because the carnal mind is enmity against God; for it is not subject to the law of God, nor indeed can be" **(ROMANS 8:7).**

"I have not departed from the commandment of His lips; I have treasured the words of His mouth more than my necessary food" **(JOB 23:12).**

"Blessed is the man who walks not in the counsel of the ungodly, nor stands in the path of sinners, nor sits in the seat of the scornful; but his delight is in the law of the LORD, and in His law he meditates day and night" **(PSALM 1:1, 2).**

"The law of the LORD is perfect, converting the soul; the testimony of the LORD is sure, making wise the simple; the statutes of the LORD are right, rejoicing the heart; the commandment of the LORD is pure, enlightening the eyes; the fear of the LORD is clean, enduring forever; the judgments of the LORD are true and righteous altogether. More to be desired are they than gold, yea, than much fine gold; sweeter also than honey and the honeycomb. Moreover by them Your servant is warned, and in keeping them there is great reward" **(PSALM 19:7–11).**

"I delight to do Your will, O my God, and Your law is within my heart" **(PSALM 40:8).**

"I will delight myself in Your statutes; I will not forget Your word" **(PSALM 119:16).**

"Your testimonies also are my delight and my counselors" **(PSALM 119:24).**

"Make me walk in the path of Your commandments, for I delight in it" **(PSALM 119:35).**

"I will delight myself in Your commandments, which I love. My hands also I will lift up to Your commandments, which I love, and I will meditate on Your statutes" **(PSALM 119:47, 48).**

"The law of Your mouth is better to me than thousands of coins of gold and silver" **(PSALM 119:72).**

"Unless Your law had been my delight, I would then have perished in my affliction" **(PSALM 119:92).**

"Oh, how I love Your law! It is my meditation all the day" **(PSALM 119:97).**

"I long for Your salvation, O LORD, and Your law is my delight" **(PSALM 119:174).**

Well-known evangelist, Billy Graham, was once asked, "Some religious people I know tell me that the Ten Commandments are part of the 'law' and do not apply to us today. They say that as Christians we are 'free from the law.' Is that right?" Mr. Graham answered, "No, it is not right, and I hope you will not be misled by these false opinions. It is very important to understand what the New Testament means when it says that Christians are 'free from the law.' It certainly does not mean that they are free from the obligations of the moral law of God and are at liberty to sin."

Conversion always leads us to "delight" to do God's will. When Christ changes our hearts—or converts us—we have one supreme desire: to obey Him. He has done so much for us that we gladly serve Him. Obedience is not a legalistic requirement. It is part of a loving heart's response to God.

13 Did Jesus teach that faith does away with keeping His law? What did the Savior teach His disciples about the importance of obedience?

Jesus gave this clear, explicit instruction to His disciples: "If you love Me, keep My commandments" **(JOHN 14:15).**

Jesus declared: "He who has My commandments and keeps them, it is he who loves Me. And he who loves Me will be loved by My Father, and I will love him and manifest Myself to him. . . . If anyone loves Me, he will keep My word; and My Father will love him, and We will come to him and make Our home with him" **(JOHN 14:21, 23).**

John, the beloved apostle, teaches, "By this we know that we love the children of God, when we love God and keep His commandments. For this is the love of God, that we keep His commandments. And His commandments are not burdensome" **(1 JOHN 5:2, 3).**

Jesus promises, "If you keep My commandments, you will abide in My love, just as I have kept My Father's commandments and abide in His love" **(JOHN 15:10).**

Jesus puts it this way: "You are My friends if you do whatever I command you" **(JOHN 15:14).**

14 Did Jesus teach that His law was done away with when He died on the cross?

"Do not think that I came to destroy the Law or the Prophets. I did not come to destroy but to fulfill. For assuredly, I say to you, till heaven and earth pass away, one jot or one tittle will by no means pass from the law till all is fulfilled" **(MATTHEW 5:17, 18).**

"Do we then make void the law through faith? Certainly not! On the contrary, we establish the law" **(ROMANS 3:31).**

"Therefore the law was our tutor to bring us to Christ, that we might be justified by faith" **(GALATIANS 3:24).**

Here Paul personifies God's law as "our tutor." The King James Version calls the law "our schoolmaster" to bring us to Christ. The law cannot save us. Its function is to *point out* our sin. Thus it drives us to the Savior who can save us! So law and grace, instead of being *opposed* to each other, are really *complementary coworkers* in God's great plan of salvation!

"Heaven and earth will pass away, but My words will by no means pass away" **(MATTHEW 24:35).**

"All flesh is as grass, and all the glory of man as the flower of the grass. The grass withers, and its flower falls away, but the word of the LORD endures forever" **(1 PETER 1:24, 25).**

15 How can we be certain that we really know God?

"By this we know that we know Him, if we keep His commandments. He who says, 'I know Him,' and does not keep His commandments, is a liar, and the truth is not in him. But whoever keeps His word, truly the love of God is perfected in him. By this we know that we are in Him" **(1 JOHN 2:3–5).**

"Whatever we ask we receive from Him, because we keep His commandments and do those things that are pleasing in His sight" **(1 JOHN 3:22).**

"For this is the love of God, that we keep His commandments. And His commandments are not burdensome" **(1 JOHN 5:3).**

"If we say that we have fellowship with Him, and walk in darkness, we lie and do not practice the truth" **(1 JOHN 1:6).**

Jesus asks His hypocritical followers who give only lip service, "Why do you call Me 'Lord, Lord,' and do not do the things which I say?" **(LUKE 6:46).**

The Master puts it plainly: "Not everyone who says to Me, 'Lord, Lord,' shall enter the kingdom of heaven, but he who does the will of My Father in heaven. Many will say to Me in that day, 'Lord, Lord, have we not prophesied in Your name, cast out demons in Your name, and done many wonders in Your name?' And then I will declare to them,

'I never knew you; depart from Me, you who practice lawlessness!' " **(MATTHEW 7:21–23).**

"Finally then, brethren, we urge and exhort in the Lord Jesus that you should abound more and more, just as you received from us how you ought to walk and to please God; for you know what commandments we gave you through the Lord Jesus" **(1 THESSALONIANS 4:1, 2).**

"He [Jesus Christ] became the author of eternal salvation to all who obey Him" **(HEBREWS 5:9).**

"Blessed are those who do His commandments, that they may have the right to the tree of life, and may enter through the gates into the city" **(REVELATION 22:14).**

"Teach me, O LORD, the way of Your statutes, and I shall keep it to the end. Give me understanding, and I shall keep Your law; indeed, I shall observe it with my whole heart" **(PSALM 119:33, 34).**

The evidence of the internal change called "conversion" is a changed life. Grace always leads to obedience. The more we love God, the more we desire to obey Him.

16 How does God describe His end-time people?

The last book of the Bible gives this description of Christ's true followers, His saints: "Here is the patience of the saints; here are those who keep the commandments of God and the faith of Jesus" **(REVELATION 14:12).**

"And the dragon [the devil] was enraged with the woman [the church], and he went to make war with the rest of her offspring, who keep the commandments of God and have the testimony of Jesus Christ" **(REVELATION 12:17).**

"Go therefore and make disciples of all the nations, baptizing them in the name of the Father and of the Son and of the Holy Spirit, teaching them to observe all things that I have commanded you; and lo, I am with you always, even to the end of the age" **(MATTHEW 28:19, 20).**

"By this we know that we love the children of God, when we love God and keep His commandments. For this is the love of God, that we keep His commandments. And His commandments are not burdensome" **(1 JOHN 5:2, 3).**

A genuine commitment to God leads to loving obedience. At the end of time God will have a group of people who reveal to the whole universe the joy of living obediently. They have been saved by grace. They love God so much that they enthusiastically obey Him. They accept His standards of conduct. They are convinced His way is best.

Commonly Asked Questions Regarding the Law of God

Didn't Jesus come to do away with the Ten Commandments and establish a new commandment of love? What about MATTHEW 22:37–40: Love God with all your heart and your neighbors as yourself? Isn't love to God and our neighbors all Jesus requires? Isn't this the "new commandment"?

It may surprise you to discover that in **MATTHEW 22,** Jesus was summarizing the law as given in the Old Testament. **DEUTERONOMY 6:5** declares, "Love the LORD your God with all your heart." **LEVITICUS 19:18** adds, "Love your neighbor as yourself." The God of the Old Testament was a God of everlasting love **(SEE JEREMIAH 31:3).** In **MATTHEW 22:40,** Jesus declared, "On these two commandments [love to God and love to our fellow man] hang all the Law and the Prophets." The first four commandments reveal how human beings tangibly demonstrate their love to their God. The last six commandments show how they demonstrate their love to their fellow man. Jesus did not come to destroy the law, but to fulfill it **(SEE MATTHEW 5:17).** He revealed how to lovingly keep the law. He came to magnify the meaning of the law **(SEE ISAIAH 42:21).** Jesus reveals how love is the fulfilling of the law **(SEE ROMANS 13:10).** He adds "If you love Me, keep My commandments" **(JOHN 14:15).**

Does Paul teach that Christians saved by faith do not have to keep the law?

Paul teaches that Christians are saved not by faith, but by grace through faith. Faith is the hand that takes the salvation freely offered by Jesus. But faith does not lead to disobedience; it leads to obedience. Paul states in no uncertain terms, "Do we then make void the law through faith? Certainly not!" **(ROMANS 3:31). ROMANS 6:15** adds, "Shall we sin [break the law] because we are not under law but under grace? Certainly not!"

Is it true that people in the Old Testament were saved by keeping the law, while salvation has been by grace since New Testament times?

In both the Old and New Testaments, salvation is by grace through faith. God does not have two methods of salvation. **TITUS 2:11** affirms, "For the grace of God that brings salvation has appeared to *all* men" **(EMPHASIS SUPPLIED).** In the Old Testament, men and women were saved by the Christ who was to come. Each lamb sacrificed pointed forward to the coming of the Messiah **(SEE GENESIS 3:21; 22:9–13).** Since the New Testament, men and women are saved by the Christ who has come. In one instance, faith looked *forward* to the Cross; in the other instance, faith looked *backward* to the Cross. Whether in the Old Testament or the New, Jesus is the only means of salvation **(SEE ACTS 4:12).**

Since we are under the new covenant, is it really necessary to keep God's law?

The new covenant is actually older than the old covenant! The new covenant was given by God Himself in the Garden of Eden when He promised that the Messiah would come to break Satan's deadly hold upon the human race. The new covenant contains the promise of redemption from sin through Jesus Christ. He saves us! He writes the principles of the law in our hearts. Love becomes the motivation for obedience. There is a new power in the life **(SEE HEBREWS 8:10; EZEKIEL 36:26; PSALM 40:8).** Under the old covenant, Israel promised to obey God's commandments in their own strength. They declared, "All that God says we will do" **(SEE EXODUS 19:8; 24:3, 7).** All attempts at external conformity to God's law lead to frustrated defeat. The law that we cannot keep in our own strength condemns us **(ROMANS 3:23; 6:23).** Under the new covenant, we belong to a new master—Jesus Christ. We have a new heart and a new standing before God **(SEE JOHN 1:12; 2 CORINTHIANS 5:17; ROMANS 8:1).**

CHAPTER 14

What the Bible Says About the Sabbath

The book of Revelation presents God's final message for a world in deep trouble. It is a message especially designed for a people living during the final, climactic hours of earth's history. It is a universal message that leaps across geographical boundaries. It is a message for all nations, tribes, languages, and peoples. It is an urgent, compelling message of good news. It is an urgent appeal for men and women everywhere to prepare for the soon return of Christ.

As we have studied in previous chapters, only in Christ are men and women capable of meeting the claims of God's law in earth's final judgment hour. God's last-day message is a message of surrender and commitment.

In this secular, materialistic age of humanistic thinking, many have dismissed the idea of a God who created the heavens and the earth. The theory of evolution has replaced the Bible teaching of creation. So it is not surprising to find a clarion call to worship God as our Creator in the Bible's last book, Revelation.

01 In an age of evolutionistic thinking, whom does God's last-day message in Revelation urgently appeal to us to worship? How do writers throughout the Bible echo this same theme?

"Then I saw another angel flying in the midst of heaven, having the everlasting gospel to preach to those who dwell on the earth—to every nation, tribe, tongue, and people—saying with a loud voice, 'Fear God and give glory to Him, for the hour of His judgment has come; and worship Him who made heaven and earth, the sea and springs of water' " **(REVELATION 14:6, 7).**

Bible writers leave no doubt that God created the heavens and the earth. There is absolutely *no* room for the evolutionary idea that this world is here simply by accident.

"By the word of the LORD the heavens were made, and all the host of them by the breath of His mouth. . . . For He spoke, and it was done; He commanded, and it stood fast" **(PSALM 33:6, 9).**

"The heavens are Yours, the earth also is Yours; the world and all its fullness, You have founded them" **(PSALM 89:11).**

"The sea is His, for He made it; and His hands formed the dry land" **(PSALM 95:5).**

"Our help is in the name of the LORD, who made heaven and earth" **(PSALM 124:8).**

The psalmist calls us to give thanks "to Him who alone does great wonders, for His mercy endures forever; to Him who by wisdom made the heavens, for His mercy endures forever; to Him who laid out the earth above the waters, for His mercy endures forever; to Him who made great lights, for His mercy endures forever—the sun to rule by day, for His mercy endures forever; the moon and stars to rule by night, for His mercy endures forever" **(PSALM 136:4–9).**

"Happy is he who has the God of Jacob for his help, whose hope is in the LORD his God, who made heaven and earth, the sea, and all that is in them; who keeps truth forever" **(PSALM 146:5, 6).**

"In the beginning God created the heavens and the earth" **(GENESIS 1:1).**

God asks Job, "Where were you when I laid the foundations of the earth? Tell Me, if you have understanding" **(JOB 38:4).**

The apostle Paul courageously told pagan worshipers of Zeus, "You should turn from these useless things to the living God, who made the heaven, the earth, the sea, and all things that are in them" **(ACTS 14:15).**

"Then Paul stood in the midst of the Areopagus and said, 'Men of Athens, I perceive that in all things you are very religious; for as I was passing through and considering the objects of your worship, I even found an altar with this inscription: TO THE UNKNOWN GOD. Therefore, the One whom you worship without knowing, Him I proclaim to you: God, who made the world and everything in it, since He is Lord of heaven and earth, does not dwell in temples made with hands. Nor is He worshiped with men's hands, as though He needed anything, since He gives to all life, breath, and all things' " **(ACTS 17:22–25).**

"You alone are the LORD; You have made heaven, the heaven of heavens, with all their host, the earth and everything on it, the seas and all that is in them, and You preserve them all. The host of heaven worships You" **(NEHEMIAH 9:6).**

"The LORD possessed me at the beginning of His way, before His works of old. I have been established from everlasting, from the beginning, before there was ever an earth. When there were no depths I was brought forth, when there were no fountains abounding with water. Before the mountains were settled, before the hills, I was brought forth; while as yet He had not made the earth or the fields, or the primal dust of the world. When He prepared the heavens, I was there, when He drew a circle on the face of the deep, when He established the clouds above, when He strengthened the fountains of the deep, when He assigned to the sea its limit, so that the waters would not transgress His command, when He marked out the foundations of the earth, then I was beside Him as a master craftsman; and I was daily His delight, rejoicing always before Him, rejoicing in His inhabited world, and my delight was with the sons of men" **(PROVERBS 8:22–31).**

"The LORD is the true God; He is the living God and the everlasting King" **(JEREMIAH 10:10).**

"Thus you shall say to them: 'The gods that have *not* made the heavens and the earth shall perish from the earth and from under these heavens.' He has made the earth by His power, He has established the world by His wisdom, and has stretched out the heavens at His discretion" **(JEREMIAH 10:11, 12).**

"He has made the earth by His power; He has established the world by His wisdom, and stretched out the heaven by His understanding" **(JEREMIAH 51:15).**

Revelation's final appeal to humanity is a call to worship the One who made heaven and earth and the fountains of waters. It is a call to worship our Creator.

02 What is the foundation of all true worship? What questions did God ask regarding the basis for worship?

"You are worthy, O Lord, to receive glory and honor and power; for You created all things, and by Your will they exist and were created" **(REVELATION 4:11).**

We should worship "Him who lives forever and ever, who created heaven and the things that are in it, the earth and the things that are in it, and the sea and the things that are in it" **(REVELATION 10:6).**

"Where were you when I laid the foundations of the earth? Tell Me, if you have understanding. Who determined its measurements? Surely you know! . . . To what were its foundations fastened? Or who laid its cornerstone, when the morning stars sang together and all the sons of God shouted for joy?" **(JOB 38:4–7).**

In these powerful passages from Revelation and Job, God Himself sets forth His wisdom, power, and supremacy over all false gods. Here He, Himself, establishes the very foundation of worship as the Creator.

03 How did God accomplish His master plan of Creation?

By inspiration, the apostle Paul wrote of "God who created all things *through Jesus Christ*" **(EPHESIANS 3:9; EMPHASIS SUPPLIED).**

"He [Jesus Christ, "the Son of His love," (verse 13)] is the image of the invisible God, the firstborn over all creation. For by Him all things were created that are in heaven and that are on earth, visible and invisible, whether thrones or dominions or principalities or powers. All things were created *through Him* and *for Him*" **(COLOSSIANS 1:15, 16; EMPHASIS SUPPLIED).**

God the Father gave His dear Son the honor of being the active Agent in the great work of Creation. This fact is easily demonstrated, first of all, by **GENESIS 1:26**: "Then God said, 'Let Us make man in Our image, according to Our likeness.' " The plural pronouns used here show that the Divine Being we call God was speaking to Someone as an equal, Someone already in His image and likeness.

JOHN 1:1, 2, 14 identifies this Divine Being as Jesus, the only-begotten Son: "In the beginning was the Word, and the Word was with God, and the Word was God. The same was in the beginning with God. . . . And the Word was made flesh, and dwelt among us . . . the only begotten of the Father" **(KJV).**

In unmistakable terms, God's Word tells us that Christ was the Creator. Note the following texts: "All things were *made by him* [that is, by Christ, the Incarnate Word], and without him was not any thing made that was made. . . . He was in the world, and the world was made by him, and the world knew him not" **(JOHN 1:3, 10, KJV; EMPHASIS SUPPLIED).** "God . . . hath in these last days spoken unto us by his Son, . . . by whom also he made the worlds. . . . Unto the Son he saith, . . . the heavens are the works of thine hands" **(HEBREWS 1:1, 2, 8–10, KJV).**

Bible verses like these clearly establish that Jesus is our Creator. How thrilling to realize that the humble Carpenter who walked the hills of Galilee was also the Almighty Creator who made, not only those very hills, but even this entire world—and "all things"! How sublime for Christians to recognize that the One whom they call "Savior" is also their Creator! Those who already feel indebted to Christ by virtue of His sacrificial act of redemption will find their love and appreciation enhanced when they acknowledge also His earlier act of divine creation!

04 How do we worship Christ as the Creator? Has He left a memorial or eternal sign of His creative activity?

"Remember the Sabbath day, to keep it holy. Six days you shall labor and do all your work, but the seventh day is the Sabbath of the LORD your God. In it you shall do no work: you, nor your son, nor your daughter, nor your male servant, nor your female servant, nor your cattle, nor your stranger who is within your gates. For in six days the LORD made the heavens and the earth, the sea, and all that is in them, and rested the seventh day. Therefore the LORD blessed the Sabbath day and hallowed it" **(EXODUS 20:8–11).**

"Speak also to the children of Israel, saying: 'Surely My Sabbaths you shall keep, for it is a sign between Me and you throughout your generations, that you may know that I am the LORD who sanctifies you" **(EXODUS 31:13).**

The Lord said to Moses, " 'Therefore the children of Israel shall keep the Sabbath, to observe the Sabbath throughout their generations as a perpetual covenant. It is a sign between Me and the children of Israel forever; for in six days the LORD made the heavens and the earth, and on the seventh day He rested and was refreshed.' And when He had made an end of speaking with him on Mount Sinai, He gave Moses two tablets of the Testimony, tablets of stone, written with the finger of God" **(EXODUS 31:16–18).**

The last book of the Bible contains a clarion call for us to worship God as Creator: "Worship Him who made heaven and earth, the sea and springs of water" **(REVELATION 14:7).**

We worship the Creator by keeping the Sabbath, which He has made in honor of Creation. The Sabbath is God's eternal memorial that He is our all-powerful Creator.

05 Was the Sabbath exclusively a Jewish institution?

"He [Jesus] said to them [the Pharisees], 'The Sabbath was made for man, and not man for the Sabbath. Therefore the Son of Man is also Lord of the Sabbath' " **(MARK 2:27, 28).**

We must be clear on the fact that Jesus did *not* say, "The Sabbath was made for the Jews." The word *man* in this text is the Greek word *anthropos,* which is a generic term and means "all mankind, irrespective of nationality or sex." It's the same Greek word translated "man" in **JOHN 1:9**, which refers to "*every* man that cometh into the world" **(EMPHASIS SUPPLIED).**

Don't let prejudice rob you of the blessing God has for you in the Sabbath. Too often Christians dispose of the Bible Sabbath with the prejudice-filled remark, "It's Jewish." How shortsighted! All the early Christians—the apostles and the Lord

Himself—were Jewish. Can we dispose of these people for the sake of prejudice? Most of the Bible was written in the Hebrew language and clothed in Jewish imagery. The "Holy Land" itself is Jewish. Can we throw all this overboard to satisfy the whims of prejudice?

Still, someone may say, "Wait a minute! I'm as unprejudiced and liberal as anyone. I have nothing against the Jews. When I say that the Sabbath is Jewish, it has nothing to do with prejudice. I'm simply stating a fact. The seventh-day Sabbath *is* Jewish, that's all. It was made for the Jews, and it has nothing whatsoever to do with Christians today. So, what's wrong with saying that?"

The thing that's wrong with this statement is this: *It's absolutely not true!*

Examine the facts. Your Bible says God gave the Sabbath as a blessing to Adam and Eve on the seventh day of Creation week, long before there were any Jews or Egyptians or Chinese or any other race or nationality **(SEE GENESIS 2:1–3)**. What is "Jewish" about the creation of the world? Remember, Abraham was the first Jew, and he lived to approximately 2000 B.C. Therefore, if we hold to a six-thousand-year period of earth's history, we see that the seventh-day Sabbath was instituted and kept some two thousand years *before* the first Jew existed!

Satan's argument that God intended only Old Testament Jews to observe the Sabbath has gained such strength that many Christians today refer to God's Sabbath as the "Jewish Sabbath." But no such expression is found in the Bible. The seventh day is called "the Sabbath of the LORD" **(EXODUS 20:10)**, but never "the Sabbath of the Jews." Luke, a Gentile writer of the New Testament, often referred to specifically Jewish things. He wrote about:

"the nation of the Jews" **(ACTS 10:22)**
"the land of the Jews" **(ACTS 10:39)**
"the people of the Jews" **(ACTS 12:11)**
"the synagogue of the Jews" **(ACTS 14:1)**

But although he mentioned the Sabbath repeatedly, Luke *never* called it "the Sabbath of the Jews"—nor did any other Bible writer. After all, as Timothy Dwight, president of Yale University, observed: "It was no more necessary for a Jew to rest after the labor of six days was ended, than for any other man. It was no more necessary for a Jew to commemorate the perfections of God, displayed in the works of creation" (*Theology Explained & Defended,* vol. III, p. 225).

The Jews kept God's holy day *not* because the Sabbath was just for them, but because *they were the only people faithful* to the true God in Old Testament times.

Our Creator gave His holy day to Adam and Eve back in Eden at the same time He gave them the institution of marriage. No one foolishly claims marriage is "just for the Jews"! The twin institutions of God's holy Sabbath and holy matrimony are like two roses plucked from the Garden of Eden; one is no more "Jewish" than the other. Both have been fiendishly attacked by Satan.

Perhaps we've already said enough to convince unprejudiced readers. But one more point may be worth making: God's holy Sabbath existed as an institution even *before* the giving of the Ten Commandments! Exodus 16 gives rather detailed instructions to God's people about the "bread from heaven" called *manna*, which the Lord provided to sustain them in the wilderness. Each day the Israelites were to gather just enough for that day; if they tried to gather extra and keep it over till the next day, it would spoil, begin to stink, and breed worms. But no manna fell on the seventh-day Sabbath, so they didn't need to gather any on that day. Instead, God told them to gather twice as much manna on Friday, the "Preparation Day," for the Sabbath. Unlike manna left over on the other days, none gathered on Friday and kept over until the seventh-day Sabbath would spoil "and it did not stink, nor were there any worms in it" **(EXODUS 16:24)**.

All of this, of course, involved many miracles on the part of God: (1) raining down the manna six days a week, (2) giving a double portion on each Preparation Day, (3) miraculously preserving the extra manna over the Sabbath, (4) providing no manna on the Sabbath so that no menial work needed to be done on God's holy day.

But some rebellious people defied the Lord's instructions and went out on the seventh day to gather manna anyway. "And the LORD said to Moses, '*How long do you refuse to keep My commandments and My laws?*' " **(EXODUS 16:28; EMPHASIS SUPPLIED)**. Yet this was quite some time before the giving of God's law of the Ten Commandments on Mount Sinai, which didn't take place until later **(SEE EXODUS 20)**. Thus God, by giving the manna in this way, not only preserved His people during their wilderness wanderings, but also preserved His Sabbath command during those forty years.

06 How did God distinguish the seventh day from all other days of the week?

"Thus the heavens and the earth, and all the host of them, were finished. And on the seventh day God ended His work which He had done, and He rested on the seventh day from all His work which He had done. Then God blessed the seventh day and sanctified it, because in it He rested from all His work which God had created and made" **(GENESIS 2:1–3)**.

The word *sanctified* means "set apart for a holy purpose," as a church building is set apart for divine worship. That's what God says He did to the seventh-day Sabbath at Creation. No other day was ever blessed by God or set aside for a holy purpose. Later, when God wrote the Ten Commandments, He said, "Remember the Sabbath day, to keep it holy" **(EXODUS 20:8)**. If we choose to disregard the Lord's command and worship on some other day, the real question is: Can we get a blessing from a day God never blessed? Can we *keep* holy a day that was never *made* holy?

Also, understand that when God "rested," it was as an example to us—*not* because He was exhausted! The prophet Isaiah quite candidly asks, "Have you not known? Have you not heard? The everlasting God, the LORD, the Creator of the ends of the earth, neither faints nor is weary" **(ISAIAH 40:28).**

07 Throughout the Old Testament, what expression, or term, does God use to describe the Sabbath?

God declares, "Moreover I also gave them My Sabbaths, to be a sign between them and Me, that they might know that I am the LORD who sanctifies them. . . . Hallow My Sabbaths, and they will be a sign between Me and you, that you may know that I am the LORD your God" **(EZEKIEL 20:12, 20).**

The Lord told Moses, "Speak also to the children of Israel, saying: 'Surely My Sabbaths you shall keep, for it is a sign between Me and you throughout your generations, that you may know that I am the LORD who sanctifies you. Therefore the children of Israel shall keep the Sabbath, to observe the Sabbath throughout their generations as a perpetual covenant. It is a sign between Me and the children of Israel forever; for in six days the LORD made the heavens and the earth, and on the seventh day He rested and was refreshed.' And when He had made an end of speaking with him on Mount Sinai, He gave Moses two tablets of the Testimony, tablets of stone, written with the finger of God" **(EXODUS 31:13, 16–18).**

"If you turn away your foot from the Sabbath, from doing your pleasure on My holy day, and call the Sabbath a delight, the holy day of the LORD honorable, and shall honor Him, not doing your own ways, nor finding your own pleasure, nor speaking your own words, then you shall delight yourself in the LORD; and I will cause you to ride on the high hills of the earth, and feed you with the heritage of Jacob your father. The mouth of the LORD has spoken" **(ISAIAH 58:13, 14).**

08 How did Jesus relate to the Sabbath? Was Jesus a Sabbath keeper? Do we find a similar example in the lives of the disciples?

If Jesus was going to establish another day for worship, He would have done it while He was still alive. He left a positive example of Sabbath keeping in His life.

"So He [Jesus] came to Nazareth, where He had been brought up. And as His custom was, He went into the synagogue on the Sabbath day, and stood up to read" **(LUKE 4:16).**

Here we have Jesus' real-life example. Why did He worship so faithfully on this special day that it became "His custom"? Some would suggest that Christ kept the Sabbath only because He found Himself in a Jewish culture. But is this true? Jesus did not allow culture to shape His thinking. He was guided by God's Word. His mind was not shaped by custom; it was molded by the Holy Spirit. He was not obedient to tradition; He was obedient to God's law. Our Lord was not a mere conformist, bowing to the expediency of "When in Rome, do as the Romans do." Jesus repeatedly healed on the Sabbath and taught that "it is lawful to do good on the Sabbath" **(MATTHEW 12:12).** He taught that we should never rest from doing good. You see, God's law had become encumbered and encrusted with regulations never found in the Ten Commandments, and Jesus made no pretense of following those man-made rules. But Jesus could truthfully say, "I have kept My Father's commandments" **(JOHN 15:10).** And that includes the Sabbath.

"It was Preparation Day [Friday, specifically "Good Friday"], and the Sabbath was about to begin. The women who had come with Jesus from Galilee followed Joseph and saw the tomb and how his body was laid in it. Then they went home and prepared spices and perfumes. *But they rested on the Sabbath in obedience to the commandment*" **(LUKE 23:54–56, NIV; EMPHASIS SUPPLIED).**

Not only did Jesus Himself honor the Sabbath by His personal example, but His closest followers—those who knew Him best—also kept the Sabbath *even after His crucifixion.* For these women were from the inner circle of Christ's disciples. If Jesus had had any instruction, any plans about changing the day of rest and worship, He surely would have shared those plans with His closest followers. But it's obvious that our Lord had given no such instruction, for this verse tells us that these women—even after Christ's crucifixion—"rested on the Sabbath in obedience to the commandment"! Furthermore, the apostles faithfully kept the Sabbath of God many years after Jesus' resurrection and ascension to heaven, as the following texts demonstrate:

The apostle Paul "came to Thessalonica, where there was a synagogue of the Jews. Then Paul, as his custom was, went in to them, and for three Sabbaths reasoned with them from the Scriptures. . . . And some of them were persuaded; and a great multitude of the devout Greeks [Gentiles]" **(ACTS 17:1, 2, 4).**

Consider the practice of Paul, the great apostle to the Gentiles. He was handpicked by God to minister specifically to the Gentile—or non-Jewish—world. The Lord told Paul, "I have set you to be a light to the Gentiles" **(ACTS 13:47).** And Paul himself, after being so soundly rejected by the Jewish brethren he loved, declared, "Lo, we turn to the Gentiles" **(ACTS 13:46, KJV).** A devout Christian, Paul felt it a privilege to follow His Lord's example in all things. Just as Christ kept the Sabbath "as His custom was," so also Paul kept the Sabbath "as his custom was" **(LUKE 4:16; ACTS 17:2).** Both Jesus and Paul obeyed all of God's commandments and provide us a good example.

Some try to argue that Paul went to the house of worship on God's holy Sabbath day only because that gave him a chance to reach the Jews. But we've already seen that Paul understood his calling as being uniquely "the apostle to the Gentiles"—not the Jews, although he loved his Jewish brethren very much. And on this occasion **(SEE ACTS 17:4)**, we're told that Paul persuaded "a great multitude" even of Gentiles!

Paul and his party traveled from Thessalonica "to Philippi, which is the foremost city of that part of Macedonia, a [Roman] colony. And we were staying in that city for some days. And on the Sabbath day we went out of the city to the riverside, where prayer was customarily made; and we sat down and spoke to the women who met there" **(ACTS 16:12, 13)**.

Philippi was a Roman colony, a Gentile city with no Jewish synagogue. And Paul was a self-supporting missionary who worked to cover his own expenses; **ACTS 18:3** says he worked as a tentmaker. But he didn't work on Sabbath. Thus, if Paul's only motive in keeping the seventh-day Sabbath had really been only to meet with Jews, as some would have us believe, then he could have skipped this Sabbath and worked on his tents. But he didn't. God says that Paul found a quiet spot where he could worship outside the city, a place where prayer was customarily made. There, before the day was over, he baptized a Gentile woman and her family **(SEE ACTS 16:14, 15)**. Paul kept the Christian Sabbath by doing God's work, not his own.

"After these things Paul departed from Athens and went to Corinth. . . . And he reasoned in the synagogue every Sabbath, and persuaded both Jews and Greeks [Gentiles]. . . . And he continued there *a year and six months*, teaching the word of God among them" **(ACTS 18:1, 4, 11; EMPHASIS SUPPLIED)**.

The divine record says that Paul religiously kept "*every* Sabbath." And since he stayed there "a year and six months," we have here a record of Paul keeping the seventh-day Sabbath for seventy-eight consecutive weeks in Corinth alone!

09 What instruction did Jesus give His closest followers regarding Sabbath observance after His death?

Knowing that years later Roman armies would come and His followers would have to flee, Jesus urged them to "pray that your flight may not be in winter or on the Sabbath" **(MATTHEW 24:20)**.

Jesus Himself clinches the case for us that His followers *were* keeping the Sabbath—and that they were *supposed* to keep it—long after the Cross. Please note: Christ foretold the destruction of Jerusalem nearly forty years before it happened, declaring that the city would be so completely devastated that even the buildings of the temple would be demolished, with not one huge stone left standing upon another **(SEE MATTHEW 24:1, 2, 5–19)**. This prophecy itself is tremendously impressive, since it deals with events that were to take place long after the Lord's crucifixion, resurrection, and ascension to heaven. He warned His disciples that when they saw armies drawing near, they must immediately "flee to the mountains" **(VERSE 16).** Then, in a most significant statement, He added, "pray that your flight may not be in winter or on the Sabbath" **(VERSE 20).**

Why pray this? Because it would be a hardship to flee in winter. And the fear, commotion, and travel involved in fleeing would be inappropriate on the Sabbath day. Christ's followers were to pray they might be able to keep the Sabbath as a day of rest and worship, because His holy day would still be just as sacred then as it was when He spoke these words on the Mount of Olives. Thus Christ gave no hint that His Sabbath would be abolished or changed, even when He discussed it in connection with an event to happen far in the future, some forty years after His death and resurrection!

So forceful is this statement from the Lord's own lips that it hits a nerve in some people. So they try to weaken it by claiming that Christ said it only because He knew *the city gates would be closed on the Sabbath*, making it difficult or impossible for Christians to flee on that day. They hope this argument will sound plausible enough to be accepted, but several facts contradict it.

In the first place, Christ, who knows the end from the beginning, knew that the Jews *would* go out through the opened city gates to battle the Romans even on the Sabbath, as recorded by the contemporary Jewish historian Josephus (see *Jewish Wars,* bk. 2, chap. 19).

Secondly, Jesus warned even those "in the field" **(MATTHEW 24:18, KJV)**, "those outside the city" **(LUKE 21:21, TLB)**, or "out in the country" **(LUKE 21:21, RSV, AMP, NKJV, NEB)** to pray they would not have to flee on the Sabbath—yet no gates or walls would hinder their flight from those areas.

Finally, the command to flee is addressed to "those who are in Judea" **(MATTHEW 24:16; LUKE 21:21).** The land of the Jews called *the province of Judea* was *not* surrounded by walls and gates! Yet Christians in all Judea were to pray that their flight would not be on the Sabbath day! Could Christ have given clearer evidence that He viewed the Sabbath as different from other days?

The Roman general Titus attacked Jerusalem and destroyed it in A.D. 70. Jesus urged His disciples to pray their flight from Jerusalem during the Roman attack would not be in the winter or on the Sabbath day. Jesus specifically gave this instruction, because He knew His closest followers would be keeping the Sabbath thirty-five years after the Crucifixion.

10 Did the apostle Paul preach only to the Jews on the Bible Sabbath?

"Paul and his party . . . came to Antioch . . . went into the synagogue on the Sabbath day," and—when asked to speak—took advantage of the opportunity to preach the gospel. "So when the Jews went out of the synagogue, the Gentiles begged that these words might be preached to them *the next Sabbath. . . . On the next Sabbath* almost the *whole city* came together to hear the word of God" **(ACTS 13:13, 14, 42, 44; EMPHASIS SUPPLIED).**

Do you see what this means? These Bible texts provide positive proof that: (1) Paul was observing the seventh-day Sabbath, and (2) he was not keeping Sunday in a religious way. For if his practice had been to worship on Sunday, Paul would have told the Gentile inquirers, "Look, you don't have to wait till next Sabbath to hear me preach. I'm holding worship services tomorrow, on the first day of the week." But Paul told them no such thing although this would have been a golden opportunity to put in a good word for Sunday sacredness—*if* the Lord had wanted to change the day of worship. Your Bible says that it wasn't until "the next Sabbath day" that the whole city gathered "to hear the word of God"! Bible facts like these speak more loudly than anything men may say, don't you think?

From his own experience, Paul could sincerely say, "Therefore let it be known to you that the salvation of God has been sent to the Gentiles, and they will hear it!" **(ACTS 28:28).**

"When they had come and gathered the church together, they reported all that God had done with them, and that He had opened the door of faith to the Gentiles" **(ACTS 14:27).**

Paul preached to the Jews on the Sabbath, convincing them Jesus was the Messiah. He also preached to the Gentiles on Sabbath—not Sunday. Eventually, the whole city listened to Paul's Sabbath preaching.

11 What does John in the book of Revelation call Jesus' special day?

John the revelator said, "I was in the Spirit on the Lord's Day, and I heard behind me a loud voice, as of a trumpet" **(REVELATION 1:10).**

Which day is "the Lord's Day"? Only God can make a day or anything else holy. Yet enthusiasts for Sunday holiness, with no warrant from the Bible, habitually call that day "the Lord's Day." But is Sunday really "the Lord's Day"? God's Word uses the phrase "the Lord's Day" only once, in the verse quoted above. But as you can see, that solitary reference gives no clue, no hint, as to which day of the week is designated by that special title. The text simply lets us know that the Lord has a day which He calls His own—"the Lord's Day." But we must look elsewhere to determine which day that is.

Rather than simply accept what any man says or what any church teaches, let's allow the Bible to be its own interpreter. Even a few texts may suffice to clarify this point. For instance, in Isaiah the Lord Himself calls "the Sabbath . . . My holy day . . . the holy day of the LORD honorable. . . . The mouth of the LORD has spoken" **(ISAIAH 58:13, 14).**

Little logic is required to see that: (1) John says the Lord has a day He calls His own; He calls it "the Lord's Day." (2) Isaiah records the Lord's own words calling the Sabbath, "My holy day." Therefore, (3) the Sabbath is "the Lord's Day."

Other texts substantiate this clear conclusion. In **GENESIS 2:3**, we read that the Sabbath was the only day the Lord "blessed . . . and sanctified." And many other passages **(FOR EXAMPLE, EXODUS 20:10; LEVITICUS 23:3; DEUTERONOMY 5:14; ETC.)** tell us that "the seventh day is the Sabbath of the LORD your God." The Holy Scriptures give no sacred title to the first day of the week. Consider, for example, **JOHN 20:1** or **JOHN 20:19**—texts written *many years after* our Lord's resurrection, and written, incidentally, by the same John who wrote **REVELATION 1:10**, referring to "the Lord's Day." In these texts, John did not call Sunday "the Lord's Day," which is strange if that's what he believed and wanted to teach. He called Sunday simply "the first day of the week." Today, individuals may mistakenly call Sunday "the Lord's Day," but that doesn't make it so.

12 According to the following texts, what is another name for the Lord's Day?

"The Son of Man is Lord even of the Sabbath" **(MATTHEW 12:8).**

"He [Jesus] said to them, 'The Sabbath was made for man, and not man for the Sabbath. Therefore the Son of Man is also Lord of the Sabbath' " **(MARK 2:27, 28).**

Jesus said, "The Son of Man is also Lord of the Sabbath" **(LUKE 6:5).**

"The seventh day is the Sabbath of the LORD your God" **(EXODUS 20:10).**

In the New Testament, we read Jesus' own words that "the Son of Man is also Lord of the Sabbath" **(MARK 2:28).** The Sabbath is the Lord's Day—it's the *only* period of time with which the Lord Jesus ever identified Himself. On the other hand, careful study of God's Word reveals that Christ never said anything about the first day of the week, either as a holy day or otherwise.

13 Today, can we really tell which day is the biblical seventh day? Does the Bible actually reveal it? What three days does the Bible mention in succession?

"That day [the day on which Jesus died] was the Preparation [Friday, specifically, "Good Friday"], and the Sabbath drew near. And the women who had come with Him [Jesus] from Galilee followed after, and they observed the tomb and how His body was laid. Then they returned [home] and prepared spices and fragrant oils. And they rested on the Sabbath according to the commandment. Now on the first day of the week [Sunday], very early in the morning, they, and certain other women with them, came to the tomb bringing the spices which they had prepared" **(LUKE 23:54–56; 24:1).**

The verses above prove from Scripture that the Bible Sabbath is the day that comes between Friday, the sixth day of the week, and Sunday, the first day of the week. What day falls between Friday and Sunday? The seventh day of the week, or what English-speaking people call Saturday.

But not only Scripture proves this. Language also identifies which day is the seventh-day Sabbath for anyone who wants to know the truth on this subject. For example, consider Greek, the language in which the New Testament was written. The Jews called the day preceding the Sabbath the "Preparation Day," because they used it to prepare for God's holy day, finishing up their work, cooking, cleaning house, etc. So the Bible speaks of "the Preparation Day, that is, the day before the Sabbath" **(MARK 15:42; SEE ALSO JOHN 19:31).** The Greek word for "preparation"—the sixth day of the week—is *paraskeue.* And two thousand years later, the day called "Friday" in our English calendar is still called *Paraskeue* ("Preparation") in the modern Greek calendar. Thus the day that follows Friday is still the Sabbath.

Or take German for another example. If you look at a calendar printed in the German language, you'll see that the day we call "Wednesday" is called *Mittwoch.* That word means "midweek," and Wednesday is the day in the middle of the week—thus proving linguistically that no mix-up of the days of the week has taken place.

A third example could be Spanish. Many of us know that the Spanish word for "Saturday"—the seventh day—is *Sábado,* which means "Sabbath." Again the message is clear: the order of the days of the week has not been changed since biblical times.

Preparation Day = sixth day = Friday

Sabbath = seventh day = Saturday

Resurrection Day = first day = Sunday

What other ways can we tell which day is the seventh day? Webster's Dictionary says: "Seventh day, Saturday, the seventh day of the week" (*Webster's New Twentieth Century Dictionary,* unabridged 2nd ed.).

Astronomy: "We have had occasion to investigate the results of the works of specialists in Chronology and we have never found one of them that has had the slightest doubt about the continuity of the weekly cycle since long before the Christian Era" (James Robertson, director, U.S. Naval Observatory, letter to F. D. Nichol, March 12, 1932).

Language: In more than 106 languages of the world, Saturday, the seventh day on our calendar, is translated as "Sabbath." There is no other word for "Saturday" in these languages; the seventh day is simply called "Sabbath."

14 What blessing does God promise those who lovingly keep His Sabbath?

"Blessed is the man who does this, and the son of man who lays hold on it; who keeps from defiling the Sabbath, and keeps his hand from doing any evil" **(ISAIAH 56:2).**

"If you turn away your foot from the Sabbath, from doing your pleasure on My holy day, and call the Sabbath a delight, the holy day of the LORD honorable, and shall honor Him, not doing your own ways, nor finding your own pleasure, nor speaking your own words. Then you shall delight yourself in the LORD; and I will cause you to ride on the high hills of the earth, and feed you with the heritage of Jacob your father. The mouth of the LORD has spoken" **(ISAIAH 58:13, 14).**

"It happened, as He [Jesus] spoke these things, that a certain woman from the crowd raised her voice and said to Him, 'Blessed is the womb that bore You, and the breasts which nursed You!' But He said, 'More than that, blessed are those who hear the word of God and keep it!' " **(LUKE 11:27, 28).**

Jesus promised, "If you know these things, blessed are you if you do them" **(JOHN 13:17).**

"Blessed are those who do His commandments, that they may have the right to the tree of life, and may enter through the gates into the city" **(REVELATION 22:14).**

God offers those who obey Him His richest blessings. The Sabbath is Christ's great sign of loyalty. It is a sign of His creative and redemptive power. On this day, in a special sense, Christians have an invitation to enter into a closer union with the Master.

15 Will God's people continue to worship Him on the Sabbath through all eternity?

" 'As the new heavens and the new earth which I will make shall remain before Me,' says the LORD, 'so shall your descendants and your name remain. And it shall come to pass that from one New Moon to another, and from one Sabbath to another, all flesh shall come to worship before Me,' says the LORD" **(ISAIAH 66:22, 23).**

God made the Sabbath in the perfect paradise of Eden, before sin entered. And after sin and sinners are eradicated from the universe, God will restore all things to those He died to redeem—including Sabbath worship. The seventh-day Sabbath of God, far from being abolished, actually spans the history of man from Paradise Lost to Paradise Regained. If we're going to keep the Sabbath in the hereafter of God's wonderful new earth, I want to begin keeping it here and now—don't you?

"O You who hear prayer, to You all flesh will come" **(PSALM 65:2).**

In the new earth, "All nations whom You have made shall come and worship before You, O Lord, and shall glorify Your name" **(PSALM 86:9).**

"But the hour is coming, and now is, when the true worshipers will worship the Father in spirit and truth; for the Father is seeking such to worship Him" **(JOHN 4:23).**

"Who shall not fear You, O Lord, and glorify Your name? For You alone are holy. For all nations shall come and worship before You, for Your judgments have been manifested" **(REVELATION 15:4).**

What a promise! Through the ceaseless ages of eternity all flesh, the entire creation, will worship God in harmony each Sabbath. If we are going to worship Him through all eternity, why not start worshiping Him on the Sabbath now? Jesus invites us to love Him with all our hearts and follow truth regardless of what others do. The book of Revelation calls us to worship Him as our Creator. The Sabbath message is part of God's urgent effort to prepare a people for earth's last hour. Pray that Jesus will fill your heart with love. Follow His example in worshiping Him on the Bible Sabbath.

The book of Revelation presents God's final message.

Commonly Asked Questions Regarding the Bible Sabbath

Since Paul declares, "Let no one judge you . . . regarding . . . sabbaths" (COLOSSIANS 2:16, 17), isn't Sabbath-keeping unnecessary?

COLOSSIANS 2:16, 17 is one of the most misunderstood passages in the Bible. One principle of Bible interpretation is not to allow a Bible passage that may be somewhat unclear keep you from following those parts of the Bible that you do understand. The Bible is plain on the topic of the Sabbath. It was given at Creation **(SEE GENESIS 2:1–3)**. Jesus observed it **(SEE LUKE 4:16)**. Paul observed it **(SEE ACTS 13:42–44)**. And it will be observed in heaven **(SEE ISAIAH 66:22, 23)**.

The key to understanding **COLOSSIANS 2:16, 17** is to recognize that the Bible mentions *two kinds of Sabbaths*—the weekly seventh-day Sabbath and the yearly sabbaths. The seventh-day Sabbath, instituted at Creation and part of the Ten Commandment law, is a weekly reminder of the loving, all-powerful Creator. The yearly sabbaths relate specifically to the history of Israel. **COLOSSIANS 2:16, 17** specifically states, "Let no one judge you in food or in drink, or regarding . . . sabbaths, *which are a shadow of things to come*" **(EMPHASIS SUPPLIED)**. The seventh-day Sabbath is a memorial of Creation, not a shadow of something to come. **HEBREWS 10:1** connects the law of shadows with animal sacrifice. **EZEKIEL 45:17** uses the exact same expressions in the exact same order as **COLOSSIANS 2:16, 17** and connects it all with the ceremonial systems of feasts and sacrifices (meat offerings, drink offerings, feasts, new moons, and sabbaths to make reconciliation for the house of Israel). **LEVITICUS 23:3** discusses the seventh-day Sabbath. **LEVITICUS 23:5–32** discusses the ceremonial (annual) sabbaths (Passover, unleavened bread, wave sheaf, first fruits, trumpets, Day of Atonement, and tabernacles). Both the feast of trumpets **(VERSE 24)** and the Day of Atonement **(VERSE 32)** are specifically called sabbaths. These annual sabbaths were intimately connected to events foreshadowing Christ's death and His second coming. They were designed by God to be shadows, pointing to the coming Messiah. **LEVITICUS 23:37** uses the language of **COLOSSIANS 2:16, 17** to describe these annual ceremonial sabbaths. **LEVITICUS 23:38** distinguishes the ceremonial sabbaths from the seventh-day Sabbath by using the expression, "besides the Sabbaths of the LORD." Since Christ has come, the shadowy sabbaths of the ceremonial law have found their fulfillment in Him. The seventh-day Sabbath continues to lead us back to the Creator God who made us. God's people will keep it as a distinguishing sign of their relationship to Him **(SEE REVELATION 14:12; EZEKIEL 20:12, 20)**.

What about ROMANS 14:5?—"One person esteems one day above another; another esteems every day alike. Let each be fully convinced in his own mind." Really, what difference does a day make?

Sometimes it's helpful to carefully notice what a Bible text does *not* say as well as what it *does* say. **ROMANS 14:5, 6** says nothing about either worship or the Sabbath. This passage simply talks about regarding a day. To say that the particular day referred to in the passage is the Sabbath is an unwarranted assumption. Verse 1 sets the tone for the entire passage, indicating that the discussion focuses on "doubtful disputations" or disputes on doubtful matters. Is the seventh-day Sabbath, set apart by God at Creation **(SEE GENESIS 2:1–3)** and placed within the heart of God's moral law **(SEE EXODUS 20:8–11)** a doubtful matter? Certainly not! The key to this passage is found in **VERSE 6**, which states, "He who observes the day, observes it to the Lord; and he who does not observe the day, to the Lord he does not observe it. He who eats, eats to the Lord, for he gives God thanks; and he who does not eat, to the Lord he does not eat, and gives God thanks." The issue Paul is discussing revolves around fast days not Sabbath days. Some Jewish Christians believed there was particular merit in fasting on certain days. They judged others by their own standard. The Pharisees fasted at least twice a week and boasted about it **(SEE LUKE 18:12)**. In **ROMANS 14**, Paul is pointing out that to fast, or not to fast, on a certain day is a matter of individual conscience, not a matter of God's command.

Didn't the disciples meet on the first day of the week? (SEE ACTS 20:7).

This meeting is mentioned in Acts because Paul was leaving the next day and worked a mighty miracle in raising Eutychus from the dead. It is clear that the meeting is a night meeting. It is the dark part of the first day of the week (SEE ACTS 20:7). In Bible times, the dark part of the day preceded the light part (SEE GENESIS 1:5). The Sabbath is observed from Friday night at sunset to Saturday night at sunset (SEE LEVITICUS 23:32; MARK 1:32). If this meeting took place on the dark part of the first day of the week, it was in fact a Saturday night meeting. Paul had met with the believers all day Sabbath. He was to depart the next day, Sunday, so the meeting continued late into Saturday night. The next day, Sunday, Paul traveled by foot to Assos, then sailed to Mitylene. The New English Bible reading of ACTS 20:7 confirms this as a Saturday night meeting, with Paul traveling on Sunday. If Paul considered Sunday sacred in honor of the Resurrection, why would he spend the entire day traveling and not worshiping? The record indicates that Paul was a seventh-day Sabbath keeper (SEE ACTS 13:42–44; 17:2; 16:12, 13; 18:4).

Can we really know which day is the biblical seventh day?

There are at least four ways that we can tell for certain that the day we know as Saturday is the biblical seventh day.

1. **The Bible** clearly reveals that Jesus was crucified on the Preparation Day (SEE LUKE 23:54). His closest followers rested on the Sabbath day as commanded by the fourth commandment (SEE LUKE 23:55, 56). And Jesus rose from the dead on the first day of the week (SEE LUKE 24:1; MARK 16:9). Most Christians recognize that Jesus died on Friday, the Preparation Day, that He rested the next day, and that He rose on the first day of the week, Sunday. The biblical seventh-day Sabbath is the day between Friday and Sunday—or Saturday.

2. **Language.** In over 106 languages of the world, the word for the seventh day, which we call "Saturday," is the word for "Sabbath." Language testifies to the Sabbath's preservation through the centuries.

3. **Astronomy.** The leading astronomers in the world testify to the fact that the weekly cycle has never changed. Centers like the U.S. Naval Observatory in the United States and the Royal Greenwich Observatory in England affirm the fact of a constant weekly cycle.

4. **History.** The Jewish people have kept an accurate record of the Sabbath through the centuries. For over four thousand years, they have preserved the true Sabbath on Saturday.

I keep Sunday in honor of the Resurrection. What's wrong with that? Didn't Jesus rise from the dead on Sunday?

Yes, Jesus certainly rose on Sunday! But He never commanded us to worship on that day in honor of the Resurrection. Just as the Communion service symbolizes His death **(SEE 1 CORINTHIANS 11:24, 26)**, baptism symbolizes His resurrection **(SEE ROMANS 6:1–6)**. The symbol of Jesus' resurrection is not worship on the day of the sun, which was adopted into Christianity from pagan Rome's sun worship, but the beautiful ceremony of baptism as a symbol of a new life transformed by the wonder-working power of the Holy Spirit. In the watery grave of baptism, the old person symbolically dies and is buried while a new life is resurrected with Christ.

Isn't one day in seven good enough? Why put so much emphasis on the Sabbath?

The issue is more than a matter of days. It is a matter of masters. Through a masterstroke of deception, Satan has worked through apostate religion to change God's law **(SEE DANIEL 7:25)**. He has cast the truth to the ground **(SEE DANIEL 8:12)**. He has made a breach in God's wall of truth. God calls us to repair the breach by keeping His Sabbath **(SEE ISAIAH 58:12, 13)**. "We ought to obey God rather than men" **(ACTS 5:29)**. To worship on the seventh day is to accept the authority of our

Creator Lord, who commanded the day to be kept **(SEE EXODUS 20:8–11)**. To knowingly accept a counterfeit day of worship is to accept an institution initiated and established solely by man in the apostasy. The real question is, then, whose servants are we—God's or man's? **(SEE ROMANS 6:16.)** All the celebrations the day before or the day after my birthday do not make these days my birthday. The world's birthday is the Bible Sabbath, the seventh day. It is a memorial to our loving Creator. No other day will do.

CHAPTER 15

What the Bible Says About the Change of the Sabbath

The prophecies of Daniel and Revelation unmask a titanic struggle between good and evil just before Jesus comes. This last battle in the great controversy centers around the law of God **(SEE REVELATION 12:17)**. Satan hates the eternal principles that are the basis of heaven's government. He desires to lead all to violate God's law and disregard the very foundation of happiness. The fourth commandment, which exalts Jesus as the Creator, is the object of the enemy's special attack. As we discovered in the last chapter, the seventh-day Sabbath is a memorial to Christ's creative authority. It is an eternal symbol of both our "rest in Christ" for salvation and our absolute loyalty to Him. The Sabbath is an eternal link to our Creator. Many sincere Christians are asking, "How was the Sabbath changed from Saturday to the first day of the week? How was the Sabbath changed from Saturday and why? Is there information in the Bible predicting an attempt to change God's law?" The answer to these questions is found in a symbolic vision given to the prophet Daniel.

01 What grand prophetic vision about the future of our world did God reveal to Daniel?

"Daniel spoke, saying, 'I saw in my vision by night, and behold, the four winds of heaven were stirring up the Great Sea. And four great beasts came up from the sea, each different from the other' " **(DANIEL 7:2, 3).**

In an earlier Bible study, we reviewed the prophetic dream of King Nebuchadnezzar, interpreted by Daniel and recorded in **CHAPTER 2** of his book. Now in **CHAPTER 7**, we see that Daniel himself had a most intriguing—and informative!—dream.

02 What is represented by the symbols of wind, sea, and beasts?

" 'Against Elam I will bring the four winds from the four quarters of heaven, and scatter them toward all those winds; there shall be no nations where the outcasts of Elam will not go. For I will cause Elam to be dismayed before their enemies and before those who seek their life. I will bring disaster upon them, My fierce anger,' says the LORD; 'and I will send the sword after them until I have consumed them' " **(JEREMIAH 49:36, 37).**

Notice carefully that Jeremiah states God will bring the four winds upon Elam, and then he says that God will bring "disaster" upon them, and they will be consumed by the sword. Evidently, winds represent disaster and destruction.

In vision, John the revelator was shown "the great harlot who sits on *many waters*. . . . Then he [the angel] said to me, '*The waters* which you saw, where the harlot sits, are *peoples, multitudes, nations, and tongues*' " **(REVELATION 17:1, 15; EMPHASIS SUPPLIED).**

" 'Those great beasts, which are four, are four kings which arise out of the earth. . . . The fourth beast shall be a fourth kingdom on earth, which shall be different from all other kingdoms, and shall devour the whole earth, trample it and break it in pieces' " **(DANIEL 7:17, 23).**

Let's summarize the meaning of these symbols. Winds blowing upon the sea indicate, or symbolize, destruction among peoples. Beasts arising out of the sea reveal nations rising up in the midst of this destruction.

03 What did Daniel actually see in vision? How many beasts were there? What did they look like?

"And four great beasts came up from the sea, each different from the other. The first was like a lion, and had eagle's wings. I watched till its wings were plucked off; and it was lifted up from the earth and made to stand on two feet like a man, and a man's heart was given to it. And suddenly another beast, a second, like a bear. It was raised up on one side, and had three ribs in its mouth between its teeth. And they said thus to it: 'Arise, devour much flesh!' After this I looked, and there was another, like a leopard, which had on its back four wings of a bird. The beast also had four heads, and dominion was given to it. After this I saw in the night visions, and behold, a fourth beast, dreadful and terrible, exceedingly strong. It had huge iron teeth; it was devouring, breaking in pieces, and trampling the residue with its feet. It was different from all the beasts that were before it, and it had ten horns" **(DANIEL 7:3–7).**

"The ten horns are ten kings who shall arise from this kingdom. And another shall rise after them; he shall be different from the first ones, and shall subdue three kings" **(DANIEL 7:24).**

In **DANIEL 7**, the prophet pictures four great beasts rising out of the sea **(SEE VERSE 3).** These beasts represent four great kingdoms that arise **(SEE VERSE 17).** As we studied in **DANIEL 2**, the four great nations that ruled in succession from Daniel's time are Babylon, Media-Persia, Greece, and Rome. The four beasts of **DANIEL 7** are a fitting description of these four great ruling powers. A lion with eagle's wings has been found on Babylonian coins and on the brickwork of ancient Babylonian buildings. The king of beasts is a fitting symbol for the king of empires. The prophet Jeremiah describes Babylon as a lion **(SEE JEREMIAH 4:7).** Media-Persia, as a dual empire, came into prominence by destroying Lydia, Babylon, and Egypt. Soon the Persians rose to ascendancy over the Medes. The Bible aptly describes this empire as a bear raising itself on one side with three ribs in its mouth. A leopard with wings clearly describes the third empire, Greece. Alexander the Great swiftly conquered the nations of his day. The dragonlike beast, dreadful, terrible, and exceedingly strong, aptly describes the fierceness of Rome.

04 How was the fourth beast, Rome, different from all the beasts before it?

"After this I saw in the night visions, and behold, a fourth beast, dreadful and terrible, exceedingly strong. It had huge iron teeth; it was devouring, breaking in pieces, and trampling the residue with its feet. It was different from all the beasts that were before it, and it had ten horns" **(DANIEL 7:7).**

The Roman Empire was not overcome by a fifth world-ruling empire. It fell from within. It was divided. The nations of Western Europe are the remains of the old Roman Empire.

05 What power arose after the ten divisions of the Roman Empire?

"I was considering the horns, and there was another horn, a little one, coming up among them, before whom three of the first horns were plucked out by the roots. And there, in this horn, were eyes like the eyes of a man, and a mouth speaking pompous words" **(DANIEL 7:8).**

In Daniel's prophecies, a horn is a symbol of power and represents a king or kingdom. This power begins small at first and subtly grows unsuspectingly into a dominant world force.

The Westminster Dictionary of the Bible says this in its article titled "Horn": "The horn is the emblem of strength and denotes political power, the image being drawn from bulls which push with their horns (Psalm 132:17; Jeremiah 48:25), and *in prophetic language signifies a kingdom or kings* (Daniel 7:8, 11, 21; Zechariah 1:18, 19; Revelation 17:12, 16)" (p. 255; emphasis supplied).

"The ten horns are ten kings who shall arise from this [fourth] kingdom. And another shall rise after them; he shall be different from the first ones, and shall subdue three kings" **(DANIEL 7:24).**

"And out of one of them came a little horn which grew exceedingly great toward the south, toward the east, and toward the Glorious Land. And it grew up to the host of heaven; and it cast down some of the host and some of the stars to the ground, and trampled them. He even exalted himself as high as the Prince of the host; and by him the daily sacrifices were taken away, and the place of His sanctuary was cast down. Because of transgression, an army was given over to the horn to oppose the daily sacrifices; and he cast truth down to the ground. He did all this and prospered" **(DANIEL 8:9–12).**

The "little" horn grew great.

06 Where did this little horn arise? What was its point of origin?

"I was considering the horns, and there was *another horn, a little one, coming up among them*, before whom three of the first horns were plucked out by the roots. And there, in this horn, were eyes like the eyes of a man, and a mouth speaking pompous words" **(DANIEL 7:8; EMPHASIS SUPPLIED).**

The little horn comes up "*among* them," that is, among "the ten horns," which **VERSE 24** says are "ten kings" or kingdoms—the ten political divisions of the Roman Empire, which became the modern nations of Western Europe. Thus we needn't look for the little horn power to arise in North or South America, Africa, Asia, or Australia. Daniel pinpoints its location as coming from within the divided Roman Empire—that is, somewhere within the nations of Italy, Germany, England, France, Spain, Portugal, Switzerland, etc.

Whoever or whatever this little horn is, it arises among the ten horns, the divisions of the Roman Empire. Arising out of Rome, it dominates the world.

07 When did this little horn arise? At what time in earth's history did this power rise?

"Thus he said: 'The fourth beast shall be a fourth kingdom on earth, which shall be different from all other kingdoms, and shall devour the whole earth, trample it and break it in pieces. The ten horns are ten kings who shall arise from this kingdom. And another shall rise after them; he shall be different from the first ones, and shall subdue three kings' " **(DANIEL 7:23, 24).**

The *time* of origin of the little horn power was marvelously foretold—it would arise "after" the breakup of the Roman Empire into ten kingdoms. The prophet Daniel was inspired to prophesy that the little horn power "shall rise *after* them" that is, after the *ten horns* or kingdoms had arisen.

History testifies that Romulus Augustulus, the last Roman emperor, fell from power in A.D. 476 after a brief reign of just one year. Rome's power as a unified empire declined until, by A.D. 476, it was divided into the ten smaller kingdoms that became Western Europe. So to fit Daniel's prophecy, the little horn had to rise to power some time after A.D. 476.

Clearly the little horn arises after the fall of the Roman Empire. It rose to prominence in the latter part of the fourth and throughout the fifth century (A.D. 351–476), when the Roman Empire was in the process of being invaded by the barbarian tribes from the north.

08 How can we be sure we identify this power correctly? What special identifying characteristics does this little horn have?

"I was considering the horns, and there was another horn, a little one, coming up among them, before whom three of the first horns were plucked out by the roots. And there, in this horn, were eyes like the eyes of a man, and a mouth speaking pompous words" **(DANIEL 7:8).**

John the revelator was shown a vision: "Then I stood on the sand of the sea. And I saw a beast rising up out of the sea, having seven heads and ten horns, and on his horns ten crowns, and on his heads a blasphemous name. . . . And he was given a *mouth speaking great things* and blasphemies, and he was given authority to continue for forty-two months. Then he opened his mouth in blasphemy against God, to blaspheme His name, His tabernacle, and those who dwell in heaven" **(REVELATION 13:1, 5, 6; EMPHASIS SUPPLIED).**

John was shown a beast that had "a mouth speaking great things." Daniel was shown a little horn that had "a mouth speaking pompous words" **(DANIEL 7:8).** Daniel repeats that thought over and over again in **CHAPTER 7**, with no concern about overdoing it or boring his readers! Daniel was fascinated because of "the pompous words which the [little] horn was speaking" **(DANIEL 7:11).** Daniel "wished to know the truth about . . . that horn which had eyes and a mouth which spoke pompous words" **(DANIEL 7:19, 20).** The little horn would even "speak pompous words against the Most High"! **(DANIEL 7:25).** Other translations render Daniel's phrase in **VERSE 20** as "a mouth speaking very great things" **(KJV)**, a "bragging mouth" **(TLB)**, "boasting proudly" **(TEV)**, "greats boasts" **(NASB)**, "spoke boastfully" **(NIV)**, and so on. They render the phrase in **REVELATION 13:5** as "proud claims" **(TEV)**, "proud words" **(NIV)**, "arrogant words" **(NASB)**, "haughty . . . words" **(RSV)**, and so on. Evidently this characteristic, common to both the antichrist/beast and the little horn, is one we should not miss.

Eyes in the Bible represent wisdom or understanding. **EPHESIANS 1:18** speaks of "the eyes of your understanding." Ancient prophets were called seers. They saw with divine wisdom into the future. This little horn power does *not* have the eyes of God's wisdom; Daniel says it has "eyes like the eyes of a man" **(DANIEL 7:8).** It substitutes human wisdom for divine truth. The little horn substitutes human authority for the eternal claims of God's law. It replaces God's law with human traditions.

09 How does this little horn power relate to God's people? What does it do to them?

Inspiration makes it clear that the little horn would be a persecuting power: "He [the little horn power] shall speak pompous words against the Most High, *shall persecute the saints of the Most High*, and shall intend to change times and law. Then *the saints shall be given into his hand* for a time and times and half a time" **(DANIEL 7:25; EMPHASIS SUPPLIED).**

John says, "It was granted to him [the beast power] to make war with the saints and to overcome them. And authority was given him over every tribe, tongue, and nation" **(REVELATION 13:7).**

Daniel says, "I was watching; and the same horn [the little horn power] was *making war* against the saints, and *prevailing against them*" **(DANIEL 7:21; EMPHASIS SUPPLIED).**

John says, "The dragon [the devil] was enraged with the woman [the church], and he went to make war with the rest of her offspring, who keep the commandments of God and have the testimony of Jesus Christ" **(REVELATION 12:17).**

The four verses quoted above, from the inspired pens of Daniel and John, again show unmistakable parallels existing between the little horn and the antichrist/beast power. Indeed, with identical points of identification, they're beginning to look like carbon copies of each other!

"I saw the woman, drunk with the blood of the saints and with the blood of the martyrs of Jesus" **(REVELATION 17:6).**

Let's make clear what the Bible is talking about when it speaks of "persecution" by this power. It doesn't mean a mere *mental* attitude such as *prejudice*. It doesn't even mean *acts of intolerance* such as prohibitions that curb or outlaw the practice of certain religious practices. Those things are all bad enough, but the Bible here is talking about persecution that touches one's *body in a very painful way:* cold-blooded *torture* and *murder*! The Bible uses words such as *war,* and *blood,* and *martyr.*

"And in her was found the blood of prophets and saints" **(REVELATION 18:24).**

"They have shed the blood of saints and prophets, and You have given them blood to drink. For it is their just due" **(REVELATION 16:6).**

"When He opened the fifth seal, I saw under the altar the souls of those who had been slain for the word of God and for the testimony which they held" **(REVELATION 6:9).**

The little horn oppresses those who do not accept its authority. It defends its traditions and persecutes those who do not conform.

10 Does God's Word tell us how long this little horn power would reign? How long would it be dominant and oppress God's people?

"He [the little horn power] shall speak pompous words against the Most High, shall persecute the saints of the Most High, and shall intend to change times and law. Then the saints shall be given into his hand for a time and times and half a time" **(DANIEL 7:25).**

What does the Bible mean by "a time and times and half a time"? At first glance, this seems like a very cryptic clue, but we can decipher it if we closely follow point by point and allow the Bible to interpret itself.

A "time" in Bible terminology means a *year.* For example, in **DANIEL 4:16, 23, 25, 32,** we read of "seven times" referring to the seven years when King Nebuchadnezzar would be driven out to dwell with the beasts of the field. The King James Version says "times," but modern translations **(TEV, NIV, TLB, AND NASB)** all say "years," either in a footnote or in the text itself. A "time" was an ancient way of expressing a year.

"Times" means specifically *two* years. The word translated "times" is *not* an ordinary *plural,* which could mean two or more, but a *dual*. Both Hebrew and Aramaic, the languages used by Daniel, had ordinary plurals, but they also had a special grammatical form known as the *dual,* used only to indicate *two*—no more, no less—such as two eyes, two ears, two children, or in this case, two years, just as in English we speak of "a pair" of gloves or "a couple."

"Half a time" indicates half a year—or six months. "The dividing of time" **(KJV)** may also be translated "half a time." So "a time and times and half a time" adds up to a total of three-and-a-half prophetic years.

Thus modern Bible versions translate **DANIEL 7:25** as follows:

- "They shall be given into his hand for a time, two times, and half a time" **(RSV).**
- "For a year, two years and half a year" (**NIV** [footnote]; **NASB** version [footnote simply has "year(s)" for "time"]).
- "For three and a half years" **(TLB; TEV).**

Another important point is that ancient calendars had 360 days to a year. For instance, the Egyptian, Hindu, and Assyrian calendars all had 360 days in a year (*Encyclopaedia Britannica,* 1967 ed., vol. 4, pp. 620, 621, 623). The Hebrews of Bible times, too, had twelve months of thirty days each. (Comparing **GENESIS 7:11, 24** with **GENESIS 8:3, 4**, we see that a five-month period lasted 150 days, showing thirty days to a month or a 360-day year.)

So three-and-a-half prophetic years would contain 1,260 days (3½ x 360 = 1,260 prophetic days).

In symbolic prophecy, which **DANIEL 7** certainly is, dealing as it does with such symbols as beasts, horns, and so on—each prophetic day stands for an actual year (**SEE NUMBERS 14:34; EZEKIEL 4:6).** On this basis, 1,260 prophetic days equal 1,260 actual years. So now we can understand Daniel's prophecy. It teaches that the little horn's period of dominance over the saints of God would last 1,260 years.

This same prophetic time period shows up in the book of Revelation as well.

"Then the woman [God's church] fled into the wilderness . . . one thousand two hundred and sixty days" **(REVELATION 12:6).**

During the Dark Ages, while the Bible was virtually a closed book, God's church had to flee persecution and go underground, so to speak, for a period of 1,260 prophetic days or 1,260 actual years.

In **REVELATION 12:14**, we read that "the woman" had to "fly into the wilderness . . . where she is nourished for a time and times and half a time, from the presence of the serpent." (The Living Bible and Today's English Version say, "for three and a half years.")

"He [the beast] was given authority to continue for forty-two months" **(REVELATION 13:5).** At thirty days to a month, this time period equals precisely 1,260 days (42 months x 30 days/month = 1,260 prophetic days or 1,260 actual years.

Apparently, because of its vital importance, the 1,260-day period is mentioned *seven* times in Daniel and Revelation—twice by Daniel and five times by John.

1. **DANIEL 7:25**. . . . . 3½ times
2. **DANIEL 12:7**. . . . . 3½ times
3. **REVELATION 11:2** . . . . 42 months
4. **REVELATION 11:3** . . . . 1,260 days
5. **REVELATION 12:6** . . . . 1,260 days
6. **REVELATION 12:14**. . . . . 3½ times
7. **REVELATION 13:5** . . . . 42 months

In conclusion, the Bible makes it plain that the supremacy of the little horn—and the beast power—would last for a specific period of time—1,260 years. In both the Old and New Testaments, God foretold that this evil, dominating power would continue more than twelve centuries.

In A.D. 538, the Roman Church became the single dominant religious power in Europe. The pagan Roman emperor, Justinian, gave to the pope of Rome civil as well as religious authority. Eventually, this resulted in severe persecution. The Dark Ages followed on the heels of this union of religious and civil authority. God's people were imprisoned, tortured, and martyred. For 1,260 years, from A.D. 538 to A.D. 1798, this union of church and state continued throughout Europe.

11 In its arrogance and pride, what would this little horn power do to the truth of God?

"Because of transgression, an army was given over to the horn [the "little horn"] to oppose the daily sacrifices; and *he cast truth down to the ground.* He did all this and *prospered*" **(DANIEL 8:12; EMPHASIS SUPPLIED).**

Quite plainly, this power *promotes teachings that are false,* for "he cast truth down to the ground." The little horn power arrogantly dares to become the adversary of God Himself! "He even exalted himself as high as *the Prince of the host.* . . . He shall even rise against the *Prince of princes* [names referring to Christ]" **(DANIEL 8:11, 25; EMPHASIS SUPPLIED).**

In spite of its wickedness, Daniel says that the little horn "prospered." As for the beast, John says, "All the world marveled and followed the beast. So they worshiped the dragon who gave authority to the beast; and they worshiped the beast, saying, 'Who is like the beast? Who is able to make war with him?' . . . All who dwell on the earth will worship him, whose names have not been written in the Book of Life of the Lamb slain from the foundation of the world" **(REVELATION 13:3, 4, 8).**

"The working of Satan [comes] . . . with all unrighteous deception among those who perish, because they did not receive the love of the truth, that they might be saved. And for this reason God will send them strong delusion, that they should believe the lie, that they all may be condemned who did not believe the truth but had pleasure in unrighteousness" **(2 THESSALONIANS 2:9–12).**

"Justice is turned back, and righteousness stands afar off; for truth is fallen in the street, and equity cannot enter" **(ISAIAH 59:14).**

"Your righteousness is an everlasting righteousness, and Your law is truth" **(PSALM 119:142).**

12 What warning did the apostle Paul give to the early church leaders regarding this apostasy in early Christianity?

"Also *from among yourselves* [that is from among the "overseers" or elders of the church, called "to shepherd the church of God," **SEE VERSES 17, 28**] men will rise up, speaking perverse things, to draw away the disciples after themselves. Therefore watch" **(ACTS 20:30, 31; EMPHASIS SUPPLIED).**

The traitor Judas came from within Christ's inner circle of disciples: "Now as they were eating, He [Jesus] said, 'Assuredly, I say to you, one of you will betray Me' " **(MATTHEW 26:21).**

In the infamous act that betrayed his Master, Judas portrayed to the world his true nature and unmasked his character for all to see. Now, of course, we know that Judas Iscariot was a scheming traitor, yet at one time *he was one of the leaders of the early church*. Jesus calls him "the son of perdition" **(JOHN 17:12).** The only other time that expression is used in Scripture, it is applied to one we may identify with the little horn and the beast power. Paul speaks of "the Man of Sin"—"the son of perdition, *who opposes and exalts himself above all that is called God or that is worshiped, so that he sits as God in the temple of God, showing himself that he is God*" **(2 THESSALONIANS 2:3, 4; EMPHASIS SUPPLIED).**

"For such are false apostles, deceitful workers, transforming themselves into apostles of Christ. And no wonder! For Satan himself transforms himself into an angel of light. Therefore it is no great thing if his ministers also transform themselves into ministers of righteousness, whose end will be according to their works" **(2 CORINTHIANS 11:13–15).**

"But there were also false prophets among the people, even as there will be false teachers among you, who will secretly bring in destructive heresies, even denying the Lord who bought them, and bring on themselves swift destruction. And many will follow their destructive ways, because of whom the way of truth will be blasphemed. By covetousness they will exploit you with deceptive words; for a long time their judgment has not been idle, and their destruction does not slumber" **(2 PETER 2:1–3).**

"Woe to you, scribes and Pharisees, hypocrites! For you travel land and sea to win one proselyte [convert], and when he is won, you make him twice as much a son of hell as yourselves" **(MATTHEW 23:15).**

The apostle Paul predicted false religious teachers would arise. **DANIEL 7:24** describes the little horn as being different from the other ten horns. The ten kingdoms of Rome were political kingdoms. The little horn is clearly an apostate religious power.

13 What would this apostate religio-political power attempt to do to the law of God?

"He shall speak pompous words against the Most High, shall persecute the saints of the Most High, and *shall intend to change times and law*. Then the saints shall be given into his hand for a time and times and half a time" **(DANIEL 7:25; EMPHASIS SUPPLIED).**

Let us ask ourselves: What power arose by destroying three of the ten tribes into which pagan Rome was divided? **(SEE DANIEL 7:8.)** Which power arose out of Rome after the division of the Roman Empire from A.D. 351 to A.D. 476 as a *religious,* not a political, power? **(SEE DANIEL 7:8.)** Which religious power arose from Rome in these early centuries and had a man as its visible head or leader? **(SEE DANIEL 7:8, 24.)** Which power made boastful, presumptuous claims about its authority? **(SEE DANIEL 7:25.)** Which has persecuted the people of God, has reigned for 1,260 years, and has attempted to change God's law? **(SEE DANIEL 7:25.)** There is only one power in history that can possibly fit this clear delineation—papal Rome. Let's note how it fits Daniel's description:

History reveals that Rome's power base expanded gradually as it uprooted that which stood in its way. It is part of human nature to want to crush opposition in an attempt to solidify one's power base. Papal Rome became dominant by bringing about the destruction of three of the ten tribes into which the Roman Empire fragmented (Heruli, A.D. 493; Vandals, A.D. 534; and Ostrogoths, A.D. 538. See Gibbons, *The History of the Decline and Fall of the Roman Empire,* vol. 4, chaps. 39, 40.)

Papal Rome was different from its predecessors. It claimed dominion over the souls, as well as the bodies, of men. It was a persecuting power. Historians of the period confirm that in the infamous Inquisition and other atrocities such as the massacre on St. Bartholomew's Day, more than fifty million people died for their faith in God's Word. The papacy reigned supreme for 1,260 years. In A.D. 533, the Roman emperor Justinian declared the bishop of Rome to be the supreme bishop of all the churches. In A.D. 538, the Roman general Belisarius drove the Ostrogoths out of Rome. The papacy was the supreme religio-political power in Europe from A.D. 538 to A.D. 1798. The French general Berthier, Napoleon's supreme commander, imprisoned the pope in 1798 and he died in exile, fulfilling the prophecy of **REVELATION 13:10**—"He who leads into captivity shall go into captivity." Daniel's prediction regarding the little horn's dominion lasting for 1,260 years met its fulfillment in the pope's captivity in 1798. People living at that time might have thought the papacy had come to an end. But Revelation's prophecy predicts that the "deadly wound" would be healed **(REVELATION 13:3)**.

And remember Daniel's prophecy that this little horn power would "think to change times and laws" **(DANIEL 7:25, KJV)**. Obviously, this amazing prophecy is speaking about the law of God. When one nation defeats another nation, laws change. The little horn power was working against God in attempting to change His law.

Does the papacy claim it changed the Sabbath?

The papacy clearly acknowledges changing the Sabbath from Saturday, the seventh day of the week, to Sunday, the first day of the week. It declares the change to be an act of its ecclesiastical authority. The statements listed below cover the last one hundred years and clearly demonstrate the consensus of the Catholic Church's thinking on the change of the Sabbath.

- "The Catholic Church for more than one thousand years before the existence of a Protestant, by virtue of her divine mission, changed the day from Saturday to Sunday" (*The Catholic Mirror,* September 1893).

- *Question:* Which day is the Sabbath day? *Answer:* Saturday is the Sabbath day. *Question:* Why do we observe Sunday instead of Saturday? *Answer:* Because the Catholic Church transferred the solemnity from Saturday to Sunday" (*The Convert's Catechism,* Peter Giereman, 1948, p. 50).

- "The Church, . . . after changing the day of rest from the Jewish Sabbath, or seventh day of the week, to the first, made the third commandment refer to Sunday as the day to be kept holy as the Lord's Day" (*Catholic Encyclopedia,* vol. 4, p. 153).

- "You may read the Bible from Genesis to Revelation, and you will not find a single line authorizing the sanctification of Sunday. The Scriptures enforce the religious observance of Saturday, a day which we never sanctify" (J. Gibbons, *Faith of Our Fathers,* p. 111).

- "The observance of Sunday by the Protestants is an homage they pay, in spite of themselves, to the authority of the Catholic Church" (*Plain Talk About Protestantism,* p. 213).

- "Fundamentalists meet for worship on Sunday, yet there is no evidence in the Bible that corporate worship was to be made on Sundays. The Jewish Sabbath, or day of rest, was, of course, Saturday. It was the Catholic Church that decided Sunday should be the day of worship for Christians, in honor of the resurrection" (Karl Keating, *Catholicism and Fundamentalism,* 1988, p. 38).

- "The sun was a foremost god with heathendom. . . . The sun has worshippers at this hour in Persia and other lands. . . . There is, in truth, something royal, kingly about the sun, making it a fit emblem of Jesus, the Sun of Justice. Hence the Church in these countries would seem to have said, 'Keep that old pagan name. It shall remain consecrated, sanctified.' And thus the pagan Sunday, dedicated to Balder, became the Christian Sunday, sacred to Jesus" (*The Catholic World,* March 1994, p. 809).

- "But since Saturday, not Sunday, is specified in the Bible, isn't it curious that non-Catholics who profess to take their religion directly from the Bible and not from the Church observe Sunday instead of Saturday? Yes, of course, it is inconsistent, but the change was made about fifteen centuries before Protestantism was born. . . . They have continued to observe the custom even though it rests upon the authority of the Catholic Church, and not upon an explicit text in the Bible. That observance remains the reminder of the Mother Church from which non-Catholic sects broke away—like a boy running away from his mother but still carrying in his pocket a picture of his mother or a lock of her hair" (Rev. John O'Brien, *The Faith of Millions,* pp. 421, 422).

- "Protestantism, in discarding the authority of the church, has no good reason for its Sunday theory, and ought, logically, to keep Saturday with the Jews" (*American Catholic Quarterly Review,* January 1883).

- "Now, every child in school knows that the Sabbath day is Saturday the seventh day of the week; and yet, with the exception of the Seventh-day Adventists, all Protestants keep Sunday instead of the Sabbath day, because the Catholic Church made this change in the first ages of Christianity" (Winnipeg [Manitoba] *Free Press,* April 21, 1884).

Human tradition can never be a substitute for divine truth. The commandments of men are no substitute for the commandments of God. No human power has the authority to change the law of God written with His own finger on tables of stone. Jesus invites us to listen to His voice alone. He says, "If you love Me, keep My commandments" **(JOHN 14:15).**

14 When we are faced with a decision between the truth of God's Word and the traditions of human beings, what counsel does Jesus give us?

The Lord Jesus prayed to His Father: "Sanctify them by Your truth. *Your Word is truth*" **(JOHN 17:17; EMPHASIS SUPPLIED).**

Christ urges us, "Seek first the kingdom of God and His righteousness, and all these things shall be added to you" **(MATTHEW 6:33).**

"You shall know the truth, and the truth shall make you free" **(JOHN 8:32).**

"The words of the LORD are pure words, like silver tried in a furnace of earth, purified seven times" **(PSALM 12:6).**

"O Lord GOD, You are God, and Your words are true" **(2 SAMUEL 7:28).**

Man-made traditions carry no weight with God. Jesus pointedly asks: "Why do you also transgress the commandment of God because of your tradition? . . . Thus you have made the commandment of God of no effect by your tradition. . . . In vain they worship Me, teaching as doctrines the commandments of men" **(MATTHEW 15:3, 6, 9; SEE ALSO MARK 7:7, 9, 13.)**

God lovingly appeals to His true followers to obey Him willingly. Our obedience is a sign of our deep love. He invites us to turn from the commandments of men to the law of God. No human being has the authority to change God's law. The Sabbath is much more than a matter of days. It is a matter of master. Jesus invites us to acknowledge Him as the supreme Lord and Master of our lives.

The Sabbath is an eternal link to our Creator.

CHAPTER 16

What the Bible Says About False Prophets and Deceptions

Cults are on the rise. False religious teachers continue to attract multitudes. Sincere people are being deceived. The stakes are high. It makes all the difference whom you follow. More than nine hundred members of the People's Temple followed their leader, Jim Jones, on a path of death into the jungles of Guyana in the late 1970s. David Koresh's followers died a fiery death in Waco, Texas. Members of Heaven's Gate evidently listened to their leader, Marshall Applewhite, and committed mass suicide in an affluent Southern California suburb.

Why were these people deceived? Are there some clear ways to identify false religious teachers? How can we distinguish between true and false religious leaders? Are there clear identifying marks of a counterfeit? How can we tell the difference?

01 What does Bible prophecy predict about false religious leaders in the last days just before the return of our Lord? What insights regarding false prophets do we gain as we trace this subject through the Bible?

"Many will come in My name, saying, 'I am the Christ,' and will deceive many. . . .Then many false prophets will rise up and deceive many. . . . For false christs and false prophets will rise and show great signs and wonders to deceive, if possible, even the elect" **(MATTHEW 24:5, 11, 24).**

Jesus warned, "Beware of false prophets, who come to you in sheep's clothing, but inwardly they are ravenous wolves" **(MATTHEW 7:15).**

Paul cautions us, "Beware lest anyone cheat you through philosophy and empty deceit, according to the tradition of men, according to the basic principles of the world, and not according to Christ" **(COLOSSIANS 2:8).**

"There were also false prophets among the people, even as there will be false teachers among you, who will secretly bring in destructive heresies, even denying the Lord who bought them, and bring on themselves swift destruction. And many will follow their destructive ways, because of whom the way of truth will be blasphemed. By covetousness they will exploit you with deceptive words; for a long time their judgment has not been idle, and their destruction does not slumber" **(2 PETER 2:1–3).**

"You therefore, beloved, since you know this beforehand, beware lest you also fall from your own steadfastness, being led away with the error of the wicked" **(2 PETER 3:17).**

"If there arises among you a prophet or a dreamer of dreams, and he gives you a sign or a wonder, and the sign or the wonder comes to pass, of which he spoke to you, saying, 'Let us go after other gods'—which you have not known—'and let us serve them,' *you shall not listen* to the words of that prophet or that dreamer of dreams, for the LORD your God is testing you to know whether you love the LORD your God with all your heart and with all your soul" **(DEUTERONOMY 13:1–3; EMPHASIS SUPPLIED).**

"The elder and honorable, he is the head; the prophet who teaches lies, he is the tail. For the leaders of this people cause them to err, and those who are led by them are destroyed" **(ISAIAH 9:15, 16).**

"Beloved, do not believe every spirit, but test the spirits, whether they are of God; because many false prophets have gone out into the world" **(1 JOHN 4:1).**

"So the great dragon was cast out, that serpent of old, called the Devil and Satan, who deceives the whole world; he was cast to the earth, and his angels were cast out with him" **(REVELATION 12:9).**

"And the LORD said to me, 'The prophets prophesy lies in My name. I have not sent them, commanded them, nor spoken to them; they prophesy to you a false vision, divination, a worthless thing, and the deceit of their heart' " **(JEREMIAH 14:14).**

"Also I have seen a horrible thing in the prophets of Jerusalem: They commit adultery and walk in lies; they also strengthen the hands of evildoers, so that no one turns back from his wickedness. All of them are like Sodom to Me, and her inhabitants like Gomorrah. Therefore thus says the LORD of hosts concerning the prophets: 'Behold, I will feed them with wormwood, and make them drink the water of gall; for from the prophets of Jerusalem profaneness has gone out into all the land.' Thus says the LORD of hosts: 'Do not listen to the words of the prophets who prophesy to you. They make you worthless; they speak a vision of their own heart, not from the mouth of the LORD. They continually say to those who despise Me, "The LORD has said, 'You shall have peace' "; and to everyone who walks according to the dictates of his own heart, they say, "No evil shall come upon you" ' " **(JEREMIAH 23:14–17).**

"Then the prophet Jeremiah said to Hananiah the prophet, 'Hear now, Hananiah, the LORD has not sent you, but you make this people trust in a lie. Therefore thus says the LORD: "Behold, I will cast you from the face of the earth. This year you shall die, because you have taught rebellion against the LORD." ' So Hananiah the prophet died the same year in the seventh month" **(JEREMIAH 28:15–17).**

"Her prophets are insolent, treacherous people; her priests have polluted the sanctuary, they have done violence to the law" **(ZEPHANIAH 3:4).**

The apostle Paul made a dire prediction: "For I know this, that after my departure savage wolves will come in among you, not sparing the flock" **(ACTS 20:29).**

"Then the beast was captured, and with him the false prophet who worked signs in his presence, by which he deceived those who received the mark of the beast and those who worshiped his image. These two were cast alive into the lake of fire burning with brimstone" **(REVELATION 19:20).**

"But I fear, lest somehow, as the serpent deceived Eve by his craftiness, so your minds may be corrupted from the simplicity that is in Christ. For if he who comes preaches another Jesus whom we have not preached, or if you receive a different spirit which you have not received, or a different gospel which you have not accepted—you may well put up with it! . . . God knows! But what I do, I will also continue to do, that I may cut off the opportunity from those who desire an opportunity to be regarded just as we are in the things of which they boast. For such are false apostles, deceitful workers, transforming themselves into apostles of Christ. And no wonder! For Satan himself transforms himself into an angel of light. Therefore it is no great thing if his ministers also transform themselves into ministers of righteousness, whose end will be according to their works" **(2 CORINTHIANS 11:3–15).**

Paul teaches that we must be alert to the danger of deception: "We should no longer be children, tossed to and fro and carried about with every wind of doctrine, by the trickery of men, in the cunning craftiness of deceitful plotting" **(EPHESIANS 4:14).**

"The Spirit expressly says that in latter times some will depart from the faith, giving heed to deceiving spirits and doctrines of demons" **(1 TIMOTHY 4:1).**

"Evil men and impostors will grow worse and worse, deceiving and being deceived" **(2 TIMOTHY 3:13).**

"For the time will come when they will not endure sound doctrine, but according to their own desires, because they have itching ears, they will heap up for themselves teachers; and they will turn their ears away from the truth, and be turned aside to fables" **(2 TIMOTHY 4:3, 4).**

02 What is our strongest defense against the subtle deceptions of the enemy?

Jesus said, "You shall know the truth, and the truth shall make you free" **(JOHN 8:32).**

"If anyone wills to do His will, he shall know concerning the doctrine, whether it is from God or whether I speak on My own authority" **(JOHN 7:17).**

"However, when He, the Spirit of truth, has come, He will guide you into all truth; for He will not speak on His own authority, but whatever He hears He will speak; and He will tell you things to come" **(JOHN 16:13).**

God points us "to the law and to the testimony! If they [false teachers] do not speak according to this word [the Word of God], it is because there is no light in them" **(ISAIAH 8:20).**

The psalmist David prayed, "Lead me in Your truth and teach me, for You are the God of my salvation; on You I wait all the day. . . . Good and upright is the LORD; therefore He teaches sinners in the way. The humble He guides in justice, and the humble He teaches His way" **(PSALM 25:5, 8, 9).**

The wisdom of God advises: "Turn at My rebuke; surely I will pour out my spirit on you; I will make my words known to you" **(PROVERBS 1:23).**

"My son, if you receive my words, and treasure my commands within you, so that you incline your ear to wisdom, and apply your heart to understanding; yes, if you cry out for discernment, and lift up your voice for understanding, if you seek her as silver, and search for her as for hidden treasures; then you will understand the fear of the LORD, and find the knowledge of God. For the LORD gives wisdom; from His mouth come knowledge and understanding" **(PROVERBS 2:1–6).**

"Study to shew thyself approved unto God, a workman that needeth not to be ashamed, rightly dividing the word of truth" **(2 TIMOTHY 2:15, KJV).**

If our consciences are enlightened and sanctified by the Word of God, they can help guide us: "Your ears shall hear a word behind you, saying, 'This is the way, walk in it,' whenever you turn to the right hand or whenever you turn to the left" **(ISAIAH 30:21).**

We must train our children to know God: "All your children shall be taught by the LORD, and great shall be the peace of your children" **(ISAIAH 54:13).**

Some truths have been lost or neglected over the years, but "thus says the LORD: 'Stand in the ways and see, and ask for the old paths, where the good way is, and walk in it; then you will find rest for your souls' " **(JEREMIAH 6:16).**

"This is the covenant that I will make with the house of Israel after those days, says the LORD: I will put My law in their minds, and write it on their hearts; and I will be their God, and they shall be My people" **(JEREMIAH 31:33).**

The loving Lord urges, "Take My yoke upon you and learn from Me, for I am gentle and lowly in heart, and you will find rest for your souls" **(MATTHEW 11:29).**

Jesus told His disciples, "It has been given to you to know the mysteries of the kingdom of heaven, but to them it has not been given. For whoever has, to him more will be given, and he will have abundance; but whoever does not have, even what he has will be taken away from him" **(MATTHEW 13:11, 12).**

03 What do the Scriptures teach about placing our trust in earthly religious leaders for salvation?

It is foolish and ultimately disappointing to follow mortal men: "Do not put your trust in princes, nor in a son of man, in whom there is no help" **(PSALM 146:3).**

"Surely men of low degree are a vapor, men of high degree are a lie; if they are weighed on the scales, they are altogether lighter than vapor" **(PSALM 62:9).**

"It is better to trust in the LORD than to put confidence in man. It is better to trust in the LORD than to put confidence in princes" **(PSALM 118:8, 9).**

When God's people distrusted Him and instead wanted to form a forbidden alliance with Egypt, the Lord reminded them: "The Egyptians are men, and not God; and their horses are flesh, and not spirit. When the LORD stretches out His hand, both he who helps will fall, and he who is helped will fall down; they all will perish together" **(ISAIAH 31:3).**

"Thus says the LORD: 'Cursed is the man who trusts in man and makes flesh his strength, whose heart departs from the LORD' " **(JEREMIAH 17:5).**

"Do not trust in a friend; do not put your confidence in a companion; guard the doors of your mouth from her who lies in your bosom. For son dishonors father, daughter rises against her mother, daughter-in-law against her mother-in-law; a man's enemies are the men of his own household. Therefore I will look to the LORD; I will wait for the God of my salvation; my God will hear me" **(MICAH 7:5–7).**

"Happy is he who has the God of Jacob for his help, whose hope is in the LORD his God" **(PSALM 146:5).**

04 In whom alone can we place confidence as the sole source of our salvation?

"There is no other God besides Me, a just God and a Savior; there is none besides Me. . . . Look to Me, and be saved, all you ends of the earth! For I am God, and there is no other" **(ISAIAH 45:21, 22).**

"Nor is there salvation in any other, for there is no other name under heaven given among men by which we must be saved" **(ACTS 4:12).**

"It is better to trust in the LORD than to put confidence in man. It is better to trust in the LORD than to put confidence in princes" **(PSALM 118:8, 9).**

"For God so loved the world that He gave His only begotten Son, that whoever believes in Him should not perish but have everlasting life" **(JOHN 3:16).**

"This is the will of Him who sent Me, that everyone who sees the Son and believes in Him may have everlasting life; and I will raise him up at the last day" **(JOHN 6:40).**

" 'I am the LORD, and there is no other; there is no God besides Me.' . . . For thus says the LORD, who created the heavens, who is God, who formed the earth and made it, who has established it, who did not create it in vain, who formed it to be inhabited: 'I am the LORD, and there is no other' " **(ISAIAH 45:5, 18).**

Jesus is the only Source of our salvation. Cult leaders focus attention upon themselves rather than Jesus. They manipulate the minds of their followers. They become substitute saviors or counterfeit messiahs.

05 What does Jesus say about placing the teachings of religious leaders and teachers above the Word of God?

"In vain they worship Me, teaching as doctrines the commandments of men. For laying aside the commandment of God, you hold the tradition of men—the washing of pitchers and cups, and many other such things you do" **(MARK 7:7, 8).**

"Woe to you lawyers! For you have taken away the key of knowledge. You did not enter in yourselves, and those who were entering in you hindered" **(LUKE 11:52).**

"Do not turn aside; for then you would go after empty things which cannot profit or deliver, for they are nothing" **(1 SAMUEL 12:21).**

"Whoever therefore breaks one of the least of these commandments, and teaches men so, shall be called least in the kingdom of heaven; but whoever does and teaches them, he shall be called great in the kingdom of heaven" **(MATTHEW 5:19).**

"Now the Spirit expressly says that in latter times some will depart from the faith, giving heed to deceiving spirits and doctrines of demons" **(1 TIMOTHY 4:1).**

In his passion for truth, Paul sometimes used strong language: "But even if we, or an angel from heaven, preach any other gospel to you than what we have preached to you, let him be accursed. As we have said before, so now I say again, if anyone preaches any other gospel to you than what you have received, let him be accursed" **(GALATIANS 1:8, 9).**

"But avoid foolish disputes, genealogies, contentions, and strivings about the law; for they are unprofitable and useless" **(TITUS 3:9).**

"If anyone among you thinks he is religious, and does not bridle his tongue but deceives his own heart, this one's religion is useless" **(JAMES 1:26).**

"I testify to everyone who hears the words of the prophecy of this book: If anyone adds to these things, God will add to him the plagues that are written in this book" **(REVELATION 22:18).**

"You shall not add to the word which I command you, nor take from it, that you may keep the commandments of the LORD your God which I command you" **(DEUTERONOMY 4:2).**

"Whatever I command you, be careful to observe it; you shall not add to it nor take away from it" **(DEUTERONOMY 12:32).**

"Do not add to His words, lest He rebuke you, and you be found a liar" **(PROVERBS 30:6).**

Paul asks: Should we follow "the commandments and doctrines of *men*? These things indeed have an appearance of wisdom in self-imposed religion, false humility, and neglect of the body, but are of no value against the indulgence of the flesh" **(COLOSSIANS 2:22, 23; EMPHASIS SUPPLIED).**

06 What practical instruction does the apostle Paul provide to keep us from being misled by false religious teachers?

"These were more fair-minded ["more noble," KJV] than those in Thessalonica, in that they received the word with all readiness, and searched the Scriptures daily to find out whether these things [that Paul preached] were so" **(ACTS 17:11).**

"Test all things; hold fast what is good" **(1 THESSALONIANS 5:21).**

God directs us "to the law and to the testimony! If they [false teachers] do not speak according to this word [the Word of God], it is because there is no light in them" **(ISAIAH 8:20).**

"You were once darkness, but now you are light in the Lord. Walk as children of light . . . finding out what is acceptable to the Lord" **(EPHESIANS 5:8–10).**

In vivid language, Jesus warned, "Beware of false prophets, who come to you in sheep's clothing, but inwardly they are ravenous wolves. You will know them by their fruits. Do men gather grapes from thornbushes or figs from thistles? Even so, every good tree bears good fruit, but a bad tree bears bad fruit. A good tree cannot bear bad fruit, nor can a bad tree bear good fruit. Every tree that does not bear good fruit is cut down and thrown into the fire. Therefore by their fruits you will know them" **(MATTHEW 7:15–20).**

"Do not be conformed to this world, but be transformed by the renewing of your mind, that you may prove what is that good and acceptable and perfect will of God" **(ROMANS 12:2).**

"Beloved, do not believe every spirit, but test the spirits, whether they are of God; because many false prophets have gone out into the world" **(1 JOHN 4:1).**

"Let us hold fast the confession of our hope without wavering, for He who promised is faithful" **(HEBREWS 10:23).**

"But hold fast what you have till I come" **(REVELATION 2:25).**

"Behold, I am coming quickly! Hold fast what you have, that no one may take your crown" **(REVELATION 3:11).**

We must endure, we must hold fast: "Jesus said to those Jews who believed Him, 'If you *abide* in My word, you are My disciples indeed' " **(JOHN 8:31; EMPHASIS SUPPLIED).**

"Cling to what is good" **(ROMANS 12:9).**

"I know your works, your labor, your patience, and that you cannot bear those who are evil. And you have tested those who say they are apostles and are not, and have found them liars" **(REVELATION 2:2).**

07 What is the only safe guide by which we can evaluate truth—the standard or yardstick by which to measure truth?

Praying to His Father, Jesus said, "Sanctify them by Your truth. *Your word is truth*" **(JOHN 17:17; EMPHASIS SUPPLIED).**

Jesus said, "You shall know the truth, and the truth shall make you free" **(JOHN 8:32).**

"Jesus said to him, 'I am the way, the truth, and the life. No one comes to the Father except through Me' " **(JOHN 14:6).**

Christians have "been born again, not of corruptible seed but incorruptible, through the word of God which lives and abides forever" **(1 PETER 1:23).**

"You are near, O LORD, and all Your commandments are truth" **(PSALM 119:151).**

"Your word is a lamp to my feet and a light to my path" **(PSALM 119:105).**

"The law of the LORD is perfect, converting the soul; the testimony of the LORD is sure, making wise the simple; the statutes of the LORD are right, rejoicing the heart; the commandment of the LORD is pure, enlightening the eyes. . . . Moreover by them Your servant is warned, and in keeping them there is great reward" **(PSALM 19: 7, 8, 11).**

"How can a young man cleanse his way? By taking heed according to Your word. . . . Your word I have hidden in my heart, that I might not sin against You!" **(PSALM 119: 9, 11).**

"O Lord GOD, You are God, and Your words are true" **(2 SAMUEL 7:28).**

God points us "to the law and to the testimony! If they [false teachers] do not speak according to this word [the Word of God], it is because there is no light in them" **(ISAIAH 8:20).**

"Lay aside all filthiness and overflow of wickedness, and receive with meekness the implanted word, which is able to save your souls" **(JAMES 1:21).**

There is only one source of truth. God's Word is a reliable guide. The old poem states it correctly when it asks:

> "What says the Bible, the blessed Bible,
> to me?
> The teachings of men so often mislead
> me.
> What says the Bible, the blessed Bible,
> to me?
> May this my only question be."

08 God respects our freedom to choose. He has created us with free will. How does the Bible emphasize the importance of our choices?

"If it seems evil to you to serve the LORD, choose for yourselves this day whom you will serve, whether the gods which your fathers served that were on the other side of the River, or the gods of the Amorites, in whose land you dwell. But as for me and my house, we will serve the LORD" **(JOSHUA 24:15).**

"And the Spirit and the bride say, 'Come!' And let him who hears say, 'Come!' And let him who thirsts come. Whoever desires, let him take the water of life freely" **(REVELATION 22:17).**

"And she [Naomi, Ruth's mother-in-law] said, 'Look, your sister-in-law has gone back to her people and to her gods; return after your sister-in-law.' But Ruth said: 'Entreat me not to leave you, or to turn back from following after you; for wherever you go, I will go; and wherever you lodge, I will lodge; your people shall be my people, and your God, my God' " **(RUTH 1:15, 16).**

"You cannot drink the cup of the Lord and the cup of demons; you cannot partake of the Lord's table and of the table of demons" **(1 CORINTHIANS 10:21).**

We need to make up our minds—no fence-sitting is allowed.

"Elijah came to all the people, and said, 'How long will you falter between two opinions? If the LORD is God, follow Him; but if Baal, follow him.' But the people answered him not a word" **(1 KINGS 18:21).**

God doesn't appreciate lukewarm, half-hearted commitments: "I know your works, that you are neither cold nor hot. I could wish you were cold or hot. So then, because you are lukewarm, and neither cold nor hot, I will vomit you out of My mouth" **(REVELATION 3:15, 16).**

"Then Jesus said to the twelve, 'Do you also want to go away?' But Simon Peter answered Him, 'Lord, to whom shall we go? You have the words of eternal life' " **(JOHN 6:67, 68).**

The devil uses deception and force. He uses lies and pressure. He uses falsehoods and coercion as his weapons. God uses the freedom of choice, the power of truth, and the attraction of love.

Certainly God can, and does, work miracles. False religious teachers exploit this truth for their benefit. They appeal to the spectacular, the sensational, as some sort of divine sign—rather than a changed life.

09 What strategy does the ultimate false religious teacher, the "beast power" of Revelation, use to deceive a majority of people on the earth?

"He performs great signs, so that he even makes fire come down from heaven on the earth in the sight of men" **(REVELATION 13:13).**

"He deceives those who dwell on the earth by those signs which he was granted to do in the sight of the beast, telling those who dwell on the earth to make an image to the beast who was wounded by the sword and lived" **(REVELATION 13:14).**

"Pharaoh also called the wise men and the sorcerers; so the magicians of Egypt, they also did in like manner with their enchantments. For every man threw down his rod, and they became serpents. But Aaron's rod swallowed up their rods. . . . Then the magicians of Egypt did so with their enchantments; and Pharaoh's heart grew hard, and he did not heed them, as the LORD had said" **(EXODUS 7:11, 12, 22).**

"And the magicians did so with their enchantments, and brought up frogs on the land of Egypt. . . . Now the magicians so worked with their enchantments to bring forth lice, but they could not. So there were lice on man and beast. Then the magicians said to Pharaoh, 'This is the finger of God.' But Pharaoh's heart grew hard, and he did not heed them, just as the LORD had said" **(EXODUS 8:7, 18, 19).**

"If there arises among you a prophet or a dreamer of dreams, and he gives you a sign or a wonder, and the sign or the wonder comes to pass, of which he spoke to you, saying, 'Let us go after other gods'—which you have not known—'and let us serve them,' you shall not listen to the words of that prophet or that dreamer of dreams, for the LORD your God is testing you to know whether you love the LORD your God with all your heart and with all your soul" **(DEUTERONOMY 13:1–3).**

"There was a certain man called Simon, who previously practiced sorcery in the city and astonished the people of Samaria, claiming that he was someone great, to whom they all gave heed, from the least to the greatest, saying, 'This man is the great power of God.' And they heeded him because he had astonished them with his sorceries for a long time" **(ACTS 8:9–11).**

The Lord curses spiritual Babylon: "The light of a lamp shall not shine in you anymore, and the voice of bridegroom and bride shall not be heard in you anymore. For your merchants were the great men of the earth, for by your sorcery all the nations were deceived" **(REVELATION 18:23).**

NOTE: As a supernatural being, Satan can perform supernatural signs. He can actually perform miracles, as we learn in the next question.

10 Can the devil actually perform miracles, supernatural signs, and marvelous wonders?

"For they are spirits of demons, performing signs, which go out to the kings of the earth and of the whole world, to gather them to the battle of that great day of God Almighty. . . . Then the beast was captured, and with him the false prophet who worked signs in his presence, by which he deceived those who received the mark of the beast and those who worshiped his image. These two were cast alive into the lake of fire burning with brimstone" **(REVELATION 16:14; 19:20).**

The Bible unequivocally states that devils can work miracles. We must not let that innocent-sounding word *signs* slip by us without realizing its full import. Other Bible versions translate **16:14** more effectively: "spirits of devils, working miracles" **(KJV)**; "demonic spirits that perform signs" **(NIV)**; "demonic spirits who work miracles" **(NLT)**. No mere illusions or amazing tricks are foretold here. Men are deceived by "those miracles which [Satan and his agents] had power to do," not which they *pretend* to do **(REVELATION 13:14, KJV).**

"False christs and false prophets will rise and show great signs and wonders to deceive, if possible, even the elect. See, I have told you beforehand" **(MATTHEW 24:24, 25).**

11 How has the devil prepared the minds of multitudes to be deceived by these false signs and miracles?

"The coming of the lawless one is according to the working of Satan, with all power, signs, and lying wonders, and with all unrighteous deception among those who perish, because they did not receive the love of the truth, that they might be saved. And for this reason God will send them strong delusion, that they should believe the lie, that they all may be condemned who did not believe the truth but had pleasure in unrighteousness" **(2 THESSALONIANS 2:9–12).**

"Now as Jannes and Jambres resisted Moses, so do these also resist the truth: men of corrupt minds, disapproved concerning the faith" **(2 TIMOTHY 3:8).**

God wants to give "eternal life to those who by patient continuance in doing good seek for glory, honor, and immortality; but to those who are self-seeking and do not obey the truth, but obey unrighteousness—indignation and wrath" **(ROMANS 2:7, 8).**

"This is the condemnation, that the light has come into the world, and men loved darkness rather than light, because their deeds were evil. For everyone practicing evil hates the light and does not come to the light, lest his deeds should be exposed. But he who does the truth comes to the light, that his deeds may be clearly seen, that they have been done in God" **(JOHN 3:19–21).**

"Because I tell the truth, you do not believe Me. Which of you convicts Me of sin? And if I tell the truth, why do you not believe Me? He who is of God hears God's words; therefore you do not hear, because you are not of God" **(JOHN 8:45–47).**

"The LORD tests the righteous, but the wicked and the one who loves violence His soul hates" **(PSALM 11:5).**

"To the wicked God says: 'What right have you to declare My statutes, or take My covenant in your mouth, seeing you hate instruction and cast My words behind you? When you saw a thief, you consented with him, and have been a partaker with adulterers. You give your mouth to evil, and your tongue frames deceit. You sit and speak against your brother; you slander your own mother's son. These things you have done, and I kept silent; you thought that I was altogether like you; but I will rebuke you, and set them in order before your eyes" **(PSALM 50:16–21).**

"You love evil more than good, lying rather than speaking righteousness. You love all devouring words, you deceitful tongue" **(PSALM 52:3, 4).**

The Lord rebukes those "who hate good and love evil; who strip the skin from My people, and the flesh from their bones" **(MICAH 3:2).**

"Then Judas Iscariot, one of the twelve, went to the chief priests to betray Him [Jesus] to them. And when they heard it, they were glad, and promised to give him money. So he sought how he might conveniently betray Him" **(MARK 14:10, 11).**

The Scriptures list a whole catalogue of sins, describing those who are "filled with all unrighteousness, sexual immorality, wickedness, covetousness, maliciousness; full of envy, murder, strife, deceit, evil-mindedness; they are whisperers, backbiters, haters of God, violent, proud, boasters, inventors of evil things, disobedient to parents, undiscerning, untrustworthy, unloving, unforgiving, unmerciful; who, knowing the righteous judgment of God, that those who practice such things are deserving of death, not only do the same but also approve of those who practice them" **(ROMANS 1:29–32).**

Quite justly, the wicked "will receive the wages of unrighteousness, as those who count it pleasure to carouse in the daytime. They are spots and blemishes, carousing in their own deceptions while they feast with you, having eyes full of adultery and that cannot cease from sin, enticing unstable souls. They have a heart trained in covetous practices, and are accursed children. They have forsaken the right way and gone astray, following the way of Balaam the son of Beor, who loved the wages of unrighteousness" **(2 PETER 2:13–15).**

"The carnal mind is enmity against God; for it is not subject to the law of God, nor indeed can be. So then, those who are in the flesh cannot please God" **(ROMANS 8: 7, 8).**

The only safeguard against deception is a love for the truth. Truth is more important than so-called supernatural signs. Satan can counterfeit signs. God's truth provides a solid foundation for our faith.

Cults flourish because they offer broken, lonely people a family atmosphere. By isolating family members, they accomplish their brainwashing tactics. Biblical Christianity calls men and women to follow Jesus and stand for truth, but it also calls them to witness to their families **(SEE 1 CORINTHIANS 7:13, 14; EPHESIANS 5:22, 23).**

12 Where can we find our ultimate security from the devil's deceptions? What does Jesus offer us?

"Behold, a king will reign in righteousness, and princes will rule with justice. A man will be as a hiding place from the wind, and a cover from the tempest, as rivers of water in a dry place, as the shadow of a great rock in a weary land" **(ISAIAH 32:1, 2).**

In Christ we are accepted. We are forgiven. We are children of God. We become members of the royal family of heaven. Jesus is a leader worthy of our allegiance. His Word is a safe guide. The greatest miracle is the miracle of a changed life. In Christ we have the greatest sense of belonging.

"To the praise of the glory of His grace, by which He made us accepted in the Beloved" **(EPHESIANS 1:6).**

We are "justified freely by His grace through the redemption that is in Christ Jesus, . . . to demonstrate at the present time His righteousness, that He might be just and the justifier of the one who has faith in Jesus" **(ROMANS 3:24, 26).**

"There is therefore now no condemnation to those who are in Christ Jesus, who do not walk according to the flesh, but according to the Spirit" **(ROMANS 8:1).**

"For He [God] made Him [Jesus] who knew no sin to be sin for us, that we might become the righteousness of God in Him" **(2 CORINTHIANS 5:21).**

"Now, therefore, you are no longer strangers and foreigners, but fellow citizens with the saints and members of the household of God" **(EPHESIANS 2:19).**

"At that time you were without Christ, being aliens from the commonwealth of Israel and strangers from the covenants of promise, having no hope and without God in the world" **(EPHESIANS 2:12).**

"You are all sons of God through faith in Christ Jesus. For as many of you as were baptized into Christ have put on Christ. There is neither Jew nor Greek, there is neither slave nor free, there is neither male nor female; for you are all one in Christ Jesus" **(GALATIANS 3:26–28).**

"Our citizenship is in heaven, from which we also eagerly wait for the Savior, the Lord Jesus Christ" **(PHILIPPIANS 3:20).**

"Behold what manner of love the Father has bestowed on us, that we should be called children of God! Therefore the world does not know us, because it did not know Him" **(1 (JOHN 3:1).**

13 What divine appeal regarding eternal allegiance to God will be preached to the entire earth before the coming of Jesus?

In vision, John the revelator saw and heard an angel "saying with a loud voice, 'Fear God and give glory to Him, for the hour of His judgment has come; and worship Him who made heaven and earth, the sea and springs of water' " **(REVELATION 14:7).**

God's last-day message is a call to give our undivided allegiance to our loving Creator. It is a call to give our total allegiance to Him. God is looking for men and women:

- Who will be sensitive to the Holy Spirit's pleading.
- Who will listen to His voice and follow Him in spite of the obstacles.

- Who will not devotedly adhere to the voice of an earthly religious leader rather than His voice.

- Who will not deny the voice of the Spirit to their heart to listen to some human voice.

- Who will be true to conscience at any cost.

"The greatest want of the world is the want of men—men who will not be bought or sold, men who in their inmost souls are true and honest, men who do not fear to call sin by its right name, men whose conscience is as true to duty as the needle to the pole, men who will stand for the right though the heavens fall" (Ellen G. White, *Education,* p. 57).

Will you be God's man, God's woman? Will you say, "Lord, I choose to listen to Your voice, and Your voice alone. I cannot, I must not, I will not allow another's voice to drown out the voice of Your Spirit. I will be loyal to You at all cost"?

Are there some clear ways to identify false religious teachers?

CHAPTER 17

What the Bible Says About Health

A growing body of scientific evidence confirms the accuracy of the Bible's teaching on health. Degenerative diseases, resulting from poor health practices, are rapidly rising. Heart disease, strokes, and cancer top the list of killer diseases taking the lives of Americans prematurely. A great proportion of these diseases are preventable. Our lifestyle makes a difference.

At Creation God surrounded Adam and Eve with all of the elements necessary for optimum health. Clear babbling brooks and flowing streams provided them with pure water. Fruits, nuts, and vegetables of all kinds grew in abundance. The natural diet God provided was packed with wholesome nutrients. As Adam and Eve exercised in the sunshine and fresh air, their bodies maintained the health with which God had created them. Evenings brought a refreshing mist, and each Sabbath they entered into an experience of deeper trust as they worshiped their Creator.

Our first parents lived in a world free of stress, anxiety, and disease. Peace and happiness walked through the land together. Their hearts were filled with love for God and for one another. It is God's intent that we discover principles from Eden to guide our lives today. Creation was not simply an act of God millenniums ago. It was a model for us in how to live today.

God is not only interested in our spiritual health. He is interested in our physical and emotional health as well. There is a close relationship between our physical and spiritual well-being.

The apostle John states it succinctly, "Beloved, I pray that you may prosper in all things and be in health, just as your soul prospers" **(3 JOHN 2).**

The Bible clearly teaches that God's message of physical health is a significant part of His last-day message for the world.

01 How does God's end-time message in the book of Revelation reveal His concern for our total health and lifestyle habits? How do other Bible writers echo this same thought?

In vision, John the revelator saw and heard an angel "saying with a loud voice, 'Fear God and give glory to Him, for the hour of His judgment has come; and worship Him who made heaven and earth, the sea and springs of water' " **(REVELATION 14:7).**

"The living creatures give glory and honor and thanks to Him who sits on the throne, who lives forever and ever, the twenty-four elders fall down before Him who sits on the throne and worship Him who lives forever and ever, and cast their crowns before the throne" **(REVELATION 4:9, 10).**

"Men were scorched with great heat, and they blasphemed the name of God who has power over these plagues; and they did not repent and give Him glory" **(REVELATION 16:9).**

Life finds its true meaning as we give glory to God in everything we do. The essence of life is giving God glory for His matchless love and infinite goodness.

"Joshua said to Achan, 'My son, I beg you, give glory to the LORD God of Israel, and make confession to Him, and tell me now what you have done; do not hide it from me' " **(JOSHUA 7:19).**

"Let them give glory to the LORD, and declare His praise in the coastlands" **(ISAIAH 42:12).**

Sometimes God's priests were unfaithful: " 'O priests, this commandment is for you. If you will not hear, and if you will not take it to heart, to give glory to My name,' says the LORD of hosts, 'I will send a curse upon you, and I will curse your blessings. Yes, I have cursed them already, because you do not take it to heart' " **(MALACHI 2:1, 2).**

"So Jesus answered and said, 'Were there not ten cleansed? But where are the nine? Were there not any found who returned to give glory to God except this foreigner?' " **(LUKE 17:17, 18).**

"Let your light so shine before men, that they may see your good works and glorify your Father in heaven" **(MATTHEW 5:16).**

"And the nations of those who are saved shall walk in its light, and the kings of the earth bring their glory and honor into it [the New Jerusalem]. . . . And they shall bring the glory and honor of the nations into it. But there shall by no means enter it anything that defiles, or causes an abomination or a lie, but only those who are written in the Lamb's Book of Life" **(REVELATION 21:24, 26, 27).**

Giving glory to God includes a complete commitment of our physical, mental, and spiritual natures to Him. It involves a commitment of our entire being.

02 How do we give glory to God? Does giving glory to God have anything to do with our physical health habits?

"Do you not know that your body is the temple of the Holy Spirit who is in you, whom you have from God, and you are not your own? For you were bought at a price; therefore glorify God in your body and in your spirit, which are God's. . . . Therefore, whether you eat or drink, or whatever you do, do all to the glory of God" **(1 CORINTHIANS 6:19, 20; 10:31).**

"Do you not know that you are the temple of God and that the Spirit of God dwells in you? If anyone defiles the temple of God, God will destroy him. For the temple of God is holy, which temple you are" **(1 CORINTHIANS 3:16, 17).**

It is *doubly true* to say that we are God's. We are His by *creation,* for He made us. Furthermore, we are His by *redemption,* for He "bought" us at the unspeakable "price" of His own blood! If these facts can't make us feel humble and grateful, nothing can.

03 What motivates us to honor God in our lifestyle and to give Him glory in each one of our choices?

"Who am I, and who are my people, that we should be able to offer so willingly as this? For all things come from You, and of Your own we have given You" **(1 CHRONICLES 29:14).**

"Know that the LORD, He is God; it is He who has made us, and not we ourselves; we are His people and the sheep of His pasture" **(PSALM 100:3).**

"You were bought at a price; do not become slaves of men" **(1 CORINTHIANS 7:23).**

Christ's own death on the cross paid the ransom price to free us from the penalty of sin.

"Therefore . . . shepherd the church of God which He purchased with His own blood" **(ACTS 20:28).**

"You were not redeemed with corruptible things, like silver or gold, from your aimless conduct received by tradition from your fathers, but with the precious blood of Christ, as of a lamb without blemish and without spot" **(1 PETER 1:18, 19).**

"They sang a new song, saying: 'You are worthy to take the scroll, and to open its seals; for You were slain, and have redeemed us to God by Your blood out of every tribe and tongue and people and nation' " **(REVELATION 5:9).**

Paul urges, "Just as you [in the past] presented your members as slaves of uncleanness, and of lawlessness leading to more lawlessness, so now present your members as slaves of righteousness for holiness" **(ROMANS 6:19).**

"Whatever you do in word or deed, do all in the name of the Lord Jesus, giving thanks to God the Father through Him. . . . Whatever you do, do it heartily, as to the Lord and not to men" **(COLOSSIANS 3:17, 23).**

The Christian life involves the whole person. It includes the entire surrender of our bodies to God. Holiness is wholeness for God.

04 What urgent appeal does the apostle Paul make regarding our bodies? How does the apostle link our lifestyle choices with our relationship to God?

"I beseech you therefore, brethren, by the mercies of God, that you present your bodies a living sacrifice, holy, acceptable to God, which is your reasonable service" **(ROMANS 12:1).**

J. B. Phillips' New Testament translates the expression, "reasonable service," as "an act of worship." In other words, when we dedicate our bodies to God to live in harmony with the Creator's principles of health, that is "an act of worship."

"Do not present your members as instruments of unrighteousness to sin, but present yourselves to God as being alive from the dead, and your members as instruments of righteousness to God" **(ROMANS 6:13).**

"Let us draw near with a true heart in full assurance of faith, having our hearts sprinkled from an evil conscience and our bodies washed with pure water" **(HEBREWS 10:22).**

"You also, as living stones, are being built up a spiritual house, a holy priesthood, to offer up spiritual sacrifices acceptable to God through Jesus Christ" **(1 PETER 2:5).**

05 Do our lifestyle choices, our physical habits, and our health practices have anything to do with preparing for the coming of Jesus? Will those who are awaiting Jesus' return surrender all their physical habits to Him?

"May the God of peace Himself sanctify you completely; and may your whole spirit, soul, and body be preserved blameless at the coming of our Lord Jesus Christ" **(1 THESSALONIANS 5:23).**

Paul's prayer was "that He [the Lord] may establish your hearts blameless in holiness before our God and Father at the coming of our Lord Jesus Christ with all His saints" **(1 THESSALONIANS 3:13).**

"This is the will of God, your sanctification: that you should abstain from sexual immorality" **(1 THESSALONIANS 4:3).**

"God be merciful to us and bless us, and cause His face to shine upon us, that Your way may be known on earth, your salvation among all nations" **(PSALM 67:2).**

God says, "I am the LORD who sanctifies you" **(LEVITICUS 20:8).**

NOTE: The word *sanctifies* means "makes holy." That's what the Lord wants to do for us.

"So now, brethren, I commend you to God and to the word of His grace, which is able to build you up and give you an inheritance among all those who are sanctified" **(ACTS 20:32).**

"Both He who sanctifies and those who are being sanctified are all of one, for which reason He is not ashamed to call them brethren" **(HEBREWS 2:11).**

"Foods for the stomach and the stomach for foods, but God will destroy both it and them. Now the body is not for sexual immorality but for the Lord, and the Lord for the body. And God both raised up the Lord and will also raise us up by His power. Do you not know that your bodies are members of Christ? Shall I then take the members of Christ and make them members of a harlot? Certainly not! Or do you not know that he who is joined to a harlot is one body with her? For 'the two,' He says, 'shall become one flesh.' But he who is joined to the Lord is one spirit with Him. Flee sexual immorality. Every sin that a man does is outside the body, but he who commits sexual immorality sins against his own body" **(1 CORINTHIANS 6:13–18).**

06 What does the Bible teach about the use of intoxicating drinks and alcoholic beverages? What effect does drinking alcohol have on our thought patterns and thinking processes?

"Wine is a mocker, strong drink is a brawler, and whoever is led astray by it is not wise. . . . Who has woe? Who has sorrow? Who has contentions? Who has complaints? Who has wounds without cause? Who has redness of eyes? Those who linger long at the wine, those who go in search of mixed wine. Do not look on the wine when it is red, when it sparkles in the cup, when it swirls around smoothly; at the last it bites like a serpent, and stings like a viper. Your eyes will see strange things, and your heart will utter perverse things" **(PROVERBS 20:1; 23:29–33).**

Scripture describes one so drunk that he's feeling no pain: "Yes, you will be like one who lies down in the midst of the sea, or like one who lies at the top of the mast, saying: 'They have struck me, but I was not hurt; they have beaten me, but I did not feel it. When shall I awake, that I may seek another drink?' " **(PROVERBS 23:34, 35).**

"It is not for kings, O Lemuel, it is not for kings to drink wine, nor for princes intoxicating drink; lest they drink and forget the law, and pervert the justice of all the afflicted" **(PROVERBS 31:4, 5).**

There is a clear relationship between drinking alcohol and forgetting God's laws. As Christians, we are kings and princes of God and need the clearest possible thought patterns. We cannot risk unclear, befuddled thoughts in these critical hours of earth's history. The Bible is very open about the damage alcohol brought to the lives of certain Bible characters through the centuries. Its lessons speak powerfully to us today.

Some time after the great Flood, "Noah began to be a farmer, and he planted a vineyard. Then he drank of the wine and was drunk, and became uncovered in his tent. And Ham, the father of Canaan, saw the nakedness of his father, and told his two brothers outside. But Shem and Japheth took a garment, laid it on both their shoulders, and went backward and covered the nakedness of their father. Their faces were turned away, and they did not see their father's nakedness. So Noah awoke from his wine, and knew what his younger son had done to him. Then he said: 'Cursed be Canaan; a servant of servants he shall be to his brethren.' And he said: 'Blessed be the LORD, the God of Shem, and may Canaan be his servant. May God enlarge Japheth, and may he dwell in the tents of Shem; and may Canaan be his servant' " **(GENESIS 9:20–27).**

Some time after the destruction of Sodom and Gomorrah, "Lot [now a widower] went up out of Zoar and dwelt in the mountains, and his two daughters were with him; for he was afraid to dwell in Zoar. And he and his two daughters dwelt in a cave. Now the firstborn said to the younger, 'Our father is old, and there is no man on the earth to come in to us as is the custom of all the earth. Come, let us make our father drink wine, and we will lie with him, that we may preserve the lineage of our father.' So they made their father drink wine that night. And the firstborn went in and lay with her father, and he did not know when she lay down or when she arose. It happened on the next day that the firstborn said to the younger, 'Indeed I lay with my father last night; let us make him drink wine tonight also, and you go in and lie with him, that we may preserve the lineage of our father.' Then they made their father drink wine that night also. And the younger arose and lay with him, and he did not know when she lay down or when she arose. Thus both the daughters of Lot were with child by their father" **(GENESIS 19:30–36)**.

"Now Abigail went to [her husband] Nabal, and there he was, holding a feast in his house, like the feast of a king. And Nabal's heart was merry within him, for he was very drunk; therefore she told him nothing, little or much, until morning light. So it was, in the morning, when the wine had gone from Nabal, and his wife had told him these things, that his heart died within him, and he became like a stone. Then it happened, after about ten days, that the LORD struck Nabal, and he died" **(1 SAMUEL 25:36–38)**.

"When David called him [Uriah, the husband of Bathsheba], he ate and drank before him; and he made him drunk. And at evening he went out to lie on his bed with the servants of his lord, but he did not go down to his house" **(2 SAMUEL 11:13)**.

"Absalom had commanded his servants, saying, 'Watch now, when Amnon's heart is merry with wine, and when I say to you, "Strike Amnon!" then kill him. Do not be afraid. Have I not commanded you? Be courageous and valiant' " **(2 SAMUEL 13:28)**.

"So they went out at noon. Meanwhile Ben-Hadad and the thirty-two kings helping him were getting drunk at the command post. The young leaders of the provinces went out first. And Ben-Hadad sent out a patrol, and they told him, saying, 'Men are coming out of Samaria!' So he said, 'If they have come out for peace, take them alive; and if they have come out for war, take them alive.' Then these young leaders of the provinces went out of the city with the army which followed them. And each one killed his man; so the Syrians fled, and Israel pursued them; and Ben-Hadad the king of Syria escaped on a horse with the cavalry. Then the king of Israel went out and attacked the horses and chariots, and killed the Syrians with a great slaughter" **(1 KINGS 20:16–21)**.

"Woe to those who rise early in the morning, that they may follow intoxicating drink; who continue until night, till wine inflames them!" **(ISAIAH 5:11)**.

"But they also have erred through wine, and through intoxicating drink are out of the way; the priest and the prophet have erred through intoxicating drink, they are swallowed up by wine, they are out of the way through intoxicating drink; they err in vision, they stumble in judgment. For all tables are full of vomit and filth; no place is clean" **(ISAIAH 28:7, 8)**.

"Harlotry, wine, and new wine enslave the heart" **(HOSEA 4:11)**.

"Woe to him who gives drink to his neighbor, pressing him to your bottle, even to make him drunk, that you may look on his nakedness! You are filled with shame instead of glory. You also—drink! And be exposed as uncircumcised! The cup of the LORD's right hand will be turned against you, and utter shame will be on your glory" **(HABAKKUK 2:15, 16)**.

Solemn words, indeed! "Do you not know that the unrighteous will not inherit the kingdom of God? Do not be deceived. Neither fornicators, nor idolaters, nor adulterers, nor homosexuals, nor sodomites, nor thieves, nor covetous, nor drunkards, nor revilers, nor extortioners will inherit the kingdom of God" **(1 CORINTHIANS 6:9, 10).**

"Now the works of the flesh are evident, which are: adultery, fornication, uncleanness, lewdness, idolatry, sorcery, hatred, contentions, jealousies, outbursts of wrath, selfish ambitions, dissensions, heresies, envy, murders, drunkenness, revelries, and the like; of which I tell you beforehand, just as I also told you in time past, that those who practice such things will not inherit the kingdom of God" **(GALATIANS 5:19–21).**

"Do not be drunk with wine, in which is dissipation; but be filled with the Spirit" **(EPHESIANS 5:18).**

Some Christians drink moderately and see little harm in it. But the Bible clearly teaches that "wine is a mocker." It deceives you. Two out of every five people who begin drinking (40 percent) end up having serious problems with alcohol. Are people who drink moderately capable of discerning when they have drunk too much? Dr. Melvin Knisley, formerly of the University of South Carolina, has clearly demonstrated that even moderate drinking destroys thousands of brain cells. It affects conscience, reason, and judgment. In this crisis hour of history, God's people need the clearest minds to make the wisest decisions. Think of the social benefits of abstinence from alcohol. Quitting alcohol would dramatically reduce absenteeism in the workplace, fatal car accidents, and multiple marriage problems. Alcohol is often the "port of entry" for the use of mind-altering drugs and other illegal substances. Dr. Knisley's advice is sound. He unashamedly says, "The only way to deal with alcohol is to quit it cold."

07 What clear warning does God give to those who knowingly defile their bodies? How important is it to make wise choices about how we treat the bodies and minds He has created?

"Do you not know that you are the temple of God and that the Spirit of God dwells in you? If anyone defiles the temple of God, God will destroy him. For the temple of God is holy, which temple you are" **(1 CORINTHIANS 3:16, 17).**

"Or do you not know that your body is the temple of the Holy Spirit who is in you, whom you have from God, and you are not your own? For you were bought at a price; therefore glorify God in your body and in your spirit, which are God's" **(1 CORINTHIANS 6:19, 20).**

"For you are the temple of the living God" **(2 CORINTHIANS 6:16).**

"The whole building, being joined together, grows into a holy temple in the Lord, in whom you also are being built together for a dwelling place of God in the Spirit" **(EPHESIANS 2:21, 22).**

08 When God created Adam and Eve, He placed them in a magnificent garden. What kind of diet did the Creator provide for them?

"And God said, 'See, I have given you every herb that yields seed which is on the face of all the earth, and every tree whose fruit yields seed; to you it shall be for food.' . . . And the LORD God commanded the man, saying, 'Of every tree of the garden you may freely eat' " **(GENESIS 1:29; 2:16).**

Consider mankind's original diet. When God created the human race, He gave us a magnificent diet of grains, nuts, and fruits—a vegetarian diet **(SEE GENESIS 1:29).** The diet God gave provides very adequate protein. Strong animals, such as the horse and cow, get all the protein they need from the oats and corn and other grains they eat. They get their protein firsthand, from the earth, and grow big and strong. The man who kills them and eats their flesh is getting his protein secondhand. It wasn't until the time of Noah's Flood that God gave people permission to eat flesh food. The average life span before the Flood was nine hundred years! **(SEE GENESIS 5:5, 27; 9:29.)**

Before Adam and Eve fell into sin by disobeying God, there was no death **(SEE ROMANS 5:12).** They would never have introduced death into Eden on their own initiative by killing animals for food while they lived in a sinless state. And in the earth made new, the redeemed from this earth will not slaughter animals in order to eat them. Once again, there shall be no death and dying in God's great hereafter **(SEE REVELATION 21:4; 1 CORINTHIANS 15:26).**

The original diet that God gave to Adam and Eve was fruits, nuts, grains, and vegetables. Our first parents and their children ate the healthful, life-giving natural products of the earth.

09 The animals that Noah brought into the ark were divided into what two classes?

"You shall take with you seven each of every *clean animal,* a male and his female; two each of *animals that are unclean,* a male and his female; also seven each of birds of the air, male and female, to keep the species alive on the face of all the earth" **(GENESIS 7:2, 3; EMPHASIS SUPPLIED).**

Ecologically, the Flood of Noah's day created an emergency crisis. Since the catastrophic deluge ripped up trees and plants and temporarily destroyed all vegetation, God gave Noah and his family permission to eat meat. And immediately man's life span was *shortened* by hundreds of years! Ever since, men have lived much shorter lives. It's not a sin to eat meat, for God gave permission to do so. But if you eat a lot of meat, you'll have more animal fat in your diet—and in your arteries. So you need to cut down on that high fat in your diet. If you want the best diet, of course, you'll choose a vegetarian one, as God intended.

Some religious teachers claim that God's distinction between clean and unclean animals applied just to the Jews. But the verses above refute that idea. God's distinction between clean and unclean animals goes back long before there was a Jewish nation. God mentioned the distinction to Noah, *centuries before* Abraham, the first Jew **(SEE GENESIS 7:2)**. Bible chronology shows that the Flood occurred around the year 2344 B.C., while Abram/Abraham was not born until around the year 2008 B.C.

When we note the anatomical characteristics God built into the animals, we realize that His distinction between the clean and unclean goes back to Creation: clean animals have split hoofs and chew the cud; clean seafood species have fins and scales **(SEE LEVITICUS 11 AND DEUTERONOMY 14)**.

This clean/unclean distinction was not just for Old Testament times. **ISAIAH 66:15–17** shows it will still be in effect when Jesus returns: "Behold, the LORD will come with fire . . . and the slain of the LORD shall be many. 'Those who sanctify themselves, . . . eating swine's flesh and the abomination and the mouse, shall be consumed together,' says the LORD." God never said we could eat unclean animals! Nor should we want to. Someone has noted, "He was a valiant man who first ate an oyster!"

Noah obviously knew of the distinction God had made, because he was told to take with him into the ark a favored few "of *clean* animals, of animals that are *unclean*, of birds, and of everything that creeps on the earth" **(GENESIS 7:8; EMPHASIS SUPPLIED)**.

"Then Noah built an altar to the LORD, and took of every clean animal and of every clean bird, and *offered burnt offerings* on the altar" **(GENESIS 8:20; EMPHASIS SUPPLIED)**.

It would be an insult to offer unclean animals as an offering to God—snakes, pigs, and other creatures He sometimes refers to as an "abomination" or "detestable"! So Noah took into the ark only *two* of the unclean animals—a male and a female—in order to preserve their species after the Flood. They were largely scavengers or God's ancient garbage disposal system. But of the clean animals, Noah was told to take *seven*, so that he and his family would have enough to eat until new vegetation grew and also enough to offer as sacrifices to God.

"Distinguish between holy and unholy, and between unclean and clean" **(LEVITICUS 10:10)**.

"And they shall teach My people the difference between the holy and the unholy, and cause them to discern between the unclean and the clean" **(EZEKIEL 44:23)**.

Some may wonder about Peter's strange vision, recorded in **ACTS 10:1–35**. In this vision, Peter saw all kinds of *unclean* animals, and God said, " 'Rise, Peter, kill and eat.' But Peter said, 'Not so, Lord! For I have never eaten anything common or unclean' " **(VERSES 13, 14)**. Peter's reply proves that during the entire three-and-a-half years he spent with Jesus, he had never heard about any change in the status of unclean foods. But what did this strange vision mean? Remember that at the very moment Peter was having this vision,

God was sending to him the Roman centurion Cornelius—a Gentile—to inquire about the true faith of Christianity. As a Jew, Peter had been taught to have no dealings or intercourse with Gentiles. See, for instance, **JOHN 4:9,** when the Samaritan woman at the well asked Jesus, " 'How is it that You, being a Jew, ask a drink from me, a Samaritan woman?' For Jews have no dealings with Samaritans."

To change the life-long lessons of his Jewish culture was apparently something very hard for Peter to do. In fact, Paul—the apostle to the Gentiles—once had to rebuke Peter, his brother in the faith, on this very point. Note what Paul says: "When Peter had come to Antioch, *I withstood him to his face, because he was to be blamed;* for before certain men came from James, he would eat with the Gentiles; but when they came, *he [Peter] withdrew and separated himself,* fearing those who were of the circumcision [that is, other Jews]" **(GALATIANS 2:11, 12; EMPHASIS SUPPLIED).**

Therefore, God sent Peter a corrective vision. Peter himself was puzzled by the vision at first. But then, enlightened by the Holy Spirit, he realized what God was trying to tell him. "God has shown me that I should not call any man common or unclean. . . . I perceive that God shows no partiality. But in every nation whoever fears Him and works righteousness is accepted by Him" **(ACTS 10:28, 34, 35).** And Peter immediately began teaching Christ and the gospel to Cornelius and his party—Gentiles, people Peter had formerly despised. Peter's vision was about *people*—not *food.* The Bible interprets itself—if we let it!

10 How can we distinguish between clean and unclean animals?

"The LORD spoke to Moses and Aaron, saying to them, 'Speak to the children of Israel, saying, "These are the animals which you *may* eat among all the animals that are on the earth: Among the animals, whatever divides the hoof, having cloven hooves and chewing the cud—that you may eat. Nevertheless these you shall *not* eat among those that chew the cud or those that have cloven hooves: the camel, because it chews the cud but does *not* have cloven hooves, is unclean to you" ' " **(LEVITICUS 11:1–4; EMPHASIS SUPPLIED).** (Other animals are listed in succeeding verses.)

"You shall not eat any detestable thing. These are the animals which you may eat: the ox, the sheep, the goat, the deer, the gazelle, the roe deer, the wild goat, the mountain goat, the antelope, and the mountain sheep. And you may eat every animal with cloven hooves, having the hoof split into two parts, and that chews the cud, among the animals. Nevertheless, of those that chew the cud or have cloven hooves, you shall *not* eat, such as these: the camel, the hare, and the rock hyrax; for they chew the cud but do not have cloven hooves; they are *unclean* for you" **(DEUTERONOMY 14:3–7; EMPHASIS SUPPLIED).**

Two complete chapters in two different books of the Bible—**LEVITICUS 11** and **DEUTERONOMY 14**—are devoted to this divine instruction on health. The Lord, the Creator who made all animals, knows which ones He made for *food* and which ones He made for *other* purposes. Some creatures were obviously designed for consumption as food, such as beef and dairy cattle, salmon and tuna, turkeys and chickens. Others He designed to be *beasts of burden*, such as horses, donkeys, and camels. Still others He designed to be *scavengers*—God's "garbage disposers"—such as swine, shellfish, and vultures. This loving Lord gives us very simple but precise anatomical guidelines in His unerring Word.

Some people eat snails and many other things never intended for human consumption. They sometimes point to Bible texts such as **1 TIMOTHY 4:3–5,** which speaks of "foods which God created to be received with thanksgiving by those who believe and know the truth. For every creature of God is good, and nothing is to be refused if it is received with thanksgiving; for it is sanctified by the word of God and prayer." We must be careful not to misunderstand what Paul is saying in this passage. In the first place, the text speaks only of "foods which God created to be received with thanksgiving by those who believe and know the truth." If we know the truth, we understand that the *only* foods God created to be received as food by believers are those from *clean* animals. The unclean animals were created by God—but for entirely *different* purposes, as noted above.

You see, the clause, "which God created to be received with thanksgiving," is grammatically a *restrictive* clause, meaning that it is a necessary, vital part of the sentence. It restricts the meaning of the rest of the sentence. For instance, if I tell you, "Bring me the book *which is on the corner table*," you cannot comply by bringing me the book *which is on the desk near the window*. When I say, "the book *which is on the corner table*," that clause restricts my meaning to a specific book. Likewise, Paul's words *restrict* his meaning *only* to those foods *which God created to be received with thanksgiving* by believers.

Some try to argue that the words "received with thanksgiving" or "sanctified by . . . prayer," nullify God's clear instructions regarding clean and unclean foods. But it would be *presumptuous* to ask God to bless what He has explicitly told us is "detestable" or "unclean"! Would you make yourself or your family some nice *cockroach* sandwiches and then have the nerve to "say grace" over them? Certainly not!

God is not trying to be dictatorial or arbitrarily restrictive in this matter. But His Book is like the manufacturer's manual that tells us what kind of fuel is best to burn in your new car. As our loving heavenly Father, God wants only the *best* for His children. "*No good thing will He withhold* from those who walk uprightly" **(PSALM 84:11; EMPHASIS SUPPLIED).**

One of the most commonly eaten unclean foods is pork or ham. What does God's Word teach about eating swine's flesh?

"The swine, though it divides the hoof, having cloven hooves, yet does not chew the cud, is *unclean* to you. *Their flesh you shall not eat*, and their carcasses you shall not touch. They are *unclean* to you" **(LEVITICUS 11:7, 8; EMPHASIS SUPPLIED).**

"Also the swine is unclean for you, because it has cloven hooves, yet does not chew the cud; you shall not eat their flesh or touch their dead carcasses" **(DEUTERONOMY 14:8).**

God was unhappy with "a people who provoke Me to anger continually to My face; who sacrifice in [pagan] gardens, and burn incense on altars of brick; who sit among the graves, and spend the night in the tombs; who eat swine's flesh, and the broth of abominable things is in their vessels" **(ISAIAH 65:3, 4).**

God's prohibition against eating unclean foods will still be in effect when Christ returns, for He warns: "Behold, the LORD will come with fire and with His chariots, like a whirlwind, to render His anger with fury, and His rebuke with flames of fire. For by fire and by His sword the LORD will judge all flesh; and the slain of the LORD shall be many. 'Those who sanctify themselves and purify themselves, to go to the gardens after an idol in the midst, eating swine's flesh and the abomination and the mouse, shall be consumed together,' says the LORD" **(ISAIAH 66:15–17).**

"If a person touches any unclean thing, whether it is the carcass of an unclean beast, or the carcass of unclean livestock, or the carcass of unclean creeping things, and he is unaware of it, he also shall be unclean and guilty" **(LEVITICUS 5:2).**

"Depart! Depart! Go out from there, touch no unclean thing; go out from the midst of her, be clean, you who bear the vessels of the LORD" **(ISAIAH 52:11).**

"Therefore 'Come out from among them and be separate, says the Lord. Do not touch what is unclean, and I will receive you' " **(2 CORINTHIANS 6:17).**

"Do not give what is holy to the dogs; nor cast your pearls before swine, lest they trample them under their feet, and turn and tear you in pieces" **(MATTHEW 7:6).**

Once when Jesus encountered a demon-possessed man, "a herd of many swine was feeding there on the mountain. So they [the demonic spirits] begged Him that He would permit them to enter them [the pigs]. And He permitted them. Then the demons went out of the man and entered the swine, and the herd ran violently down the steep place into the lake and drowned" **(LUKE 8:32, 33).**

"It has happened to them according to the true proverb: 'A dog returns to his own vomit,' and, 'a sow, having washed, to her wallowing in the mire' " **(2 PETER 2:22).**

God's counsel applies to all pork products, including bacon, ham, and pork-based sandwich meats. Pork is extremely high in fat, contributing to coronary artery disease. It is a well-established fact that trichinosis comes from eating contaminated pork products. Bacon and ham cured with nitrates are seriously suspected as a contributing factor to cancer. The scientific evidence in favor of God's diet is continually growing in the twenty-first century.

12 What general principles does God give regarding seafood? How can we be certain that the fish we eat are clean according to God's Word?

"These you may eat of all that are in the water: whatever in the water has *fins* and *scales*, whether in the seas or in the rivers—that you may eat. But all in the seas or in the rivers that do not have fins and scales, all that move in the water or any living thing which is in the water, they are an *abomination* to you. They shall be an abomination to you; you shall *not* eat their flesh, but you shall regard their carcasses as an abomination" **(LEVITICUS 11:9–11; EMPHASIS SUPPLIED).**

As to fish or "seafood" in general, God made a very simple, systematic distinction. All that have *scales* and *fins* are clean, but all others are unclean. This rules out all shellfish such as crabs, lobsters, shrimp, oysters, clams, and so on. It also rules out catfish, which have fins but lack scales. Fish without fins and scales characteristically are scavengers of the sea, mostly "bottom-feeders" that feed on the feces and filth of other fish. When I decided to invest in a nice fish aquarium, I knew nothing about it so relied on the expert—the salesman—for advice on size, temperature, filters, and so on. After telling me what varieties of colorful, tropical fish I might enjoy having, he added one more suggestion. He suggested adding a very small, young catfish to the tank "to help keep it clean." I did, and watching that little guy eat the droppings of the other fish verified the Bible for me. Here again, "Father knows best."

God's Word declares that any living creature in the sea without fins and scales is unclean. All shellfish, such as crabs, clams, oysters, shrimp, and lobsters are scavengers. They are unclean. Since the God who made our bodies desires us to be in health, He has given us these instructions to preserve our health.

13 What amazing promise did God make to Israel if they followed His principles of health?

The Lord of all the earth tested His people in these words: "If you diligently heed the voice of the LORD your God and do what is right in His sight, give ear to His commandments and keep all His statutes, I will put none of the diseases on you which I have brought on the Egyptians. For I am the LORD who heals you" **(EXODUS 15:26).**

In **LEVITICUS 26:3**, God says, "If you walk in My statutes and keep My commandments, and perform them . . ." and then follows *a whole catalogue* of divine blessings. And the same promise is stated in **DEUTERONOMY 28:1**. "Now it shall come to pass, if you diligently obey the voice of the LORD your God, to observe carefully all His commandments which I command you today, that the LORD your God will set you high above all nations of the earth."

"Then it shall come to pass, because you listen to these judgments, and keep and do them, that the LORD your God will keep with you the covenant and the mercy which He swore to your fathers. And He will love you and bless you and multiply you; He will also bless the fruit of your womb and the fruit of your land, your grain and your new wine and your oil, the increase of your cattle and the offspring of your flock, in the land of which He swore to your fathers to give you. . . . And the LORD will take away from you all sickness, and will afflict you with none of the terrible diseases of Egypt which you have known, but will lay them on all those who hate you" **(DEUTERONOMY 7:12, 13, 15)**.

There is credible evidence that many Egyptians died of heart disease, cancer, diabetes, and sexually transmitted diseases. Obesity was common. Recent evidence also shows indication of trichinosis likely due to poorly cooked pork. Following God's principles of health made a dramatic difference for Israel, and following them will make a dramatic difference in our health as well.

14 What will be the ultimate fate of those who continue to rebel against God by defiling their bodies, although they know better?

God solemnly warns: " 'Those who sanctify themselves and purify themselves, to go to the gardens after an idol in the midst, eating swine's flesh and the abomination and the mouse, shall be consumed together,' says the LORD" **(ISAIAH 66:17)**.

God is disappointed with "a people . . . who eat swine's flesh, and the broth of abominable things is in their vessels" **(ISAIAH 65:3, 4)**.

The issue here is not a God who is authoritative or arbitrary. The issue is simply this: If individuals openly rebel against God by refusing to present their bodies to Him as a living sacrifice, God will withdraw His blessing from them.

15 Often we may feel powerless to overcome lifestyle habits that have gripped us for years. What Bible promises does God give to those who desire victory over physical habits that have consistently defeated them?

"Abide in Me, and I in you. As the branch cannot bear fruit of itself, unless it abides in the vine, neither can you, unless you abide in Me. I am the vine, you are the branches. He who abides in Me, and I in him, bears much fruit; for without Me you can do nothing. . . . If you abide in Me, and My words abide in you, you will ask what you desire, and it shall be done for you" **(JOHN 15:4. 5, 7)**.

"I can do all things through Christ who strengthens me" **(PHILIPPIANS 4:13)**.

"We have such trust through Christ toward God. Not that we are sufficient of ourselves to think of anything as being from ourselves, but our sufficiency is from God" **(2 CORINTHIANS 3:4, 5)**.

Praying to God, Paul desires "that He would grant you, according to the riches of His glory, to be strengthened with might through His Spirit in the inner man" **(EPHESIANS 3:16)**.

"Finally, my brethren, be strong in the Lord and in the power of His might" **(EPHESIANS 6:10)**.

Paul prays that we may be "strengthened with all might, according to His glorious power, for all patience and longsuffering with joy" **(COLOSSIANS 1:11)**.

The Almighty God "gives power to the weak, and to those who have no might He increases strength. Even the youths shall faint and be weary, and the young men shall utterly fall, but those who wait on the LORD shall renew their strength; they shall mount up with wings like eagles, they shall run and not be weary, they shall walk and not faint" **(ISAIAH 40:29–31)**.

"Fear not, for I am with you; be not dismayed, for I am your God. I will strengthen you, yes, I will help you, I will uphold you with My righteous right hand" **(ISAIAH 41:10)**.

16 What is the source of our power for victory over these habits? How do we receive this power into our own lives?

"But as many as received Him, to them He gave the right to become children of God, to those who believe in His name" **(JOHN 1:12)**.

"Jesus came and spoke to them, saying, 'All authority has been given to Me in heaven and on earth' " **(MATTHEW 28:18)**.

"And do not lead us into temptation, but deliver us from the evil one. For Yours is the kingdom and the power and the glory forever. Amen" **(MATTHEW 6:13)**.

Paul speaks of "the exceeding greatness of His power toward us who believe, according to the working of His mighty power" **(EPHESIANS 1:19)**.

"Thanks be to God, who gives us the victory through our Lord Jesus Christ" **(1 CORINTHIANS 15:57)**.

We can conquer through Jesus, "who has gone into heaven and is at the right hand of God, angels and authorities and powers having been made subject to Him" **(1 PETER 3:22)**.

"For whatever is born of God overcomes the world. And this is the victory that has overcome the world—our faith" **(1 JOHN 5:4).**

We can learn to control our appetites. We can *eat to live* rather than *live to eat*. We don't have to be among those God speaks of in **PHILIPPIANS 3:19,** "whose end is destruction, whose god is their belly." The Lord will gladly help us sanctify our tastes if we ask Him. Instead of junk food, we can learn to enjoy the premium fuel our bodies deserve.

Our health comes to us as a sacred trust. Failure to care for the priceless machinery of our body is an insult to the Creator. Jesus wants us well! He can help us change our careless, self-destructive lifestyle to one that heaven can approve. In **JOHN 15:5,** Jesus says, "Without Me you can do nothing." On the other hand, the apostle Paul triumphantly proclaims in **PHILIPPIANS 4:13,** "I can do all things through Christ who strengthens me." Without Christ, we can do *nothing*. With Him, we can do *all* things! Jesus says, "Surrender all, and let Me work miracles in your life. Put your life on the altar and give Me your heart. My welcoming arms are out for you!"

Although we may feel weak, in Christ we are strong. God's promise is sure. The power of Christ is stronger than our physical desires or cravings. In Jesus we can be overcomers.

Whatever your physical craving or habit, however great your desire or inclination, there is victory for you in Christ. Heaven's power is available for you today. Our Lord may not take your craving away immediately, but if you trust Him, relying on His promises, He will give you the victory.

God is deeply interested in our physical health.

Commonly Asked Questions Regarding Health

Didn't Jesus say, "It is not what goes into a man but it's what goes out which defiles him" (SEE MARK 7:18–20)? Why put so much emphasis on health? Does it really make much difference?

What issues are involved here? The New Testament plainly declares, "Do you not know that your body is the temple of the Holy Spirit . . . glorify God in your body" **(1 CORINTHIANS 6:19, 20)**. "If anyone defiles the temple of God, God will destroy him. For the temple of God is holy, which temple you are" **(1 CORINTHIANS 3:17)**. "Therefore, whether you eat or drink, or whatever you do, do all to the glory of God" **(1 CORINTHIANS 10:31)**. The Scriptures are consistent. They don't tell us in one place to carefully consider what we eat and drink, and then tell us somewhere else that it doesn't matter what we eat or drink.

Let's summarize **MARK 7** in its entirety. The Pharisees had very strict laws regarding ceremonial cleanliness. They believed that to touch a Gentile (non-Jew) in the market place was defiling. All cooking utensils, such as pots, cups, and plates, must be washed thoroughly in case some Gentile had touched them, thereby defiling them **(SEE MARK 7:1–5)**. The object of discussion in **MARK 7** is not the Levitical health laws **(SEE LEVITICUS 11)** given by a loving God to preserve the health of His people, but the Jewish "tradition of the elders" **(MARK 7:5)**. The Pharisees believed that to eat with unwashed hands was to absorb or take in defilement from the Gentiles. The question here is not *what* one eats, but *how* one eats. In **MARK 7**, Jesus is not repudiating the health laws which our Lord Himself gave, but rather He is rejecting the idea of ceremonial defilement by touching Gentiles. In this context, nothing from outside you can produce defilement or sin. All sin results in the mind. The Jews rejected God's commandments in order to maintain their tradition of exclusiveness **(SEE VERSE 9)**.

Some have felt that in **MARK 7** Jesus is doing away with the distinction between clean and unclean animals because in **VERSE 19**, in the King James Version, He speaks of "purging all meats." Actually, the word *meats* is the Greek word *broma,* meaning "food"—not necessarily flesh foods, but all food. Most recent Bible translations use the word *food* in **VERSE 19**. Besides, the discussion in **MARK 7** is not about health or dietary concerns; it is dealing with the issue of ceremonial uncleaness. Jesus is saying in **VERSE 19** that no food is ceremonially unclean. No food carries sin within it. Sin arises not from without, but from within **(SEE VERSE 21)**. Jesus did not consider unclean animals as food. They were scavengers never to be eaten. The issue in **MARK 7** is not whether disease comes by eating unclean animals, but whether ceremonial defilement comes by touching Gentiles and transferring it through foods into the body.

Didn't the apostle Paul say, "Meat doesn't commend us to God, we are no better or worse if we eat" (SEE 1 CORINTHIANS 8:8)? Didn't he also declare, "Whatever is sold in the market place eat, asking no question for conscience sake" (SEE 1 CORINTHIANS 10:25)?

The background for the answer to these thoughtful questions is provided in **1 CORINTHIANS 8:1**, where Paul introduces the passage by saying, "Now as touching things offered to idols . . . " **(KJV)**. So there will be no misunderstanding, he emphasizes this point again in **VERSE 4**: "concerning the eating of things offered to idols." Again, at the end of the discussion, he speaks of meat "offered to idols" **(1 CORINTHIANS 10:28)**. Portions of the animals which were sacrificed in idol worship at pagan temples in Corinth were sold in the marketplaces. This led some very strict Jews to become vegetarians **(SEE ROMANS 14:2–4)**.

The issue at stake here is not clean versus unclean meat. The issue is whether it is morally wrong to eat meat that has been sacrificed to an idol. In eating such meat, will one be participating in idol worship? Paul's response is that idols are nothing at all **(SEE 1 CORINTHIANS 8:4)**. We are no better or worse if we eat meat that has been offered to an idol **(SEE VERSE 8)**. However, Paul says, if doing so would be a stumbling block to someone else, offending their weak conscience, don't eat any meat offered to idols **(SEE VERSES 11–13)**. At stake here is not unclean foods, but food offered to idols. Jesus did not come to cleanse pigs. He came to cleanse sinners. Unclean animals which are unhealthful in the Old Testament are still unhealthful in the New Testament. Since our Lord will not withhold from us any good thing **(SEE PSALM 84:11)**, unclean animals are not good things.

Aren't the health laws part of the Jewish Old Testament rituals which Christ did away with at the Cross?

When Jesus died, He gave His life to redeem mankind. His death did not affect in any way what is healthful food and what is not. It only makes sense that if pork, for example, was unhealthful because pigs were scavengers before the Cross, it is unhealthy because pigs are still scavengers after the Cross. Contrary to popular opinion, the biblical health laws are not for the Jews alone. When Noah entered the ark, he was instructed to bring in the clean animals by sevens and the unclean by twos. Since the clean animals would be eaten due to the shortage of vegetation after the Flood, they were brought by sevens. In **LEVITICUS 11**, God distinguishes between clean and unclean animals for all mankind. **ISAIAH 65:2–5** describes those who have rebelled against God as worshiping idols and eating swine's flesh. The prophet Isaiah reveals that the rebellious will be destroyed like those "eating swine's flesh." God knows best. He desires our bodies to be in good health. He invites us to give up anything that harms His temple.

Since God told Noah, "Every moving thing that lives shall be food for you. I have given you all things, even as the green herbs" (GENESIS 9:3), isn't it permissible to eat whatever we want?

We might ask: Was God giving Noah permission to eat snakes, rats, alligators, lizards, worms, and cockroaches? Certainly not! Noah already knew the difference between clean and unclean foods **(SEE GENESIS 7:2)**. God was simply making a statement. He was saying, "Noah, you may now eat flesh foods." The evidence for this is that God clearly forbade unclean animals later in both **LEVITICUS 11** and

DEUTERONOMY 14. Since God does not change His moral standards **(SEE PSALM 89:34)** and since God's character does not change **(MALACHI 3:6)**, He did not give permission to Noah to do something He forbade Moses to do. All God's laws, including those relating to health, were given in love to reduce disease and increase happiness **(SEE EXODUS 15:26)**. Many in the scientific community recognize that the health principles of the Bible can significantly assist in reducing both heart disease and cancer. God's ways are best.

Doesn't the Bible say to beware of those who command you to abstain from meat (SEE 1 TIMOTHY 4:3)?

This text describes a group who depart from the biblical faith in the last days. According to the text, they teach two twin errors: (1) they forbid marriage, and (2) command abstaining from "meats" **(KJV)** or "foods" (the Greek word is *broma*), which God has created to be received with thanksgiving. The word *meat* here refers not to animals in particular, but to food in general. The same word is used in the Greek version of the Old Testament in **GENESIS 1:29**: "Every herb that yields seed which is on the face of all the earth, and every tree whose fruit yields seed; to you it shall be for food." Throughout the centuries, certain ascetics, monks, and priests, have declared the world to be evil. Both marriage and food are created by God. They are both part of God's good plan for the human race. According to **1 TIMOTHY 4:4, 5**, those creatures sanctified by the Word of God are good and not to be refused when received with thanksgiving. Paul here is arguing against the fanaticism that declares all physical pleasure is evil. He reveals that God's creation is good. God desires that His creatures heartily enjoy the food He has created for them. The issue here is not clean or unclean foods, but whether food itself is part of the material world and thus should be rejected as evil. Paul says, "No! God's creation is good."

What difference does it make what we eat and drink, isn't God interested in our spiritual life only?

Human beings are a unit. Whatever affects us physically also affects us mentally and spiritually. Our physical habits affect the quality of blood that passes through the brain. A poor quality of blood supplied to the brain makes us less capable of comprehending spiritual truth. In **1 THESSALONIANS 5:23**, Paul states, "May the God of peace Himself sanctify you completely." In **ROMANS 12:1**, he adds, "I beseech you therefore, brethren . . . that you present your bodies a living sacrifice . . . to God." John adds that Jesus' desire for all His children is "that you may prosper in all things and be in health, just as your soul prospers" **(3 JOHN 2)**. God's Word declares that it does make a difference what we take into our bodies.

What did Paul mean when He instructed Timothy to take "a little wine for your stomach's sake" (1 TIMOTHY 5:23)?

It's obvious that Paul was not advocating social drinking in this passage. He clearly states, "No longer drink only water, but use a little wine for your stomach's sake and your frequent infirmities" **(1 TIMOTHY 5:23)**. Anyone who has traveled in the Middle East knows the difficulty of getting pure, unpolluted water. And whatever kind of wine Paul was talking about (fermented or unfermented), it is quite plain that the purpose of his counsel to Timothy was due to Timothy's stomach ailments. Paul's counsel relates to a medicinal use, not a social enjoyment.

What kind of wine was Paul recommending? Would the apostle encourage the moderate use of a drink about which **PROVERBS 23:31** says, "Do not look on the wine when it is red"? A drink which brings woe, sorrow, babbling, and wounds **(SEE PROVERBS 23:29)**? A drink which is deceptive **(SEE PROVERBS 20:1)**? A drink that perverts the judgment, causing our eyes to behold strange things and our hearts to utter strange things **(SEE PROVERBS 23:32, 33)**? Certainly not! The Bible uses the word *wine* to refer to both an alcoholic, fermented beverage as well as unfermented grape juice. According to **ISAIAH 65:8**, the new wine is found in a cluster, and there is blessing in it. This is obviously the unfermented, freshly squeezed juice of the grape. Referring to the Communion wine, Jesus told His disciples that He would not participate in the service again until He drank it new with them in the Father's kingdom **(SEE MATTHEW 26:29)**. The Communion wine, representing Christ's pure, undefiled blood, must be unfermented since fermentation is a sign of sin. In **1 TIMOTHY 5:23,** Paul encourages Timothy to use a little wine, or grape products, for his stomach's sake. Unfermented grape juice has healthful properties for the body. Indeed, there is blessing in the freshly squeezed juice of the grape.

CHAPTER 18

What the Bible Says About Death

Death has intrigued men and women from the beginning of time. When Cain killed Abel, our first parents experienced the pain of death deeply. They were heart-broken and filled with sorrow over the death of their son. They, too, had many unanswered questions, but they clung to the hope of a coming Messiah who would ultimately defeat death and its originator, the devil.

You may be filled with questions yourself. You may be wondering, "What happens five minutes after death? Do the dead go to heaven, hell, or some intermediate place called purgatory?" You may be confused about the different ideas and theories regarding death. With so many conflicting opinions, how can you be certain what happens when you die? The Bible writers clearly reveal what happens when we die. God's Word provides clear, sensible answers. It unlocks the secret of the grave. It pulls the curtain aside and reveals the mystery of death. As you study the Bible passages in this chapter, your heart will be filled with hope and confidence. To really understand what the Bible teaches about death, it is necessary to understand Creation. So let's start at the beginning.

01 What does the Bible teach about how we were created?

"The LORD God formed man [Adam] of the dust of the ground, and breathed into his nostrils the breath of life; and man became a living being" **(GENESIS 2:7).**

This statement is not only biblically sound, but scientifically accurate. Scientists now know the chemical composition of our bodies. Physically, we are made up of the very elements found in the earth; we contain carbon, calcium, phosphorus, iron, and so on. Moses, God's penman for Genesis, didn't have to rely on unaided human reason, and his record of Creation is scientifically accurate. The Bible was not written to be a scientific textbook, but it always tells the truth!

In creating Adam, the first man, God also used a second ingredient—"breath," or "spirit," which we'll discuss under question number 10. But right now, please notice the marvelous result of God's combination of these two ingredients: DUST + BREATH = A LIVING BEING! Instead of "a living being," the King James Version of the Bible says, "a living soul." Note carefully what the Bible says—and, just as importantly, what it does *not* say. It says, "Man *became* a living soul." It does not say, "Man *has* a soul"—as if a man is one thing and a soul is something separate that he possesses. Man does not *have* a soul. Man *is* a soul, a living being, a person.

In fact, the most accurate definition of the word *soul* is "person," "being," "life," or "creature." Modern versions of the Bible recognize this and translate the phrase, "a living soul" **(GENESIS 2:7, KJV)**, more clearly for us. Note the following examples:

"a living being" **(NKJV)**

"a living being" **(NASB)**

"a living being" **(NAB)**

"a living being" **(NIV)**

"a living being" **(RSV)**

"a living being" **(NRSV)**

"a living creature" **(REB)**

"a living person" **(TLB)**

Once again, note that man does not *have* a person or a soul. Man *is* a person or a being or a soul. So it's theologically correct to say, "That poor *soul* is struggling along on a fixed income," meaning, "That unfortunate person." A person is a soul. You are a soul.

In the Bible, the word *soul* may also mean "life." For instance, in **MATTHEW 16:25, 26,** Jesus taught, "Whoever desires to save his life will lose it, but whoever loses his life for My sake will find it. For what profit is it to a man if he gains the whole world, and loses his own soul? Or what will a man give in exchange for his soul?" In writing this passage, Matthew wrote the Greek word *psuche* four times, but the translators twice rendered it "life" and twice as "soul." You can see for yourself that the two words are interchangeable. And you can see, further, that "life" is not something naturally and irrevocably ours. We can lose it, for we're not inherently immortal.

We don't have enough space in this chapter to look at all the numerous examples that could be given to clarify the meanings of the word *soul* as used in the King James Version, so let's look at only two. In the Old Testament, the following texts all say that "souls" were "destroyed" by "the edge of the sword"—**JOSHUA 10:28, 30, 32, 35, 37, 39; 11:11 (KJV)**! This means that *persons* were *killed*—not some invisible "essence," which a sword could not harm. In the New Testament, Peter says that "eight souls" were saved in Noah's ark **(SEE 1 PETER 3:20)**. He means that eight persons, or eight lives, were saved—and modern Bible translations render it that way.

The Bible has much to say about God as our Creator and how He made us.

"Know that the LORD, He is God; it is He who has made us, and not we ourselves; we are His people and the sheep of His pasture" **(PSALM 100:3)**.

"I will praise You, for I am fearfully and wonderfully made; marvelous are Your works, and that my soul knows very well" **(PSALM 139:14)**.

"O LORD, You are our Father; we are the clay, and You our potter; and all we are the work of Your hand" **(ISAIAH 64:8)**.

"In the sweat of your face you shall eat bread till you return to the ground, for out of it you were taken; for *dust you are, and to dust you shall return*. . . . Therefore the LORD God sent him [Adam] out of the garden of Eden to till the ground from which he was taken" **(GENESIS 3:19, 23; EMPHASIS SUPPLIED)**.

Let us all recognize and admit that "I also have been formed out of clay" **(JOB 33:6)**.

"For He [God] knows our frame; He remembers that we are dust" **(PSALM 103:14)**.

"It is written, 'The first man Adam became a living being.' The last Adam [Jesus Christ, the Creator] became a life-giving spirit" **(1 CORINTHIANS 15:45)**.

"The first man [Adam] was of the earth, made of dust; the second Man [Jesus] is the Lord from heaven" **(1 CORINTHIANS 15:47)**.

"But indeed, O man, who are you to reply against God? Will the thing formed say to him who formed it, 'Why have you made me like this?' " **(ROMANS 9:20)**.

"We have this treasure in earthen vessels, that the excellence of the power may be of God and not of us" **(2 CORINTHIANS 4:7)**.

Death is very democratic—king and commoner, beasts and humans—all share the same fate: "All go to one place: all are from the dust, and all return to dust" **(ECCLESIASTES 3:20; SEE ALSO VERSE 19)**.

02 If God breathed the "breath of life"—not a soul—into Adam at creation, is it possible for the soul to die?

"Behold, all souls are Mine; the soul of the father as well as the soul of the son is Mine; the soul who sins shall die" **(EZEKIEL 18:4).**

"The soul who sins shall die" **(EZEKIEL 18:20).**

Why did the Holy Spirit inspire Ezekiel to write these words (twice in one chapter!) if the pagan Greeks were right in asserting that the soul of man is "imperishable"? Of course, this verse is problematic for those who believe in the immortal soul. But God simply uses the word *soul* in the way we've just learned: A soul is a person, and if a person sins, he or she will die.

"The wages of sin is death, but the gift of God is eternal life in Christ Jesus our Lord" **(ROMANS 6:23).**

"Do not fear those who kill the body but cannot kill the soul. But rather fear Him who is able to destroy both soul and body in hell" **(MATTHEW 10:28).**

This passage clearly explains that not only the body, but also the soul—our very life—can be destroyed and totally annihilated in the fires of hell. Our God is a consuming fire to sin, wherever it is found **(SEE HEBREWS 12:29).**

03 Who only has immortality?

The apostle Paul speaks of "the blessed and only Potentate, the King of kings and Lord of lords, *who alone has immortality*, dwelling in unapproachable light, whom no man has seen or can see, to whom be honor and everlasting power. Amen" **(1 TIMOTHY 6:15, 16; EMPHASIS SUPPLIED).**

Let's define our terms: *mortal* means "subject to death or destined to die." *Immortal* means "exempt from the liability of death, undying, imperishable." It's fashionable today, in many popular churches, to speak of "the immortal soul." Fashionable, yes—but scriptural? No. So much pulpit pounding is done in the attempt to impress congregations that they're "immortal" and possess "immortal souls"—that it may surprise many to learn that, according to the Bible, *only God Himself* is immortal or has immortality.

The inspired theologian Paul explicitly declares that God, "the King of kings and Lord of lords . . . *alone* has immortality" **(1 TIMOTHY 6:15, 16; EMPHASIS SUPPLIED).** Or "alone possesses immortality" **(NASB).** The KJV says, "The King of kings, and Lord of lords . . . *only* hath immortality" **(EMPHASIS SUPPLIED).**

Not everything in life—or even in the Bible—is as plain as that. The primary fact we must nail down on the authority of the Word of God is that the Lord alone is immortal. Turn to those texts and read them with your own eyes in your own Bible! When the Bible plainly declares that God alone is immortal, that "[He] only hath immortality," we needn't spend our time trying to find Bible verses telling us that man is immortal now or that he has an immortal soul—for we won't find them. God's Holy Spirit never contradicts Himself!

"Now to the King eternal, immortal, invisible, to God who alone is wise, be honor and glory forever and ever. Amen" **(1 TIMOTHY 1:17).**

Bible scholar James Strong performed a great service to all students of God's Word by producing his monumental work, *Strong's Exhaustive Concordance.* This is perhaps *the* standard reference used for word study in the Holy Scriptures, and serves as an "index" to the entire Bible, since it systematically lists every single word used in the King James Version. But *Strong's Concordance* demonstrates that, in the Bible, the term "immortal" is reserved exclusively to refer to God. In fact, that word, *immortal,* occurs only once in the entire Bible—in the verse just quoted above, **1 TIMOTHY 1:17.** The phrase "immortal soul" does not appear even once in the Word of God.

Despite the strong current of popular theology and the official stance of his own church, one Roman Catholic scholar at St. Ambrose College observed: "There is no such phrase in Scripture as 'immortal soul' or 'immortality of the soul' or its equivalent; there is only the *promise* of immortality" (Father Joseph E. Kokjohn, "A HELL of a Question," *Commonweal,* January 15, 1971, p. 368).

"Mortal" means subject to death. "Immortal" means not subject to death, imperishable. The Bible never uses the term "immortal" to describe human beings. It uses the word only to describe who God is. Immortality is a gift that God will give to us.

04 How does the Bible use the term "immortality"? Is immortality something we have today or do we seek for it? When do we receive immortality?

When Jesus returns, He will give "eternal life to those who by patient continuance in doing good *seek* for glory, honor, and *immortality*" **(ROMANS 2:7; EMPHASIS SUPPLIED).**

At least three scriptural facts should be stressed at this point:

1. Man is told to *seek* for *immortality* in **ROMANS 2:7,** as noted above. But we need not seek for something we already have.

2. Man is *not naturally* immortal. That's why "our Savior Jesus Christ . . . has abolished death and *brought life and immortality to light through the gospel*" **(2 TIMOTHY 1:10; EMPHASIS SUPPLIED).**

3. If mankind were inherently immortal by nature, then all

persons—good or bad, saint or sinner—would have eternal life. But the Bible says, "Whoever hates his brother is a murderer, and you know that no murderer has eternal life abiding in him" **(1 JOHN 3:15)**.

"Can a mortal be more righteous than God? Can a man be more pure than his Maker?" **(JOB 4:17)**.

Man is always referred to as "mortal," meaning "subject to death."

05 How do multiple Bible writers describe our current condition?

"Therefore do not let sin reign in your *mortal* body, that you should obey it in its lusts" **(ROMANS 6:12; EMPHASIS SUPPLIED)**.

"If the Spirit of Him who raised Jesus from the dead dwells in you, He who raised Christ from the dead will also give life to your mortal bodies through His Spirit who dwells in you" **(ROMANS 8:11)**.

"We who live are always delivered to death for Jesus' sake, that the life of Jesus also may be manifested in our mortal flesh" **(2 CORINTHIANS 4:11)**.

06 What glorious, climactic event will crown the saved with immortality?

"Behold, I tell you a mystery: We shall not all sleep, but we shall all be changed—in a moment, in the twinkling of an eye, at the last trumpet. For the trumpet will sound, and the dead will be raised incorruptible, and we shall be changed. For *this corruptible must put on incorruption*, and *this mortal must put on immortality*. So when this corruptible has put on incorruption, and this mortal has put on immortality, then shall be brought to pass the saying that is written: 'Death is swallowed up in victory' " **(1 CORINTHIANS 15:51–54; EMPHASIS SUPPLIED)**.

These wonderful verses from the inspired pen of Paul tell us that it is only *at Christ's glorious return* that He will give us immortality. It is *then* that "we shall be *changed*" from our present mortal natures and "put on immortality." **ROMANS 6:23** promises us that "the gift of God is eternal life." But it's a gift He hasn't given yet. The apostle Paul in **2 TIMOTHY 4:8** said that his "crown" will be bestowed "on that Day"—the great day of Christ's "appearing" at the Second Coming. All believers can look forward with calm assurance to receiving that gift. For "this is the promise that He has promised us—eternal life" **(1 JOHN 2:25)**.

"The Lord Himself will descend from heaven with a shout, with the voice of an archangel, and with the trumpet of God. And the dead in Christ will rise first" **(1 THESSALONIANS 4:16)**.

07 How do Solomon and the Old Testament prophets describe what happens at death?

When we die, "then the *dust* will return to the earth as it was, and the *spirit* [breath] will return to God who gave it" **(ECCLESIASTES 12:7; EMPHASIS SUPPLIED).**

Let's consider the word *spirit,* as used in the Bible. Its basic root meaning is "breath," seen in such words as *re**spira**tion.* Our English word *spirit* is from the Latin *spiritus,* which of course is not found in the original Bible manuscripts since they were written in Hebrew and Greek. Instead, the New Testament uses the Greek word *pneuma,* from which we get such English words as *pneumonia,* a disease that obstructs breath and *pneumatic* tires that are blown up with "breath" or compressed air.

GENESIS 2:7 tells us that when God first made Adam, He used two components: "the *dust* of the ground" and "the *breath* of life." When our Creator combined those two elements, "man became a living soul"—a living, breathing person.

The miraculous process just described is called *creation,* and the opposite process is called *death.* Note how the Bible describes these two processes and also how the parallel structure in the very same verse shows the terms "spirit" and "breath" to be synonymous, equivalent terms:

- "You send forth Your Spirit, they are created. . . . You take away their breath, they die and return to their dust" **(PSALM 104:30, 29).**
- "The Spirit of God has made me, and the breath of the Almighty gives me life" **(JOB 33:4).**
- "If He should gather to Himself His Spirit and His breath, all flesh would perish together, and man would return to dust" **(JOB 34:14, 15).**

Keep in mind two obvious facts about our breath or spirit:

- First, our breath/spirit does not exist apart from our body. Take away our body and lungs, and we stop breathing.
- Second, our breath/spirit is not the conscious part of us that thinks. Our brain does that.

Those who believe humans are naturally immortal or have immortal souls are reluctant to accept these basic facts. But they need to remember *where* God's spirit is in each of us. I am alive "all the while my *breath* is in me, and *the spirit of God is in my nostrils*" **(JOB 27:3, KJV; EMPHASIS SUPPLIED).** That's where our Creator placed it in the beginning. "The LORD God formed man . . . and *breathed into his nostrils the breath of life*" **(GENESIS 2:7; EMPHASIS SUPPLIED).** We should understand that this "breath of life" is more than just air. It's the life-giving power of God! Hospital emergency rooms don't have it. When we die, or "breathe our last" and expire, God takes this life-giving power back to Himself.

Read the wise man Solomon's inspired description: "Then [at death] the dust will return to the earth as it was: and the spirit [breath] will return to God who gave it" **(ECCLESIASTES 12:7)**. At least three points should be observed about this verse:

1. There's no implication that man's breath or spirit is the same as his personality or "essence"—"the man himself." On the contrary, the Bible here uses the neuter pronoun "it." Remember that when Jesus died, He committed His spirit (*pneuma*) into His Father's hands **(SEE LUKE 23:46)**. If the body were a mere shell and the spirit "the real man," how strange that "three days" later Christ explicitly declared: "I have not yet ascended to My Father" **(JOHN 20:17)**. Those who teach that the spirit is a person's "very essence" contradict Christ and claim He had ascended to His Father on Friday afternoon! However, we must take Christ at His word and conclude that the spirit (*pneuma*), which leaves the body at death, is *not* "the real man."

2. Also, there's no implication that man's breath or spirit is a conscious entity. Since Solomon says the dust returns to earth "as it was," we can assume that the breath or spirit also returns to God the same "as it was" before. Adam's breath was not conscious *before* God created him by breathing into his nostrils, so why should we assume that it is conscious after death? No Bible student believes in the pre-existence of the human soul or person before life on earth; that concept was voiced by Plato and accepted by the pagan religions of the East. (Latter-day Saints—Mormons—do teach the idea of man's existence before birth, but of course they make no claim to get that doctrine from the Holy Bible.)

3. Finally, this biblical description of death provides no comfort to those holding the traditional view of conscious, immortal souls. For it makes no distinction between good men and bad men. It says the spirits of all the dead go back to God at the moment of death—everyone from the apostle Paul to Adolf Hitler. If the traditional view were true, then this verse would put even Judas himself consciously, joyously, actually in the presence of God! But Universalism is a heresy few Christians will accept.

The Bible does not teach that the soul returns to God. The Bible mentions the word *soul* approximately eighteen hundred times. However, it never once uses the expression "immortal soul." For Bible-believing Christians, their great hope is the resurrection at the second coming of Christ.

08 What happens to our conscious thoughts at death? How much does a person know after death? Do we know more five minutes before we die or five minutes afterwards?

"The living know that they will die; but the dead know nothing, and they have no more reward, for the memory of them is forgotten. Also their love, their hatred, and their envy have now perished; nevermore will they have a share in anything done under the sun" **(ECCLESIASTES 9:5, 6).**

The Bible teaches that the dead are not conscious. Those who believe humans are naturally immortal admit that the *body* dies but argue that the "real man," his mind and personality—his soul—can never die. Yet this verse speaks of a man's mind, not his body. Physically, man's brain dies with the rest of his body. Intellectually, "the dead know nothing." Emotionally, their love, hatred, and envy are "perished." Today's English Version of the Bible says, "Their loves, their hates, their passions, all died with them" **(ECCLESIASTES 9:6).**

"Whatever your hand finds to do, do it with your might; for there is no . . . knowledge or wisdom in the grave where you are going" **(ECCLESIASTES 9:10).** Those who contend that only one's body goes into the grave will find no comfort in this verse, for it does not say "in the grave where *your body* is going" but "where *you* are going." Again, no mental activity or consciousness is ascribed to the dead.

When a man dies, he knows nothing about anything that happens on earth—even to those nearest and dearest to him; their successes and failures alike are not perceived by him: "His sons come to honor, and he does not know it; they are brought low, and he does not perceive it" **(JOB 14:21).**

When a man dies, "His spirit departs, he returns to his earth; *in that very day his plans perish*" **(PSALM 146:4; EMPHASIS SUPPLIED).**

The Bible teaches that the dead are not conscious. This verse is so plain it is difficult to misunderstand it. Obviously, God is using strong language to indicate absolutely *no mental activity.* If the dead man's "thoughts perish," then he's not conscious of any thoughts and is therefore not conscious, period.

09 Is the spirit that returns to God a conscious entity? What is it?

"As the body without the spirit is dead, so faith without works is dead also" **(JAMES 2:26).**

This text reads, "the body without the breath" in the New English Bible, the Revised English Bible, and the margin of the King James Version. The breath/spirit from God is our source of life, and the two words may be considered equivalent.

When the Flood of Noah's day came, "All in whose nostrils was the breath of the spirit of life, all that was on the dry land, died" **(GENESIS 7:22).**

I will live "all the while my breath is in me, and the spirit of God is in my nostrils" **(JOB 27:3, KJV).**

"When He [Jesus] had said this, He breathed on them, and said to them, 'Receive the Holy Spirit' " **(JOHN 20:22).**

"Nor is He [God] worshiped with men's hands, as though He needed anything, since He gives to all life, breath, and all things" **(ACTS 17:25).**

It is the great Creator, "the LORD, who stretches out the heavens, lays the foundation of the earth, and forms the spirit of man within him" **(ZECHARIAH 12:1).**

Throughout Scripture the spirit and the breath are the same thing. When a person dies, it is God's life-giving power, His breath, that returns. The psalmist David states it this way: "His breath [spirit] goeth forth" **(PSALM 146:4, KJV).** The spirit is not some conscious entity. It is not some immortal soul. The Hebrew word for "breath" throughout Old Testament Scripture is *ruach.* This Hebrew word means "air," "wind," or "spirit." **JOB 27:3** talks about God's spirit, or breath, in our nostrils. At death, this spirit, or breath, returns to God.

10 Do believers who die go directly to heaven? Are they worshiping Him before His throne now?

"The dead *do not praise* the LORD, nor any who go down into silence" **(PSALM 115:17; EMPHASIS SUPPLIED).**

But the righteous dead would indeed praise God devoutly and fervently—*if* they were conscious!

"For in death there is no remembrance of You; in the grave who will give You thanks?" **(PSALM 6:5).**

If the righteous dead were really conscious and taken to heaven at the moment of death, they wouldn't need to *remember* God—they'd see Him face-to-face. But that's not true. The dead are *not* conscious. In death "there is no remembrance"—even of God!

"What profit is there in my blood, when I go down to the pit? Will the dust praise You? Will it declare Your truth?" **(PSALM 30:9).**

"*While I live* I will praise the LORD; I will sing praises to my God while I have my being" **(PSALM 146:2; EMPHASIS SUPPLIED).**

According to this text, after we die, we not only are unable to praise the Lord, but we don't even have any "being"!

"Sheol [the grave] cannot thank You, death cannot praise You; those who go down to the pit cannot hope for Your truth. The living, the living man, he shall praise You, as I do this day" **(ISAIAH 38:18, 19)**.

The psalmist asks God, "Will You work wonders for the dead? Shall the dead arise and praise You? Shall Your lovingkindness be declared in the grave? Or Your faithfulness in the place of destruction? Shall Your wonders be known in the dark? And Your righteousness in the land of forgetfulness?" **(PSALM 88:10–12)**.

In this text—with profound implications—the Bible calls the grave, where the dead abide, "the land of *forgetfulness*," a most appropriate name for the place where inhabitants "know nothing," where one's "thoughts perish," where "there's no remembrance" and no "praise" and no "thanks" even of God. Forgetfulness, indeed!

God mercifully shuts our eyes at death to all of the sorrow, heartache, and disappointment on earth. Since the "dead know nothing" **(ECCLESIASTES 9:5)** and "in death there is no remembrance of You" **(PSALM 6:5)**, it is only logical that "the dead do not praise the LORD" **(PSALM 115:17)**.

11 What comforting assurance do Jesus and the Bible writers give us about the nature of death?

When Mary and Martha, the sisters of Lazarus, sent word to Jesus that their brother—who was Jesus' close friend—was sick, Jesus did nothing. Instead, He waited two more days. "And after that He said to them [His disciples], 'Our friend Lazarus sleeps, but I go that I may wake him up.' Then His disciples said, 'Lord, if he sleeps he will get well.' However, Jesus spoke of his death, but they thought that He was speaking about taking rest in sleep. Then Jesus said to them plainly, 'Lazarus is dead' " **(JOHN 11:11–14)**.

The words of the Master Himself should settle the matter beyond all dispute. But this clear statement in John's Gospel is not a rare or isolated case. God, the only One who knows everything—including what death is like—tells us over and over again in both the Old and New Testament that death is a "sleep." Note these consistent statements:

Writing under inspiration, the psalmist David prayed to God lest he "sleep the sleep of death" **(PSALM 13:3)**.

"Now shall I sleep in the dust; and thou shalt seek me in the morning, but I shall not be" **(JOB 7:21, KJV)**.

When God's leader, Moses, had finished his work, "the LORD said unto Moses, Behold, thou shalt sleep with thy fathers" **(DEUTERONOMY 31:16, KJV)**.

"Now the days of David drew nigh that he should die. . . . So David slept with his fathers, and was buried" **(1 KINGS 2:1, 10, KJV)**.

"And Solomon slept with his fathers, and was buried in the city of David his father" **(1 KINGS 11:43, KJV).**

"And many of those who sleep in the dust of the earth shall awake, some to everlasting life, some to shame and everlasting contempt" **(DANIEL 12:2).**

When Jesus was about to raise a dead girl miraculously back to life, "He said to them, 'Make room, for the girl is not dead, but sleeping.' And they ridiculed Him" **(MATTHEW 9:24).**

When Stephen was stoned to death as the first Christian martyr, the Bible says, "he fell asleep" **(ACTS 7:60).**

The apostle Paul teaches that "if there is no resurrection of the dead, then Christ is not risen. . . . Then also those who have fallen asleep in Christ have perished" **(1 CORINTHIANS 15:13, 18).**

In these words, Paul not only teaches that *death is a sleep,* he also emphasizes the absolute need of the resurrection as opposed to the unscriptural belief that Christians go directly to heaven when they die. For if that misconception were true, believers would instantly be walking the streets of gold in heavenly bliss the moment they breathe their last breath. Here, however, Inspiration teaches that *without the resurrection*, they would have "perished."

Paul encourages us: "Behold, I tell you a mystery: We shall not all sleep [the sleep of death before Jesus returns, for some will be alive on that great day], but we shall all be changed [from mortal to immortal]" **(1 CORINTHIANS 15:51).**

"Awake, you who sleep, arise from the dead" **(EPHESIANS 5:14).**

Interestingly enough, even today we call a burial ground a "cemetery"—from the Greek word, *koimeterion*, a "sleeping place."

Paul encourages believers not to sorrow for "those who sleep in Jesus. For this we say to you by the word of the Lord, that we who are alive and remain until the coming of the Lord will by no means precede those who are asleep [believers who are dead]" **(1 THESSALONIANS 4:14, 15).**

Paul tells us not to worry, for whether we're alive or dead when Jesus comes, "whether we wake or sleep, we should live together with Him" **(1 THESSALONIANS 5:10).**

Speaking of death as a sleep is an appropriate, beautiful metaphor. But when the Word of God uses that term so consistently, it becomes *more* than a convenient euphemism for an unpleasant subject. For all who take the Bible seriously, it becomes fact. And death itself becomes nothing to fear. It's comforting to realize that just as drowsy slumber comes at the end of day, so death's quiet, restful sleep comes at the end of life. Psychiatrists know that death holds a terror for many people. But men fear death as children fear the dark—because it is unknown. Once we know the truth about death, that it's simply a sleep, its horror is dispelled.

Poet John Donne's famous sonnet "Death, Be Not Proud," ends with these lines, using the same metaphor:

"One short sleep past, we wake eternally, And Death shall be no more: Death, thou shalt die."

Further proof that death is a state of complete oblivion and total unconsciousness is seen in the fact that the Bible records several cases of dead people who *did* come back to life. What did they know? What could they tell us of that unique and wonderful experience? Nothing—*absolutely not one thing*! When Jesus' friend Lazarus died, the Master miraculously resurrected him. **JOHN 11:17** tells us that "when Jesus came, He found that he [Lazarus] had already been in the tomb four days." His body had begun to decompose. When Jesus ordered the stone to be taken away from the grave, Lazarus's sister cautioned, "Lord, by this time there is a stench, for he has been dead four days" **(VERSE 39).**

Think of it! Four glorious days to spend amid the beauties of heaven! Surely Lazarus would have much to tell about the dazzling experience—*if* he had really gone to heaven and *if* he had even been conscious. If that miracle happened today, Lazarus would be overwhelmed by reporters, hounded by talk-show hosts to describe his experience in great depth, and his book would be an instant bestseller. Instead, Lazarus was strangely silent. He had no message from beyond the grave. Not a single word is recorded in Scripture about even one thing he'd seen or heard during those four days. His reaction is incredible if he were conscious and aware of his after-death experience. But it's exactly what we'd expect from one who had slept an unconscious, dreamless sleep.

The silent reaction of Lazarus is not unique. Your Bible records *seven* instances of dead people brought back to life—besides Jesus' own resurrection. *None* of those favored individuals said as much as a single syllable about their remarkable experience!

The Bible compares death to a sleep more than fifty times. To the Bible-believing Christian, death is no more to be feared than a sound sleep. When we are sleeping soundly, we are not aware of time passing at all. We are at rest—complete rest.

Not only does Scripture teach that death is an unconscious sleep, but it teaches that the dead sleep *until the resurrection.* None of the Bible writers believed that death is the time of eternal rewards. Jesus said: "Behold, I am coming quickly, and My reward is with Me, to give to every one according to his work" **(REVELATION 22:12).** "For the Son of Man will come . . . and then He will reward each according to his works" **(MATTHEW 16:27).**

For example, Peter stresses the fact that David did not go to heaven when he died: "Men and brethren, let me speak freely to you of the patriarch David, that he is both dead and buried, and his tomb is with us to this day. . . . For David did not ascend into the heavens" **(ACTS 2:29, 34).**

Could language be clearer than that? Those words are from Peter's Pentecost sermon, but clergymen intent on teaching man's innate immortality seldom quote them. Instead, such preachers argue, "Of course David's *body* is dead and buried; we never said his body is ascended into heaven. But his soul is in heaven." However, this explanation is less than convincing to all who note that Peter spoke not of "David's body" but of "David," the man himself. Christ will resurrect the whole person.

12 Besides sleep, what other word does the Bible use to describe death?

John the revelator reports, "Then I heard a voice from heaven saying to me, 'Write: " 'Blessed are the dead who die in the Lord from now on.' 'Yes,' says the Spirit, 'that they may rest from their labors, and their works follow them' " ' " **(REVELATION 14:13).**

"Then a white robe was given to each of them; and it was said to them that they should rest a little while longer, until both the number of their fellow servants and their brethren, who would be killed as they were, was completed" **(REVELATION 6:11).**

In overwhelming despair, Job asks, "Why did I not die at birth? Why did I not perish when I came from the womb? . . . For now I would have lain still and been quiet, I would have been asleep; then I would have been at rest. . . . There the wicked cease from troubling, and there the weary are at rest. There the prisoners rest together; they do not hear the voice of the oppressor. The small and great are there, and the servant is free from his master" **(JOB 3:11, 13, 17–19).**

"The righteous perishes, and no man takes it to heart; merciful men are taken away [by death], while no one considers that the righteous is taken away from evil. He shall enter into peace; they shall rest in their beds [the grave]" **(ISAIAH 57:1, 2).**

13 How does Jesus take away the fear of death? What gives us assurance when we die?

Jesus Christ says, "I am He who lives, and was dead, and behold, I am alive forevermore. Amen. *And I have the keys of Hades* [the abode of the dead, the grave] *and of Death*" **(REVELATION 1:18); EMPHASIS SUPPLIED).**

The term "hell" in the Bible is usually translated from three ancient words: the Hebrew *she'ol,* in the Old Testament and the Greek *Hades* or *Gehenna,* in the New Testament. Of these, only *Gehenna* implies a place of burning. Both *Hades* and *she'ol* refer to the grave. In the Septuagint—the Greek translation of the Hebrew Old Testament—*Hades* is the usual translation for the Hebrew *she'ol,* "grave." The word *Hades* appears on many ancient tombstones in Asia Minor, denoting the "grave" of such and such a person.

"To the angel of the church in Philadelphia write, 'These things says He who is holy, He who is true, "He who has the key of David, He who opens and no one shuts, and shuts and no one opens" ' " **(REVELATION 3:7).**

"Our God is the God of salvation; and to GOD the Lord belong escapes from death" **(PSALM 68:20).**

"Therefore He is also able to save to the uttermost those who come to God through Him, since He always lives to make intercession for them" **(HEBREWS 7:25).**

14 What events will take place when Jesus comes?

"The Lord Himself will descend from heaven with a shout, with the voice of an archangel, and with the trumpet of God. And *the dead in Christ will rise first.* Then we who are alive and remain shall be caught up together with them in the clouds to meet the Lord in the air. And thus we shall always be with the Lord" **(1 THESSALONIANS 4:16, 17; EMPHASIS SUPPLIED).**

"This we say to you by the word of the Lord, that we who are alive and remain until the coming of the Lord will by no means precede those who are asleep" **(1 THESSALONIANS 4:15).**

"As in Adam all die, even so in Christ all shall be made alive. But each one in his own order: Christ the firstfruits, afterward those who are Christ's at His coming" **(1 CORINTHIANS 15:22, 23).**

"Behold, I tell you a mystery: We shall not all sleep, but we shall all be changed—in a moment, in the twinkling of an eye, at the last trumpet. For the trumpet will sound, and the dead will be raised incorruptible, and we shall be changed. For this corruptible must put on incorruption, and this mortal must put on immortality. So when this corruptible has put on incorruption, and this mortal has put on immortality, then shall be brought to pass the saying that is written: 'Death is swallowed up in victory' " **(1 CORINTHIANS 15:51–54).**

"Blessed and holy is he who has part in the first resurrection. Over such the second death has no power, but they shall be priests of God and of Christ, and shall reign with Him a thousand years" **(REVELATION 20:6).**

"God will redeem my soul from the power of the grave, for He shall receive me" **(PSALM 49:15).**

"You will guide me with Your counsel, and afterward receive me to glory" **(PSALM 73:24).**

Jesus solemnly promised, "I will come again and receive you to Myself; that where I am, there you may be also" **(JOHN 14:3).**

"Father, I desire that they also whom You gave Me may be with Me where I am, that they may behold My glory which You have given Me; for You loved Me before the foundation of the world" **(JOHN 17:24).**

John the revelator was shown a vision of our heavenly future: "I looked, and behold, a great multitude which no one could number, of all nations, tribes, peoples, and tongues, standing before the throne and before the Lamb, clothed with white robes. . . . 'These are the ones who come out of the great tribulation, and washed their robes and made them white in the blood of the Lamb. Therefore they are before the throne of God, and serve Him day and night in His temple. And He who sits on the throne will dwell among them. They shall neither hunger anymore nor thirst anymore; the sun shall not strike them, nor any heat; for the Lamb who is in the midst of the throne will shepherd them and lead them to living fountains of waters. And God will wipe away every tear from their eyes' " **(REVELATION 7:9, 14–17).**

15 Since Jesus is immortal and will grant us immortality when He returns, how can we be sure to receive this priceless gift He offers?

Read the following passages written by the apostle John. They reveal how we can be sure of receiving eternal life.

"This is the testimony: that God has given us eternal life, and this life is in His Son. He who has the Son has life; he who does not have the Son of God does not have life" **(1 JOHN 5:11, 12).**

"Whoever denies the Son does not have the Father either; he who acknowledges the Son has the Father also. Therefore let that abide in you which you heard from the beginning. If what you heard from the beginning abides in you, you also will abide in the Son and in the Father. And this is the promise that He has promised us—eternal life" **(1 JOHN 2:23–25).**

"These things I have written to you who believe in the name of the Son of God, that you may know that you have eternal life, and that you may continue to believe in the name of the Son of God" **(1 JOHN 5:13).**

"And this is eternal life, that they may know You, the only true God, and Jesus Christ whom You have sent" **(JOHN 17:3).**

Jesus promises "that whoever believes in Him should not perish but have eternal life. For God so loved the world that He gave His only begotten Son, that whoever believes in Him should not perish but have everlasting life" **(JOHN 3:15, 16).**

"He who believes in the Son has everlasting life; and he who does not believe the Son shall not see life, but the wrath of God abides on him" **(JOHN 3:36).**

"This is the will of Him who sent Me, that everyone who sees the Son and believes in Him may have everlasting life; and I will raise him up at the last day. . . . Most assuredly, I say to you, he who believes in Me has everlasting life" **(JOHN 6:40, 47).**

Jesus, the good Shepherd, says, "My sheep hear My voice, and I know them, and they follow Me. And I give them eternal life, and they shall never perish; neither shall anyone snatch them out of My hand" **(JOHN 10:27, 28).**

Death is a peaceful sleep until the return of Jesus. There is no consciousness of the passage of time in the grave. For the righteous, the next event after death is the resurrection. Death for the believer is no more to be feared than a rest in the arms of a loving Savior. When we accept Jesus, we receive the gift of eternal life and the promise of immortality.

Can the dead communicate with the living?

Commonly Asked Questions Regarding Death

What does Paul mean by the expression "absent from the body and . . . present with the Lord" (2 CORINTHIANS 5:8)?

In **2 CORINTHIANS 5:1–11,** Paul contrasts the earthly perishable body, subject to sickness, diseases, and death, with the glorious, eternal, immortal body which God has prepared for us in the heavens. The expression "absent from the body" means absent from the mortal body with its earthly infirmities. The expression "present with the Lord" means present in the glorious immortal body received at Jesus' second coming. **VERSE 4** gives us a clue to Paul's thinking when the apostle longs for "mortality to be swallowed up by life." These words echo the words Paul wrote earlier in **1 CORINTHIANS 15:51–54,** we shall "put on incorruption, and this mortal must put on immortality." In **2 CORINTHIANS 5,** as well as **1 CORINTHIANS 15,** Paul longs for the immortality bestowed at Jesus' second coming **(SEE ALSO 2 TIMOTHY 4:6–8).**

If the dead are asleep, how could the Witch of Endor bring the prophet Samuel back from the dead to speak to King Saul (SEE 1 SAMUEL 28:15)?

There are three important facts to observe about this story:

1. God's clear command through the entire Old Testament period was that spiritualists were to be driven out of the land of Israel and be put to death. The Word of God unmasks all spiritualism as the work of demonic, satanic forces **(SEE DEUTERONOMY 18:10–15, ISAIAH 47:13, 14).**

2. Saul had already rejected the prophet Samuel's counsel. He had inquired of God and received no answer **(SEE 1 SAMUEL 28:6)**. Saul specifically sought out the Witch of Endor because he had received no answer from the Lord. What Saul saw was not Samuel. Notice carefully that the Bible declares the witch saw "a spirit ascending out of the earth" **(VERSE 13)**, and Saul "perceived" he saw Samuel **(VERSE 14)**. Since the "dead know nothing" **(ECCLESIASTES. 9:5)**, Satan masquerades as the form of dead loved ones imitating both their forms and voices **(SEE REVELATION 16:14)**.

3. The ultimate result of Saul's visit to the Witch of Endor was not repentance, confession of sin, and life—but despair, discouragement and death **(SEE 1 SAMUEL 28:16, 20, 21; 31:3, 4, 9, 10)**. Deceived by Satan, Saul surrendered his soul to demons.

Doesn't Paul imply that an individual goes directly to heaven at death by stating that he "desire[s] to depart and be with Christ" and death "is gain" (PHILIPPIANS 1:21, 23)?

The Bible does not contradict itself. Paul doesn't state one thing in one place and another somewhere else. The apostle is clear. At the second coming of Jesus, the righteous dead are resurrected to receive their eternal reward **(SEE 1 THESSALONIANS 4:16, 17; 1 CORINTHIANS 15:51–54)**. In **PHILIPPIANS 3:20, 21**, the apostle points out that "our citizenship is in heaven, from which we also eagerly wait for the Savior, the Lord Jesus Christ, who will transform our lowly body that it may be conformed to His glorious body." Again, Paul's desire is the second coming of our Lord. Writing to his friend, Timothy, the apostle declares from this same Roman prison, "I have fought a good fight, I have finished the race, I have kept the faith. Finally, there is laid up for me a crown of righteousness, which the Lord, the righteous Judge, will give to me on that Day, and not to me only but also to all who have loved His appearing" **(2 TIMOTHY 4:7, 8)**. Paul longed for the return of Jesus when he would see his Lord face-to-face and be ushered into eternity. Yes, death is gain! For the apostle, it meant freedom from the pain of a weary body, deliverance from the bondage of a Roman prison, and security from the temptation of Satan. To Paul, death was a sleep with no awareness of the passage of time. The next event after closing his eyes in the sleep of death would be "to depart and be with Christ." Since there is no conscious passage of time from death to the Second Coming, for Paul, death meant closing his eyes in sleep and waking up to be with his Lord.

In the parable of the rich man and Lazarus, at death the rich man goes immediately to hell and Lazarus to heaven. How do you explain this parable if the dead are sleeping (LUKE 16:19–31)?

It's important to notice this is *a parable.* It is the fifth in a series of parables—the lost sheep, the lost coin, the lost boy **(LUKE 15)**, and the unjust steward **(LUKE 16:1–11)**. Parables are designed to teach great moral principles. Each feature of the parable is not to be taken literally. For example, we do not have wool and four feet like sheep. We are not metal like a silver coin. The question in each parable is: What are the great moral lessons being taught by this parable? We get in deep trouble if we attempt to take each detail of the parable literally rather than seeking the lesson Jesus is trying to teach.

But let's assume that the parable of the rich man and Lazarus *is* a literal story. Do people actually have conversations between heaven and hell? Can those in heaven see people burning in hell? Can they hear their screams? Do souls actually have fingers and tongues as described in the parable? Abraham must have a large bosom to contain all the individuals who go there! To take the parable literally is to create huge problems. Heaven would be a terrible place if we beheld the constant, ever present suffering of our friends.

Why did Jesus tell this story? What lessons was He trying to teach? The Jews had a common story describing death as passing through a valley of darkness and picturing salvation as fleeing to the security of Abraham's bosom, while eternal loss meant going to destruction. Jesus used this story to teach three lessons:

Riches gained by greed, dishonesty, or oppressing the poor are not a sign of God's favor at all. The Jews believed riches were a sign of God's favor and that poverty a sign of His displeasure. In the story, the rich man, whom the Jews thought was blessed of God, ends up in hell. And the poor man is in heaven. Jesus reversed the expected outcomes.

The parable describes a great gulf fixed between heaven and hell. Jesus clearly communicated that there is no second chance after death. The decisions made in life determine our eternal destiny.

Jesus points out that if the Pharisees rejected the clear teachings of God's Word regarding salvation, they would also reject a mighty, supernatural spectacular miracle such as one rising from the dead.

The Jews were always asking Jesus for a sign. He gave them the greatest sign by raising Lazarus from the dead shortly after telling this parable **(SEE JOHN 11:11–14, 43, 44)**. As the result, the Jews became threatened and attempted to kill Lazarus **(SEE JOHN 12:10)**. They also became so angry at Jesus—they were so deceived—that they plotted to destroy Jesus as well. They had read the Bible with a veil over their eyes **(SEE 2 CORINTHIANS 3:14–16)**. They had failed to understand that all the scriptures testify of Jesus **(SEE JOHN 5:39)**. When Jesus raised Lazarus from the dead, they did not believe. Jesus' words in **LUKE 16:31** were prophetic: "If they do not hear Moses and the prophets, neither will they be persuaded though one rise from the dead." What an appeal! What an urgent warning. Scripture is our final authority. Jesus used a popular Jewish story to illustrate this powerful truth. Thus all the Bible harmonizes beautifully.

What does REVELATION 6:9–11 mean when it describes the souls under the altar crying with a loud voice saying, "How long, O Lord, holy and true, until You judge and avenge our blood?"

Personification is a common biblical method of describing situations with symbolic language. After Cain killed Abel, the Lord said to Cain, "The voice of your brother's blood cries to Me from the ground" **(GENESIS 4:10)**. Was Abel's blood really speaking? No! Not literally. The language communicates God's faithful, loving, tender concern for His martyr, Abel, and Cain's accountability for his sinful act. According to **HEBREWS 12:24**, "The blood . . . [of Jesus] speaks better things than that of Abel." It communicates forgiveness, mercy, and redemption. Certainly the blood of Jesus is not literally speaking. The language communicates God's message of redemption.

In **REVELATION 6,** God clearly communicates that He has not forgotten His faithful martyrs through the centuries. Their blood symbolically cries out for God to bring justice upon their persecutors and to reward these faithful ones with eternity. In the Bible, the word *soul* often means "person or people" **(SEE ROMANS 13:1; EZEKIEL 18:4; ACTS 27:37).** It also means "life" **(SEE HEBREWS 13:17; 1 PETER 4:19; MATTHEW 10:28).** Thus **REVELATION 6:9** could read: "The lives of those people martyred for Jesus, symbolically like Abel's blood, cry out from the ground for justice." There will be a final judgment, and God Himself will set all things right!

Is the soul immortal?

The Bible uses the word *soul* approximately sixteen hundred times, but never once uses the expression "immortal soul." The word *mortal* means "subject to death." The word *immortal* means "not subject to death." The Bible expressly states, "The soul who sins shall die" **(EZEKIEL 18:4).** Jesus declared that both the body and the soul could be destroyed in hell **(SEE MATTHEW 10:28).** Immortality is an attribute of Divinity. Only God is naturally immortal **(SEE 1 TIMOTHY 6:15, 16).** Satan's first lie in the Garden of Eden was regarding death. The evil one stated that the result of disobedience was not death, but life. He said, "You will not surely die" **(GENESIS 3:4).** God's Word says, "The wages of sin is death" **(ROMANS 6:23).** Death is the absence of life. Sin brings forth not eternal life in hell, but total, absolute banishment from the presence of God by annihilation. The Bible is clear. Man is mortal **(SEE JOB 4:17).** We seek for immortality **(SEE ROMANS 2:7).** The righteous receive immortality as a gift from our Lord at His second coming **(SEE 1 CORINTHIANS 15:51–54).** Sinners receive their eternal reward at the Second Coming as well. "Sin, when it is finished, bringeth forth death" **(JAMES 1:15, KJV).** The choice, then, is between eternal life and eternal death.

What does Peter mean when he talks about Christ preaching to the spirits in prison (1 PETER 3:19)?

To understand this text it is necessary to read the entire passage—**1 PETER 3:18–22. VERSE 18** reveals that Jesus, the Divine Son of God who was put to death for our sins, was "made alive" through the power of the Holy Spirit. **VERSE 19** makes a transition and declares that it was by this same Holy Spirit that Christ spoke to the spirits in prison. When did He preach to these spirits in prison? Who are the spirits in prison? **VERSE 20** tells us! In the days of Noah, the hearts of men and women were only evil continually. They were in bondage to evil spirits. The same Holy Spirit who raised Jesus from literal death appealed to men and women possessed by evil spirits who were spiritually dead in the day of Noah to bring them to spiritual life. The Spirit of Christ spoke through the prophet preaching the gospel to men and women trapped in spiritual prisons **(SEE 1 PETER 1:10–12).** The mighty power of the Spirit opens the prison of sin so the captives go free **(SEE ISAIAH 61:1).** The illustration becomes even clearer in **1 PETER 3:21.** The experience of the Flood is compared to baptism. Just as the Holy Spirit raised Jesus from death to life, and just as the Holy Spirit led Noah's family into the ark, preserving them from death and leading them to life, so the Holy Spirit works to awaken spiritual life, convicting men and women of sin, providing power for a changed life, and leading them through the waters of baptism. In Noah's day, the Spirit led men and women from death to life. Today, the Spirit delivers men and women from spiritual prisons, leading them from death to life—all because of the mighty power of the resurrected Christ.

What does the Bible teach about reincarnation?

Belief in reincarnation is based upon two premises, neither of which is true. First, human beings purify themselves through their own righteous acts. Second, we each have an immortal soul that survives bodily death. The Bible teaches that salvation is through faith in Christ **(SEE EPHESIANS 2:8; ROMANS 3:24–31).** Death is a sleep until the glorious resurrection **(SEE 1 THESSALONIANS 4:15, 16; 1 CORINTHIANS 15:51, 54).** There is no second chance after death **(SEE HEBREWS 9:27).** Now is the time for salvation **(SEE 2 CORINTHIANS 6:2).**

A Hope Stronger Than Death

In China during the Boxer uprising, in August of 1900, a young mother and missionary, Lizzie Atwater, had to face the prospect of a brutal death at the hands of Boxer fanatics who had sworn vengeance on all foreigners. She had to wait in agonizing suspense as the bands of marauders closed in on her compound. And she waited, clutching a baby to her breast.

But in this time of terror, Lizzie found a way to hope. This is what she wrote to her sister and her family shortly before her death:

"I long for a sight of your dear faces, but I fear we shall not meet on earth. I am preparing for the end very quietly and calmly. The Lord is wonderfully near, and He will not fail me. I was very restless and excited while there seemed a chance of life, but God has taken away that feeling, and now I just pray for grace to meet the terrible end bravely. The pain will soon be over, and oh the sweetness of the welcome above!"

In Ecuador, in January of 1956, Roj Youderian was killed while trying to share the gospel with Auca Indians in the jungle. Days after his body was found, Roj's wife, Barbara, wrote this in her private journal: "God gave me this verse in Psalm 48 two days ago: 'For this is God, Our God forever and ever; He will be our guide Even to death' (Psalm 48:14, NKJV). I wrote a letter to the mission family, trying to explain the peace I have."

In the Belgian Congo, in September of 1956, missionary Lois Carlson had to face her husband's death listening to the static from a shortwave radio. Dr. Paul Carlson's hospital had been overrun by Simba nationalists. Once in a while, he could sneak out a brief message on the shortwave. Lois caught this sentence, "Where I go from here I know not, only that it will be with Him."

Days later, another message: "I know I'm ready to meet my Lord, but my thought for you makes this more difficult. I trust that I might be a witness for Christ."

When they found Dr. Carlson's body, slain at the hospital, there was a New Testament in his jacket pocket. In its pages, the doctor had written the date—it was the day before he was shot—and he'd penned a single word: "Peace."

Peace in the face of the worst of circumstances. Peace in the face of death. That only happens when people have a profound sense of security, a profound sense of trust in the One who will be with them in the end.

People experience peace when they know which resurrection awaits them. They know that they are going to awaken to see Jesus coming through the clouds, lighting up the sky. They know that they will be transformed. They know that they will never again experience heartache and pain and death. They know that they will spend eternity with Jesus.

CHAPTER 19

What the Bible Says About Hell

On July 8, 1741, Jonathan Edwards preached his now famous sermon, "Sinners in the Hands of an Angry God." Throughout the sermon, Pastor Edwards urged his congregation to avoid the "horror of hell" by turning to Jesus. Describing the agony of hell, he thundered, "The God that holds you over the pit of hell, much as one holds a spider, or loathsome insect over the fire, abhors you, and is dreadfully provoked; his wrath toward you burns like fire; he looks upon you as worthy of nothing else. . . . There will be no end to the exquisite horrible misery."

Is this the God of the Bible? If you were God, would you delight in tormenting sinners in hell for millions and millions of years? How could a loving God burn sinners in hell for eternity? And how could we be happy if we knew our loved ones were burning in hell, suffering incredibly, forever? Is it logical that a loving God would keep the lost in a state of continual suffering for all eternity? Is hell some fiery inferno in the center of the earth with millions crying out for deliverance right now?

This is no small matter. Robert Ingersoll, one of the most prominent agnostics of the nineteenth century, declared, "The myth of hell represents all the meanness, all the revenge, all the selfishness, all the cruelty, all the hatred, all the infamy of which the heart of man is capable." Tens of thousands of people have become atheists, because they could not believe in a God who would torment people in hell for millions of years. For them, this God does not exist. And they are right. He doesn't. The Bible portrays a completely different picture of God and a completely different description of hell.

The Bible presents a clear answer for the question of how God's love can coexist with the fires of hell.

01 Does God delight in destroying the wicked? How do the Old Testament prophets view this final act of God?

"The LORD will rise up as at Mount Perazim, He will be angry as in the Valley of Gibeon—that He may do His work, His awesome work, and bring to pass His act, His unusual act" **(ISAIAH 28:21).**

God does all He can to save each rebellious individual, but in the end He respects each one's own freedom of choice. Reluctantly, like a parent who hates to punish a beloved child, God goes about His strange work of destruction—strange because for *Him* it's completely out of character. Note how our loving heavenly Father describes it: "The LORD will rise up . . . He will be angry . . . that He may do His work, His awesome work; and bring to pass His act, His unusual act" **(ISAIAH 28:21).**

"For He does not afflict willingly, nor grieve the children of men" **(LAMENTATIONS 3:33).**

" 'As I live,' says the Lord GOD, 'I have no pleasure in the death of the wicked, but that the wicked turn from his way and live. Turn, turn from your evil ways! For why should you die, O house of Israel?' " **(EZEKIEL 33:11).**

When ancient Israel rebelled against God, He allowed their enemies to destroy them. God withdrew His protecting power and allowed them to experience the result of their own choices. The destruction of Israel was God's "awesome work" or "an unusual act" **(ISAIAH 28:21).** God's final destruction of the wicked is not the result of His anger. It is the result of the sinner's rebellion. It is called "awesome" or "unusual" because the heart of a loving God longs to save.

02 Where do the fires of hell originate? With what—or whom—do the Bible prophets associate this fire?

"Our God is a consuming fire" **(HEBREWS 12:29).**

"If we sin willfully after we have received the knowledge of the truth, there no longer remains a sacrifice for sins, but a certain fearful expectation of judgment, and fiery indignation which will devour the adversaries" **(HEBREWS 10:26, 27).**

The resurrected wicked from all ages of this world's history, "whose number is as the sand of the sea . . . went up on the breadth of the earth and surrounded the camp of the saints and the beloved city. And fire came down from God out of heaven and devoured them" **(REVELATION 20:8, 9).**

"The sight of the glory of the LORD was like a consuming fire on the top of the mountain [Mount Sinai] in the eyes of the children of Israel" **(EXODUS 24:17).**

"Now when the people complained, it displeased the LORD; for the LORD heard it, and His anger was aroused. So the fire of the LORD burned among them, and consumed some in the outskirts of the camp. Then the people cried out to Moses, and when Moses prayed to the LORD, the fire was quenched. So he called the name of the place Taberah, because the fire of the LORD had burned among them" **(NUMBERS 11:1–3).**

"A fire came out from the LORD and consumed the two hundred and fifty men who were offering [rebellious] incense" **(NUMBERS 16:35).**

"The LORD your God is a consuming fire, a jealous God" **(DEUTERONOMY 4:24).**

"Understand today that the LORD your God is He who goes over before you as a consuming fire. He will destroy them and bring them down before you; so you shall drive them out and destroy them quickly, as the LORD has said to you" **(DEUTERONOMY 9:3).**

"Our God shall come, and shall not keep silent; a fire shall devour before Him, and it shall be very tempestuous all around Him" **(PSALM 50:3).**

"A fire goes before Him, and burns up His enemies round about" **(PSALM 97:3).**

"Behold, the LORD will come with fire and with His chariots, like a whirlwind, to render His anger with fury, and His rebuke with flames of fire" **(ISAIAH 66:15).**

"I watched till thrones were put in place, and the Ancient of Days was seated; His garment was white as snow, and the hair of His head was like pure wool. His throne was a fiery flame, its wheels a burning fire" **(DANIEL 7:9).**

"It is a righteous thing with God to repay with tribulation those who trouble you, and to give you who are troubled rest with us when the Lord Jesus is revealed from heaven with His mighty angels, in flaming fire taking vengeance on those who do not know God, and on those who do not obey the gospel of our Lord Jesus Christ" **(2 THESSALONIANS 1:6–8).**

Since our God is a consuming fire, the fires of hell that destroy the wicked originate in His righteous character. God is a consuming fire to sin. When a sinner clings to his sin, God becomes a consuming fire to him.

03 Where do both the righteous and wicked ultimately receive their final reward?

"Blessed are the meek, for they shall inherit *the earth*" **(MATTHEW 5:5; EMPHASIS SUPPLIED).**

"If the righteous will be recompensed on the earth, how much more the ungodly and the sinner" **(PROVERBS 11:31).**

"Who is the man that fears the LORD? . . . He himself shall dwell in prosperity, and his descendants shall inherit the earth" **(PSALM 25:12, 13).**

"Evildoers shall be cut off; but those who wait on the LORD, they shall inherit the earth. . . . But the meek shall inherit the earth, and shall delight themselves in the abundance of peace. . . . Those blessed by Him shall inherit the earth, but those cursed by Him shall be cut off. . . . The righteous shall inherit the land, and dwell in it forever. . . . Wait on the LORD, and keep His way, and He shall exalt you to inherit the land; when the wicked are cut off, you shall see it" **(PSALM 37:9, 11, 22, 29, 34).**

"Your people shall all be righteous; they shall inherit the land forever, the branch of My planting, the work of My hands, that I may be glorified" **(ISAIAH 60:21).**

"If you are Christ's, then you are Abraham's seed, and heirs according to the promise" **(GALATIANS 3:29).**

The Divine Judge pronounces the doom of the devil: "Thou hast defiled thy sanctuaries by the multitude of thine iniquities, by the iniquity of thy traffick; therefore will I bring forth a fire from the midst of thee, it shall devour thee, and I will bring thee to ashes upon the earth in the sight of all them that behold thee" **(EZEKIEL 28:18, KJV).**

"They [the armies of the resurrected wicked] went up on the breadth of the earth and surrounded the camp of the saints and the beloved city. And fire came down from God out of heaven and devoured them" **(REVELATION 20:9).**

"The day of the Lord will come as a thief in the night, in which the heavens will pass away with a great noise, and the elements will melt with fervent heat; both the earth and the works that are in it will be burned up. Therefore, since all these things will be dissolved, what manner of persons ought you to be in holy conduct and godliness, looking for and hastening the coming of the day of God, because of which the heavens will be dissolved, being on fire, and the elements will melt with fervent heat? Nevertheless we, according to His promise, look for new heavens and a new earth in which righteousness dwells" **(2 PETER 3:10–13).**

04 When do the wicked and the righteous receive their final reward? Is hell a hot spot burning in the center of the earth now with the devil in charge?

"For if God did not spare the angels who sinned, but cast them down to hell and delivered them into chains of darkness, *to be reserved for judgment;* then the Lord knows how to deliver the godly out of temptations and *to reserve* the unjust under punishment for the day of judgment" **(2 PETER 2:4, 9; EMPHASIS SUPPLIED).**

"The wicked are reserved for the day of doom; they shall be brought out on the day of wrath" **(JOB 21:30).**

"The LORD will take vengeance on His adversaries, and He reserves wrath for His enemies" **(NAHUM 1:2).**

"The angels who did not keep their proper domain, but left their own abode, He has reserved in everlasting chains under darkness for the judgment of the great day . . . wandering stars for whom is reserved the blackness of darkness forever" **(JUDE 6, 13).**

"The heavens and the earth which are now preserved by the same word, are reserved for fire until the day of judgment and perdition of ungodly men" **(2 PETER 3:7).**

"In accordance with your hardness and your impenitent heart you are treasuring up for yourself wrath in the day of wrath and revelation of the righteous judgment of God" **(ROMANS 2:5).**

There *is* a heaven to win and a hell to shun. The fires of hell will be real, literal, and very hot! There will be excruciating *physical pain* and unbearable *mental anguish* from realizing what one has lost. But here's the point we must grasp: Hell is not burning *now*! The theme running through the verses quoted above is that punishment and rewards are *reserved* for that great day in the future. Not even the devils are burning now. If Satan and his devils were confined to a place of burning now, who'd carry on their evil work? The punishment of Satan and his demons is reserved till the judgment, and redeemed saints will even take part in that trial. The apostle Paul says, "Do you not know that we shall judge angels [fallen angels like Lucifer]?" **(1 CORINTHIANS 6:3).**

Evidently, the devils themselves understand that their punishment is reserved for some future time because when Jesus met two demon-possessed men, the devils "cried out, saying, 'What have we to do with You, Jesus, You Son of God? Have You come here to torment us before the time?' " **(MATTHEW 8:29).**

Furthermore, Jesus plainly taught in **MATTHEW 5:30, NIV,** that a sinner goes into hell not as a mere spirit, but bodily. The Savior said, "If your right hand causes you to stumble, cut it off and throw it away. It is better for you to lose one part of your body than for your whole body to go into hell." But a dead person's body is in the grave and will remain there till the resurrection. Therefore hell cannot be burning now. The fact is, *hell hasn't happened yet.*

05 How complete is God's final destruction of the wicked? Do the unsaved burn for millions of years without end? If they do, how does this harmonize with God's loving character?

" 'Behold, the day is coming, burning like an oven, and all the proud, yes, all who do wickedly will be stubble. And the day which is coming shall *burn them up*,' says the LORD of hosts, 'That will leave them *neither root nor branch*. But to you who fear My name the Sun of Righteousness [Jesus Christ] shall arise with healing in His wings; and you shall go out and grow fat like stall-fed calves. You shall trample the wicked, for they shall be *ashes* under the soles of your feet on the day that I do this,' says the LORD of hosts" **(MALACHI 4:1–3; EMPHASIS SUPPLIED).**

Several statements in this scripture should be noticed: (1) "Stubble" is the short stubs or stumps of grain, left after the harvest, which burns very fast. (2) When the Bible says that the day of God's judgment on the wicked will not just "burn them" but will "burn them up," it means total destruction by flames. (3) Satan is the "root" of rebellion and evil. His demons and human followers are the "branches." (4) Our God, "the Lord of hosts" Himself, says that "the wicked . . . shall be ashes"—denoting complete annihilation, *not* eternal torment.

"For yet a little while and the wicked shall be no more; indeed, you will look carefully for his place, but it shall be no more" **(PSALM 37:10).**

Here, again, the destruction to come is described as being complete as can be imagined: "The wicked shall be no more." When the flames of hell finally go out, God will have a clean universe. The wicked shall have "no more" a "place" in it. They shall, in fact, cease to exist.

Do we realize "that the triumphing of the wicked is short, and the joy of the hypocrite is but for a moment? Though his haughtiness mounts up to the heavens, and his head reaches to the clouds, yet *he will perish forever* like his own refuse; those who have seen him will say, 'Where is he?' He will fly away like a dream, and *not be found;* yes, he will be chased away like a vision of the night. *The eye that saw him will see him no more, nor will his place behold him anymore*" **(JOB 20:5–9; EMPHASIS SUPPLIED).**

"When the whirlwind passes by, the wicked is no more, but the righteous has an everlasting foundation" **(PROVERBS 10:25).**

"Behold, they shall be as stubble, the fire shall burn them; they shall not deliver themselves from the power of the flame; it shall not be a coal to be warmed by, nor a fire to sit before!" **(ISAIAH 47:14).**

Yes, indeed, "the fire shall burn them; they shall not deliver themselves from the power of the flame." But when the fires of hell finally die down and eventually go out, the cleansing conflagration will be forever over. There "shall not be a coal to be warmed by, nor a fire to sit before!"

"The wicked shall perish; and the enemies of the LORD, like the splendor of the meadows, shall vanish. Into smoke they shall vanish away" **(PSALM 37:20).**

"The destruction of transgressors and of sinners shall be together, and those who forsake the LORD shall be consumed. . . . The strong shall be as tinder, and the work of it as a spark; both will burn together, and no one shall quench them" **(ISAIAH 1:28, 31).**

"The transgressors shall be destroyed together; the future of the wicked shall be cut off" **(PSALM 37:38).**

God's Word makes it plain that the fate of the wicked is "destruction"—*not* eternal torment—for "the wicked shall *perish* . . . shall *vanish away* . . . shall be *consumed*." But notice also that the punishment of all "the wicked . . . of transgressors and of sinners shall be together"—*not* one by one as they individually happen to die, for hell is not burning now.

Furthermore, the concept of endless burning is inconsistent with the teaching of Jesus. In the most familiar verse in all the Bible, **JOHN 3:16**, Jesus said that whoever believes in Him will "have everlasting life" and whoever does not believe in Him will "perish." The word *perish*—a correct translation of the Greek—means "to cease to exist" and describes an *end* to the punishment rather than eternal torment.

Dr. Richard Weymouth, the first to translate the New Testament into modern English and esteemed as the most accomplished Greek scholar of his day, strongly declared, "My mind fails to conceive a grosser *misrepresentation* of language than when five or six of the strongest words which the Greek tongue possesses, signifying *to destroy* or *destruction*, are translated to mean 'maintaining an everlasting but wretched existence.' To translate *black* as *white* is nothing compared to this" (Richard Francis Weymouth, quoted in Edward White, *Life in Christ,* 3rd ed., revised and enlarged, 1878, p. 365).

06 What terms or expressions does the Bible use to describe the destruction of the wicked? What do these expressions mean?

Jesus said of the wicked, "these will go away into *everlasting punishment,* but the righteous into eternal life" **(MATTHEW 25:46; EMPHASIS SUPPLIED).**

Do the Master's words, "everlasting punishment," contradict Scripture's clear and consistent teaching on the punishment of the wicked? Absolutely not, as careful study will now show.

The Bible uses such phrases as "eternal," "everlasting," and "forever and ever" in connection with the fate of the wicked. These expressions show that the overthrow of the wicked is a complete overthrow, that there will never be any hope of recovery from their fate, for it is eternal. Their *torment* is not eternal. Their *grief* and *anguish* are not eternal. But their *destruction* is eternal. **PSALM 92:7, KJV**, declares that "the wicked

. . . shall be destroyed for ever." And because the sinner's destruction is so complete, God says the wicked "shall be as though they had never been" **(OBADIAH 16)**.

In **2 THESSALONIANS 1:9**, the apostle Paul explicitly points out this complete annihilation of the wicked by saying that they "shall be punished with everlasting destruction." This agrees with what Jesus said: "These will go away into everlasting punishment" **(MATTHEW 25:46)**. However, note carefully that "everlasting punish*ment*" is not endless punish*ing.*

The apostle Paul spoke of "the enemies of the cross of Christ: whose end is destruction"—*not* eternal burning **(PHILIPPIANS 3:18, 19)**.

"Enter by the narrow gate; for wide is the gate and broad is the way that leads to destruction, and there are many who go in by it. Because narrow is the gate and difficult is the way which leads to life, and there are few who find it" **(MATTHEW 7:13, 14)**.

In this memorable passage from Jesus' own lips, the Master speaks of the "broad" and "narrow" ways and contrasts "life" with "destruction"—*not* with eternal burning.

Jesus said, "The hour is coming in which all who are in the graves will hear His voice and come forth—those who have done good, to the resurrection of life, and those who have done evil, to the resurrection of condemnation" **(JOHN 5:28, 29)**.

"Those who sleep in the dust of the earth shall awake, some to everlasting life, some to shame and everlasting contempt" **(DANIEL 12:2)**.

"But the cowardly, unbelieving, abominable, murderers, sexually immoral, sorcerers, idolaters, and all liars shall have their part in the lake which burns with fire and brimstone, which is the second death" **(REVELATION 21:8)**.

The destruction of the wicked is everlasting. Sinners do not remain alive in the fires of hell forever. God, in one act, destroys them forever. This destruction never needs to be repeated. An everlasting punishment is not an everlasting punishing. An everlasting punishment completely destroys. The wicked are not in a state of everlasting "punishing."

07 How does the Bible explain the meaning of its own terms—"everlasting punishment" and "eternal fire"?

"Sodom and Gomorrah, and the cities around them in a similar manner to these, having given themselves over to sexual immorality and gone after strange flesh, are set forth as an example, suffering the vengeance of eternal fire" **(JUDE 7)**.

The Word of God says that the punishment of the wicked in Sodom and Gomorrah is "set forth as an example"—a biblical example—of what the punishment of the wicked of all time will be. It explicitly says that those wicked people and those wicked cities suffered "the vengeance of eternal fire." But are Sodom and Gomorrah burning today, burning forever? Of course not! That "eternal fire" did its work of everlasting destruction and went out thousands of years ago—two thousand years, in fact, before Jude was inspired to write this verse in the first century A.D.!

"The sinners in Zion are afraid; fearfulness has seized the hypocrites: Who among us shall dwell with the devouring fire? Who among us shall dwell with everlasting burnings?" **(ISAIAH 33:14).**

"Then He will also say to those on the left hand, 'Depart from Me, you cursed, into the everlasting fire prepared for the devil and his angels' " **(MATTHEW 25:41).**

This fire, it should be noticed, was never intended for men and women created by the God of love. Jesus says it is "prepared for the devil and his angels." Also, the words *everlasting* and *eternal* are interchangeable, and come from the very same Greek word. In fact, **MATTHEW 25:46** contains both words, each translated from the same original Greek word, *aeonian.* Christ's expression, "everlasting fire," is synonymous with Jude's expression, "eternal fire"—which we know did not burn forever.

Note what Dr. William Temple, the late archbishop of Canterbury, primate of Great Britain, says about this everlasting (*aeonian*) fire: "One thing we can say with confidence: everlasting torment is to be *ruled out*. If men had not imported the Greek and unbiblical notion [from Plato], of the natural indestruction of the individual soul, and then read the New Testament with that already in their minds, they would have drawn from it a belief, not in everlasting torment, but in annihilation. It is the *fire* that is called *aeonian,* not the life cast into it" (*Christian Faith and Life,* 1954, p. 81).

Dr. Temple wrote further: "Are there not, however, many passages which speak of the endless torment of the lost? No; as far as my knowledge goes there is none at all. . . . After all, annihilation *is* an everlasting punishment though it is not unending torment" (*Nature, God, and Man,* 1953, p. 464).

Sodom and Gomorrah are not burning now! In fact, they were completely destroyed and, some believe, are under the Dead Sea. The eternal fire of the Bible is one that destroys so completely that it fully consumes.

08 How complete was the destruction of Sodom and Gomorrah by Heaven's eternal fire?

The Lord turned "the cities of Sodom and Gomorrah into ashes, condemned them to destruction, making them an example to those who afterward would live ungodly" **(2 PETER 2:6).**

God, through the apostle Peter, corroborates what we have been saying when he speaks of Sodom and Gomorrah being turned into *ashes,* implying utter and complete destruction.

And, evidently, *it does not take long f*or "eternal fire" to reduce whatever it attacks to mere "ashes," for Jesus said that "the same day that Lot went out of Sodom it rained fire and brimstone from heaven, and destroyed them all" **(LUKE 17:29, KJV).** Then Jeremiah tells us that "Sodom . . . was overthrown in a moment" **(LAMENTATIONS 4:6).** Evidently, that wicked city did not have to burn on and on and on. Here again, "eternal" means an everlasting *result,* not an endless *process.*

"The LORD rained brimstone and fire on Sodom and Gomorrah, from the LORD out of the heavens. So He overthrew those cities, all the plain, all the inhabitants of the cities, and what grew on the ground. . . . Then he [Abraham] looked toward Sodom and Gomorrah, and toward all the land of the plain; and he saw, and behold, the smoke of the land which went up like the smoke of a furnace" **(GENESIS 19:24, 25, 28).**

" 'As God overthrew Sodom and Gomorrah and their neighbors,' says the LORD, 'so no one shall reside there [in Babylon], nor son of man dwell in it' " **(JEREMIAH 50:40).**

" 'Therefore, as I live,' says the LORD of hosts, the God of Israel, 'surely Moab shall be like Sodom, and the people of Ammon like Gomorrah—overrun with weeds and saltpits, and a perpetual desolation. The residue of My people shall plunder them, and the remnant of My people shall possess them' " **(ZEPHANIAH 2:9).**

"All these things happened to them as examples, and they were written for our admonition, upon whom the ends of the ages have come" **(1 CORINTHIANS 10:11).**

As Sodom and Gomorrah were turned to ashes and destroyed forever, the wicked will be completely destroyed, never to live again.

09 How do the Old Testament prophets describe the destruction of Jerusalem by fire? What expressions do they use to picture complete destruction?

" 'But if you will not heed Me to hallow the Sabbath day, such as not carrying a burden when entering the gates of Jerusalem on the Sabbath day, then I will kindle a fire in its gates, and it shall devour the palaces of Jerusalem, and it shall not be quenched' " **(JEREMIAH 17:27).**

Another adjective the Bible uses to describe hellfire is "unquenchable." Jesus warns in **MARK 9:43–45** that the fire which punishes the wicked "shall never be quenched." Is that true? Will hellfire never be quenched? You'd better believe it! But let's understand what that means. To *quench* a fire means to *put it out.* A fire that shall never be quenched is *not* one that shall never *go* out, but one that cannot be *put* out. In 1871, the Great Chicago Fire destroyed that city. If we describe that fire by saying that the flames could not be quenched, would you conclude that Chicago was still burning? No, you'd simply understand that the fire couldn't be put out and raged till it devoured everything within reach—and then died out.

The verse above says Jerusalem would be burned with a fire that could "not be quenched." The literal fulfillment of this prophecy came when the Babylonians put the torch to Jerusalem **(SEE 2 CHRONICLES 36:19–21).** But is that fire still burning? Are those Jewish palaces ever burning, yet never quite consumed? No, but this unquenchable fire brought Jerusalem to destruction and ashes, just as hellfire will bring the wicked to destruction and ashes. The fire that destroys the wicked must of necessity be unquenchable; if it weren't, the wicked would put it out.

Some believe that **MARK 9:43–48** proves the truth of the doctrine of eternal torment, for there Jesus warns the wicked against being cast into hell, "where 'their worm does not die and the fire is not quenched.' " The last part of this text poses no problem, since we've just seen what "unquenchable fire" means. So let's focus on the first part, which says, "Their worm does not die."

First, we need to understand that "their worm" does not refer to a soul, but rather to a maggot, feeding upon a dead body—not inhabiting a living one. Jesus' words echo those of the prophet Isaiah, who says the redeemed "shall go forth and look upon the corpses of the men who have transgressed against Me. For their worm does not die, and their fire is not quenched" **(ISAIAH 66:24).** Again, the picture is one of maggots preying on dead bodies.

The worm—a gnawing, carrion-eating destroyer—causes no suffering to the insensible carcass, but simply hastens the disappearance of dead bodies. The worm and the fire together, as agents of destruction, actually indicate the utter impossibility of this text referring to eternal life in torment. This awesome warning stands for dissolution, disintegration, and final disappearance. So this text does *not* support the theory of eternal, conscious suffering of the living damned. The work of the "worm" and the "fire" is eternal in *results,* but not in process or duration.

In this text, Jesus is unmistakably alluding to the ghastly scenes of the ancient Valley of Hinnom, a ravine south of Jerusalem, just outside the city wall. It was a place of fire and destruction used as a vast refuse pit. All that was worthless was cast into the Gehenna fires—refuse, animal carcasses, even the corpses of criminals so wicked as to be judged unworthy of burial. Here fires were kept burning to consume the corruption, and worms preyed upon the putrefying flesh. Whatever the fire failed to consume along the outer edges of the pit, the worms would devour.

The "Valley of Hinnom" in Hebrew is *Ge Hinnom*, which the Greek transliterates into *Gehenna*, the term for "hell" that Christ used here. Jesus, the Master Teacher, knew His listeners were familiar with this place where refuse was burned up, having seen it with their own eyes. So in using *Gehenna* to designate the final fires of God's destructive judgments, He achieved instant communication.

But in so doing, He offered no support to the doctrine of eternal torment. For the ancient fire of Gehenna was not a fire into which living persons were cast, to be kept alive under torture, but one into which corpses were cast to be consumed. Any part remaining unburned was devoured by worms, so nothing was left. Bible scholar Dr. Richard Weymouth tells us: "*Gehenna of Fire* Or 'Hell.' The severest punishment inflicted by the Jews upon any criminal. The corpse (after the man had been stoned to death) was thrown out into the Valley of Hinnom (*Ge Hinnom*) and was devoured by the worm or the flame" (*The New Testament in Modern Speech,* 3rd ed., 1902, Matthew 5:22, note 12).

As a place of burning, especially for the punishment of the wicked, *Gehenna* fits our idea of hell—except that *Gehenna* is not presently burning, but simply symbolizes the coming "lake of fire" mentioned in Revelation. Instead of supporting the theory of the eternal torment of the damned, Christ again portrayed the doom of the wicked as destruction. The "worm," like the "unquenchable fire," is a symbol of death and destruction.

"Therefore thus says the Lord GOD: 'Behold, My anger and My fury will be poured out on this place—on man and on beast, on the trees of the field and on the fruit of the ground. And it will burn and not be quenched' " **(JEREMIAH 7:20).**

God warned, "Because they have forsaken Me and burned incense to other gods, that they might provoke Me to anger with all the works of their hands. Therefore My wrath shall be aroused against this place and shall not be quenched" **(2 KINGS 22:17).**

"The destruction of transgressors and of sinners shall be together, and those who forsake the LORD shall be consumed. . . . The strong shall be as tinder, and the work of it as a spark; both will burn together, and no one shall quench them" **(ISAIAH 1:28, 31).**

"Say to the forest of the South, 'Hear the word of the LORD! Thus says the Lord GOD: "Behold, I will kindle a fire in you, and it shall devour every green tree and every dry tree in you; the blazing flame shall not be quenched, and all faces from the south to the north shall be scorched by it" ' " **(EZEKIEL 20:47).**

"They [the armies of the resurrected wicked] went up on the breadth of the earth and surrounded the camp of the saints and the beloved city [New Jerusalem]. And fire came down from God out of heaven and devoured them" **(REVELATION 20:9).**

Devoured is a strong word. When a child devours his or her meal there is nothing left.

Jerusalem was destroyed by an unquenchable fire that human hands could not put out. It totally destroyed Jerusalem. It was unquenchable, yet Jerusalem is not burning today. An unquenchable fire is one that totally destroys. It devours. It consumes. It leaves nothing. It burns up everything in its path.

10 How does the Bible use the word *forever* in relationship to the destruction of the wicked? What happens to the wicked who are consumed in the fires of hell?

"The devil, who deceived them, was cast into the lake of fire and brimstone where the beast and the false prophet are. And they will be tormented day and night forever and ever. . . . And anyone not found written in the Book of Life was cast into the lake of fire" **(REVELATION 20:10, 15).**

Let's consider the word *forever.* We've just read that the wicked will be "tormented day and night for ever and ever." What's the explanation? How do we know from that very chapter of **REVELATION 20** that "for ever and ever" in **VERSE 10** does not mean "without end"? Because **VERSE 9** says, "And fire . . . devoured them," and because **VERSE 14** says, "The lake of fire . . . is the second *death*" **(EMPHASIS SUPPLIED).** The Bible never contradicts itself. It consistently describes the end of the wicked as ultimate destruction. For instance, **PSALM 21:9** says of God's enemies that "the fire shall devour them" **(KJV).** Or "consume them" **(RSV, NRSV, NIV).** Both expressions are as powerful a statement as one can use to signify complete destruction or annihilation.

Now, in regard to the word *forever*, English readers must remember that the Hebrew, *olam,* and the Greek, *aionios,* both translated "forever" in the Bible, are idioms which don't always mean what we think they mean. So let's ask the Bible itself what it means by "forever." Let's apply the acid test of usage to find the Bible meaning of this word.

- **EXODUS 21:6** describes the custom to be followed if a man was willing to be the slave of another man for the rest of his life. "His master shall pierce his ear with an awl; and he shall serve him forever." But how long is "forever" in this case? Another translation says, "for the rest of his life." That's as long as he could serve him, of course. But the text says, "forever"! "Forever," in this case, simply means *as long as he lives.*

- And what about Samuel? His mother dedicated him to the Lord. She was barren of children, so she promised that if the Lord would give her a son, she'd let him serve God all his life. As soon as the boy was weaned, she brought him to the temple, "that he may appear before the LORD and remain there forever" **(1 SAMUEL 1:22).** How could that be? The context itself explains: "*As long as he lives* he shall be lent to the LORD" **(VERSE 28, EMPHASIS SUPPLIED).** After all, Samuel could serve the Lord only as long as he lived. Here again, the word *forever* means for the rest of a man's life.

- Paul, writing to Philemon regarding the return of his runaway servant Onesimus, told Philemon to "receive him forever" **(PHILEMON 15).** What does that mean? Obviously, Philemon could receive Onesimus back only as long as either of them lived. So "forever" here means "as long as life

> lasts." Commenting on this verse, the scholarly reference, *The Cambridge Bible for Schools and Colleges,* says that *forever* in biblical usage "tends to mark duration as long as the nature of the subject allows."

Thus the time involved in "forever" depends upon the subject to which the word *forever,* or *everlasting,* is applied. When used to describe God or the gift of life that God gives, it naturally means "without an end, eternal." Applied to something transitory, such as mortal man, it means a relatively short period of time—the lifetime of that person. Please remember these simple words of Scripture: "He who has the Son has life; he who does not have the Son of God does not have life" **(1 JOHN 5:12).** For example, "No murderer has eternal life abiding in him" **(1 JOHN 3:15).** Could God make it plainer than that?

We often use the word *forever* in the same way ourselves. For instance, when we receive a gift or award, we often say, "I'll treasure it forever!" What does this really mean? It menas "as long as I live." This idea of "forever" meaning a period of time limited in duration by the subject to which it applies is reflected in some of our other English usage.

At least fifty-six times the Bible uses the word *forever* for things that have already come to an end! A Catholic professor at St. Ambrose College explains: "As for the frequently used word *eternal,* its meaning is often the same as that in many secular writings—a period of long duration, not necessarily time without end" (Father Joseph E. Kokjohn, "A HELL of a Question," *Commonweal,* January 15, 1971, p. 368). The familiar expression "forever and ever" means literally "to the ages of the ages" and is an idiomatic expression meaning "to the end of the age," "to the end of life," or "to the end of any particular experience." And that's exactly how it's used in the Bible.

Speaking of the fate of those who worship the beast power and receive his mark, **REVELATION 14:11** says, "The smoke of their torment ascends forever and ever; and they have no rest day or night." It's true that no night's rest will interrupt the suffering of the wicked: it will continue until they're annihilated. But those who claim that this passage teaches eternal torment overlook the fact that it does *not* say their torment will continue forever—rather, it is the "smoke" of their torment that drifts on endlessly.

PSALM 37:20 says of the wicked: "Into smoke they shall vanish away." That this is not endless burning is evident from the fact that the same expression is used concerning mystical "Babylon," called "the great harlot." The Bible says, "Her smoke rises up forever and ever!" **(REVELATION 17:1, 5, 18; 19:3).**

This means complete and total destruction, for God says, "She will be utterly burned with fire . . . and shall not be found anymore" **(REVELATION 18:8, 21).**

Bible scholars know that this phrase about smoke rising up forever and ever is derived from **ISAIAH 34:10.** The context in **ISAIAH 34** disproves any contention about endless burning. Isaiah predicted that "the sword of the Lord" would fall upon the idolatrous city of Bozrah, twenty miles southeast of the Dead Sea. God's curse on Bozrah says, "Its land shall become burning pitch. It shall not be quenched night or day; its smoke shall ascend forever. From generation to generation it shall lie waste; . . . the pelican and the porcupine shall possess it. . . . And thorns shall come up in its palaces, nettles and brambles in its fortresses. . . . The wild beasts of the desert shall also meet with the jackals . . . there" **(ISAIAH 34:6, 9–14).**

Thus God's Word in Isaiah proves that fire, which makes smoke ascend "forever and ever," does not burn forever. If it did, how could thorns, nettles, and brambles grow up and wild animals take possession of Bozrah?

God repeats that city's fate: " 'I have sworn by Myself,' says the LORD, 'that Bozrah shall become a desolation, a reproach, a waste, and a curse. And all its cities shall be perpetual wastes' " **(JEREMIAH 49:13).** This same destiny befalls the wicked: when they're burned up as Bozrah was, their complete annihilation will last through all eternity.

"The cowardly, unbelieving, abominable, murderers, sexually immoral, sorcerers, idolaters, and all liars shall have their part in the lake which burns with fire and brimstone, which is the second death" **(REVELATION 21:8).**

Christ will come as a mighty Conqueror, "in flaming fire taking vengeance on those who do not know God, and on those who do not obey the gospel of our Lord Jesus Christ. These shall be punished with everlasting destruction from the presence of the Lord and from the glory of His power" **(2 THESSALONIANS 1:8, 9).**

Some Christians misunderstand the expression "forever and ever" in **REVELATION 20:10.** In the Bible the expression "forever and ever" does not mean endless existence; it literally means until the end of the age or the end of a given period of time. Here are some biblical examples of "forever": The slave was to serve his master "forever" **(EXODUS 21:6)** or as long as he lived. Samuel was to serve in the temple forever **(1 SAMUEL 1:22, 28)** or as long as he lived. Jonah was in the belly of the whale forever **(JONAH 2:6).** The Bible does not contradict itself. The wicked are consumed or totally devoured. They exist in the flames as long as they can live. A new age dawns when suffering and sorrow are no more.

11 If hell literally burned forever, someplace in the universe, could there ever be true happiness anywhere? How does the Bible picture the ultimate state of the earth and the joy of the redeemed?

"Nevertheless we, according to His promise, look for new heavens and a new earth in which righteousness dwells" **(2 PETER 3:13).**

This old world, so corrupt, so infected with the sickness of sin, so polluted by weeds and disease and death, will be completely cleansed by fire and made over anew.

"The day of the Lord will come as a thief in the night, in which the heavens will pass away with a great noise, and the elements will melt with fervent heat; both the earth and the works that are in it will be burned up. Therefore, since all these things will be dissolved, what manner of persons ought you to be in holy conduct and godliness, looking for and hastening the coming of the day of God, because of which the heavens will be dissolved, being on fire, and the elements will melt with fervent heat?" **(2 PETER 3:10–12).**

"The earth melted" **(PSALM 46:6).**

"The mountains melt like wax at the presence of the LORD, at the presence of the Lord of the whole earth" **(PSALM 97:5).**

"The Lord GOD of hosts, He who touches the earth and it melts" **(AMOS 9:5).**

"The mountains quake before Him, the hills melt, and the earth heaves at His presence, yes, the world and all who dwell in it" **(NAHUM 1:5).**

"The earth and all its inhabitants are dissolved" **(PSALM 75:3).**

"Behold, the LORD is coming out of His place; He will come down and tread on the high places of the earth. The mountains will melt under Him, and the valleys will split like wax before the fire, like waters poured down a steep place" **(MICAH 1:3, 4).**

"Behold, I create new heavens and a new earth; and the former shall not be remembered or come to mind" **(ISAIAH 65:17).**

" 'As the new heavens and the new earth which I will make shall remain before Me,' says the LORD, 'so shall your descendants and your name remain' " **(ISAIAH 66:22).**

"Now I saw a new heaven and a new earth, for the first heaven and the first earth had passed away. Also there was no more sea. . . . Then He who sat on the throne said, 'Behold, I make all things new.' And He said to me, 'Write, for these words are true and faithful' " **(REVELATION 21:1, 5).**

12 Will the flames of hell consume this planet forever? What will God finally do with sorrow, suffering, and pain?

"God will wipe away every tear from their eyes; there shall be no more death, nor sorrow, nor crying. There shall be no more pain, for the former things have passed away" **(REVELATION 21:4, 5).**

"The Lamb [Jesus] who is in the midst of the throne will shepherd them and lead them to living fountains of waters. And God will wipe away every tear from their eyes" **(REVELATION 7:17).**

"He will swallow up death forever, and the Lord GOD will wipe away tears from all faces; the rebuke of His people He will take away from all the earth; for the LORD has spoken" **(ISAIAH 25:8).**

"Then Death and Hades [the grave] were cast into the lake of fire. This is the second death" **(REVELATION 20:14).**

We are promised that "the last enemy that will be destroyed is death" **(1 CORINTHIANS 15:26)**.

"So when this corruptible has put on incorruption, and this mortal has put on immortality, then shall be brought to pass the saying that is written: 'Death is swallowed up in victory.' 'O Death, where is your sting? O Hades [grave], where is your victory?' " **(1 CORINTHIANS 15:54, 55)**.

"And the ransomed of the LORD shall return, and come to Zion with singing, with everlasting joy on their heads. They shall obtain joy and gladness, and sorrow and sighing shall flee away" **(ISAIAH 35:10)**.

"Your sun shall no longer go down, nor shall your moon withdraw itself; for the LORD will be your everlasting light, and the days of your mourning shall be ended" **(ISAIAH 60:20)**.

God longs "to console those who mourn in Zion, to give them beauty for ashes, the oil of joy for mourning, the garment of praise for the spirit of heaviness" **(ISAIAH 61:3)**.

"Behold, I create new heavens and a new earth; and the former shall not be remembered or come to mind. But be glad and rejoice forever in what I create; for behold, I create Jerusalem as a rejoicing, and her people a joy. I will rejoice in Jerusalem, and joy in My people; the voice of weeping shall no longer be heard in her, nor the voice of crying" **(ISAIAH 65:17–19)**.

David declared with assurance in his prayer to God: "In Your presence is fullness of joy; at Your right hand are pleasures forevermore" **(PSALM 16:11)**.

13 Will this great controversy between sin and righteousness, good and evil, ever be repeated?

"What do you conspire against the LORD? He will make an utter end of it. Affliction will not rise up a second time" **(NAHUM 1:9)**.

The "affliction" of sin will never again trouble God's universe. Never again will evil arise, for the whole creation will have witnessed the terrible nature and results of sin.

14 What is the final fate of Satan and his followers? What is God's attitude toward the destruction of the wicked?

"They shall drink, and swallow, and they shall be as though they had never been" **(OBADIAH 16)**.

"Behold, they shall be as stubble, the fire shall burn them; they shall not deliver themselves from the power of the flame; it shall not be a coal to be warmed by, nor a fire to sit before!" **(ISAIAH 47:14).**

God says of Lucifer/Satan: "Thine heart was lifted up because of thy beauty, thou hast corrupted thy wisdom by reason of thy brightness: I will cast thee to the ground, I will lay thee before kings, that they may behold thee. Thou hast defiled thy sanctuaries by the multitude of thine iniquities, by the iniquity of thy traffick; therefore will I bring forth a fire from the midst of thee, it shall devour thee, and I will bring thee to ashes upon the earth in the sight of all them that behold thee" **(EZEKIEL 28:17, 18, KJV).**

" 'Behold, the day is coming, burning like an oven, and all the proud, yes, all who do wickedly will be stubble. And the day which is coming shall burn them up,' says the LORD of hosts, 'that will leave them neither root nor branch. . . . You shall trample the wicked, for they shall be ashes under the soles of your feet on the day that I do this,' says the LORD of hosts" **(MALACHI 4:1, 3).**

"Then the beast was captured, and with him the false prophet who worked signs in his presence, by which he deceived those who received the mark of the beast and those who worshiped his image. These two were cast alive into the lake of fire burning with brimstone" **(REVELATION 19:20).**

"The devil, who deceived them, was cast into the lake of fire and brimstone where the beast and the false prophet are. And they will be tormented day and night forever and ever" **(REVELATION 20:10).**

In deep anguish, the Lord of love cries out, " 'I have no pleasure in the death of one who dies,' says the Lord GOD. 'Therefore turn and live!' " **(EZEKIEL 18:32).**

" 'Do I have any pleasure at all that the wicked should die?' says the Lord GOD, 'and not that he should turn from his ways and live?' " **(EZEKIEL 18:23).**

" 'As I live,' says the Lord GOD, 'I have no pleasure in the death of the wicked, but that the wicked turn from his way and live. Turn, turn from your evil ways! For why should you die, O house of Israel?' " **(EZEKIEL 33:11).**

" 'Therefore I will judge you, O house of Israel, every one according to his ways,' says the Lord GOD. 'Repent, and turn from all your transgressions, so that iniquity will not be your ruin. Cast away from you all the transgressions which you have committed, and get yourselves a new heart and a new spirit. For why should you die, O house of Israel?' " **(EZEKIEL 18:30, 31).**

"For He does not afflict willingly, nor grieve the children of men" **(LAMENTATIONS 3:33).**

"The Lord is not slack concerning His promise, as some count slackness, but is longsuffering toward us, not willing that any should perish but that all should come to repentance" **(2 PETER 3:9).**

God "desires all men to be saved and to come to the knowledge of the truth" **(1 TIMOTHY 2:4).**

The God we serve is a God of mercy and justice. "The LORD, the LORD God, merciful and gracious, longsuffering, and abounding in goodness and truth, keeping mercy for thousands, forgiving iniquity and transgression and sin, by no means clearing the guilty, visiting the iniquity of the fathers upon the children and the children's children to the third and the fourth generation" **(EXODUS 34:6, 7).**

"Who is a God like You, pardoning iniquity and passing over the transgression of the remnant of His heritage? He does not retain His anger forever, because He delights in mercy" **(MICAH 7:18).**

"But he who sins against me [wisdom, personified as an attribute of God] wrongs his own soul; all those who hate me love death" **(PROVERBS 8:36).**

"Seek the LORD while He may be found, call upon Him while He is near. Let the wicked forsake his way, and the unrighteous man his thoughts; let him return to the LORD, and He will have mercy on him; and to our God, for He will abundantly pardon" **(ISAIAH 55:6, 7).**

"Repent therefore and be converted, that your sins may be blotted out, so that times of refreshing may come from the presence of the Lord" **(ACTS 3:19).**

The apostle Paul "declared first to those in Damascus and in Jerusalem, and throughout all the region of Judea, and then to the Gentiles, that they should repent, turn to God, and do works befitting repentance" **(ACTS 26:20).**

A loving God longs for His children to turn to Him for salvation. He does not want one person to be lost. He reaches out in tender mercy to save you today. The choice is yours! Where will you spend eternity? Every man, woman, and child must decide. There is only one sensible choice. Choose today to spend eternity with Christ, rejoicing in the new earth.

Commonly Asked Questions Regarding the Destruction of the Wicked

Is hell a hot spot burning in the center of the earth now?

According to the Bible, the final destruction of the wicked comes at the end of time. The wicked are reserved unto judgment **(SEE 2 PETER 2:4)**. Our God is a consuming fire to sin wherever it is found **(SEE HEBREWS 12:29)**. The fires of hell originate from heaven at the end of time, not some hot spot in the earth **(SEE REVELATION 20:9)**. The wicked will be totally consumed. They shall be cut off from the earth **(SEE PROVERBS 10:25; PSALM 37:10, 11, 20, 34, 38)**. They shall be consumed to ashes **(SEE MALACHI 4:1, 3)**. This final destruction will occur after the thousand-year millennium **(SEE REVELATION 20:5)** at the resurrection of damnation **(SEE JOHN 5:28, 29)**.

What about texts such as REVELATION 20:10, which declare the wicked will burn forever?

The word *forever* in the Bible can be literally translated "until the end of the age" or "as long as he shall live." The wicked are consumed, burned up, turned to ashes **(SEE MALACHI 4:1, 3)**. The old age of sin and death ends, and God ushers in a new age **(SEE REVELATION 21:1–4)**. God creates a new heavens and new earth with no more crying, death, sickness, or pain. In the Old Testament, a slave was to serve his master forever **(SEE EXODUS 21:6)**. Hannah brought her son Samuel to the temple forever **(SEE 1 SAMUEL 1:22)**. In both these instances, the time period was "as long as they lived." Regarding Hannah's son, **1 SAMUEL 1:28** clearly states, "as long as he lives he shall be lent to the LORD." Jonah even uses the expression "forever" to describe his experience in the belly of the whale **(SEE JONAH 2:6)**. "Forever" was a limited, not an unending, time. It was as long as the Lord decreed, until the end of the age, or as long as Jonah could live in that environment. The punishment of the wicked will be everlasting **(SEE MATTHEW 25:46)**. They will be consumed. Burned to ashes, they will be gone forever. Hell is not everlasting "punishing" or a continued state of torment. The idea of an eternally burning hell would make God a cosmic monster, delighting in destroying His creatures. A loving God must blot sin out of the universe or it will destroy the entire planet. Like a cancer surgeon, He must cut out the disease, however painful.

What about the expression "eternal fire"?

Sodom and Gomorrah, two ancient cities filled with sin, were consumed with fire from heaven. The Bible states that they were burned with an "eternal fire" **(SEE JUDE 7).** They are not burning today. These two cities are in ruins under the Dead Sea. According to **2 PETER 2:6,** they were turned into ashes. An eternal fire is one whose effects are eternal, one which totally consumes forever.

Doesn't the Bible speak about the fire which cannot "be quenched" (MARK 9:43, 48)?

The fire which cannot be quenched is one which no human hands can put out. It utterly, totally consumes. As a result of the Jews' disobedience, Jerusalem was destroyed by Nebuchadnezzar in 586 B.C. The city was burned with an unquenchable fire. You may read the prophecy of this destruction in **JEREMIAH 17:27.** The fire consuming Jerusalem "shall not be quenched." Yet Jerusalem is not burning today. The fire has done a complete work.

What Could Have Been

Did you ever read the sad saga of Gary Gilmore? It is an absolutely amazing story. Gary Gilmore was a murderer. A petty thief at first, imprisoned for eighteen of his final twenty-one years for his brutal crimes. Even when he was out on parole, he murdered a couple of people in the state of Utah. When Gary Gilmore went to death row and was finally executed, he made this statement just before his death: "I don't want to come back and live anymore because mine was a life that was never lived."

The tragedy of the Gary Gilmore story is the tragedy of a life missed out. Eighteen of his final twenty-one years were spent in prison. He never really lived.

And the tragedy of the wicked, the tragedy of men and women who are ultimately lost, devoured in hell's final flames, is that they have never really truly, genuinely lived.

And the Bible says that there is weeping, crying, and gnashing of teeth—a life never lived.

Matthew's Gospel describes it this way: "and will cast them into the furnace of fire. There will be wailing and gnashing of teeth" **(MATTHEW 13:42).** Why? Why this mental agony? Because they know what they could have had; they know that they could have lived, but now they are lost.

"Then the king said to the servants, 'Bind him hand and foot, take him away, and cast him into outer darkness; there will be weeping and gnashing of teeth' " **(MATTHEW 22:13).**

In those final moments when the wicked are totally and completely and absolutely destroyed, they will say, "God, we could have lived. God, You reached out to save us. God, You wanted to redeem us. But oh God, we are lost forever, and ever, to be consumed and burned up."

Christ has made provision to save every human being. Christ walked into the fires of hell. What are the fires of hell? They are God's judgment upon sin. And it was on a cross that Christ was Godforsaken. It was there that Jesus cried out, "My God, why have You forsaken Me?"

There He experienced pain.

There He experienced the suffering.

There He experienced the aloneness.

There He experienced the agony.

There He experienced the condemnation.

There He experienced the wailing and the gnashing of teeth that the lost will experience at the end of time.

And so from that cross, from the One who bears our guilt, from the One who bears our condemnation, from the One who walked into hell itself for us on the cross, from the One who took the fire of hell in His own body, from the One who hung there for us, comes heaven's strongest appeal. Our Lord wants us saved not lost. The prophet Ezekiel echoes this thought in **EZEKIEL 18:23:** " 'Do I have any pleasure at all that the wicked should die?' says the Lord GOD, 'and not that he should turn from his ways and live?' "

What a question!

Before the whole universe, He asks it, "Do I have any pleasure at all that the wicked should die?"

And then He answers it, " 'For I have no pleasure in the death of one who dies,' says the Lord GOD. 'Therefore turn and live!' " **(EZEKIEL 18:32).** He says "I have no pleasure. My fiery presence will consume and burn up sin, at the end of time." Sin will be no more, at the end of time, and there will be a new heavens and a new earth.

But God says, "I have no pleasure in men and women being destroyed." They destroy themselves. They destroy themselves by their choices. They destroy themselves by their decisions. They destroy themselves by turning their backs on Him.

Thank God that He offers us life. Thank God that not one man, not one woman, not one boy nor girl need be lost. You and I do not have to experience what the Bible calls that weeping and gnashing of teeth.

We don't have to experience that agony of being consumed in the flames. We don't have to experience that mental torture of what could have been. We don't have to have a life with a tragic ending, utterly consumed, burnt up and turned to ashes.

We can dance for joy. We can celebrate with gladness. We can rejoice through all eternity. We can live the lives we were meant to live from the beginning with eternal happiness, free from all sickness, sorrow, suffering, and death. There He experienced pain.

CHAPTER 20

What the Bible Says About Baptism

Baptism is one of the most important subjects in the New Testament. It is mentioned over eighty times. Before His ascension to heaven, Jesus commissioned His disciples to "go therefore and make disciples of all the nations, baptizing them in the name of the Father and of the Son and of the Holy Spirit" **(MATTHEW 28:19, 20).** The book of Acts records that the disciples followed their Lord's instructions, and tens of thousands of people were baptized.

The earliest Christian churches on record have baptistries where believers were baptized. It might surprise you to discover that churches like St. Mary's in Ephesus, St. John of Lateran in Rome, and the cathedral at Pisa all had baptistries where adult believers were baptized. It was not until the Catholic Council of Vienne in A.D. 1311 that sprinkling and pouring were officially accepted by the Roman Church as equally valid with baptism by immersion. The New Testament church baptized adult believers who committed their lives to Christ, repented of their sins, and obeyed His Word.

Final words are extremely important. Parting words are usually significant. Picture a family gathered around a hospital bed eagerly trying to catch every word of a dying loved one. Last words make a difference.

Christ's last words were some of the most significant He ever uttered. His final command to His disciples was: "Go into all the world and preach the gospel to every creature" **(MARK 16:15).**

Christ commissioned His disciples to instruct people in the principles of the Christian life. When they accepted the claims of His love and became disciples, the sign of their allegiance to a new life was baptism.

The subject of baptism raises many questions. How important is Bible baptism? Is baptism essential to our salvation? Does it make any difference how a person is baptized? How many kinds of baptism are there? Are sprinkling, pouring, and immersion all the same? This chapter answers these questions directly from the Bible.

01 What importance did Christ place upon baptism? Is baptism a nonessential or is it vital to the Christian life?

Jesus declared: "He who believes and is baptized will be saved; but he who does not believe will be condemned" **(MARK 16:16).**

It should not escape our attention that in these words the Master is specifying not just one, but two important things—*believing* and *being baptized.* It's as if a friend who admires your car asks, "What would I have to give you to trade cars with me?" You know he has a nice car, but one less expensive than yours. So you think it over and finally say, "Give me your car and five thousand dollars, and I'll do it." Notice that you specify two things. If he delivers only the five thousand dollars but not the car (or vice versa), will you make the trade? Of course not, because your friend has failed to fulfill the contract.

Those who try to minimize the importance of baptism often overlook the implications of Jesus' words. Theoretically, circumstances beyond one's control may sometimes prevent someone from being baptized. The thief on the cross comes to mind. But from a practical standpoint, such cases are few and far between. Prisoners behind penitentiary walls have been granted the opportunity to be immersed in makeshift baptismal fonts. Persons who are very ill, perhaps on their deathbed, have been carried to the bathtub and baptized. Baptism often depends more on the person's *will* than on circumstances. If we believe and have the opportunity, Jesus teaches we *should* seal our faith in baptism.

At Pentecost, the people asked the apostles, " 'Men and brethren, what shall we do?' Then Peter said to them, 'Repent, and let every one of you be baptized in the name of Jesus Christ for the remission of sins; and you shall receive the gift of the Holy Spirit.' . . . Then those who gladly received his word were baptized; and that day about three thousand souls were added to them" **(ACTS 2:37, 38, 41).**

Once again, the Word of God tells "every one of [us]" to do two important things—*repent* and be *baptized*. This apostolic directive, clearly given at the birth of the church on the Day of Pentecost, should carry some weight in the minds and hearts of all believers. Few spiritual leaders, if any, question the importance of either believing or repenting as steps to be taken by us sinners on the path to becoming a Christian. Yet some vacillate and hesitate, hedging their words carefully, when asked about the matter of baptism. Peter, however, under the strong influence of God's Holy Spirit, did not.

"There is also an antitype which now saves us—baptism (not the removal of the filth of the flesh, but the answer of a good conscience toward God), through the resurrection of Jesus Christ" **(1 PETER 3:21).**

The terms *type* and *antitype* are not often used today, but they're still helpful to describe two things that share common features of characteristics so that one symbolizes, corresponds to, or prefigures the other. The *American Heritage Dictionary* gives as one meaning of *type* "a figure, representation, or symbol of something to come, as an event in the Old Testament that foreshadows another in the New Testament." That source defines *antitype* as "one that is foreshadowed by or identified with an earlier symbol or type, as a figure in the New Testament that has a counterpart in the Old Testament."

In the preceding verse, **1 PETER 3:20**, the apostle mentions "Noah" and "the ark" and recalls how the patriarch and his family were preserved alive from the waters of the great Flood. Then he uses the Greek word *antitupos*, "antitype," to state that as they "were saved through water," so we are saved by "baptism."

However, lest any accuse him of teaching salvation by works, Peter hastens to explain in **VERSE 21** that, actually, salvation comes to all people "through the resurrection of Jesus Christ." All of this is in perfect harmony with his clear statement in **VERSE 18** that "Christ also suffered once for sins, the just for the unjust, that He might bring us to God, being put to death in the flesh but made alive by the Spirit." Yet it does point out the importance of baptism.

02 What counsel did Jesus give Nicodemus regarding the significance of baptism?

Baptism is much more than a lifeless ritual. It is a deeply spiritual symbol of complete, total commitment to Christ, the burial of the old life and a resurrection to new life in Christ.

"Jesus answered, 'Most assuredly, I say to you, unless one is born of water and the Spirit, he cannot enter the kingdom of God' " **(JOHN 3:5).**

"Jesus answered and said to him [Nicodemus], 'Most assuredly, I say to you, unless one is born again, he cannot see the kingdom of God' " **(JOHN 3:3).**

God promises, "I will sprinkle clean water on you, and you shall be clean; I will cleanse you from all your filthiness and from all your idols. I will give you a new heart and put a new spirit within you; I will take the heart of stone out of your flesh and give you a heart of flesh. I will put My Spirit within you and cause you to walk in My statutes, and you will keep My judgments and do them" **(EZEKIEL 36:25–27).**

"Christ also loved the church and gave Himself for her, that He might sanctify and cleanse her with the washing of water by the word" **(EPHESIANS 5:25, 26).**

"When the kindness and the love of God our Savior toward man appeared, not by works of righteousness which we have done, but according to His mercy He saved us, through the washing of regeneration and renewing of the Holy Spirit, whom He poured out on us abundantly through Jesus Christ our Savior, that having been justified by His grace we should become heirs according to the hope of eternal life" **(TITUS 3:4–7).**

"For as many of you as were baptized into Christ have put on Christ" **(GALATIANS 3:27).**

03 How many methods of baptism does the Bible recognize?

There is "One Lord, one faith, one baptism" **(EPHESIANS 4:5).**

There is one Lord, the Savior Jesus Christ. There is one faith, one true Bible religion. There is one true method of Bible baptism. Some religious leaders have compromised the biblical pattern by adopting many different modes or methods of baptism. Sprinkling, pouring, and immersion are not all the same. The method of baptism makes a difference. God's Word approves and recognizes only *one* method, as stated in this verse.

04 What does Jesus' own baptism teach us about the nature of biblical baptism?

"It came to pass in those days that Jesus came from Nazareth of Galilee, and was baptized by John [the Baptist] in the Jordan [River]. And immediately, *coming up from the water,* He saw the heavens parting and the Spirit descending upon Him like a dove" **(MARK 1:9, 10; EMPHASIS SUPPLIED).**

"Then Jesus came from Galilee to John [the Baptist] at the Jordan to be baptized by him. . . . When He had been baptized, Jesus *came up immediately from the water*" **(MATTHEW 3:13, 16; EMPHASIS SUPPLIED).**

When Scripture tells us that Jesus "came up" out of the water, we know that He was fully immersed. This word picture is clear and instructive. On the other hand, beautiful paintings that show John the Baptist merely pouring a little water over Christ's head from a sea shell are misleading. Those paintings were done centuries after the event by artists paid by religious leaders who wished to reinforce their teachings in the minds of illiterate people.

"Now John [the Baptist] also was baptizing in Aenon near Salim, *because there was much water there*. And they came and were baptized" **(JOHN 3:23; EMPHASIS SUPPLIED).**

Why did John the Baptist choose this particular place for his work of baptizing the people? The Bible tells us that it was "because there was much water there." But there'd be no reason to require a place where there was "much water" if a mere sprinkling or pouring were the method used. Multiple Bible references to baptism throughout the New Testament show plainly that immersion was the one method used in the days of Christ and His apostolic church.

Considering this matter from the point of view of language, the very word *baptism* is from the Greek word *baptisma* derived from the Greek verb *baptizo* meaning "to dip" or "to immerse." The term *baptize* was used anciently to describe the complete immersing of cloth in dye and the submerging of a cup or a bowl in order to fill it with water. The term *baptize* conveys the meaning of "immersion," and no other. John Calvin, the Protestant Reformer who founded the Presbyterian Church, though he felt that the exact mode of baptism was of little importance, nevertheless commented as follows on the meaning of the term: "The very word *baptize*, however, signifies to immerse; and it is certain that immersion was the practice of the ancient church" (*Institutes of the Christian Religion,* bk. 4, chap. 15, sec. 19, vol. 2, p. 434).

The records of history also help illuminate this question about the method of baptism. For instance, consider a few authoritative quotations:

- John Wesley was the founder of the Methodist Church, which does not practice baptism by immersion. But Wesley himself did. When he was forty years of age, he prepared a statement in his own handwriting, which reads as follows: "I believe [myself] it is a duty to observe, so far as I can . . . to baptize by immersion" (quoted by J. H. Blunt, *Dictionary of Sects, Heresies, Ecclesiastical Parties, and Schools of Religious Thought,* p. 320).

- Cardinal James Gibbons, Roman Catholic archbishop of Baltimore, speaks frankly in his best-selling book *The Faith of Our Fathers:* "For several centuries after the establishment of Christianity, baptism was usually conferred by immersion; but since the twelfth century, the practice of baptising by infusion [merely pouring a bit of water on the head] has prevailed in the Catholic church, as this manner is attended with less inconvenience than baptism by immersion. . . . Immersion was the more common practice in the primitive church" (p. 317).

- "Less inconvenience," he says. Yet even in the Roman Catholic Church, "No known council ever enacted a canon condemning baptism by immersion, nor has any pope condemned it. Immersion continued to be the most common and accepted form of baptism for 1,300 years" (Henry F. Brown, *Baptism Through the Centuries,* p. 36).

- Respected historian Arthur P. Stanley reports that "for the first thirteen centuries the almost universal practice of baptism was that of which we read in the New Testament, and which is the very meaning of the word 'baptize'—that those who were baptized were plunged, submerged, immersed into the water. The practice is still, as we have seen, continued in Eastern Churches [Greek Orthodox and Russian Orthodox]. In the Western Church [based at the Vatican] it still lingers amongst Roman Catholics in the solitary instance of the cathedral of Milan" (*Christian Institutions,* p. 21).

Changes in the architecture of baptismal fonts make it possible to trace the changing attitudes of spiritual leaders toward baptism through the centuries. Travelers in Europe know that for many centuries a Roman Catholic church complex was comprised of three buildings: the magnificent cathedral, the tall bell tower, or campanile, and a third building—the baptistry. This latter structure was not quite so large as the cathedral, but it was a separate building of good size, usually octagonal in shape and topped with a dome.

Splendid examples of these are seen by visitors to such Italian cities as Florence and Pisa (where the campanile is the famous "Leaning Tower"), and many others. Inside the third building, the baptistry, is a large, deep font or receptacle for the water. This is beautifully carved of marble, often set with tiles, and capable of accommodating adult believers—somewhat like today's hot tub, only deeper and much more ornate.

The *Encyclopaedia Britannica* testifies that up to the eleventh century, baptistries were commonly separate buildings, often large and richly decorated. The fact that an entire, separate building was built for the full-size baptismal font confirms what we've already learned: that baptism by immersion was practiced even in the Roman Catholic Church for many centuries. "The original font in Florence, Italy, for example, is twelve feet wide and nearly five feet deep. It was built in 1371" (*Encyclopaedia Britannica,* vol. 3, p. 139, article "Baptistery").

05 How was the treasurer of the Queen of Ethiopia baptized by Philip?

"So he [the Ethiopian eunuch, treasurer to the Ethiopian queen] commanded the chariot to stand still. And both Philip and the eunuch *went down into the water,* and he baptized him. Now *when they came up out of the water,* the Spirit of the Lord caught Philip away, so that the eunuch saw him no more; and he went on his way rejoicing" **(ACTS 8:38, 39; EMPHASIS SUPPLIED).**

These verses show that both men *went down into* the water, then they *came up out* of the water—certainly for the purpose of baptism by immersion. Here, then, we have a clear indication of the method of baptism employed by the early church, even on such an unexpected, rather informal occasion.

06 When Jesus was baptized by John in the Jordan River, what two significant things happened?

"When He had been baptized, Jesus came up immediately from the water; and behold, the heavens were opened to Him, and He saw the Spirit of God descending like a dove and alighting upon Him. And suddenly a voice came from heaven, saying, 'This is My beloved Son, in whom I am well pleased' " **(MATTHEW 3:16, 17).**

"It came to pass in those days that Jesus came from Nazareth of Galilee, and was baptized by John in the Jordan. And immediately, coming up from the water, He saw the heavens parting and the Spirit descending upon Him like a dove. Then a voice came from heaven, 'You are My beloved Son, in whom I am well pleased' " **(MARK 1:9–11).**

"When all the people were baptized, it came to pass that Jesus also was baptized; and while He prayed, the heaven was opened. And the Holy Spirit descended in bodily form like a dove upon Him, and a voice came from heaven which said, 'You are My beloved Son; in You I am well pleased' " **(LUKE 3:21, 22).**

That wonderful voice from heaven was heard again while Jesus was on the Mount of Transfiguration with Peter, James, and John: "While he [Peter] was still speaking, behold, a bright cloud overshadowed them; and suddenly a voice came out of the cloud, saying, 'This is My beloved Son, in whom I am well pleased. Hear Him!' " **(MATTHEW 17:5).**

Later Peter recalled and reported this experience when Christ was transfigured on the Mount: "We did not follow cunningly devised fables when we made known to you the power and coming of our Lord Jesus Christ, but were eyewitnesses of His majesty. For He received from God the Father honor and glory when such a voice came to Him from the Excellent Glory: 'This is My beloved Son, in whom I am well pleased' " **(2 PETER 1:16, 17).**

When Jesus was baptized, the Spirit of God descended upon Him, giving Him strength for the temptations to come. His Father spoke these words from heaven, "This is my beloved Son, in whom I am well pleased" **(MATTHEW 3:17).** When people are baptized today, God gives them new power for living and the assurance they are pleasing Him.

07 Can we expect a greater infilling of the Holy Spirit at baptism? Why would God give to those being baptized an extra measure of His Holy Spirit?

"Peter said to them, 'Repent, and let every one of you be baptized in the name of Jesus Christ for the remission of sins; and you shall receive the gift of the Holy Spirit. For the promise is to you and to your children, and to all who are afar off, as many as the Lord our God will call' " **(ACTS 2:38, 39).**

"Now when the apostles who were at Jerusalem heard that Samaria had received the word of God, they sent Peter and John to them, who, when they had come down, prayed for them that they might receive the Holy Spirit. For as yet He had fallen upon none of them. They had only been baptized in the name of the Lord Jesus. Then they laid hands on them, and they received the Holy Spirit" **(ACTS 8:14–17).**

"While Peter was still speaking these words, the Holy Spirit fell upon all those who heard the word. And those of the circumcision who believed were astonished, as many as came with Peter, because the gift of the Holy Spirit had been poured out on the Gentiles also. For they heard them speak with tongues and magnify God. Then Peter answered, 'Can anyone forbid water, that these should not be baptized who have received the Holy Spirit just as we have?' And he commanded them to be baptized in the name of the Lord. Then they asked him to stay a few days" **(ACTS 10:44–48).**

"I will pour water on him who is thirsty, and floods on the dry ground; I will pour My Spirit on your descendants, and My blessing on your offspring" **(ISAIAH 44:3).**

"I will sprinkle clean water on you, and you shall be clean; I will cleanse you from all your filthiness and from all your idols. I will give you a new heart and put a new spirit within you; I will take the heart of stone out of your flesh and give you a heart of flesh. I will put My Spirit within you and cause you to walk in My statutes, and you will keep My judgments and do them" **(EZEKIEL 36:25–27).**

08 How does the New Testament's teaching on baptism give us assurance regarding God's forgiveness of our past lives of sin?

"Now why are you waiting? Arise and be baptized, and wash away your sins, calling on the name of the Lord" **(ACTS 22:16).**

"And such [evil sinners] were some of you. But you were washed, but you were sanctified, but you were justified in the name of the Lord Jesus and by the Spirit of our God" **(1 CORINTHIANS 6:11).**

We are saved, "not by works of righteousness which we have done, but according to His mercy He saved us, through the washing of regeneration and renewing of the Holy Spirit" **(TITUS 3:5).**

"Let us draw near with a true heart in full assurance of faith, having our hearts sprinkled from an evil conscience and our bodies washed with pure water" **(HEBREWS 10:22).**

"There is also an antitype which now saves us—baptism (not the removal of the filth of the flesh, but the answer of a good conscience toward God), through the resurrection of Jesus Christ" **(1 PETER 3:21).**

"And he [the jailer at Philippi] brought them [Paul and Silas] out and said, 'Sirs, what must I do to be saved?' So they said, 'Believe on the Lord Jesus Christ, and you will be saved, you and your household.' Then they spoke the word of the Lord to him and to all who were in his house. And he took them the same hour of the night and washed their stripes [their wounds from having their backs beaten]. And immediately he and all his family were baptized" **(ACTS 16:30–33).**

"Then Crispus, the ruler of the synagogue, believed on the Lord with all his household. And many of the Corinthians, hearing, believed and were baptized" **(ACTS 18:8).**

God blessed Paul's efforts with success wherever he went, as the verses above, among many others, show. The jailer at Philippi was a Gentile convert, whereas Crispus was a Jew from the secular city of Corinth—and not just a Jew but a rabbi—"the ruler of the synagogue." They and their families "believed and were baptized."

Baptism is a symbol of spiritual cleansing. The water of baptism itself does not save us, but it does signify that we accept the blood of Christ, which does save us.

09 How can a person know if he or she is ready to be baptized? What are the conditions God desires us to meet before baptism?

Repentance. "Then Peter said to them, 'Repent, and let every one of you be baptized in the name of Jesus Christ for the remission of sins; and you shall receive the gift of the Holy Spirit' " **(ACTS 2:38).**

Repentance is a deep sorrow for sin. It means a conscious desire to turn from those things that violate God's will and sadden His heart.

Belief. "Now as they went down the road, they came to some water. And the [Ethiopian] eunuch said, 'See, here is water. What hinders me from being baptized?' Then Philip said, 'If you believe with all your heart, you may.' And he answered and said, 'I believe that Jesus Christ is the Son of God' " **(ACTS 8:36, 37).**

This belief is more than simply an intellectual assent to a particular creed. It is a heart commitment to Jesus and His Word. It is a turning to Him with all the heart, a belief that He is the Savior, who alone can forgive sin and give victory in your life.

Instruction. "Go therefore and make disciples of all the nations, baptizing them in the name of the Father and of the Son and of the Holy Spirit, teaching them to observe all things that I have commanded you; and lo, I am with you always, even to the end of the age" **(MATTHEW 28:19, 20).**

Learning is a lifelong process, and one should never wait to be baptized until they feel they have grasped all truth. However, it is necessary to understand basic scriptural truths before making such a significant decision.

These biblical conditions God has given for baptism are beyond the ability of any baby to meet, thus precluding infant baptism. For an infant cannot repent of any sins. How can we attribute sinful acts to an innocent baby who hasn't reached the age of accountability? Also, no infant can intelligently believe in Christ or commit his life to the Lord. And no infant can be taught the great truths and principles of faith. For these reasons, careful students of the Bible have long insisted upon believers' baptism, not infant baptism.

Yale University Professor Jaroslav Jan Pelikan, a prominent theologian writing for *Encyclopaedia Britannica*, asserts that many Christians expect "a pure church, into which one would come, not automatically by birth and infant baptism, but consciously by the decision of faith. . . . The church is composed of true believers who have made personal confession of their faith. . . . The decision of faith may be neither anticipated nor taken away from the child by its parents and the church. Therefore baptism must be postponed until such a time as the child becomes capable of making this decision personally. . . . The earliest Christian literature makes no explicit reference to the custom of baptizing infants" (*Encyclopaedia Britannica,* vol. 3, pp. 138, 139, article "Baptism").

The Baby Jesus was brought to the temple to be dedicated to God **(SEE LUKE 2:22–24),** but there is no mention in Scripture of His being baptized as an infant. Indeed, there is no mention in the Bible of *any* infant being baptized. Thus Bible baptism is specifically intended and designed for *instructed adult believers.*

10 What does baptism signify spiritually in the life of each believer?

"Do you not know that as many of us as were baptized into Christ Jesus were baptized into His death? Therefore we were buried with Him through baptism into death, that just as Christ was raised from the dead by the glory of the Father, even so we also should walk in newness of life" **(ROMANS 6:3, 4).**

In these verses, Paul teaches plainly that baptism is a fitting symbol of each Christian's act of:

- *Dying* to his old sinful way of life—just as Christ died on the cross.
- *Burying* his sins in the watery grave of baptism—just as Christ was buried in the tomb.
- *Rising* again out of the water to walk a new life—just as Christ arose in His triumphant resurrection.

We see God's wisdom in instituting such a perfectly fitting memorial of His Son's death and resurrection—but this symbolism is seen only in the baptism of believing adults by immersion as taught in the Bible. The so-called baptism of uninstructed infants by sprinkling—as changed by man—can offer no such parallels to Christ's monumental acts in achieving our salvation. But Bible baptism does commemorate Christ's death and resurrection.

Even though the Lutheran Church he founded does not practice baptism by immersion, Martin Luther's own comments regarding baptism by immersion are revealing: "On this account (as a symbol of death and resurrection), I could wish that such as are to be baptized should be completely immersed into the water, according to the meaning of the word, and to the significance of the ordinance, not because I think it necessary, but because it would be beautiful to have a full and perfect sign of so perfect a thing; as also, without doubt, it was instituted by Christ" (*Luther's Works,* 1551 ed., vol. 2, p. 76. Quoted in Henry F. Brown, *Baptism Through the Centuries,* p. 40).

Furthermore, Luther—who translated the Bible into the German language—said, "Then also without doubt, in German tongues, the little word 'Tauf' [baptism] comes from the word 'tief' [deep], because what one baptizes he sinks deep into the water" (*Werke,* Irmischeid ed., vol. 21, p. 229. Cited in T. J. Conant, *The Meaning and Use of Baptism,* p. 146).

Church historian Dr. Philip Schaff says that "Luther sought to restore immersion, but without effect" (*History of the Christian Church,* vol. 2, p. 251, footnote).

"For if we have been united together in the likeness of His death, certainly we also shall be in the likeness of His resurrection, knowing this, that our old man was crucified with Him, that the body of sin might be done away with, that we should no longer be slaves of sin" **(ROMANS 6:5, 6).**

"Buried with Him in baptism, in which you also were raised with Him through faith in the working of God, who raised Him from the dead. And you, being dead in your trespasses and the uncircumcision of your flesh, He has made alive together with Him, having forgiven you all trespasses" **(COLOSSIANS 2:12, 13).**

"If then you were raised with Christ, seek those things which are above, where Christ is, sitting at the right hand of God. Set your mind on things above, not on things on the earth. For you died, and your life is hidden with Christ in God" **(COLOSSIANS 3:1–3).**

"If we died with Christ, we believe that we shall also live with Him. . . . Likewise you also, reckon yourselves to be dead indeed to sin, but alive to God in Christ Jesus our Lord" **(ROMANS 6:8, 11).**

"I have been crucified with Christ; it is no longer I who live, but Christ lives in me; and the life which I now live in the flesh I live by faith in the Son of God, who loved me and gave Himself for me" **(GALATIANS 2:20).**

"Those who are Christ's have crucified the flesh with its passions and desires" **(GALATIANS 5:24).**

"God forbid that I should boast except in the cross of our Lord Jesus Christ, by whom the world has been crucified to me, and I to the world" **(GALATIANS 6:14).**

Paul prayed "that you put off, concerning your former conduct, the old man which grows corrupt according to the deceitful lusts, and be renewed in the spirit of your mind, and that you put on the new man which was created according to God, in true righteousness and holiness" **(EPHESIANS 4:22–24).**

"You have put off the old man with his deeds, and have put on the new man who is renewed in knowledge according to the image of Him who created him" **(COLOSSIANS 3:9, 10).**

Baptism symbolizes a death to sin and a resurrection to a new life in Jesus Christ. Living for Jesus, we are fully alive. Baptism by full immersion is the true symbol that we accept the death, burial, and resurrection of our Lord. Through baptism we acknowledge that we are now walking in the "newness of life."

Both Philip and the Ethiopian entered the water. Philip then placed the Ethiopian completely under the water. The baptismal candidate must enter into the water, be completely covered by the water, and rise from the water in order to correctly symbolize the death of the old man of sin, burial with Christ, and resurrection in Christ to a new life. Baptism by immersion is the only biblical method.

11 Although baptism is a symbol of union with Christ, does it also symbolize union with His church? What is the relationship of baptism to Christ's church? Can an individual be baptized into Christ without uniting with His church?

"Then those who gladly received his [Peter's] word were baptized; and that day about three thousand souls were added to them. And they continued steadfastly in the apostles' doctrine and fellowship, in the breaking of bread, and in prayers . . . praising God and having favor with all the people. And the Lord added to the church daily those who were being saved" **(ACTS 2:41, 42, 47).**

"As the body is one and has many members, but all the members of that one body, being many, are one body, so also is Christ. For by one Spirit we were all baptized into one *body*—whether Jews or Greeks, whether slaves or free—and have all been made to drink into one Spirit. . . . Now you are *the body of Christ,* and members individually" **(1 CORINTHIANS 12:12, 13, 27; EMPHASIS SUPPLIED).**

"And believers were increasingly added to the Lord, multitudes of both men and women" **(ACTS 5:14).**

"For he [Barnabas] was a good man, full of the Holy Spirit and of faith. And a great many people were added to the Lord" **(ACTS 11:24).**

"However, many of those who heard the word believed; and the number of the men came to be about five thousand" **(ACTS 4:4).**

"For as we have many members in one body, but all the members do not have the same function, so we, being many, are one body in Christ, and individually members of one another" **(ROMANS 12:4, 5).**

"He put all things under His feet, and gave Him to be head over all things to the church, which is His body" **(EPHESIANS 1:22, 23).**

God gives gifts and talents and abilities "for the equipping of the saints for the work of ministry, for the edifying of the body of Christ" **(EPHESIANS 4:12).**

"The husband is head of the wife, as also Christ is head of the church; and He is the Savior of the body. . . . For we are members of His body, of His flesh and of His bones" **(EPHESIANS 5:23, 30).**

"He is the head of the body, the church, who is the beginning, the firstborn from the dead, that in all things He may have the preeminence" **(COLOSSIANS 1:18).**

"I now rejoice in my sufferings for you, and fill up in my flesh what is lacking in the afflictions of Christ, for the sake of His body, which is the church" **(COLOSSIANS 1:24).**

In the New Testament, baptism was into the body of Christ, or the church. Bible baptism is the doorway to the church, the God-given rite of entry, the initiation into the body of Christ and the family of God. What an unspeakable privilege!

12 Is rebaptism ever necessary? If a person has been baptized once, should he ever be baptized again?

"It happened, while Apollos was at Corinth, that Paul, having passed through the upper regions, came to Ephesus. And finding some disciples he said to them, 'Did you receive the Holy Spirit when you believed?' So they said to him, 'We have not so much as heard whether there is a Holy Spirit.' And he said to them, 'Into what then were you baptized?' So they said, 'Into John's baptism.' Then Paul said, 'John indeed baptized with a baptism of repentance, saying to the people that they should believe on Him who would come after him, that is, on Christ Jesus.' When they heard this, they were baptized in the name of the Lord Jesus" **(ACTS 19:1–5).**

In this instance, Paul rebaptized believers who had been baptized by John the Baptist in the Jordan River but who had never heard of the Holy Spirit. As the truth about New Testament Christianity dawned upon their minds, they were rebaptized as a symbol of following all of this new truth. There are some Christians who have a new deep experience with Jesus as they discover new truths in the plan of salvation. They desire to become part of Christ's church and choose to be rebaptized.

"Then Peter said to them, 'Repent, and let every one of you be baptized in the name of Jesus Christ for the remission of sins; and you shall receive the gift of the Holy Spirit' " **(ACTS 2:38).**

"But when they believed Philip as he preached the things concerning the kingdom of God and the name of Jesus Christ, both men and women were baptized" **(ACTS 8:12).**

"Each of you says, 'I am of Paul,' or 'I am of Apollos,' or 'I am of Cephas,' or 'I am of Christ.' Is Christ divided? Was Paul crucified for you? Or were you baptized in the name of Paul? I thank God that I baptized none of you except Crispus and Gaius, lest anyone should say that I had baptized in my own name" **(1 CORINTHIANS 1:12–15).**

"Go therefore and make disciples of all the nations [the KJV says, "teach all nations"], baptizing them in the name of the Father and of the Son and of the Holy Spirit" **(MATTHEW 28:19).**

Many new Christian believers, having studied and learned the full significance of Bible baptism, choose to be "buried in the watery grave" of full immersion even though they've been told they were sprinkled as an infant many years before. They may or may not consider this a "rebaptism," but they now wish to seal their newfound commitment to Christ by the conscious act of going down into the waters of baptism, thus following the example of Jesus.

13 What gracious appeal does Jesus make for us to accept the salvation He so freely offers?

"And the Spirit and the bride say, 'Come!' And let him who hears say, 'Come!' And let him who thirsts come. Whoever desires, let him take the water of life freely" **(REVELATION 22:17).**

"Ho! Everyone who thirsts, come to the waters; and you who have no money, come, buy and eat. Yes, come, buy wine and milk without money and without price. Why do you spend money for what is not bread, and your wages for what does not satisfy?

Listen carefully to Me, and eat what is good, and let your soul delight itself in abundance. Incline your ear, and come to Me. Hear, and your soul shall live; and I will make an everlasting covenant with you—the sure mercies of David" **(ISAIAH 55:1–3).**

"Come and let us walk in the light of the LORD" **(ISAIAH 2:5).**

"Oh, taste and see that the LORD is good; blessed is the man who trusts in Him!" **(PSALM 34:8).**

"All that the Father gives Me will come to Me, and the one who comes to Me I will by no means cast out" **(JOHN 6:37).**

Everyone is invited! Won't you come and join the family of God? Jesus invites us to come to Him. Baptism is a symbol we are coming without reservation. We are coming completely. We are coming in total surrender to His will. As we come, He promises to cleanse us from our past and give us a new life. We become part of His family, the church.

Have you been baptized by immersion? Do you have the assurance your guilt is completely gone? Is your past buried? Are you new in Christ? Why not make this decision now?

CHAPTER 21

What the Bible Says About Money

In the sixth century before Christ, the wealthiest man in the world was Croesus. Croesus was the king of Lydia from 560 to 547 B.C. He is credited with issuing the first true gold coins with a standardized purity for general circulation. One day King Croesus asked the philosopher Salon, "Who is the happiest man in the world?" Salon's answer, as recorded by the Greek historian Herodotus, went something like this: "To live well you must prepare to die well."

There is something tragically wrong with a society that is obsessed with making money. Seeking happiness in material things leads us down the road to nowhere. Attempting to fill our lives with things only leaves us empty. Salon was right. There is more to life than simply making money.

Norman Cousins, editor of the *Saturday Review,* made a very perceptive statement forty years ago. It was true then, but it is even truer now. "We are so busy extending ourselves and increasing the size and ornamentation of our personal kingdom that we have hardly considered that no age in history has had so many loose props under it as our own." We are so busy buying that we have failed to realize there are some moral screws loose in our society. The foundation is cracking. We just might be investing our money in the wrong places.

The Bible presents eternal financial principles that make sense. It reveals financial secrets that most of the world does not know. It encourages us to reevaluate our priorities—to seek the eternal rather than the earthly. God's Word leads us to make investments that will pay off in the long run.

01 What is the foundational principle that should guide all of our stewardship? Who really owns this world and everything in it?

"Every beast of the forest is Mine, and the cattle on a thousand hills. I know all the birds of the mountains, and the wild beasts of the field are Mine. If I were hungry, I would not tell you; for the world is Mine, and all its fullness" **(PSALM 50:10–12).**

" 'The silver is Mine, and the gold is Mine,' says the LORD of hosts" **(HAGGAI 2:8).**

"O LORD, how manifold are Your works! In wisdom You have made them all. The earth is full of Your possessions—this great and wide sea, in which are innumerable teeming things, living things both small and great" **(PSALM 104:24, 25).**

"Out of the ground the LORD God formed every beast of the field and every bird of the air, and brought them to Adam to see what he would call them. And whatever Adam called each living creature, that was its name" **(GENESIS 2:19).**

"But who am I, and who are my people, that we should be able to offer so willingly as this? For all things come from You, and of Your own we have given You. For we are aliens and pilgrims before You, as were all our fathers; our days on earth are as a shadow, and without hope. O LORD our God, all this abundance that we have prepared to build You a house for Your holy name is from Your hand, and is all Your own" **(1 CHRONICLES 29:14–16).**

"He [God] sends the springs into the valleys; they flow among the hills. They give drink to every beast of the field; the wild donkeys quench their thirst. By them the birds of the heavens have their home; they sing among the branches. . . . He causes the grass to grow for the cattle, and vegetation for the service of man, that he may bring forth food from the earth" **(PSALM 104:10–12, 14).**

"Look at the birds of the air, for they neither sow nor reap nor gather into barns; yet your heavenly Father feeds them. Are you not of more value than they?" **(MATTHEW 6:26).**

The Creator declares, "All the earth is Mine" **(EXODUS 19:5).**

"Indeed heaven and the highest heavens belong to the LORD your God, also the earth with all that is in it" **(DEUTERONOMY 10:14).**

"Everything under heaven is Mine" **(JOB 41:11).**

A little poem by Marcella Hooe is called "What Do You Owe?"

> What do you owe God, you ask? Suppose He sent you this bill:
>
> One hundred thousand dollars for the sun upon the hill;
>
> Two thousand for the little brook that runs along the way;
>
> Five hundred for the night time, and a thousand for the day.
>
> Six hundred for the little birds that trill and chirp and sing;
>
> Six hundred for the tiny flowers which tell us that it's Spring;
>
> These are the bills which everyone of every clime forget.
>
> If God should charge you what you owe, you'd always be in debt.

God is the Owner of this world. Everything in it rightfully belongs to Him.

02 What is the basis for God's ownership of this world? How do the Bible prophets establish and confirm the claim that this world and everything in it belongs to God?

"The earth is the LORD'S, and all its fullness, the world and those who dwell therein" **(PSALM 24:1).**

"Thus says the LORD, who created you, O Jacob, and He who formed you, O Israel: 'Fear not, for I have redeemed you; I have called you by your name; you are Mine' " **(ISAIAH 43:1).**

"Indeed My hand has laid the foundation of the earth, and My right hand has stretched out the heavens" **(ISAIAH 48:13).**

"Of old You laid the foundation of the earth, and the heavens are the work of Your hands" **(PSALM 102:25).**

"In the beginning God created the heavens and the earth" **(GENESIS 1:1).**

"Thus says the LORD, who created the heavens, who is God, who formed the earth and made it, who has established it, who did not create it in vain, who formed it to be inhabited: 'I am the LORD, and there is no other' " **(ISAIAH 45:18).**

"Thus says God the LORD, who created the heavens and stretched them out, who spread forth the earth and that which comes from it, who gives breath to the people on it, and spirit to those who walk on it" **(ISAIAH 42:5).**

"Lift up your eyes on high, and see who has created these things, who brings out their host by number; He calls them all by name, by the greatness of His might and the strength of His power; not one is missing" **(ISAIAH 40:26).**

"So he [Jonah] said to them [the ship's crew], 'I am a Hebrew; and I fear the LORD, the God of heaven, who made the sea and the dry land' " **(JONAH 1:9).**

The Bible teaches that the Father, Son, and Holy Spirit participated in the process of creation together **(SEE EPHESIANS 3:9; COLOSSIANS 1:15, 16).** The earth is His. He made it.

03 In addition to being our Creator, what other reason does the Bible give for Christ's ownership of this world?

"You were not redeemed with corruptible things, like silver or gold . . . but with the precious blood of Christ, as of a lamb without blemish and without spot" **(1 PETER 1:18, 19).**

"Those who trust in their wealth and boast in the multitude of their riches, none of them can by any means redeem his brother, nor give to God a ransom for him—for the redemption of their souls is costly" **(PSALM 49:6–8).**

"You were bought at a price; do not become slaves of men" **(1 CORINTHIANS 7:23).**

Our salvation comes from Christ "who Himself bore our sins in His own body on the tree, that we, having died to sins, might live for righteousness—by whose stripes you were healed" **(1 PETER 2:24).**

"For Christ also suffered once for sins, the just for the unjust, that He might bring us to God" **(1 PETER 3:18).**

Christ is the One "who loved us and washed us from our sins in His own blood" **(REVELATION 1:5).**

"The Son of Man did not come to be served, but to serve, and to give His life a ransom for many" **(MATTHEW 20:28).**

Jesus said, "This is My blood of the new covenant, which is shed for many for the remission of sins" **(MATTHEW 26:28).**

Paul told the church leaders, "The Holy Spirit has made you overseers, to shepherd the church of God which He purchased with His own blood" **(ACTS 20:28).**

"We have redemption through His blood, the forgiveness of sins" **(COLOSSIANS 1:14).**

"Not with the blood of goats and calves, but with His own blood He entered the Most Holy Place once for all, having obtained eternal redemption. For if the blood of bulls and goats and the ashes of a heifer, sprinkling the unclean, sanctifies for the purifying of the flesh, how much more shall the blood of Christ, who through the eternal Spirit offered Himself without spot to God, cleanse your conscience from dead works to serve the living God?" **(HEBREWS 9:12–14).**

"If we walk in the light as He is in the light, we have fellowship with one another, and the blood of Jesus Christ His Son cleanses us from all sin" **(1 JOHN 1:7).**

"He Himself is the propitiation for our sins, and not for ours only but also for the whole world" **(1 JOHN 2:2).**

Often when we run up a bill for service of any kind, we'll ask, "How much do I owe you?" The following anonymous poem directs our thoughts to this profound question and its sublime answer—

> When this passing world is done,
> When has sunk the glaring sun,
> When we stand with Christ in glory,
> Looking o'er life's finished story,
>   Then, Lord, shall I fully know—
>   Not till then—how much I owe.
>
> When I stand before the throne,
> Dressed in beauty not my own;
> When I see Thee as Thou art,
> Love Thee with unsinning heart,
>   Then, Lord, shall I fully know—
>   Not till then—how much I owe!

When our Lord created this world, He entrusted it to Adam. God gave Adam dominion over the entire creation **(SEE GENESIS 1:26).** At the Fall, Adam surrendered his right of dominion. Lucifer, the fallen angel, usurped the dominion and claimed the Lordship of the earth. Bible writers often refer to Lucifer as the "prince of this world" or "the prince of the power of the air" **(EPHESIANS 2:2; SEE ALSO JOHN 12:31; 14:30).** Christ's sinless life and substitutionary death fully paid the ransom for our sins. The Cross sealed Satan's fate and pledged complete restoration for this planet **(SEE EPHESIANS 1:14; 1 CORINTHIANS 6:19, 20; JOHN 12:31, 32).** God is the true Owner of this world, both by creation and redemption. Everything we have is a gift of His grace. We are stewards of goods entrusted to us by God. We are, and were, Christ's. He created us, and He redeemed us. This world is His. He made it in the first place and shed His blood to redeem it.

04 Since God owns the world and everything in it, what does the Bible declare regarding our responsibility for everything He has graciously entrusted us with?

The apostle Paul states, "It is required in stewards that one be found faithful" **(1 CORINTHIANS 4:2).**

A steward is one who manages another person's property, finances, or other affairs. And that is what we are—stewards—under God. For we do not own this world or anything in it; God, as Creator, owns it all. Yet He placed Adam and Eve and their descendants in charge of it all by giving them "dominion" over the other creatures and by placing them "in the Garden of Eden to tend and keep it" **(GENESIS 1:28; 2:15).** Paul's verse above teaches that as stewards, we are required to be "found faithful" in everything we manage, including finances.

"He who is faithful in what is least is faithful also in much; and he who is unjust in what is least is unjust also in much" **(LUKE 16:10).**

The Lord repeats His praise twice in these verses: "His Lord said to him, 'Well done, good and faithful servant; you were faithful over a few things, I will make you ruler over many things. Enter into the joy of your Lord.' " And then, "His Lord said to him, 'Well done, good and faithful servant; you have been faithful over a few things, I will make you ruler over many things. Enter into the joy of your Lord' " **(MATTHEW 25:21, 23).**

"And the Lord said, 'Who then is that faithful and wise steward, whom his master will make ruler over his household, to give them their portion of food in due season?' " **(LUKE 12:42).**

"But one of His disciples, Judas Iscariot, Simon's son, who would betray Him, said 'Why was this fragrant oil not sold for three hundred denarii and given to the poor?' This he said, not that he cared for the poor, but because he was a thief, and had the money box; and he used to take what was put in it" **(JOHN 12:4–6).**

The grasping greed that made Judas a thief was put into his heart by the devil. But then Satan went even further: "The devil having already put it into the heart of Judas Iscariot, Simon's son, to betray Him [Jesus]. . . . Satan entered him. Then Jesus said to him, 'What you do, do quickly' " **(JOHN 13:2, 27).**

God entrusts each of us with a portion of His goods to manage. Everything we have is a trust from the King of the universe. God is testing us with earthly possessions to see if we can be entrusted with heavenly riches.

05 Who is the giver of all good gifts? Who provides us with the opportunity to receive all of life's blessings? In reality, where do all our possessions come from? What is the origin of all our wealth?

We should beware of the temptation to "say in your heart, 'My power and the might of my hand have gained me this wealth.' And you shall remember the LORD your God, for it is He who gives you power to get wealth, that He may establish His covenant which He swore to your fathers, as it is this day" **(DEUTERONOMY 8:17, 18).**

"All this came upon King Nebuchadnezzar. At the end of the twelve months he was walking about the royal palace of Babylon. The king spoke, saying, 'Is not this great Babylon, that I have built for a royal dwelling by my mighty power and for the honor of my majesty?' " **(DANIEL 4:28–30).**

"Every good gift and every perfect gift is from above and comes down from the Father of lights, with whom there is no variation or shadow of turning" **(JAMES 1:17).**

"For who makes you differ from another? And what do you have that you did not receive? Now if you did indeed receive it, why do you boast as if you had not received it?" **(1 CORINTHIANS 4:7).**

We cannot give to God anything that He has not first given us. Everything we have—our health and strength and energy, our time and talents and abilities, our very life itself—comes from God, our Maker. It is written: "He gives to all life, breath, and all things **(ACTS 17:25).** So we can afford to be generous. Jesus said, "Freely you have received, freely give" **(MATTHEW 10:8).**

"Unless the LORD builds the house, they labor in vain who build it; unless the LORD guards the city, the watchman stays awake in vain. It is vain for you to rise up early, to sit up late, to eat the bread of sorrows; for so He gives His beloved sleep" **(PSALM 127:1, 2).**

"The blessing of the LORD makes one rich, and He adds no sorrow with it" **(PROVERBS 10:22).**

This text contains a wonderful lesson. So often people are tempted to cut corners, to cheat, lie, or steal in an attempt to make themselves rich. But their ill-gotten gains bring deep sorrow to their lives in the form of everything from loss of self-respect and guilty consciences to prison terms. But when *the blessing of the Lord* makes us rich, "He adds no sorrow with it."

06 How do we acknowledge that God is the Owner of all we have? What is one of the ways that we express our appreciation to Him for all of life's blessings?

" 'Will a man rob God? Yet you have robbed Me! But you say, "In what way have we robbed You?" In tithes and offerings. You are cursed with a curse, for you have robbed Me, even this whole nation. Bring all the tithes into the storehouse, that there may be food in My house, and try Me now in this,' says the LORD of hosts, 'if I will not open for you the windows of heaven and pour out for you such blessing that there will not be room enough to receive it' " **(MALACHI 3:8–10; EMPHASIS SUPPLIED).**

God says, "If you're faithful in paying your tithe—the one-tenth which is holy—I'll make the other nine-tenths go further than if you kept the whole ten-tenths." God says, "If you have a hundred dollars, and you return to Me ten dollars of that money, a tithe, you show you believe that I'm the Lord of all. You also show you believe I've given you the power to get wealth; you show you believe you're just a steward taking care of the other ninety dollars. If you are faithful in tithing, I will open the windows of heaven and pour you out such a blessing there won't even be room enough to receive it!"

Certainly you need to eat, you need clothes, you need to make house payments or pay your rent. God knows all that. But what *else* does God say? He says, "Try Me, prove Me, test Me." This is the only place in the Bible where God makes it this explicit. He says, "Try Me. Put Me to the test. If you'll return 10 percent, and prove Me, trying it out to see if it works, I promise you'll never be sorry." God is asking you for a chance to prove His promise.

When Jesus asked whose likeness was imprinted on the Roman coins, "they said to Him, 'Caesar's.' And He said to them, 'Render therefore to Caesar the things that are Caesar's, and to God the things that are God's' " **(MATTHEW 22:21; SEE ALSO MARK 12:17).**

The tithe is definitely among "the things that are God's," which every believer should "render" to Him. God allows us to keep and use for ourselves the other nine-tenths He gives us, but "*the tithe . . . is the LORD's.* It is *holy* to the LORD" **(LEVITICUS 27:30; EMPHASIS SUPPLIED).**

Faithful believers were taught to offer perfect animals without blemish as a sacrifice to God. So the Lord asks, " 'When you offer the blind [animal] as a sacrifice, is it not evil? And when you offer the lame and sick [animal, which you couldn't sell at market], is it not evil? Offer it then to your governor! Would he be pleased with you? Would he accept you favorably?' says the LORD of hosts. . . . 'And you bring the stolen, the lame, and the sick; thus you bring an offering! Should I accept this from your hand?' says the LORD" **(MALACHI 1:8, 13).**

In other words: Don't give God second best; always give of your best to the Master.

" 'If you will not hear, and if you will not take it to heart, to give glory to My name,' says the LORD of hosts, 'I will send a curse upon you, and I will curse your blessings. Yes, I have cursed them already, because you do not take it to heart' " **(MALACHI 2:2).**

Picture this scene: God's temple is lying in ruins, and His selfish people are lax in contributing toward its rebuilding, so the Lord tells the prophet Haggai, " 'This people says, "The time has not come, the time that the LORD's house should be built." ' Then the word of the LORD came by Haggai the prophet, saying, 'Is it time for you yourselves to dwell in your paneled houses, and this temple to lie in ruins?' Now therefore, thus says the LORD of hosts: 'Consider your ways! You have sown much, and bring in little; you eat, but do not have enough; you drink, but you are not filled with drink; you clothe yourselves, but no one is warm; and he who earns wages, earns wages to put into a bag with holes.' Thus says the LORD of hosts: 'Consider your ways! Go up to the mountains and bring wood and build the temple, that I may take pleasure in it and be glorified,' says the LORD. 'You looked for much, but indeed it came to little; and when you brought it home, I blew it away. Why?' says the LORD of hosts. 'Because of My house that is in ruins, while every one of you runs to his own house. Therefore the heavens above you withhold the dew, and the earth withholds its fruit. For I called for a drought on the land and the mountains, on the grain and the new wine and the oil, on whatever the ground brings forth, on men and livestock, and on all the labor of your hands' " **(HAGGAI 1:2–11).**

When Israel was openly disobedient to God, He withheld His blessings. God's richest blessings are poured out on unselfish hearts.

God's blessing can make a little go a long way: "The word of the LORD came to him [Elijah], saying, 'Arise, go to Zarephath, which belongs to Sidon, and dwell there. See, I have commanded a widow there to provide for you.' So he arose and went to Zarephath. And when he came to the gate of the city, indeed a widow was there gathering sticks. And he called to her and said, 'Please bring me a little water in a cup, that I may drink.' And as she was going to get it, he called to her and said, 'Please bring me a morsel of bread in your hand.' So she said, 'As the LORD your God lives, I do not have bread, only a handful of flour in a bin, and a little oil in a jar; and see, I am gathering a couple of sticks that I may go in and prepare it for myself and my son, that we may eat it, and die.' And Elijah said to her, 'Do not fear; go and do as you have said, but make me a small cake from it first, and bring it to me; and afterward make some for yourself and your son. For thus says the LORD God of Israel: "The bin of flour shall not be used up, nor shall the jar of oil run dry, until the day the LORD sends rain on the earth." ' So she went away and did according to the word of Elijah; and she and he and her household ate for many days. The bin of flour was not used up, nor did the jar of oil run dry, according to the word of the LORD which He spoke by Elijah" **(1 KINGS 17:8–16).**

God makes wonderful promises to those who are faithful: "Trust in the LORD, and do good; dwell in the land, and feed on His faithfulness. Delight yourself also in the LORD, and *He shall give you the desires of your heart. Commit your way to the LORD, trust also in Him, and He shall bring it to pass*" **(PSALM 37:3–5; EMPHASIS SUPPLIED).**

Jesus Himself tells us, "I say to you, do not worry about your life, what you will eat or what you will drink; nor about your body, what you will put on. Is not life more than food and the body more than clothing? Look at the birds of the air, for they neither sow nor reap nor gather into barns; yet your heavenly Father feeds them. Are you not of more value than they? Which of you by worrying can add one cubit to his stature? So why do you worry about clothing? Consider the lilies of the field, how they grow: they neither toil nor spin; and yet I say to you that even Solomon in all his glory was not arrayed like one of these. Now if God so clothes the grass of the field, which today is, and tomorrow is thrown into the oven, will He not much more clothe you, O you of little faith? Therefore do not worry, saying, 'What shall we eat?' or 'What shall we drink?' or 'What shall we wear?' For after all these things the Gentiles seek. For your heavenly Father knows that you need all these things. But seek first the kingdom of God and His righteousness, and all these things shall be added to you" **(MATTHEW 6:25–33).**

"Then Jesus said to them, 'Children, have you any food?' They answered Him, 'No.' And He said to them, 'Cast the net on the right side of the boat, and you will find some.' So they cast, and now they were not able to draw it in because of the multitude of fish. . . . Simon Peter went up and dragged the net to land, full of large fish, one hundred and fifty-three; and although there were so many, the net was not broken" **(JOHN 21:5, 6, 11).**

"When He [Jesus] had stopped speaking, He said to Simon [Peter], 'Launch out into the deep and let down your nets for a catch.' But Simon answered and said to Him, 'Master, we have toiled all night and caught nothing; nevertheless at Your word I will let down the net.' And when they had done this, they caught a great number of fish, and their net was breaking. So they signaled to their partners in the other boat to come and help them. And they came and filled both the boats, so that they began to sink" **(LUKE 5:4–7).**

Jesus easily solved the problem of those frustrated, disappointed fishermen. He is the One who has the capacity to meet all of our needs. There is nothing too hard for God. There is no problem too great for Him to solve.

"He [Jesus] said to them, 'Take heed and beware of covetousness, for one's life does not consist in the abundance of the things he possesses.' Then He spoke a parable to them, saying: 'The ground of a certain rich man yielded plentifully. And he thought within himself, saying, "What shall I do, since I have no room to store my crops?" So he said, "I will do this: I will pull down my barns and build greater, and there I will store all my crops and my goods. And I will say to my soul, 'Soul, you have many goods laid up for many years; take your ease; eat, drink, and be merry.' " But God said to him, "Fool! This night your soul will be required of you; then whose will those things be which you have provided?" So is he who lays up treasure for himself, and is not rich toward God' " **(LUKE 12:15–21).**

The experience of the rich fool in Jesus' parable illustrates the fundamental truth that "You can't take it with you when you die." How sad, then, that so many place an inordinate value on earthly riches and try to hoard them rather than use them for good and for God in this life. When one fabulously wealthy business leader died, people asked, "How much did he leave?" The answer was: "*All* of it!"

Any way you look at it, the tithing system given by God is a *heavenly* financial arrangement. No mere man could devise a plan as perfect.

07 How does the Bible define tithe? What is its purpose? Is tithing part of God's plan for His people today?

"All the tithe of the land, whether of the seed of the land or of the fruit of the tree, is the LORD'S. It is holy to the LORD. . . . And concerning the tithe of the herd or the flock, of whatever passes under the rod, the tenth one shall be holy to the LORD" **(LEVITICUS 27:30, 32).**

Simply put, the tithe is "a tenth part of one's income consecrated to God" (*The Westminster Dictionary of the Bible,* p. 609). "Tithing in one form or another was practiced . . . by worshipers of the true God at a very early time" (*Seventh-day Adventist Bible Dictionary,* p. 1127.)

The tithe is a divine idea! Proof of its heavenly origin is seen with just a moment's reflection. First of all, we know that the gospel ministry must be supported—but it's beautiful to think that we can pay the minister of God *with the Lord's own money*!

Second, the tithing system is eminently equitable and fair to all. Those who earn more, pay more. And those who earn a little, pay only a little. And because the tithe is a *fixed* percentage—10 percent for everyone—no one is in a "higher bracket" and charged a greater proportion of his income.

The Scripture texts quoted above, and others, tell us that the tenth we call the "tithe" is not ours to keep. "All the tithe . . . is the Lord's. It is holy to the Lord." To keep it for ourselves would be stealing, robbing from God Himself! So we don't "give" tithe—we "return" tithe back to God to show we can be trusted. God gives us the ability to get wealth. He places ten-tenths into our hands to see if we'll acknowledge His ownership of all by returning the one-tenth He claims as His. Then, if we're faithful to return our tithe to God, He *blesses* the nine-tenths so that it goes far beyond our expectations.

"Then Melchizedek king of Salem brought out bread and wine; he was the priest of God Most High. And he blessed him [Abram] and said: 'Blessed be Abram of God Most High, possessor of heaven and earth; and blessed be God Most High, who has delivered your enemies into your hand.' And he [Abram] gave him a tithe of all" **(GENESIS 14:18–20).**

God appointed the Levites—those of the tribe of Levi—to serve Him as ministering priests and to be supported by the tithe funds instead of getting a portion of the land as an inheritance. "Behold, I have given the children of Levi all the tithes in Israel as an inheritance in return for the work which they perform, the work of the tabernacle of meeting" **(NUMBERS 18:21–24).**

"You shall truly tithe all the increase of your grain that the field produces year by year. And you shall eat before the LORD your God, in the place where He chooses to make His name abide, the tithe of your grain and your new wine and your oil, of the firstborn of your herds and your flocks, that you may learn to fear the LORD your God always" **(DEUTERONOMY 14:22–25).**

"As soon as the commandment was circulated, the children of Israel brought in abundance the firstfruits of grain and wine, oil and honey, and of all the produce of the field; and they brought in abundantly the tithe of everything. And the children of Israel and Judah, who dwelt in the cities of Judah, brought the tithe of oxen and sheep; also the tithe of holy things which were consecrated to the LORD their God they laid in heaps" **(2 CHRONICLES 31:5, 6).**

"Then all Judah brought the tithe of the grain and the new wine and the oil to the storehouse" **(NEHEMIAH 13:12).**

Jesus said, "Woe to you, scribes and Pharisees, hypocrites! For you pay tithe of mint and anise and cummin, and have neglected the weightier matters of the law: justice and mercy and faith. These you ought to have done, without leaving the others undone" **(MATTHEW 23:23).**

"Indeed those who are of the sons of Levi, who receive the priesthood, have a commandment to receive tithes from the people according to the law, that is, from their brethren, though they have come from the loins of Abraham; but he whose genealogy is not derived from them received tithes from Abraham and blessed him who had the promises. Now beyond all contradiction the lesser is blessed by the better. Here mortal men receive tithes, but there he receives them, of whom it is witnessed that he lives. Even Levi, who receives tithes, paid tithes through Abraham, so to speak" **(HEBREWS 7:5–9)**.

Although all our money belongs to God, the tithe is holy. It is an acknowledgment of God's ownership. It reveals that we really believe He owns all we have.

08 What promises did God give the Israelites who made Him "first" in their giving? Do these promises apply to us today?

"Honor the LORD with your possessions, and with the firstfruits of all your increase; so your barns will be filled with plenty, and your vats will overflow with new wine" **(PROVERBS 3:9, 10)**.

"The first of the firstfruits of your land you shall bring into the house of the LORD your God" **(EXODUS 23:19)**.

God told Moses, "Speak to the children of Israel, and say to them: 'When you come into the land which I give to you, and reap its harvest, then you shall bring a sheaf of the firstfruits of your harvest to the priest' " **(LEVITICUS 23:10)**.

"There is one who scatters, yet increases more; and there is one who withholds more than is right, but it leads to poverty. The generous soul will be made rich, and he who waters will also be watered himself" **(PROVERBS 11:24, 25)**.

"He who has pity on the poor lends to the LORD, and He will pay back what he has given" **(PROVERBS 19:17)**.

"He who has a generous eye will be blessed, for he gives of his bread to the poor" **(PROVERBS 22:9)**.

" 'Bring all the tithes into the storehouse, that there may be food in My house, and try Me now in this,' says the LORD of hosts, 'if I will not open for you the windows of heaven and pour out for you such blessing that there will not be room enough to receive it. And I will rebuke the devourer for your sakes, so that he will not destroy the fruit of your ground, nor shall the vine fail to bear fruit for you in the field,' says the LORD of hosts" **(MALACHI 3:10, 11)**.

"Whoever gives one of these little ones only a cup of cold water in the name of a disciple, assuredly, I say to you, he shall by no means lose his reward" **(MATTHEW 10:42)**.

"But this I say: He who sows sparingly will also reap sparingly, and he who sows bountifully will also reap bountifully" **(2 CORINTHIANS 9:6)**.

09 Who are some outstanding biblical examples of faithfulness in tithing? Are there some well-known examples of tithing in the business community as well?

"Then Jacob made a vow, saying, 'If God will be with me, and keep me in this way that I am going, and give me bread to eat and clothing to put on.... This stone which I have set as a pillar shall be God's house, and of all that You give me I will surely give a tenth to You' " **(GENESIS 28:20, 22).**

"Then Melchizedek king of Salem brought out bread and wine; he was the priest of God Most High. And he blessed him [Abram] and said: 'Blessed be Abram of God Most High, possessor of heaven and earth; and blessed be God Most High, who has delivered your enemies into your hand.' And he [Abram] gave him a tithe of all" **(GENESIS 14:18–20).**

"Now consider how great this man [Melchizedek] was, to whom even the patriarch Abraham gave a tenth of the spoils" **(HEBREWS 7:4).**

I daresay that not only the patriarchs Jacob and Abraham were faithful in paying God an honest tithe, but so were Moses and David, Peter and Paul, and all the other heroes of faith. But beyond the pages of the Bible, many Christians have found real-life blessings in honoring God by obeying His Word in this respect. Some of our country's greatest business leaders have put God's plan to the test and found that tithing does pay financially as well as spiritually. A few examples may suffice to illustrate their successful experiences:

- ***William Colgate:*** builder of the prosperous Colgate-Palmolive Company.
- ***John D. Rockefeller Sr.:*** founder of Standard Oil Company.
- ***Henry John Heinz:*** of H. J. Heinz "57 Varieties" pickle and ketchup fame.
- ***James Cash Penney:*** founder of the J. C. Penney stores.
- ***Henry P. Crowell:*** founder of the Quaker Oats Company.
- ***John Wanamaker:*** builder of Wanamaker's Department Stores.
- ***Matthias W. Baldwin:*** founder of the Baldwin Locomotive Works.
- ***R. G. LeTourneau:*** builder of LeTourneau's heavy equipment for road building.
- ***James L. Kraft:*** founder of the Kraft Cheese Company.
- ***Milton Snavely Hershey:*** builder of the world's largest chocolate factory.

10 What did Jesus say about the importance of faithfulness in tithing?

Jesus said, "Woe to you, scribes and Pharisees, hypocrites! For you pay tithe of mint and anise and cummin, and have neglected the weightier matters of the law: justice and mercy and faith. These you ought to have done, without leaving the others undone" **(MATTHEW 23:23).**

Jesus said, "Woe to you Pharisees! For you tithe mint and rue and all manner of herbs, and pass by justice and the love of God. These you ought to have done, without leaving the others undone" **(LUKE 11:42).**

In discussing tithe, Jesus said, "This ye ought to have done," but He condemned the Pharisees for neglecting mercy, justice, and compassion. The tithe is sacred. It is set apart to accomplish God's goal of spreading the gospel message to the ends of the earth. And in addition to this, the local congregation as well as the church at large has expenses not provided for in the tithe.

11 The tithe—the first 10 percent of our income—is set apart as holy, but what does the Bible teach about offerings?

"Every man shall give as he is able, according to the blessing of the LORD your God which He has given you" **(DEUTERONOMY 16:17).**

"On the first day of the week let each one of you lay something aside, storing up as he may prosper, that there be no collections when I come" **(1 CORINTHIANS 16:2).**

"If there is first a willing mind, it is accepted according to what one has, and not according to what he does not have" **(2 CORINTHIANS 8:12).**

The Lord asks, "Will a man rob God? Yet you have robbed Me! But you say, 'In what way have we robbed You?' In tithes and offerings" **(MALACHI 3:8).**

The tithe is the Lord's tenth, holy to the Lord and sacred to His treasury. But freewill offerings also serve as a good barometer of our character and spiritual condition. And in this text, the Lord says we can "rob" Him in both tithes and offerings. Selfishness on our part is also looked on as robbery of God when He enables us, through His blessings, to be benevolent to His cause and to others. Thomas Fuller rightly observed that "he who gives his heart to God will not withhold his money." For when the heart is converted, the purse will be inverted.

When the Lord blesses us, our thankful hearts lead us to ask, "What shall I render to the LORD for all His benefits toward me?" **(PSALM 116:12).**

The psalmist tells us, "Give to the LORD the glory due His name; bring an offering, and come into His courts" **(PSALM 96:8).**

"Then Isaac sowed in that land, and reaped in the same year a hundredfold; and the LORD blessed him" **(GENESIS 26:12).**

"Remember the LORD your God, for it is He who gives you power to get wealth, that He may establish His covenant which He swore to your fathers, as it is this day" **(DEUTERONOMY 8:18).**

"For the poor will never cease from the land; therefore I command you, saying, 'You shall open your hand wide to your brother, to your poor and your needy, in your land' " **(DEUTERONOMY 15:11).**

When Mary Magdalene brought some very expensive perfumed oil to Jesus and began to anoint Him with it, others "criticized her sharply." But the Master defended her in these words: "She has done what she could. She has come beforehand [that is, before My death] to anoint My body for burial" **(MARK 14:5, 8).**

"He who is faithful in what is least is faithful also in much; and he who is unjust in what is least is unjust also in much" **(LUKE 16:10).**

"Moreover, brethren, we make known to you the grace of God bestowed on the churches of Macedonia: that in a great trial of affliction the abundance of their joy and their deep poverty abounded in the riches of their liberality. For I bear witness that according to their ability, yes, and beyond their ability, they were freely willing" **(2 CORINTHIANS 8:1–3).**

12 Each of us has different giving capacities. Our ability to give is different. What is more important to God—the amount we give or the attitude with which we give?

"Let each one give as he purposes in his heart, not grudgingly or of necessity; for God loves a cheerful giver" **(2 CORINTHIANS 9:7).**

"He [Jesus] looked up and saw the rich putting their gifts into the treasury, and He saw also a certain poor widow putting in two mites. So He said, 'Truly I say to you that this poor widow has put in more than all; for all these out of their abundance have put in offerings for God, but she out of her poverty put in all the livelihood that she had' " **(LUKE 21:1–4).**

"If there is among you a poor man of your brethren, within any of the gates in your land which the LORD your God is giving you, you shall not harden your heart nor shut your hand from your poor brother, but you shall open your hand wide to him and willingly lend him sufficient for his need, whatever he needs. . . . You shall surely give to him, and your heart should not be grieved when you give to him, because for this thing the LORD your God will bless you in all your works and in all to which you put your hand" **(DEUTERONOMY 15:7, 8, 10, 11).**

"Be hospitable to one another without grumbling" **(1 PETER 4:9).**

"Speak to the children of Israel, that they bring Me an offering. From everyone who gives it willingly with his heart you shall take My offering" **(EXODUS 25:2).**

'Take from among you an offering to the Lord. Whoever is of a willing heart, let him bring it as an offering to the Lord: gold, silver, and bronze" **(EXODUS 35:5).**

A young professional once asked his pastor, "When will the church stop asking for my money?" The pastor responded, "When God stops giving to you." The poem below reflects this thought:

"What—*giving* again?"

I asked in dismay.

"And must I keep *giving*

And *giving* away?"

"Oh, no," said the angel,

Piercing me through.

"Just give till the Master

Stops *giving* to you!"

"I know also, my God, that You test the heart and have pleasure in uprightness. As for me, in the uprightness of my heart I have willingly offered all these things; and now with joy I have seen Your people, who are present here to offer willingly to You" **(1 CHRONICLES 29:17).**

"He who has a generous eye will be blessed, for he gives of his bread to the poor" **(PROVERBS 22:9).**

Here is Paul's personal example: "I have coveted no one's silver or gold or apparel. Yes, you yourselves know that these hands have provided for my necessities, and for those who were with me. I have shown you in every way, by laboring like this, that you must support the weak. And remember the words of the Lord Jesus, that He said, 'It is more blessed to give than to receive' " **(ACTS 20:33–35).**

Paul strongly urges that "he who gives" should do so "with liberality" **(ROMANS 12:8).**

"But this I say: He who sows sparingly will also reap sparingly, and he who sows bountifully will also reap bountifully" **(2 CORINTHIANS 9:6).**

God has promised to supply the needs of all who are faithful in returning His tithes and offerings. In **PHILIPPIANS 4:19**, we have an eternal pledge: "And my God shall supply all your need according to His riches in glory by Christ Jesus." To all who are faithful stewards, God gives the assurance that He will supply their needs. The needs of God's children are already underwritten by the bank of heaven. Jesus stated, "Therefore do not worry, saying, 'What shall we eat?'. . . or 'What shall we wear?' . . . But seek first the kingdom of God and His righteousness, and all these things shall be added to you" **(MATTHEW 6:31–33).**

13 What promise does God make to His people who are faithful in their giving?

"There is one who scatters, yet increases more; and there is one who withholds more than is right, but it leads to poverty. The generous soul will be made rich, and he who waters will also be watered himself" **(PROVERBS 11:24, 25; EMPHASIS SUPPLIED).**

"He who has pity on the poor lends to the LORD, and He will pay back what he has given" **(PROVERBS 19:17).**

"And the LORD restored Job's losses when he prayed for his friends. Indeed the LORD gave Job twice as much as he had before.... Now the LORD blessed the latter days of Job more than his beginning; for he had fourteen thousand sheep, six thousand camels, one thousand yoke of oxen, and one thousand female donkeys. He also had seven sons and three daughters" **(JOB 42:10, 12, 13).**

If you encounter a poor man, "You shall surely give to him, and your heart should not be grieved when you give to him, because for this thing the LORD your God will bless you in all your works and in all to which you put your hand" **(DEUTERONOMY 15:10).**

"But this I say: He who sows sparingly will also reap sparingly, and he who sows bountifully will also reap bountifully.... Now may He who supplies seed to the sower, and bread for food, supply and multiply the seed you have sown and increase the fruits of your righteousness, while you are enriched in everything for all liberality, which causes thanksgiving through us to God" **(2 CORINTHIANS 9:6, 10, 11).**

"If I have made gold my hope, or said to fine gold, 'You are my confidence;' if I have rejoiced because my wealth was great, and because my hand had gained much.... 'Then let thistles grow instead of wheat, and weeds instead of barley' " **(JOB 31:24, 25, 40).**

"The schemes of the schemer are evil; he devises wicked plans to destroy the poor with lying words, even when the needy speaks justice. But a generous man devises generous things, and by generosity he shall stand" **(ISAIAH 32:7, 8).**

Some people pride themselves on their piety—how they fast and pray, and so on. But here God describes the "fast that I have chosen.... Is it not to share your bread with the hungry, and that you bring to your house the poor who are cast out; when you see the naked, that you cover him, and not hide yourself from your own flesh? Then your light shall break forth like the morning, your healing shall spring forth speedily, and your righteousness shall go before you; the glory of the LORD shall be your rear guard. Then you shall call, and the LORD will answer; you shall cry, and He will say, 'Here I am.' If you take away the yoke from your midst, the pointing of the finger, and speaking wickedness, if you extend your soul to the hungry and satisfy the afflicted soul, then your light shall dawn in the darkness, and your darkness shall be as the noonday.

The LORD will guide you continually, and satisfy your soul in drought, and strengthen your bones; you shall be like a watered garden, and like a spring of water, whose waters do not fail" **(ISAIAH 58:6–11).**

When Jesus comes in His glory, "then the King will say to those on His right hand, 'Come, you blessed of My Father, inherit the kingdom prepared for you from the foundation of the world: for I was hungry and you gave Me food; I was thirsty and you gave Me drink; I was a stranger and you took Me in; I was naked and you clothed Me; I was sick and you visited Me; I was in prison and you came to Me.' Then the righteous will answer Him, saying, 'Lord, when did we see You hungry and feed You, or thirsty and give You drink? When did we see You a stranger and take You in, or naked and clothe You? Or when did we see You sick, or in prison, and come to You?' And the King will answer and say to them, 'Assuredly, I say to you, inasmuch as you did it to one of the least of these My brethren, you did it to Me' " **(MATTHEW 25:34–40).**

"Give, and it will be given to you: good measure, pressed down, shaken together, and running over will be put into your bosom. For with the same measure that you use, it will be measured back to you" **(LUKE 6:38).**

You *can't* outgive God! For He'll give it right back to you. Now as a final thought, consider these anonymous words on how much we ought to give:

Give as you would if an *angel*

Awaited your gift at the door.

Give as you would if tomorrow

Found you where giving was o'er.

Give as you would to the Master

If you met *His* loving look.

Give as you would of your substance

If *His hand* your offering took.

Our heavenly Father owns the world and takes the responsibility of providing for His children. Thank God, the promise to the faithful steward is certain!

The Bible presents eternal financial principles that make sense. It reveals financial secrets that most of the world does not know. It encourages us to re-evaluate our priorities—to seek the eternal rather than the earthly. God's Word leads us to make investments that will pay off in the long run.

CHAPTER 22

What the Bible Says About Growing as a Christian

Proud parents are very conscious of every part of their child's growth. They note each important milestone in their child's life whether it is rolling over for the first time, taking that first step, or speaking the first complete sentence. Each one of these "firsts" is an indicator of growth. Growth patterns are important to parents, and they are important to God too!

The Christian life involves both coming to Jesus and growing in Jesus. It involves forgiveness and restoration. Jesus longs to forgive our sins, removing the guilt and condemnation of the past. His acceptance, forgiveness, and love help us to grow in Him. He desires to rebuild our lives. In this chapter, we will learn God's way of making us whole again.

01 What miraculous change occurs when we surrender our lives to Jesus?

"Then I will give them one heart, and I will put a new spirit within them, and take the stony heart out of their flesh, and give them a heart of flesh, that they may walk in My statutes and keep My judgments and do them; and they shall be My people, and I will be their God" **(EZEKIEL 11:19, 20).**

"This is the covenant that I will make with the house of Israel after those days, says the Lord: I will put My laws in their mind and write them on their hearts; and I will be their God, and they shall be My people" **(HEBREWS 8:10).**

The Almighty God of heaven puts His laws into our *minds* so we will know what is right, and He writes them in our *hearts,* so we will *love* to do what is right. He transforms our characters and changes us from within—if we let Him.

"I will give you a new heart and put a new spirit within you; I will take the heart of stone out of your flesh and give you a heart of flesh. I will put My Spirit within you and cause you to walk in My statutes, and you will keep My judgments and do them" **(EZEKIEL 36:26, 27).**

The first successful human heart transplant was performed by Dr. Christiaan Barnard of South Africa, but it is our loving Lord—the Creator and Divine Physician—who specializes in spiritual heart transplants.

"Then I will give them a heart to know Me, that I am the LORD; and they shall be My people, and I will be their God, for they shall return to Me with their whole heart" **(JEREMIAH 24:7).**

"Create in me a clean heart, O God; and renew a right spirit within me" **(PSALM 51:10, KJV).**

"The LORD your God will circumcise your heart and the heart of your descendants, to love the LORD your God with all your heart and with all your soul, that you may live" **(DEUTERONOMY 30:6).**

"Then I will give them one heart and one way, that they may fear Me forever, for the good of them and their children after them. And I will make an everlasting covenant with them, that I will not turn away from doing them good; but I will put My fear in their hearts so that they will not depart from Me" **(JEREMIAH 32:39, 40).**

"Cast away from you all the transgressions which you have committed, and get yourselves a new heart and a new spirit. For why should you die, O house of Israel?" **(EZEKIEL 18:31).**

"You [faithful believers] are our epistle [letter] written in our hearts, known and read by all men; clearly you [yourself] are an epistle of Christ, ministered by us, written not with ink but by the Spirit of the living God, not on tablets of stone but on tablets of flesh, that is, of the heart" **(2 CORINTHIANS 3:2, 3).**

God promises to do something for us that we cannot do for ourselves. He says, "I will give you a heart of flesh." God promises to work miracles inside of us.

02 As we read His Word prayerfully, what promise does our Lord make regarding what will happen deep within our hearts and minds?

"His divine power has given to us all things that pertain to life and godliness, through the knowledge of Him who called us by glory and virtue, by which have been given to us *exceedingly great* and *precious promises, that through these you may be partakers of the divine nature,* having escaped the corruption that is in the world through lust" **(2 PETER 1:3, 4; EMPHASIS SUPPLIED).**

"But he [Lazarus] said to him [the rich man], 'If they do not hear Moses and the prophets, neither will they be persuaded though one rise from the dead' " **(LUKE 16:31).**

How true were the words of Jesus in this parable. For the hardhearted ones who rejected Him refused to be persuaded even when not just one, but two—Lazarus and Christ Himself—rose from the dead!

"For this reason we also thank God without ceasing, because when you received the word of God which you heard from us, you welcomed it not as the word of men, but as it is in truth, the word of God, which also effectively works in you who believe" **(1 THESSALONIANS 2:13).**

"Of His own will He brought us forth by *the word of truth,* that we might be a kind of firstfruits of His creatures. So then, my beloved brethren, let every man be swift to hear, slow to speak, slow to wrath; for the wrath of man does not produce the righteousness of God. Therefore lay aside all filthiness and overflow of wickedness, and receive with meekness the implanted word, which is able to save your souls" **(JAMES 1:18–21).**

The apostle Peter tells us that we have "been born again, not of corruptible seed but incorruptible, through the word of God which lives and abides forever, because 'All flesh is as grass, and all the glory of man as the flower of the grass. The grass withers, and its flower falls away, but the word of the LORD endures forever' " **(1 PETER 1:23–25).**

"Therefore, laying aside all malice, all deceit, hypocrisy, envy, and all evil speaking, as newborn babes, desire the pure milk of the word, that you may grow thereby" **(1 PETER 2:1, 2).**

As Jesus preached in different villages, "His mother and brothers came to Him, and could not approach Him because of the crowd. And it was told Him by some, who said, 'Your mother and Your brothers are standing outside, desiring to see You.' But He answered and said to them, 'My mother and My brothers are these who hear the word of God and do it' " **(LUKE 8:19–21).**

"It happened, as He spoke these things, that a certain woman from the crowd raised her voice and said to Him, 'Blessed is the womb that bore You, and the breasts which nursed You!' But He said, 'More than that, blessed are those who hear the word of God and keep it!' " **(LUKE 11:27, 28).**

"For the word of God is living and powerful, and sharper than any two-edged sword, piercing even to the division of soul and spirit, and of joints and marrow, and is a discerner of the thoughts and intents of the heart" **(HEBREWS 4:12).**

"As God is faithful, our word to you was not Yes and No. For the Son of God, Jesus Christ, who was preached among you by us—by me, Silvanus, and Timothy—was not Yes and No, but in Him was Yes. For all the promises of God in Him are Yes, and in Him Amen, to the glory of God through us" **(2 CORINTHIANS 1:18–20).**

"You search *the Scriptures,* for in them you think you have eternal life; and these are they which *testify of Me*" **(JOHN 5:39; EMPHASIS SUPPLIED).**

The "Scriptures" Jesus was referring to were the Old Testament—the only Scriptures of the Bible available at that time, for the New Testament had not yet been written. Bible scholars have found in the Old Testament Scriptures dozens and dozens of remarkable prophecies pertaining to Jesus that foreshadow many details of His life and ministry as the Messiah—including His great sacrifice on the cross. Christ is the center of both the Old and New Testaments. For example, Jesus is represented throughout the Old Testament sanctuary. He is symbolized in the seven-branched candlestick, the altar of incense, and the table of shewbread. He is a dying sacrifice and the living Priest.

God's counsel is, "Study to shew thyself approved unto God, a workman that needeth not to be ashamed, rightly dividing the word of truth" **(2 TIMOTHY 2:15, KJV).**

"All Scripture is given by inspiration of God, and is profitable for doctrine, for reproof, for correction, for instruction in righteousness, that the man of God may be complete, thoroughly equipped for every good work" **(2 TIMOTHY 3:16, 17).**

John Greenleaf Whittier, the Quaker poet, wrote the following lines:

> We search the world for truth, we cull
> The good, the pure, the beautiful,
>
> From graven stone and written scroll,
> From the old flower-fields of the soul,
>
> And, weary seekers of the best,
> We come back laden from our quest,
>
> To find that all the sages said
> *"Is in the Book our mothers read."*

03 Is it possible to study the Bible and still receive very little benefit? Why are some people not changed when they study the Bible?

"Indeed the gospel was preached to us as well as to them; but the word which they heard did not profit them, not being mixed with faith in those who heard it" **(HEBREWS 4:2).**

"Beware, brethren, lest there be in any of you an evil heart of unbelief in departing from the living God" **(HEBREWS 3:12).**

"Without faith it is impossible to please Him, for he who comes to God must believe that He is, and that He is a rewarder of those who diligently seek Him" **(HEBREWS 11:6).**

"For this reason we also thank God without ceasing, because when you received the word of God which you heard from us, you welcomed it not as the word of men, but as it is in truth, the word of God, which also effectively works in you who believe" **(1 THESSALONIANS 2:13).**

"That they all may be condemned who did not believe the truth but had pleasure in unrighteousness" **(2 THESSALONIANS 2:12).**

"Therefore lay aside all filthiness and overflow of wickedness, and receive with meekness the implanted word, which is able to save your souls" **(JAMES 1:21).**

To receive benefit from reading the Bible, it must be personally applied by faith. Place yourself in every story. Believe that God will accomplish miraculous changes in your life as you read His Word.

04 What do both the Old and New Testaments teach about what it really means to be a genuine follower of God? What is true spirituality?

"This is eternal life, that they may know You, the only true God, and Jesus Christ whom You have sent" **(JOHN 17:3).**

"They [the Pharisees] said to Him [Jesus], 'Where is Your Father?' Jesus answered, 'You know neither Me nor My Father. If you had known Me, you would have known My Father also' " **(JOHN 8:19).**

King David said, "As for you, my son Solomon, know the God of your father, and serve Him with a loyal heart and with a willing mind" **(1 CHRONICLES 28:9).**

"Those who know Your name will put their trust in You; for You, LORD, have not forsaken those who seek You" **(PSALM 9:10).**

"Thus says the LORD: 'Let not the wise man glory in his wisdom, let not the mighty man glory in his might, nor let the rich man glory in his riches; but let him who glories glory in this, that he understands and knows Me, that I am the LORD, exercising lovingkindness, judgment, and righteousness in the earth. For in these I delight,' says the LORD" **(JEREMIAH 9:23, 24).**

"But this is the covenant that I will make with the house of Israel after those days, says the LORD: I will put My law in their minds, and write it on their hearts; and I will be their God, and they shall be My people. No more shall every man teach his neighbor, and every man his brother, saying, 'Know the LORD,' for they all shall know Me, from the least of them to the greatest of them, says the LORD. For I will forgive their iniquity, and their sin I will remember no more" **(JEREMIAH 31:33, 34).**

"None of them shall teach his neighbor, and none his brother, saying, 'Know the LORD,' for all shall know Me, from the least of them to the greatest of them. For I will be merciful to their unrighteousness, and their sins and their lawless deeds I will remember no more" **(HEBREWS 8:11, 12).**

"Let us know, let us pursue the knowledge of the LORD" **(HOSEA 6:3).**

Christ will return, "in flaming fire taking vengeance on those who do not know God, and on those who do not obey the gospel of our Lord Jesus Christ" **(2 THESSALONIANS 1:8).**

"We know that the Son of God has come and has given us an understanding, that we may know Him who is true; and we are in Him who is true, in His Son Jesus Christ. This is the true God and eternal life" **(1 JOHN 5:20).**

When the people found Jesus, "They said to Him, 'What shall we do, that we may work the works of God?' Jesus answered and said to them, 'This is the work of God, that you believe in Him whom He sent' " **(JOHN 6:28, 29).**

05 When we know Jesus, what are our inner desires? What characterizes the attitude of one who really loves Jesus?

"He [Jesus] went a little farther and fell on His face, and prayed, saying, 'O My Father, if it is possible, let this cup pass from Me; nevertheless, not as I will, but as You will' " **(MATTHEW 26:39).**

Speaking of His heavenly Father, Jesus said, "He who sent Me is with Me. The Father has not left Me alone, for I always do those things that please Him" **(JOHN 8:29).**

Jesus declared, "I do not seek My own will but the will of the Father who sent Me" **(JOHN 5:30).**

Christ said, "I have come down from heaven, not to do My own will, but the will of Him who sent Me" **(JOHN 6:38).**

Jesus' desire is "that the world may know that I love the Father, and as the Father gave Me commandment, so I do" **(JOHN 14:31).**

Jesus Christ, the Lord from heaven, "being found in appearance as a man, He humbled Himself and became obedient to the point of death, even the death of the cross" **(PHILIPPIANS 2:8).**

"Jesus said to them, 'My food is to do the will of Him who sent Me, and to finish His work' " **(JOHN 4:34).**

Jesus said, "If you keep My commandments, you will abide in My love, just as I have kept My Father's commandments and abide in His love" **(JOHN 15:10).**

Christ declared, "I have glorified You on the earth. I have finished the work which You have given Me to do" **(JOHN 17:4).**

Longing to do God's will is at the heart of true spirituality. The Christian faith is not based on attempting to force God to do what we want; it is seeking to discover what He wants. It is not pursuing our will; it is pursuing His.

06 What is a major obstacle to a close relationship with Jesus? What hinders our growth in Christ?

Known sin is an obstacle to a full relationship with Jesus. When we continually turn our backs on Him, we cannot fully see His face.

"Behold, the LORD's hand is not shortened, that it cannot save; nor His ear heavy, that it cannot hear. But your iniquities have separated you from your God; and your sins have hidden His face from you, so that He will not hear" **(ISAIAH 59:1, 2).**

"If I regard iniquity in my heart, the Lord will not hear" **(PSALM 66:18).**

"The LORD is far from the wicked, but He hears the prayer of the righteous" **(PROVERBS 15:29).**

"Your iniquities have turned these things away, and your sins have withheld good from you" **(JEREMIAH 5:25).**

"Then My anger shall be aroused against them in that day, and I will forsake them, and I will hide My face from them, and they shall be devoured. And many evils and troubles shall befall them, so that they will say in that day, 'Have not these evils come upon us because our God is not among us?' And I will surely hide My face in that day because of all the evil which they have done, in that they have turned to other gods" **(DEUTERONOMY 31:17, 18).**

"And He said: 'I will hide My face from them, I will see what their end will be, for they are a perverse generation, children in whom is no faith' " **(DEUTERONOMY 32:20).**

"When you spread out your hands, I will hide My eyes from you; even though you make many prayers, I will not hear. Your hands are full of blood" **(ISAIAH 1:15).**

"Now we know that God does not hear sinners; but if anyone is a worshiper of God and does His will, He hears him" **(JOHN 9:31).**

"You ask and do not receive, because you ask amiss, that you may spend it on your pleasures" **(JAMES 4:3).**

"The Gentiles shall know that the house of Israel went into captivity for their iniquity; because they were unfaithful to Me, therefore I hid My face from them. I gave them into the hand of their enemies, and they all fell by the sword. According to their uncleanness and according to their transgressions I have dealt with them, and hidden My face from them" **(EZEKIEL 39:23, 24).**

"Then they will cry to the LORD, But He will not hear them; He will even hide His face from them at that time, because they have been evil in their deeds" **(MICAH 3:4).**

"The sacrifice of the wicked is an abomination to the LORD, but the prayer of the upright is His delight. The way of the wicked is an abomination to the LORD, but He loves him who follows righteousness. . . . The LORD is far from the wicked, but He hears the prayer of the righteous" **(PROVERBS 15:8, 9, 29).**

"One who turns away his ear from hearing the law, even his prayer is an abomination" **(PROVERBS 28:9).**

07 Where do all our temptations originate? Does God tempt us? Or do our temptations come from another source?

"You are of your father the devil, and the desires of your father you want to do. He was a murderer from the beginning, and does not stand in the truth, because there is no truth in him. When he speaks a lie, he speaks from his own resources, for he is a liar and the father of it" **(JOHN 8:44).**

"Now the serpent was more cunning than any beast of the field which the LORD God had made. And he said to the woman [Eve], 'Has God indeed said, "You shall not eat of every tree of the garden?" ' And the woman said to the serpent, 'We may eat the fruit of the trees of the garden; but of the fruit of the tree which is in the midst of the garden, God has said, "You shall not eat it, nor shall you touch it, lest you die." ' Then the serpent said to the woman, 'You will not surely die. For God knows that in the day you eat of it your eyes will be opened, and you will be like God, knowing good and evil' " **(GENESIS 3:1–5).**

A farmer planted good seeds in his field, but his enemy came by night and planted weeds in his field. When the farm hands noticed all the weeds and asked where they came from, "he said to them, 'An enemy has done this.' The servants said to him, 'Do you want us then to go and gather them up?' . . . He [Jesus, in explaining the parable] answered and said to them [the disciples]: 'He who sows the good seed is the Son of Man. The field is the world, the good seeds are the sons of the kingdom, but the tares [weeds] are the sons of the wicked one. The enemy who sowed them is the devil, the harvest is the end of the age, and the reapers are the angels' " **(MATTHEW 13:28, 37–39).**

Ananias and his wife Sapphira promised to sell a piece of land and give the proceeds to the church, but then they kept part of it. "Peter said, 'Ananias, why has Satan filled your heart to lie to the Holy Spirit and keep back part of the price of the land for yourself?' " **(ACTS 5:3).**

Paul, filled with the Holy Spirit, boldly confronted Elymas the sorcerer "and said, 'O full of all deceit and all fraud, you son of the devil, you enemy of all righteousness, will you not cease perverting the straight ways of the Lord?' " **(ACTS 13:10).**

When God praised the integrity of His servant Job to Satan, the latter responded with this challenge: "But now, stretch out Your hand and touch all that he has [that is, his great possessions], and he will surely curse You to Your face!" **(JOB 1:11).**

When Job withstood the test and remained faithful, Satan challenged God still further: "But stretch out Your hand now, and touch his bone and his flesh, and he will surely curse You to Your face!" **(JOB 2:5).**

With great concern, the apostle Paul said, "I fear, lest somehow, as the serpent deceived Eve by his craftiness, so your minds may be corrupted from the simplicity that is in Christ" **(2 CORINTHIANS 11:3).**

"He who sins is of the devil, for the devil has sinned from the beginning. For this purpose the Son of God was manifested, that He might destroy the works of the devil" **(1 JOHN 3:8).**

"Satan stood up against Israel, and moved David to number Israel [that is, to take a census to see how strong his people or his troops were]. . . . And God was displeased with this thing; therefore He struck Israel" **(1 CHRONICLES 21:1, 7).**

"Be sober, be vigilant; because your adversary the devil walks about like a roaring lion, seeking whom he may devour" **(1 PETER 5:8).**

08 How can we handle the sometimes overwhelming temptations of the evil one? What powerful assurance does Jesus give us when we face temptation?

"No temptation has overtaken you except such as is common to man; but God *is faithful, who will not allow you to be tempted beyond what you are able,* but with the temptation will also make the way of escape, that you may be able to bear it" **(1 CORINTHIANS 10:13; EMPHASIS SUPPLIED).**

"But where sin abounded, grace abounded much more" **(ROMANS 5:20).**

"I can do all things through Christ who strengthens me" **(PHILIPPIANS 4:13).**

"Through whom we have received grace and apostleship for obedience" **ROMANS 1:5).**

Jesus prayed, in what came to be known as "The Lord's Prayer": "Do not lead us into temptation, but deliver us from the evil one" **(LUKE 11:4).**

"The Lord said, 'Simon, Simon! Indeed, Satan has asked for you, that he may sift you as wheat. But I have prayed for you, that your faith should not fail; and when you have returned to Me, strengthen your brethren' " **(LUKE 22:31, 32).**

Paul cautions us to "put on the whole armor of God, that you may be able to stand against the wiles of the devil. For we do not wrestle against flesh and blood, but against principalities, against powers, against the rulers of the darkness of this age, against spiritual hosts of wickedness in the heavenly places. Therefore take up the whole armor of God, that you may be able to withstand in the evil day, and having done all, to stand" **(EPHESIANS 6:11–13).**

"My brethren, take the prophets, who spoke in the name of the Lord, as an example of suffering and patience. Indeed we count them blessed who endure. You have heard of the perseverance of Job and seen the end intended by the Lord—that the Lord is very compassionate and merciful" **(JAMES 5:10, 11).**

09 Where will we find strength to meet the temptations of the enemy? Since Jesus met all the temptations of Satan on our behalf, what does He invite us to do?

"Seeing then that we have a great High Priest who has passed through the heavens, Jesus the Son of God, let us hold fast our confession. For we do not have a High Priest who cannot sympathize with our weaknesses, but was in all points tempted as we are, yet without sin. *Let us therefore come boldly to the throne of grace,* that we may obtain mercy and find grace to help in time of need" **(HEBREWS 4:14–16; EMPHASIS SUPPLIED).**

"Therefore, brethren, having boldness to enter the Holiest by the blood of Jesus, by a new and living way which He consecrated for us, through the veil, that is, His flesh, and having a High Priest over the house of God, let us draw near with a true heart in full assurance of faith, having our hearts sprinkled from an evil conscience and our bodies washed with pure water. Let us hold fast the confession of our hope without wavering, for He who promised is faithful" **(HEBREWS 10:19–23).**

Think of "Christ as a Son over His own house, whose house we are if we hold fast the confidence and the rejoicing of the hope firm to the end" **(HEBREWS 3:6).**

"Through Him [Christ] we both have access by one Spirit to the Father" **(EPHESIANS 2:18).**

Paul speaks of Jesus, "in whom we have boldness and access with confidence through faith in Him" **(EPHESIANS 3:12).**

"Be anxious for nothing, but in everything by prayer and supplication, with thanksgiving, let your requests be made known to God; and the peace of God, which surpasses all understanding, will guard your hearts and minds through Christ Jesus" **(PHILIPPIANS 4:6, 7).**

10 How can we continue to grow in our Christian lives?

"Now this is the confidence that we have in Him, that if we ask anything according to His will, He hears us. And if we know that He hears us, whatever we ask, we know that we have the petitions that we have asked of Him" **(1 JOHN 5:14, 15)**.

Jesus taught us to pray with faith: "I say to you, ask, and it will be given to you; seek, and you will find; knock, and it will be opened to you. For everyone who asks receives, and he who seeks finds, and to him who knocks it will be opened. If a son asks for bread from any father among you, will he give him a stone? Or if he asks for a fish, will he give him a serpent instead of a fish?" **(LUKE 11:9–11)**.

"I sought the LORD, and He heard me, and delivered me from all my fears. . . . The eyes of the LORD are on the righteous, and His ears are open to their cry. . . . The righteous cry out, and the LORD hears, and delivers them out of all their troubles" **(PSALM 34:4, 15, 17)**.

"Call upon Me in the day of trouble; I will deliver you, and you shall glorify Me" **(PSALM 50:15)**.

"If I regard iniquity in my heart, the LORD will not hear. But certainly God has heard me; He has attended to the voice of my prayer" **(PSALM 66:18, 19)**.

"The LORD is near to all who call upon Him, to all who call upon Him in truth. He will fulfill the desire of those who fear Him; He also will hear their cry and save them" **(PSALM 145:18, 19)**.

"The LORD is far from the wicked, but He hears the prayer of the righteous" **(PROVERBS 15:29)**.

"If any of you lacks wisdom, let him ask of God, who gives to all liberally and without reproach, and it will be given to him. But let him ask in faith, with no doubting, for he who doubts is like a wave of the sea driven and tossed by the wind. For let not that man suppose that he will receive anything from the Lord; he is a double-minded man, unstable in all his ways" **(JAMES 1:5–8)**.

"The effective, fervent prayer of a righteous man avails much" **(JAMES 5:16)**.

The Lord God promises, "Call to Me, and I will answer you, and show you great and mighty things, which you do not know" **(JEREMIAH 33:3)**.

Jesus said, "Whatever things you ask in prayer, believing, you will receive" **(MATTHEW 21:22)**.

"Therefore I say to you, whatever things you ask when you pray, believe that you receive them, and you will have them" **(MARK 11:24)**.

"Now we know that God does not hear sinners; but if anyone is a worshiper of God and does His will, He hears him" **(JOHN 9:31)**.

"Whatever you ask in My name, that I will do, that the Father may be glorified in the Son. If you ask anything in My name, I will do it" **(JOHN 14:13, 14)**.

"Most assuredly, I say to you, whatever you ask the Father in My name He will give you. Until now you have asked nothing in My name. Ask, and you will receive, that your joy may be full" **(JOHN 16:23, 24).**

No one knows exactly *how* the priceless privilege of prayer works—but we know it works! Notice a few principles: First, we must *ask* God—this presumes we believe that He exists and that He loves us. Second, we must *believe* that God hears us and that He wants what is best for us, so we must ask in faith. Third, experienced Christians have found that our prayers are *always answered*—but this does not mean that God, in His wisdom, always answers, "Yes." Sometimes He answers, "Wait." So we must be diligent and persevering in prayer. And sometimes He answers, "No," because He knows that what we request would not be best for us. A little baby in her infant seat may cry for the pretty bumble bee that's buzzing around, but her mother won't let her have it. So God, our loving heavenly Father, must sometimes deny our requests—often because He has *something better* in store for us!

A fourth principle of prayer is seen in the verses just above, where Jesus teaches that we should *ask in His name.* Jesus' name is powerful. At the name of Jesus all of the hosts of hell tremble. At Jesus' name, demons flee. At Jesus' name, the angelic armies of heaven come to the aid of God's children.

Prayer is not magic; it's not some mystical spell from the likes of young Harry Potter. Instead, it's a direct line to heaven designed by the God who loves us—and who loves to hear from us. Prayer does not bring God down to us; it brings us up to Him. He knows our needs before we ask. But He wants us to ask because it shows we recognize our dependence on Him.

One Christian writer asks, "Why should the sons and daughters of God be reluctant to pray, when prayer is the key in the hand of faith to unlock heaven's storehouse, where are treasured the boundless resources of Omnipotence?" (Ellen G. White, *Steps to Christ,* p. 94).

"If you abide in Me, and My words abide in you, you will ask what you desire, and it shall be done for you" **(JOHN 15:7).**

"Whatever we ask we receive from Him, because we keep His commandments and do those things that are pleasing in His sight" **(1 JOHN 3:22).**

Our Lord promises to provide us with the power for Christian living. We can have absolute confidence that when we ask for His power and His Spirit to do His will, He will gladly give us what we long for **(SEE LUKE 11:13).**

11 What example has Jesus left us for victorious Christian living? What "how tos" has He given us?

"Now in the morning, having risen a long while before daylight, He went out and departed to a solitary place; and there He prayed" **(MARK 1:35).**

No other life was ever so crowded with labor and responsibility as was that of Jesus, yet how often was He found in prayer! How constant was His communion with God!

"Great multitudes came together to hear, and to be healed by Him of their infirmities. So He Himself often withdrew into the wilderness and prayed" **(LUKE 5:15, 16).**

"Now it came to pass in those days that He went out to the mountain to pray, and continued all night in prayer to God" **(LUKE 6:12).**

"And when He had sent them away, He departed to the mountain to pray" **(MARK 6:46).**

"And whatever things you ask in prayer, believing, you will receive" **(MATTHEW 21:22).**

Like Jesus, Paul urges us to be "praying always with all prayer and supplication in the Spirit, being watchful to this end with all perseverance and supplication for all the saints" **(EPHESIANS 6:18).**

"And it happened as He was alone praying that His disciples joined Him" **(LUKE 9:18).**

"Now it came to pass, as He was praying in a certain place, when He ceased, that one of His disciples said to Him, 'Lord, teach us to pray, as John also taught his disciples' " **(LUKE 11:1).**

"Let this mind be in you which was also in Christ Jesus" **(PHILIPPIANS 2:5).**

We discover strength for Christian living by seeking God in prayer. Prayer opens our hearts to God to receive His strength.

12 What Bible promises for victory over temptation can we claim as our own?

"Being confidant of this very thing, that He who has begun a good work in you will complete it until the day of Jesus Christ" **(PHILIPPIANS 1:6).**

"My God shall supply all your need according to His riches in glory by Christ Jesus" **(PHILIPPIANS 4:19).**

"The LORD is my shepherd; I shall not want" **(PSALM 23:1).**

Paul's prayer is "that He would grant you, according to the riches of His glory, to be strengthened with might through His Spirit in the inner man" **(EPHESIANS 3:16).**

"Be anxious for nothing, but in everything by prayer and supplication, with thanksgiving, let your requests be made known to God; and the peace of God, which surpasses all understanding, will guard your hearts and minds through Christ Jesus" **(PHILIPPIANS 4:6, 7).**

13 When we feel we are too weak or the struggle seems too great, what encouraging Bible promises are ours?

"I can do all things through Christ who strengthens me" **(PHILIPPIANS 4:13).**

Christ taught us, saying, "I am the vine, you are the branches. He who abides in Me, and I in him, bears much fruit; for without Me you can do nothing. If anyone does not abide in Me, he is cast out as a branch and is withered; and they gather them and throw them into the fire, and they are burned. If you abide in Me, and My words abide in you, you will ask what you desire, and it shall be done for you" **(JOHN 15:5–7).**

NOTE: The stark contrast between those last two Scripture passages is indeed remarkable. One text declares that through Christ, we "can do all things." The other asserts that without Christ, we "can do nothing." It's time we learned where our true strength lies.

"We have such trust through Christ toward God. Not that we are sufficient of ourselves to think of anything as being from ourselves, but our sufficiency is from God" **(2 CORINTHIANS 3:4, 5).**

"Finally, my brethren, be strong in the Lord and in the power of His might" **(EPHESIANS 6:10).**

May we be "strengthened with all might, according to His glorious power, for all patience and longsuffering with joy" **(COLOSSIANS 1:11).**

"He gives power to the weak, and to those who have no might He increases strength. Even the youths shall faint and be weary, and the young men shall utterly fall, but those who wait on the LORD shall renew their strength" **(ISAIAH 40:29, 30, 31).**

God gives this wonderful assurance:"Fear not, for I am with you; be not dismayed, for I am your God. I will strengthen you, yes, I will help you, I will uphold you with My righteous right hand" **(ISAIAH 41:10).**

Paul tells us that when he prayed to God for healing from some unnamed affliction (many Bible scholars believe it was trouble with his eyes), "He [God] said to me, 'My grace is sufficient for you, for My strength is made perfect in weakness.' Therefore most gladly I will rather boast in my infirmities, that the power of Christ may rest upon me. Therefore I take pleasure in infirmities, in reproaches, in needs, in persecutions, in distresses, for Christ's sake. For when I am weak, then I am strong" **(2 CORINTHIANS 12:9, 10).**

14 What does Christ desire to accomplish in our lives through His Holy Spirit? What is His ultimate goal in our lives?

"Behold what manner of love the Father has bestowed on us, that we should be called children of God! Therefore the world does not know us, because it did not know Him.

"Beloved, now we are children of God; and it has not yet been revealed what we shall be, but we know that when He is revealed, we shall be like Him, for we shall see Him as He is. And everyone who has this hope in Him purifies himself, just as He is pure" **(1 JOHN 3:1–3).**

Paul says God "made no distinction between us and them [that is, between Gentiles and Jews], purifying their hearts by faith" **(ACTS 15:9).**

"Therefore, having these promises, beloved, let us cleanse ourselves from all filthiness of the flesh and spirit, perfecting holiness in the fear of God" **(2 CORINTHIANS 7:1).**

God has "given to us exceedingly great and precious promises, that through these you may be partakers of the divine nature, having escaped the corruption that is in the world through lust" **(2 PETER 1:4).**

"Therefore, beloved, looking forward to these things, be diligent to be found by Him in peace, without spot and blameless" **(2 PETER 3:14).**

"He who says he abides in Him ought himself also to walk just as He walked" **(1 JOHN 2:6).**

15 Where do we discover the strength, righteousness, and power to be more like Jesus?

"Therefore we also, since we are surrounded by so great a cloud of witnesses, let us lay aside every weight, and the sin which so easily ensnares us, and let us run with endurance the race that is set before us, looking unto Jesus, the author and finisher of our faith, who for the joy that was set before Him endured the cross, despising the shame, and has sat down at the right hand of the throne of God" **(HEBREWS 12:1, 2).**

"By one offering [that is, by the sacrifice of Himself on the cross] He [Jesus] has perfected forever those who are being sanctified" **(HEBREWS 10:14).**

Our Lord Jesus "is able to keep you from stumbling, and to present you faultless before the presence of His glory with exceeding joy" **(JUDE 24).**

Our wonderful Savior, "the Author and Finisher of our faith," is also rightfully portrayed as "the Alpha and the Omega, the Beginning and the End" and "the First and the Last." He is Jesus, the "KING OF KINGS AND LORD OF LORDS" **(REVELATION 1:8, 11; 19:16).**

Jesus declares that He is "the Author and Finisher of our faith." What a promise! We may stumble, but He will never let us go. We may falter, but He will remain steadfast. As we continue trusting, believing, praying, and fellowshiping with God in His Word, we will continue to grow in Christ. As we share His love with others and witness to our family and friends, our own faith will increase.

The more we know Jesus, the more we long to be like Him.

CHAPTER 23

What the Bible Says About God's Last-Day Church

The church has fallen out of favor with many people today. Tens of thousands have dropped out of Christian churches throughout North America in recent years. They have concluded that the church is a large, bureaucratic institution driven by politics, and they want no part of it. These honest, clear thinking people are tired of hypocrisy and formalism. Many of them long for genuine New Testament Christianity. They ask themselves, "Where are the people of God today?"

Does God have a church on earth? With hundreds of churches battling among themselves over who is right, does God have a true church today? And if He does, can you find it?

The average person is confused by this bewildering array of churches. Some people have even concluded that the discovery of truth is extremely personal. They argue that truth is a matter of opinion. "You have your truth, and I have mine," they say. "You look at it your way, and I will look at it mine."

This leads us to some important questions. Is finding truth a matter of chance? Does God have a true church today? Does it make any difference which church I attend? If God has a true church, how can I find it?

This chapter will help you answer these important questions directly from the Bible itself. Throughout the history of the world, God has always had a people who followed Him. This group of loyal and committed followers have composed His church in every age.

01 What key characteristic did God's genuine followers possess throughout the Old Testament era?

Just as He had earlier promised Abraham **(SEE GENESIS 15:5; 22:16–18)**, God also assured Jacob, "I will make your descendants multiply as the stars of heaven; I will give to your descendants all these lands; and in your seed all the nations of the earth shall be blessed; *because Abraham obeyed My voice and kept My charge, My commandments, My statutes, and My laws*" **(GENESIS 26:4, 5; EMPHASIS SUPPLIED).**

God says He plans to bless Abraham immensely, "for I know him, that he will command his children and his household after him, and they shall keep the way of the LORD, to do justice and judgment; that the LORD may bring upon Abraham that which he hath spoken of him" **(GENESIS 18:18, 19, KJV).**

As a supreme test of obedience, God told Abraham to sacrifice his son, Isaac, to Him. Painfully, reluctantly, but in great faith, Abraham at once proceeded to obey—only to find that the Lord intervened and prevented Isaac's death at the last moment. Then God told Abraham, "Because you have done this thing, and have not withheld your son, your only son—blessing I will bless you, and multiplying I will multiply your descendants as the stars of the heaven and as the sand which is on the seashore; and your descendants shall possess the gate of their enemies. In your seed all the nations of the earth shall be blessed, *because* you have obeyed My voice" **(GENESIS 22:16–18; EMPHASIS SUPPLIED).**

Abraham was "called out" from his homeland to share God's goodness and glory through his obedience. As such he is a symbol of God's church in every age.

"By faith Abraham obeyed when he was called to go out to the place which he would receive as an inheritance. And he went out, not knowing where he was going. . . . By faith Abraham, when he was tested, offered up Isaac, and he who had received the promises offered up his only begotten son" **(HEBREWS 11:8, 17).**

"Faith by itself, if it does not have works, is dead. But someone will say, 'You have faith, and I have works.' Show me your faith without your works, and I will show you my faith by my works. You believe that there is one God. You do well. Even the demons believe—and tremble! But do you want to know, O foolish man, that faith without works is dead? Was not Abraham our father justified by works when he offered Isaac his son on the altar? Do you see that faith was working together with his works, and by works faith was made perfect? And the Scripture was fulfilled which says, 'Abraham believed God, and it was accounted to him for righteousness.' And he was called the friend of God. You see then that a man is justified by works, and not by faith only. . . . For as the body without the spirit is dead, so faith without works is dead also" **(JAMES 2:17–24, 26)**.

Because Abraham was faithful to Him, God planned to acquaint the nations of this world with a knowledge of Himself through the family (or church) of Abraham. Abraham's son, Isaac, passed on God's blessing to his son, Jacob. Jacob's twelve sons became the founders of the nation of Israel. Israel was the church of the Old Testament. God desired to reveal a knowledge of His glory to the world through His church, Israel.

"Blessed is the man who fears the LORD, who delights greatly in His commandments. His descendants will be mighty on earth; the generation of the upright will be blessed" **(PSALM 112:1, 2)**.

"Blessed is every one who fears the LORD, who walks in His ways. When you eat the labor of your hands, you shall be happy, and it shall be well with you. Your wife shall be like a fruitful vine in the very heart of your house, your children like olive plants all around your table. Behold, thus shall the man be blessed who fears the LORD. The LORD bless you out of Zion, and may you see the good of Jerusalem all the days of your life. Yes, may you see your children's children. Peace be upon Israel!" **(PSALM 128:1–6)**.

Jesus taught us, "Whoever therefore breaks one of the least of these commandments, and teaches men so, shall be called least in the kingdom of heaven; but whoever does and teaches them, he shall be called great in the kingdom of heaven" **(MATTHEW 5:19)**.

The Master condemns not only those who *break* one of God's commandments but also those who *teach* men to do so. This puts a terrible responsibility on spiritual leaders, of course—but not upon them alone. Some may think, "I'm not a preacher. I don't teach religion one way or the other." But those who think that way are mistaken. For each of us does indeed teach. When He uttered these words, the Master knew that we cannot escape teaching by our example, by our lifestyle, by our everyday actions and attitudes toward sacred things—and often far more eloquently than we could teach by mere words alone. We are responsible for our witness, responsible even for the unintended lessons we give to others.

Evidently, the Master expects us to obey, for He says quite plainly, "Not everyone who says to Me, 'Lord, Lord,' shall enter the kingdom of heaven, but he who does the will of My Father in heaven. Many will say to Me in that day, 'Lord, Lord, have we not prophesied in Your name, cast out demons in Your name, and done many wonders in Your name?' And then I will declare to them, 'I never knew you; depart from Me, you who practice lawlessness!' " **(MATTHEW 7:21–23).**

Jesus tried to get His lessons across through illustrative stories: "Therefore whoever hears these sayings of Mine, and does them, I will liken him to a wise man who built his house on the rock: and the rain descended, the floods came, and the winds blew and beat on that house; and it did not fall, for it was founded on the rock. But everyone who hears these sayings of Mine, and does not do them, will be like a foolish man who built his house on the sand: and the rain descended, the floods came, and the winds blew and beat on that house; and it fell. And great was its fall" **(MATTHEW 7:24–27).**

02 How does God describe His covenant relationship with Israel? There are two key points to keep in mind as you read the passages below—God's faithfulness and His people's obedience.

"You are a holy people to the LORD your God; the LORD your God has chosen you to be a people for Himself, a special treasure above all the peoples on the face of the earth. . . . Therefore know that the LORD your God, He is God, the faithful God who keeps covenant and mercy for a thousand generations with those who love Him and keep His commandments" **(DEUTERONOMY 7:6, 9).**

"The LORD will establish you as a holy people to Himself, just as He has sworn to you, if you keep the commandments of the LORD your God and walk in His ways" **(DEUTERONOMY 28:9).**

"Now therefore, if you will indeed obey My voice and keep My covenant, then you shall be a special treasure to Me above all people; for all the earth is Mine. And you shall be to Me a kingdom of priests and a holy nation" **(EXODUS 19:5, 6).**

The Lord delights in "showing mercy to thousands, to those who love Me and keep My commandments" **(DEUTERONOMY 5:10).**

"You shall have no other gods before Me. You shall not make for yourself a carved image—any likeness of anything that is in heaven above, or that is in the earth beneath, or that is in the water under the earth; you shall not bow down to them nor serve them. For I, the LORD your God, am a jealous God, visiting the iniquity of the fathers on the children to the third and fourth generations of those who hate Me, but showing mercy to thousands, to those who love Me and keep My commandments" **(EXODUS 20:3–6).**

Nehemiah described God in these words: "O great and awesome God, You who keep Your covenant and mercy with those who love You and observe Your commandments" **(NEHEMIAH 1:5).**

The prophet Daniel said, "I prayed to the LORD my God, and made confession, and said, 'O Lord, great and awesome God, who keeps His covenant and mercy with those who love Him, and with those who keep His commandments' " **(DANIEL 9:4).**

Although at times the Israelites were unfaithful to God, they remained His chosen people (or church) throughout the Old Testament. God's people, or church, are described as "those who love Him and keep His commandments" **(DEUTERONOMY 7:9).**

03 Is obedience an Old Testament phenomenon only? What role does obedience to God's commandments play in the New Testament? What instructions did Jesus give to His followers?

The Lord Jesus said, "If you love Me, keep My commandments" **(JOHN 14:15).**

Note how closely Jesus ties *love* for Him to willing *obedience*. "He who has My commandments and keeps them, it is he who loves Me. And he who loves Me will be loved by My Father, and I will love him and manifest Myself to him.... If anyone loves Me, he will keep My word; and My Father will love him, and We will come to him and make Our home with him. He who does not love Me does not keep My words; and the word which you hear is not Mine but the Father's who sent Me" **(JOHN 14:21, 23, 24).**

Again, Jesus taught: "If you keep My commandments, you will abide in My love, just as I have kept My Father's commandments and abide in His love.... You are My friends if you do whatever I command you" **(JOHN 15:10, 14).**

The apostle John speaks very plainly: "By this we know that we know Him, if we keep His commandments. He who says, 'I know Him,' and does not keep His commandments, is a liar, and the truth is not in him. But whoever keeps His word, truly the love of God is perfected in him. By this we know that we are in Him" **(1 JOHN 2:3–5).**

"We love Him because He first loved us. If someone says, 'I love God,' and hates his brother, he is a liar; for he who does not love his brother whom he has seen, how can he love God whom he has not seen? And this commandment we have from Him: that he who loves God must love his brother also" **(1 JOHN 4:19–21).**

"By this we know that we love the children of God, when we love God and keep His commandments. For this is the love of God, that we keep His commandments. And His commandments are not burdensome" **(1 JOHN 5:2, 3).**

In this text John gives a Bible definition of "the love of God," telling us that it means living a life of obedience to His will. And he adds that God's commandments are not grievous or burdensome. If we truly love God, it won't be hard to have no other gods before Him. We won't bow down to images, take His name in vain, or desecrate the day

He sanctified for us. If we truly love our fellow man, it won't be hard to honor our parents or refrain from murder. We won't steal from another, and we won't steal his or her spouse—or betray our own—by committing adultery. If we love our fellow man, we won't lie to him or greedily covet what he has.

In both the Old and New Testaments, God identifies His followers as those *who love Him and keep His commandments.* Love always leads to obedience, and obedience is the visible fruit of a loving relationship with God.

04 What clear identifying characteristics of the true church does Jesus outline in the Bible's last book, Revelation?

"The dragon [the devil] was enraged with the woman [the church], and he went to make war with the rest of her offspring, who keep the commandments of God and have the testimony of Jesus Christ" **(REVELATION 12:17).**

The King James Version of the Bible uses the word *remnant* instead of "the rest of her offspring" to picture God's true church in the last days. The word *remnant* literally means "those who are left." In the setting of **REVELATION 12:17**, the remnant are those who are left and who remain faithful to God. In both the Old and New Testaments, from the beginning of time to the end of time, God has a group of people who lovingly obey Him by keeping His commandments. They are the faithful ones, the ones that are left. Like the New Testament church, their allegiance to God's truth is uncompromising.

"Here is the patience of the saints; here are those who keep the commandments of God and the faith of Jesus" **(REVELATION 14:12).**

When Scripture identifies the "saints" of God's true church, symbolized by the "woman," as those "who keep the commandments of God," we know it means all of the Ten Commandments. For virtually everyone keeps some of His commandments. Even criminals may keep some of the commandments while flagrantly breaking others. If the identifying earmark God gives in these verses is to be of any specific meaning at all, it must denote God's special people who keep *all ten* of His Ten Commandments.

"Blessed are those who do His commandments, that they may have the right to the tree of life, and may enter through the gates into the city" **(REVELATION 22:14).**

Some Christians act as if *law* and *obedience* were merely legalistic requirements from the Old Testament that need to be shed as quickly as possible, but Scripture says, "One who turns away his ear from hearing the law, even his prayer is an abomination" **(PROVERBS 28:9).**

The apostle James says that if we break one of God's Ten Commandments, it is as if we have broken all ten. "Whoever shall keep the whole law, and yet stumble in one point, he is guilty of all. For He who said, 'Do not commit adultery,' also said, 'Do not murder.' Now if you do not commit adultery, but you do murder, you have become a transgressor of the law. So speak and so do as those who will be judged by the law of liberty" **(JAMES 2:10–12).**

The Ten Commandments are like a chain with ten links. If we break even one link, the whole chain is broken.

In Christ's great commission to the church, He said that we are to go to all nations, "teaching them to observe all things that I have commanded you; and lo, I am with you always, even to the end of the age" **(MATTHEW 28:20).**

05 How do the New Testament writers describe Christ's church?

Paul calls it "the church of the living God, the pillar and ground of the truth" **(1 TIMOTHY 3:15).**

In His prayer to His heavenly Father, Jesus asked God to "sanctify them by Your truth. Your word [the Bible] is truth" **(JOHN 17:17).**

"Jesus said to him [Thomas], 'I am the way, the truth, and the life. No one comes to the Father except through Me' " **(JOHN 14:6).**

In Jesus' trial before Pilate, the Roman governor asked Him, " 'Are You a king then?' Jesus answered, 'You say rightly that I am a king. For this cause I was born, and for this cause I have come into the world, that I should bear witness to the truth. Everyone who is of the truth hears My voice.' Pilate said to Him, 'What is truth?' " **(JOHN 18:37, 38).**

Unfortunately, Pilate never waited for Jesus' answer. Jesus was more than willing to unfold the truths of His Word to this Roman ruler.

The apostle Paul says you have a "hope which is laid up for you in heaven, of which you heard before in the word of the truth of the gospel" **(COLOSSIANS 1:5).**

The New Testament church is based on the "word" or "truth" of God. Jesus promised, "I will build My church, and the gates of Hades shall not prevail against it" **(MATTHEW 16:18).** Christ has a church, an organized group of faithful, obedient believers.

06 Is Christ's last-day church universal or local? How widely will His end-time message be preached?

John says, "Then I saw another angel flying in the midst of heaven, having the everlasting gospel to preach to those who dwell on the earth—*to every nation, tribe, tongue, and people*" **(REVELATION 14:6; EMPHASIS SUPPLIED).**

"And he [the mighty angel] said unto me [John, as a representative of God's last-day people], Thou must prophesy again before many peoples, and nations, and tongues, and kings" **(REVELATION 10:11, KJV).**

"And this gospel of the kingdom shall be preached in all the world as a witness to all the nations, and then the end will come" **(MATTHEW 24:14).**

"Go into all the world and preach the gospel to every creature" **(MARK 16:15).**

Just as Jesus longs for His message to go to all the world, Satan desires to enslave the minds of millions through his cunning deceptions.

"It was granted to him [the beast power] to make war with the saints and to overcome them. And authority was given him over every tribe, tongue, and nation" **(REVELATION 13:7).**

"Then King Darius wrote: To all peoples, nations, and languages that dwell in all the earth: Peace be multiplied to you. I make a decree that in every dominion of my kingdom men must tremble and fear before the God of Daniel. For He is the living God, and steadfast forever; His kingdom is the one which shall not be destroyed, and His dominion shall endure to the end" **(DANIEL 6:25, 26).**

God's passionate desire is that all mankind accept His truth, unite with His people, and be saved through all eternity.

God "desires all men to be saved and to come to the knowledge of the truth" **(1 TIMOTHY 2:4).**

"Then the master said to the servant, 'Go out into the highways and hedges, and compel them to come in, that my house may be filled' " **(LUKE 14:23).**

"Is He the God of the Jews only? Is He not also the God of the Gentiles? Yes, of the Gentiles also" **(ROMANS 3:29).**

"The grace of God that brings salvation has appeared to all men" **(TITUS 2:11).**

"The Lord is not slack concerning His promise, as some count slackness, but is longsuffering toward us, not willing that any should perish but that all should come to repentance" **(2 PETER 3:9).**

"For God did not send His Son into the world to condemn the world, but that the world through Him might be saved" **(JOHN 3:17).**

God's last-day church, preaching His final message, must be an international movement proclaiming His truth to the world.

07 What is at the heart of the message of Christ's last-day church?

"Then I saw another angel flying in the midst of heaven, having the everlasting gospel to preach to those who dwell on the earth—to every nation, tribe, tongue, and people" **(REVELATION 14:6).**

The things of God are built to last. We read of:

God's everlasting covenant **(2 SAMUEL 23:5; HEBREWS 13:20).**

God's everlasting righteousness **(PSALM 119:142).**

God's everlasting way **(PSALM 139:24).**

God's everlasting kingdom **(PSALM 145:13).**

God's everlasting word **(ISAIAH 40:8).**

God's everlasting salvation **(ISAIAH 45:17).**

God's everlasting purpose **(EPHESIANS 3:11).**

God's everlasting gospel **(REVELATION 14:6).**

There is only one gospel—the gospel of Christ. The apostle Paul testified, "I am not ashamed of the gospel of Christ, for it is the power of God to salvation for everyone who believes" **(ROMANS 1:16).** With earnest conviction he warns, "I marvel that you are turning away so soon from Him who called you in the grace of Christ, to a different gospel, which is not another; but there are some who trouble you and want to pervert the gospel of Christ. But even if we, or an angel from heaven, preach any other gospel to you than what we have preached to you, let him be accursed. As we have said before, so now I say again, if anyone preaches any other gospel to you than what you have received, let him be accursed" **(GALATIANS 1:6–9).**

This "gospel of Christ" is the "everlasting" gospel, as John puts it in **REVELATION 14:6.**

It was first announced in Eden when God told the diabolical serpent, "I will put enmity between you [Satan] and the woman [Eve], and between your seed and her Seed [Christ]; He shall bruise your head, and you shall bruise His heel" **(GENESIS 3:15).**

It was preached to Abraham. "And the Scripture, foreseeing that God would justify the Gentiles by faith, preached the gospel to Abraham beforehand, saying, 'In you all the nations shall be blessed' " **(GALATIANS 3:8).**

It was preached to the children of Abraham. "Therefore, since a promise remains of entering His rest, let us fear lest any of you seem to have come short of it. For indeed the gospel was preached to us as well as to them; but the word which they heard did not profit them, not being mixed with faith in those who heard it" **(HEBREWS 4:1, 2).**

It has since been proclaimed anew to every generation. The gospel is the "good news" that Jesus has forgiven our sins, that through His death we can become the children of God, and that through His power we can live transformed, obedient lives.

08 What time period does God's last-day church announce to the world? Is this business as usual? Where are we in the stream of time?

John hears the angel "saying with a loud voice, 'Fear God and give glory to Him, for *the hour of His judgment* has come; and worship Him who made heaven and earth, the sea and springs of water' " **(REVELATION 14:7; EMPHASIS SUPPLIED).**

A pre-Advent judgment taking place before Christ's return sounds strange to us who are accustomed to think of God's final judgment taking place *all at once*—in a *flash.* The reality is that even in human legal proceedings, a case is not disposed of that way. In fact, there are several consecutive *steps* or *stages* to the whole judicial process as follows:

- Step 1. First, there is the investigation of all pertinent facts. We call this a *trial.*
- Step 2. Then there is the rendering of a decision based on the evidence—the *verdict.*
- Step 3. Then there is deliberation over how severe the sentence should be; this is the *penalty phase.*
- Step 4. Then there is often an assessment of the verdict, or a *judicial review.*
- Step 5. Finally, there is a carrying out of the verdict; this is the *execution of the sentence.*

Apparently, the same process holds true in God's final judgment of mankind. God's judgment has similar stages. The pre-Advent judgment is the investigative phase, like the courtroom *trial,* which must precede the rendering of the *verdict,* when Jesus pronounces each person either unjust and filthy or righteous and holy. This takes place just *before* He comes again **(SEE REVELATION 22:11, 12).**

The whole universe witnesses this phase of God's judgment with great interest. Paul tells us that "we have been made a spectacle to the world, both to angels and to men" **(1 CORINTHIANS 4:9).** The word here translated as *spectacle* is the Greek word *theatron,* which gives us our word *theater.* And the word translated as *world* is the Greek word *kosmos,* which has been taken into English as *cosmos,* implying "the whole universe of unfallen worlds and angels" who look on with inexpressible interest to see how you and I choose to live. It's far more fascinating than any soap opera! That's why the author of Hebrews cautions us: "Since we are surrounded by such a cloud of witnesses [including the Monarch of heaven Himself], let us lay aside every weight, and the sin which so easily ensnares us" **(HEBREWS 12:1).**

The Bible teaches a pre-Advent judgment in such texts as **DANIEL 7:9, 10**: "I watched till thrones were put in place, and the Ancient of Days [God the Father] was seated; His garment was white as snow, and the hair of His head was like pure wool. His throne was a fiery flame, its wheels a burning fire; a fiery stream issued and came forth from before Him. A thousand thousands ministered to Him; ten thousand times ten thousand stood before Him. The court was seated, and the books were opened."

Note that this judgment scene—when "the [record] books were opened" in heaven—takes place while on earth an evil power is "making war against the saints, and prevailing against them, until the Ancient of Days came, and a judgment was made in favor of the saints of the Most High, and the time came for the saints to possess the kingdom" **(DANIEL 7:21, 22).**

Other passages which teach the pre-Advent judgment—in addition to **REVELATION 14:7 AND DANIEL 7:9, 10**—include the judgment scene in heaven described in **REVELATION 11:18:** "The nations were angry, and Your wrath has come, and the time of the dead, that they should be judged, and that You should reward Your servants the prophets and the saints, and those who fear Your name, small and great, and should destroy those who destroy the earth."

In the very next verse, John tells us, "Then the temple of God was opened in heaven, and the ark of His covenant was seen in His temple" **(REVELATION 11:19).** The golden ark contained the two tables of stone inscribed with the Ten Commandments by God's own finger. Thus this vision and this text directs our attention to God's law, the standard in the judgment, according to **JAMES 2:10–12.**

In this investigative judgment of God's people taking place in heaven before He returns, Christ will be our Mediator **(SEE 1 TIMOTHY 2:5)**, our powerful Advocate **(SEE 1 JOHN 2:1)**, to speak in our behalf. He's a defense attorney who's never lost a case!

The true church teaches we are living in the judgment hour preliminary to the coming of Christ. It has an urgent message for the world. It is an "Adventist" church. It teaches that Christ came once, and that He is coming again. *Advent* means "coming," as in Christ's first advent, which believers celebrate at Christmas time, and His second advent, which believers eagerly anticipate.

09 In the light of the urgent message of the judgment hour, what three specific truths does God's Word reveal at the end time?

John hears the angel "saying with a loud voice, 'Fear God and give glory to Him, for the hour of His judgment has come; and worship Him who made heaven and earth, the sea and springs of water' " **(REVELATION 14:7).**

Fear God

"As the heavens are high above the earth, so great is His mercy toward those who fear Him" **(PSALM 103:11).**

"He will bless those who fear the LORD, both small and great" **(PSALM 115:13).**

"The LORD takes pleasure in those who fear Him, in those who hope in His mercy" **(PSALM 147:11).**

"Though a sinner does evil a hundred times, and his days are prolonged, yet I surely know that it will be well with those who fear God, who fear before Him" **(ECCLESIASTES 8:12).**

"Let us hear the conclusion of the whole matter: Fear God and keep His commandments, for this is man's all" **(ECCLESIASTES 12:13).**

"His mercy is on those who fear Him from generation to generation" **(LUKE 1:50).**

"Therefore, whether you eat or drink, or whatever you do, do all to the glory of God" **(1 CORINTHIANS 10:31).**

To "fear God" means to respect, reverence, and obey Him. God's end-time message is an urgent appeal to respect Him by listening to His commands and living in harmony with them.

Give glory to Him

"Let your light so shine before men, that they may see your good works and glorify your Father in heaven" **(MATTHEW 5:16).**

To give glory to God is to honor Him in all that we do, including eating and drinking. It is a message of obedience to God's physical and moral laws. We give Him glory through our lifestyle.

Worship Him as Creator

The very basis of worship is the fact that God created us. John the revelator pictures an amazing scene in heaven with the heavenly host crying out, "You are worthy, O Lord, to receive glory and honor and power; for You created all things, and by Your will they exist and were created" **(REVELATION 4:11).** Since He created us, God is worthy of our worship. Has our Lord left us a sign of His creative authority? How do we worship Him as Creator? Let's go back to the beginning.

When God created the heavens and the earth, He left the Sabbath as a memorial of Creation. He blessed, sanctified, and rested upon the Sabbath **(SEE GENESIS 2:1–3).** The Sabbath is God's perpetual reminder of His love. It is the eternal symbol of His creative power. It is the perpetual sign of His creative authority. In **EXODUS 20:8,** God commands all of His people to "remember the Sabbath day, to keep it holy." "For in six days the LORD made the heavens and the earth, the sea, and all that is in them, and rested the seventh day. Therefore the LORD blessed the Sabbath day and hallowed it" **(EXODUS 20:11).** In an age of evolution, the Sabbath speaks of our incalculable worth in God's sight. Revelation's call to worship the Creator is a call to all people to return to the true Bible Sabbath.

The true church calls men and women to worship on the Bible Sabbath as a memorial of Creation **(SEE REVELATION 4:11; EXODUS 20:8, 11).** It is an invitation to return to the Bible Sabbath of the seventh day, Saturday.

10 What crucial announcement is made in REVELATION 14:8? Who or what is spiritual Babylon? What does this prophetic term mean? Where does it originate?

"And another angel followed, saying, 'Babylon is fallen, is fallen, that great city, because she has made all nations drink of the wine of the wrath of her fornication' " **(REVELATION 14:8).**

"After these things I [John] saw another angel coming down from heaven, having great authority, and the earth was illuminated with his glory. And he cried mightily with a loud voice, saying, 'Babylon the great is fallen, is fallen, and has become a dwelling place of demons, a prison for every foul spirit, and a cage for every unclean and hated bird! For all the nations have drunk of the wine of the wrath of her fornication, the kings of the earth have committed fornication with her, and the merchants of the earth have become rich through the abundance of her luxury.' And I heard another voice from heaven saying, 'Come out of her, My people, lest you share in her sins, and lest you receive of her plagues' " **(REVELATION 18:1–4).**

Evidently, God considers the message of Christian *apostasy*—that is, a *falling away* from the truth—of vital importance, for He has mighty angels twice proclaim and John twice record it in two separate chapters of the Bible's last book. Even within those urgent, repeated warnings, God uses repetition for emphasis. He says "Babylon is fallen, is fallen." So we may conclude that God really wants to tell us something here about this fallen, apostate religious power called Babylon. Then He lovingly adds this tender appeal: "Come out of her, My people," showing that many of His people are still within the confines of that false religious organization, but He desperately calls them to "Come out of her!"

John speaks of a false religious power. " 'The great harlot . . . with whom the kings of the earth committed fornication, and the inhabitants of the earth were made drunk with the wine of her fornication.' . . . And on her forehead a name was written: MYSTERY, BABYLON THE GREAT, THE MOTHER OF HARLOTS AND OF THE ABOMINATIONS OF THE EARTH" **(REVELATION 17:1, 2, 5).**

Throughout the Old and New Testaments, the Lord refers to His faithful people under the symbol of a woman. Christ is the Bridegroom; His church is His bride. And unfaithfulness to God is depicted as spiritual adultery **(SEE ISAIAH 54:5, 6; 62:5; JEREMIAH 3:1, 8, 14, 20; 31:32; EZEKIEL 16:28, 32; 23:1–49; MATTHEW 9:14, 15; 2 CORINTHIANS 11:2; REVELATION 19:7–9).** Thus a pure woman represents God's true church; a corrupt woman represents a corrupt church. Here John is given a vision of a corrupt church referred to in various Bible versions in no uncertain terms as a "whore," "harlot," or "prostitute."

Furthermore, the two Scripture passages quoted above predict *an illicit alliance* between *church* and *state*—an ecclesiastical power "with whom the kings of the earth committed fornication." This prophecy was sadly fulfilled when, for centuries during the Middle Ages, the fallen church—having departed from God—relied upon the strong arm of the state's civil power to enforce her edicts and to punish, torture, and execute so-called heretics. When ecclesiastical leaders have ready access to the powers of the state, they are "armed and dangerous"! That's why, when God used Christopher Columbus to open up a whole continent in the New World, our pilgrim forefathers fled from such persecutions as the infamous Inquisition and came to America to worship in God-given freedom of conscience.

God will avenge the blood of His saints who were martyred by the harlot for their faith. "True and righteous are His judgments, because He has judged the great harlot who corrupted the earth with her fornication; and He has avenged on her the blood of His servants shed by her" **(REVELATION 19:2).**

"Then he answered and said, 'Babylon is fallen, is fallen! And all the carved images of her gods He has broken to the ground' " **(ISAIAH 21:9).**

When John the revelator wrote about the fall of Babylon, the ancient Babylon of history had fallen centuries before, as Isaiah mentions here. That empire had suffered God's judgment long ago. That great city lay in ruins at the time John wrote his prophecy about Babylon falling. He was referring, instead, *not* to the *literal* Babylon of history but to *spiritual* Babylon of prophecy—a false religious system that opposes God's truth. Chapter 16, "What the Bible Says About False Prophets and Deceptions," identifies Babylon and her false religious teachings.

But here is the principle. Babylon is a symbol of religious confusion. Wine is a symbol of false doctrines that confuse the mind. God's last-day message calls us from falsehood to truth.

11 What is the message of the third angel of REVELATION 14? Who is Revelation's message a warning against worshiping?

John the revelator sees yet *another* angel bearing a vital message: "Then a third angel followed them, saying with a loud voice, 'If anyone worships the beast and his image, and receives his mark on his forehead or on his hand, he himself shall drink of the wine of the wrath of God, which is poured out full strength into the cup of His indignation' " **(REVELATION 14:9, 10).**

God's message of dire warning, seen in the passage above, is not a needless one, for incredibly enough, many people are misled to worship this false religious power. "They worshiped the dragon [Satan, **SEE REVELATION 12:9; 20:2**] who gave authority to the beast; and they worshiped the beast, saying, 'Who is like the beast? Who is able to make war with him?'... Then I saw another beast coming up out of the earth, and he . . . causes the earth and those who dwell in it to worship the first beast. . . . He was granted power to give breath to the image of the beast, that the image of the beast should both speak and cause as many as would not worship the image of the beast to be killed" **(REVELATION 13:4, 11, 12, 15).**

12 How can we avoid worshiping the beast? What is the difference between true and false worship?

"Here is the patience of the saints [God's true followers]; here are those who *keep the commandments of God and the faith of Jesus*" **(REVELATION 14:12; EMPHASIS SUPPLIED).**

In the verses immediately preceding this one **(REVELATION 14:9–11)**, God issues through the third angel the most fearful warning ever given to mankind. It can be no accident or coincidence that immediately following this warning to those who might accept the mark of the beast, a commendation is given to those who "keep the commandments of God and the faith of Jesus" as opposed to the man-made directives and the corrupted faith of the beast power.

"The dragon [the devil] was enraged with the woman [God's true church], and he went to make war with the rest of her offspring, who keep the commandments of God and have the testimony of Jesus Christ" **(REVELATION 12:17)**.

When Satan tempted Jesus in the wilderness, "the devil took Him up on an exceedingly high mountain, and showed Him all the kingdoms of the world and their glory. And he said to Him, 'All these things I will give You if You will fall down and worship me' " **(MATTHEW 4:8, 9)**.

Above everything else, the devil wants to be worshiped. God's end-time message makes this point abundantly clear. The final conflict over worship will find its focal point in the commandments of God. One group worships the Creator, and the other group worships the beast power. While one group keeps the commandments of God, the other group follows the tradition of men. While one group keeps the true Bible Sabbath, the other accepts a counterfeit day of worship.

Jesus taught that "no one can serve two masters; for either he will hate the one and love the other, or else he will be loyal to the one and despise the other. You cannot serve God and mammon [an Aramaic word meaning *wealth* or *property*]" **(MATTHEW 6:24)**.

"You cannot drink the cup of the Lord and the cup of demons; you cannot partake of the Lord's table and of the table of demons" **(1 CORINTHIANS 10:21)**.

"I [John] fell at his [the angel's] feet to worship him. But he said to me, 'See that you do not do that! I am your fellow servant, and of your brethren who have the testimony of Jesus. Worship God!' " **(REVELATION 19:10)**.

"I, John, saw and heard these things. And when I heard and saw, I fell down to worship before the feet of the angel who showed me these things. Then he said to me, 'See that you do not do that. For I am your fellow servant, and of your brethren the prophets, and of those who keep the words of this book. Worship God' " **(REVELATION 22:8, 9)**.

The last two scriptures quoted above teach an important lesson to those who will receive it. Notwithstanding the fact that God's second commandment absolutely forbids bowing down to any idol or statue, one religious organization has placed such statues in every church, every university, every school, every hospital it owns and teaches its faithful believers to bow down to them. Yet in the passages above, God makes it clear that not only should we not bow down to to *lifeless statues,* we should not bow down even to *living angels*! The Scriptures say we must reverence God and Him alone.

The true church warns men and women not to accept the counterfeit worship of the beast. In a future chapter, we will study the subject of the mark of the beast. The final crisis will be over worship. God calls us from the false to the true. He graciously invites us to worship the Creator on the seventh-day Sabbath as a sign of our allegiance to Him.

13 Interest in spiritualism and communication with the dead is rapidly growing around the world. According to Revelation's end-time predictions, what will the true church teach about death?

"I [John] heard a voice from heaven saying to me, 'Write: Blessed are the dead who die in the Lord from now on.' 'Yes,' says the Spirit, 'that they may rest from their labors, and their works follow them' " **(REVELATION 14:13).**

The psalmist David prayed, "O LORD my God; enlighten my eyes, lest I sleep the sleep of death" **(PSALM 13:3).**

"Now the days of David drew near that he should die. . . . So David rested with his fathers, and was buried in the City of David" **(1 KINGS 2:1, 10).**

When Stephen, the first Christian martyr, was stoned to death, "he knelt down and cried out with a loud voice, 'Lord, do not charge them with this sin.' And when he had said this, he fell asleep" **(ACTS 7:60).**

The Lord Jesus Himself spoke of death as a "sleep" when Lazarus grew sick and died. "He said to them, 'Our friend Lazarus sleeps, but I go that I may wake him up.' Then His disciples said, 'Lord, if he sleeps he will get well.' However, Jesus spoke of his death, but they thought that He was speaking about taking rest in sleep. Then Jesus said to them plainly, 'Lazarus is dead' " **(JOHN 11:11–14).**

Daniel prophesied, "Those who sleep in the dust of the earth shall awake, some to everlasting life, some to shame and everlasting contempt" **(DANIEL 12:2).**

Jesus taught that "the hour is coming in which all who are in the graves will hear His voice and come forth—those who have done good, to the resurrection of life, and those who have done evil, to the resurrection of condemnation" **(JOHN 5:28, 29).**

"As in Adam all die, even so in Christ all shall be made alive. But each one in his own order: Christ the firstfruits, afterward those who are Christ's at His coming" **(1 CORINTHIANS 15:22, 23).**

In his sermon on the Day of Pentecost, Peter said, "Men and brethren, let me speak freely to you of the patriarch David, that he is both dead and buried, and his tomb is with us to this day. . . . For David did not ascend into the heavens" **(ACTS 2:29, 34).**

"If the dead do not rise, then Christ is not risen. And if Christ is not risen, your faith is futile; you are still in your sins! Then also those who have fallen asleep in Christ have perished" **(1 CORINTHIANS 15:16–18)**.

Peter states, "David did not ascend into the heavens" when he died. "He is both dead and buried," awaiting the call of the Life-Giver at the resurrection. If the faithful really went to heaven when they died, they'd be walking the streets of gold and praising God with immortal tongues. But Paul tells us that without the resurrection, "those who have fallen asleep [or died] in Christ have perished." The Bible makes clear the mystery of death and shows believers that it's not a horror to fear, but a deep, dreamless sleep from which we'll awake at the resurrection!

The true church teaches the truth about death. It clearly reveals that death is a peaceful rest until Jesus returns **(SEE 1 THESSALONIANS 4:16, 17; 1 CORINTHIANS 15:51–54)**.

Characteristics of God's true church

- It is a worldwide movement.
- It proclaims the everlasting gospel.
- It teaches that we are living in the judgment hour and emphasizes that Jesus is coming soon.
- It leads men and women to obey God's commandments.
- It teaches men and women to give glory to God in what they eat or drink. It helps them to understand the necessity of refraining from alcohol, tobacco, and unclean foods.
- It explains the significance of worshiping our loving Creator on the seventh-day Sabbath.
- It leads men and women out of religious confusion to God's truths.
- It warns against accepting any sign of human authority (the mark of the beast) in the place of God's Word.
- It teaches that death is a peaceful rest until the resurrection.

There is only one religious movement in all the world that is preaching these heaven-sent messages of **REVELATION 14**. There is only one church in all the world that is urgently proclaiming the truths of the three angels of **REVELATION 14**—the Seventh-day Adventist Church. The Seventh-day Adventist Church is not merely another denomination. It is not merely another religious body littering the landscape of churches. It is a divine movement of destiny raised up by God. It is a prophetic movement proclaiming God's last-day truth.

Does it make any difference which church I attend?

God's Special People

The tributaries of a major river in the Philippines were swollen from the spring rains. As the river overflowed, the Filipino feast of crucifixion was occurring. The year was 1993. A barge swiftly sailed down a narrow tributary that got larger and larger. It was joined by a second and third barge. Each of these barges had a large crucifix and hundreds of Filipinos on board. During this special holy day, the barges floated down the river in a religious procession. More people from the banks of the river began to swim out to join the procession. As they climbed onto the barges, the barges began to sink. The marshals, in an attempt to calm the panicking crowd aboard the barges, began throwing people into the water.

But it was too late.

First one barge tipped over, then the second and then the third. Three hundred people drowned. Three hundred people drowned because they grasped the wrong thing.

Whatever one's religious convictions may be about worshiping the crucifix, these people grasped something that couldn't hold them up. They grasped something that would not bear their weight. Unfortunately, on a religious pilgrimage, they lost their lives.

I wonder, Is it possible for us to grasp beliefs in the name of religion and sink spiritually? Does God have a church on earth today that is solidly based on the Bible and that won't sink? What does the Bible teach about discovering God's truth for today?

There certainly is a hunger for genuine Christianity in the hearts of thousands.

There is a longing for something more than they have. That hunger isn't merely for a church; that hunger is for a Bible-believing people.

That hunger is for the living Christ and His truth. That hunger is for a people that base their lives on the Word of God. There is a hunger for authentic Christianity and the truth of God worldwide today. Let me give you a few examples of this spiritual longing.

After the fall of communism, people lined up for hours to get a seat at meetings where the Bible was being preached. They longed to hear the Word of God. When Russian army trucks delivered cases of Bibles to the series, the people rushed the host and hostess. It was almost bedlam. These dear Russian people, who had been denied the opportunity for so long, were eager to get their hands on the Word of God.

There is something deep within the human spirit that wants to know God. There is a hunger for truth in our society. Materialism has not satisfied. Pleasure has not satisfied. Technology has not satisfied. Men and women are longing for truth. They are longing for something real. Something that will not let them down in a crisis. Something that fills the longing emptiness in their souls.

There is that hunger for the Word of God. There is that hunger for spiritual principles and biblical values. There is that hunger for truth that men and women can hang on to. There is an inner compulsion for something solid, something that won't sink when we cling to it.

Does God have a people on earth today called "His church"?

As you look down the history of the Christian church, God has always had a people proclaiming His truth to that generation. In the days of Noah, God called a man. Noah appealed to men and women to enter into the ark of safety. The majority rejected God's call but God still had a few faithful people who entered the ark. They were His church. The ark was an ark of safety. There was a call to step out from the majority.

There was a call from the popular masses. There was a call to take a step in faith. There was a call to get into the ark.

Today there is a call to obey God and get into God's ark of safety, His church.

In the Old Testament, God called Abraham out of the popular majority. "Then the LORD appeared to him and said: 'Do not go down to Egypt; live in the land of which I shall tell you' " **(GENESIS 26:2)**. God called Abraham out of the popular culture to follow Him completely.

Notice the features of God's people: "because Abraham obeyed My voice and kept My charge, My commandments, My statutes, and My laws" **(GENESIS 26:5).**

God chose Abraham to be faithful to Him and to lead his family to keep God's commandments. In the days of ancient Israel, God called out a faithful obedient group. "Therefore you shall love the LORD your God, and keep His charge, His statutes, His judgments, and His commandments always" **(DEUTERONOMY 11:1).**

In the days of Noah, a people loved God, kept His commandments, and got into the ark. In the days of Abraham, a people loved God, stepped out from the majority, and kept His commandments. In the days of ancient Israel, a people loved God and kept His commandments. God called them His chosen, His special people.

In the days of the New Testament, Peter preached powerfully. Three thousand were baptized on the Day of Pentecost. As they were baptized, they stepped out and became God's special people to keep His commandments. "But you are a chosen generation, a royal priesthood, a holy nation, His own special people, that you may proclaim the praises of Him who called you out of darkness into His marvelous light **(1 PETER 2:9).**

In the days of Noah, did God have a special people? Certainly.

In the days of Abraham, did God have a special people? Certainly.

In the days of Moses, did God have a special people? Certainly.

In the days of Peter, did He have a special people? Yes, certainly.

God's special people were always characterized by obedience. They loved Him enough to obey Him. They were carved out from the majority. They were a commandment-keeping people. God called them from darkness to light—from error to truth—from commandment-breaking to commandment-keeping.

Throughout the centuries, God has had men and women who have been faithful to Him. They have been called His church. It was never God's intent for the Christian church to be divided into different denominations, with each one teaching something different. God's Word teaches something else. Now here's an eternal principle:

You do not go to church to find the truth; you go to the Bible to find the truth. And when you find a church teaching the eternal principles of God's Word, you have discovered God's people for today. Just as in every generation God has had a special people, He has a special chosen people today.

CHAPTER 24

What the Bible Says About Prophecy, Visions, and Dreams

Throughout biblical times, God has guided His church through the gift of prophecy. He has spoken through visions and dreams to instruct, correct, and enlighten His people. The Lord spoke to Israel in these words, "If there is a prophet among you, I, the LORD, make Myself known to him in a vision; I speak to him in a dream" **(NUMBERS 12:6)**. The gift of prophecy was God's prime channel of communication with His people from the writing of Genesis by Moses to the writing of Revelation by John. For sixteen hundred years God revealed His will through the Bible prophets in the sixty-six books of the Old and New Testaments.

The prophets were spokesmen and spokeswomen for God. Many people wonder, "Did God withdraw the gift of prophecy at the end of the biblical period? Did prophecy cease with the completion of the New Testament? Does prophecy have a role in the church today? If it does, how can we distinguish between the true and false gift of prophecy?"

In this chapter, we will examine the most significant passages in the Bible on the gift of prophecy and discover from these multiple passages God's strategy for guiding His church today.

01 One of Jesus' favorite and most important themes was the Holy Spirit. What amazing promises regarding the ministry of the Holy Spirit did Jesus give to His church just before His crucifixion, resurrection, and ascension to heaven? How do New Testament authors describe the work of the Holy Spirit?

When Jesus told His saddened disciples that He must soon leave them, He also promised, "I will pray the Father, and He will give you another Helper, that He may abide with you forever. . . . The Helper, the Holy Spirit, whom the Father will send in My name, He will teach you all things, and bring to your remembrance all things that I said to you" **(JOHN 14:16, 26).**

Jesus promised to send "the Spirit of truth, whom the world cannot receive, because it neither sees Him nor knows Him; but you know Him, for He dwells with you and will be in you" **(JOHN 14:17).**

"When the Helper comes, whom I shall send to you from the Father, the Spirit of truth who proceeds from the Father, He will testify of Me" **(JOHN 15:26).**

Jesus said, "Nevertheless I tell you the truth. It is to your advantage that I go away; for if I do not go away, the Helper will not come to you; but if I depart, I will send Him to you. And when He has come, He will convict the world of sin, and of righteousness, and of judgment: of sin, because they do not believe in Me; of righteousness, because I go to My Father and you see Me no more; of judgment, because the ruler of this world is judged. I still have many things to say to you, but you cannot bear them now. However, when He, the Spirit of truth, has come, He will guide you into all truth; for He will not speak on His own authority, but whatever He hears He will speak; and He will tell you things to come. He will glorify Me, for He will take of what is Mine and declare it to you. All things that the Father has are Mine. Therefore I said that He will take of Mine and declare it to you" **(JOHN 16:7–15).**

"Therefore, when He had risen from the dead, His disciples remembered that He had said this to them; and they believed the Scripture and the word which Jesus had said" **(JOHN 2:22).**

"His disciples did not understand these things at first; but when Jesus was glorified, then they remembered that these things were written about Him and that they had done these things to Him" **(JOHN 12:16).**

The two passages above show that the Holy Spirit, the promised Helper or Comforter, did indeed "bring things to the remembrance" of Christ's disciples after His death.

The apostle Peter, who earlier had been culturally prejudiced against Gentiles, reasoned, "If therefore God gave them [believing Gentiles] the same gift [of the Holy Spirit] as He gave us when we believed on the Lord Jesus Christ, who was I that I could withstand God?" **(ACTS 11:17).**

"The disciples were filled with joy and with the Holy Spirit" **(ACTS 13:52).**

"Hope does not disappoint, because the love of God has been poured out in our hearts by the Holy Spirit who was given to us" **(ROMANS 5:5).**

"Likewise the Spirit also helps in our weaknesses. For we do not know what we should pray for as we ought, but the Spirit Himself makes intercession for us with groanings which cannot be uttered. Now He who searches the hearts knows what the mind of the Spirit is, because He makes intercession for the saints according to the will of God" **(ROMANS 8:26, 27).**

"The kingdom of God is not eating and drinking, but righteousness and peace and joy in the Holy Spirit" **(ROMANS 14:17).**

Paul prayed that wonderful, priceless gifts would be bestowed upon us: "May the God of hope fill you with all joy and peace in believing, that you may abound in hope by the power of the Holy Spirit" **(ROMANS 15:13).**

"The fruit of the Spirit is love, joy, peace, longsuffering, kindness, goodness, faithfulness, gentleness, self-control" **(GALATIANS 5:22, 23).**

Anyone who exhibits "the fruit of the Spirit" is the kind of person we really want to be around and spend time with—just a great human being, and slightly more than human!

Some things we can't learn from earthly teachers, "But God has revealed them to us through His Spirit. For the Spirit searches all things, yes, the deep things of God. For what man knows the things of a man except the spirit of the man which is in him? Even so no one knows the things of God except the Spirit of God. Now we have received, not the spirit of the world, but the Spirit who is from God, that we might know the things that have been freely given to us by God. These things we also speak, not in words which man's wisdom teaches but which the Holy Spirit teaches, comparing spiritual things with spiritual" **(1 CORINTHIANS 2:10–13).**

Paul desired for us "that the God of our Lord Jesus Christ, the Father of glory, may give to you the spirit of wisdom and revelation in the knowledge of Him" **(EPHESIANS 1:17).**

02 What are some of the special gifts the Holy Spirit places in the church so that it can proclaim the gospel to the world?

"He Himself gave some to be apostles, some prophets, some evangelists, and some pastors and teachers" **(EPHESIANS 4:11)**.

"When He [Christ] ascended on high, He . . . gave gifts to men" **(EPHESIANS 4:8)**.

When the Lord Jesus ascended to heaven, He didn't leave the church destitute—as if to say, "You're on your own. Do the best you can." Not at all. Instead, we read that He "gave gifts" to His people. Those gifts are special talents and abilities to equip them for ministry in many different lines of endeavor. The Greek word for "gift" is *charisma*. So when we speak of a "charismatic person," we mean one who is especially gifted in one or more ways. You'll notice, as you peruse "God's Catalog of Gifts" in **EPHESIANS 4:11** that these God-given talents are designed, *not* for self-glorification, as the gift of beauty may sometimes be perverted and profaned. Rather, they're given to equip the one so favored to advance the work of God.

The church has "been built on the foundation of the apostles and prophets, Jesus Christ Himself being the chief cornerstone" **(EPHESIANS 2:20)**.

Paul says that the mystery of Christ "in other ages was not made known to the sons of men, as it has now been revealed by the Spirit to His holy apostles and prophets" **(EPHESIANS 3:5)**.

"Having then gifts differing according to the grace that is given to us, let us use them: if prophecy, let us prophesy in proportion to our faith; or ministry, let us use it in our ministering; he who teaches, in teaching" **(ROMANS 12:6, 7)**.

Paul shows how necessary are these gifts: "How then shall they call on Him in whom they have not believed? And how shall they believe in Him of whom they have not heard? And how shall they hear without a preacher?" **(ROMANS 10:14)**.

"God has appointed these in the church: first apostles, second prophets, third teachers, after that miracles, then gifts of healings, helps, administrations, varieties of tongues" **(1 CORINTHIANS 12:28)**.

"On the next day we . . . entered the house of Philip the *evangelist,* who was one of the seven [deacons], and stayed with him" **(ACTS 21:8; EMPHASIS SUPPLIED)**.

The seasoned apostle Paul told young Timothy, "Be watchful in all things, endure afflictions, do the work of an evangelist, fulfill your ministry" **(2 TIMOTHY 4:5)**.

"For a long time Israel has been without the true God, without a teaching priest, and without law" **(2 CHRONICLES 15:3)**.

"I will give you shepherds according to My heart, who will feed you with knowledge and understanding" **(JEREMIAH 3:15)**.

Teachers are needed who will minister by "teaching them to observe all things that I have commanded you" **(MATTHEW 28:20).**

"In the church that was at Antioch there were certain prophets and teachers" **(ACTS 13:1).**

"The elders who are among you I exhort, I who am a fellow elder and a witness of the sufferings of Christ, and also a partaker of the glory that will be revealed: Shepherd the flock of God which is among you, serving as overseers, not by compulsion but willingly, not for dishonest gain but eagerly; nor as being lords over those entrusted to you, but being examples to the flock" **(1 PETER 5:1–3).**

Each of the gifts of the Spirit is designed by God to nurture, build up, and equip God's church to reach the world with the gospel. The gifts of the Spirit are not ends in themselves. They are means to the greater end of Christian growth and service.

03 Would the gifts of the Holy Spirit cease at the end of the New Testament period? How long would the gift of prophecy continue in the church?

These God-given talents and gifts are bestowed "for the equipping of the saints for the work of ministry, for the edifying of the body of Christ, till we all come to the unity of the faith and of the knowledge of the Son of God, to a perfect man, to the measure of the stature of the fullness of Christ" **(EPHESIANS 4:12, 13).**

Since none can say we have reached the state of perfection Paul describes in this verse—and we won't reach that ideal till Jesus comes—the implication is that all these gifts will continue in the church until that great day.

04 What promise does God give to His church awaiting the Advent?

Paul prays and desires "that ye come behind in no gift; waiting for the coming of our Lord Jesus Christ" **(1 CORINTHIANS 1:7, KJV).**

The church is still waiting for the coming of the Lord. And the church still needs the Spirit-empowered ministries provided in these gifts. Heaven knows we still need pastors and teachers and evangelists—and God has provided them. We still need apostles, which literally means "one who is sent"—as on a mission, like a foreign missionary. And God still provides those brave missionaries. The words *apostle* and *missionary* are very similar in meaning. The

English word *apostle* comes from the Greek word *apostolos*, which is made up of two words—*apo,* meaning "off" or "away," and *stello,* meaning "to send" or "to dispatch." Thus *apostolos* literally means "one sent forth"—"a messenger" or "an ambassador" or "a missionary." The Jewish historian Josephus uses the word *apostolos* when speaking of the ambassadors whom the Jews sent as their representatives to Rome.

The English word *mission* is from the Latin word *missio* or *mittere,* meaning "to send." Thus a "missionary" is one sent on a mission; a "missile" is a rocket sent into space; a "missive" is a letter or message sent to someone; and an "emissary," like an ambassador, is an official agent sent to represent or advance the interests of another. Thus the words *apostle* and *missionary* are very similar in their meaning, notwithstanding the fact that the original apostles were privileged to walk with and learn from Christ in person.

And just as God has provided His church with apostles (missionaries), He has also sent prophets at critical junctures in sacred history. He sent Noah at the time of the Flood, Moses at the time of the Exodus, and John the Baptist at the time of Christ's first advent. Thus He may well choose to provide a special prophetic messenger just before the all-important Second Coming. After all, in this verse—**1 CORINTHIANS 1:7**—God promises that the church will "come behind in no gift"—not a single one—as we wait and watch and work.

The Hebrew word for "prophet" is *nabi,* meaning "one called [by God]." (The Greek word is *prophetes.*) Thus a prophet is a person supernaturally called and qualified as a *spokesperson for God.* A prophet first received instruction from God and then conveyed it to the people. The prophet was chiefly a teacher of righteousness and spirituality, a moral reformer, bearing messages of counsel and warning, whose work often included the prediction of future events.

05 What two specific characteristics of God's last-day church are described in Revelation?

"The dragon [the devil] was enraged with the woman [the church], and he went to make war with the rest of her offspring, who *keep the commandments of God and have the testimony of Jesus Christ*" **(REVELATION 12:17; EMPHASIS SUPPLIED).** These two identifying marks are critical in our understanding of God's true church. God's last-day church will keep the commandments of God, including the Bible Sabbath, and have the "testimony of Jesus."

Here John uses his inspired pen to give us not just one, but two, very specific marks of identification that pinpoint God's last-day church. Those two earmarks are that (1) His church will keep all of God's commandments, and that (2) it will have "the testimony of Jesus."

06 How does the Bible define the "testimony of Jesus"?

John writes, "I fell at his [the angel's] feet to worship him. But he said to me, 'See that you do not do that! I am your fellow servant, and of your brethren who have the testimony of Jesus. Worship God! *For the testimony of Jesus is the spirit of prophecy*' " **(REVELATION 19:10; EMPHASIS SUPPLIED).**

"I, John, saw and heard these things. And when I heard and saw, I fell down to worship before the feet of the angel who showed me these things. Then he said to me, 'See that you do not do that. For I am your fellow servant, and of your brethren the prophets, and of those who keep the words of this book. Worship God' " **(REVELATION 22:8, 9).**

These two verses from the pen of inspiration make plain the Bible meaning of "the testimony of Jesus." Carefully compare what the angel says:

"I am your fellow servant, and of your brethren who have the testimony of Jesus."

"I am your fellow servant, and of your brethren the prophets."

To avoid any possible misunderstanding, the angel offers us an explicit definition: "The testimony of Jesus is the spirit of prophecy" **(REVELATION 19:10).** The prophets are those who have the spirit of prophecy, that is, the gift of prophecy.

"There are diversities of gifts, but the same Spirit. There are differences of ministries, but the same Lord. And there are diversities of activities, but it is the same God who works all in all. But the manifestation of the Spirit is given to each one for the profit of all: for to one is given the word of wisdom through the Spirit, to another the word of knowledge through the same Spirit, to another faith by the same Spirit, to another gifts of healings by the same Spirit, to another the working of miracles, to another prophecy, to another discerning of spirits, to another different kinds of tongues, to another the interpretation of tongues. But one and the same Spirit works all these things, distributing to each one individually as He wills" **(1 CORINTHIANS 12:4–11).**

"Though I have the gift of prophecy, and understand all mysteries and all knowledge, and though I have all faith, so that I could remove mountains, but have not love, I am nothing" **(1 CORINTHIANS 13:2).**

When one of heaven's messengers descended to bring John the gift of prophecy, the aged apostle knelt to worship the angel. The angel stopped him, explaining that he was testifying for Jesus in giving to John the spirit, or gift, of prophecy **(SEE ALSO REVELATION 22:8, 9). REVELATION 12:17** tells us that the gift of prophecy, or the testimony of Jesus, would be revealed again in God's last-day church. God will have a last–day remnant people, or church, who keep the commandments of God, and are guided by the prophetic gift. His church faithfully obeys Him and receives divine direction from Him. Of course the devil tries to counterfeit the genuine gift of prophecy by inspiring false prophets.

To protect us from being deceived, Scripture gives several biblical tests of a true prophet. These biblical tests help us distinguish between the true and false gift of prophecy.

07 Anyone can claim to be a true prophet. They may purport to have visions and dreams, some of which may seem to be true. What does the Bible teach regarding the accuracy of a true prophet?

"When the word of the prophet comes to pass, the prophet will be known as one whom the LORD has truly sent" **(JEREMIAH 28:9).**

"They have also healed the hurt of My people slightly, saying, 'Peace, peace!' when there is no peace" **(JEREMIAH 6:14; SEE ALSO JEREMIAH 8:11).**

"Then I said, 'Ah, Lord GOD! Behold, the prophets say to them, "You shall not see the sword, nor shall you have famine, but I will give you assured peace in this place." ' And the LORD said to me, 'The prophets prophesy lies in My name. I have not sent them, commanded them, nor spoken to them; they prophesy to you a false vision, divination, a worthless thing, and the deceit of their heart. Therefore thus says the LORD concerning the prophets who prophesy in My name, whom I did not send, and who say, "Sword and famine shall not be in this land"—By sword and famine those prophets shall be consumed!' " **(JEREMIAH 14:13–15).**

"Son of man, prophesy against the prophets of Israel who prophesy, and say to those who prophesy out of their own heart, 'Hear the word of the LORD!' Thus says the Lord GOD: 'Woe to the foolish prophets, who follow their own spirit and have seen nothing! . . . They have envisioned futility and false divination, saying, "Thus says the LORD!" But the LORD has not sent them; yet they hope that the word may be confirmed. Have you not seen a futile vision, and have you not spoken false divination? You say, "The LORD says," but I have not spoken.' Therefore thus says the Lord GOD: 'Because you have spoken nonsense and envisioned lies, therefore I am indeed against you,' says the Lord GOD. 'My hand will be against the prophets who envision futility and who divine lies; they shall not be in the assembly of My people, nor be written in the record of the house of Israel, nor shall they enter into the land of Israel. Then you shall know that I am the Lord GOD. Because, indeed, because they have seduced My people, saying, "Peace!" when there is no peace—and one builds a wall, and they plaster it with untempered mortar' " **(EZEKIEL 13:2, 3, 6–10).**

" 'The prophet who presumes to speak a word in My name, which I have not commanded him to speak, or who speaks in the name of other gods, that prophet shall die.' And if you say in your heart, 'How shall we know the word which the LORD has not spoken?'—when a prophet speaks in the name of the LORD, if the thing does not happen or come to pass, that is the thing which the LORD has not spoken; the prophet has spoken it presumptuously; you shall not be afraid of him" **(DEUTERONOMY 18:20–22).**

In prophecies that are not conditional, that is, prophecies that depend on a personal response to determine their fulfillment, the true prophet is 100 percent accurate. The so-called prophets of our day miss the mark completely on this test. A few of their predictions may come to pass, but most are never fulfilled.

08 Is it possible that the devil may counterfeit the true gift of prophecy? What if a prophet is apparently accurate, but leads people away from the truths of Scripture?

"If there arises among you a prophet or a dreamer of dreams, and he gives you a sign or a wonder, and the sign or the wonder comes to pass, of which he spoke to you, saying, 'Let us go after other gods'—which you have not known—'and let us serve them,' you shall not listen to the words of that prophet or that dreamer of dreams, for the LORD your God is testing you to know whether you love the LORD your God with all your heart and with all your soul. You shall walk after the LORD your God and fear Him, and keep His commandments and obey His voice, and you shall serve Him and hold fast to Him" **(DEUTERONOMY 13:1–4).**

In the two passages from Deuteronomy quoted above, God is giving us two major principles about how we should relate to those who claim to be prophets.

First, if a prophet's prediction *fails to come true,* you can know that the Lord did not send him, for God's predictions always come true—not 10 percent of the time. Not 50 percent of the time. *But 100 percent of the time.* Remember that even a clock that doesn't run is correct twice a day. But divine prophecy is more than a lucky guess. God doesn't have to guess—He knows!

Second, if a prophet makes a prediction, and it *does* come true, but then he suggests that you violate or disobey God's commands or instructions, you can know that prophet is not from God. A genuine prophet will *never* lead anyone away from the true God or from true Bible teachings.

"He said to him [the man of God], 'I too am a prophet as you are, and an angel spoke to me by the word of the LORD, saying, "Bring him back with you to your house, that he may eat bread and drink water." ' (He was lying to him)" **(1 KINGS 13:18).**

"The elder and honorable, he is the head; the prophet who teaches lies, he is the tail" **(ISAIAH 9:15).**

"But there were also false prophets among the people, even as there will be false teachers among you, who will secretly bring in destructive heresies, even denying the Lord who bought them, and bring on themselves swift destruction. And many will follow their destructive ways, because of whom the way of truth will be blasphemed. By covetousness they will exploit you with deceptive words; for a long time their judgment has not been idle, and their destruction does not slumber" **(2 PETER 2:1–3).**

"These [in Berea] were more fair-minded than those in Thessalonica, in that they received the word with all readiness, and searched the Scriptures daily to find out whether these things [even the things that the apostle Paul taught] were so" **(ACTS 17:11).**

"We should no longer be children, tossed to and fro and carried about with every wind of doctrine, by the trickery of men, in the cunning craftiness of deceitful plotting" **(EPHESIANS 4:14).**

" 'Both prophet and priest are profane; yes, in My house I have found their wickedness' says the LORD" **(JEREMIAH 23:11).**

Israel had been especially plagued by false prophets **(SEE JEREMIAH 23:9–40; EZEKIEL 13:1–23).** False prophets lead *away* from Bible truth, not *to* Bible truth. They distort God's word. At times their teachings may appear true, but they are based on false doctrine.

"Beloved, do not believe every spirit, but test the spirits, whether they are of God; because many false prophets have gone out into the world" **(1 JOHN 4:1).**

"The coming of the lawless one is according to the working of Satan, with all power, signs, and lying wonders, and with all unrighteous deception among those who perish, because they did not receive the love of the truth, that they might be saved. And for this reason God will send them strong delusion, that they should believe the lie, that they all may be condemned who did not believe the truth but had pleasure in unrighteousness" **(2 THESSALONIANS 2:9–12).**

"They went out from us, but they were not of us; for if they had been of us, they would have continued with us; but they went out that they might be made manifest, that none of them were of us" **(1 JOHN 2:19).**

God says, "My people have been lost sheep. Their shepherds [that is, their pastors or spiritual leaders] have led them astray" **(JEREMIAH 50:6).**

Jesus warned, "Beware of false prophets, who come to you in sheep's clothing, but inwardly they are ravenous wolves" **(MATTHEW 7:15).**

"Many false prophets will rise up and deceive many. . . . False christs and false prophets will rise and show great signs and wonders to deceive, if possible, even the elect. See, I have told you beforehand" **(MATTHEW 24:11, 24, 25).**

"Many will say to Me in that day, 'Lord, Lord, have we not prophesied in Your name, cast out demons in Your name, and done many wonders in Your name?' And then I will declare to them, 'I never knew you; depart from Me, you who practice lawlessness!' " **(MATTHEW 7:22, 23).**

"When they [Barnabas and Saul] had gone through the island to Paphos, they found a certain sorcerer, a false prophet, a Jew whose name was Bar-Jesus, who was with the proconsul, Sergius Paulus, an intelligent man. This man called for Barnabas and Saul and sought to hear the word of God. But Elymas the sorcerer (for so his name is translated) withstood them, seeking to turn the proconsul away from the faith" **(ACTS 13:6–8).**

"The time will come when they will not endure sound doctrine, but according to their own desires, because they have itching ears, they will heap up for themselves teachers; and they will turn their ears away from the truth, and be turned aside to fables" **(2 TIMOTHY 4:3, 4).**

Note: Paul does *not* say that the time *may* come when individuals will turn from sound doctrine and the truth. He says that the time *will* come.

The true gift of prophecy does not lead us away from the Bible; it leads us back to it. The Bible is always supreme. It is the sole criterion for the establishment of doctrine.

09 If the genuine gift of prophecy is the testimony of Jesus—or Jesus' message to His people—how will a true prophet relate to Jesus?

"Every spirit that confesses that Jesus Christ has come in the flesh is of God, and every spirit that does not confess that Jesus Christ has come in the flesh is not of God" **(1 JOHN 4:2, 3).**

"When He, the Spirit of truth, has come, He will guide you into all truth; for He will not speak on His own authority, but whatever He hears He will speak; and He will tell you things to come. He will glorify Me, for He will take of what is Mine and declare it to you" **(JOHN 16:13, 14).**

"Therefore I make known to you that no one speaking by the Spirit of God calls Jesus accursed, and no one can say that Jesus is Lord except by the Holy Spirit" **(1 CORINTHIANS 12:3).**

"Simon Peter answered and said, 'You are the Christ, the Son of the living God.' Jesus answered and said to him, 'Blessed are you, Simon Bar-Jonah, for flesh and blood has not revealed this to you, but My Father who is in heaven' " **(MATTHEW 16:16, 17).**

All true prophets revere Jesus, as Peter speaks of "the precious blood of Christ, as of a lamb without blemish and without spot" **(1 PETER 1:19).**

The Bible declares that the true gift of prophecy exalts Jesus. The poet summarized it well in these words:

Lord, make me a nail upon the wall,
And from this thing so humble and so small
Hang a lovely picture of Thy face.

Jesus said, "You search the Scriptures, for in them you think you have eternal life; and these are they which testify of Me" **(JOHN 5:39).**

"If you believed Moses, you would believe Me; for he wrote about Me. But if you do not believe his writings, how will you believe My words?" **(JOHN 5:46, 47).**

The function of the gift of prophecy is continually to exalt and uplift Jesus. Since the Spirit of prophecy exalts Jesus, it is called "the testimony of Jesus."

10 Biblical prophets led to obedience of God's law. They were generally raised up at a time of moral decay and lawlessness to lead God's people back to faithfulness to His revealed will. How will the last-day gift of prophecy relate to God's law and God's Word?

God points us "To the law and to the testimony! If they [supposed prophets] do not speak according to this word [the Word of God], it is because there is no light in them" **(ISAIAH 8:20).**

"Bind up the testimony, seal the law among my disciples" **(ISAIAH 8:16).**

The law of God and the Word of God are the anchors of our faith. Christ is the center. Our allegiance is to Jesus. His word and His law provide spiritual direction.

"These [in Berea] were more fair-minded than those in Thessalonica, in that they received the word with all readiness, and searched the Scriptures daily to find out whether these things [Paul said] were so" **(ACTS 17:11).**

Paul praised the Scriptures to young Timothy in these words: "From childhood you have known the Holy Scriptures, which are able to make you wise for salvation through faith which is in Christ Jesus. All Scripture is given by inspiration of God, and is profitable for doctrine, for reproof, for correction, for instruction in righteousness, that the man of God may be complete, thoroughly equipped for every good work" **(2 TIMOTHY 3:15–17).**

"The wise men are ashamed, they are dismayed and taken. Behold, they have rejected the word of the LORD; so what wisdom do they have?" **(JEREMIAH 8:9).**

"Jesus answered and said to them, 'You are mistaken, not knowing the Scriptures nor the power of God' " **(MATTHEW 22:29).**

The Lord Jesus declared in His sermon on the mount: "Assuredly, I say to you, till heaven and earth pass away, one jot or one tittle will by no means pass from the law till all is fulfilled. Whoever therefore breaks one of the least of these commandments, and teaches men so, shall be called least in the kingdom of heaven; but whoever does and teaches them, he shall be called great in the kingdom of heaven" **(MATTHEW 5:18, 19).**

All Bible prophets exalt God's law. Elijah called Israel from idolatry to the true God. Nehemiah preached a reform in Sabbath keeping. John the Baptist condemned Herod's adultery. All true Bible prophets exalt God's Word. The true gift of prophecy does not take the place of the Bible—it exalts it.

11 Each of the Bible prophets manifested certain physical characteristics while receiving visions from God. How does the Bible describe these?

When the prophet Daniel was visited by a heavenly being and taken off in vision, he felt very humble, awe-struck, and physically weak. He said, "How can this servant of my lord [that is, himself] talk with you, my lord? As for me, no strength remains in me now, nor is any breath left in me" **(DANIEL 10:17).**

"Therefore I was left alone when I saw this great vision, and no strength remained in me; for my vigor was turned to frailty in me, and I retained no strength. Yet I heard the sound of his words; and while I heard the sound of his words I was in a deep sleep on my face, with my face to the ground" **(DANIEL 10:8, 9).**

"Suddenly, one having the likeness of the sons of men [an angel] touched my lips; then I opened my mouth and spoke, saying to him who stood before me, 'My lord, because of the vision my sorrows have overwhelmed me, and I have retained no strength' " **(DANIEL 10:16).**

"As he [the angel Gabriel] was speaking with me, I was in a deep sleep with my face to the ground; but he touched me, and stood me upright" **(DANIEL 8:18).**

"And I, Daniel, fainted and was sick for days; afterward I arose and went about the king's business. I was astonished by the vision, but no one understood it" **(DANIEL 8:27).**

"Then again, the one having the likeness of a man [the angel] touched me and strengthened me. And he said, 'O man greatly beloved, fear not! Peace be to you; be strong, yes, be strong!' So when he spoke to me I was strengthened, and said, 'Let my lord speak, for you have strengthened me' " **(DANIEL 10:18, 19).**

The prophet Habakkuk describes a similar experience: "When I heard, my body trembled; my lips quivered at the voice; rottenness entered my bones [I felt weak]; and I trembled in myself, that I might rest in the day of trouble" **(HABAKKUK 3:16).**

When Peter, James, and John were on the Mount of Transfiguration with Jesus, they heard the voice of God Himself. "And when the disciples heard it, they fell on their faces and were greatly afraid" **(MATTHEW 17:6).**

John the revelator saw the resurrected Christ in His majesty. "And when I saw Him, I fell at His feet as dead. But He laid His right hand on me, saying to me, 'Do not be afraid; I am the First and the Last' " **(REVELATION 1:17).**

A prophet who is taken off in vision keeps his eyes wide open. "And Balaam raised his eyes, and saw Israel encamped according to their tribes; and the Spirit of God came upon him. Then he took up his oracle and said: 'The utterance of Balaam the son of Beor, the utterance of the man whose eyes are opened, the utterance of him who hears the words of God, who sees the vision of the Almighty, who falls down, with eyes wide open" **(NUMBERS 24:2–4; SEE ALSO VERSES 15, 16).**

To summarize these scriptural descriptions of the physical phenomena experienced by a prophet while in vision, we've learned that:

- The prophet retains *no strength* of his own.
- The prophet is then *supernaturally strengthened.*
- The prophet often *does not breathe* while inspired by God's Holy Spirit.
- The prophet has his eyes *wide open.*

12 The fruits of the prophet's life are a reliable test of the genuineness of his claims. How did Jesus Himself tell us to distinguish between the true and counterfeit gifts of prophecy?

The Master cautions us, "Beware of false prophets, who come to you in sheep's clothing, but inwardly they are ravenous wolves. You will know them by their fruits. Do men gather grapes from thornbushes or figs from thistles? Even so, every good tree bears good fruit, but a bad tree bears bad fruit. . . . Therefore by their fruits you will know them" **(MATTHEW 7:15–17, 20).**

"A tree is known by its fruit" **(MATTHEW 12:33).**

The wise words of Christ have been proved true many times. The fruit of God's true prophets has been good throughout all sacred history, guiding the faithful and building the church. But the fruit of false prophets, such as Jim Jones, David Koresh, and the Heaven's Gate cult, has been tragic, causing the death of all their followers.

When Jewish leaders planned to kill the apostles, Gamaliel, a wise and respected teacher, cautioned against it in these words: "I say to you, keep away from these men and let them alone; for if this plan or this work is of men, it will come to nothing; but if it is of God, you cannot overthrow it—lest you even be found to fight against God" **(ACTS 5:38, 39).**

The faithful man is described thus: "He shall be like a tree planted by the rivers of water, that brings forth its fruit in its season, whose leaf also shall not wither; and whatever he does shall prosper" **(PSALM 1:3).**

"The righteous shall flourish like a palm tree, He shall grow like a cedar in Lebanon. Those who are planted in the house of the LORD shall flourish in the courts of our God. They shall still bear fruit in old age; they shall be fresh and flourishing" **(PSALM 92:12–14).**

"A good man out of the good treasure of his heart brings forth good things, and an evil man out of the evil treasure brings forth evil things" **(MATTHEW 12:35).**

"To console those who mourn in Zion, to give them beauty for ashes, the oil of joy for mourning, the garment of praise for the spirit of heaviness; that they may be called trees of righteousness, the planting of the LORD, that He may be glorified" **(ISAIAH 61:3).**

"But the wisdom that is from above is first pure, then peaceable, gentle, willing to yield, full of mercy and good fruits, without partiality and without hypocrisy. Now the fruit of righteousness is sown in peace by those who make peace" **(JAMES 3:17, 18).**

"Blessed is the man who trusts in the LORD, and whose hope is the LORD. For he shall be like a tree planted by the waters, which spreads out its roots by the river, and will not fear when heat comes; but its leaf will be green, and will not be anxious in the year of drought, nor will cease from yielding fruit" **(JEREMIAH 17:7, 8).**

There are two major issues to consider when considering the fruits of the Spirit in the life of a true prophet. First, how does he revel these fruits in his personal life? Is he arrogant, headstrong, dictatorial, undisciplined, and un-Christian? The second consideration has to do with the results of his ministry, the spiritual fruitage in the life of the church. Has his ministry dramatically blessed God's church and people? What impact has his teaching had upon God's church?

Paul's prayer is that we be "filled with the fruits of righteousness which are by Jesus Christ, to the glory and praise of God" **(PHILIPPIANS 1:11).**

"Walk worthy of the Lord, fully pleasing Him, being fruitful in every good work and increasing in the knowledge of God" **(COLOSSIANS 1:10).**

13 If God has promised that He would guide His people through the genuine gift of prophecy, where should we look to find it today?

"God has appointed these *in the church:* first apostles, second prophets, third teachers, after that miracles, then gifts of healings, helps, administrations, varieties of tongues" **(1 CORINTHIANS 12:28; EMPHASIS SUPPLIED).**

"Now in the church that was at Antioch there were certain prophets and teachers: Barnabas, Simeon who was called Niger, Lucius of Cyrene, Manaen who had been brought up with Herod the tetrarch, and Saul" **(ACTS 13:1).**

"Having then gifts differing according to the grace that is given to us, let us use them: if prophecy, let us prophesy in proportion to our faith; or ministry, let us use it in our ministering; he who teaches, in teaching; he who exhorts, in exhortation; he who gives, with liberality; he who leads, with diligence; he who shows mercy, with cheerfulness" **(ROMANS 12:6–8).**

God's church, "having been built on the foundation of the apostles and prophets, Jesus Christ Himself being the chief cornerstone, in whom the whole building, being fitted together, grows into a holy temple in the Lord, in whom you also are being built together for a dwelling place of God in the Spirit" **(EPHESIANS 2:20–22).**

The mystery of Christ "in other ages was not made known to the sons of men, as it has now been revealed by the Spirit to His holy apostles and prophets" **(EPHESIANS 3:5).**

"When He [Christ] ascended on high, He led captivity captive, and gave gifts to men. . . . He Himself gave some to be apostles, some prophets, some evangelists, and some pastors and teachers, for the equipping of the saints for the work of ministry, for the edifying of the body of Christ, till we all come to the unity of the faith and of the knowledge of the Son of God, to a perfect man, to the measure of the stature of the fullness of Christ" **(EPHESIANS 4:8, 11–13).**

"To the church of God which is at Corinth, to those who are sanctified in Christ Jesus, called to be saints, with all who in every place call on the name of Jesus Christ our Lord, both theirs and ours . . . even as the testimony of Christ was confirmed in you, so that you come short in no gift, eagerly waiting for the revelation of our Lord Jesus Christ" **(1 CORINTHIANS 1:2, 6, 7).**

When we discover God's faithful commandment-keeping church, we should also look within the church for the gift of prophecy. Prophecy is one of God's last-day gifts to His church, so we should expect to find it within the church. The gift of prophecy is not a doctrine contrary to the Bible, but rather it is one of the gifts that God says will remain in the church.

What a joy it is to know that God has a commandment-keeping church on earth today. It has been raised up to prepare a people for the coming of the Lord. God promised to place the gift of prophecy within His true church. It is one of the identifying characteristics of the true church **(SEE REVELATION 12:17; 19:10).**

Seventh-day Adventists believe that God has again raised up the genuine gift of prophecy in the life and teachings of Ellen G. White, who was born in a humble home in Gorham, Maine. When she was only a child, she had a tragic accident, so she completed only a few grades of education. She thought of herself as "the weakest of the weak."

When she was a young woman, God revealed Himself to her in visions and dreams. She wrote down God's messages as counsel to His church. Her books on health and education are world renowned. Her thousands of pages about Jesus are spiritual masterpieces. Books such as *Steps to Christ, The Desire of Ages,* and *The Great Controversy* have run through millions of copies. Ellen G. White was a humble woman who exalted Jesus and always led her readers back to the Bible. She claimed her writings were "a lesser light" to lead men and women to "the greater light," the Bible.

14 Why did God give His church the gift of prophecy? What is the result of following the prophets' counsels?

"Jehoshaphat [king of Judah] stood and said, 'Hear me, O Judah and you inhabitants of Jerusalem: Believe in the LORD your God, and you shall be established; believe His prophets, and you shall prosper' " **(2 CHRONICLES 20:20).**

"If you will not believe, surely you shall not be established" **(ISAIAH 7:9).**

"Thus Israel saw the great work which the LORD had done in Egypt; so the people feared the LORD, and believed the LORD and His servant Moses" **(EXODUS 14:31).**

"But he said to him, 'If they do not hear Moses and the prophets, neither will they be persuaded though one rise from the dead' " **(LUKE 16:31).**

The Master declared, "If you believed Moses, you would believe Me; for he wrote about Me. But if you do not believe his writings, how will you believe My words?" **(JOHN 5:46, 47).**

Jesus said, "Most assuredly, I say to you, he who receives whomever I send receives Me; and he who receives Me receives Him who sent Me" **(JOHN 13:20).**

God has given His church the gift of prophecy. Following God's counsel brings greater joy to our lives. Accepting heaven's wisdom saves us from a great deal of heartache and sorrow. The prophets' messages are heaven's blessings on our lives.

People are looking for alternative answers.

People are looking for alternative answers.

CHAPTER 25

What the Bible Says About End-Time Delusions

The Bible's last book, Revelation, reveals the plans of God and unmasks the plans of Satan. It especially focuses upon the conflict between good and evil, Christ and Satan, in earth's final hour. The overarching theme in Revelation is Christ's victory over the forces of hell. Although His people will be caught in the grip of a titanic struggle, they will triumph at last.

In these final, climactic hours of earth's history, Satan will pull out all the stops to deceive God's people. He will do everything he can to lead them astray.

In Revelation's prophecies, a pure, chaste woman represents the true church **(SEE REVELATION 12:1, 2)**. An impure woman represents the fallen church. The bride of Christ, the true church, radiates the glory of God, revealing His truth to the world. The apostate church, pictured as a harlot, offers her wine of false doctrines, confusing the mind and leading multitudes to destruction.

In this chapter, we will especially notice the characteristics of this false system of worship so we can keep from being deceived by it. We will also discover the characteristics of true worship so we can embrace it.

Spiritual Babylon revealed

The Bible's last book, Revelation identifies God's true church—His end-time people—in a variety of ways. How does God describe His true church in Revelation 12? How are these symbols explained by the Bible itself?

"A great sign appeared in heaven: a woman clothed with the sun, with the moon under her feet, and on her head a garland of twelve stars" **(REVELATION 12:1)**.

Throughout the Old and New Testaments, the Lord refers to His faithful people under the symbol of a woman. Christ is the Bridegroom; His church is His bride. And unfaithfulness to God is depicted as spiritual adultery **(SEE ISAIAH 54:5, 6; 62:5; JEREMIAH 3:1, 8, 14, 20; 31:32; EZEKIEL 16:28, 32; 23:1–49; MATTHEW 9:14, 15; 2 CORINTHIANS 11:2; REVELATION 19:7–9)**.

In **REVELATION 12:1**, God's true church is depicted in dazzling brightness—"clothed with the sun," representing the glory of God. Her "garland of twelve stars" could symbolize either the patriarchs of the twelve tribes of Israel or the twelve apostles or both.

" 'For your Maker is your husband, the LORD of hosts is His name; and your Redeemer is the Holy One of Israel; He is called the God of the whole earth. For the LORD has called you like a woman forsaken and grieved in spirit, like a youthful wife when you were refused,' says your God" **(ISAIAH 54:5, 6)**.

God says to His people, "I will betroth you to Me forever; yes, I will betroth you to Me in righteousness and justice, in lovingkindness and mercy; I will betroth you to

Me in faithfulness, and you shall know the LORD" **(HOSEA 2:19, 20)**.

Paul speaks of God's people, the church, as the bride of Christ: "I am jealous for you with godly jealousy. For I have betrothed you to one husband, that I may present you as a chaste virgin to Christ" **(2 CORINTHIANS 11:2)**.

Note how "wife and husband" parallels "church and Christ": "Wives, submit to your own husbands, as to the Lord. For the husband is head of the wife, as also Christ is head of the church; and He is the Savior of the body. Therefore, just as the church is subject to Christ, so let the wives be to their own husbands in everything. Husbands, love your wives, just as Christ also loved the church and gave Himself for her" **(EPHESIANS 5:22–25)**.

"As a young man marries a virgin, so shall your sons marry you; and as the bridegroom rejoices over the bride, so shall your God rejoice over you" **(ISAIAH 62:5)**.

" 'Return, O backsliding children,' says the LORD; 'for I am married to you. I will take you, one from a city and two from a family, and I will bring you to Zion' " **(JEREMIAH 3:14)**.

A woman is the biblical symbol of the church, for God says, "I have likened the daughter of Zion [a follower of the true God] to a lovely and delicate woman" **(JEREMIAH 6:2)**.

Jesus speaks of Himself as "the bridegroom" and John the Baptist and his disciples as "friends of the bridegroom": "The disciples of John [the Baptist] came to Him [Jesus], saying, 'Why do we and the Pharisees fast often, but Your disciples do not fast?' And Jesus said to them, 'Can the friends of the bridegroom mourn as long as the bridegroom is with them? But the days will come when the bridegroom will be taken away from them, and then they will fast' " **(MATTHEW 9:14, 15)**.

"He who has the bride is the bridegroom; but the friend of the bridegroom, who stands and hears him, rejoices greatly because of the bridegroom's voice. Therefore this joy of mine is fulfilled" **(JOHN 3:29)**.

When Christ returns, it will be said, " 'Let us be glad and rejoice and give Him glory, for the marriage of the Lamb [Jesus] has come, and His wife [the church] has made herself ready.' And to her it was granted to be arrayed in fine linen, clean and bright, for the fine linen is the righteous acts of the saints. Then he [the angel] said to me, 'Write: "Blessed are those who are called to the marriage supper of the Lamb!" ' " **(REVELATION 19:7–9)**.

John the revelator saw the church flee from persecution: "Then the woman fled into the wilderness, where she has a place prepared by God, that they should feed her there one thousand two hundred and sixty days" **(REVELATION 12:6)**.

The woman, God's true church, "fled into the wilderness," going underground, so to speak, to escape persecution during the Dark Ages for a period of 1,260 prophetic days—or 1,260 actual years, following the scriptural principle that one prophetic day equals one actual year **(SEE NUMBERS 14:34; EZEKIEL 4:6).**

"When the dragon [the devil] saw that he had been cast to the earth, he persecuted the woman who gave birth to the male Child. But the woman was given two wings of a great eagle, that she might fly into the wilderness to her place, where she is nourished for a time and times and half a time, from the presence of the serpent. So the serpent spewed water out of his mouth like a flood after the woman, that he might cause her to be carried away by the flood. But the earth helped the woman, and the earth opened its mouth and swallowed up the flood which the dragon had spewed out of his mouth. And the dragon was enraged with the woman, and he went to make war with the rest of her offspring, who keep the commandments of God and have the testimony of Jesus Christ" **(REVELATION 12:13–17).**

Here we read again of the woman (the church) being persecuted "for a *time* and *times* and *half* a time." In the Bible, the term "time" is used for a year **(COMPARE DANIEL 11:13** in the **KJV** with the **NKJV**, or **DANIEL 4:16, 23, 25, 32** in the **KJV** with the **NASB)**. Ancient calendars—such as those of the Egyptians, Hindus, Assyrians, and Hebrews—all had 360 days per year. So "a time and times and half a time" figures out to be: 3½ (years) x 360 (days each) = 1,260 prophetic days—or 1,260 actual years. But the text says that after this period of persecution, the earth helps the woman by opening its mouth and swallowing up the flood of persecution which the dragon had spewed out against her. God used Columbus to open up a whole new continent as a way of escape and refuge for God's people—the Pilgrims and others who fled from religious persecution in the Old World.

In **ISAIAH 54:5, 6; HOSEA 2:19; 2 CORINTHIANS 11:2; EPHESIANS 5:22–26,** God describes His people as His bride. So the woman, clothed with the sun in **REVELATION 12:1,** represents the church, the bride of Christ.

02 What is the foundation, the very essence, of God's true church?

"But if I am delayed, I write so that you may know how you ought to conduct yourself in the house of God, which is the church of the living God, *the pillar and ground of the truth*" **(1 TIMOTHY 3:15; EMPHASIS SUPPLIED).**

In His prayer to His heavenly Father, Jesus asked God to "sanctify them by Your truth. Your word [the Bible] is truth" **(JOHN 17:17).**

"Jesus said to him [Thomas], 'I am the way, the truth, and the life. No one comes to the Father except through Me' " **(JOHN 14:6).**

The apostle Paul says you have a "hope which is laid up for you in heaven, of which you heard before in the word of the truth of the gospel" **(COLOSSIANS 1:5).**

Speaking to church leaders, Paul says, "the Holy Spirit has made you overseers, to shepherd the church of God which He purchased with His own blood" **(ACTS 20:28).**

03 What characterizes all false religious movements? How does the Bible picture the fallen church?

"Then one of the seven angels who had the seven bowls [containing the seven last plagues] came and talked with me, saying to me, 'Come, I will show you the judgment of the great harlot who sits on many waters, with whom the kings of the earth committed fornication, and the inhabitants of the earth were made drunk with the wine of her fornication.' So he carried me away in the Spirit into the wilderness. And I saw a woman sitting on a scarlet beast which was full of names of blasphemy, having seven heads and ten horns. The woman was arrayed in purple and scarlet, and adorned with gold and precious stones and pearls, having in her hand a golden cup full of abominations and the filthiness of her fornication. And on her forehead a name was written: MYSTERY, BABYLON THE GREAT, THE MOTHER OF HARLOTS AND OF THE ABOMINATIONS OF THE EARTH" **(REVELATION 17:1–5).**

In Bible symbolism, a *pure* woman represents God's true church; a *corrupt* woman represents a corrupt church. Here John is given a vision of a corrupt church referred to in no uncertain terms in various Bible versions as a "whore," "harlot," or "prostitute."

This woman is not only a *corrupt* church, a harlot who prostitutes God's truth, but she is also a remarkably *rich* one—she's "adorned with gold and precious stones and pearls, having in her hand a golden cup."

Furthermore, this passage predicts *an illicit alliance between church and state*—an ecclesiastical power "with whom the kings of the earth committed fornication." Sadly, this prophecy was fulfilled when, for centuries during the Middle Ages, the false church departed from God and relied upon the strong arm of the state's civil power to enforce her edicts and to punish, torture, and execute so-called heretics, often by burning them alive at the stake. When church and state unite, persecution often follows. That's why, when God used Christopher Columbus to open up a whole continent in the New World, our religious forefathers fled from such persecutions as the infamous Inquisition and came to America to worship in God-given freedom of conscience. So this corrupt church is depicted also as a persecuting church, as the following verses show.

John continues, "I saw the woman, drunk with the blood of the saints and with the blood of the martyrs of Jesus" **(REVELATION 17:6).**

"And in her was found the blood of prophets and saints" **(REVELATION 18:24).**

"True and righteous are His judgments, because He has judged the great harlot who corrupted the earth with her fornication; and He has avenged on her the blood of His servants shed by her" **(REVELATION 19:2).**

"Babylon was a golden cup in the LORD's hand, that made all the earth drunk. The nations drank her wine; therefore the nations are deranged" **(JEREMIAH 51:7).**

"And another angel followed, saying, 'Babylon is fallen, is fallen, that great city, because she has made all nations drink of the wine of the wrath of her fornication' " **(REVELATION 14:8).**

"For all the nations have drunk of the wine of the wrath of her fornication, the kings of the earth have committed fornication with her, and the merchants of the earth have become rich through the abundance of her luxury" **(REVELATION 18:3).**

"Do not look on the wine when it is red, when it sparkles in the cup, when it swirls around smoothly; at the last it bites like a serpent, and stings like a viper" **(PROVERBS 23:31, 32).**

Wine affects the forebrain, where conscience, reason, and judgment are located. So Babylon's "wine" signifies the confusion of her false doctrine. **PSALM 116:13** speaks of the "cup of salvation." Babylon's wine cup, full of lies, may be called the cup of death.

Revelation's "Babylon" represents a false religious system, which brings the principles of Old Testament Babylon into religious worship in the Christian era. An understanding of Old Testament Babylon lets us positively identify New Testament Babylon and flee its errors.

04 Who is behind all false teaching? Where does all false doctrine originate?

Jesus told the scheming Pharisees, "You are of your father the devil, and the desires of your father you want to do. He was a murderer from the beginning, and does not stand in the truth, because there is no truth in him. When he speaks a lie, he speaks from his own resources, for he is a liar and the father of it" **(JOHN 8:44).**

"Now the serpent was more cunning than any beast of the field which the LORD God had made. And he said to the woman [Eve], 'Has God indeed said, "You shall not eat of every tree of the garden?" ' And the woman said to the serpent, 'We may eat the fruit of the trees of the garden; but of the fruit of the tree which is in the midst of the garden, God has said, "You shall not eat it, nor shall you touch it, lest you die." ' Then the serpent said to the woman, 'You will not surely die. For God knows that in the day you eat of it your eyes will be opened, and you will be like God, knowing good and evil.' So when the woman saw that the tree was good for food, that it was pleasant to the eyes, and a tree desirable to make one wise, she took of its fruit and ate. She also gave to her husband with her, and he ate. . . . [Then God said,] 'I will put enmity between you [the serpent] and the woman, and between your seed [Satan's followers] and her Seed [the Messiah, Christ]; He shall bruise your head, and you shall bruise His heel' " **(GENESIS 3:1–6, 15).**

A farmer planted good seeds in his field, but his enemy came by night and planted weeds in his field. When the farm hands noticed all the weeds and asked where they came from, "he said to them, 'An enemy has done this.' The servants said to him, 'Do you want us then to go and gather them up?' . . . He [Jesus, in explaining the parable] answered and said to them: 'He who sows the good seed is the Son of Man. The field is the world, the good seeds are the sons of the kingdom, but the tares [weeds] are the sons of the wicked one. The enemy who sowed them is the devil, the harvest is the end of the age, and the reapers are the angels' " **(MATTHEW 13:28, 37–39).**

Paul, filled with the Holy Spirit, boldly confronted Elymas the sorcerer and said, 'O full of all deceit and all fraud, you son of the devil, you enemy of all righteousness, will you not cease perverting the straight ways of the Lord?" **(ACTS 13:10).**

With great concern, the apostle Paul said, "I fear, lest somehow, as the serpent deceived Eve by his craftiness, so your minds may be corrupted from the simplicity that is in Christ" **(2 CORINTHIANS 11:3).**

"He who sins is of the devil, for the devil has sinned from the beginning. For this purpose the Son of God was manifested, that He might destroy the works of the devil" **(1 JOHN 3:8).**

"Be sober, be vigilant; because your adversary the devil walks about like a roaring lion, seeking whom he may devour" **(1 PETER 5:8).**

"Do not fear any of those things which you are about to suffer. Indeed, the devil is about to throw some of you into prison, that you may be tested, and you will have tribulation ten days. Be faithful until death, and I will give you the crown of life" **(REVELATION 2:10).**

Satan, the father of lies, counterfeits truth. He attempts to deceive us. He desires to capture the minds of thousands through religious deceit.

05 Old Testament Babylon originated at the Tower of Babel. It was built on the site of man's rebellion against God after the worldwide Flood. What happened at Babel, and how can this apply to the confusion in the religious world today?

Even though the Lord pledged His solemn promise that He would never again destroy the world with water **(SEE GENESIS 9:8–17)**, there were those who chose, instead, to trust a do-it-yourself salvation by attempting to build a tower tall enough to save themselves if another flood came. It came to be called the Tower of Babel. "The LORD came down to see the city and the tower which the sons of men had built. And the LORD said, 'Indeed the people are one and they all have one language, and this is what they begin to do; now nothing that they propose to do will be withheld from them. Come, let Us go down and there confuse their language, that they may not understand one another's speech.' So the LORD scattered them abroad from there over the face of all the earth, and they ceased building the city. Therefore its name is called Babel, because there the LORD confused the language of all the earth; and from there the LORD scattered them abroad over the face of all the earth" **(GENESIS 11:5–9).**

The passage above is a perfect example of the verses below:

"He [God] frustrates the devices of the crafty, so that their hands cannot carry out their plans" **(JOB 5:12).**

"He deprives the trusted ones of speech, and takes away the discernment of the elders" **(JOB 12:20).**

"The LORD brings the counsel of the nations to nothing; He makes the plans of the peoples of no effect" **(PSALM 33:10).**

"Destroy, O Lord, and divide their tongues, for I have seen violence and strife in the city" **(PSALM 55:9).**

"And they [the apostles] were all filled with the Holy Spirit and began to speak with other tongues [other languages], as the Spirit gave them utterance. And there were dwelling in Jerusalem Jews, devout men, from every nation under heaven. And when this sound occurred, the multitude came together, and were confused, because everyone heard them speak in his own language. Then they were all amazed and marveled, saying to one another, 'Look, are not all these who speak Galileans? And how is it that we hear, each in our own language in which we were born? Parthians and Medes and Elamites, those dwelling in Mesopotamia, Judea and Cappadocia, Pontus and Asia, Phrygia and Pamphylia, Egypt and the parts of Libya adjoining Cyrene, visitors from Rome, both Jews and proselytes, Cretans and Arabs—we hear them speaking in our own tongues the wonderful works of God' " **(ACTS 2:4–11).**

On the Day of Pentecost—the "birthday" of the church—the Almighty God, in a marvelous display of divine power, *reversed* for His apostles what He did earlier at the Tower of Babel, thus equipping them to spread the gospel everywhere.

The Tower of Babel was built shortly after God destroyed the earth with a flood. Filled with rebellion, proud people determined to build a monument to their own egos. If the world was ever destroyed again by a flood, they would survive. God demonstrated their folly by confusing the languages of the workers. The Tower of Babel is a monument to their confusion. It demonstrates the foolishness of human wisdom. It reveals the folly of substituting human ideas for divine truth. Old

Testament Babylon was built on the site of the Tower of Babel. It represents confusion or humanity's way in opposition to God's way. It represents arrogance, pride, and self-inflated ego in contrast to God's plan of humble obedience.

06 Where did Old Testament Babylon find the source of its religio-political power? What was at the foundation of its teaching?

"The king [Nebuchadnezzar] spoke, saying, 'Is not this great Babylon, that I have built for a royal dwelling by my mighty power and for the honor of my majesty?' " **(DANIEL 4:30).**

"But when his [Nebuchadnezzar's] heart was lifted up, and his spirit was hardened in pride, he was deposed from his kingly throne, and they took his glory from him" **(DANIEL 5:20).**

The wise man Solomon wrote, "Pride goes before destruction, and a haughty spirit before a fall" **(PROVERBS 16:18).**

"Whoever exalts himself will be humbled, and he who humbles himself will be exalted" **(LUKE 14:11).**

"God resists the proud, but gives grace to the humble" **(1 PETER 5:5).**

"Yours, O LORD, is the greatness, the power and the glory, the victory and the majesty; for all that is in heaven and in earth is Yours; Yours is the kingdom, O LORD, and You are exalted as head over all. Both riches and honor come from You, and You reign over all. In Your hand is power and might; in Your hand it is to make great and to give strength to all" **(1 CHRONICLES 29:11, 12).**

"The word of the LORD came to me again, saying, 'Son of man, say to the prince of Tyre, "Thus says the Lord GOD: 'Because your heart is lifted up, and you say, "I am a god, I sit in the seat of gods, in the midst of the seas," yet you are a man, and not a god, though you set your heart as the heart of a god' " ' " **(EZEKIEL 28:1, 2).**

God said, "Behold, I will stir up the Medes against them [the Babylonians]. . . . And Babylon, the glory of kingdoms, the beauty of the Chaldeans' pride, will be as when God overthrew Sodom and Gomorrah" **(ISAIAH 13:17, 19).**

Old Testament Babylon was established in direct opposition to the plain commands of God. It was a system of religion based on the traditions and authority of human beings rather than God's authority. It was human-centered rather than God-centered. Any system of worship that places the word of human leaders above God's Word is part of the Babylonian system. Any system that substitutes human religious leaders for Christ is a false system.

07 According to the Bible, what is the foundation of our faith? Who alone is the source of our salvation?

"Nor is there salvation in any other [than Jesus Christ], for *there is no other name under heaven* given among men by which we must be saved" **(ACTS 4:12; EMPHASIS SUPPLIED).**

"He commanded us to preach to the people, and to testify that it is He who was ordained by God to be Judge of the living and the dead. To Him all the prophets witness that, through His name, whoever believes in Him will receive remission of sins" **(ACTS 10:42, 43).**

"She [Jesus' mother, Mary] will bring forth a Son, and you shall call His name JESUS, for He will save His people from their sins" **(MATTHEW 1:21).**

"He who believes in the Son has everlasting life; and he who does not believe the Son shall not see life, but the wrath of God abides on him" **(JOHN 3:36).**

"Jesus said to him, 'I am the way, the truth, and the life. No one comes to the Father except through Me' " **(JOHN 14:6).**

"No other foundation can anyone lay than that which is laid, which is Jesus Christ" **(1 CORINTHIANS 3:11).**

"There is one God and one Mediator between God and men, the Man Christ Jesus, who gave Himself a ransom for all" **(1 TIMOTHY 2:5, 6).**

"How shall we escape if we neglect so great a salvation, which at the first began to be spoken by the Lord, and was confirmed to us by those who heard Him" **(HEBREWS 2:3).**

"This is the testimony: that God has given us eternal life, and this life is in His Son. He who has the Son has life; he who does not have the Son of God does not have life" **(1 JOHN 5:11, 12).**

"Look to Me, and be saved, all you ends of the earth! For I am God, and there is no other" **(ISAIAH 45:22).**

Salvation comes not from the rites and ceremonies of the church. It comes from looking to Jesus. Salvation is a gift received by faith. It is based in Jesus' death on the cross, not on our good works. The false Babylonian system is based on human teachings, human works, and human accomplishments.

08 What was the visible manifestation of Babylon's defiance against the true God?

God warns Jerusalem, "Your altars shall be desolate, your incense altars shall be broken, and I will cast down your slain men before your idols" **(EZEKIEL 6:4).**

When Israel drifted from God, they participated in the idolatry of Babylon. The apostasy of God's chosen people was so blatant that they built altars for pagan idols.

God warns His rebellious people, "In all your dwelling places the cities shall be laid waste, and the high places shall be desolate, so that your altars may be laid waste and made desolate, your idols may be broken and made to cease, your incense altars may be cut down, and your works may be abolished" **(EZEKIEL 6:6).**

Good King Josiah was young, but he faithfully led the people back to God. "They broke down the altars of the Baals in his [Josiah's] presence, and the incense altars which were above them he cut down; and the wooden images, the carved images, and the molded images he broke in pieces, and made dust of them and scattered it on the graves of those who had sacrificed to them" **(2 CHRONICLES 34:4).**

"Their heart is divided; now they are held guilty. He will break down their altars; He will ruin their sacred pillars" **(HOSEA 10:2).**

Pagan cultures throughout the Old Testament period were distinguished by idol worship. Turning from the Creator, they worshiped the objects of His creation.

"He shall also break the sacred pillars of Beth Shemesh that are in the land of Egypt; and the houses of the gods of the Egyptians he shall burn with fire" **(JEREMIAH 43:13).**

'Thus says the Lord GOD: 'I will also destroy the idols, and cause the images to cease from Noph; there shall no longer be princes from the land of Egypt; I will put fear in the land of Egypt' " **(EZEKIEL 30:13).**

"All her [Samaria's] carved images shall be beaten to pieces, and all her pay as a harlot shall be burned with the fire; all her idols I will lay desolate, for she gathered it from the pay of a harlot, and they shall return to the pay of a harlot" **(MICAH 1:7).**

God told His people, "Your carved images I will also cut off, and your sacred pillars from your midst; you shall no more worship the work of your hands" **(MICAH 5:13, 14).**

"The idols He shall utterly abolish. . . . In that day a man will cast away his idols of silver and his idols of gold, which they made, each for himself to worship, to the moles and bats" **(ISAIAH 2:18, 20).**

"Therefore by this the iniquity of Jacob will be covered; and this is all the fruit of taking away his sin: When he makes all the stones of the altar like chalkstones that are beaten to dust, wooden images and incense altars shall not stand" **(ISAIAH 27:9).**

" 'It shall be in that day,' says the LORD of hosts, 'that I will cut off the names of the idols from the land, and they shall no longer be remembered' " **(ZECHARIAH 13:2).**

Modern Babylon is a system of religion that uses idols in its worship. Its statues, images, and religious icons revive the idolatry of ancient Babylon. Any system that incorporates images into its worship service is part of spiritual Babylon.

09 What clear, explicit command did God give His people? Why did God give this command?

In His Ten Commandments, God says clearly, "You shall not make for yourself a carved image—any likeness of anything that is in heaven above, or that is in the earth beneath, or that is in the water under the earth; you shall not bow down to them nor serve them. For I, the LORD your God, am a jealous God, visiting the iniquity of the fathers upon the children to the third and fourth generations of those who hate Me" **(EXODUS 20:4, 5).**

"When the people saw that Moses delayed coming down from the mountain, the people gathered together to Aaron, and said to him, 'Come, make us gods that shall go before us; for as for this Moses, the man who brought us up out of the land of Egypt, we do not know what has become of him.' . . . And the LORD said to Moses. . . . 'They have turned aside quickly out of the way which I commanded them. They have made themselves a molded calf, and worshiped it and sacrificed to it, and said, "This is your god, O Israel, that brought you out of the land of Egypt!" ' . . . [Aaron excused himself in these words:] 'They said to me, "Make us gods that shall go before us; as for this Moses, the man who brought us out of the land of Egypt, we do not know what has become of him." And I said to them, "Whoever has any gold, let them break it off." So they gave it to me, and I cast it into the fire, and this calf came out' " **(EXODUS 32:1, 7, 8, 23, 24).**

The Lord commanded, "You shall make no molded gods for yourselves" **(EXODUS 34:17).**

The Lord God said, "Do not turn to idols, nor make for yourselves molded gods: I am the LORD your God" **(LEVITICUS 19:4).**

"You shall not make idols for yourselves; neither a carved image nor a sacred pillar shall you rear up for yourselves; nor shall you set up an engraved stone in your land, to bow down to it; for I am the LORD your God" **(LEVITICUS 26:1).**

"Professing to be wise, they became fools, and changed the glory of the incorruptible God into an image made like corruptible man—and birds and four-footed animals and creeping things" **(ROMANS 1:22, 23).**

"But the rest of mankind, who were not killed by these plagues, did not repent of the works of their hands, that they should not worship demons, and idols of gold, silver, brass, stone, and wood, which can neither see nor hear nor walk" **(REVELATION 9:20).**

"Take heed to yourselves, lest you forget the covenant of the LORD your God which He made with you, and make for yourselves a carved image in the form of anything which the LORD your God has forbidden you. For the LORD your God is a consuming fire, a jealous God. When you beget children and grandchildren and have grown old in the land, and act corruptly and make a carved image in the form of anything, and do evil in the sight of the LORD your God to provoke Him to anger" **(DEUTERONOMY 4:23–25).**

"You shall not make for yourself a carved image—any likeness of anything that is in heaven above, or that is in the earth beneath, or that is in the water under the earth; you shall not bow down to them nor serve them. For I, the LORD your God, am a jealous God, visiting the iniquity of the fathers upon the children to the third and fourth generations of those who hate Me, but showing mercy to thousands, to those who love Me and keep My commandments" **(DEUTERONOMY 5:8–10).**

" 'Cursed is the one who makes a carved or molded image, an abomination to the LORD, the work of the hands of the craftsman, and sets it up in secret.' And all the people shall answer and say, 'Amen!' " **(DEUTERONOMY 27:15).**

"Therefore the king asked advice, made two calves of gold, and said to the people, 'It is too much for you to go up to

Jerusalem [to worship in God's temple there]. Here are your gods, O Israel, which brought you up from the land of Egypt!' " **(1 KINGS 12:28).**

Israel's wicked King Jeroboam invented a political religion and instituted feasts according to his own times, different from those of Jehovah. He gave the people idolatrous objects of adoration, and pretended to think it would be inconvenient for them to go up to Jerusalem to worship. Those calves were doubtless of the same kind as the calf set up by Aaron, and it's remarkable that in introducing them to the people, he used the same words that the people in Aaron's day used on that occasion: "This is your god, O Israel, that brought you out of the land of Egypt!" **(EXODUS 32:4, 8).** Will people never learn?

"So I went in and saw, and there—every sort of creeping thing, abominable beasts, and all the idols of the house of Israel, portrayed all around on the walls" **(EZEKIEL 8:10).**

"Therefore, since we are the offspring of God, we ought not to think that the Divine Nature is like gold or silver or stone, something shaped by art and man's devising" **(ACTS 17:29).**

The prophet Daniel was called in to decipher the handwriting on the wall which brought to a dramatic halt the drunken feast of Babylonian King Belshazzar and a thousand of his lords. But before he did so, he told the king, "You have lifted yourself up against the Lord of heaven. They have brought the [sacred] vessels of His house [God's temple in Jerusalem] before you, and you and your lords, your wives and your concubines, have drunk wine from them. And you have praised the [heathen] gods of silver and gold, bronze and iron, wood and stone, which do not see or hear or know; and the God who holds your breath in His hand and owns all your ways, you have not glorified" **(DANIEL 5:23).**

Wicked King Manasseh of Judah "even set a carved image, the idol which he had made, in the house of God, of which God had said to David and to Solomon his son, 'In this house and in Jerusalem, which I have chosen out of all the tribes of Israel, I will put My name forever' " **(2 CHRONICLES 33:7).**

"Let all be put to shame who serve carved images, who boast of idols. Worship Him, all you gods" **(PSALM 97:7).**

"But our God is in heaven; He does whatever He pleases. Their idols are silver and gold, the work of men's hands. They have mouths, but they do not speak; eyes they have, but they do not see; they have ears, but they do not hear; noses they have, but they do not smell; they have hands, but they do not handle; feet they have, but they do not walk; nor do they mutter through their throat. Those who make them are like them; so is everyone who trusts in them" **(PSALM 115:3–8).**

"The idols of the nations are silver and gold, the work of men's hands. They have mouths, but they do not speak; eyes they have, but they do not see; they have ears, but they do not hear; nor is there any breath in their mouths. Those who make them are like them; so is everyone who trusts in them" **(PSALM 135:15–18).**

"To whom then will you liken God? Or what likeness will you compare to Him? The workman molds an image, the goldsmith overspreads it with gold, and the silversmith casts silver chains. Whoever is too impoverished for such a contribution chooses a tree that will not rot; he seeks for himself a skillful workman to prepare a carved image that will not totter" **(ISAIAH 40:18–20).**

"I am the LORD, that is My name; and My glory I will not give to another, nor My praise to carved images. . . . They shall be turned back, they shall be greatly ashamed, who trust in carved images, who say to the molded images, 'You are our gods' " **(ISAIAH 42:8, 17).**

"They shall be ashamed and also disgraced, all of them; they shall go in confusion together, who are makers of idols" **(ISAIAH 45:16).**

"To whom will you liken Me, and make Me equal and compare Me, that we should be alike? They lavish gold out of the bag, and weigh silver on the scales; they hire a goldsmith, and he makes it a god; they prostrate themselves, yes, they worship. They bear it on the shoulder, they carry it and set it in its place, and it stands; from its place it shall not move. Though one cries out to it, yet it cannot answer nor save him out of his trouble" **(ISAIAH 46:5–7).**

Reading these passages describing pagan idolatry leaves us amazed that these practices influenced God's chosen people. Israel's prophets condemned these idolatrous practices and called the nation back to faithfulness to God's commands. It might be even more amazing that in subtle ways idolatry has penetrated many Christian churches. The historical statements below tell the sad, tragic story.

"The church did everything it could to stamp out such 'pagan' rites, but had to capitulate and allow the rites to continue with only the name of the local deity changed to some Christian saint's name" (Dr. Edwin Goodenough, *Religious Tradition and Myth,* pp. 56, 57).

"The Christian calendar of saints replaced the Roman 'fasti' [gods]; ancient divinities dear to the people were allowed to revive under the names of 'Christian saints' " (Will Durant, *The Age of Faith,* pp. 745, 746).

"Confiding then in the power of Christianity to resist the infection of evil, and to transmit the instruments and appendages of demon worship to an evangelical use . . . the rulers of the church from early times were prepared, should occasion arise, to adopt or imitate, or sanction the existing rites and customs of the populace" (Cardinal Newman, *The Development of Christian Doctrine,* p. 372).

10 How did the Babylonians view death? What strange ritual occurred at the very door of the Old Testament sanctuary?

"So He [a heavenly being] brought me to the door of the north gate of the LORD's house [the temple]; and to my dismay, women were sitting there weeping for Tammuz" **(EZEKIEL 8:14).**

Tammuz was a pagan god of Sumerian origin whose heathen worship was spread throughout the ancient world, especially in Babylonia, Assyria, Phoenicia, and Palestine. He was the god of pastures and flocks, the heavenly shepherd who supposedly died annually and rose to new life every year after the pagan goddess Ishtar, his wife and sister, descended into the underworld and brought him up again. His departure was mourned in public festivities of grieving and singing dirges. His awakening and return were supposed to cause vegetation to flourish again. The Tammuz cult found entrance into Judah, and God's Word describes Hebrew women weeping for that god at the temple gates, performing the religious rites connected with his annual death.

The myth of Tammuz and Ishtar, described in many Babylonian texts and praised in songs, was known in Phoenicia as that of Adonis (from the Semitic word *adon*, meaning "lord"), and from there it was carried to Greece and Rome and found its expression there in the mythological story of Venus and Adonis. But the worship of Adonis was only one form of the widespread worship of Tammuz.

Tammuz, the god of vegetation, was one of the many deities of Babylon. The Babylonians believed that in the winter, Tammuz died. In the season of abundant crops, they believed, he lived again. This worship of the dead was common in Babylon.

The concept of the immortal soul was at the heart of Babylonian worship. The thought that the soul leaves the body at death comes directly from paganism.

11 What does the Bible teach regarding death and communication with those who have died? The following Bible passages outline the Bible teaching on death and the pagan origin of the idea of the immortality of the soul and the worship of dead loved ones.

The Bible teaches: "the living know that they will die; but the dead know nothing, and they have no more reward, for the memory of them is forgotten" **(ECCLESIASTES 9:5).**

"The dead do not praise the LORD, nor any who go down into silence" **(PSALM 115:17).**

"His breath goeth forth, he returneth to his earth; in that very day his thoughts perish" **(PSALM 146:4, KJV).**

After a man dies, "his sons come to honor, and he does not know it; they are brought low, and he does not perceive it" **(JOB 14:21).**

"Man dies and is laid away; indeed he breathes his last and where is he?" **(JOB 14:10).**

"In death there is no remembrance of You; in the grave who will give You thanks?" **(PSALM 6:5).**

"Will You work wonders for the dead? Shall the dead arise and praise You? Shall Your lovingkindness be declared in the grave? Or Your faithfulness in the place of destruction? Shall Your wonders be known in the dark? And Your righteousness in the land of forgetfulness?" **(PSALM 88:10–12).**

"What profit is there in my blood, when I go down to the pit? Will the dust praise You? Will it declare Your truth?" **(PSALM 30:9).**

"While I live I will praise the LORD; I will sing praises to my God while I have my being" **(PSALM 146:2).**

"You hide Your face, they are troubled; You take away their breath, they die and return to their dust" **(PSALM 104:29).**

"For Sheol cannot thank You, death cannot praise You; those who go down to the pit cannot hope for Your truth. The living, the living man, he shall praise You, as I do this day" **(ISAIAH 38:18, 19).**

"In the sweat of your face you shall eat bread till you return to the ground, for out of it you were taken; for dust you are, and to dust you shall return" **(GENESIS 3:19).**

"Then the dust will return to the earth as it was, and the spirit will return to God who gave it" **(ECCLESIASTES 12:7).**

"My days are past, my purposes are broken off, even the thoughts of my heart" **(JOB 17:11).**

Any system of religion that teaches the doctrine of the immortal soul is part of Old Testament Babylon. Immortality of the soul was at the very heart of pagan worship.

12 The prophet saw further abominations in Israel. Babylonian practices and pagan influences were incorporated by some worshipers into the very worship of God's people at the door of the temple. What false worship practices were brought into Israel's worship from Babylon?

God brought the prophet Ezekiel, in vision, "into the inner court of the LORD's house; and there, at the door of the temple of the LORD, between the porch and the altar, were about twenty-five men with their backs toward the temple of the LORD and their faces toward the east, and they were worshiping the sun toward the east" **(EZEKIEL 8:16).**

Three things about this verse are worthy of special notice. First, those pictured were not only *worshiping the sun,* but they turned "their *backs* toward the temple of the LORD" to do it. Second, the fact that they stood in the inner court of the temple implies that they were probably *priests.* If they were the supposed spiritual leaders of the true religion, their sin was a most flagrant insult to God. Third, the divine record declares this *rebellious act of sun worship* to be, in God's eyes, the *greatest of abominations* **(COMPARE EZEKIEL 8:6, 9, 13, 15, 17, 18).**

The Creator of all things cautions us, "Take heed, lest you lift your eyes to heaven, and when you see the sun, the moon, and the stars, all the host of heaven, you feel driven to worship them and serve them, which the LORD your God has given to all the peoples under the whole heaven as a heritage" **(DEUTERONOMY 4:19).**

To see just how great an abomination sun worship is in the eyes of God, we need only recall that ancient people commonly worshiped the sun as their supreme deity—for it gave them light and warmth and food by making their crops grow. But Paul says they "exchanged the truth of God for a lie, and worshiped and served the creature [and the sun is just a "creature" or creation of God] rather than the Creator" **(ROMANS 1:25).** Many honest, sincere, but misguided, people have "exchanged the truth of God for a lie," and many have been led to worship on Sunday instead of on the day honoring our Creator, God's holy Sabbath.

"If there is found among you, within any of your gates which the LORD your God gives you, a man or a woman who has been wicked in the sight of the LORD your God, in transgressing His covenant, who has gone and served other gods and worshiped them, either the sun or moon or any of the host of heaven, which I have not commanded, and it is told you, and you hear of it, then you shall inquire diligently" **(DEUTERONOMY 17:2–4).**

So deep and widespread was the abomination of sun worship that faithful King Josiah had to institute reforms. "He removed the idolatrous priests whom the kings of Judah had ordained to burn incense on the high places in the cities of Judah and in the places all around Jerusalem, and those who burned incense to Baal, to the sun, to the moon, to the constellations, and to all the host of heaven. . . . Then he removed the horses that the kings of Judah had dedicated to the sun, at the entrance to the house of the LORD, by the chamber of Nathan-Melech, the officer who was in the court; and he burned the chariots of the sun with fire" **(2 KINGS 23:5, 11).**

The patriarch Job examines himself: "If I have observed the sun when it shines, or the moon moving in brightness, so that my heart has been secretly enticed, and my mouth has kissed my hand; this also would be an iniquity deserving of judgment, for I would have denied God who is above" **(JOB 31:26–28).**

Sun worship was widespread in the East and in Egypt from a very early date, but Job means to say that he never participated in such idolatry. The words "if . . . my mouth has kissed my hand" refer to the fact that it was customary to kiss idols **(SEE 1 KINGS 19:18; HOSEA 13:2).** But the heavenly bodies were so remote that the worshipers could not have access to them, so they expressed their adoration for them by kissing their hand.

The Lord is patient and long-suffering, but finally "God turned and gave them up to worship the host of heaven, as it is written in the book of the Prophets: 'Did you offer Me slaughtered animals and sacrifices during forty years in the wilderness, O house of Israel? You also took up the tabernacle of Moloch, and the star of your god Remphan, images which you made to worship; and I will carry you away beyond Babylon' " **(ACTS 7:42, 43).**

"Remphan" was a star-god worshiped by the ancient Israelites (compare **AMOS 5:26,** which speaks of "your idols, the star of your gods, which you made for yourselves").

The sun, moon, and stars were worshiped from the earliest centuries. Sun worship was ingrained in pagan culture. The Edomites, the Egyptians, the Babylonians, the Persians, and the Romans all revered or worshiped the sun.

13 What eternal sign has God given His people to distinguish true worship from counterfeit worship for all time?

"Moreover I also gave them My Sabbaths, to be a sign between them and Me, that they might know that I am the LORD who sanctifies them. . . . Hallow My Sabbaths, and they will be a sign between Me and you, that you may know that I am the LORD your God" **(EZEKIEL 20:12, 20).**

"And on the seventh day God ended His work which He had done, and He rested on the seventh day from all His work which He had done. Then God blessed the seventh day and sanctified it, because in it He rested from all His work which God had created and made" **(GENESIS 2:2, 3).**

" 'See! For the LORD has given you the Sabbath; therefore He gives you on the sixth day bread for two days. Let every man remain in his place; let no man go out of his place on the seventh day.' So the people rested on the seventh day" **(EXODUS 16:29, 30).**

God's holy Sabbath existed as an institution even *before* the giving of the Ten Commandments! The sixteenth chapter of the book of Exodus gives detailed instructions to God's people about the "bread from heaven," called *manna,* which the Lord provided to sustain them in the wilderness. Each day they were to gather just enough for that day. If they tried to gather extra and keep it over till the next day, it would spoil, begin to stink, and breed worms. But no manna fell on the seventh-day Sabbath. So God told them to gather *twice* as much on Friday, the "Preparation Day," for the Sabbath and save the extra for use on the Sabbath. None of the manna saved over on the Sabbath would spoil "and it did not stink, nor were there any worms in it" **(EXODUS 16:24).**

All of this, of course, involved many miracles on the part of God: (1) raining down the manna six days a week, (2) giving a double portion on each Preparation Day, (3) miraculously preserving the extra manna over the Sabbath, (4) providing no manna on the Sabbath so that no menial work needed to be done on God's holy day. But note that some rebellious people defied the Lord's instructions and went out on the seventh day to gather manna anyway. "And the LORD said to Moses, *'How long do you refuse to keep My commandments and My laws?'* " **(EXODUS 16:28; EMPHASIS SUPPLIED).** Yet this was quite some time *before* the giving of God's law of the Ten Commandments on Mount Sinai. Thus God, by giving the manna in this way, not only preserved His people during their wilderness wanderings, but also preserved His Sabbath command during those forty years.

"Remember the Sabbath day, to keep it holy. Six days you shall labor and do all your work, but the seventh day is the Sabbath of the LORD your God. In it you shall do no work: you, nor your son, nor your daughter, nor your male servant, nor your female servant, nor your cattle, nor your stranger who is within your gates. For in six days the LORD made the heavens and the earth, the sea, and all that is in them, and rested the seventh day. Therefore the LORD blessed the Sabbath day and hallowed it" **(EXODUS 20:8–11).**

"Work shall be done for six days, but the seventh day shall be a holy day for you, a Sabbath of rest to the LORD. Whoever does any work on it shall be put to death" **(EXODUS 35:2).**

So often today, in the rat-race and stress of our pressure-cooker society, we hear people frankly comment, "I'm so busy working, I don't go to church. I don't have time to study my Bible. It seems I don't have time to spend with my family or quiet moments to spend with God." The Master knew it would be like this. He knew our physical frame, having made it, and He foresaw our need for rest. He knew our personalities, often triggered by greed or ambition, and He realized that, if left to ourselves, we'd find no time for spiritual things of lasting value—no time for fellowship with Him. That's why the Divine Physician wrote the *prescription* we call the Sabbath. That's why He gave us a gift that only He could give—a gift of time.

When the Lord wanted to give mankind a test, a sign that would demonstrate their obedience and commemorate His great work of Creation, with infinite wisdom He made this test a simple one that was within the ability of all. Girls and women, as well as boys and men, can rest. Elderly folks, as well as youth, can rest. The poor people, as well as the wealthy, can rest. Sick people, as well as the healthy and vigorous, can rest. The uneducated and unsophisticated, as well as the learned and brilliant, can rest. All it takes is a willing and submissive heart.

Nehemiah says of the Lord God: "You came down also on Mount Sinai, and spoke with them [Your people] from heaven, and gave them just ordinances and true laws, good statutes and commandments. You made known to them Your holy Sabbath, and commanded them precepts, statutes and laws, by the hand of Moses Your servant" **(NEHEMIAH 9:13, 14).**

The seventh-day Sabbath was actually made known to the human race when the Creator—Jesus—gave it to our first parents in the Garden of Eden at the end of Creation week. But after God's people spent over four hundred years in bondage as slaves in Egypt, God once again "made known to them [His] holy Sabbath" after liberating them.

Jesus declared, "The Son of Man is Lord even of the Sabbath" **(MATTHEW 12:8).**

"He [Jesus] said to them, 'The Sabbath was made for man, and not man for the Sabbath. Therefore the Son of Man is also Lord of the Sabbath' " **(MARK 2:27, 28).**

God told His servant Moses, "Speak also to the children of Israel, saying: 'Surely My Sabbaths you shall keep, for it is a sign between Me and you throughout your generations, that you may know that I am the LORD who sanctifies you' " **(EXODUS 31:13).**

But not even God's chosen people, the Jews, were always careful about obeying the Lord. Nehemiah reports: "In those days I saw people in Judah treading wine presses on the Sabbath, and bringing in sheaves, and loading donkeys with wine, grapes, figs, and all kinds of burdens, which they brought into Jerusalem on the Sabbath day. And I warned them about the day on which they were selling provisions. Men of Tyre dwelt there also, who brought in fish and all kinds of goods, and sold them on the Sabbath to the children of Judah, and in Jerusalem. Then I contended with the nobles of Judah, and said to them, 'What evil thing is this that you do, by which you profane the Sabbath day? Did not your fathers do thus, and did not our God bring all this disaster on us and on this city? Yet you bring added wrath on Israel by profaning the Sabbath.' So it was, at the gates of Jerusalem, as it began to be dark before the Sabbath, that I commanded the gates to be shut, and charged that they must not be opened till after the Sabbath. Then I posted some of my servants at the gates, so that no burdens would be brought in on the Sabbath day. Now the merchants and sellers of all kinds of wares lodged outside Jerusalem once or twice. Then I warned them, and said to them, 'Why do you spend the night around the wall? If you do so again, I will lay hands on you!' From that time on they came no more on the Sabbath. And I commanded the Levites [the priests] that they should cleanse themselves, and that they should go and guard the gates, to sanctify the Sabbath day. Remember me, O my God, concerning this also, and spare me according to the greatness of Your mercy!" **(NEHEMIAH 13:15–22).**

The Lord of the Sabbath lovingly tells us, "If you turn away your foot from [desecrating] the Sabbath, from doing your pleasure on My holy day, and call the Sabbath a delight, the holy day of the LORD honorable, and shall honor Him, not doing your own ways, nor finding your own pleasure, nor speaking your own words, then you shall delight yourself in the LORD; and I will cause you to ride on the high hills of the earth, and feed you with the heritage of Jacob your father. The mouth of the LORD has spoken" **(ISAIAH 58:13, 14).**

God directed His people that they should not " 'carry a burden out of your houses on the Sabbath day, nor do any work, but hallow the Sabbath day, as I commanded your fathers. . . . And it shall be, if you heed Me carefully,' says the LORD, 'to bring no burden through the gates of this city on the Sabbath day, but hallow the Sabbath day, to do no work in it, then . . . this city shall remain forever. . . . But if you will not heed Me to hallow the Sabbath day, such as not carrying a burden when entering the gates of Jerusalem on the Sabbath day, then I will kindle a fire in its gates, and it shall devour the palaces of Jerusalem, and it shall not be quenched' " **(JEREMIAH 17:22, 24, 25, 27).**

The following historical quotations enable us to discover how the pagan day of worship gradually slipped into the Christian church:

"[Constantine's] coins bore on the one side the letters of the name of Christ; on the other the figure of the Sun-god, . . . as if he could not bear to relinquish the patronage of the bright luminary" (Arthur B. Stanley, *Lectures on the History of the Eastern Church,* p. 184).

Absolutely amazing! On Constantine's coins Christ was on one side, and the sun-god on the other side! A wedding took place, a wedding between Christianity and paganism. A wedding between the church of Rome and the pagan emperors of Rome.

Stanley also says: "The retention of the old pagan name of 'Dies Solis,' or 'Sunday,' for the weekly is, in great measure, owing to the union of pagan and Christian sentiment with which the first day of the week was recommended by Constantine to his subjects, pagan and Christian alike, as the 'venerable day of the Sun' " (Ibid.).

"In ancient Babylonia the sun was worshipped from immemorial antiquity" (James G. Frazer, *The Worship of Nature,* vol. 1, p. 529).

"What a pity that it [Sunday] comes branded with the mark of paganism, and christened with the name of the sun god, then adopted and sanctioned by the papal apostasy, and bequeathed as a sacred legacy to Protestantism" (Dr. Edward Hiscox, "The Baptist Manual," November 13, 1893).

"To conciliate pagans to nominal Christianity, Rome, pursuing its usual policy, took measures to get the Christian and pagan festivals amalgamated, and to get paganism and Christianity—now far sunk in idolatry—in this as in so many other things to shake hands" (Alexander Hislop, *The Two Babylons*, p. 195).

14 Why was false worship so widespread? How did many religious leaders relate to this union of true and false religion in Bible times?

Speaking of the spiritual leaders of His people, God says: "Her priests have violated My law and profaned My holy things; they have not distinguished between the holy and unholy, nor have they made known the difference between the unclean and the clean; and they have hidden their eyes from My Sabbaths, so that I am profaned among them" **(EZEKIEL 22:26)**.

Sadly, this indictment has a striking parallel in our own day. Men—even members of the religious establishment—hide their eyes from the obligation to keep the true Sabbath. They close their eyes to plain Scriptural evidences and claim, "I can't see it."

God says, "You have despised My holy things and profaned My Sabbaths" **(EZEKIEL 22:8)**.

People ignore God and His wishes, then turn to Him only in a crisis: "The priests did not say, 'Where is the LORD?' And those who handle the law did not know Me; the rulers also transgressed against Me; the prophets prophesied by Baal, and walked after things that do not profit. . . . As the thief is ashamed when he is found out, so is the house of Israel ashamed; they and their kings and their princes, and their priests and their prophets, saying to a tree, 'You are my father,' and to a stone 'You gave birth to me.' For they have turned their back to Me, and not their face. But in the time of their trouble they will say, 'Arise and save us' " **(JEREMIAH 2:8, 26, 27)**.

Jeremiah writes of "the sins of her prophets and the iniquities of her priests" **(LAMENTATIONS 4:13)**.

"Her heads judge for a bribe, her priests teach for pay, and her prophets divine for money. Yet they lean on the LORD, and say, 'Is not the LORD among us? No harm can come upon us' " **(MICAH 3:11)**.

"Her princes in her midst are roaring lions; her judges are evening wolves that leave not a bone till morning. Her prophets are insolent, treacherous people; her priests have polluted the sanctuary, they have done violence to the law" **(ZEPHANIAH 3:3, 4).**

Of course, there are many godly, committed spiritual leaders who are faithful to God and dedicated to His Word. Some of these are "blind" to the fullness of His truth. This was true in Jesus' day, and it is true today. Many of the Jewish priests who opposed Jesus' ministry accepted His message shortly after His death. The Bible records that "many of the priests were obedient to the faith" **(ACTS 6:7).**

However, not all religious teachers and spiritual leaders are safe to follow. The Lord's most determined enemies were the Pharisees and Sadducees—the religious leaders of His day. And Judas, who betrayed Christ, was one in the inner circle of disciples, to all appearances a pious man and model Christian. Our only safe guide is *not man* but the Word of God.

God says, "My people have been lost sheep. *Their shepherds have led them astray*. . . . They have forgotten their resting place" **(JEREMIAH 50:6; EMPHASIS SUPPLIED).**

The Sabbath of the Lord may well be considered our "resting place." But many people don't know this Bible truth, because "their shepherds [or pastors] have led them astray."

" 'The lips of a priest should keep knowledge, and people should seek the law from his mouth; for he is the messenger of the LORD of hosts. But you have departed from the way; you have caused many to stumble at the law. You have corrupted the covenant of Levi,' says the LORD of hosts. 'Therefore, I also have made you contemptible and base before all the people, because you have not kept My ways but have shown partiality in the law' " **(MALACHI 2:7–9).**

Instead of being faithful shepherds to the flock, some clergy themselves "have caused many to stumble at the law" and "have shown partiality in the law" by teaching that perhaps *nine* of the Ten Commandments are still valid, but *one*—namely, the fourth commandment respecting God's Sabbath—is no longer in effect but has been abolished. Still other clergy teach their believers, by precept and example, that they should bow down to religious statues, reverencing them and praying before them Thus people are often misled by those whom they trust.

15 What physical habits characterized the Babylonian lifestyle? How does this harmonize with the biblical teaching of the body as the temple of the Holy Spirit?

"They drank wine, and praised the gods of gold and silver, bronze and iron, wood and stone" **(DANIEL 5:4).**

The prophet Daniel was called in to decipher "the handwriting on the wall," which brought to a dramatic halt the drunken feast of Babylonian King Belshazzar and a thousand of his lords. But before he did so, he told the king, "You have lifted yourself up against the Lord of heaven. They have brought the [sacred] vessels of His house [God's temple in Jerusalem] before you, and you and your lords, your wives and your concubines, have drunk wine from them. And you have praised the [heathen] gods of silver and gold, bronze and iron, wood and stone, which do not see or hear or know; and the God who holds your breath in His hand and owns all your ways, you have not glorified" **(DANIEL 5:23).**

Here are solemn, sobering words: "The works of the flesh are evident, which are: adultery, fornication, uncleanness, lewdness, idolatry, sorcery, hatred, contentions, jealousies, outbursts of wrath, selfish ambitions, dissensions, heresies, envy, murders, drunkenness, revelries, and the like; of which I tell you beforehand, just as I also told you in time past, that those who practice such things will not inherit the kingdom of God" **(GALATIANS 5:19–21).**

"Do you not know that the unrighteous will not inherit the kingdom of God? Do not be deceived. Neither fornicators, nor idolaters, nor adulterers, nor homosexuals, nor sodomites, nor thieves, nor covetous, nor drunkards, nor revilers, nor extortioners will inherit the kingdom of God" **(1 CORINTHIANS 6:9, 10).**

"You cannot drink the cup of the Lord and the cup of demons; you cannot partake of the Lord's table and of the table of demons" **(1 CORINTHIANS 10:21).**

"Therefore, whether you eat or drink, or whatever you do, do all to the glory of God" **(1 CORINTHIANS 10:31).**

This drunken feast is a typical example of Babylon's desire to gratify the physical senses.

16 What powerful appeal do the Bible writers give regarding our body temples?

The apostle Paul pleads, "I beseech you therefore, brethren, by the mercies of God, that you present your bodies a living sacrifice, holy, acceptable to God, which is your reasonable service" **(ROMANS 12:1).**

"Therefore do not let sin reign in your mortal body, that you should obey it in its lusts. And do not present your members as instruments of unrighteousness to sin, but present yourselves to God as being alive from the dead, and your members as instruments of righteousness to God. . . . Do you not know that to whom you present yourselves slaves to obey, you are that one's slaves whom you obey, whether of sin leading to death, or of obedience leading to righteousness? **(ROMANS 6:12, 13, 16).**

"Or do you not know that your body is the temple of the Holy Spirit who is in you, whom you have from God, and you are not your own? For you were bought at a price; therefore glorify God in your body and in your spirit, which are God's" **(1 CORINTHIANS 6:19, 20).**

Spiritual Babylon's principles run through many religious organizations today. They include:

- Looking to a visible, earthly head rather than Christ.
- Any form of idol/image worship.
- A misunderstanding of what happens to people when they die, prayers to saints, veneration of dead loved ones, etc.
- A departure from God's commands and substituting Sunday worship for Sabbath worship.
- A misunderstanding of the body as God's temple, use of alcohol, tobacco, and unclean foods.

17 Is it possible to reform Babylon? What about conscientious Christians who are in churches which teach Babylon's doctrines? What final appeal does God give to those still in Babylon?

God knows He must soon destroy Babylon, so these words given through John the revelator are His fearful warning as well as His loving invitation—all rolled into one urgent appeal: "I heard another voice from heaven saying, '*Come out of her, my people*, lest you share in her sins, and lest you receive of her plagues' " **(REVELATION 18:4; EMPHASIS SUPPLIED).**

Throughout biblical history, God in His mercy has sent urgent messages to leave or flee from judgment-bound cities on the verge of destruction. When God was about to destroy Sodom and Gomorrah, He sent a warning to Abraham's nephew, Lot: "Then the men [the angels] said to Lot, 'Have you anyone else here? Son-in-law, your sons, your daughters, and whomever you have in the city—take them out of this place! For we will destroy this place, because the outcry against them has grown great before the face of the LORD, and the LORD has sent us to destroy it' " **(GENESIS 19:12, 13).**

When God was about to destroy Korah, Dathan, and Abiram for attempting to undermine Moses' leadership, He warned all the people through Moses, saying, " 'Depart now from the tents of these wicked men! Touch nothing of theirs, lest you be consumed in all their sins.' So they got away from around the tents of Korah, Dathan, and Abiram; and Dathan and Abiram came out and stood at the door of their tents, with their wives, their sons, and their little children" **(NUMBERS 16:26, 27).**

Jesus, knowing that Roman armies would destroy Jerusalem some forty years hence, gave this warning to His followers: "When you see the 'abomination of desolation,' spoken of by Daniel the prophet, standing in the holy place (whoever reads, let him understand), then let those who are in Judea flee to the mountains. Let him who is on the housetop not go down to take anything out of his house. And let him who is in the field not go back to get his clothes. But woe to those who are pregnant and to those who are nursing babies in those days! And pray that your flight may not be in winter or on the Sabbath" **(MATTHEW 24:15–20).**

"Therefore 'Come out from among them and be separate, says the Lord. Do not touch what is unclean, and I will receive you. I will be a Father to you, and you shall be My sons and daughters, says the LORD Almighty' " **(2 CORINTHIANS 6:17, 18).**

"Depart! Depart! Go out from there, touch no unclean thing; go out from the midst of her, be clean, you who bear the vessels of the LORD" **(ISAIAH 52:11).**

God warned His people, "Move from the midst of Babylon, go out of the land of the Chaldeans" **(JEREMIAH 50:8).**

"Flee from the midst of Babylon, and every one save his life! Do not be cut off in her iniquity, for this is the time of the LORD's vengeance; He shall recompense her. . . . My people, go out of the midst of her! And let everyone deliver himself from the fierce anger of the LORD" **(JEREMIAH 51:6, 45).**

God doesn't call us to stay in Babylon and reform it, but to come out of Babylon. Soon the plagues will fall on all inhabitants of Babylon. In love, God has sent you a message to come completely out of Babylon and be separate.

Spiritual Babylon faces the judgments of God. Revelation's message is clear: "Come out of her my people." God's people by the tens of thousands are still in churches that have accepted the principles of Old Testament Babylon. They have incorporated idols, Sunday worship, and the immortality of the soul into their worship. God's earnest appeal is to leave them, to come out of every church that still clings to the teachings of Babylon!

CHAPTER 26

What the Bible Says About the Unpardonable Sin

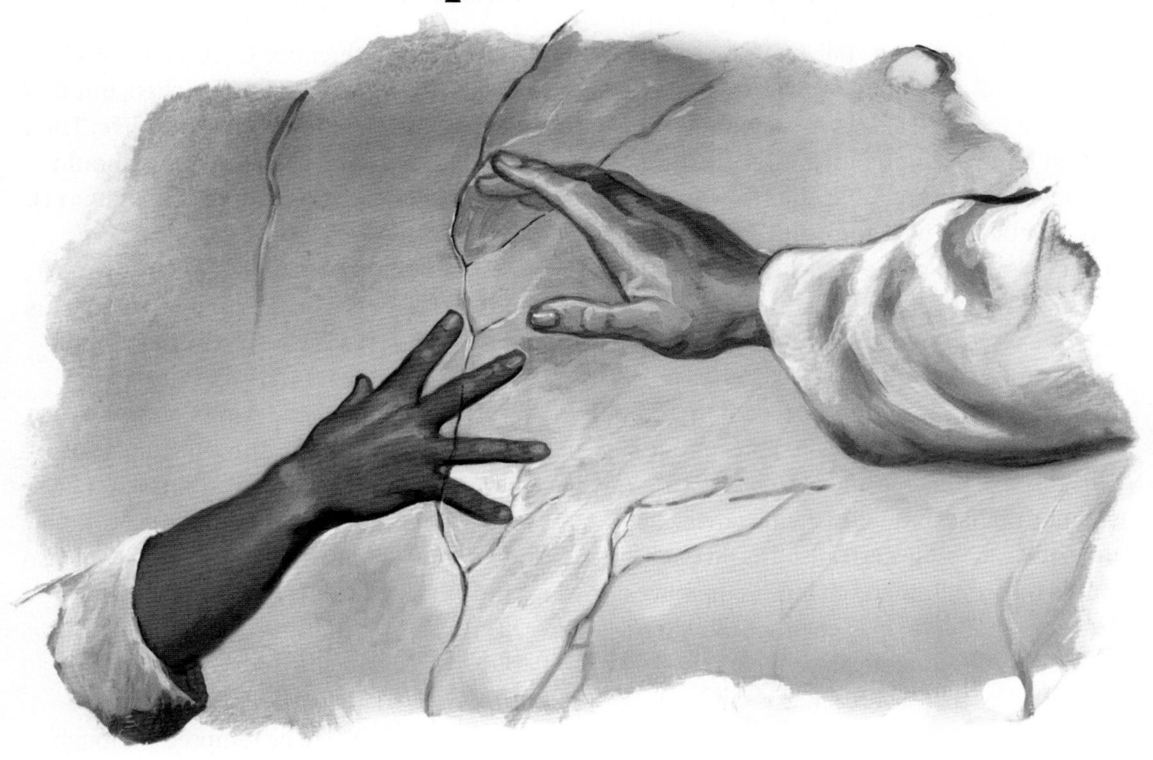

The young woman in her early twenties trembled as she approached her pastor. She was extremely nervous. With tears in her eyes she asked, "Pastor, can I speak privately with you?" As she shared her heart's secrets, a sordid tale of sin and guilt, she wondered aloud, "Is there any hope for me? Have I committed the unpardonable sin? Am I beyond God's mercy?" This young woman's questions are certainly not hers alone. Many people wonder about the very same thing. They long for a ray of hope. They feel guilty and condemned and wonder whether God can ever forgive them. They wonder, *Is it possible I have committed the unpardonable sin?*

What is the unpardonable sin? Is there a sin so great that even God cannot forgive it? Will a person know if he or she has committed it? Why is it unforgiveable?

Since the unpardonable sin involves our relationship with the Holy Spirit, it is vital to know how the Holy Spirit works in our lives. This chapter will reveal how the Holy Spirit works in our lives and what it means to resist His working and how to avoid committing the unpardonable sin.

01 Is there a sin that Jesus declares is unpardonable? How does He describe it? What does it consist of?

Jesus said, "Therefore I say to you, every sin and blasphemy will be forgiven men, but the blasphemy against the Spirit will not be forgiven men" **(MATTHEW 12:31).**

"Anyone who speaks a word against the Son of Man, it will be forgiven him; but whoever speaks against the Holy Spirit, it will not be forgiven him, either in this age or in the age to come" **(MATTHEW 12:32).**

This is a fascinating Bible passage. The Pharisees attributed Jesus' miracle-working power to Beelzebub (another name for Satan) rather than to God. Why did they do this? For one simple reason. If they accepted Christ's miracles as genuine manifestations of divine power, then they must accept Jesus Himself as divine. This would mean a dramatic change in their lives. The unpardonable sin is not a specific sin such as adultery, murder, stealing, or cursing. Jesus clearly states that "every sin" can, and will, be forgiven if we truly repent and ask for forgiveness. The unpardonable sin, then, is the refusal to accept Jesus for who He is—our loving, forgiving, life-changing Savior. As we shall discover in this chapter, the unpardonable sin has to do with a hardened, unrepentant heart.

" 'Come now, and let us reason together,' says the LORD, 'though your sins are like scarlet, they shall be as white as snow; though they are red like crimson, they shall be as wool' " **(ISAIAH 1:18).**

"Let the wicked forsake his way, and the unrighteous man his thoughts; let him return to the LORD, and He will have mercy on him; and to our God, for He will abundantly pardon" **(ISAIAH 55:7).**

" 'As I live,' says the Lord GOD, 'I have no pleasure in the death of the wicked, but that the wicked turn from his way and live. Turn, turn from your evil ways! For why should you die, O house of Israel?' " **(EZEKIEL 33:11).**

"If we confess our sins, He is faithful and just to forgive us our sins and to cleanse us from all unrighteousness" **(1 JOHN 1:9).**

"My little children, these things I write to you, so that you may not sin. And if anyone sins, we have an Advocate with the Father, Jesus Christ the righteous. And He Himself is the propitiation for our sins, and not for ours only but also for the whole world" **(1 JOHN 2:1, 2).**

Part of the good news of the gospel is that Christ has lived in this sinful world, and He knows what it's like to be tempted—though He never sinned, not even once. "For we do not have a High Priest who cannot sympathize with our weaknesses, but was in all points tempted as we are, yet without sin" **(HEBREWS 4:15).** Now in the verse quoted above, John says that if we sin, "we have an Advocate with the Father, Jesus Christ the righteous." The Lord Jesus Himself is our Advocate—our Defense Lawyer, our Intermediary, the Spokesman on our behalf with the Father. And He's a Lawyer who has never lost a case!

But don't mistakenly feel that "I *need* a good defense, because the heavenly Father is awfully mean and vindictive, just *itching* to *punish* me like some sadistic monster!" The devil would like us to think that, but Jesus sets the matter straight with these comforting words: "I do not say to you that I shall pray the Father for you; for *the Father Himself loves you*, because you have loved Me, and have believed that I came forth from God" **(JOHN 16:26, 27; EMPHASIS SUPPLIED).**

Before he was converted on the road to Damascus, the apostle Paul was Saul—an absolute terror to the church of Christ. He gives this testimony: "I was formerly a blasphemer, a persecutor, and an insolent man; but I obtained mercy because I did it ignorantly in unbelief. And the grace of our Lord was exceedingly abundant, with faith and love which are in Christ Jesus. This is a faithful saying and worthy of all acceptance, that Christ Jesus came into the world to save sinners, of whom I am chief" **(1 TIMOTHY 1:13–15).**

Jesus said, "Assuredly, I say to you, all sins will be forgiven the sons of men, and whatever blasphemies they may utter; but he who blasphemes against the Holy Spirit never has forgiveness, but is subject to eternal condemnation" **(MARK 3:28, 29).**

The unpardonable sin is not a specific *type of sin,* such as murder, adultery, or stealing. It is a *degree in sin* in which the heart becomes hardened against the prompting of the Holy Spirit. Another way to describe it is that the unpardonable sin is the sin we will not confess. Any sin we confess is pardonable. But if we refuse to yield to the claims of the Holy Spirit, we deny God the ability to work in our lives.

"You stiff-necked and uncircumcised in heart and ears! You always resist the Holy Spirit; as your fathers did, so do you" **(ACTS 7:51).**

"If anyone sees his brother sinning a sin which does not lead to death, he will ask, and He [God] will give him life for those who commit sin not leading to death. There is sin leading to death. I do not say that he should pray about that. All unrighteousness is sin, and there is sin not leading to death" **(1 JOHN 5:16, 17).**

02 Unpardonable sins are the ones we cling to and refuse to confess. If we resist the pleadings of the Holy Spirit long enough, we will build a wall of separation between us and God. What are the conditions that God's Word outlines for the forgiveness of sins?

"Then Peter said to them, '*Repent*, and let every one of you be baptized in the name of Jesus Christ for the remission of sins; and you shall receive the gift of the Holy Spirit' " **(ACTS 2:38; EMPHASIS SUPPLIED).**

"Repent therefore and be converted, that your sins may be blotted out, so that times of refreshing may come from the presence of the Lord" **(ACTS 3:19).**

"Truly, these times of ignorance God overlooked, but now commands all men everywhere to repent" **(ACTS 17:30).**

Paul was "testifying to Jews, and also to Greeks, repentance toward God and faith toward our Lord Jesus Christ" **(ACTS 20:21).**

Paul "declared first to those in Damascus and in Jerusalem, and throughout all the region of Judea, and then to the Gentiles, that they should repent, turn to God, and do works befitting repentance" **(ACTS 26:20).**

John the Baptist came "saying, 'Repent, for the kingdom of heaven is at hand!' . . . Therefore bear fruits worthy of repentance" **(MATTHEW 3:2, 8).**

"Repentance and remission of sins should be preached in His name to all nations, beginning at Jerusalem" **(LUKE 24:47).**

King Solomon prayed, "When they come to themselves in the land where they were carried captive, and repent, and make supplication to You in the land of those who took them captive, saying, 'We have sinned and done wrong, we have committed wickedness' " **(1 KINGS 8:47; SEE ALSO VERSES 46–50; 2 CHRONICLES 6:36–39).**

We're saved "not by works of righteousness which we have done, but according to His mercy He saved us, through the washing of regeneration and renewing of the Holy Spirit" **(TITUS 3:5).**

"If we confess our sins, He is faithful and just to forgive us our sins and to cleanse us from all unrighteousness" **(1 JOHN 1:9).**

"He who covers his sins will not prosper, but whoever confesses and forsakes them will have mercy" **(PROVERBS 28:13).**

In Daniel's beautiful and humble prayer, he confesses, "we have sinned and committed iniquity, we have done wickedly and rebelled, even by departing from Your precepts and Your judgments. Neither have we heeded Your servants the prophets, who spoke in Your name to our kings and our princes, to our fathers and all the people of the land" **(DANIEL 9:5, 6; SEE ALSO 4–21).**

Here is a wonderful prayer of confession to God: "Please let Your ear be attentive and Your eyes open, that You may hear the prayer of Your servant which I pray before You now, day and night, for the children of Israel Your servants, and confess the sins of the children of Israel which we have sinned against You. Both my father's house and I have sinned. We have acted very corruptly against You, and have not kept the commandments, the statutes, nor the ordinances which You commanded Your servant Moses" **(NEHEMIAH 1:6, 7).**

"I acknowledged my sin to You, and my iniquity I have not hidden. I said, 'I will confess my transgressions to the LORD,' and You forgave the iniquity of my sin" **(PSALM 32:5).**

"Have mercy upon me, O God, according to Your lovingkindness; according to the multitude of Your tender mercies, blot out my transgressions. Wash me thoroughly from my iniquity, and cleanse me from my sin. For I acknowledge my transgressions, and my sin is always before me. Against You, You only, have I sinned, and done this evil in Your sight—that You may be found just when You speak, and blameless when You judge. . . . Purge me with hyssop, and I shall be clean; wash me, and I shall be whiter than snow. . . . Create in me a clean heart, O God, and renew a steadfast spirit ["a right spirit," KJV] within me" **(PSALM 51:1–4, 7, 10).**

The Bible labels **PSALM 51**, "A Psalm of David when Nathan the prophet went to him, after he had gone in to Bathsheba."

All sins that are repented of and confessed will be forgiven. When a person refuses to repent, he or she has closed the mind to the inner working of the Holy Spirit. The unpardonable sin is a state of open rebellion in which the promptings of the Holy Spirit are at first ignored, then resisted, and finally rejected totally until they are no longer perceived.

03 Is the Holy Spirit merely a divine force or is the Holy Spirit a divine personality? How does the Bible describe the Holy Spirit?

Jesus promised the Holy Spirit in these words: "Nevertheless I tell you the truth. It is to your advantage that I go away; for if I do not go away, the Helper [the Holy Spirit] will not come to you; but if I depart, I will send Him to you. And when He has come, He will convict the world of sin, and of righteousness, and of judgment" **(JOHN 16:7, 8).**

"I [Jesus] will pray the Father, and He will give you another Helper, that He may abide with you forever—the Spirit of truth, whom the world cannot receive, because it neither sees Him nor knows Him; but you know Him, for He dwells with you and will be in you. . . . But the Helper, the Holy Spirit, whom the Father will send in My name, He will teach you all things, and bring to your remembrance all things that I said to you" **(JOHN 14:16, 17, 26).**

The Bible calls the Holy Spirit our "Helper." In this passage, Scripture refers to the Holy Spirit as "Him" or "He." The Holy Spirit is not an "it." The Holy Spirit is not an impersonal force. The Holy Spirit is the Third Person of the Godhead.

"But when the Helper comes, whom I shall send to you from the Father, the Spirit of truth who proceeds from the Father, He will testify of Me" **(JOHN 15:26).**

"However, when He, the Spirit of truth, has come, He will guide you into all truth; for He will not speak on His own authority, but whatever He hears He will speak; and He will tell you things to come" **(JOHN 16:13).**

"The Spirit Himself bears witness with our spirit that we are children of God" **(ROMANS 8:16).**

"Likewise the Spirit also helps in our weaknesses. For we do not know what we should pray for as we ought, but the Spirit Himself makes intercession for us with groanings which cannot be uttered. Now He who searches the hearts knows what the mind of the Spirit is, because He makes intercession for the saints according to the will of God" **(ROMANS 8:26, 27).**

04 How does the New Testament reveal the Holy Spirit as the Third Person of the Godhead?

Jesus said, "Go therefore and make disciples of all the nations, baptizing them in the name of the Father and of the Son and of the Holy Spirit" **(MATTHEW 28:19).**

Paul prayed, "The grace of the Lord Jesus Christ, and the love of God, and the communion of the Holy Spirit be with you all. Amen" **(2 CORINTHIANS 13:14).**

The Holy Spirit knows the things of God. "For what man knows the things of a man except the spirit of the man which is in him? Even so no one knows the things of God except the Spirit of God" **(1 CORINTHIANS 2:11).**

Scripture equates the Holy Spirit with God. "Peter said, 'Ananias, why has Satan filled your heart to lie to the Holy Spirit and keep back part of the price of the land for yourself? While it remained, was it not your own? And after it was sold, was it not in your own control? Why have you conceived this thing in your heart? You have not lied to men but to God' " **(ACTS 5:3, 4).**

The Holy Spirit was present at Creation. "The earth was without form, and void; and darkness was on the face of the deep. And the Spirit of God was hovering over the face of the waters" **(GENESIS 1:2).**

Blasphemy is defined as a sin against God alone, but Jesus warns us not to commit blasphemy against the Holy Spirit. "Therefore I say to you, every sin and blasphemy will be forgiven men, but the blasphemy against the Spirit will not be forgiven men. Anyone who speaks a word against the Son of Man, it will be forgiven him; but whoever speaks against the Holy Spirit, it will not be forgiven him, either in this age or in the age to come" **(MATTHEW 12:31, 32).**

05 What is the prime function of the Holy Spirit? What is His work? What does He do in the life of each Christian?

Jesus declared: "When He [the Holy Spirit] has come, He will convict the world of sin, and of righteousness, and of judgment" **(JOHN 16:8).**

We may classify the work of the Holy Spirit under at least four headings:

1. Teaching

"But the Helper, the Holy Spirit, whom the Father will send in My name, He will teach you all things, and bring to your remembrance all things that I said to you" **(JOHN 14:26).**

"When He, the Spirit of truth, has come, He will guide you into all truth" **(JOHN 16:13).**

2. Convicting and converting

"Jesus answered and said to him [Nicodemus], 'Most assuredly, I say to you, unless one is born again, he cannot see the kingdom of God. . . . The wind blows where it wishes, and you hear the sound of it, but cannot tell where it comes from and where it goes. So is everyone who is born of the Spirit' " **(JOHN 3:3, 8).**

"When He has come, He will convict the world of sin, and of righteousness, and of judgment" **(JOHN 16:8).**

3. Imparting spiritual gifts

"The manifestation of the Spirit is given to each one for the profit of all: for to one is given the word of wisdom through the Spirit, to another the word of knowledge through the same Spirit, to another faith by the same Spirit, to another gifts of healings by the same Spirit, to another the working of miracles, to another prophecy, to another discerning of spirits, to another different kinds of tongues, to another the interpretation of tongues. But one and the same Spirit works all these things, distributing to each one individually as He wills" **(1 CORINTHIANS 12:7–11).**

4. Revealing truth

John records how Jesus broke the sad news to His inner circle of disciples that He would be leaving them to return to His Father in heaven. Then, to soften the blow of His leaving, He added, "I will pray the Father, and He will give you another Helper, that He may abide with you forever—the Spirit of truth" **(JOHN 14:16, 17).** When John recorded Jesus as saying that the Father would give us "*another* Helper," he could choose from two different Greek words—*heteros* and *allos*—meaning "another." The word *heteros* usually implies "another of a different kind," like our English word *heterosexual* refers to the difference between the sexes—the opposite sex. On the other hand, *allos* usually implies "another of the same kind," as we might say, "Paul was *another* apostle of Jesus, along with Peter."

So which word did John use? Did he use *heteros,* implying that Jesus would ask the Father to send us a Helper who was *different* than Himself? Or did John use *allos,* suggesting that the promised Helper would be *like* Jesus and would remain with us, not temporarily, but "forever"? No one but a Being who is equal to Christ can fully represent Him. Thus it is fitting that John used the word *allos,* implying that the promised Helper would be *Another of the same quality and ranking* as the Son Himself. Like Christ, the Holy Spirit is not only a Person, but He is also a *Divine* Person. Thus He is admirably qualified to represent Jesus perfectly. It is the Spirit who acts as a Regent for Christ on earth and who is the true Vicar of Jesus Christ. The office and authority of the Son of God can be held only by another Person of the Trinity.

"However, when He, the Spirit of truth, has come, He will guide you into all truth; for He will not speak on His own authority, but whatever He hears He will speak, and He will tell you things to come" **(JOHN 16:13).**

06 When sin is cherished and the convicting power of the Holy Spirit is repeatedly rejected, what ultimately occurs?

As a Person, the Holy Spirit can be *grieved.* "Do not grieve the Holy Spirit of God, by whom you were sealed for the day of redemption" **(EPHESIANS 4:30).**

"How often they provoked Him in the wilderness, and grieved Him in the desert!" **(PSALM 78:40).**

God sadly reminisces, "For forty years I was grieved with that generation, and said, 'It is a people who go astray in their hearts, and they do not know My ways' " **(PSALM 95:10).**

Jesus, "when He had looked around at them [the Pharisees] with anger, being grieved by the hardness of their hearts, He said to the man, 'Stretch out your hand.' And he stretched it out, and his hand was restored as whole as the other" **(MARK 3:5).**

King Ahaz said, "Hear now, O house of David! Is it a small thing for you to weary men, but will you weary my God also?" **(ISAIAH 7:13).**

"But they rebelled and grieved His Holy Spirit; so He turned Himself against them as an enemy, and He fought against them" **(ISAIAH 63:10).**

"You stiff-necked and uncircumcised in heart and ears! You always resist the Holy Spirit; as your fathers did, so do you" **(ACTS 7:51).**

Paul pleads, "Do not quench the Spirit" **(1 THESSALONIANS 5:19).**

07 Was there ever a time when nearly the entire human race rejected the promptings of the Holy Spirit? When that happens, what is the attitude and condition of the mind?

"And the LORD said, 'My Spirit shall not strive with man forever, for he is indeed flesh; yet his days shall be one hundred and twenty years.' There were giants on the earth in those days, and also afterward, when the sons of God came in to the daughters of men and they bore children to them. Those were the mighty men who were of old, men of renown. Then the LORD saw that the wickedness of man was great in the earth, and that *every intent of the thoughts of his heart was only evil continually.* And the LORD was sorry that He had made man on the earth, and He was grieved in His heart. So the LORD said, 'I will destroy man whom I have created from the face of the earth, both man and beast, creeping thing and birds of the air, for I am sorry that I have made them.' But Noah found grace in the eyes of the LORD" **(GENESIS 6:3–8; EMPHASIS SUPPLIED).**

During the time of the Flood, a whole generation rejected the pleading of the Holy

Spirit. Consequently, there was nothing more God could do. After He appealed through Noah for 120 years and sent His Spirit in mighty power, men and women made their final, irrevocable decision. The Holy Spirit convicts us of sin. The Holy Spirit leads us to repentance and confession. Whenever we resist the convicting power of the Holy Spirit, we are hardening our hearts. Whenever we refuse to surrender sin, the Holy Spirit points out that we are hardening our hearts.

"From within, out of the heart of men, proceed evil thoughts, adulteries, fornications, murders, thefts, covetousness, wickedness, deceit, lewdness, an evil eye, blasphemy, pride, foolishness. All these evil things come from within and defile a man" **(MARK 7:21–23).**

The patriarch Job describes man as one "who is abominable and filthy, who drinks iniquity like water!" **(JOB 15:16).**

Solomon said, "Truly the hearts of the sons of men are full of evil; madness is in their hearts while they live, and after that they go to the dead" **(ECCLESIASTES 9:3).**

Jeremiah echoed, "The heart is deceitful above all things, and desperately wicked; who can know it?" **(JEREMIAH 17:9).**

Even converted Christians must admit that "we ourselves were also once foolish, disobedient, deceived, serving various lusts and pleasures, living in malice and envy, hateful and hating one another" **(TITUS 3:3).**

08 What role did the Holy Spirit play in the writing of the Bible? Is the Bible merely a collection of human ideas about God or is it the inspired, authoritative Word of God?

"Prophecy never came by the will of man, but holy men of God spoke as they were moved by the Holy Spirit" **(2 PETER 1:21).**

"All Scripture is given by inspiration of God, and is profitable for doctrine, for reproof, for correction, for instruction in righteousness" **(2 TIMOTHY 3:16).**

"When they did not agree among themselves, they departed after Paul had said one word: 'The Holy Spirit spoke rightly through Isaiah the prophet to our fathers' " **(ACTS 28:25).**

"Men and brethren, this Scripture had to be fulfilled, which the Holy Spirit spoke before by the mouth of David concerning Judas, who became a guide to those who arrested Jesus" **(ACTS 1:16).**

David humbly said, "The Spirit of the LORD spoke by me, and His word was on my tongue" **(2 SAMUEL 23:2).**

The prophets inquired and searched diligently, "searching what, or what manner of time, the Spirit of Christ who was in them was indicating when He testified beforehand the sufferings of Christ and the glories that would follow" **(1 PETER 1:11)**.

"Therefore, as the Holy Spirit says: 'Today, if you will hear His voice . . .' " **(HEBREWS 3:7)**. Then follows a quotation from **PSALM 95:7–11**: "For He is our God, and we are the people of His pasture, and the sheep of His hand. Today, if you will hear His voice: 'Do not harden your hearts, as in the rebellion, as in the day of trial in the wilderness, when your fathers tested Me; they tried Me, though they saw My work. For forty years I was grieved with that generation, and said, "It is a people who go astray in their hearts, and they do not know My ways." So I swore in My wrath, "They shall not enter My rest." ' "

09 How does the Holy Spirit guide us today? What role does the Holy Spirit have in leading us into truth?

"When He, the Spirit of truth, has come, He will guide you into all truth; for He will not speak on His own authority, but whatever He hears He will speak; and He will tell you things to come" **(JOHN 16:13)**.

"But the Helper, the Holy Spirit, whom the Father will send in My name, He will teach you all things, and bring to your remembrance all things that I said to you" **(JOHN 14:26)**.

"But when the Helper comes, whom I shall send to you from the Father, the Spirit of truth who proceeds from the Father, He will testify of Me" **(JOHN 15:26)**.

"We are of God. He who knows God hears us; he who is not of God does not hear us. By this we know the spirit of truth and the spirit of error" **(1 JOHN 4:6)**.

"But you have an anointing from the Holy One, and you know all things. . . . But the anointing which you have received from Him abides in you, and you do not need that anyone teach you; but as the same anointing teaches you concerning all things, and is true, and is not a lie, and just as it has taught you, you will abide in Him" **(1 JOHN 2:20, 27)**.

The term "anointing" often implies the Holy Spirit.

"God has revealed them to us through His Spirit. For the Spirit searches all things, yes, the deep things of God. For what man knows the things of a man except the spirit of the man which is in him? Even so no one knows the things of God except the Spirit of God. Now we have received, not the spirit of the world, but the Spirit who is from God, that we might know the things that have been freely given to us by God. These things we also speak, not in words which man's wisdom teaches but which the Holy Spirit teaches, comparing spiritual things with spiritual" **(1 CORINTHIANS 2:10–13)**.

"All Scripture is given by inspiration of God, and is profitable for doctrine, for reproof, for correction, for instruction in righteousness" **(2 TIMOTHY 3:16)**.

The Holy Spirit revealed the truth of the Scriptures to the Bible writers. The Holy Spirit leads us to understand these truths. It is extremely dangerous to reject any truth in God's Word. To do so is to resist the Holy Spirit, who leads us into truth. Since the Bible was written by men and women under the influence of the Holy Spirit, to resist any clear teaching of the Bible is to harden the heart against the influence of God's Spirit.

10 When the Holy Spirit impresses us with new truths in the Bible, what response does God desire us to have? If we reject new light and truth when God reveals them to us, whose promptings are we rejecting? Whose convicting power are we turning our backs upon?

"Then Jesus said to them, 'A little while longer the light is with you. Walk while you have the light, lest darkness overtake you; he who walks in darkness does not know where he is going' " **(JOHN 12:35).**

"Then Jesus said to them, 'I shall be with you a little while longer, and then I go to Him who sent Me' " **(JOHN 7:33).**

The Lord Jesus said, "I must work the works of Him who sent Me while it is day; the night is coming when no one can work. As long as I am in the world, I am the light of the world" **(JOHN 9:4, 5).**

Jesus urges, "While you have the light, believe in the light, that you may become sons of light. . . . I have come as a light into the world, that whoever believes in Me should not abide in darkness" **(JOHN 12:36, 46).**

"In Him [Jesus, the Word of God] was life, and the life was the light of men. And the light shines in the darkness, and the darkness did not comprehend it. There was a man sent from God, whose name was John [the Baptist]. This man came for a witness, to bear witness of the Light, that all through him might believe. He was not that Light, but was sent to bear witness of that Light. That was the true Light which gives light to every man coming into the world" **(JOHN 1:4–9).**

"Then Jesus spoke to them again, saying, 'I am the light of the world. He who follows Me shall not walk in darkness, but have the light of life' " **(JOHN 8:12).**

"O house of Jacob, come and let us walk in the light of the LORD" **(ISAIAH 2:5).**

"I, the LORD, have called You in righteousness, and will hold Your hand; I will keep You and give You as a covenant to the people, as a light to the Gentiles, to open blind eyes, to bring out prisoners from the prison, those who sit in darkness from the prison house" **(ISAIAH 42:6, 7).**

"The night is far spent, the day is at hand. Therefore let us cast off the works of darkness, and let us put on the armor of light" **(ROMANS 13:12).**

"You were once darkness, but now you are light in the Lord. Walk as children of light. . . . But all things that are exposed are made manifest by the light, for whatever makes manifest is light. Therefore He says: 'Awake, you who sleep, arise from the dead, and Christ will give you light.' See then that you walk circumspectly, not as fools but as wise" **(EPHESIANS 5:8, 13–15).**

"You are all sons of light and sons of the day. We are not of the night nor of darkness. Therefore let us not sleep, as others do, but let us watch and be sober. For those who sleep, sleep at night, and those who get drunk are drunk at night. But let us who are of the day be sober, putting on the breastplate of faith and love, and as a helmet the hope of salvation" **(1 THESSALONIANS 5:5–8).**

"If we say that we have fellowship with Him, and walk in darkness, we lie and do not practice the truth. But if we walk in the light as He is in the light, we have fellowship with one another, and the blood of Jesus Christ His Son cleanses us from all sin" **(1 JOHN 1:6, 7).**

Jesus said, "If one walks in the night, he stumbles, because the light is not in him" **(JOHN 11:10).**

11 To whom does God promise to give the fullness of His Holy Spirit? When can we expect to receive the Spirit's power?

"We are His witnesses to these things, and so also is the Holy Spirit whom God has given to those who obey Him" **(ACTS 5:32).**

The Holy Spirit reveals light or truth to us and prompts us to walk in it. As we follow the convictions God places in our hearts through the Holy Spirit, we will continue to walk in the light of truth.

"If you love Me, keep My commandments. And I will pray the Father, and He will give you another Helper [the Holy Spirit], that He may abide with you forever" **(JOHN 14:15, 16).**

In these verses of Scripture, God's Word makes an interesting and important connection between our obedience and receiving the Holy Spirit. The fullness of the Holy Spirit is given especially to those who lovingly obey God.

12 How does the Holy Spirit change our lives? What difference in our attitudes and actions does the Holy Spirit make?

"I say then: Walk in the Spirit, and you shall not fulfill the lust of the flesh. . . . But the fruit of the Spirit is love, joy, peace, longsuffering, kindness, goodness, faithfulness, gentleness, self-control. Against such there is no law. And those who are Christ's have crucified the flesh with its passions and desires. If we live in the Spirit, let us also walk in the Spirit. Let us not become conceited, provoking one another, envying one another" **(GALATIANS 5:16, 22–26)**.

"He who sows to his flesh will of the flesh reap corruption, but he who sows to the Spirit will of the Spirit reap everlasting life" **(GALATIANS 6:8)**.

"There is therefore now no condemnation to those who are in Christ Jesus, who do not walk according to the flesh, but according to the Spirit. . . . That the righteous requirement of the law might be fulfilled in us who do not walk according to the flesh but according to the Spirit. For those who live according to the flesh set their minds on the things of the flesh, but those who live according to the Spirit, the things of the Spirit" **(ROMANS 8:1, 4, 5)**.

"Therefore, brethren, we are debtors—not to the flesh, to live according to the flesh. For if you live according to the flesh you will die; but if by the Spirit you put to death the deeds of the body, you will live. For as many as are led by the Spirit of God, these are sons of God" **(ROMANS 8:12–14)**.

"Since you have purified your souls in obeying the truth through the Spirit in sincere love of the brethren, love one another fervently with a pure heart" **(1 PETER 1:22)**.

The Master stated, "It is the Spirit who gives life; the flesh profits nothing. The words that I speak to you are spirit, and they are life" **(JOHN 6:63)**.

The Holy Spirit makes a dramatic difference in our lives. Through the Spirit we are convicted of sin and led into truth. The Spirit transforms our hearts, giving us a new desire to serve God. New power flows into our lives through the Spirit, and we are resurrected from spiritual death to spiritual life.

13 Where does the Holy Spirit indelibly write God's law? How does the Holy Spirit empower us to live obedient lives?

"For this is the covenant that I will make with the house of Israel after those days, says the LORD: I will put My laws in their mind and write them on their hearts; and I will be their God, and they shall be My people" **(HEBREWS 8:10)**.

"You are our epistle written in our hearts, known and read by all men; clearly you are an epistle of Christ, ministered by us, written not with ink but by the Spirit of the living God, not on tablets of stone but on tablets of flesh, that is, of the heart. . . . But if the ministry of death, written and engraved on stones, was glorious, so that the children of Israel could not look steadily at the face of Moses because of the glory of his countenance, which glory was passing away, how will the ministry of the Spirit not be more glorious?" **(2 CORINTHIANS 3:2, 3, 7, 8)**.

"Then I will give them one heart, and I will put a new spirit within them, and take the stony heart out of their flesh, and give them a heart of flesh, that they may walk in My statutes and keep My judgments and do them; and they shall be My people, and I will be their God" **(EZEKIEL 11:19, 20)**.

14 What promises does God give to all who open their hearts to receive His Holy Spirit? What gracious invitation does the Holy Spirit give to each one of us?

Everyone is invited! "And the Spirit and the bride say, 'Come!' And let him who hears say, 'Come!' And let him who thirsts come. Whoever desires, let him take the water of life freely" **(REVELATION 22:17)**.

"Ho! Everyone who thirsts, come to the waters; and you who have no money, come, buy and eat. Yes, come, buy wine and milk without money and without price. Why do you spend money for what is not bread, and your wages for what does not satisfy? Listen carefully to Me, and eat what is good, and let your soul delight itself in abundance. Incline your ear, and come to Me. Hear, and your soul shall live; and I will make an everlasting covenant with you— the sure mercies of David" **(ISAIAH 55:1–3)**.

Jesus faithfully promises, "I will give of the fountain of the water of life freely to him who thirsts" **(REVELATION 21:6)**.

"On the last day, that great day of the feast, Jesus stood and cried out, saying, 'If anyone thirsts, let him come to Me and drink' " **(JOHN 7:37)**.

The loving Lord Jesus knows how we feel. He knows that we long—that we hunger and thirst—for something that is missing in our lives. And He knows that only He can fulfill all our longings.

Jesus proclaimed: "Blessed are those who hunger and thirst for righteousness, for they shall be filled" **(MATTHEW 5:6)**.

"Therefore with joy you will draw water from the wells of salvation" **(ISAIAH 12:3)**.

"Jesus answered and said to her [the woman at the well], 'If you knew the gift of God, and who it is who says to you, "Give Me a drink," you would have asked Him, and He would have given you living water. . . . Whoever drinks of this water will thirst again, but whoever drinks of the water that I shall give him will never thirst. But the water that I shall give him will become in him a fountain of water springing up into everlasting life' " **(JOHN 4:10, 13, 14)**.

The Holy Spirit invites us to give ourselves totally to God. He invites us to come with all of our guilt, our weakness, and our doubts. When we come, He promises to give us a fresh new start in a new life.

What is the unpardonable sin?

A Commonly Asked Question Regarding the Holy Spirit

What does the Bible teach about tongues?

The following points should be carefully noted when considering the gift of tongues.

1. In **ACTS 2,** "tongues" was a real language used to break the language barrier, communicate the gospel, and authenticate truth **(ACTS 2:4–8).**

2. The word *glossalalia* means languages **(SEE REVELATION 14:6).**

3. There are only three mentions of "tongues" in Acts **(SEE ACTS 2; 10; 19).** In each instance, people of other language groups are present.

    a. In **ACTS 2,** "tongues" are a real language **(VERSES 8, 11).**

    b. In **ACTS 10,** Cornelius and his household upon accepting Jesus spoke with tongues. Peter was a Jew; Cornelius was a Greek. Cornelius spoke in a real language which Peter understood. This confirmed in Peter's mind the reality of Cornelius's conversion. (**ACTS 11:17** says it was the same gift the disciple received.)

    c. Paul, the international apostle, witnessed tongues in Ephesus **(ACTS 19).** Every time the Bible mentions "tongues" in Acts there is more than one language group present.

4. The Corinthian church was Paul's problem church. It was often involved in strife and conflict. In Corinth, Paul attempted to control the abuse of the genuine gift. He set forth the following guidelines:

    a. Only one person should speak at a time **(1 CORINTHIANS 14:27).**

    b. There should always be an interpreter **(1 CORINTHIANS 14:28).**

    c. At most, two or three should speak in a single

service **(1 CORINTHIANS 14:27).**

d. The speaker understands and is in control of what is being said **(1 CORINTHIANS 14:32).**

e. "God is not the author of confusion" **(1 CORINTHIANS 14:33).**

5. Paul's appeal was for intelligent communication **(1 CORINTHIANS 14:9, 19).**

6. Since the Holy Spirit interprets our prayers into the language of heaven, interceding for us at God's throne, it is unnecessary to speak a language we do not understand **(ROMANS 8:26).**

7. Since the highest faculty God has given us is our mind, it is dangerous to allow any power to control our mind. The mind is the seat of intelligence. It is with the mind that we worship God. Any form of worship which bypasses the mind can become emotional manipulation **(PHILIPPIANS 2:5).**

8. Tongues is only one of the spiritual gifts. It is not the sign of the infilling of the Holy Spirit—witnessing is **(ACTS 1:6–8)**! Not everyone will receive the gift of tongues (real language) to preach the gospel. When it is needed to further God's work, He will give it **(1 CORINTHIANS 12:6–11, 18, 29, 30).**

CHAPTER 27

What the Bible Says About the Miraculous Rise of God's People

The Bible's last book, Revelation, clearly unfolds God's end-time message. It outlines the future. One of the specific focal points of Revelation's message is its description of God's last-day church. In **REVELATION 12**, the Bible gives us the identifying features of the true church. It will keep the commandments of God and be guided by the gift of prophecy **(SEE VERSE 17)**.

In **REVELATION 14**, God reveals the message of the true church. He pictures His last-day church as preaching the everlasting gospel to the entire earth in the context of the three angels' messages proclaiming our Lord's soon return and calling men and women to obedience in earth's final judgment hour.

REVELATION 10 is one of the most thrilling chapters in all of the Bible. It accurately describes the rise of God's end-time people. It reveals that God's last-day church is a direct fulfillment of prophecy. It distinguishes God's true church from all counterfeit movements.

Just as the New Testament church arose after the disciples' great disappointment at the cross, God's end-time people were to arise after another end-time disappointment. **REVELATION 10** tells this incredible story.

01 During Jesus' trial, Pilate asked, "What is truth?" Unfortunately, he never waited for an answer. This leads us to ask the same question. Is it possible to know truth? And if it is, *how* can we know it?

Jesus said, "You shall know the truth, and the truth shall make you free" **(JOHN 8:32).**

Jesus reveals this key to really understanding truth: "If anyone *wills* to do His will, he shall *know* concerning the doctrine, whether it is from God or whether I speak on My own authority" **(JOHN 7:17; EMPHASIS SUPPLIED).**

This verse is most instructive to sincere believers. If we're serious, if we truly *want to do His will,* Jesus promises that we will *know* His truth and *understand* His doctrine, His teaching. Other versions of the Bible render this text as:

> "Anyone who resolves to do the will of God will know" **(NRSV).**
>
> "Anyone who chooses to do the will of God will find out" **(NIV).**
>
> "If anyone is willing to do His will, he will know" **(NASB).**
>
> "If anyone desires to do His will, he shall know" **(MKJV).**

"Jesus said to him, 'I am the way, the truth, and the life. No one comes to the Father except through Me' " **(JOHN 14:6).**

In His beautiful prayer to His heavenly Father, Jesus prayed for His people: "Sanctify them by Your truth. Your word [the Bible] is truth" **(JOHN 17:17).**

The Lord promised that "when He, the Spirit of truth, has come, He will guide you into all truth" **(JOHN 16:13).**

Some people are "always learning and never able to come to the knowledge of the truth" **(2 TIMOTHY 3:7).**

With fervent desire, David prayed, "Show me Your ways, O LORD; teach me Your paths. Lead me in Your truth and teach me, for You are the God of my salvation; on You I wait all the day. . . . Good and upright is the LORD; therefore He teaches sinners in the way. The humble He guides in justice, and the humble He teaches His way" **(PSALM 25:4, 5, 8, 9).**

"Turn at my rebuke; surely I will pour out my spirit on you; I will make my words known to you" **(PROVERBS 1:23).**

The wise man, Solomon, gives this loving counsel: "My son, if you receive my words, and treasure my commands within you, so that you incline your ear to wisdom, and apply your heart to understanding; yes, if you cry out for discernment, and lift up your voice for understanding, if you seek her as silver, and search for her as for hidden treasures; then you will understand the fear of the LORD, and find the knowledge of God. For the LORD gives wisdom; from His mouth come knowledge and understanding; He stores up sound wisdom for the upright; He is a shield to those who walk uprightly" **(PROVERBS 2:1–7).**

Our knowledge of God can progressively increase and grow ever brighter as we walk with Him. "The path of the just is like the shining sun, that shines ever brighter unto the perfect day" **(PROVERBS 4:18).**

02 Some people have a lot of questions, but very few answers. The skeptics place a premium on uncertainty. What counsel does Luke give Theophilus regarding the certainty of the gospel? How do other Bible writers champion this same theme?

Dr. Luke, a Gentile physician **(SEE COLOSSIANS 4:14)**, author of the third Gospel and of the book of Acts, told his friend, "It seemed good to me also, having had perfect understanding of all things from the very first, to write to you an orderly account, most excellent Theophilus, that you may know the certainty of those things in which you were instructed" **(LUKE 1:3, 4).**

Luke himself was a contemporary of Christ and a traveling companion of Paul: "just as those who from the beginning were eyewitnesses and ministers of the word delivered them to us" **(LUKE 1:2).** Luke was also with Paul in Rome just before the apostle was beheaded as a martyr, apparently after all others had forsaken him. Just before his death, Paul wrote, "Only Luke is with me" **(2 TIMOTHY 4:11).**

The apostle Peter, who with James and John witnessed firsthand the breathtaking glorification of Christ on the Mount of Transfiguration **(SEE MATTHEW 17:1–8; MARK 9:2–10; LUKE 9:28–36)**, wholeheartedly declares that "we did not follow cunningly devised fables when we made known to you the power and coming of our Lord Jesus Christ, but were eyewitnesses of His majesty" **(2 PETER 1:16).**

The apostle John testifies that "truly Jesus did many other signs in the presence of His disciples, which are not written in this book; but these are written that you may believe that Jesus is the Christ, the Son of God, and that believing you may have life in His name" **(JOHN 20:30, 31).**

Solomon reminds us, "So that your trust may be in the LORD; I have instructed you today, even you. Have I not written to you excellent things of counsels and knowledge, that I may make you know the certainty of the words of truth, that you may answer words of truth to those who send to you?" **(PROVERBS 22:19–21).**

In the previous verse, Solomon says, "That you may answer . . . those who send to you." As Christians, we are studying God's "words of truth" not just for our *own* sakes but the for sakes of *others* whom we may teach—others who ask us questions. Peter said we should "be ready always to give an answer to every man that asketh you a reason of the hope that is in you with meekness and fear" **(1 PETER 3:15, KJV).**

03 REVELATION 10 pictures an angel descending from the throne of God with a message of critical importance for the inhabitants of the earth. What does this angel have in his hand?

In vision, John saw a mighty angel: "He had a little book open in his hand. And he set his right foot on the sea and his left foot on the land" **(REVELATION 10:2).**

The word *angel* in this verse is from the Greek word *angelos,* meaning "messenger."

Since the words *sea* and *earth* repeatedly are used together to designate the world as a whole **(SEE EXODUS 20:4, 11; PSALM 69:34),** the fact that the angel stands upon both sea and earth implies the worldwide nature of his message and its widespread proclamation.

04 The angel holds a "little book" or "small scroll" in his hand. The little book is opened. What is the only Bible book ever said to be closed or sealed until the time of the end?

As the prophet Daniel brought his little book to a close, he was told, "But you, Daniel, *shut up the words, and seal the book* until the time of the end; many shall run to and fro, and knowledge shall increase" **(DANIEL 12:4; EMPHASIS SUPPLIED).**

"And he [the angel] said, 'Go your way, Daniel, for the words are closed up and sealed till the time of the end' " **(DANIEL 12:9).**

The book John saw in the angel's hand is repeatedly described as "a little book" **(SEE REVELATION 10:2, 8, 9, 10).** The prophetic book of Daniel, containing only twelve chapters, is "a little book." Furthermore, we've just read that it was to be "sealed"—but only "till the time of the end." Daniel had been instructed to "shut up the words, and seal the book until the time of the end" **(DANIEL 12:4).** Now, in his inspired glimpse into the end-time future, John sees the "little book open" **(REVELATION 10:2).** The vision spotlights the vital importance of the prophecies in the little book of Daniel—the only book in the Bible Christ urges us to "understand" **(MATTHEW 24:15).**

05 Bible students have studied Daniel's prophecies for centuries. What aspect of Daniel's message was "sealed" until the time of the end? What particular portion of prophecy does the angel of REVELATION 10 emphasize?

The mighty angel "swore by Him who lives forever and ever, who created heaven and the things that are in it, the earth and the things that are in it, and the sea and the things that are in it, that there should be delay no longer" **(REVELATION 10:6).**

The awesome heavenly messenger "raised up his hand to heaven" **(VERSE 5)** in a gesture characteristic of the utterance of an oath. In the most *solemn* of oaths—swearing by the eternal Creator Himself—the angle then "swore . . . that there should be delay no longer." That is, there shall be no longer delay in fulfilling the predictions of this little book held by the angel.

The fact that the little book was opened reveals that "there should be delay no longer." It clearly focuses on the time prophecies of Daniel. Since no one knows the day or hour of Christ's coming **(SEE MATTHEW 24:36),** the expression "delay no longer" cannot relate to a literal date for Christ's return.

06 Where in the book of Daniel do we find a time prophecy that points to the time of the end?

"And he ["a holy one,"] said to me [Daniel], 'For two thousand three hundred days; then the sanctuary shall be cleansed.' . . . So he [the angel Gabriel] came near where I stood, and when he came I was afraid and fell on my face; but he said to me, 'Understand, son of man, that the vision refers to the time of the end' " **(DANIEL 8:14, 17).**

"And the vision of the [2,300] evenings and mornings which was told is true; therefore seal up the vision, for it refers to many days in the future" **(DANIEL 8:26).**

"And he [Gabriel] said, 'Look, I am making known to you what shall happen in the latter time of the indignation; for at the appointed time the end shall be' " **(DANIEL 8:19).**

"Now I have come to make you understand what will happen to your people in the latter days, for the vision refers to many days yet to come" **(DANIEL 10:14).**

"The vision is yet for an appointed time; but at the end it will speak, and it will not lie. Though it tarries, wait for it; because it will surely come, it will not tarry" **(HABAKKUK 2:3).**

As we have studied in a previous chapter, the 2,300 prophetic days of **DANIEL 8:14** equal 2,300 literal years. The expression "then the sanctuary shall be cleansed" refers to the opening of the judgment in the year 1844.

07 How would a study of the time prophecies of Daniel affect the lives of those who studied these prophecies? When the book was assimilated by study, particularly the 2,300-year prophecy pointing to 1844, what experience would occur for those who studied these prophecies?

"Then I [John] took the little book out of the angel's hand and ate it, and it was as sweet as honey in my mouth. But when I had eaten it, my stomach became bitter. And he said to me, 'You must prophesy again about many peoples, nations, tongues, and kings' " **(REVELATION 10:10, 11).**

REVELATION 10:9, 10 uses a familiar form of parallelism:

> "It will make your stomach bitter."
>
> "It will be as sweet as honey in your mouth."
>
> "It was as sweet as honey in my mouth."
>
> "My stomach became bitter."

When did this bittersweet experience occur? In the late 1700s and early 1800s, independently of one another, scores of religious leaders around the world began a renewed study of the prophecies of Daniel. This interest in prophecy led honest-hearted men and women of God to abandon the popular belief that the world would soon enter a thousand-year period of peace known as the millennium. They saw that prophecy clearly taught that the destinies of all were to be decided before Christ's return. Consequently, they understood that there is no second chance for salvation when Jesus comes.

Overjoyed with prophecies that seemed to indicate the coming of Jesus, they went forth to warn the world. Among them were people such as Edward Irving and seven hundred preachers of the church of England; Joseph Wolff, missionary to India; Manuel Lacunza, a serious Bible student from South America; Johann Bengel of Germany; and many others. Foremost in the United States was a Baptist preacher, William Miller. In a period of personal despair, he began to study the Scriptures. There Miller found new hope and courage as an uplifted Savior was presented before him. Accepting Jesus as his personal Savior, he began to study the Scriptures carefully.

Dispensing with all Bible commentaries and using only his Bible and a concordance, William Miller began at Genesis and studied the Scriptures verse by verse, comparing scripture with scripture. As he studied the prophetic portions of Daniel, he arrived at the same conclusion as did a host of other serious Bible students. Independently of each other, they arrived at the conclusion that Jesus was coming, and coming soon.

As Miller studied the 2,300-year prophecy of **DANIEL 8,** he saw that it was explained in **DANIEL 9.** Amazed at the precision of **DANIEL 9:24–27,** he concluded that **DANIEL 8:14** was just as accurate. When he discovered, according to **DANIEL 9:24–27**, that Jesus was to be baptized in A.D. 27, crucified in A.D. 31, and that the gospel was to go to the Gentiles in A.D. 34, and that these events had been fulfilled exactly on time, he marveled. He reasoned that since these events had been fulfilled, and since **DANIEL 9** is an explanation of **DANIEL 8**, both prophecies start at the same time.

Since **DANIEL 8** begins at the commandment to restore and build Jerusalem in 457 B.C., **DANIEL 9** begins there also. Figuring 2,300 years from 457 B.C., Miller arrived at the date of A.D. 1844 for the end of the prophecy. Misunderstanding the subject of the sanctuary, he thought the words "then the sanctuary shall be cleansed" referred to the cleansing of the earth by fire. He thought Christ would return in 1844.

This preaching of a specific date for Christ's return sparked one of the greatest religious revivals in American history. Thousands were converted. Church bells throughout America tolled for noon prayer meetings. In anticipation of the coming of the Lord, debts were paid, family differences settled, and saloons closed. The moving of the Spirit of God led to deep repentance for sin, earnest prayer, and serious Bible study.

As multitudes anticipated the arrival of Jesus, Miller and his followers settled on the date October 22, 1844. As **REVELATION 10** predicted, a study of Daniel's prophecy was "sweet . . . in my mouth," yet when Jesus did not return, it was "bitter" **(VERSE 10)**. This bitter disappointment of 1844 left them downhearted and discouraged. As they rechecked the prophetic evidence, they could find no mistake in their reckoning. They were convinced the date was right. But why had Jesus not come?

The hour of their disappointment was the hour of God's appointment. They came to see that the sanctuary to be cleansed was not the earth, but rather the heavenly sanctuary. The prediction "then the sanctuary shall be cleansed" refers to Christ's work of judgment preliminary to His return to earth. This was a fulfillment of God's urgent end-time message, "The hour of His judgment has come" **(REVELATION 14:7)**.

08 According to the prophet Daniel, what special ministry do the Father and Son participate in together before Jesus' return?

"I watched till thrones were put in place, and the Ancient of Days [God the Father] was seated; His garment was white as snow, and the hair of His head was like pure wool. His throne was a fiery flame, its wheels a burning fire; a fiery stream issued and came forth from before Him. A thousand thousands ministered to Him; ten thousand times ten thousand stood before Him. The court was seated, and the books were opened" **(DANIEL 7:9, 10)**.

This passage in **DANIEL 7**—as well as the whole chapter!—deserves careful study and analysis. It tells us that God's prophet Daniel was privileged to witness the opening of judgment in the heavenly court. Yet the context of surrounding verses shows events still continuing on earth while this divine court convened. In fact, the scenes shown Daniel here seem to alternate back and forth between heaven and earth. For instance, consider the following:

Verses 9, 10. Judgment scene in heaven. Innumerable angels or other heavenly beings stand before "the Ancient of Days. . . . The court was seated, and the books [of record] were opened."

Verses 7, 8, 11. Turmoil on earth. In the verses immediately surrounding the judgment scene in heaven, Daniel saw on earth a "dreadful" beast with "ten horns" and watched as "another horn, a little one" came "up among them." It had "eyes like the eyes of a man, and a mouth speaking pompous words." This wicked power Daniel calls "the little horn" is the same one that John calls "the beast" in **REVELATION 13:1–10** and the "antichrist" in **1 JOHN 4:2, 3 AND 2 JOHN 7**, and that Paul calls "the man of sin" in **2 THESSALONIANS 2:3, 4**. And it is a wicked power that does its evil work *on earth*. After watching the court convene in heaven, Daniel again hears "the sound of the pompous words which the horn was speaking" on earth.

Verses 13, 14. Judgment scene in heaven. Jesus, "the Son of Man," joins His Father. He is seen coming *not to this earth* but to His Father—"He came to the Ancient of Days." When Jesus returns to give His "rewards"—punishment for the lost, redemption for the saved—all cases have *already* been decided. "He who is unjust, let him be unjust still; he who is filthy, let him be filthy still; he who is righteous, let him be righteous still; he who is holy, let him be holy still. And behold, I am coming quickly, and *My reward is with Me,* to give to every one according to his work" **(REVELATION 22:11, 12; EMPHASIS SUPPLIED).** Daniel describes the pre-Advent judgment that determines those rewards.

Verses 19–21. Turmoil on earth. After the vision of the heavenly court fades, Daniel's attention is again back on earthly affairs. "Then I wished to know the truth about . . . that horn which had eyes and a mouth which spoke pompous words. . . . I was watching; and the same horn was making war against the saints, and prevailing against them." Obviously, this religious persecution is taking place here on earth while the pre-Advent investigation of the heavenly books proceeds above.

Sometimes investigative reporters grill a politician with probing questions about his personal life, and if the politician feels he has nothing to hide, he'll say, "My life is an open book." Like it or not, that will be the situation of all of us in the heavenly judgment because Daniel says, "The books were opened."

This careful judgment is *not* for the purpose of enlightening the Lord God, for He already knows all things. But remember that Lucifer/Satan rebelled against his Maker by spreading lies about God, "And war broke out in heaven. . . . So the great dragon was cast out, that serpent of old, called the Devil and Satan, who deceives the whole world; he was cast to the earth, and his angels were cast out with him" **(REVELATION 12:7–9)**. Many, many "angels were cast out with him" because they *believed* Satan's lies that God was an unfair, unjust tyrant. Therefore God chooses not to conduct this judgment simply in His head, in His own infinite mind—with the instant "snap judgment" of which He is capable. He chooses not simply to announce to the unfallen beings throughout the universe that *some* humans will burn in hell while *others* will be their next-door neighbors through all eternity, "Just because I say so!"

Instead, God wisely chooses to conduct this judgment with great deliberation and quite openly, as the innumerable multitudes of heavenly beings look on, so it's clear to everyone's satisfaction that He is indeed lovingly fair and righteously just. You see, there is a sense in which *God Himself* is on trial here. That's why **REVELATION 14:7** says, "The hour of *His* judgment has come" **(EMPHASIS SUPPLIED)**—another verse, by the way, which proves a pre-Advent judgment, because events continue on earth even after this awesome announcement. Christ has already shown His infinite, perfect love by dying for us. Now He wants to show His infinite, perfect justice to all. And, evidently, God's *openness* in this judgment succeeds in demonstrating that justice to the satisfaction of every mind in Creation, for heavenly voices ring out with glorious praise, saying, "Great and marvelous are Your works, Lord God Almighty! Just and true are Your ways, O King of the saints! Who shall not fear You, O Lord, and glorify Your name? For You alone are holy. For all nations shall come and worship before You, for Your judgments have been manifested" **(REVELATION 15:3, 4)**.

Daniel says, "I was watching in the night visions, and behold, One like the Son of Man, coming with the clouds of heaven! He came to the Ancient of Days, and they brought Him near before Him. Then to Him was given dominion and glory and a kingdom, that all peoples, nations, and languages should serve Him. His dominion is an everlasting dominion, which shall not pass away, and His kingdom the one which shall not be destroyed" **(DANIEL 7:13, 14)**.

In vision, Daniel watched "until the Ancient of Days came, and a judgment was made in favor of the saints of the Most High, and the time came for the saints to possess the kingdom. . . . 'But the court shall be seated, and they shall take away his [the little horn's or antichrist's] dominion, to consume and destroy it forever. Then the kingdom and dominion, and the greatness of the kingdoms under the whole heaven, shall be given to the people, the saints of the Most High. His kingdom is an everlasting kingdom, and all dominions shall serve and obey Him' " **(DANIEL 7:22, 26, 27)**. The heavenly judgment deals with the final solution to the sin problem. As the heavenly record books are opened, God's mercy and justice, His love and law, will eventually be seen in His dealing with every human being.

Just as the early disciples anticipated that Christ would set up an earthly kingdom in A.D. 31 and were bitterly disappointed at His crucifixion, so His last-day followers anticipated He would come to earth in 1844 and were bitterly disappointed. Notice these striking similar parallels:

New Testament Church	***Last-Day Church***
1. Students of prophecy	*1. Students of prophecy*
2. Believed Christ would set up an earthly kingdom	*2. Believed Christ would set up an earthly kingdom*
3. Bitterly disappointed	*3. Bitterly disappointed*
4. Directed attention to ministry of Christ in sanctuary	*4. Directed attention to ministry of Christ in sanctuary*
5. Preached message of Christ's ministry to world	*5. Preached message of Christ's ministry to world*

According to Scripture, this disappointed group that looked for Jesus to come in 1844 would be molded into Christ's last-day church to carry His message to the world.

09 Where did these early Adventists find the key to unlock the mystery of their disappointment?

" 'The nations were angry, and Your wrath has come, and the time of the dead, that they should be judged, and that You should reward Your servants the prophets and the saints, and those who fear Your name, small and great, and should destroy those who destroy the earth.' Then the temple of God was opened in heaven, and the ark of His covenant was seen in His temple" **(REVELATION 11:18, 19).**

Like the scene described in **DANIEL 7:9, 10,** this scene, opened to the inspired view of John the revelator, is clearly

1. a judgment scene, for it speaks of "the time of the dead, that they should be judged, and that You should reward Your servants the prophets and the saints." But it is also

2. a judgment scene taking place in the courts of heaven, for "the temple of God was opened in heaven," and within it John even sees "the ark" containing God's holy law. And it is also

3. a pre-Advent occurrence, taking place while events were still happening on earth, for it states that "the nations were angry," as usual.

After Jesus did not appear in 1844, these disappointed followers sensed that the temple of God was opened in heaven. Jesus had begun a special work in the heavenly sanctuary preliminary to His return to earth.

10 When the temple in heaven was opened, what did Jesus' disappointed followers see? What did the ark of the covenant in the heavenly sanctuary contain?

"Then the temple of God was opened in heaven, and the ark of His covenant was seen in His temple. And there were lightnings, noises, thunderings, an earthquake, and great hail" **(REVELATION 11:19).**

The "ark of His covenant [or "testimony," KJV]" was a beautiful golden chest adorned with two angels sculpted of gold. It was the sacred receptacle designed by God Himself **(SEE EXODUS 25:10–21)**, which contained the two stone tablets on which the Lord inscribed His law with His own finger **(SEE EXODUS 31:18; 32:16).** This moral law of the Ten Commandments will serve as the God-appointed standard in all phases of the final judgment **(SEE JAMES 2:10–12).**

The sanctuary in heaven is the great original. In the days of Israel, God instructed Moses to build a sanctuary "according to the pattern" revealed on the Mount **(EXODUS 25:8, 40).** The earthly sanctuary is a copy of the great original in heaven. It helps us understand God's eternal plan of salvation. Notice God's clear instructions to Moses to place the Ten Commandments in the ark of the covenant.

The Lord told Moses: "I will write on the tablets the words that were on the first tablets, which you broke; and you shall put them in the ark" **(DEUTERONOMY 10:2).**

"Then I [Moses] turned and came down from the mountain [Mount Sinai], and put the tablets [the engraved tables of stone] in the ark which I had made; and there they are, just as the LORD commanded me" **(DEUTERONOMY 10:5).**

God told Moses, "You shall put into the ark the Testimony [the law of Ten Commandments] which I will give you" **(EXODUS 25:16).**

"He [Moses] took the Testimony [God's law, written with His own hand] and put it into the ark, inserted the poles [for carrying purposes] through the rings of the ark, and put the mercy seat on top of the ark" **(EXODUS 40:20).**

These Advent believers understood for the first time that we are living in the judgment hour. They sensed God's call for obedience. The ark of the covenant in heaven's sanctuary revealed God's law. Love leads to obedience. The law which Jesus died to preserve would be enshrined in the hearts of His followers through grace.

11 What message of encouragement did Jesus give these disappointed believers?

"And he [the "mighty angel"] said to me [John], 'You must prophesy again about many peoples, nations, tongues, and kings' " **(REVELATION 10:11).**

"Then I [John] saw another angel flying in the midst of heaven, having the everlasting gospel to preach to those who dwell on the earth—to every nation, tribe, tongue, and people" **(REVELATION 14:6).**

God's last warning message is of such urgency and importance that it must be proclaimed worldwide, to everyone everywhere.

12 What promises does God give to His end-time people?

"And this gospel of the kingdom will be preached in all the world as a witness to all the nations, and then the end will come" **(MATTHEW 24:14).**

"After these things I saw another angel coming down from heaven, having great authority and the earth was illuminated with His glory" **(REVELATION 18:1).**

"For the earth will be filled with the knowledge of the glory of the LORD, as the waters cover the sea" **(HABAKKUK 2:14).**

"For My house shall be called a house of prayer for all nations" **(ISAIAH 56:7).**

Following the disappointment in 1844, Jesus raised up a dynamic, divine movement on earth, a movement that ultimately would span the globe. It would proclaim that Jesus is coming again and urge men and women to surrender their lives to Him and respond in loving obedience. It is indeed thrilling to sense that God has such a divine movement of destiny in the last days of earth's history. This unique prophetic movement has been especially raised up by God to prepare a world for His soon return. Today in more than two hundred nations of the world, in every major language, the message of God's love and truth is being proclaimed in the Advent movement. God has especially raised up the Seventh-day Adventist Church as a powerful last-day prophetic movement to make an impact on the world. The Seventh-day Adventist Church is not just another denomination; it is a God-ordained—divinely called—prophetic movement for these last days.

Does God have a true church on earth today?

The Surprise of a Lifetime

She was the pride of the twenty-two-ship Townsend Thoresen fleet—a magnificent vessel christened the *Herald of Free Enterprise.* The ship ferried passengers and vehicles across the English Channel in first-class comfort. At 433 feet long and a displacement of about eight thousand tons, she could weather most any storm.

And yet, on the night of March 6, 1987, the passengers on the *Herald* experienced a terrifying surprise, one in which 193 men, women, and children lost their lives in a matter of seconds. How could such a tragedy happen just because someone forgot to close a couple of doors?

Everything about the ship's preparations for the crossing from Belgium to England went routinely. The crew had done it all countless times before. The *Herald of Free Enterprise* was a RORO—a roll-on, roll-off ferry. Hundreds of vehicles and passengers could come aboard very quickly through the massive steel doors in the bow of the ship.

At 7:05 P.M. on that gray winter evening, the *Herald* began backing out of her dock at Zeebrugge Harbor. The sea was calm, and the easterly wind light.

Loading officer Leslie Sabel stood at a control panel on G deck, where the vehicles were parked. Across the dimly lit deck, he spotted someone in orange overalls weaving between the cars and trucks toward the bow. He thought it was Mark Stanley, the crewmember whose job it was to close the twelve-ton, hydraulically operated bow doors. Satisfied that the job would be done, Sabel climbed a stairway toward the bridge.

Stanley, however, was in his quarters—fast asleep. Like the rest of the crew, he was working a twenty-four-hour shift. That afternoon, after doing some maintenance, he had decided to make himself some tea in his cabin. Then, feeling very tired, he sat down on his bunk, opened a book—and fell asleep almost immediately. And he slept through the call to "harbor stations."

The captain of the ship, David Lewry, might have noticed that the bow doors were still open—bright dockside lights were shining on them, and they were just visible below the bridge. But he was backing the ship out of her berth, so the captain was facing the stern. And by the time the *Herald* swung around, she was in darkness.

At 7:20 P.M., the ship accelerated into the main shipping channel, and a bow wave began to pile up under her blunt prow. As the *Herald* continued to pick up speed, churning white water broke over the top of the car deck, rushing in at the rate of two hundred tons per minute. The vehicle deck ran from one end of the ship to the other, so there was nothing to interrupt the flow of the sea into the *Herald.*

While the vehicle deck was flooding, most of the passengers were either sitting in the restaurants on board, lining up at the duty-free shop, or relaxing comfortably in the lounges, chatting or dozing off. Everyone was feeling quite warm and safe. But at 7:27 P.M., the *Herald* began to roll over on its port side. While the crew and passengers wondered what on earth was going on, the ship righted itself briefly and then rolled completely onto its side. Seawater rushed in through windows in the upper decks, and the ship began to sink. Those who weren't crushed to death or drowned tried to climb to safety, clutching at lighting fixtures and ledges as they tried to work their way to what was now the top of the ship.

What happened so suddenly to the *Herald* that night was the worst British peacetime marine disaster since the sinking of the *Iolaire* in 1919. It was completely unexpected. In a matter of seconds, the world inside the *Herald* had been completely upset. At one instant, passengers were chewing on deli sandwiches, and at the next, they were crashing through tables toward the port side. At one instant, passengers were paying for souvenirs, and at the next, they'd been wrenched away by a rush of icy seawater.

How could anyone be prepared for that?

You know, the Bible speaks of another soon-coming event that will seem like a sudden disaster to many people. It tells us that the tragedies striking the world today are building up to the great climax of history. It's actually a glorious event, but that event will strike some people with all the terror of a thief breaking into your home at midnight.

Look at how the apostle Paul describes it in **1 THESSALONIANS:** "For you yourselves know perfectly that the day of the Lord so comes as a thief in the night. For when they say, 'Peace and safety!' then sudden destruction comes upon them, as labor pains upon a pregnant woman. And they shall not escape" **(1 THESSALONIANS 5:2, 3).**

What is this "day of the Lord"? It's the second coming of Jesus Christ. It's what Jesus promised to do before He left this earth. He said He would be preparing a place for His followers in heaven, and that He would come back again to take them home.

The Second Coming is a glorious event. But for some people, it's like a thief in the night. While everyone's saying, "Peace and safety!" sudden destruction comes.

It is as traumatic as labor pains.

But it doesn't have to be that way. Your world doesn't have to turn upside down when Jesus comes. It can, in fact, turn right side up. Look at the rest of this passage in **1 THESSALONIANS:** "But you, brethren, are not in darkness, so that this Day should overtake you as a thief. You are all sons of light and sons of the day. We are not of the night nor of darkness. Therefore let us not sleep, as others do, but let us watch and be sober" **(1 THESSALONIANS 5:4–6).**

People who've made a commitment to Jesus Christ, the Light of the world, are called children of light. They're not groping about in the dark anymore. They have a Friend who guides them toward a secure future and they are joined by other "truth seekers" united in one last-day people of God.

CHAPTER 28

What the Bible Says About the Mark of the Beast

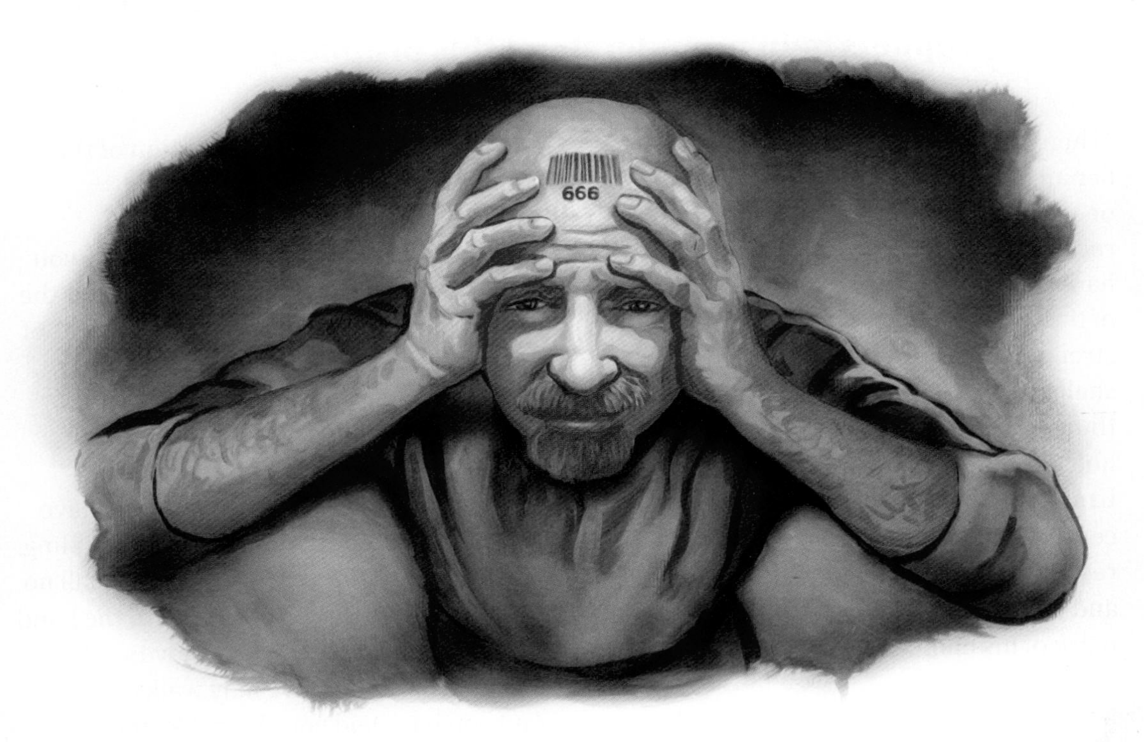

God's heart is full of love for this planet. A loving God sent His Son to redeem us. A loving God reaches out to us in daily concern. A loving God is coming again for us. He will put an end to sickness, disease, sorrow, hunger, pain, and death.

God's love is revealed in gentle pleadings to our heart. It is also revealed in solemn warnings. Just as a loving father warns his children about danger, our loving heavenly Father warns us about the coming perils ahead.

The most solemn warning ever given to humanity is found in **REVELATION 13.** A crucial test is coming. The conflict will revolve around true and false worship. The central issue is the law of God. Church and state will unite. God's people will be ridiculed, mocked, and imprisoned. An economic boycott will be imposed and, according to prophecy, those who are faithful to God will be unable to buy or sell.

The book of Revelation reveals the plans of God and unmasks the delusions of the enemy. Every person has a choice. Our eternal destiny hinges upon the choice we make. **REVELATION 13** focuses upon the final issue in the great controversy between good and evil.

01 What urgent warning does Jesus give His people in the Bible's last book—Revelation? How do the Old Testament prophets help us understand this prophecy?

"Then a third angel followed them [two earlier angels], saying with a loud voice, 'If anyone worships the beast and his image, and receives his mark on his forehead or on his hand, he himself shall also drink of the wine of the wrath of God, which is poured out full strength into the cup of His indignation. He shall be tormented with fire and brimstone [burning sulphur] in the presence of the holy angels and in the presence of the Lamb. And the smoke of their torment ascends forever and ever; and they have no rest day or night, who worship the beast and his image, and whoever receives the mark of his name' " **(REVELATION 14:9–11).**

God is a God of love. Nevertheless, the most fearfully threatening words in all the Bible are uttered by an angel in this awesome warning from God Himself. Here God calls us to avoid, at all costs, "the mark" of the beast—the emblem of the authority of a false, counterfeit religious power.

"In the hand of the LORD there is a cup, and the wine is red; it is fully mixed, and He pours it out; surely its dregs shall all the wicked of the earth drain and drink down" **(PSALM 75:8).**

"Upon the wicked He will rain coals; fire and brimstone [burning sulphur] and a burning wind shall be the portion of their cup" **(PSALM 11:6).**

"Awake, awake! Stand up, O Jerusalem, you who have drunk at the hand of the LORD the cup of His fury; you have drunk the dregs of the cup of trembling, and drained it out. . . . Therefore please hear this, you afflicted, and drunk but not with wine. Thus says your Lord, the LORD and your God, who pleads the cause of His people: 'See, I have taken out of your hand the cup of trembling, the dregs of the cup of My fury; you shall no longer drink it. But I will put it into the hand of those who afflict you, who have said to you, "Lie down, that we may walk over you." And you have laid your body like the ground, and as the street, for those who walk over' " **(ISAIAH 51:17, 21–23).**

Christ's final judgments fall on a world that has spurned His love and turned its back on His mercy. He has given people multiple opportunities to repent, but they have rejected them all. The cup of His mercy is now the cup of His judgment. Sin's wages are disaster, destruction, and eventually death. God's wrath is His final judgment on sin. Sin and sinners will finally be destroyed and righteousness will reign forever.

02 As the final crisis breaks upon this world as an overwhelming surprise, what great challenge will the righteous face? What civil penalties will eventually be inflicted upon those who do not receive the mark of the beast?

"He was granted power to give breath to the image of the beast, that the image of the beast should both speak and cause as many as would not worship the image of the beast *to be killed.* He causes all, both small and great, rich and poor, free and slave, to receive a mark on their right hand or on their foreheads, and that *no one may buy or sell* except one who has the mark or the name of the beast, or the number of his name" **(REVELATION 13:15–17; EMPHASIS SUPPLIED).**

A law "that no one may buy or sell" is a terrible economic boycott: a businessman could not sell to anyone; a mother could not buy food for her family or milk for her baby. Then there is the ultimate coercion: *the death penalty* against all who refuse to worship this false power.

Once before, God's people faced a similar crisis: "Then a herald cried aloud: 'To you it is commanded, O peoples, nations, and languages, that at the time you hear the sound of the horn, flute, harp, lyre, and psaltery, in symphony with all kinds of music, you shall fall down and worship the gold image that King Nebuchadnezzar has set up; and whoever does not fall down and worship shall be cast immediately into the midst of a burning fiery furnace.' So at that time, when all the people heard the sound of the horn, flute, harp, and lyre, in symphony with all kinds of music, all the people, nations, and languages fell down and worshiped the gold image which King Nebuchadnezzar had set up" **(DANIEL 3:4–7; SEE ALSO VERSES 8–30).** These three Hebrew worthies stood faithful to God. They would not yield to the king's coercive decree. When they were thrown into the flames, Jesus miraculously delivered them. God was with them in their time of greatest trial, and He will be with us in the coming time of trial.

John says, "I saw the woman [the harlot or corrupt church], drunk with the blood of the saints and with the blood of the martyrs of Jesus. And when I saw her, I marveled with great amazement" **(REVELATION 17:6).**

"And in her [the false church] was found the blood of prophets and saints, and of all who were slain on the earth" **(REVELATION 18:24).**

"Then the beast was captured, and with him the false prophet who worked signs in his presence, by which he deceived those who received the mark of the beast and those who worshiped his image. These two were cast alive into the lake of fire burning with brimstone" **(REVELATION 19:20).**

"I saw thrones, and they sat on them, and judgment was committed to them. Then I saw the souls of those who had been beheaded for their witness to Jesus and for the word of God, who had not worshiped the beast or his image, and had not received his mark on their foreheads or on their hands. And they lived and reigned with Christ for a thousand years" **(REVELATION 20:4).**

A great crisis is approaching in which everyone will be coerced, through an economic boycott or by the threat of death, to receive the mark of the beast. Those who yield to these pressures, both religious and economic, will do so with the clear understanding that they are violating the commandments of God. But God at last will deliver His faithful people, and they will live with Him forever.

03 What will those who receive the mark of the beast also receive? What is the result of turning one's back on God and giving allegiance to the beast power?

"Then I saw another sign in heaven, great and marvelous: seven angels having the seven last plagues, for in them the wrath of God is complete ["filled up," KJV]" **(REVELATION 15:1).**

"Then I heard a loud voice from the temple saying to the seven angels, 'Go and pour out the bowls of the wrath of God [the seven last plagues] on the earth.' So the first went and poured out his bowl upon the earth, and a foul and loathsome sore came upon the men who had the mark of the beast and those who worshiped his image" **(REVELATION 16:1, 2).**

"Then the third angel poured out his bowl on the rivers and springs of water, and they became blood. And I heard the angel of the waters saying: 'You are righteous, O Lord, the One who is and who was and who is to be, because You have judged these things. For they have shed the blood of saints and prophets, and You have given them blood to drink. For it is their just due.' And I heard another from the altar saying, 'Even so, Lord God Almighty, true and righteous are Your judgments' " **(REVELATION 16:4–7).**

God's judgments are indeed altogether righteous, a perfect mixture of both mercy and justice. In this case, notice that the text says this plague on the wicked "is their just due." In other words, "they deserve it." Notice also that even in the face of these terrible plagues, the wicked are so hardened in sin that they not only stubbornly refuse to repent but actually blaspheme God's name! "And men were scorched with great heat, and they blasphemed the name of God who has power over these plagues; and they did not repent and give Him glory. . . . They blasphemed the God of heaven because of their pains and their sores, and did not repent of their deeds. . . . And great hail from heaven fell upon men, each hailstone about the weight of a talent. Men blasphemed God because of the plague of the hail, since that plague was exceedingly great" **(REVELATION 16:9, 11, 21).**

04 How does God identify His sign, which stands in opposition to Satan's mark?

"After these things I [John] saw four angels standing at the four corners of the earth, holding the four winds of the earth, that the wind should not blow on the earth, on the sea, or on any tree. Then I saw another angel ascending from the east, having the seal of the living God. And he cried with a loud voice to the four angels to whom it was granted to harm the earth and the sea, saying, 'Do not harm the earth, the sea, or the trees till we have sealed the servants of our God on their foreheads' " **(REVELATION 7:1–3).**

"Now He who establishes us with you in Christ and has anointed us is God, who also has sealed us and given us the Spirit in our hearts as a guarantee" **(2 CORINTHIANS 1:21, 22).**

"In Him you also trusted, after you heard the word of truth, the gospel of your salvation; in whom also, having believed, you were sealed with the Holy Spirit of promise" **(EPHESIANS 1:13).**

"And do not grieve the Holy Spirit of God, by whom you were sealed for the day of redemption" **(EPHESIANS 4:30).**

"Bind up the testimony, seal the law among my disciples. . . . To the law and to the testimony! If they [false teachers] do not speak according to this word [the Word of God], it is because there is no light in them" **(ISAIAH 8:16, 20).**

God's seal relates to His law **(SEE ISAIAH 8:16, 20).** As an ancient king's seal contained his title and dominion, giving authority to his decrees and letters and making them official, so God's seal contains His name, title, and area of authority. It is the Holy Spirit who convicts us of sin and leads to obedience. The Holy Spirit is the agency God uses to seal His law in our hearts. In ancient times, a seal would authenticate a document. We discover God's seal, which authenticates His Ten Commandment law, in the fourth commandment.

"For in six days the LORD [His name], made [His title: Maker or Creator] the heavens and the earth [His dominion], the sea, and all that is in them, and rested the seventh day. Therefore the LORD blessed the Sabbath day and hallowed it" **(EXODUS 20:11).** The Sabbath is a special sign, or seal, between God and His people.

These signs—the seal of God and the mark of the beast—represent two systems of religion. One is initiated by God, and one is initiated by human beings. One is the way of truth! One is the way of error! To every soul will come the crucial test: Shall I obey God or shall I obey human authority?

Who is the beast?

05 From whom does the beast power, this religio-political system, receive its power, throne, and great authority?

"Then I [John] stood on the sand of the sea. And I saw a beast rising up out of the sea, having seven heads and ten horns, and on his horns ten crowns, and on his heads a blasphemous name. Now the beast which I saw was like a leopard, his feet were like the feet of a bear, and his mouth like the mouth of a lion. *The dragon gave him his power, his throne,* and *great authority*" **(REVELATION 13:1, 2; EMPHASIS SUPPLIED).**

"So *the great dragon* was cast out [of heaven], that serpent of old, called the Devil and Satan, who deceives the whole world; he was cast to the earth, and his angels were cast out with him" **(REVELATION 12:9).**

"He laid hold of the dragon, that serpent of old, who is the Devil and Satan, and bound him for a thousand years" **(REVELATION 20:2).**

The dragon is identified clearly in these verses. In simple language stripped of all symbolism, God's Word tells us that the dragon is the devil or Satan. None other than the archenemy of God and man is behind the human instrumentality called the beast power.

But the devil works through *human* agents. Just as God works through His church, the devil works through fallen religious institutions that have rejected God's truth and turned their backs on his law. Although the dragon is *primarily* Satan, as we've just learned, the dragon in a secondary sense was the pagan Roman Empire.

This "dragon"—the devil—attempted to destroy "as soon as it was born" the "male Child [Jesus]" who was later "caught up to God and His throne" **(REVELATION 12:3–5).** Satan used pagan Rome in this attempt on Jesus' life, for **MATTHEW 1:1–20** tells us that King Herod, Rome's agent, tried to destroy the Babe. Later, Satan used pagan Rome to crucify Christ:

- A Roman governor, Pilate, condemned Christ to die **(SEE MATTHEW 27:2, 17–26).**
- A Roman executioner nailed Him to the cruel cross **(SEE MATTHEW 27:27, 35).**
- A Roman soldier pierced His heart with a spear **(SEE JOHN 19:34).**
- A Roman seal was affixed to His tomb **(SEE MATTHEW 27:66).**
- A Roman squad of soldiers guarded His tomb **(SEE MATTHEW 27:62–65).**

Still later, the dragon, through pagan Rome, gave the beast his seat or throne (the original language of **REVELATION 13:2** uses the Greek word *thronos*). This happened when the Roman emperor Constantine decided to move his capital from Rome to what came to be called Constantinople, in what today is Turkey, leaving a power vacuum at the imperial city of Rome, the former throne, or seat, of the Caesars. Therefore, careful Bible students expect to find the beast power located in Rome.

It was the dragon, or the devil, working through pagan Rome, who tried to destroy Christ. And it was that same power that gave the beast its seat, or capital city, power, and authority. Nations don't do that very often! To whom did pagan Rome give its seat of government? How did it take place? History is clear.

Professor Labianca of the University of Rome stated, "To the succession of the Caesars came the succession of the pontiffs in Rome. When Constantine left Rome, he gave the seat to the pontiff."

"By retiring to the East he [Constantine] left the field clear for the Bishops of Rome."

"The Papacy is but 'the ghost' of the deceased Roman Empire, sitting crowned upon the 'grave thereof' " (Arthur P. Stanley, *Lectures on the History of the Eastern Church,* p. 197).

The papal system of religion is the one mentioned in **REVELATION 13** as the beast power. We must remember here that we are talking about a system, not about individual members of that system. The beast is not a person; it is a false religious organization.

06 How widespread would this power be? Would it be a local or universal power?

John the revelator says, "I saw one of his [the beast's] heads as if it had been mortally wounded, and his deadly wound was healed. And all the world marveled and followed the beast. . . . And he was given a mouth speaking great things and blasphemies, and he was given authority to continue for forty-two months" **(REVELATION 13:3, 5).**

ACTS 8:9–11 gives us an example of Satan's power to deceive. "There was a certain man called Simon, who previously practiced sorcery in the city and astonished the people of Samaria, claiming that he was someone great, to whom they all gave heed, from the least to the greatest, saying, 'This man is the great power of God.' And they heeded him because he had astonished them with his sorceries for a long time."

"The coming of the lawless one is according to the working of Satan, with all power, signs, and lying wonders, and with all unrighteous deception among those who perish, because they did not receive the love of the truth, that they might be saved. And for this reason God will send them strong delusion, that they should believe the lie, that they all may be condemned who did not believe the truth but had pleasure in unrighteousness" **(2 THESSALONIANS 2:9–12).**

07 What kind of words would proceed out of the mouth of this beast power?

"Then he opened his mouth in blasphemy against God, to blaspheme His name, His tabernacle, and those who dwell in heaven" **(REVELATION 13:6).**

"I [John] stood on the sand of the sea. And I saw a beast rising up out of the sea, having seven heads and ten horns, and on his horns ten crowns, and on his heads a blasphemous name" **(REVELATION 13:1).**

"So he carried me away in the Spirit into the wilderness. And I saw a woman [a harlot or corrupt church] sitting on a scarlet beast which was full of names of blasphemy, having seven heads and ten horns" **(REVELATION 17:3).**

"I [Daniel] was considering the horns, and there was another horn, a little one, coming up among them, before whom three of the first horns were plucked out by the roots. And there, in this horn [the little horn power], were eyes like the eyes of a man, and a mouth speaking pompous words" **(DANIEL 7:8).**

"I watched then because of the sound of the pompous words which the horn [the little horn power] was speaking; I watched till the beast was slain, and its body destroyed and given to the burning flame" **(DANIEL 7:11).**

Daniel wondered about "the other horn [the little horn power] which came up, before which three fell, namely, that horn which had eyes and a mouth which spoke pompous words, whose appearance was greater than his fellows" **(DANIEL 7:20).**

"He shall speak pompous words against the Most High, shall persecute the saints of the Most High, and shall intend to change times and law. Then the saints shall be given into his hand for a time and times and half a time" **(DANIEL 7:25).**

08 How does the Bible define blasphemy? Does blasphemy include something much deeper than merely claiming that God does not exist?

"The Jews answered Him [Jesus], saying, 'For a good work we do not stone You, but for blasphemy, and because You, being a Man, make Yourself God' " **(JOHN 10:33).**

"And the scribes and the Pharisees began to reason, saying, 'Who is this who speaks blasphemies? Who can forgive sins but God alone?' " **(LUKE 5:21).**

On two occasions the Lord Jesus was unjustly accused of blasphemy, thus giving us two examples from the Bible of what is meant by that sin: blasphemy occurs when

(1) any human pretends to be, or claims to be, God, and (2) any human claims the power to forgive sins. In Jesus' case, the accusations were unjust because He truly was, and is, God and holds all the powers and prerogatives of God—including the right to forgive us our sins.

Now that we understand specifically how the Word of God defines blasphemy, let's discover how blasphemy was revealed in the apostate church of the Middle Ages. The Roman Church has two distinctive doctrines that fall under the Bible's definition of blasphemy. One is its claim to have the power to forgive sins. The other is attributing to the pope the position of God on earth. We'll examine each of these in turn.

First, the Roman Church claims that the power of forgiveness or absolution is vested in her human priests.

"Seek where you will, through heaven and earth, and you will find but one created being who can forgive the sinner, who can free him from the chains of hell, that extraordinary being is the priest, the Catholic priest. 'Who can forgive sins except God?' was the question which the Pharisees sneeringly asked. 'Who can forgive sins?' is the question which the Pharisees of the present day also ask, and I answer there is a man on earth that can forgive sins and that man is the Catholic priest. Yes, beloved brethren, the priest not only declares that the sinner is forgiven, but he really forgives him. The priest raises his hand, he pronounces the word of absolution, and in an instant, quick as a flash of light, the chains of hell are burst asunder, and the sinner becomes a child of God. So great is the power of the priest that the judgments of heaven itself are subject to his decision" (Michael Muller, *The Catholic Priest,* pp. 78, 79).

In reality, however, when a priest raises his hand over the penitent and dares to pronounce the words, "I absolve thee," he himself is guilty of blasphemy! Furthermore, in the Roman Catholic priesthood, a multitude of human mediators are substituted for Christ, when the Bible says that there is only "one Mediator between God and men, the Man Christ Jesus" **(1 TIMOTHY 2:5)**.

The Vatican not only keeps its priestly army of mediators interposed between the repentant sinner and the forgiving God, it even insists that sinners *cannot* approach God for forgiveness on their own, but must go through a Roman Catholic priest! Proof of this fact is seen in a news item in the *Los Angeles Times* (December 12, 1984, part 1, p. 11) announcing "an authoritative papal statement" under the headline "No Forgiveness Directly from God, Pope Says."

Now, let's turn to the second Bible definition of blasphemy, the claim by any human to be God or to stand in the place of God. Here are just a few statements from authoritative Catholic sources:

"The Pope is of so great dignity and so exalted that he is not a mere man, but as it were God, and the vicar of God. . . . Hence the pope is crowned with a triple crown, as king of heaven and of earth and of the lower regions. . . . The pope is as it were God on earth. . . . Chief King of kings, . . . to whom has been entrusted by the omnipotent God direction . . . of the heavenly kingdom" (Lucius Ferraris, *Prompta Bibliotheca* [*Handy Library*], vol. 6, "Papa," article 2, pp. 26–29, reprinted 1899).

"All names which in the Scriptures are applied to Christ, by virtue of which it is established that He is over all the church, all the same names are applied to the Pope" (Cardinal Robert Bellarmine, *On the Authority of Councils*, vol. II, bk. 2, chap. 17, p. 266).

"For thou [the pope] art the shepherd, thou art the physician, thou art the director, thou art the husbandman; finally, thou art another god on earth" (Archbishop Christopher Marcellus, "Oration to the Pope in the Fifth Lateran Council," session IV [1512], quoted in J. D. Mansi, ed., *Sacrorum Conciliorum Nova et Amplissa Collectio,* vol. 32, col. 761). Marcellus was a Roman Catholic priest and the archbishop of Corcyra.

Pope Leo XIII urged "complete submission and obedience of will to the Church and to the Roman Pontiff, as to God himself" ("On the Chief Duties of Christians as Citizens," January 10, 1890, translated in *The Great Encyclical Letters of Pope Leo XIII,* p. 193). The same proud pontiff also boasted, "We [the popes] hold upon this earth the place of God Almighty" (Ibid., p. 304).

Much more evidence could be given, but perhaps this will suffice. Aware of how the papal hierarchy assumes prerogatives that belong only to God, Adam Clarke, three times Methodist conference president, wrote:

"To none can this [prophetic clue] apply so well or so fully as to the popes of Rome. They have assumed infallibility, which belongs only to God. They profess to forgive sins, which belongs only to God. They profess to open and shut heaven, which belongs only to God. They profess to be higher than all the kings of the earth, which belongs only to God. And they go beyond God in pretending to loose whole nations from their oath of allegiance to their kings, when such kings do not please them! And they go against God when they give indulgences for sin. This is the worst of all blasphemies!" (Adam Clarke, *Commentary on the Bible,* one-volume edition, p. 699, note on Daniel 7:25). Clarke's *Commentary* has long been considered among the most perceptive ever published. The book jacket remarks that "Adam Clarke's monumental commentary on the Bible has been a standard reference work for over a century and . . . has won for the author the accolade, 'Prince of Commentators.' "

"The priest holds the place of the Saviour himself, when, by saying 'Ego te absolvo,' he absolves from sin" (Alphonsus de Liguori, *Dignities and Duties of the Priest,* p. 34).

Paul warns us, "Let no one deceive you by any means; for that Day [Christ's second coming] will not come unless the falling away [from the truth] comes first, and the man of sin is revealed, the son of perdition, who opposes and exalts himself above all that is called God or that is worshiped, so that he sits as God in the temple of God, showing himself that he is God" **(2 THESSALONIANS 2:3, 4).**

The devil himself aspired to take God's place! "How you are fallen from heaven, O Lucifer, son of the morning! How you are cut down to the ground, you who weakened the nations! For you have said in your heart: 'I will ascend into heaven, I will exalt my throne above the stars of God; I will also sit on the mount of the congregation on the farthest sides of the north; I will ascend above the heights of the clouds, I will be like the Most High' " **(ISAIAH 14:12–14).**

As we have seen, if anyone claims to be God, that person has committed an act of blasphemy. We have also seen that an earthly religious leader who claims the ability to forgive our sins has committed blasphemy. Such a leader usurps the authority that belongs to God alone!

09 How will the beast power of REVELATION 13 relate to the true people of God?

"It was granted to him [the beast power] to make war with the saints and to overcome them. And authority was given him over every tribe, tongue, and nation" **(REVELATION 13:7).**

"I was watching; and the same horn [the little horn power] was making war against the saints, and prevailing against them" **(DANIEL 7:21).**

"He [the little horn power] shall speak pompous words against the Most High, shall persecute the saints of the Most High, and shall intend to change times and law. Then the saints shall be given into his hand for a time and times and half a time" **(DANIEL 7:25).**

"I saw the woman [the harlot or corrupt church], drunk with the blood of the saints and with the blood of the martyrs of Jesus" **(REVELATION 17:6).**

"And in her was found the blood of prophets and saints" **(REVELATION 18:24).**

"True and righteous are His [God's] judgments, because He has judged the great harlot who corrupted the earth with her fornication; and He has avenged on her the blood of His servants shed by her" **(REVELATION 19:2).**

"When they finish their testimony, the beast that ascends out of the bottomless pit will make war against them, overcome them, and kill them" **(REVELATION 11:7).**

"The dragon [the devil] was enraged with the woman [the true church], and he went to make war with the rest of her offspring, who keep the commandments of God and have the testimony of Jesus Christ" **(REVELATION 12:17).**

It is a well-known fact that millions of martyrs have paid with their blood the price for faithfulness to God. Church history is filled with examples of such persecution. During the Middle Ages when church and state were united, persecution followed. Faithful believers were fiercely persecuted.

10 How long would the beast power continue to persecute the people of God?

"He [the beast power] was given a mouth speaking great things and blasphemies, and he was given authority to continue for forty-two months" **(REVELATION 13:5).**

The beast power would continue for a period of specific duration. As we study this clue, keep in mind the important scriptural principle that in symbolic time prophecies, a prophetic day equals an actual year.

Applying the biblical principle of counting a day for a year, **NUMBERS 14:34** says, "for each day . . . a year." And again, God says, "I have appointed thee each day for a year" **(EZEKIEL 4:6, KJV).** This principle has proven itself in actual practice over and over again:

"42 months" = 3½ years = 1,260 days/years **(REVELATION 13:5).**

"one thousand two hundred and sixty days" = 1,260 days/years **(REVELATION 12:6).**

"a time and times and half a time" = 3½ years = 1,260 days/years **(REVELATION 12:14).**

"a time and times and half a time" = 3½ years = 1,260 days/years **(DANIEL 7:25).**

- In Bible prophecy, the term "time" is used for a year **(COMPARE DANIEL 11:13 IN THE KJV WITH THE NKJV, OR DANIEL 4:16, 23, 25, 32 IN THE KJV WITH THE NASB).**

- The word translated as *times* is not an ordinary plural (which could mean several), but a *dual*. Both Hebrew and Aramaic, the languages used by Daniel, had ordinary plurals, but they also had a special grammatical form for duals, used to mean only *two*—no more, no less—such as *two* eyes, *two* ears, *two* children, or in this case, *two* years, just as in English we speak of a "pair" (of gloves) or a "couple."

- Ancient calendars of the Egyptians, Hindus, Assyrians, and Hebrews all had 360 days per year. So "a time and times and half a time" is figured as 3½ years x 360 days each = 1,260 prophetic days, or once again, 1,260 actual years.

The bishop of Rome gained supreme power—given him by Emperor Justinian—in A.D. 538. And Napoleon's General Berthier took the pope captive in 1798—*exactly* 1,260 years later!

One or two further observations may be in order here. First, the act of General Berthier taking the pope captive—wittingly or unwittingly—fulfilled God's prophecy: "He who leads into captivity shall go into captivity" **(REVELATION 13:10).** But the same verse adds: "He who kills with the sword must be killed with the sword," and the pope was not killed by the sword. Still, it was the sword of Berthier and his military might that captured Pope

Pius VI and unceremoniously removed him from the papal throne. The aged pontiff was hurried from prison to prison in France and at length confined in a fortress at the top of the Alps. He was later removed to Valence, France, where in 1799, he died—alone and in exile.

Second, someone may ask, "How can the papacy be identified as the beast power since it is *alive and well,* and the Bible says the beast incurred 'a deadly wound' "? The answer is that in **REVELATION 13:3** the Bible actually says:

> "the beast *seemed to have had* a fatal wound" **(NIV; EMPHASIS SUPPLIED).**
>
> "*as it were* wounded to death" **(KJV; EMPHASIS SUPPLIED).**
>
> "*as if it had been* mortally wounded" **(NKJV; EMPHASIS SUPPLIED).**
>
> "*as if it had been* slain" **(NASB; EMPHASIS SUPPLIED).**
>
> "*seemed to have* a mortal wound" **(RSV; EMPHASIS SUPPLIED).**
>
> "*seemed to have* received a death-blow" **(NRSV; EMPHASIS SUPPLIED).**
>
> "*appeared to have* been wounded to death" **(PHILLIPS; EMPHASIS SUPPLIED).**
>
> "*seemed* wounded beyond recovery" **(NLT; EMPHASIS SUPPLIED).**

So the deadly nature of the wound was more apparent than real. The blow to the papacy was extremely serious, but not fatal, though to all appearances it seemed so. In fact, at the time it happened, many observers joked about Pope Pius VI being "Pius the Last." Moreover, *all* the Bible versions make clear that, later, the beast's deadly wound was "healed" **(SEE REVELATION 13:3, 12).** Since history steps in and verifies this prediction as well, it seems that *we can certainly trust the Bible*! God knows the end from the beginning.

In A.D. 538, Justinian, the pagan Roman emperor, officially granted the Roman bishop the role of defender of the emperor's empire, the definer of heretics, and defender of the faith. The papacy exercised great influence from A.D. 538 to A.D. 1798.

11 What identifying number is associated with the beast? What is the number of his name?

The beast and his image decrees "and that no one may buy or sell except one who has the mark or the name of the beast, or the number of his name. Here is wisdom. Let him who has understanding calculate the number of the beast, for it is the number of a man: His number is 666" **(REVELATION 13:17, 18).**

Let's see what Catholic translators of the Douay Version of the Bible say about this mystic number. The Douay Bible, called "the most venerable English version printed under Catholic auspices," has the following comment on **REVELATION 13:18** in a special footnote on that verse: "*Six hundred sixty-six*. The numeral letters of his name shall make up this number."

Over the years, individual popes have had many names, such as John, Paul, John Paul, Gregory, and so on. But what is the *official* title used by the papacy which, like an umbrella, covers the whole dynasty of popes? Several general titles are used, such as "Holy Father" and "Roman Pontiff," but the main one—the one on which the other titles are based—is "Vicar of the Son of God," along with its variations, "Vicar of Christ," "Vicar of Jesus Christ," and "Vicar of God." In Latin, that official title is "VICARIUS FILII DEI." Literally translated, the title, *Vicarius Filii Dei,* means "vicar of the Son of God." The pope claims to stand in the place of Jesus as His substitute, since the latter has returned to heaven.

This exalted title, *Vicarius Filii Dei,* or some equivalent form of it, has appeared so frequently in Roman Catholic literature and rituals for centuries that it scarcely seems necessary to add further proof of its validity and importance. In the earliest collection of Roman Catholic canon law, we read: "Beatus Petrus in terris Vicarius Filii Dei esse videtur constitutus" ("Decretum Gratiani," prima pars, dist. xcvi). The English translation reads: "Blessed Peter is seen to have been constituted Vicar of the Son of God on the earth" ("Decretum of Gratian," part 1, div. 96).

This title is in Latin—not only the language of the Roman Empire, but also the official language of the Roman Catholic Church itself. Consequently, the Latin language would naturally be used in computing the number 666. Latin's alphabetic letters have numeric values. We sometimes call these "Roman numerals." **REVELATION 13:17, 18** says quite plainly that "the number of the beast . . . is the number of a man." More specifically, it's "the number of his name." And we've found that in the Catholic Douay Bible, in a footnote comment to **VERSE 18** reads: "*Six hundred sixty-six.* The numeral letters of his name shall make up this number." So let's investigate the possibility that the pope's name, his official title, fits this clue. Let's count the letters in his "name" that have Roman numeric values.

Title: VICARIUS FILII DEI

V =	5	
I =	1	
C =	100	
A =	0	(no numeric value)
R =	0	(no numeric value)
I =	1	
U =	5	(formerly interchangeable with V)
S =	0	(no numeric value)
F =	0	(no numeric value)
I =	1	
L =	50	
I =	1	
I =	1	
D =	500	
E =	0	(no numeric value)
I =	1	
Total =	666	

As you can see, this convincing computation totals 666 exactly—no more, no less. Some may inquire why the letter *U* in the calculation above is counted like the letter *V* and given the Roman numeral value of 5. A critic may complain that this is forcing things to come out to the preconceived total. But that's a groundless complaint, for the fact is that the letter *V* was interchangeable with *U* until recent centuries.

The Romans used the letter *V* for both *U* and *V* sounds, just as today we still write the letter *C* for both *K* and *S* sounds in words like *calculate* and *certainty*. Later, medieval scholars began writing *U* for a vowel and *V* for a consonant. Encyclopedias confirm this fact. For instance: "The history of this letter [*V*] is identical with that of U, from which it was not differentiated till the 15th to 17th century. . . . The pointed form V became identified with the consonant, the rounded form with the vowel" (*Encyclopaedia Britannica,* vol. 22, p. 832, article, "V."

"V is the twenty-second letter of our alphabet. Its history is the same as that of the letter U. . . . During the 1400's to 1600's, the rounded form U came to be used only to represent the vowel, and the pointed form V only to represent the consonant" (*World Book Encyclopedia,* vol. 17, p. 8417, article "V."

Besides this documentation, think of our letter *W.* It looks like two letter *V*s written together. But when we pronounce its name, we call it a "double-U"—not a "double-V." And sometimes a building has its name engraved above the entrance, like this: PVBLIC LIBRARY. These things are a throwback to the days when *U* and *V* were interchangeable.

Some try to blunt the force of this striking numeric fulfillment by pointing out that other names may also add up to 666. That may be, but remember: This computation is *only one* of many God-given clues identifying the beast power, and when considered in connection with them, it *is* significant. It certainly adds weight and strength to the long list of other identifying points found in Scripture.

Putting all the evidence together, it becomes clear that the papal power is the beast power of **REVELATION 13.**

12 How does the change of the Sabbath relate to the final conflict? What does the papacy claim as its sign of authority?

God foresaw and predicted the attempted change of His holy law! **DANIEL 7:25** says the little horn power "shall intend to change times and law." At least *three points* should be noticed about this important verse:

1. First, this text warns about a change in *divine* law, not human law, for human laws are routinely changed every day. So a change in merely human law would not be a subject for

prophecy. The Revised Standard Version of the Bible says that the little horn power "shall *think* to change times and the law"—that is, God's law. And since the two preceding statements in this verse **(DANIEL 7:25)** declare what the little horn would do against the Most High ("he shall speak pompous words against the Most High, and shall persecute the saints of the Most High"), we must conclude that it is also the "times and the law" of the Most High that the little horn would attempt to change.

2. Second, the expression "intend to change" (or "think to change") denotes only an *attempted* change in the law God wrote in stone with His own finger, for no mere man or even the devil himself could really change it. God's divine law is *beyond our reach,* and it's pure presumption and blasphemy for anyone even to think he could change it. But Daniel's text says the little horn power would attempt that very thing!

3. Third, the word *times* calls our attention specifically to the fourth commandment, since the Sabbath commandment is the only one of the ten that deals with any element of time.

We know the Roman Catholic Church is responsible for this predicted attempt to change the fourth commandment for two reasons: (1) it's the only institution that could have done so, and (2) it admits doing so! In *The Convert's Catechism of Catholic Doctrine,* a set of questions and answers used as an official training manual to instruct new church members, we read:

"QUESTION: Which is the Sabbath day?

"ANSWER: Saturday is the Sabbath day.

"QUESTION: Why do we observe Sunday instead of Saturday?

"ANSWER: We observe Sunday instead of Saturday because the Catholic Church transferred the solemnity from Saturday to Sunday" (p. 50).

"The Pope is of so great authority and power that he can modify, explain, or interpret even divine laws. . . . Petrus de Ancharano [died 1416] very clearly asserts this in Consil. 373, No. 3, verso: 'The Pope can modify divine law, since his power is not of man, but of God, and he acts in the place of God upon earth' " (Lucius Ferraris, *Prompta Bibliotheca* [*Handy Library*], "Papa," article 2, vol. 6, p. 29. Reprinted 1899).

Please note the following pertinent quotations from Roman Catholic sources:

- "Reason and sense demand the acceptance of one or the other of these alternatives: either Protestantism and the keeping holy of Saturday, or Catholicity and the keeping holy of Sunday. Compromise is impossible" (Cardinal James Gibbons, *The Catholic Mirror,* December 23, 1893).

- "Like two sacred rivers flowing from Paradise, the Bible and divine Tradition contain the Word of God, the precious gems of revealed truths. Though these two divine streams are in themselves, on account of their divine origin, of equal sacredness, and are both full of revealed truths, still, of the two, Tradition is to us more clear and safe" (Father Joseph Faà di Bruno, *Catholic Belief,* p. 45). Do you agree that tradition—the customs and practices of man—is more safe than the Bible? Rome baptizes tradition with the word *divine* and dares to hold it above the Bible.

- "Sunday is our mark of authority. . . . The church is above the Bible, and this transference of Sabbath observance is proof of that fact" (*Catholic Record,* September 1, 1923).

- "The Bible says, remember that thou keep holy the Sabbath day. The Catholic Church says, No! By my divine power I abolish the Sabbath day, and command you to keep holy the first day of the week. And lo! The entire civilized world bows down in reverent obedience to the command of the holy Catholic Church" (Father Enright, president, Redemptorist College).

- On January 18, 1563, "the Archbishop of Reggio made a speech in which he openly declared that tradition stood above the Scriptures because the church had changed the Sabbath into Sunday—not by a command of Christ, but by its own authority" (*Canon and Tradition,* p. 263). The basis of papal authority, he declared, was founded upon the right to change the Sabbath from Saturday, the seventh day, to Sunday, the first day.

- "Of course the Catholic Church claims that the change [of the Sabbath from the seventh-day of the week, Saturday, to the first day of the week, Sunday] was her act. . . . And the act is a mark of her ecclesiastical power and authority in religious matters" (Letter from Chancellor H. R. Thomas to Cardinal James Gibbons, November 11, 1895).

Rome claims that the change of the Sabbath from Saturday to Sunday is a mark of its authority. In the future, church and state will unite once again in an attempt to enforce this mark. It is only at this point in the future—when the issues are clear—that the mark of the beast will be enforced. No one has the mark of the beast now.

13 How does God distinguish His faithful followers from those who receive the mark of the beast?

"Here is the patience of the saints; here are those who keep the commandments of God and the faith of Jesus" **(REVELATION 14:12).**

These two points of identification are sufficient to narrow the field specifically to those alone who are loyal to God. Consider that keeping "the faith of Jesus" eliminates at once the Jew, the Muslim, the Buddhist, the Hindu, and all atheists. There are many wonderful, godly people in each religious community, but God's last-day people are clearly identified with two twin characteristics: (1) the faith of Jesus, and (2) obedience to the commandments of God.

The second identifying point, describing the saints as "those who keep the commandments of God," eliminates Christian groups who violate the second commandment by bowing down to religious figures or statues. This inspired definition of God's "saints" also rules out the religious establishment that violates—every week—the fourth commandment by observing, and proclaiming the observance of, another day in place of the Bible Sabbath. This single Scripture—**REVELATION 12:17**—is as clear as day and is of great import and significance. It enables us to identify God's true, last-day people.

14 What is the central issue in the final crisis at the close of this earth's history?

The issue here involves *far more* than a matter of *days*—it's a choice of *masters*! It's a battle for the minds and souls of men and women, a life-and-death struggle for their allegiance. And it focuses on and revolves around worship—*the one thing Satan wants most*!

"Choose for yourselves this day whom you will serve. . . . But as for me and my house, we will serve the LORD" **(JOSHUA 24:15).**

Jesus said, "No one can serve two masters; for either he will hate the one and love the other, or else he will be loyal to the one and despise the other. You cannot serve God and mammon" **(MATTHEW 6:24).**

"God be thanked that though you were slaves of sin, yet you obeyed from the heart that form of doctrine to which you were delivered" **(ROMANS 6:17).**

The issues we have dealt with in this chapter are weighty. They require a change in our thinking. They call us from following tradition to being faithful to God's Word. Will you fall upon your knees and ask God to give you the strength and courage to follow this truth?

CHAPTER 29

What the Bible Says About the United States in Prophecy

"America the Beautiful" is one of America's most popular patriotic songs. The lyrics were written by Katherine Lee Bates, and the music was composed by church organist Samuel A. Ward. In 1893, at the age of thirty-three, Katherine Bates journeyed by train across the heartland of America to Colorado Springs to teach a short English course at Colorado College. The scenes of her trip so inspired her that she wrote the magnificent, moving poem about the beauty and greatness of America.

When Richard Nixon visited China in 1972, the Chinese welcomed the president with this moving piece of music. The second verse captures the essence of what America stands for. It speaks of liberty and freedom for all.

"O beautiful for Pilgrim feet
Whose stern impassioned stress
A thoroughfare for freedom beat
Across the wilderness.

"America! America!
God mend thine every flaw
Confirm thy soul in self-control
Thy liberty in law."

Will America always be the "thoroughfare for freedom" that Katherine Bates's famed "America the Beautiful" speaks about? Will America continue to champion the principles of religious freedom? Or will it one day repudiate its rich heritage, unite with the beast, and become a persecuting power? What is America's future?

Throughout the centuries, the Bible has revealed the rise and fall of nations with amazing accuracy. Their destinies were predicted in advance, but the Bible is not primarily a history book! Not every world power is mentioned.

Nations are brought into the biblical picture, not because of their political power, but in the light of their role in God's overall plan. The Bible reveals the role of nations in the long-standing controversy between Christ and Satan. In the last days of earth's history, the final conflict will center upon the question of loyalty to God as manifested by obedience to His law.

Working through both religious and state powers, Satan will attempt to coerce God's people—with economic boycotts, fines, and threats of imprisonment and death—to ignore God's law by accepting a substitute Sabbath.

REVELATION 13 refers to two beasts, or powers. The first beast, arising from the sea, represents an apostate religious system arising out of Rome. The second beast does not arise out of the sea, but out of the earth. Note the contrast in the verses below.

01 From where do these two separate beasts, or world powers, originate? Notice the two contrasting places from which each beast rises. What does this tell us about each power? How do these two distinct locations help us identify the two powers?

"Then I [John] stood on the sand of the sea. And I saw a beast rising up out of the sea, having seven heads and ten horns, and on his horns ten crowns, and on his heads a blasphemous name" **(REVELATION 13:1).**

"Then I saw another beast coming up out of the earth, and he had two horns like a lamb and spoke like a dragon" **(REVELATION 13:11).**

"Then he [the angel] said to me, 'The waters which you saw, where the harlot sits, are peoples, multitudes, nations, and tongues' " **(REVELATION 17:15).**

The Amplified Bible makes **REVELATION 13:11** clear by saying, "I saw another beast rising up out of the land [itself]." Absence of water denotes a scarcity of people. The wilderness of this vast American continent—unpopulated but for a few scattered Indian tribes—marvelously fits the Bible description of unpopulated, "dry" ground, and fulfills this prophecy in a remarkable way.

"Daniel spoke, saying, 'I saw in my vision by night, and behold, the four winds of heaven were stirring up the Great Sea. And four great beasts came up from the sea, each different from the other' " **(DANIEL 7:2, 3).**

These "four great beasts"—or kingdoms, see **DANIEL 7:23**—representing Babylon, Media-Persia, Greece, and Rome, all arose out of the sea of humanity in *populated* areas. On the other hand, the second beast that John the revelator saw was "coming up out of the earth," a relatively *unpopulated* area. To recap: The first beast arises from the sea; the second beast arises from the land.

In chapter 28 of this book, we clearly identified the first beast as the papacy.

According to **REVELATION 13,** this beast received its seat of government from pagan Rome, became a universal system of worship, persecuted the people of God, claimed the power to forgive sins, and reigned supreme for 1,260 years during the Middle Ages.

In Bible prophecy, the sea represents a populated area of the earth **(SEE REVELATION 17:15).** So the beast rising out of the sea represents a power arising out of the populated areas of the world. The papal system rose out of the populated areas of Europe. The earth, on the other hand, represents the opposite—an unpopulated, or sparsely populated, area. The second beast rises out of the sparsely populated area of the New World.

02 How does this second beast of REVELATION 13 (the lamblike beast) unite with the first beast (the papacy)?

"And he [the second beast] exercises all the authority of the first beast in his presence, and CAUSES the earth and those who dwell in it to worship the first beast, whose deadly wound was healed" **(REVELATION 13:12; EMPHASIS SUPPLIED).**

That word, *causes,* is repeated in **VERSE 16** and denotes force, *coercion of the worst kind.* Other versions of the English Bible render it as "compels," "makes," "requires," and "forces."

"And I saw one of his [the first beast's] heads as if it had been mortally wounded, and his deadly wound was healed. And all the world marveled and followed the beast. So they worshiped the dragon who gave authority to the beast; and they worshiped the beast, saying, 'Who is like the beast? Who is able to make war with him?' " **(REVELATION 13:3, 4).**

03 What are some of the clear evidences that this second beast power of REVELATION 13 represents the United States?

"Then I saw another beast coming up out of the earth, and he had two horns like a lamb and spoke like a dragon. And he exercises all the authority of the first beast in his presence, and causes the earth and those who dwell in it to worship the first beast, whose deadly wound was healed" **(REVELATION 13:11, 12).**

"He [the first beast] was given authority to continue for forty-two months" **(REVELATION 13:5).**

"He [the first beast] who leads into captivity shall go into captivity" **(REVELATION 13:10).**

God gives us enough facts to place the prophecy in its proper time frame. Reading **REVELATION 13:10, 11,** we see that this second beast was arising or "coming up" around the time that the first beast (the papacy) was led "into captivity," having received its deadly wound after forty-two prophetic months (1,260 actual years) of supremacy.

When was this? We have already noted that the pope died in exile soon after being taken "into captivity" by Napoleon's general in 1798. As we scan the horizon of history, we discover only one world power "coming up" around 1798—the United States of America.

The American colonies began their struggle for independence in 1775. In 1776, they declared themselves a free and independent nation. In 1777, delegates from the thirteen original states adopted the Articles of Confederation. In 1783, the Revolutionary War closed in a peace treaty with Great Britain. In 1787, the Constitution was framed; and in March of 1789, it was ratified and went into effect. George Washington served as the country's first president until 1797. Thus we come to the pivotal year 1798, when this nation is introduced in prophecy—"coming up" at just the right time!

Also, the government symbolized by this second beast is introduced in the early part of its career, that is, while still a *youthful* power. John says, "I beheld another beast coming up out of the earth; and he had two horns like a lamb." Why doesn't John simply say, "He had two horns?" Why does he add "like a *lamb*"? Obviously, he wants to emphasize not only this second beast's innocent and harmless character, but also its youthful nature. For a lamb's horns are horns that have barely begun to grow.

Not only the lamblike horns, but the phrase, "coming up," must signify that this political power was newly organized and just then arising. With our gaze still fixed on the year 1798, we again ask: What notable power was at that time coming into prominence, but still in its youth? Again, there is only one answer: the new nation of the United States!

In 1754, John Wesley, founder of the Methodist Church, said of this second prophetic beast: "He has not yet come, though he cannot be far off. For he is to appear at the end of the forty-two months of the first beast [which ended in 1798]" (*Explanatory Notes Upon the New Testament,* p. 1010, comment on Revelation 13:11). In looking for a nation to arise in a very short time as a fulfillment of this prophecy, Wesley was correct.

"Then I saw another beast coming up out of the earth, and he had two horns like a lamb and spoke like a dragon" **(REVELATION 13:11).**

Jesus is often depicted as a Lamb. For example, John the Baptist announced Jesus in these words: "Behold! The Lamb of God who takes away the sin of the world!" **(JOHN 1:29).** Here are some texts in the book of **REVELATION** that also refer to Jesus as "Lamb."

REVELATION 5:6

REVELATION 5:8

REVELATION 5:12

REVELATION 5:13

REVELATION 6:1

REVELATION 6:16

REVELATION 7:9

REVELATION 7:10

REVELATION 7:14

REVELATION 7:17

REVELATION 12:11

REVELATION 13:8

REVELATION 14:1

REVELATION 14:4

REVELATION 14:10

REVELATION 15:3

REVELATION 17:14

REVELATION 19:7

REVELATION 19:9

REVELATION 21:14

REVELATION 21:22

REVELATION 21:23

REVELATION 22:1

REVELATION 22:3

The perceptive student of Scripture will note that the first beast in **REVELATION 13:1** had ten horns with "ten crowns." Those multiple crowns represent "the crowned heads of Europe" (England, France, Germany, Italy, Portugal, Spain, etc.). By way of strong contrast, the second beast had no crowns on his lamblike horns. Since a crown is the fitting symbol of a monarchy, the notable absence of crowns in this case clearly indicates a democratic government vesting its power in the hands of the people—not in any ruling king.

Revelation reveals the form of government the United States has always had, and this constitutes another strong link in the chain of evidence that this prophecy denotes the United States of America. Had the second beast in John's vision been depicted wearing a crown, no one could maintain that the prophecy represented the United States, for that country has never had a king. In fact, early American patriots, applauding their "experiment in democracy," were proud to point out that on this side of the Atlantic there is "a church without a pope, a state without a king!"

But this is not the most conclusive proof that the new nation symbolized here is democratic in government. A democracy, by definition, is "government of the people, by the people, for the people." **REVELATION 13:14 (KJV)** makes plain that this power says to the *people* "that they should make an image to the beast, which had the wound by the sword, and did live." Thus it has a democratic form of government rather than an absolute monarchy or dictatorship. A dictator or powerful king can pass laws without asking anyone's permission. But the president of the United States cannot act unilaterally and autocratically. He must ask the people's representatives in Congress to make and pass a law.

So when the prophet depicts the second beast as "saying to them that dwell on the earth, that they should make an image to the beast," God clearly foretells a form of government in which the legislative power rests with the people.

Let's summarize.

This lamblike beast with two horns arose precisely when the first beast was going into captivity. The papacy received its deadly wound in 1798 when the French general, Berthier, took the pope captive. Ultimately, the pope died in captivity.

The first beast arose out of or from the sea—"peoples, multitudes, nations, and tongues" **(REVELATION 17:15).** It arose out of Rome from the populated masses of Europe. The second beast arose from an unpopulated area of the world. The Greek word for "coming up" is *anabaino,* meaning "springing up." This power arises like a silent seed growing from the quiet earth. It arises rapidly from obscurity to become a world superpower.

Lamblike qualities indicate gentleness, innocence, and freedom. Throughout the book of Revelation, Jesus is described as a Lamb. Jesus gives each of His followers the freedom of choice. This lamblike power grants its citizens the opportunity to worship freely in harmony with the dictates of their consciences.

Furthermore, note that a lamb is a meek, peaceful creature, in contrast to the rapacious, aggressive, warlike animals such as the lion, bear, leopard, and fierce beast of **DANIEL 7.** A lamb is a fitting symbol of a peace-loving nation like the United States, as opposed to the imperialistic nations of Babylon, Media-Persia, Greece, and Rome, which continuously had to expand to satisfy their dreams of empire **(SEE DANIEL 7:3–7; REVELATION 13:2).**

We should also notice that a lamb is a young animal. The lion, the bear, the leopard, and the dragon described earlier in the chapter are full-grown animals, indicating older, established nations. The youthful lamb represents a nation just born.

Crowns indicate kingly authority. This new power has no crown or king! Horns are symbols of power. Here the power comes from another source—from the people. The two horns represent a democratic, republican form of government.

The United States established two separate authorities—political and religious. The principle of complete separation between church and state was represented by the "two horns like a lamb."

04 What remarkable, striking events does Bible prophecy predict will occur in the United States of America? Although this is surprising and seems unlikely at a time of tolerance and freedom for all, Revelation predicts a time of future crisis in which rapid changes to America's fundamental principles of religious liberty will take place.

"Then I saw another beast coming up out of the earth, and he had two horns like a lamb and *spoke like a dragon*. And he exercises all the authority of the first beast in his presence, and causes the earth and those who dwell in it to worship the first beast, whose deadly wound was healed" **(REVELATION 13:11, 12; EMPHASIS SUPPLIED).**

The various points already covered unmistakably identify the second beast as the United States—no one could reasonably apply all these prophetic clues to any other nation.

How I wish we could stop right here in our study, for so far the prophecy paints a positive picture of the United States, a picture of which all patriotic Americans can be proud. But sad to say, the picture will change, as we shall now see. The lamblike beast begins to speak "like a dragon"! Also, **REVELATION 13:14, 15** says that this second beast—the United States—will make "an image to the beast" or "an image *of* the beast" **(EMPHASIS SUPPLIED).**

So what is meant by "an image"? An image of anything is something that looks like, or resembles, it. John tells us that this image would be just like the papal power—that is, it would be just like "the first beast, whose deadly wound was healed . . . the beast who was wounded by the sword and lived" **(REVELATION 13:12, 14).**

The image of the beast won't be a literal image like a statue or idol. Instead, it will be a reverberating echo of the first beast. It will be almost an exact replica—a repeat performance, of what the world suffered centuries ago during the Dark Ages. To learn what the "image" will be like, we must first recall what the papal beast was like, especially during the heyday of its power.

The papacy was a church clothed with civil power—an ecclesiastical body having absolute authority to threaten and punish all dissenters with confiscation of goods, imprisonment, torture, and death. It was a union of church and state. So what would be an "image" of such a religious and civil power? It would be another ecclesiastical establishment clothed with political power—in other words, a modern-day union of church and state.

How could such an image be formed in the United States? Consider this: God warns that just before Christ returns, "there shall be a time of trouble, such as never was" **(DANIEL 12:1).** We all know that the "Christian lobby" in Washington has already grown strong. Let a crisis come—"a time of trouble" such as multiple terrorist attacks, worldwide economic depression, or nuclear war—and hear the voices cry, "This is a *judgment from God* because we've wandered so far from His ways! We've got to get back to God! Let's make this a Christian nation. This is our last chance!"

And well-meaning Americans—whether church members, ministers, or legislators—will seek a political solution to a spiritual problem. They will compromise the Bill of Rights under the guise of preserving public morality. They will band together to pass laws trying to force people through civil power to do what the church has failed to persuade them to do through preaching and teaching.

In order for the United States to form an "image" of the beast, the religious power must once again so control the civil government that the strong arm of the state will be employed by the church to accomplish her own ends. History shows that whenever the church obtains civil power, she employs it to punish dissent from her doctrines and restrict liberty of conscience. A sample of papal philosophy is seen in this quotation from Pope Leo XIII: "It is quite unlawful to demand, to defend, or to grant unconditional freedom of thought, of speech, of writing, or of worship, as if these were so many rights given by nature to man" ("Human Liberty," translated in *The Great Encyclical Letters of Pope Leo XIII,* 3rd ed., p. 161).

REVELATION 13:12 declares that the United States will exercise the same power as the papacy: "He [the lamblike beast] exercises all the authority of the first beast" before him. The first beast was Papal Rome, and during the centuries of its supremacy, the papacy was dictatorial and very intolerant—especially in matters of religion. It persecuted any and all who disagreed with its dogmatic teachings, and used the civil arm—the armies of the state—to carry out its commands and enforce its edicts.

Those who are understandably reluctant to accept this fact, who say, "It can't happen here!" need to remember Thomas Jefferson's wisely prophetic words: "The spirit of the times may alter, will alter. Our rulers will become corrupt, our people careless. A single zealot may commence persecution, and better men be his victims" ("Notes on Virginia," Query 17, *The Writings of Thomas Jefferson,* vol. VIII, p. 402).

05 How will the lamblike beast—the United States—attempt to coerce everyone to worship the image of the beast and receive the mark of the beast?

The lamblike beast decrees "that no one may buy or sell except one who has the mark or the name of the beast, or the number of his name" **(REVELATION 13:17).**

"He was granted power to give breath to the image of the beast, that the image of the beast should both speak and cause as many as would not worship the image of the beast to be killed" **(REVELATION 13:15).**

When the early church was corrupted by departing from the simplicity of the gospel, it lost the Spirit and power of God.

Consequently, in order to control the consciences of the people, the church sought the support of the secular power.

In order for the United States to form an image of the beast, a religious power must control the civil government. The church will use the authority of the state to coerce conscience once again.

An image is a "likeness to" something that it resembles.

The papacy claims, as the sign of its authority, a substitute day of worship. Sunday is a "likeness" to the Sabbath, but it is not the Sabbath. It is a substitute, or counterfeit, day of worship.

In this astounding prophecy, the United States of America establishes a likeness to the papacy by using the power of government to enforce a religious day of worship. In a time of great crisis, the people and their religious leaders put enormous pressure on their legislators to enforce a common day of religious worship.

06 What agencies will Satan use to deceive thousands to put pressure on their local political officials and civil authorities to form an image to the beast?

In a period of social upheaval, economic difficulty, natural disasters, and international tension, church and state will unite in an attempt to establish peace. Satan will use false miracles to establish his claims.

"He performs great signs, so that he even makes fire come down from heaven on the earth in the sight of men. And he deceives those who dwell on the earth by those signs ["miracles," KJV] which he was granted to do in the sight of the beast, telling those who dwell on the earth to make an image to the beast who was wounded by the sword and lived" **(REVELATION 13:13, 14).**

Satan was a powerful angel—a supernatural being created by God. As such, he possesses supernatural powers. It's instructive to see that this verse **(REVELATION 13:14, KJV)** speaks of "miracles which he had power to do"—not miracles which he *appeared* to do, as if it's a mere trick or illusion. **REVELATION 16:14, KJV,** also speaks of "the spirits of devils, working miracles."

"They are the spirits of devils, working miracles, which go forth unto the kings of the earth and of the whole world, to gather them to the battle of that great day of God Almighty" **(REVELATION 16:14, KJV).**

Paul predicted, "The coming of the lawless one is according to the working of Satan, with all power, signs, and lying wonders" **(2 THESSALONIANS 2:9).**

Jesus warned, "False christs and false prophets will rise and show great signs and wonders to deceive, if possible, even the elect. See, I have told you beforehand" **(MATTHEW 24:24, 25).**

07 In every generation God has had a faithful group of people who have not yielded to Satan's sophistries. They have remained loyal to Jesus and faithful to His Word. The Bible predicts that in the last days there will be a marvelous outpouring of the Holy Spirit on these faithful followers of Jesus. How does the Bible describe this group of people upon whom Jesus will abundantly pour out His Spirit?

"And we are His witnesses to these things, and so also is the Holy Spirit whom God has given to those who obey Him" **(ACTS 5:32).**

"If you love Me, keep My commandments. And I will pray the Father, and He will give you another Helper [the Holy Spirit], that He may abide with you forever" **(JOHN 14:15, 16).**

"And having been perfected, He [Christ] became the author of eternal salvation to all who obey Him" **(HEBREWS 5:9).**

"But Peter and the other apostles answered and said: 'We ought to obey God rather than men' " **(ACTS 5:29).**

"Then Samuel said: 'Has the LORD as great delight in burnt offerings and sacrifices, as in obeying the voice of the LORD? Behold, to obey is better than sacrifice, and to heed than the fat of rams' " **(1 SAMUEL 15:22).**

In these verses of Scripture, God's Word makes an interesting and important connection between obedience on our part and the reception of the Holy Spirit.

The faithful people of God are neither impressed nor deceived by Satan's miracles. They know that *supernatural acts are not the test of spiritual truth*. God's Word—and God's Word alone—is the test. That's why the Lord points us "to the law and to the testimony! If they [would-be religious teachers] do not speak according to this Word [the Word of God], it is because there is no light in them" **(ISAIAH 8:20).**

08 What are the identifying characteristics of those who have gained the victory over the beast and who are ready for the coming of Christ and eternity?

"The dragon [the devil] was enraged with the woman [the true church], and he went to make war with the rest of her offspring, who keep the commandments of God and have the testimony of Jesus Christ" **(REVELATION 12:17).**

"Here is the patience of the saints; here are those who keep the commandments of God and the faith of Jesus" **(REVELATION 14:12).**

"He who is unjust, let him be unjust still; he who is filthy, let him be filthy still; he who is righteous, let him be righteous still; he who is holy, let him be holy still. And behold, I am coming quickly, and My reward is with Me, to give to every one according to his work. I am the Alpha and the Omega, the Beginning and the End, the First and the Last. *Blessed are those who do His commandments, that they may have the right to the tree of life, and may enter through the gates into the city*" **(REVELATION 22:11–14; EMPHASIS SUPPLIED).**

Ages ago, Lucifer in heaven refused to remain obedient to God and rebelled against His government, His authority, His law. Today, we hear supposed ministers of the gospel preaching from the pulpit that God's law has been abolished and that New Testament Christians need not keep the commandments anymore. Yet God, in the last book of the Bible, lovingly tells us in verses like those above that we should follow Him and His way as spelled out in His Book.

Jesus said, "If you love Me, keep My commandments" **(JOHN 14:15).**

The apostle John puts it plainly: "He who says, 'I know Him,' and does not keep His commandments, is a liar, and the truth is not in him" **(1 JOHN 2:4).**

"For this is the love of God, that we keep His commandments. And His commandments are not burdensome" **(1 JOHN 5:3).**

The conflict will soon intensify beyond our imagination. Through the power of Jesus Christ, you can remain loyal through these last days. John saw in vision the triumphal celebration given in heaven for those who have been victorious over the beast and his image: "I saw . . . those who have the victory over the beast, over his image and over his mark and over the number of his name, standing on the sea of glass, having harps of God. They sing the song of Moses . . . and the song of the Lamb, saying: 'Great and marvelous are Your works, Lord God Almighty! Just and true are Your ways, O King of the saints' " **(REVELATION 15:2, 3).**

Praise God! His faithful followers will triumph with Him at last. One day they will rejoice around His throne forever secure from the assault of the enemy.

Nations in Prophecy

In Philadelphia at the Continental Congress on July 2, 1776, a debate raged that would determine the future of America. The debate was over whether or not the United States should declare its independence from England. The discussion was intense. Both sides presented their arguments. The debate went on most of the night.

When the vote was taken it was deadlocked. Delaware had three votes. One of the Delaware delegates voted for independence. One of the Delaware delegates voted against independence.

The third Delaware delegate was at home on his farm. It was raining and the roads were filled with mud. He couldn't get there.

A message went out from that Continental Congress and it spread like wildfire throughout the eastern seaboard. The vote is deadlocked! This one delegate sensed, "I have to get there." He mounted his horse and rode through the mud and rain. He rode all that night arriving the next day to cast the deciding vote for independence.

There was a little boy sent by his grandfather to look through the keyhole in the door to see if the delegates signed the document. As the story goes, the grandfather was a bell-ringer. If they signed, Grandpa was going to ring for liberty. As the delegate from Delaware arrived, the little boy looked through the keyhole in the closed, locked door. As he peered in, his grandpa kept muttering, "They're not going to sign it; they're not going to sign it."

But the little boy watched as the deciding vote was cast. He watched the historic vote for independence. And he then began to shout to his grandfather the bell-ringer: "Ring, Grandpa! Ring, Grandpa! Ring for liberty!"

The liberty bell sounded that day and for the first time in history, a nation was born on the principles of religious freedom.

The United States Constitution guarantees both civil and religious freedom to all of its citizens. According to the First Amendment, the free exercise of religion is every individual's God-given right.

Will these historic freedoms ever be challenged?

Will church and state ever unite in the United States of America?

Does the Bible mention United States in prophecy?

Wouldn't it be strange indeed if the Bible did not mention the United States?

Wouldn't it be rather odd if a nation born on the principles of religious liberty—the cradle of religious tolerance—was not mentioned in prophecy?

Wouldn't it be strange for God to raise up a nation committed to the ideal of democracy and not to mention that at all in Bible prophecy? The book of Revelation describes those great empires that have an impact on Christian history. The Bible does not mention every nation in the world. The Bible is not primarily a history book. Where nations dramatically affect God's people and ultimate plans, the Scripture mentions them.

The Bible brought Babylon into view because Nebuchadnezzar, the king of Babylon, attacked Jerusalem, God's people. The Bible brought Media-Persia into view because Media-Persia would overthrow Babylon and let God's people go free. Greece and Rome were foretold because of their relationship to God's people. Greece united the empire with a common language for the gospel to be proclaimed. The entire New Testament was written in Greek.

Jesus was born in the days of Rome. He lived, ministered, and died in a Roman society.

The church-state union, under the Roman Church in the early centuries, compromised truth, persecuted God's people, and opposed the true gospel.

The Bible brings nations into view not because they are a political power but if they have a significant part to play in the plan and purposes of God. Revelation's prophecies clearly describe the rise of America and its role in earth's final events.

CHAPTER 30

What the Bible Says About the Seven Last Plagues

The battle of Armageddon described in the Bible's last book, Revelation, has fascinated Bible students, historians, politicians, and theologians for centuries. News commentators often use the term to describe some unusual natural or political disaster. It has especially been used to describe the conflict in the Middle East. There is a certain mystique or intrigue about the battle of Armageddon. Where will it be fought? Who will be involved? When will it occur? Will it result in universal destruction? Who will survive earth's last war? And what about the seven last plagues? What relationship do they have to Armageddon and the coming Tribulation?

These are good questions and demand solid biblical answers.

Thousands are stunned with bewilderment regarding the future. They wander in a maze of confusion.

God reveals through prophecy an outline of coming events for the informed Christian. According to Bible prophecy, the crisis at the close of time is not merely a military struggle. It is the last battle in the long-standing spiritual conflict between Christ and Satan.

The seven last plagues and the battle of Armageddon focus on the end of human history and the coming of Christ.

01 How does the Bible's last book, Revelation, describe the final crisis at the close of this earth's history?

An ungodly union of church and state "causes [compels] all, both small and great, rich and poor, free and slave, to receive a mark on their right hand or on their foreheads, and that no one may buy or sell except one who has the mark or the name of the beast, or the number of his name" **(REVELATION 13:16, 17).**

"He was granted power to give breath to the image of the beast, that the image of the beast should both speak and cause as many as would not worship the image of the beast to be killed" **(REVELATION 13:15).**

"At that time Michael shall stand up, the great prince who stands watch over the sons of your people; and there shall be a time of trouble, such as never was since there was a nation, even to that time. And at that time your people shall be delivered, every one who is found written in the book" **(DANIEL 12:1).**

02 God's character is one of immense love. He desires only the best for all humanity. His actions are totally, only, and always loving. Love is not passive. At times it must be very active and deal with evil. What is the fate of those who have turned their backs on God's love and receive the mark of the beast?

"Then a third angel followed them, saying with a loud voice, 'If anyone worships the beast and his image, and receives his mark on his forehead or on his hand, he himself shall also drink of the wine of the wrath of God, which is poured out full strength into the cup of His indignation. He shall be tormented with fire and brimstone in the presence of the holy angels and in the presence of the Lamb' " **(REVELATION 14:9, 10).**

"Great Babylon was remembered before God, to give her the cup of the wine of the fierceness of His wrath" **(REVELATION 16:19).**

"In the hand of the LORD there is a cup, and the wine is red; it is fully mixed, and He pours it out; surely its dregs shall all the wicked of the earth drain and drink down" **(PSALM 75:8).**

03 How does the Bible define the "wrath of God, poured out full strength"? As we shall see from the passages below, God's wrath is not vindictive anger; it is righteous judgment.

"Then I [John] saw another sign in heaven, great and marvelous: seven angels having the seven last plagues, for in them the wrath of God is complete" **(REVELATION 15:1).**

"Then one of the four living creatures gave to the seven angels seven golden bowls full of the wrath of God" **(REVELATION 15:7).**

The seven last plagues, which contain "the wrath of God," do *not* fall on God's followers. They fall only upon those "who had the mark of the beast and those who worshiped his image" **(REVELATION 16:2).**

This situation is a perfect parallel to the situation long ago in Egypt when God sent ten plagues to punish Pharaoh and the Egyptians when they would not let His people go **(SEE EXODUS 7:16–12:30).** The first three plagues affected everyone in all the land of Egypt, but the *last seven plagues* affected only the Egyptians—not God's faithful people **(SEE, FOR EXAMPLE, EXODUS 8:20–24; 9:3–7; 9:18–26; 10:21–23; 11:57; 12:29, 30).**

The seven last plagues are part of the Tribulation of the last days, but obviously *God does not need to remove His people from this world in order to protect them* any more than He needed to remove the three faithful Hebrew children from the fiery furnace or Daniel from the lions' den to protect them!

Satan hates God and desires all men and women to receive the mark of the beast power rather than God's seal. When every person has chosen between the mark of the beast and the seal of God, the plagues will fall. All who knowingly give allegiance to the beast, accepting a human decree for a command of God, will receive the seven last plagues.

REVELATION 16:2–15 lists the first six plagues:

1. a grievous sore
2. a sea of blood
3. rivers and springs of waters turning to blood
4. the sun scorching people
5. darkness on seat of the beast
6. "the battle of that great day of God Almighty"

04 What remarkable end-time event follows the outpouring of these first six plagues?

"Behold, *I am coming* as a thief. Blessed is he who watches, and keeps his garments, lest he walk naked and they see his shame" **(REVELATION 16:15; EMPHASIS SUPPLIED).**

"Remember therefore how you have received and heard; hold fast and repent. Therefore if you will not watch, I will come upon you as a thief, and you will not know what hour I will come upon you" **(REVELATION 3:3).**

"Watch therefore, for you do not know what hour your Lord is coming. But know this, that if the master of the house had known what hour the thief would come, he would have watched and not allowed his house to be broken into. Therefore you also be ready, for the Son of Man is coming at an hour you do not expect" **(MATTHEW 24:42–44).**

"You yourselves know perfectly that the day of the Lord so comes as a thief in the night. For when they say, 'Peace and safety!' then sudden destruction comes upon them, as labor pains upon a pregnant woman. And they shall not escape. But you, brethren, are not in darkness, so that this Day should overtake you as a thief" **(1 THESSALONIANS 5:2–4).**

"But the day of the Lord will come as a thief in the night, in which the heavens will pass away with a great noise, and the elements will melt with fervent heat; both the earth and the works that are in it will be burned up" **(2 PETER 3:10).**

Please note what these last two Scripture texts make clear. It's not *the Lord* who comes as a thief; it's the *day* of the Lord, the *time* of His return, that sneaks up and surprises those who fail to watch. Paul explicitly states in **1 THESSALONIANS 5:1** that this passage deals with "the times and the seasons." He's discussing here not the *manner,* but the time of Christ's return. He's giving insight into *when* Christ will return, not *how.*

Notice the apostle Paul's clear statement: "The day of the Lord so comes as a thief in the night" **(1 THESSALONIANS 5:2).** Rules of elementary grammar dictate that the subject of the sentence is *day*—not *Lord*! And the words, "of the Lord," are simply a prepositional phrase used to identify which "day" is meant.

The apostle Peter puts it the same way in **2 PETER 3:10**: "The day of the Lord will come as a thief in the night." Here Peter agrees with Paul in saying that it's the *day* of the Lord that comes as unexpectedly as a thief to most people. But the *event itself,* when it happens, will be anything but secret! In fact, Peter's text eloquently disproves the idea that the coming of Jesus will be quiet like a thief entering a house. Peter says, "But the day of the Lord will come as a thief in the night; in the which the heavens shall pass away with *a great noise.*"

When the Japanese attacked Pearl Harbor and propelled the United States into World

War II, America was not expecting it. December 7, 1941, the "day of infamy," did sneak upon the country as a thief. But the attack itself was anything but secret; it was like "the shot heard round the world." In the same way, Jesus said that the *time* of His return is *top secret:* "Of that day and hour no one knows, not even the angels of heaven, but My Father only" **(MATTHEW 24:36).** But the momentous, awesome event itself will be breathtaking beyond all belief, a cataclysmic climax to human history that will be of dazzling majesty and unimaginable glory!

At the end time, the seven last plagues fall only on the wicked, while the righteous, still on earth, are protected. Jesus comes as a thief *after* the plagues, not before.

05 What promises of divine protection and hope does God give His people to give them courage during the time of the plagues?

"I will say of the LORD, 'He is my refuge and my fortress; my God, in Him I will trust.' Surely He shall deliver you from the snare of the fowler and from the perilous pestilence. He shall cover you with His feathers, and under His wings you shall take refuge; His truth shall be your shield and buckler. You shall not be afraid of the terror by night, nor of the arrow that flies by day, nor of the pestilence that walks in darkness, nor of the destruction that lays waste at noonday. A thousand may fall at your side, and ten thousand at your right hand; but it shall not come near you. Only with your eyes shall you look, and see the reward of the wicked. Because you have made the LORD, who is my refuge, even the Most High, your dwelling place, no evil shall befall you, nor shall any plague come near your dwelling" **(PSALM 91:2–10).**

"Seek the LORD, all you meek of the earth, who have upheld His justice. Seek righteousness, seek humility. It may be that you will be hidden in the day of the LORD's anger" **(ZEPHANIAH 2:3).**

"My people will dwell in a peaceful habitation, in secure dwellings, and in quiet resting places, though hail comes down on the forest, and the city is brought low in humiliation" **(ISAIAH 32:18, 19).**

06 How will God's people be fed during this time? What assurance does our Lord give that He will care for them?

"He will dwell on high; his place of defense will be the fortress of rocks; bread will be given him, his water will be sure" **(ISAIAH 33:16).**

God pledges His tender care to the one who loves Him. "Because he has set his love upon Me, therefore I will deliver him; I will set him on high, because he has known My name. He shall call upon Me, and I will answer him; I will be with him in trouble; I will deliver him and honor him" **(PSALM 91:14, 15).**

"Do not seek what you should eat or what you should drink, nor have an anxious mind. For all these things the nations of the world seek after, and your Father knows that you need these things. But seek the kingdom of God, and all these things shall be added to you. Do not fear, little flock, for it is your Father's good pleasure to give you the kingdom" **(LUKE 12:29–32).**

07 As the world falls apart around us with natural, political, and economic disasters on every hand, where will God's people find lasting security?

"God is our refuge and strength, a very present help in trouble. Therefore we will not fear, even though the earth be removed, and though the mountains be carried into the midst of the sea" **(PSALM 46:1, 2).**

"In the fear of the LORD there is strong confidence, and His children will have a place of refuge" **(PROVERBS 14:26).**

"The name of the LORD is a strong tower; the righteous run to it and are safe" **(PROVERBS 18:10).**

"The LORD is near to all who call upon Him, to all who call upon Him in truth. He will fulfill the desire of those who fear Him; He also will hear their cry and save them. The LORD preserves all who love Him, but all the wicked He will destroy" **(PSALM 145:18–20).**

08 What does the Bible call earth's last war? Who will fight in this final battle? Who will win? How will Satan attempt to unite all nations to destroy God's people?

"They are the spirits of devils, working miracles, which go forth unto the kings of the earth and of the whole world, to gather them to the battle of that great day of God Almighty" **(REVELATION 16:14, KJV).**

"The coming of the lawless one is according to the working of Satan, with all power, signs, and lying wonders, and with all unrighteous deception among those who perish, because they did not receive the love of the truth, that they might be saved" **(2 THESSALONIANS 2:9, 10).**

The devil used signs and wonders in an attempt to deceive Pharaoh, and he will use them in our day as well. His strategy is the same throughout the centuries. Notice the devil's cunning deceptions in the texts below.

The Lord God told Moses, "When Pharaoh speaks to you, saying, 'Show a miracle for yourselves,' then you shall say to Aaron, 'Take your rod and cast it before Pharaoh, and let it become a serpent.' So Moses and Aaron went in to Pharaoh, and they did so, just as the LORD commanded. And Aaron cast down his rod before Pharaoh and before his servants, and it became a serpent. But Pharaoh also called the wise men and the sorcerers; so the magicians of Egypt, they also did in like manner with their enchantments. For every man threw down his rod, and they became serpents. But Aaron's rod swallowed up their rods. And Pharaoh's heart grew hard, and he did not heed them, as the LORD had said" **(EXODUS 7:9–13).**

God cautions that we must beware. "If there arises among you a prophet or a dreamer of dreams, and he gives you a sign or a wonder, and the sign or the wonder comes to pass, of which he spoke to you, saying, 'Let us go after other gods'—which you have not known—'and let us serve them, you shall not listen to the words of that prophet' " **(DEUTERONOMY 13:1–3).**

Jesus warned, "False christs and false prophets will rise and show great signs and wonders to deceive, if possible, even the elect. See, I have told you beforehand" **(MATTHEW 24:24, 25).**

Of the lamblike beast, we read, "He doeth great wonders, so that he maketh fire come down from heaven on the earth in the sight of men, and deceiveth them that dwell on the earth by the means of those miracles which he had power to do in the sight of the beast; saying to them that dwell on the earth, that they should make an image to the beast, which had the wound by a sword, and did live" **(REVELATION 13:13, 14, KJV).**

God tells Babylon, "by your sorcery all the nations were deceived" **(REVELATION 18:23).**

"And they gathered them together to the place called in Hebrew, Armageddon" **(REVELATION 16:16).**

The word *Armageddon* comes from the Hebrew *Har Megiddo*, meaning "Mount Megiddo," or "Hill of Megiddo," or "mount of assembly." It was at Megiddo, during one of Israel's greatest crises when it appeared that doom was certain, that God intervened and sent reinforcements at precisely the right moment **(SEE JUDGES 5:19, 20).** During the last days of earth's history, infuriated by the plagues, the whole world will be turned into a vast battlefield as the wicked attempt to destroy God's people. It will appear as if their doom is certain.

The battle of Armageddon is the final conflict between good and evil. It is not limited to a single geographical location. It is a universal struggle. Satan marshals all of his evil forces to ruthlessly destroy God's commandment-keeping people wherever they may be found.

09 As the whole world unites against God's commandment-keeping people, what divine act climaxes all of history?

John the revelator reports: "Then the seventh angel poured out his bowl into the air, and a loud voice came out of the temple of heaven, from the throne, saying, 'It is done!' And there were noises and thunderings and lightnings; and there was *a great earthquake,* such a mighty and great earthquake as had not occurred since men were on the earth. Now the great city was divided into three parts, and the cities of the nations fell. And great Babylon was remembered before God, to give her the cup of the wine of the fierceness of His wrath. Then every island fled away, and the mountains were not found. And great hail from heaven fell upon men, each hailstone about the weight of a talent. Men blasphemed God because of the plague of the hail, since that plague was exceedingly great" **(REVELATION 16:17–21; EMPHASIS SUPPLIED).**

The earthquake will be horrendous, and the hail will be devastating. A Hebrew "talent" was a unit of weight or money equivalent to 3,000 shekels. Most authorities estimate the weight of the ancient talent as slightly over sixty-six pounds! Hailstones of that weight can pulverize a building! The earth will be left in ruins, but this is the seventh and final plague, so the Lord will be on His way to rescue His faithful people.

"Then the sky receded as a scroll when it is rolled up, and every mountain and island was moved out of its place" **(REVELATION 6:14).**

"The lofty looks of man shall be humbled, the haughtiness of men shall be bowed down, and the LORD alone shall be exalted in that day. . . . The loftiness of man shall be bowed down, and the haughtiness of men shall be brought low; the LORD alone will be exalted in that day, but the idols He shall utterly abolish. They shall go into the holes of the rocks, and into the caves of the earth, from the terror of the LORD and the glory of His majesty, when He arises to shake the earth mightily. In that day a man will cast away his idols of silver and his idols of gold, which they made, each for himself to worship, to the moles and bats, to go into the clefts of the rocks, and into the crags of the rugged rocks, from the terror of the LORD and the glory of His majesty, when He arises to shake the earth mightily" **(ISAIAH 2:11, 17–21).**

Once again God will intervene. When the enemy is ready to pounce on God's people, like a lion stalking her prey to destroy it, God will powerfully manifest His hand to deliver them.

10 What divine announcement does the seventh angel make at the close of time?

"Then the seventh angel poured out his bowl into the air, and a loud voice came out of the temple of heaven, from the throne, saying, 'It is done!' " **(REVELATION 16:17).**

"And He [Jesus Christ] said to me [John], 'It is done! I am the Alpha and the Omega, the Beginning and the End. I will give of the fountain of the water of life freely to him who thirsts' " **(REVELATION 21:6).**

"So when Jesus had received the sour wine, He said, 'It is finished!' And bowing His head, He gave up His spirit" **(JOHN 19:30).**

At Jesus' death, He stated, "It is finished." The plan of salvation was complete. A door of salvation was open for all. Once again the words, "It is finished," will echo throughout the universe. The Lord of both Creation and Redemption, who provided such a beautiful beginning in the Garden of Eden and provided ransom for the entire human race, now rescues us in triumph to provide a happy ending for a world caught in the grip of sin and death.

It is finished! Life's trials and heartaches are over. Now it is time for God to deliver His people.

In the last moments of time, Jesus returns as King of kings and Lord of lords and finally and completely destroys Satan and his work. Christ's followers triumph; right conquers.

" 'I will call for a sword against Gog throughout all My mountains,' says the Lord GOD. 'Every man's sword will be against his brother. And I will bring him to judgment with pestilence and bloodshed; I will rain down on him, on his troops, and on the many peoples who are with him, flooding rain, great hailstones, fire, and brimstone' " **(EZEKIEL 38:21, 22).**

"And men were scorched with great heat, and they blasphemed the name of God who has power over these plagues; and they did not repent and give Him glory" **(REVELATION 16:9).**

"They blasphemed the God of heaven because of their pains and their sores, and did not repent of their deeds" **(REVELATION 16:11).**

11 How does all of human history on this planet in rebellion come to one glorious, triumphant close?

"Now I saw heaven opened, and behold, a white horse. And He who sat on him was called Faithful and True, and in righteousness He judges and makes war. His eyes were like a flame of fire, and on His head were many crowns. He had a name written that no one knew except Himself. He was clothed with a robe dipped in blood, and His name is called The Word of God. And the armies in heaven, clothed in fine linen, white and clean, followed Him on white horses. Now out of His mouth goes a sharp sword, that with it He should strike the nations. And He Himself will rule them with a rod of iron. He Himself treads the winepress of the fierceness and wrath of Almighty God. And He has on His robe and on His thigh a name written: KING OF KINGS AND LORD OF LORDS" **(REVELATION 19:11–16).**

"And I [John] looked, and behold, a white horse. He who sat on it had a bow; and a crown was given to him, and he went out conquering and to conquer" **(REVELATION 6:2).**

"In the beginning was the Word, and the Word was with God, and the Word was God. . . . And the Word became flesh and dwelt among us, and we beheld His glory, the glory as of the only begotten of the Father, full of grace and truth" **(JOHN 1:1, 14).**

Like a protective "big brother," the Almighty God promises His people: "It is a righteous thing with God to repay with tribulation those who trouble you, and to give you who are troubled rest with us when the Lord Jesus is revealed from heaven with His mighty angels" **(2 THESSALONIANS 1:6, 7).**

Speaking of the pure woman who represents God's true church, John wrote: "To her it was granted to be arrayed in fine linen, clean and bright, for the fine linen is the righteous acts of the saints" **(REVELATION 19:8).**

"The rest [the wicked] were killed with the sword which proceeded from the mouth of Him who sat on the horse. And all the birds were filled with their flesh" **(REVELATION 19:21).**

Jesus came as a babe in Bethlehem, but now His appearance is awesome! "He had in His right hand seven stars, out of His mouth went a sharp two-edged sword, and His countenance was like the sun shining in its strength" **(REVELATION 1:16).**

The ten kings who give their power and authority to the beast "will make war with the Lamb, and the Lamb will overcome them, for He is Lord of lords and King of kings; and those who are with Him are called, chosen, and faithful" **(REVELATION 17:14).**

Of Jesus Christ it can be truly said, "Yes, all kings shall fall down before Him; all nations shall serve Him" **(PSALM 72:11).**

The God who is in complete control says, "By me kings reign, and rulers decree justice. By me princes rule, and nobles, all the judges of the earth" **(PROVERBS 8:15, 16).**

"King [Nebuchadnezzar] answered Daniel, and said, 'Truly your God is the God of gods, the Lord of kings, and a revealer of secrets, since you could reveal this secret' " **(DANIEL 2:47).**

Jesus Christ shall be *universally worshiped* by every being in all creation. "Therefore God also has highly exalted Him [Jesus] and given Him the name which is above every name, that at the name of Jesus every knee should bow, of those in heaven, and of those on earth, and of those under the earth, and that every tongue should confess that Jesus Christ is Lord, to the glory of God the Father" **(PHILIPPIANS 2:9–11).**

Paul speaks of our Lord Jesus Christ's appearing, "which He will manifest in His own time, He who is the blessed and only Potentate, the King of kings and Lord of lords" **(1 TIMOTHY 6:15).**

Friend, the outcome of the battle is certain. No matter how discouraging the future appears, Jesus and His people will triumph. If you have not yet decided to place your confidence in Jesus by inviting Him into your life, why not do it right now before it is forever too late?

CHAPTER 31

What the Bible Says About the Millennium

Many Christians are confused about the future. The prophecies of Revelation baffle them. They are perplexed by Revelation's mystic symbols, wild beasts, and mysterious images. In reality we need not be confused regarding the future. The book of Revelation begins with these words, "The Revelation of Jesus Christ . . ." **(REVELATION 1:1).** The same Jesus who inspired the apostle John to write Revelation unlocks its mysteries for each one of us. The Bible clearly explains the meaning of its own symbols. As we allow the Bible to explain itself, the picture becomes clear.

One of the most fascinating topics of the Bible is the millennium. The word *millennium* is not found in the Bible. It comes from two Latin words, *mille,* meaning "one thousand," and *annum,* meaning "year." There are many different ideas taught about this thousand-year period. Some people believe that the second coming of Christ will usher in a golden age of one thousand years for mankind on earth. Others believe that the thousand years will be a time of distress, hardship, chaos, and destruction.

A third view is that the millennium occurs after Christ returns and the righteous ascend to heaven. In this view, Satan and his angels are the only ones left on earth during the thousand years. At the end of the thousand years, the Holy City descends from heaven, the wicked are resurrected to fight against God and receive their final judgment, and evil is ultimately completely destroyed.

This chapter will reveal the real truth about the millennium as we let the Bible interpret itself and explain the meaning of its own symbols. So let's begin.

01 What marvelous promise do the Bible prophets give to the righteous who die before Jesus returns? What is the fate of the unsaved, or the wicked, when Christ returns?

"The Lord Himself will descend from heaven with a shout, with the voice of an archangel, and with the trumpet of God. And the *dead in Christ will rise first.* Then we [believers] who are *alive* and remain shall be caught up together with them in the clouds to meet the Lord in the air. And thus we shall always be with the Lord" **(1 THESSALONIANS 4:16, 17; EMPHASIS SUPPLIED).**

"But each one in his own order: Christ the firstfruits, afterward those who are Christ's [will rise to new life] at His coming" **(1 CORINTHIANS 15:23).**

"Behold, I tell you a mystery: We shall not all sleep [the sleep of death], but we shall all be changed—in a moment, in the twinkling of an eye, at the last trumpet. For the trumpet will sound, and the dead will be raised incorruptible, and we shall be changed. For this corruptible must put on incorruption, and this mortal must put on immortality. So when this corruptible has put on incorruption, and this mortal has put on immortality, then shall be brought to pass the saying that is written: 'Death is swallowed up in victory' " **(1 CORINTHIANS 15:51–54).**

"Blessed and holy is he who has part in the first resurrection. Over such the second death has no power, but they shall be priests of God and of Christ, and shall reign with Him a thousand years" **(REVELATION 20:6).**

"You will be blessed, because they cannot repay you; for you shall be repaid at the resurrection of the just" **(LUKE 14:14).**

Jesus said, "The hour is coming in which all who are in the graves will hear His voice and come forth—those who have done good, to the resurrection of life, and those who have done evil, to the resurrection of condemnation" **(JOHN 5:28, 29).**

"And many of those who sleep in the dust of the earth shall awake, some to everlasting life, some to shame and everlasting contempt" **(DANIEL 12:2).**

02 How many general resurrections does the Bible describe?

Jesus said, "The hour is coming in which all who are in the graves will hear His voice and come forth—those who have done good, to the resurrection of life, and those who have done evil, to the resurrection of condemnation" **(JOHN 5:28, 29).**

There are *two* separate and distinct resurrections of the dead—one for the righteous and one for the wicked. This comes as no surprise to Bible students familiar with the texts to that effect which are sprinkled throughout Scripture. The *first* resurrection raises to life God's faithful followers and occurs *at the second coming of Christ* and the beginning of the millennium. The second resurrection raises to life the lost who have rejected God's forgiveness, and this resurrection occurs *one thousand years later,* at the end of the millennium.

03 What is the eventual fate of the unsaved? What is their destiny?

"It is a righteous thing with God to repay with tribulation those who trouble you, and to give you who are troubled rest with us when the Lord Jesus is revealed from heaven with His mighty angels, in flaming fire taking vengeance on those who do not know God, and on those who do not obey the gospel of our Lord Jesus Christ. These shall be punished with everlasting destruction from the presence of the Lord and from the glory of His power, when He comes, in that Day, to be glorified in His saints and to be admired among all those who believe, because our testimony among you was believed" **(2 THESSALONIANS 1:6–10).**

"Then the lawless one will be revealed, whom the Lord will consume with the breath of His mouth and destroy with the brightness of His coming" **(2 THESSALONIANS 2:8).**

It's a theological fiction—one of many—that when the Lord comes to rapture His church the wicked will be left alive and that life on earth will go on for seven more years. The verses above show that the lawless wicked will be *consumed* by the breath of the Lord's mouth and *destroyed* by the brightness of His coming. Unredeemed sinners cannot survive in the presence of a holy God.

"For our God is a consuming fire" **(HEBREWS 12:29).**

"Our God shall come, and shall not keep silent; a fire shall devour before Him, and it shall be very tempestuous all around Him. He shall call to the heavens from above, and to the earth, that He may judge His people: 'Gather My saints together to Me, those who have made a covenant with Me by sacrifice' " **(PSALM 50:3–5).**

"For if we sin willfully after we have received the knowledge of the truth, there no longer remains a sacrifice for sins, but a certain fearful expectation of judgment, and fiery indignation which will devour the adversaries" **(HEBREWS 10:26, 27).**

"Of how much worse punishment, do you suppose, will he be thought worthy who has trampled the Son of God underfoot, counted the blood of the covenant by which he was sanctified a common thing, and insulted the Spirit of grace?" **(HEBREWS 10:29).**

"The heavens and the earth which are now preserved by the same word, are reserved for fire until the day of judgment and perdition of ungodly men" **(2 PETER 3:7).**

"But the day of the Lord will come as a thief in the night, in which the heavens will pass away with a great noise, and the elements will melt with fervent heat; both the earth and the works that are in it will be burned up. Therefore, since all these things will be dissolved, what manner of persons ought you to be in holy conduct and godliness, looking for and hastening the coming of the day of God, because of which the heavens will be dissolved, being on fire, and the elements will melt with fervent heat?" **(2 PETER 3:10–12).**

"Then the sky receded as a scroll when it is rolled up, and every mountain and island was moved out of its place. And the kings of the earth, the great men, the rich men, the commanders, the mighty men, every slave and every free man, hid themselves in the caves and in the rocks of the mountains, and said to the mountains and rocks, 'Fall on us and hide us from the face of Him who sits on the throne and from the wrath of the Lamb! For the great day of His wrath has come, and who is able to stand?' " **(REVELATION 6:14–17).**

Of the wicked lost, we read: "He himself shall also drink of the wine of the wrath of God, which is poured out full strength into the cup of His indignation. He shall be tormented with fire and brimstone in the presence of the holy angels and in the presence of the Lamb" **(REVELATION 14:10).**

04 In REVELATION 20, the Bible describes what some Bible scholars call the millennium, which simply means "one thousand years." Where will Satan be during this thousand-year time period?

"Then I [John] saw an angel coming down from heaven, having the key to the *bottomless pit* and a great chain in his hand. He laid hold of the dragon, that serpent of old, who is the Devil and Satan, and bound him for a thousand years; and he cast him into *the bottomless pit,* and shut him up, and set a seal on him, so that he should deceive the nations no more till the thousand years were finished. But after these things he must be released for a little while" **(REVELATION 20:1–3; EMPHASIS SUPPLIED).**

"Now when the thousand years have expired, Satan will be released from his prison" **(REVELATION 20:7).**

What does all this mean? This passage comes into sharp focus if we clarify two key terms: (1) the "great chain" that binds Satan and (2) "the bottomless pit" that forms the "prison" where he spends the thousand years. Can these things be literal? Will Satan literally be bound with a chain in a bottomless pit for a thousand years?

The devil himself is certainly real and literal enough. Jesus said, "I saw Satan fall like lightning from heaven" **(LUKE 10:18).** But the dazzling angel Lucifer, who made himself into the devil called Satan, is a supernatural being. As Paul put it: "We do not wrestle against flesh and blood, but against principalities, against powers, against the rulers of the darkness of this age, against spiritual hosts of wickedness in the heavenly places" **(EPHESIANS 6:12).**

Simple reason tells us that no actual, literal "chain" or "pit" or "prison" could secure a supernatural being. More importantly, Sacred Scripture tells us the same thing. You may recall Christ's experience one day after sailing across the Sea of Galilee:

"Then they [Jesus and His disciples] came to the other side of the sea [of Galilee], to the country of the Gadarenes. And when He had come out of the boat, immediately there met Him out of the tombs a man with an unclean spirit [a devil or demon], who had his dwelling among the tombs; and no one could bind him, not even with chains, because he had often been bound with shackles and chains. And the chains had been pulled apart by him, and the shackles broken in pieces; neither could anyone tame him" **(MARK 5:1–4).**

Now ask yourself if a devil-possessed *man* can easily break asunder a chain with superhuman strength, is it likely that the prince of devils himself could be bound with one? So what kind of "chain" is it that God uses to effectively bind Satan?

It's a chain of circumstances which binds the devil more securely than any literal chain ever forged. Note the circumstances in which Satan finds himself at this point in the stream of time. In the first place, all the righteous have been taken to heaven. And they were unwilling to listen to his temptations anyway. All the wicked have been struck dead. Thus the entire earth is de-populated, with no one left for Satan to tempt!

The term "bottomless pit" is identical in meaning to the description, "without form and void," of **JEREMIAH 4:23**. These terms also parallel the description of the world at the beginning of Creation—a place of desolation and darkness. These parallels clearly show that Satan is bound to the uninhabited earth, unable to tempt anyone. The Bible uses the term "chains" not as literal chains, but as chains of darkness and circumstances.

"For if God did not spare the angels who sinned, but cast them down to Hell and delivered them into chains of darkness, to be reserved for judgment" **(2 PETER 2:4).**

The word *hell* in this verse is translated from the Greek word *tartaros,* which means simply "a dark abyss." This is the only use of *tartaros* in the entire Bible, and nothing in this Greek word even implies a place of fire or burning. Like **JUDE 6,** quoted here afterward, this verse speaks not of fire, but of "chains of darkness" and says judgment is "reserved" or future.

"The angels who did not keep their proper domain, but left their own abode, He [God] has reserved in everlasting chains under darkness for the judgment of the great day" **(JUDE 6).**

05 Where are the wicked, or unsaved, during this thousand-year period?

"At that day [of Christ's second coming] the slain of the LORD shall be from one end of the earth even to the other end of the earth. They shall not be lamented, or gathered, or buried; they shall become refuse ["dung," KJV] on the ground" **(JEREMIAH 25:33).**

"The slain of the Lord" are all of the wicked who are alive when Christ returns. They're struck dead by the brightness of His coming, and their bodies litter the entire earth. But usually when people die, they're lamented by survivors who care about them. Dead bodies are always gathered from the site of an accident or other tragedy. And of course they're buried out of respect and for sanitary reasons. So why does inspiration say *none* of these things will be true in the day of this worldwide, wholesale slaughter? Simply because *there are no survivors around* to do any of these things! For all the righteous are raptured to heaven at Christ's second coming, and all the wicked perish to the very last person.

The prophet Isaiah echoes Jeremiah's thought with this promise to believers:

"Your dead shall live; together with my dead body they shall arise. Awake and sing, you who dwell in dust. . . . For behold, the LORD comes out of His place to punish the inhabitants of the earth for their iniquity; the earth . . . will no more cover her slain" **(ISAIAH 26:19, 21).**

"Behold, the LORD makes the earth empty and makes it waste. . . . The land shall be entirely emptied . . . for the LORD has spoken this word" **(ISAIAH 24:1, 3).**

"They shall spread them before the sun and the moon and all the host of heaven, which they have loved and which they have served and after which they have walked, which they have sought and which they have worshiped. They shall not be gathered nor buried; they shall be like refuse on the face of the earth" **(JEREMIAH 8:2).**

"They shall die gruesome deaths; they shall not be lamented nor shall they be buried, but they shall be like refuse on the face of the earth. They shall be consumed by the sword and by famine, and their corpses shall be meat for the birds of heaven and for the beasts of the earth" **(JEREMIAH 16:4).**

The Old Testament prophets often described conditions that would occur as the result of Israel's rebellion against God. As the result of disobedience, God would allow heathen armies to destroy thousands of Israelites. However, Jeremiah's prophecy goes far beyond ancient Israel. It reaches into the future. It describes a universal destruction from one end of the earth to the other of those who rebel against God.

06 This thousand-year period begins at the second coming of Christ. What is the condition of the earth during the millennium?

"Then the seventh angel poured out his bowl into the air, and a loud voice came out of the temple of heaven, from the throne, saying, 'It is done!' And there were noises and thunderings and lightnings; and there was a great earthquake, such a mighty and great earthquake as had not occurred since men were on the earth. Now the great city was divided into three parts, and the cities of the nations fell. And great Babylon was remembered before God, to give her the cup of the wine of the fierceness of His wrath. Then every island fled away, and the mountains were not found" **(REVELATION 16:17–20).**

"I beheld the earth, and indeed it was without form, and void; and the heavens, they had no light. I beheld the mountains, and indeed they trembled, and all the hills moved back and forth. I beheld, and indeed there was no man, and all the birds of the heavens had fled. I beheld, and indeed the fruitful land was a wilderness, and all its cities were broken down at the presence of the LORD, by His fierce anger. For thus says the LORD: 'The whole land shall be desolate; yet I will not make a full end' " **(JEREMIAH 4:23–27).**

Jeremiah's prediction fitly describes Israel's destruction at the hand of the Babylonians. As the language of the passage clearly portrays, it also describes the complete devastation of earth at the second coming of Christ.

"And there were lightnings, noises, thunderings, an earthquake, and great hail" **(REVELATION 11:19).**

"The LORD will cause His glorious voice to be heard, and show the descent of His arm, with the indignation of His anger and the flame of a devouring fire, with scattering, tempest, and hailstones" **(ISAIAH 30:30).**

"Then the sky receded as a scroll when it is rolled up, and every mountain and island was moved out of its place" **(REVELATION 6:14).**

"And the foundations of the earth are shaken. The earth is violently broken, the earth is split open, the earth is shaken exceedingly. The earth shall reel to and fro like a drunkard, and shall totter like a hut; its transgression shall be heavy upon it, and it will fall, and not rise again. It shall come to pass in that day that the LORD will punish on high the host of exalted ones, and on the earth the kings of the earth" **(ISAIAH 24:18–21).**

07 How many people will be alive on earth during this time? Will there be people living on earth during the millennium?

"Then I saw an angel standing in the sun; and he cried with a loud voice, saying to all the birds that fly in the midst of heaven, 'Come and gather together for the supper of the great God, that you may eat the flesh of kings, the flesh of captains, the flesh of mighty men, the flesh of horses and of those who sit on them, and the flesh of all people, free and slave, both small and great' " **(REVELATION 19:17, 18).**

"And the rest were killed with the sword which proceeded from the mouth of Him [the returning Jesus] who sat on the horse. And all the birds were filled with their flesh" **(REVELATION 19:21).**

The sword is obviously figurative, yet very real. Most Bible scholars feel, on the basis of the following texts, that the "sword" which proceeds from Jesus' mouth is the Word of God.

- **EPHESIANS 6:17.** Paul speaks of "the sword of the Spirit, which is the word of God."
- **HEBREWS 4:12.** "The word of God is living and powerful, and sharper than any two-edged sword."
- **REVELATION 1:16.** "Out of His [Christ's] mouth went a sharp two-edged sword."
- **ISAIAH 11:4.** "With the breath of His lips He shall slay the wicked."
- **2 THESSALONIANS 2:8.** "Then the lawless one will be revealed, whom the Lord will consume with the breath of His mouth and destroy with the brightness of His coming."

"At that day the slain of the LORD shall be from one end of the earth even to the other end of the earth. They shall not be lamented, or gathered, or buried; they shall become refuse on the ground" **(JEREMIAH 25:33).**

"Behold, the LORD makes the earth empty and makes it waste, distorts its surface and scatters abroad its inhabitants. And it shall be: as with the people, so with the priest; as with the servant, so with his master; as with the maid, so with her mistress; as with the buyer, so with the seller; as with the lender, so with the borrower; as with the creditor, so with the debtor. The land shall be entirely emptied and utterly plundered, for the LORD has spoken this word" **(ISAIAH 24:1–3).**

All the redeemed—both those resurrected from death and those living when Jesus returns—have been taken to heaven by Jesus at His second coming. And all of the living wicked have been struck dead. So not one living person remains on the earth.

08 When Christ returns at the beginning of this thousand-year period, will He set up His kingdom on earth? Where will He take the redeemed?

Jesus told His disciples, "Let not your heart be troubled; you believe in God, believe also in Me. In My Father's house are many mansions; if it were not so, I would have told you. I go to prepare a place for you. And if I go and prepare a place for you, I will come again and receive you to Myself; that where I am, there you may be also" **(JOHN 14:1–3).**

"If anyone serves Me, let him follow Me; and where I am, there My servant will be also. If anyone serves Me, him My Father will honor" **(JOHN 12:26).**

"Father, I desire that they also whom You gave Me may be with Me where I am, that they may behold My glory which You have given Me; for You loved Me before the foundation of the world" **(JOHN 17:24).**

"Then we who are alive and remain shall be caught up together with them in the clouds to meet the Lord in the air. And thus we shall always be with the Lord" **(1 THESSALONIANS 4:17).**

During the millennium, the righteous have an opportunity to observe firsthand the justice and love of God in dealing with the sin problem. In a new way, more forcefully than ever before, they grasp His powerful attempts to save all people. They realize anew that all who are lost are lost because of their own personal rejection of the appeals of Christ.

09 If the righteous dead are resurrected and receive immortal bodies at the return of our Lord and are translated to heaven along with the righteous living, what will all the righteous be doing during the thousand years in heaven?

"I [John] saw thrones, and they [the redeemed saints] sat on them, *and judgment was committed to them*. Then I saw the souls of those who had been beheaded for their witness to Jesus and for the word of God, who had not worshiped the beast or his image, and had not received his mark on their foreheads or on their hands. *And they lived and reigned with Christ for a thousand years"* **(REVELATION 20:4; EMPHASIS SUPPLIED).**

"Dare any of you, having a matter against another, go to law before the unrighteous, and not before the saints? Do you not know that the saints will judge the world? And if the world will be judged by you, are you unworthy to judge the smallest matters? Do you not know that we shall judge angels [fallen angels who followed Satan and became devils]? How much more, things that pertain to this life?" **(1 CORINTHIANS 6:1–3).**

"Jesus said to them, 'Assuredly I say to you, that in the regeneration, when the Son of Man sits on the throne of His glory, you who have followed Me will also sit on twelve thrones, judging the twelve tribes of Israel" **(MATTHEW 19:28).**

Jesus promised "that you may eat and drink at My table in My kingdom, and sit on thrones judging the twelve tribes of Israel" **(LUKE 22:30).**

"If we endure, we shall also reign with Him. If we deny Him, He also will deny us" **(2 TIMOTHY 2:12).**

"God did not spare the angels who sinned, but cast them down to hell and delivered them into chains of darkness, to be reserved for judgment" **(2 PETER 2:4).**

10 When will the final resurrection of the wicked take place? When do they receive their final reward?

"But the rest of the dead [the wicked] did not live again until the thousand years were finished. This is the first resurrection. Blessed and holy is he who has part in the first resurrection. Over such the second death has no power" **(REVELATION 20:5, 6).**

Something about this verse makes it a bit confusing. Let's look at it more closely. Have you ever been chatting with a friend, mentioning topics A, B, C, and then as you begin talking about topic D, you suddenly remember something you want to add about topic C? We all do that at times. And John the revelator did it here in **REVELATION 20.** In **VERSE 4,** John is discussing the *redeemed.* He mentions how "they came to life, and reigned with Christ a thousand years" **(REVELATION 20:4, RSV).** Then, in contrast to the redeemed, he mentions a new topic, the *wicked,* and says, "But the rest of the dead [the wicked] did not live again until the thousand years were finished" **(REVELATION 20:5).** So far, so good.

But after having brought into discussion this new topic of the wicked, John suddenly thinks of *one or two more* remarks he wishes to make about the *redeemed,* so he adds in reference to them: "This is the first resurrection. Blessed and holy is the one who has a part in the first resurrection; over these the second death has no power, but they will be priests of God and of Christ and will reign with Him for a thousand years" **(REVELATION 20:5, 6, NASB).**

In other words, John's brief statement that "the rest of the dead [those who do *not* "come to life and reign with Christ a thousand years," those who are *not* "blessed and holy"] did not live again until the thousand years were finished" was *inserted parenthetically* into his larger discussion of the redeemed. And modern Bible versions often print it that way for the sake of clarification. Please note how some modern Bible versions have phrased **REVELATION 20:4–6.**

- "They came to life and reigned with Christ a thousand years. (The rest of the dead did not come to life until the thousand years were ended.) This is the first resurrection. Blessed and holy are those who share in the first resurrection" **(NRSV).**
- "They came to life and reigned with Christ for a thousand years. (The rest of the dead did not come to life until the thousand years were ended.) This is the first resurrection. Blessed and holy are those who share in the first resurrection" **(NIV).**
- "They came to life and reigned with Christ for a thousand years. (The rest of the dead did not come to life until the thousand years were over.) This is the first resurrection. Happy and holy is the one who shares in the first resurrection!" **(PHILLIPS).**
- "They came to life and ruled as kings with Christ for a thousand years. (The rest of the dead did not come to life until the thousand years were over.) This is the first raising of the dead. Happy and greatly blessed are those who are included in this first raising of the dead" **(TEV).**

11 The devil senses that it is his last chance for world control. After the millennium, rather than repent he is further hardened in his evil ways. His devious mind and rebellious heart have one object—to dominate the world by casting Christ off His throne. What events unfold at the end of the thousand years?

"Now when the thousand years have expired, Satan will be released from his prison and will go out to deceive the nations [that is, all the resurrected wicked from all ages] which are in the four corners of the earth, Gog and Magog, to gather them together to battle, whose number is as the sand of the sea. They went up on the breadth of the earth and surrounded the camp of the saints and the beloved city" **(REVELATION 20:7–9).**

Satan will be bound for a thousand years because he'll have no one to tempt, with all the redeemed beyond his reach in heaven and all the wicked dead upon the earth. But **REVELATION 20:5** tells us that the wicked will live again when the thousand years are finished.

This change in circumstances—this second resurrection—will release Satan from his divinely imposed prison.

With the resurrection of the wicked, the great deceiver will have the rebels of all time at his disposal. Satan rallies his troops and urges them to surround and attack the Holy City. He builds their confidence with the thought that their wicked forces far outnumber the righteous within the city. He's right about that, but do you suppose God will allow them to attack or even vanquish "the beloved city"? Absolutely not!

12 From where does the Holy City—New Jerusalem—descend?

"Then I, John, saw the holy city, New Jerusalem, coming down out of heaven from God, prepared as a bride adorned for her husband" **(REVELATION 21:2).**

"And he [the angel] carried me away in the Spirit to a great and high mountain, and showed me the great city, the holy Jerusalem, descending out of heaven from God" **(REVELATION 21:10).**

"He who overcomes, I will make him a pillar in the temple of My God, and he shall go out no more. And I will write on him the name of My God and the name of the city of My God, the New Jerusalem, which comes down out of heaven from My God. And I will write on him My new name" **(REVELATION 3:12).**

"This Hagar is Mount Sinai in Arabia, and corresponds to Jerusalem which now is, and is in bondage with her children—but the Jerusalem above is free, which is the mother of us all" **(GALATIANS 4:25, 26).**

"He [Abraham] waited for the city which has foundations, whose builder and maker is God" **(HEBREWS 11:10).**

"But you have come to Mount Zion and to the city of the living God, the heavenly Jerusalem, to an innumerable company of angels" **(HEBREWS 12:22).**

"Here we have no continuing city, but we seek the one to come" **(HEBREWS 13:14).**

13 As Satan mobilizes his forces to attack the Holy City, how does God prevent him from doing so? What is the ultimate fate of Satan and all his followers?

"They [the armies of the resurrected wicked] went up on the breadth of the earth and surrounded the camp of the saints and the beloved city. And fire came down from God out of heaven and devoured them" **(REVELATION 20:9).**

If a boy devours a candy bar, he eats it up till there's nothing left; it's all gone. That's what God's Word says this fire does to all the wicked of all time.

"Then the LORD rained brimstone and fire on Sodom and Gomorrah, from the LORD out of the heavens" **(GENESIS 19:24).**

"So fire went out from the LORD and devoured them, and they died before the LORD" **(LEVITICUS 10:2).**

"And a fire came out from the LORD and consumed the two hundred and fifty men who were offering incense" **(NUMBERS 16:35).**

"A fire goes before Him, and burns up His enemies round about" **(PSALM 97:3).**

"Our God is a consuming fire" **(HEBREWS 12:29).**

"But the wicked shall perish: and the enemies of the LORD like the splendor of the meadows, shall vanish. Into smoke they shall vanish away" **(PSALM 37:20).**

"A fire was kindled in their company; the flame burned up the wicked" **(PSALM 106:18).**

"On the day that Lot went out of Sodom it rained fire and brimstone from heaven and destroyed them all" **(LUKE 17:29).**

Paul speaks of "flaming fire taking vengeance on those who do not know God, and on those who do not obey the gospel of our Lord Jesus Christ" **(2 THESSALONIANS 1:8).**

14 Once Satan and the wicked are destroyed, what does God do to this world?

"Nevertheless we, according to His promise, look for new heavens and a new earth in which righteousness dwells" **(2 PETER 3:13).**

"Behold, I create new heavens and a new earth; and the former shall not be remembered or come to mind" **(ISAIAH 65:17).**

" 'As the new heavens and the new earth which I will make shall remain before Me,' says the LORD, 'so shall your descendants and your name remain. And it shall come to pass that from one New Moon to another, and from one Sabbath to another, all flesh shall come to worship before Me,' says the LORD" **(ISAIAH 66:22, 23).**

"Now I saw a new heaven and a new earth, for the first heaven and the first earth had passed away. Also there was no more sea" **(REVELATION 21:1).**

"But there shall by no means enter it [the holy city, New Jerusalem] anything that defiles, or causes an abomination or a lie, but only those who are written in the Lamb's Book of Life" **(REVELATION 21:27).**

The great challenge of the millennium is that men and women must choose today where they will spend eternity. There is no second chance after Jesus comes. The Bible clearly states, "Behold, now is the accepted time; behold, now is that day of salvation" **(2 CORINTHIANS 6:2).** Thousands will be lost because they are looking forward to a future time to make a decision for Jesus Christ. Jesus invites you to give Him your whole life today. If you have not done so, why not do it now?

CHAPTER 32

What the Bible Says About Heaven

God's plans for us are more amazing than we can possibly imagine. His ultimate goal for this planet in rebellion is beyond our comprehension. His dream for us is far beyond our wildest imagination. Whatever you imagine heaven to be like, the reality is more magnificent, more beautiful, more glorious.

In this chapter, we will discover the destiny of the redeemed in the earth made new. In **2 PETER 3:13,** we read, "We, according to His promise, look for new heavens and a new earth in which righteousness dwells." Jesus said, "The meek . . . shall inherit the earth" **(MATTHEW 5:5).**

When the earth came forth from the hand of the Creator, it was beautiful beyond description. God will eventually destroy sin and sinners and restore earth to its Edenic splendor.

In His Word, God has given us a preview of the glories of the new earth as an appetizer to create within us the desire to be there, but He has not answered every question we might have on the subject. We do well to remember Paul's words: "Eye has not seen, nor ear heard, nor have entered into the heart of man the things which God has prepared for those who love Him" **(1 CORINTHIANS 2:9)**.

Although we cannot understand everything about heaven, we can find answers to some of our most fundamental questions directly from the Bible.

01 This world belongs to Christ by virtue of creation and redemption. Our Creator and Redeemer is our coming King. Christians need not fear the future, because we know the final outcome of history. History is really "His Story." How will the great controversy between good and evil end?

"Then the seventh angel sounded: And there were loud voices in heaven, saying, 'The kingdoms of this world have become the kingdoms of our Lord and of His Christ, and He shall reign forever and ever!' " **(REVELATION 11:15)**.

"Who shall not fear You, O Lord, and glorify Your name? For You alone are holy. For all nations shall come and worship before You, for Your judgments have been manifested" **(REVELATION 15:4)**.

"All the ends of the world shall remember and turn to the LORD, and all the families of the nations shall worship before You. For the kingdom is the LORD's, and He rules over the nations" **(PSALM 22:27, 28)**.

"Yes, all kings shall fall down before Him; all nations shall serve Him" **(PSALM 72:11)**.

"All nations whom You have made shall come and worship before You, O Lord, and shall glorify Your name" **(PSALM 86:9)**.

"It shall come to pass in the latter days that the mountain of the LORD's house shall be established on the top of the mountains, and shall be exalted above the hills; and all nations shall flow to it" **(ISAIAH 2:2)**.

"Thus says the Lord GOD: 'Behold, I will lift My hand in an oath to the nations, and set up My standard for the peoples; they shall bring your sons in their arms, and your daughters shall be carried on their shoulders; kings shall be your foster fathers, and their queens your nursing mothers; they shall bow down to you with their faces to the earth, and lick up the dust of your feet. Then you will know that I am the LORD, for they shall not be ashamed who wait for Me' " **(ISAIAH 49:22, 23)**.

"In the days of these kings [the nations of Western Europe] the God of heaven will set up a kingdom which shall never be destroyed; and the kingdom shall not be left to other people; it shall break in pieces and consume all these kingdoms, and it shall stand forever. Inasmuch as you saw that the stone was cut out of the mountain without hands, and that it broke in pieces the iron, the bronze, the clay, the silver, and the gold—the great God has made known to the king what will come to pass after this. The dream is certain, and its interpretation is sure" **(DANIEL 2:44, 45).**

"Then to Him [Jesus] was given dominion and glory and a kingdom, that all peoples, nations, and languages should serve Him. His dominion is an everlasting dominion, which shall not pass away, and His kingdom the one which shall not be destroyed. . . . But the saints of the Most High shall receive the kingdom, and possess the kingdom forever, even forever and ever" **(DANIEL 7:14, 18).**

Daniel watched "until the Ancient of Days came, and a judgment was made in favor of the saints of the Most High, and the time came for the saints to possess the kingdom. . . . Then the kingdom and dominion, and the greatness of the kingdoms under the whole heaven, shall be given to the people, the saints of the Most High. His kingdom is an everlasting kingdom, and all dominions shall serve and obey Him" **(DANIEL 7:22, 27).**

"And the LORD shall be King over all the earth. In that day it shall be—'The LORD is one,' and His name one" **(ZECHARIAH 14:9).**

02 What title does the Bible give Jesus—the Ruler of this new heaven and earth?

"These [the ten kings who ally themselves with the beast power] will make war with the Lamb [Jesus], and the Lamb will overcome them, for He is Lord of lords and King of kings; and those who are with Him are called, chosen, and faithful" **(REVELATION 17:14).**

"And He has on His robe and on His thigh a name written: KING OF KINGS AND LORD OF LORDS" **(REVELATION 19:16).**

"Yes, all kings shall fall down before Him; all nations shall serve Him" **(PSALM 72:11).**

"The king [Nebuchadnezzar] answered Daniel, and said, 'Truly your God is the God of gods, the Lord of kings, and a revealer of secrets, since you could reveal this secret' " **(DANIEL 2:47).**

"Therefore God also has highly exalted Him [Jesus] and given Him the name which is above every name, that at the name of Jesus every knee should bow, of those in heaven, and of those on earth, and of those under the earth, and that every tongue should confess that Jesus Christ is Lord, to the glory of God the Father" **(PHILIPPIANS 2:9–11).**

Paul speaks of the appearing of our Lord Jesus Christ, "which He will manifest in His own time, He who is the blessed and only Potentate, the King of kings and Lord of lords" **(1 TIMOTHY 6:15).**

03 In one of the most magnificent visions in the entire Bible, John saw the Holy City descending from heaven. An angelic being with a great voice announces the transfer of Christ's capital. When Jesus reigns as the King of planet Earth, where will His capital city, New Jerusalem, be located?

"Then I, John, saw the holy city, New Jerusalem, coming down out of heaven from God, prepared as a bride adorned for her husband. And I heard a loud voice from heaven saying, 'Behold, the tabernacle of God is with men, and He will dwell with them, and they shall be His people. God Himself will be with them and be their God' " **(REVELATION 21:2, 3).**

"Therefore they [the redeemed] are before the throne of God, and serve Him day and night in His temple. And He who sits on the throne will dwell among them" **(REVELATION 7:15).**

"I will set My tabernacle among you, and My soul shall not abhor you. I will walk among you and be your God, and you shall be My people" **(LEVITICUS 26:11, 12).**

"Jesus answered and said to him, 'If anyone loves Me, he will keep My word; and My Father will love him, and We will come to him and make Our home with him" **(JOHN 14:23).**

04 What are the dimensions of this fantastic city? What is it like?

"The city is laid out as a square; its length is as great as its breadth. And he measured the city with the reed: twelve thousand furlongs. Its length, breadth, and height are equal. Then he measured its wall: one hundred and forty-four cubits, according to the measure of a man, that is, of an angel. The construction of its wall was of jasper; and the city was pure gold, like clear glass. The foundations of the wall of the city were adorned with all kinds of precious stones: the first foundation was jasper, the second sapphire, the third chalcedony, the fourth emerald, the fifth sardonyx, the sixth sardius, the seventh chrysolite, the eighth beryl, the ninth topaz, the tenth chrysoprase, the eleventh jacinth, and the twelfth amethyst. The twelve gates were twelve pearls: each individual gate was of one pearl. And the street of the city was pure gold, like transparent glass" **(REVELATION 21:16–21).**

A furlong is about one-eighth of a mile. Thus, the city is about fourteen hundred miles in circumference, or 345 miles on each side. A cubit is approximately eighteen inches. This would make the walls of the New Jerusalem approximately 210 feet high. This fantastic city, the capital of the universe, will descend to earth. The redeemed planet, once fallen in sin, will become the master control center of the entire universe.

Everything about this magnificent city will be superlatively glorious, beyond all comparison with anything else ever seen on earth. Jesus will lead the redeemed to the gate of the golden city, and His own nail-scarred hand will lay hold of the gate, swing it back on its glittering hinges, and bid us enter in. O matchless love!

05 Since the New Jerusalem is a real city, upon a real planet, will the redeemed have real, immortal bodies?

Paul speaks of Christ, "who will transform our lowly body that it may be conformed to His glorious body, according to the working by which He is able even to subdue all things to Himself" **(PHILIPPIANS 3:21).**

Jesus was recognizable in His glorious immortal body after the Resurrection. Mary recognized His voice at the tomb; the disciples recognized His physical features when He appeared in the upper room; His followers on the Emmaus road eventually recognized His unique mannerisms. We, too, will recognize one another in heaven even in our new immortal bodies. God longs to save *you*—not some unrecognizable, disembodied spirit. He will preserve your unique identity throughout the ages of eternity.

"Behold, I tell you a mystery: We shall not all sleep, but we shall all be changed—in a moment, in the twinkling of an eye, at the last trumpet. For the trumpet will sound, and the dead will be raised incorruptible, and we shall be changed. For this corruptible must put on incorruption, and this mortal must put on immortality. So when this corruptible has put on incorruption, and this mortal has put on immortality, then shall be brought to pass the saying that is written: 'Death is swallowed up in victory' " **(1 CORINTHIANS 15:51–54).**

"Beloved, now we are children of God; and it has not yet been revealed what we shall be, but we know that when He is revealed, we shall be like Him, for we shall see Him as He is" **(1 JOHN 3:2).**

"Thomas, called the Twin, one of the twelve, was not with them when Jesus came. The other disciples therefore said to him, 'We have seen the Lord.' So he said to them, 'Unless I see in His hands the print of the nails, and put my finger into the print of the nails, and put my hand into His side, I will not believe.' . . . Then He [Jesus] said to Thomas, 'Reach your finger here, and look at My hands; and reach your hand here, and put it into My side. Do not be unbelieving, but believing' " **(JOHN 20:24, 25, 27).**

"As they said these things, Jesus Himself stood in the midst of them, and said to them, 'Peace to you.' But they were terrified and frightened, and supposed they had seen a spirit. And He said to them, 'Why are you troubled? And why do doubts arise in your hearts? Behold My hands and My feet, that it is I Myself. Handle Me and see, for a spirit does not have flesh and bones as you see I have.' When He had said this, He showed them His hands and His feet. But while they still did not believe for joy, and marveled, He said to them, 'Have you any food here?' So they gave Him a piece of a broiled fish and some honeycomb. And He took it and ate in their presence" **(LUKE 24:36–43).**

Job had faith! "For I know that my Redeemer lives, and He shall stand at last on the earth; and after my skin is destroyed, this I know, that in my flesh I shall see God, whom I shall see for myself, and my eyes shall behold, and not another" **(JOB 19:25–27).**

"In this [earthly body] we groan, earnestly desiring to be clothed with our habitation which is from heaven, if indeed, having been clothed, we shall not be found naked. For we who are in this tent groan, being burdened, not because we want to be unclothed, but further clothed, that mortality may be swallowed up by life" **(2 CORINTHIANS 5:2–4).**

"We who live are always delivered to death for Jesus' sake, that the life of Jesus also may be manifested in our mortal flesh" **(2 CORINTHIANS 4:11).**

"If the Spirit of Him who raised Jesus from the dead dwells in you, He who raised Christ from the dead will also give life to your mortal bodies through His Spirit who dwells in you" **(ROMANS 8:11).**

The word *mortal* means subject to disease, decay, and death. The word *immortal* means not subject to death. It means imperishable or eternal. Just as Jesus received a glorious, immortal body at His resurrection, we, too, will receive a glorious, immortal body when Jesus comes again. Just as Jesus was recognized by His voice, His unique mannerisms, and physical features, so we will recognize our loved ones in heaven.

06 What will these immortal bodies be like? Will they be subject to sickness, pain, or death?

"God will wipe away every tear from their eyes; there shall be no more death, nor sorrow, nor crying. There shall be no more pain, for the former things have passed away" **(REVELATION 21:4).**

"Then the eyes of the blind shall be opened, and the ears of the deaf shall be unstopped. Then the lame shall leap like a deer, and the tongue of the dumb sing. For waters shall burst forth in the wilderness, and streams in the desert" **(ISAIAH 35:5–7).**

"And the inhabitant shall not say 'I am sick'; the people who dwell in it will be forgiven their iniquity" **(ISAIAH 33:24).**

Will the new earth be a place of idle euphoria? Will our minds and bodies remain active throughout the ceaseless ages of eternity? How will we keep from getting bored?

"For behold, I create a new heavens and a new earth; and the former shall not be remembered or come to mind. But be glad and rejoice forever in what I create" **(ISAIAH 65:17, 18).**

"They shall build houses and inhabit them; they shall plant vineyards and eat their fruit. They shall not build and another inhabit; they shall not plant and another eat; for as the days of a tree so shall be the days of my people, and My elect shall long enjoy the work of their hands" **(ISAIAH 65:21, 22).**

"And you, O tower of the flock, the stronghold of the daughter of Zion, to you shall it come, even the former dominion shall come, the kingdom of the daughter of Zion" **(MICAH 4:8).**

In the Bible, Zion is a symbol of God's people or His church. Jeremiah the prophet states, "I have likened the daughter of Zion to a lovely and delicate woman" **(JEREMIAH 6:2).** In Bible prophecy, a woman represents the church **(SEE REVELATION 12:17; EPHESIANS 5:28–33; 2 CORINTHIANS 11:2).** The former dominion or, as some translations say, "the first dominion," is a clear reference to the dominion God gave Adam and Eve over the rest of His creation at the Garden of Eden. When God created Adam, He declared, "Let us make man in Our image, according to Our likeness; let them have dominion" **(GENESIS 1:26).**

"The meek . . . shall inherit the earth" **(MATTHEW 5:5).**

This earth will be made over into the Edenic splendor that was lost by sin. Peter affirms, "Nevertheless we, according to His promise, look for new heavens and a new earth in which righteousness dwells" **(2 PETER 3:13).** Once again joy and happiness will reign. The redeemed will find their delight in their garden home just as Adam and Eve did in the beginning. The secrets of the laboratories of nature will be revealed to them. They will unite with the unfallen beings of varied planets to study the mysteries of the universe. They will travel from star to star and planet to planet proclaiming the everlasting love of Jesus.

08 Here on earth our greatest joy comes from wholesome, positive relationships with our families and friends. Where will we find our greatest joy in heaven? What will our relationships be like there?

"They shall not labor in vain, nor bring forth children for trouble; for they shall be the descendants of the blessed of the LORD, and their offspring with them" **(ISAIAH 65:23).**

"And I say to you that many will come from east and west and sit down with Abraham, Isaac, and Jacob in the kingdom of heaven" **(MATTHEW 8:11).**

Relationships bring life's greatest joy. Think of the incredible joy of rejoicing with family and friends meeting with the great heroes of faith down through the ages in the earth made new. We will have the glorious privilege of fellowshiping with Bible luminaries such as Moses, Joseph, David, Esther, Peter, Paul, Mary, and a host of others.

Everybody worth knowing will be there. But there will be one divine personage who stands head and shoulders above all of the rest.

"And there shall be no more curse, but the throne of God and of the Lamb shall be in it, and His servants shall serve Him. They shall see His face, and His name shall be on their foreheads. There shall be no night there: They need no lamp nor the light of the sun, for the Lord God gives them light. And they shall reign forever and ever" **(REVELATION 22:3–5).**

Our greatest joy through the ceaseless ages of eternity will be fellowship with Jesus. Our hearts will delight in worshiping Him. We will join with all of heaven in singing redemption's song.

"You are worthy to take the scroll, and to open its seals, for you were slain, and have redeemed us to God by your blood out of every tribe and tongue and people and nation, And have made us kings and priests to our God; and we shall reign on earth" **(REVELATION 5:9).**

From Sabbath to Sabbath the redeemed of earth will join with all of the hosts of heaven in a symphony of praise and worship **(SEE ISAIAH 66:22, 23).** The joy we will experience is indescribable. Would you like to make a new commitment to Jesus and dedicate your life to Him anew? He longs for you to enjoy fellowship with Him throughout eternity. Will you accept His gracious invitation? He is reaching out to you right now. There is nothing He desires more than to have you with Him through all eternity. Why not bow your head right now wherever you are and accept His gracious invitation?